# BASEBALL
# AND THE
# AMERICAN
# LEGAL MIND

# BASEBALL AND THE AMERICAN LEGAL MIND

Edited with introductions by

SPENCER WEBER WALLER
NEIL B. COHEN
PAUL FINKELMAN

GARLAND PUBLISHING, INC.
New York & London
1995

**Library of Congress Cataloging-in-Publication Data**

Baseball and the American legal mind / edited with introductions
by Spencer Weber Waller, Neil B. Cohen, Paul Finkelman.
  p.   cm.
  Includes bibliographical references.
  ISBN 0-8153-1954-1 (hardcover). — ISBN 0-8153-2057-4
(paperback).
  1. Baseball—Law and legislation—United States.   I. Waller,
Spencer Weber, 1957–   . II. Cohen, Neil B., 1952–   .
III. Finkelman, Paul, 1949–   .
KF3989. A75B37   1995
796.357'0973—dc20                                        94-39340
                                                            CIP

Paperback cover design by Karin Badger

Printed on acid-free, 250-year-life paper
Manufactured in the United States of America

# CONTENTS

# INTRODUCTION

Americans are a particularly legalistic people. It should come as no surprise that baseball, the great American pastime, intersects with the law in a variety of ways. Most obviously, baseball is a highly legalistic game with a far more elaborate set of rules than any other sport. Every pitch and every play require a ruling. The rulings are made either individually or, occasionally, *en banc*[1] by adjudicators (known, of course, as umpires) who, like their judicial brethren, wear special clothing designed to distinguish them from the combatants and imbue them with a more transcendent authority.

Like legal jurists, umpires shape baseball according to a written code but inevitably place their own interpretative gloss on the governing rules. Just as some judges are "strict constructionists" while others employ a more flexible approach, some umpires allow a higher, lower, or wider strike zone than others. Just as some judges allow great leeway for the antics of attorneys while others more quickly resort to contempt citations, some umpires allow players and managers to vent their spleens extravagantly while others quickly banish such a malcontent to the bench or even the showers.

Moreover, the culture of baseball parallels the culture of our legal system. It turns every sandlot batter and baserunner into a litigator. We learn at an early age to argue the call and appeal to another umpire. We know that such arguments and appeals rarely succeed, but we persevere nonetheless. Furthermore, there is something therapeutic about arguing with the umpire. It may be no wonder that the United States leads the world in the production of lawyers—we learn legal culture and process in youth league and schoolyard baseball!

To press these parallels even further, it should be noted that in baseball, as in real life, there are outlaws who, nonetheless, become folk heroes. Fans have adored many pitchers who were notorious for throwing spitballs, knowing full well that those pitchers were violating the letter of the baseball law. Similarly, violations of the spirit of the baseball rules are also often fondly remembered.[2] There is even a play in baseball that glorifies "criminal" conduct—stealing a base.

Given the extensive parallels between legal culture and baseball culture, the breadth and depth of the baseball/law nexus is only to be expected. This nexus results not only in mine-run litigation arising out of the business of baseball (although there is plenty of that, some of which is illustrated in this book) but also in the considerable use of legal insights to inform the world of baseball and baseball insights to inform the world of law. Is there any other "game" about which this can be said?

This collection explores the baseball/law nexus. Neither the close reader nor the casual peruser can escape the conclusion that the relationship between baseball and the American legal mind is truly synergistic.

Part 1 collects articles examining the surprising (to the uninitiated) parallels between baseball rules and the development of rules of law. A classic "aside" from the *University of Pennsylvania Law Review*, "The Common Law Origins of the Infield Fly Rule," introduces this topic. Several additional asides and commentaries continue the point. The chapter concludes with wisdom drawn from the most famous statutory interpretation decision of the 1980s (yes, even more famous than Justice Scalia's musings in this area)—the saga of George Brett and the pine tar bat.

Part 2 collects six of the most important court decisions concerning baseball's status under the antitrust laws. Most notable are *Federal Baseball Club v. National League*, one of Justice Holmes's least insightful opinions, and *Flood v. Kuhn*, famous for Justice Blackmun's paean to baseball players of bygone days (and the curmudgeony refusal of Justices White and Burger to join that part of the Court's opinion). Also in the chapter are excerpts from congressional hearings about the antitrust status of baseball, including Casey Stengel's hilarious testimony to the Senate Judiciary Committee and some scholarly commentary on the issue.

Part 3 contains the current Uniform Players' Contract as well as four notable turn-of-the-century decisions about early player contracts. The chapter also includes a selection of five pieces from the scores of scholarly exegeses of this topic.

Parts 4 and 5 provide both judicial and scholarly commentary on franchise relocation and intellectual property, respectively.

Part 6 collects cases and commentary analyzing liability for the inevitable injuries that accompany playing and watching baseball.

Part 7 presents a selection of expositions of legal theory, both formal and informal, that draw their inspiration from the wisdom gained from baseball. Articles such as "Dennis Martinez and the Uses of Theory," "Strict Constructionism and the Strike Zone," "Error Behind the Plate and in the Law," and "What Do Babe Ruth and John Marshall Have in Common?" represent contributions to the wealth of legal theory that would not exist without baseball.

Part 8 represents either the heart of this book or a parochial and self-indulgent yearning for one's erstwhile home, depending on which editor you ask.

Finally, Part 9 is a list of recommended reading, containing valuable and entertaining appraisals of baseball and the law that would have been included in this collection but for space limitations.

## NOTES

1.  In baseball's ultimate forum, the World Series, the addition of extra umpires creates an exceptionally large tribunal not unlike the Supreme Court.

2.  The pinch-hit appearance of midget Eddie Gaedel for the hapless St. Louis Browns, which guaranteed both a walk for the team and publicity (presumably translating into increased team attendance) for Bill Veeck, its owner, is a good example of this phenomenon.

# Baseball and the American Legal Mind

# PART 1

## BASEBALL RULES AND THE PATH OF THE LAW: THE INFIELD FLY AND PINE TAR CONTROVERSIES

The legal mind and the baseball mind have quite a bit in common. Indeed, some of baseball's best strategists, such as Branch Rickey, Miller Huggins, and Tony LaRussa, were trained as lawyers. Thus, it should come as no surprise that there are parallels between the development of baseball jurisprudence and rules of law. Indeed, the two have had a synergistic relationship; baseball has informed the law, and the law has informed baseball.

Baseball's influence on the development of American jurisprudential thought is best exemplified in a classic "aside" from the *University of Pennsylvania Law Review*, "The Common Law Origins of the Infield Fly Rule." This piece, and several commentaries inspired by it, provides an excellent example of the use of baseball wisdom to inform the development of legal thought.

Of course, legal thought also has had a significant impact on the development of baseball rules. Jurisprudential thought regarding modes of statutory interpretation, including strict construction, purposive construction, and noninterpretivism, have informed legal decisionmaking on a number of occasions. Perhaps the most famous such occasion is the notorious pine tar decision of a decade ago.

This section presents several examples of the synergistic relationship between the law of baseball and the law of the land. Certainly no other sport has such influence on the legal mind.

# ASIDE

## THE COMMON LAW ORIGINS
## OF THE INFIELD FLY RULE

The[1] Infield Fly Rule[2] is neither a rule of law nor one of equity; it is a rule of baseball.[3] Since the[4] 1890's it has been a part of the body of the official rules of baseball.[5] In its inquiry

---

[1] 11 Oxford English Dictionary 257-60 (1961).

[2] Off. R. Baseball 2.00 & 6.05(e). Rule 2.00 is definitional in nature and provides that:

> An INFIELD FLY is a fair fly ball (not including a line drive nor an attempted bunt) which can be caught by an infielder with ordinary effort, when first and second, or first, second and third bases are occupied, before two are out. The pitcher, catcher, and any outfielder who stations himself in the infield on the play shall be considered infielders for the purpose of this rule.
>
> When it seems apparent that a batted ball will be an Infield Fly, the umpire shall immediately declare "Infield Fly" for the benefit of the runners. If the ball is near the baselines, the umpire shall declare "Infield Fly, if Fair."
>
> The ball is alive and runners may advance at the risk of the ball being caught, or retouch and advance after the ball is touched, the same as on any fly ball. If the hit becomes a foul ball, it is treated the same as any foul.
>
> NOTE: If a declared Infield Fly is allowed to fall untouched to the ground, and bounces foul before passing first or third base, it is a foul ball. If a declared Infield Fly falls untouched to the ground outside the baseline, and bounces fair before passing first or third base, it is an Infield Fly.

Rule 6.05(e) gives operational effect to the definition, by providing that the batter is out when an Infield Fly is declared.

Depending upon the circumstances, other rules which may or may not apply to a particular situation include, *inter alia*, Fed. R. Civ. P., Rule Against Perpetuities, and Rule of *Matthew* 7:12 & *Luke* 6:31 (Golden).

[3] Although referred to as "Rules" both officially and in common parlance, if the analogy between the conduct-governing strictures of baseball and a jurisprudential entity on the order of a nation-state is to be maintained, the "rules" of baseball should be considered to have the force, effect, and legitimacy of the statutes of a nation-state. The analogy would continue to this end by giving the "ground rules" of a particular baseball park the same status as the judge-made rules of procedure of a particular court.

[4] Note 1 *supra*.

[5] It is only with the greatest hesitation that one hazards a guess as to *the* year of origin of the Infield Fly Rule. Seymour considers it to have been 1893. 1 H. Seymour, Baseball 275 (1960). Richter, on the other hand, in an opinion which *The Baseball Encyclopedia* joins, considers the rule to have entered the game in 1895. F. Richter, Richter's History and Records of Baseball 256 (1914); The Baseball Encyclopedia 1526-27 (1974). Finally, Voigt considers 1894 the correct year. 1 D. Voigt, American Baseball 288 (1966).

Although independent investigation of primary sources has led to the belief that the

into the common law origins[6] of the rule, this Aside does not seek to find a predecessor to the rule in seventeenth-century England. The purpose of the Aside is rather to examine whether the same types of forces that shaped the development of the common law[7] also generated the Infield Fly Rule.

As a preliminary matter, it is necessary to emphasize that baseball is a game of English origin, rooted in the same soil from which grew Anglo-American law and justice.[8] In this respect it is like American football and unlike basketball, a game that sprang fully developed from the mind of James Naismith.[9] The story of Abner Doubleday, Cooperstown, and 1839, a pleasant tribute to American ingenuity enshrined in baseball's Hall of Fame, is not true.[10] The myth reflects a combination of economic opportunism,[11] old friendship,[12] and not a small element of anti-British feeling.[13] The true birthplace of the game is England;

---

rule first developed in 1894 and 1895, notes 25-35 *infra* & accompanying text, a certain sense of justice would be satisfied if the rule developed as a result of play during the 1894 season. For that season was the first of the championship seasons of the Baltimore Orioles, the team that developed what is now known as "inside baseball," including such plays as the Baltimore chop and the hit-and-run. The Orioles not only played smart baseball; they played dirty baseball. "Although they may not have originated dirty baseball they perfected it to a high degree. In a National League filled with dirty players they were undoubtedly the dirtiest of their time and may have been the dirtiest the game has ever known." D. WALLOP, BASEBALL: AN INFORMAL HISTORY 88 (1969); *accord*, L. ALLEN, THE NATIONAL LEAGUE STORY 68 (1961); *see* R. SMITH, BASEBALL 136-46 (1947). Even if the Infield Fly Rule was not developed as a result of the event of the 1894 season, perhaps it should have been.

[6] For a discussion of origins, *see generally* Scopes v. State, 154 Tenn. 105, 289 S.W. 363 (1927); *Genesis* 1:1-2:9. *But see even more generally* Epperson v. Arkansas, 393 U.S. 97 (1968); R. ARDREY, AFRICAN GENESIS (1961); C. DARWIN, THE DESCENT OF MAN (1871); C. DARWIN, THE ORIGIN OF SPECIES (1859).

[7] For a discussion of common law in a non-baseball context, see W. HOLDSWORTH, A HISTORY OF ENGLISH LAW (1903-1938); O.W. HOLMES, THE COMMON LAW (1881).

[8] *Cf.* Palko v. Connecticut, 302 U.S. 319, 325 (1937).

[9] R. BRASCH, HOW DID SPORTS BEGIN? 41 (1970).

[10] R. HENDERSON, BAT, BALL AND BISHOP 170-94 (1947). The Doubleday theory of origin is outlined in 84 CONG. REC. 1087-89 (1939) (remarks of Congressman Shanley) (*semble*). Congressional approval of the theory, however, was never forthcoming. H.R.J. Res. 148, 76th Cong., 1st Sess. (1939), seeking to designate June 12, 1939, National Baseball Day, was referred to the Committee on the Judiciary, never again to be heard from. 84 CONG. REC. 1096 (1939). Nor did the Supreme Court formally adopt the Doubleday theory. Flood v. Kuhn, 407 U.S. 258, 260-61 (1972) (opinion of Blackmun, J.) (not explicitly rejecting the theory either). An interesting, if unlikely, explanation, offerable as an alternative to both the Doubleday and English theories of origin, is found in J. HART, HEY! B.C. 26 from the back (unpaginated, abridged & undated ed.).

[11] R. BRASCH, *supra* note 9, at 31-32.

[12] R. HENDERSON, *supra* note 10, at 179. The chairman of the commission suggested by A.G. Spalding to investigate the origins of the game was A.G. Mills, who had belonged to the same military post as Abner Doubleday.

[13] R. SMITH, *supra* note 5, at 31.

thence it was carried to the western hemisphere, to develop as an American form.[14]

The original attitude toward baseball developed from distinctly English origins as well. The first "organized" games were played in 1845 by the Knickerbocker Base Ball Club of New York City,[15] and the rules which governed their contests clearly indicate that the game was to be played by gentlemen. Winning was not the objective; exercise was.[16] "The New York club players were 'gentlemen in the highest social sense'—that is, they were rich. . . . The earliest clubs were really trying to transfer to our unwilling soil a few of the seeds of the British cricket spirit."[17] This spirit, which has been variously described as the attitude of the amateur, of the gentleman, and of the sportsman,[18] would have kept the rules simple and allowed moral force to govern the game.[19] Such an attitude, however, was unable to prevail.

As baseball grew, so did the influence of values that saw winning, rather than exercise, as the purpose of the game.[20] Victory was to be pursued by any means possible within the language of the rules, regardless of whether the tactic violated the spirit of the rules.[21] The written rules had to be made more and more specific, in order to preserve the spirit of the game.[22]

The Infield Fly Rule is obviously not a core principle of baseball. Unlike the diamond itself or the concepts of "out" and "safe," the Infield Fly Rule is not necessary to the game. Without the Infield Fly Rule, baseball does not degenerate into bladderball[23] the way the collective bargaining process degener-

---

[14] See generally H. SEYMOUR, supra note 5; D. VOIGT, supra note 5. The American qualities of the game are also revealed in other than historical or legal contexts. Cf. M. GARDNER, THE ANNOTATED CASEY AT THE BAT (1967); B. MALAMUD, THE NATURAL (1952).

[15] R. SMITH, supra note 5, at 32-35.

[16] KNICKERBOCKER BASE BALL CLUB R. 1 (1845), reprinted in R. HENDERSON, supra note 10, at 163-64, and in F. RICHTER, supra note 5, at 227.

[17] R. SMITH, supra note 5, at 37.

[18] Keating, Sportsmanship as a Moral Category, 75 ETHICS 25, 33 (1964).

[19] R. SMITH, supra note 5, at 68-69.

[20] 1 D. VOIGHT, supra note 5, at xvii; cf. Hearings on S. 3445, Federal Sports Act of 1972, Before the Senate Committee on Commerce, 92d Cong., 2d Sess. 94-95 (1973) (statement of H. Cosell). See generally Keating, supra note 18, at 31-34.

[21] Perhaps the most glaring example of this attitude is contained in the career of Mike "King" Kelly. When the rules permitted substitutions on mere notice to the umpire, Kelly inserted himself into the game after the ball was hit in order to catch a ball out of reach of any of his teammates. R. SMITH, supra note 5, at 89-90.

[22] Cf. id. 68-69; 1 D. VOIGT, supra note 5, at 204-05.

[23] See Yale Daily News, Oct. 29, 1966, at 1, col. 1.

ates into economic warfare when good faith is absent.[24] It is a technical rule, a legislative response to actions that were previously permissible, though contrary to the spirit of the sport.

Whether because the men who oversaw the rules of baseball during the 1890's were unwilling to make a more radical change than was necessary to remedy a perceived problem in the game, or because they were unable to perceive the need for a broader change than was actually made, three changes in the substantive rules, stretching over a seven-year period, were required to put the Infield Fly Rule in its present form. In each legislative response to playing field conduct, however, the fundamental motive for action remained the same: "To prevent the defense from making a double play by subterfuge, at a time when the offense is helpless to prevent it, rather than by skill and speed."[25]

The need to enforce this policy with legislation first became apparent in the summer of 1893. In a game between New York and Baltimore, with a fast runner on first, a batter with the "speed of an ice wagon"[26] hit a pop fly. The runner stayed on first, expecting the ball to be caught. The fielder, however, let the ball drop to the ground, and made the force out at second.[27] The particular occurrence did not result in a double play, but that possibility was apparent; it would require only that the ball not be hit as high. Although even the Baltimore Sun credited the New York Giant with "excellent judgment,"[28] the incident suggested that something should be done, because by the play the defense obtained an advantage that it did not deserve and that the offense could not have prevented. Umpires could handle the situation by calling the batter out,[29] but this was not a satisfactory solution; it could create as many problems as it solved.[30] The 1894 winter meeting responded with adoption of the "trap ball"

---

[24] NLRB v. Insurance Agents Int'l Union, 361 U.S. 477, 488-90 (1960).

[25] 1 H. SEYMOUR, *supra* note 5, at 276.

[26] Baltimore Sun, May 24, 1893, at 6, col. 2. Raised by this statement is the issue of the speed of an ice wagon in both relative and absolute terms. Such inquiry is beyond the scope of this Aside.

[27] *Id.* The fielder who made the play was Giant shortstop and captain John Montgomery Ward, who became a successful attorney after his playing days ended. 1 D. VOIGT, *supra* note 5, at 285.

[28] Baltimore Sun, May 24, 1893, at 6, col. 2.

[29] *E.g.*, the Chicago-Baltimore game of June 8, 1893. "In the second inning . . . Kelley hit a pop fly to short-stop. Dahlen caught the ball, then dropped it and threw to second base, a runner being on first. The muff was so plain that Umpire McLaughlin refused to allow the play and simply called the batsman out." Baltimore Sun, June 9, 1893, at 6, col. 2.

[30] Text accompanying notes 45-46 *infra*.

rule, putting the batter out if he hit a ball that could be handled by an infielder while first base was occupied with one out.[31]

The trap ball rule of 1894, however, did not solve all problems. First, although the rule declared the batter out, there was no way to know that the rule was in effect for a particular play. The umpire was not required to make his decision until after the play, and, consequently, unnecessary disputes ensued.[32] Second, it became apparent that the feared unjust double play was not one involving the batter and one runner, but one that, when two men were on base, would see two baserunners declared out.[33] The 1895 league meeting ironed out these difficulties through changes in the rules.[34] The third problem with the trap ball rule of 1894, one not perceived until later, was that it applied only when one man was out. The danger of an unfair double play, however, also exists when there are no men out. This situation was corrected in 1901, and the rule has remained relatively unchanged since that time.[35]

The Infield Fly Rule, then, emerged from the interplay of four factors, each of which closely resembles a major force in the development of the common law. First is the sporting approach to baseball. A gentleman, when playing a game, does not act in a manner so unexpected as to constitute trickery;[36] in particular he does not attempt to profit by his own unethical conduct.[37]

---

[31] Baltimore Sun, Feb. 27, 1894, at 6, col. 3. The rule stated that "the batsman is out if he hits a fly ball that can be handled by an infielder while first base is occupied and with only one out." Id. Apr. 26, 1894, at 6, col. 2.

[32] Baltimore Sun, Apr. 26, 1894, at 6n col. 2.

[33] 1 H. Seymour, supra note 5, at 275-76. Seymour developed yet another reason for the change in the rule: that "teams got around it by having outfielders come in fast and handle the pop fly." Id. 276. This does not appear to be a valid thesis because, from the beginning, the rule referred not to whether an infielder, as opposed to an outfielder, did handle the chance, but to whether an infielder could handle it. Note 31 supra.

[34] Baltimore Sun, Feb. 18, 1895, at 6, col. 4. Id. Feb. 28, 1895, at 6, col. 5.

[35] The Baseball Encyclopedia 1527 (1974). The current rule is set forth in note 2 supra.

[36] See, e.g., Pluck (the wonder chicken).

[37] In the law, this belief is reflected in the clean hands doctrine, which "is rooted in the historical concept of [the] court of equity as a vehicle for affirmatively enforcing the requirements of conscience and good faith." Precision Instrument Mfg. Co. v. Automotive Maintenance Mach. Co., 324 U.S. 806, 814 (1945). For a statutory codification of the clean hands rule, see Cal. Health & Safety Code § 28548, ¶ 2 (West 1967) (requiring food service employees to "clean hands" before leaving restroom). See generally Z. Chafee, Some Problems of Equity, chs. 1-3 (1950).

To be contrasted with the doctrine of "clean hands" is the "sticky fingers" doctrine. The latter embodies the reaction of the baseball world to the excitement caused by the emergence of the home run as a major aspect of the game. Applying to the ball a foreign substance, such as saliva, made the big hit a difficult feat to achieve. As a result, in 1920, the spitball was outlawed. L. Allen, supra note 5, at 167. The banning of the spitball was

The gentleman's code provides the moral basis for the rule; it is the focal point of the rule, just as the more general precept of fair play provides a unifying force to the conduct of the game. The principle of Anglo-American law analogous to this gentleman's concept of fair play is the equally amorphous concept of due process, or justice[38] itself.

Baseball's society, like general human society, includes more than gentlemen, and the forces of competitiveness and professionalism required that the moral principle of fair play be codified so that those who did not subscribe to the principle would nonetheless be required to abide by it.[39] Thus the second factor in the development of the Infield Fly Rule—a formal and legalistic code of rules ensuring proper conduct—was created.[40] In the common law, this development manifested itself in the formalism of the writ system.[41] Conduct was governed by general principles; but to enforce a rule of conduct, it was necessary to find a remedy in a specific writ.[42] The common law plaintiff had no remedy if the existing writs did not encompass the wrong complained of; and the baseball player who had been the victim of a "cute" play could not prevail until the umpire could be shown a rule of baseball squarely on point.

To the generalization set forth in the preceding sentence there is an exception, both at common law and at baseball. At common law, the exception was equity, which was able to aid the plaintiff who could not find a form of action at law.[43] At baseball, the exception was the power of the umpire to make a

---

not, however, absolute. Seventeen pitchers were given lifetime waivers of the ban, *id.*, possibly because the spitball had become an essential element of their stock-in-trade, and depriving them of the pitch would in effect deny them the right to earn a living. *See* Adams v. Tanner, 244 U.S. 590 (1917); McDermott v. City of Seattle, 4 F. Supp. 855, 857 (W.D. Wash. 1933); Winther v. Village of Weippe, 91 Idaho 798, 803-04, 430 P.2d 689, 694-95 (1967); *cf.* RESTATEMENT (SECOND) OF CONTRACTS § 90 (Tent. Drafts Nos. 1-7, 1973). *But see* Ferguson v. Skrupa, 372 U.S. 726, 730-31 (1963).

[38] *See generally, e.g.,* U.S. CONST. amends. V & XIV and cases citing thereto; Poe v. Ullman, 367 U.S. 497, 539-55 (1961) (Harlan, J., dissenting); J. RAWLS, A THEORY OF JUSTICE (1971); Bentley, *John Rawls: A Theory of Justice,* 121 U. PA. L. REV. 1070 (1973); Michelman, *In Pursuit of Constitutional Welfare Rights: One View of Rawls' Theory of Justice,* 121 U. PA. L. REV. 962 (1973); Scanlon, *Rawls' Theory of Justice,* 121 U. PA. L. REV. 1020 (1973); *cf., e.g.,* Byron R. "Whizzer" White (1962- ), Hugo L. Black (1937-71), & Horace Gray (1881-1902) (Justices). *But cf., e.g.,* Roger B. Taney (1836-64) (Chief Justice).

[39] Keating, *supra* note 18, at 30. *See also* R. SMITH, *supra* note 5, at 68-69.

[40] Text accompanying notes 25-35 *supra.*

[41] 2 F. MAITLAND, COLLECTED PAPERS 477-83 (1911).

[42] F. POLLOCK, THE GENIUS OF THE COMMON LAW 13 (1912); 2 F. POLLOCK, & F. MAITLAND, HISTORY OF ENGLISH LAW 558-65 (2d ed. 1952).

[43] F. MAITLAND, EQUITY 4-5 (1909).

call that did not fit within a particular rule.[44] The powers of equity and of the umpire, however, were not unlimited. The law courts circumscribed the power of the chancellor to the greatest extent possible, and this process of limitation has been defended.[45] Likewise, the discretionary power of the umpire has been limited: Additions to the written rules have reduced the area within which the umpire has discretion to act. Strong policy reasons favor this limitation upon the umpire's discretionary power. Because finality of decision is as important as correctness of decision, an action that invites appeal, as broad discretion in the umpire does, is not valued. The umpire must have the status of an unchallengeable finder of fact.[46] Allowing challenges to his authority on matters of rules admits the possibility that he may be wrong, and encourages a new generation of challenges to findings of fact.

The fourth element in the development of the Infield Fly Rule is demonstrated by the piecemeal approach that rules committees took to the problem. They responded to problems as they arose; the process of creating the Infield Fly Rule was incremental, with each step in the development of the rule merely a refinement of the previous step. Formalism was altered to the extent necessary to achieve justice in the particular case; it was not abandoned and replaced with a new formalism. Anglo-American law has two analogies to this process. The first is the way in which common law precedents are employed to mold existing remedies to new situations. Although the rigid structure of the common law was slow to change, it did change. The substantive change took place not only as a result of judicial decision; it was also caused by legislation, which is the second analogy. The legislation, however, was to a great extent directed at specific defects perceived to exist in the system.[47] Adjustment of the law, not its reform, was the goal of the legislative process. The rules of baseball and of Anglo-American jurisprudence are thus to be contrasted with the continental system of complete codes designed to remedy society's ills with a single stroke of the legislative brush.[48]

The dynamics of the common law and the development of one of the most important technical rules of baseball, although

---

[44] Note 29 *supra.*

[45] 2 F. MAITLAND, *supra* note 41, at 491-94.

[46] OFF. R. BASEBALL 4.19.

[47] F. POLLOCK, *supra* note 42, at 72.

[48] *Cf.* H. GUTTERIDGE, COMPARATIVE LAW 77-78 (2d ed. 1949).

on the surface completely different in outlook and philosophy, share significant elements. Both have been essentially conservative, changing only as often as a need for change is perceived, and then only to the extent necessary to remove the need for further change. Although problems are solved very slowly when this attitude prevails, the solutions that are adopted do not create many new difficulties. If the process reaps few rewards, it also runs few risks.

# FURTHER ASIDE

## A Comment on "The Common Law
## Origins of The Infield Fly Rule"

*John J. Flynn\**

Many analogies limp, others stumble and a few march with the machine-like cadence of the Phillies doing exercises before a ball game. The analogy between the evolution of the Infield Fly Rule and the common law, to be found in Volume 123 past of the *University of Pennsylvania Law Review* and reprinted in this volume of the *Journal*,[1] falls into the "limp" category and might even descend to the "stumble" category when viewed from some perspectives. For example, the author totally ignores the impact of economic analysis in the evolution of both the Infield Fly Rule and the common law. Psychological analysis is given short shrift; and the insights of sociology, anthropology, political "science" and statistical analysis are totally ignored. One is left with the impression that both the Infield Fly Rule and common law were largely fashioned by common sense human reactions to reality;[2] surely a disturbing conclusion to the followers of S. Freud, C.W. Mills, B.F. Skinner, A. Smith, H. Spencer, L. Keynes, J. Bentham, M. Freidman, and countless other leaders of modern social "science."

It is not enough to suggest that an infielder would intentionally drop

---

\* Professor of Law, University of Utah.

[1] Page 1474, Anno domini 1975. Citation form will not necessarily follow the form dictated by the White Book since it has not been empirically shown what, if any, value is achieved by doing so.

[2] For example, the author suggests that the fact that the batsman in an 1893 game between New York and Baltimore had the "speed of an ice wagon" while the runner on first was fast indicated the necessity for the Infield Fly Rule once a "pop up" to an infielder was hit. 123 Penn. L. Rev. 1474 at 1477. Aside from the fact that the rule as it finally evolved would not apply to this situation, (Off.R. Baseball 2.00) it is important to ask why the players involved were motivated to act as they did. There are at least three variables: the batter with the speed of an ice wagon (N.Y.B.I.W.), the fast runner on first (S.N.Y.F.B.R.), and the allegedly ungentlemanly respondent to the pop fly (R.B.O.2B). Thus, should we seek the motivation of the parties (M.O.P.) to the transaction, the equation might be: Let $M^1$ = the respondent's (R.B.O.2B) motive; $M^2$ = the batter's (N.Y.B.I.W.) motive; and, $M^3$ = the speedy first base runner's (S.N.Y.F.B.R.) motive. Then M.O.P. = $[M^2$ (N.Y.B.I.W.) x (S.N.Y.F.B.R.)] ÷ $M^1$(R.B.O. 2B); or is it M.O.P. x $M^1$ (R.B.O.2B) = (N.Y.B.I.W.) x $M^3$ (S.N.Y.F.B.R.). Well whatever, this would give us an M.O.P. which would clearly dictate whether to adopt and in what form to adopt an Infield Fly Rule, absent the meaningless standard of common sense which should never govern the development of legal rules. One could also draw good charts and graphs with such information, which surely would enhance the intellectual prestige of the article and render the article unintelligible to all but the initiated. In addition, it would suggest to New York Management that the "ice wagon" be traded for a first base coach and cash.

a fly ball so as to accomplish a "double play" simply for the sake of achieving a double play. One must consider the economic implications of the decision-making involved. Behavior must be measured on the assumption that "the people involved with the legal [baseball] system act as rational maximizers of their satisfactions."[3] Every effort must be made to construct a viable theory through statistically based empirical evidence as to why the participants behave as they do; then quantify and hold constant all the variables; construct a model which can maximize the efficiency of the system; and, proceed with the machine-like logic of a gumball dispenser to dictate the rule which does, in "reality", govern. Players, fans, umpires and any others who may be interested can rest assured that such a "scientific"[4] and empirically based process will produce "truth,"[5] maximize economic effi-

---

[3] R. Posner, *The Economic Approach to Law*, 53 Tex. L. Rev. 757, 761 (1975).

[4] The word science is derived from the Latin Scientia or knowledge. It is, of course, used in many conflicting ways; including a body of systematized knowledge, or systematized knowledge verifiable by observation, or a field of verifiable general rules equalling truth or quite simply knowledge which can be called truths. It is used here in the sense of establishing general rules through empirical research and inductive reasoning which are the "truth", so long as assumptions are not reexamined, variables can be ignored and intellectual humility can be suppressed. This enables one to claim "Economics is logically positivistic, scientifically rigorous, and generally indifferent to normative issues." H. MANNE, THE ECONOMICS OF LEGAL RELATIONSHIPS, p. VII (1975). Some academics even believe this proposition and devote considerable effort based on the presumption. See BORK, THE ANTITRUST PARADOX: A POLICY AT WAR WITH ITSELF (1978).

The implication that the concept "scientific" equals immutable and eternal "truth" may come as a surprise to those who have studied the history of science and its process of thinking. *See, e.g.,* T. KUHN, THE STRUCTURE OF SCIENTIFIC REVOLUTIONS (2d Ed. 1962). Many philosophers may find these claims somewhat naive as well. *See, e.g.,* W. QUINE, TWO DOGMA'S OF EMPIRICISM, FROM A LOGICAL POINT OF VIEW, p. 20 (1961); F.S. Cohen, *Field Theory and Judicial Logic*, 59 YALE L.J. 238 (1950). Felix Cohen, *ibid,* even had the temerity to suggest: "Lawyers . . . have special opportunities to learn what many logicians have not yet recognized: That truth on earth is a matter of degree, and that, whatever may be the case in Heaven a terrestrial major league batting average above .300 is nothing to be sneezed at." While many economists feverently repeat "ours is a science," trans. "we have truth," it must be conceded that one would readily settle for an economist with a .250 batting average, ice wagon speed, and minimal fielding ability. Most teams would probably be willing to give up a psychologist, two sociologists and future draft choices for a statistician to get an economist with those qualifications.

[5] So long as the basic assumptions are not re-examined and such non-scientific factors as perception, language, reasoning and humanistic or ethical values are excluded from the equation. All this is justified since a "law" is a "law" is a "law." *See generally,* H. Kelsen, *The Pure Theory of Law,* 50 L.Q.REV. 474 (1934). Any first year law student knows, particularly after experiencing the first set of law school examinations, that law like the "science" of economics is nothing but pure deduction consisting of the "stating of a rule applicable to certain facts, a finding that the facts of a particular case are those certain facts and [that therefore] the application of the rule is a logical necessity." J.M. Zane, *German Legal Philosophy,* 16 MICH. L. REV. 288, 337 (1918). As for the claims of O.W. Holmes that law is "the prophecies of what the courts will do in fact," *The Path of the Law,* 10 HARV. L. REV. 457, (1897) and that the "life of the law has not been logic: it has been experience," THE COMMON LAW p. 5 (1881), everyone knows that Holmes was severely injured in the Civil War, spent his formative years in Cambridge and was often observed attending burlesque theatres in Washington, D. C. Moreover, Holmes believed baseball to be a game and a sport and not a commercial venture in interstate commerce. Federal Baseball Club

ciency, and reflect reality — though the resulting rule dictating behavior may be bizarre and amoral.

Moreover, any reasonably sophisticated[6] technician[7] can demonstrate that the evolution of common law doctrines like those of baseball were exclusively determined by the inexorable force of economic analysis — even where the parties were not aware of what they were doing.[8] For example, the lawyers who created the concepts of common law property and future interests may have believed that they were engaged in a political struggle with the monarchy; while in reality they were maximizing the long term efficiency of a private property system within the constraints of the culture and political system of the day.[9] Some followers of antitrust policy, a contentious lot,[10] may believe that Congress and the courts have been seeking to control the arbitrary exercise of economic power for political and social reasons as well as economic ones. In reality, they have been or should have been searching for the holy grail of economic "efficiency" which governs us all in

---

v. National League, 259 U.S. 200 (1922). Even economic research has concluded this is not the case. *See generally,* R.G. NOLL, GOVERNMENT AND THE SPORTS BUSINESS (1974). As for those who believe "law" to be primarily an analytical process involving inductive and deductive reasoning deeply dependent on complex variables and value judgments, what can you say. They are probably against Restatements, do not join the ABA, and indulge in astronomy too.

[6] "Sophisticated": Makes the appropriate assumptions and excludes pesky facts that destroy mathematical symmetry so that the model of deductive logic can function in the finest traditions of German legal philosophy. *See* Zane, *supra,* note 5. The further one can hide assumptions and ignore non-quantifiable factors, the better. *See* G. TULLOCK, THE LOGIC OF THE LAW (1971) for an excellent example of the art. There, ethics is made the end of the law rather than the beginning of law and is treated in four and one-half pages at the end of the book.

[7] For an analysis of the concept "technician" see Leff, *Economic Analysis of Law: Some Realism About Nominalism,* 60 VA. L. REV. 451 (1974).

[8] Or, if one prefers, the "rational maximizers of satisfactions" were ignorant of what they were doing but were forced to do what they did by economic models governing their behavior. Although theological truths about the eternal verities of economic models like Pareto optimality, the Phillips curve, marginal costs and so on are clearly relevant here, extensive analysis of such truths would only reopen old wounds and encourage doubt in the infallibility of *"science."* Such doubt might encourage revolutions, *see generally,* T. KUHN, THE STRUCTURE OF SCIENTIFIC REVOLUTIONS (2d Ed. 1970), a decided threat to existing institutions by encouraging progress in the improvement of the human condition. Who needs all that; and besides, the whole thing would soon degenerate into a debate over moral and ethical value judgments. Such a process can produce such monstrosities as a "progressive" income tax, due process, equal protection of the laws and all those other rules which interfere with the rational maximization of satisfaction — particularly the satisfactions of those in control of the existing order. Moreover, it might suggest that moral values be at the bottom of legal decision-making. *See* F. COHEN, THE ETHICAL BASIS OF LEGAL CRITICISM (1959), a decidedly dangerous doctrine which might open the door to humanism and give credence to the notion that the objective of a legal system is the attainment of "justice."

[9] *See generally,* H. MAINE, ANCIENT LAW (1871); B. ACKERMAN, ECONOMIC FOUNDATIONS OF PROPERTY LAW pp vii-xvi (1975).

[10] *See generally, Hearings on S. 1284, The Antitrust Improvements Act of 1975,* Subcommittee on Antitrust and Monopoly, Senate Judiciary Committee, 94th Cong. 1st Sess. (1975); H. GOLDSCHMID, H. M. MANN, J. F. WESTEN (Ed.) INDUSTRIAL CONCENTRATION: THE NEW LEARNING (1974).

accord with the immutable rules of theoretical models.[11] To this day, lawyers are indebted to the genius of these forebearers for creating a complex system guaranteed to generate misunderstanding, litigation and fees thereby curing solicitor unemployment difficulties.

Surely the Infield Fly Rule was developed by a similar group of creative pathfinders motivated by the goal of economic "efficiency." The author of the "Aside" did not assuage this possibility. No charts of players salaries, attendance records, statistical measures of performance and other empirical evidence is to be found. Theoretical models are lacking — there is not even a sloping demand curve or any attempt to graphically demonstrate the impact of the before and after marginal costs of adopting the Infield Fly Rule. One searches in vain for a Phillips curve, and Pareto optimality receives not a mention! The article is even understandable and readable by the average lawyer; surely a commentary on the intellectual quality of the article.

The author's analytical approach is hopelessly flawed by the way the issue is stated: "To prevent the defense from making a double play by subterfuge, at a time when the offense is helpless to prevent it, rather than by skill and speed."[12] Employing the pejorative term "subterfuge" not only mires the inquiry in a morass of unmeasurable value judgments, but also signals that unexamined political, moral and social goals for the game have been pre-determined. Other than acknowledging the English origins of the game, and the evolution of the values of the game from gentlemanly exercise to "winning,"[13] no effort is made to plumb the empirical depths which would justify the employment of a concept like "subterfuge." While there may be doubt in some circles as to the utility of defining organizational goals as a tool of analysis,[14] right thinking deductivists all follow the ancient maxim: "Ya can't tell the players without a program." The program in this case requires a clear enunciation of the organizational goals of baseball. Those goals, even though they may have been undergoing a Darwinian evolutionary process of natural selection favoring those best able to employ the pre-defined "subterfuge," may have been discovered by a careful analysis of the·empirical evidence of the day. Clearly the pre-conditioning of all involved is highly relevant; as is a statistical attitude analysis of any survivor's opinions. The author rejects a scientific basis to explain the adoption of the rule but rather attributes the basis of the rule to a felt need for a moral principle of

---

[11] For a debate on this question, *see, Antitrust Jurisprudence: A Symposium on the Economic, Political and Social Goals of Antitrust Policy,* 125 U. PENN. L. REV. 1182 (1977).

[12] 123 U. PENN. L. REV. at 1477, citing The Baltimore Sun, May 24, 1893, at 6, Col. 2.

[13] 123 U. PENN. L. REV. at 1475.

[14] *See,* L. B. Mohr, *The Concept of Organizational Goal,* 67 AM. POL. SCI. REV. 470 (1973).

fair play to govern the game. If true, the conditioning required to call for a mass consensus condemning as unfair what is otherwise good sense, would surely have been a fruitful source of research. Although the paucity of grant money in late 19th Century America perhaps makes historical collections of such information scant, there can be no excuse for at least indicating the overriding role that psychological conditioning must have played in the development of the rule. The behaviorist conditioning by the resource persons[15] of the day is a crucial fact to be determined. Nowhere is the attempt made to search out these eternal verities; surely a sorry exhibition of a failure to employ modern interdisciplinary research and a missed golden opportunity to tap government research funds, foundation support or other sources of funds devoted to the pursuit of "truth."

By the same token, the cultural and genetic influences upon the development of the rule are generally ignored. Surely the race, religion and volksgeist of those immediately involved in the development of the rule during the period from 1890 - 1901 is of great relevance. The only reference to such factors is the acknowledgement that the Baltimore teams of this era were noted for not only playing "smart baseball," but also for playing "dirty baseball."[16] Why such a tradition should develop in Baltimore and not in New York, Boston or Philadelphia is an unexamined conundrum which may contain the key to explaining currency of devious conduct in Baltimore to obtain an advantage during the game. For example, it is well known that Maryland was first settled by Catholics and had long been the center of Papist culture in America; while New York still suffered the remains of a Calvinist heritage of self-righteousness and rigid moralism bequeathed

---

[15] "Resource person" is a concept of art in modern day grantsmanship. Grantsmanship, of course, is the great driving force behind the "scientizing" of the humanities — or as they are called in some circles, the "social sciences." Successful grantsmanship requires the development of a complex vocabulary and the conviction that a field of knowledge has become a "profession" — much like the ancient professions of the clergy, medicine, law and prostitution. The status of being a "profession" is usually achieved by the practitioners of the art repeating over and over; "We are a profession." The benefits, of course, are enormous. It makes price fixing and other anticompetitive behavior defensible on ethical grounds. In addition, there are intangible values to be gained in pride and the knowledge that one is better than the rest of society. In the evolution of a movement from an area of knowledge to an academic discipline to a profession there is a period of linquistic confusion engendered by the search for common definitions for the jargon being developed by the priesthood of the nascent profession. "Resource person" is one such word in need of definition by many of the emerging "social sciences." Of course, some concepts of a "profession" are better left undefined; like "property" in law, "ethics" in medicine, "God" in religion, and the customer's real name in prostitution.

[16] 123 U. PENN. L. REV. at 1475, n. 5. The concept "dirty" is also a value ridden term not examined. How one could reach such a conclusion without establishing fixed first principles of "dirty" and "non-dirty" is beyond rational analysis. Perhaps "dirty" is like pornography and one knows it when he sees it. See, Jacobelles v. Ohio, 378 U.S. 184, (1964) (Stewart, J. concurring).

by Dutch settlers. Philadelphia benefitted from the quaint but uplifting moral sentiments of Quaker beliefs, extolling self integrity and a gentle disposition toward others. Boston on the other hand, was an odd melting pot of Puritanism, tempered with Yankee materialism, Unitarianism, Catholicism, and various sects espousing divers forms of idealism. It is apparent why Baltimore's cultural heritage might produce a team willing to play fast and loose with gentlemanly standards so long as the letter of existing rules was not violated; while teams from Philadelphia and New York might look askance at such conduct. Freudian analysis might show that Boston's peculiar blend of religious heritage may have produced a tradition of loudly condemning such conduct since it took place in public, but a secret desire to engage in similar sinful activity if there were only a way to hide it.

The short of the matter is that the author ignored several avenues of scientific inquiry which could have established the "true" reasons for the adoption of the Infield Fly Rule. A view of law claiming it to be based on human value judgments rather than the inexorable force of discoverable scientific rules — the truth — obviously led the author astray. How one can expect to efficiently manage a society, much less a baseball contest, on this basis must be truly appalling to the modern devotee of "interdisciplinary research." The next thing one can expect through the law review floodgates is the advocacy of humanism, compassion and morality in the development and administration of our law. Next, "they"[17] will want to outlaw the intentional pass, Fenway Park's Wall, baseball cards, C. O. Finley, the reserve clause and baseball's antitrust exemption. Then we will be but a short step from the anarchy to be realized by the abandonment of legal and economic positivism. The *desideratum*[18] of legal decision-making will no longer

---

[17] "They" can be anyone the reader may be paranoid about. For example; for conservatives, "they" can be liberals and vice-versa; for positivists, "they" can be realists and vice-versa; and, for the Philadelphia Phillies, "they" can be the Cincinnati Reds or the Los Angeles Dodgers, but hardly vice-versa.

[18] *Desideratum* was a favorite word for Law Review editors when I was a lad. Scarcely a page would go by without that word in the best reviews and even lesser publications would insert it with some regularity. It ranked right up there with *sine qua non*, privity, *op. cit.*, *supra*, *inter alia*, proximate cause, and *ratio decidendi*. All the style and "class" has gone out of law review writing. Brevity, clarity, and sterility command the writing style in the pages of our reviews. As Fred Rodell has observed: "There are two things wrong with almost all legal writing. One is its style. The other is its content." F. Rodell, *Goodbye to Law Reviews*, 23 VA. L. REV. 38 (1937), reprinted in 1 J. CONTEMP. L. 4 (1974). The author of the Aside is not to be completely faulted on either of these counts. The style is impeccable, although one could have wished for a couple of *desideratums* or *sine qua nons* (there is an *inter alia*, 123 U. PENN. L. REV. 1474, n. 2). The topic is of great import since it concerns a vital aspect of what some consider the "national pastime." While the Editors of the *Review* and the *Journal* are to be congratulated on their courage in publishing such a controversial article inviting the wrath of good empiricists everywhere, there is no indication that this act of Law Review statesmanship signals a trend toward

be fixed truths modestly supplied by "science" and deductive analysis, but mushy value judgments premised on non-verifiable assumptions about the ought of the human condition. Government economic policy will no longer be planned by Wharton's computer; the judicial function will no longer be controlled by the efficient utilization of personpower and the invocation of immutable rubrics to cut down clogged calendars without regard to the justice of particular decisions; political campaigns will begin focusing on the irrelevancies of issues dealing with felt human needs rather than the psychologically planned imagery of Madison Avenue; and, "the law" will continue to be plagued by the injection of human values into the process. Who knows where it will all lead; decisions of war and peace and in international relations may be made on some basis other than the immutable principles of game theory. By rejecting the modern theology of scientific analysis and empirical research, the author of the "Aside" has established a dangerous precedent which can only return to haunt the Editors of the *University of Pennsylvania Law Review* and this *Journal*. May the Phillies continue to lose the race for a National League Pennant each year; by virtue of judgment calls by umpires mired in the morality of a bygone era, if not by ice wagons on the basepaths.

---

a free flowing style and better topic selection elsewhere. For example, creative scholarship could undertake a study of the balk, the intentional pass, or why a batter is given three strikes or four balls. Even a serious study of the origins of law reviews and the way they are numbered, if not a re-examination of the non-pedagogical goals of law reviews, would be a welcome relief from the average subjects of "lead articles," "notes or comments" and "case notes."

The courage of the *Journal* staff in reprinting "The Common Law Origins of The Infield Fly Rule," as well as printing this comment, should not go unnoticed nor should it be praised. Incalculable harm may come from spreading the inference that law is not a "science" even if it might illuminate the quaint history of what is obviously a pre-ordained rule which must govern the game. It is to be fervently hoped, that the fan's trust in the immutable nature of the game and the wisdom of Bowie Kuhn has not been undermined by re-publication of the Aside.

# THE INFIELD FLY RULE AND THE INTERNAL REVENUE CODE: AN EVEN FURTHER ASIDE

Mark W. Cochran*

Life,[1] we are told, imitates the World Series.[2] This *Even Further Aside*[3] tests the validity of that premise by exploring certain similarities and differences between the Official Baseball Rules[4] and rules of somewhat broader application. Specifically, this *Even Further Aside* will compare baseball's infield fly rule[5] with functionally similar provisions of the Internal Revenue Code[6] in order to

---

* Associate Professor of Law, St. Mary's University. The author gratefully acknowledges the contributions of Michael Ariens, a colleague and fellow baseball fan, and Carl Bjerre, a law student at Cornell University.

1. On the meaning of life, or more specifically on the problem of defining the commencement thereof, see Roe v. Wade, 410 U.S. 113, 129-152 (1973). *Cf.* Welch v. Helvering, 290 U.S. 111 (1933), in which Justice Cardozo suggested that "[l]ife in all its fullness must supply the answer to the riddle" of which business expenses are "ordinary and necessary" and therefore deductible. *Id.* at 115.

2. T. Boswell, How Life Imitates the World Series (1982). A. Bartlett Giamatti, president of the National League of Professional Baseball Clubs, has been quoted as saying that baseball "is more than just a sport. It is life itself." Chadwick, *Baseball's Academician*, Am. Way, June 15, 1987, at 46. Although Mr. Giamatti's statement raises interesting philosophical issues, this *Even Further Aside* will pursue Mr. Boswell's more conservative assertion. The premise that life imitates baseball is, of course, a variation on the familiar truism that life imitates art (and vice versa). If life imitates both art and baseball, does it follow that baseball imitates art? Apparently not, according to the United States Court of Appeals for the Ninth Circuit. In Wills v. Commissioner, 411 F.2d 537 (9th Cir. 1969), the court held that a famous baseball player could not exclude from his gross income the value of awards he had received by claiming they were awards for "artistic achievement." *Id.* at 542.

3. *See* Flynn, *Further Aside: A Comment on "The Common Law Origins of The Infield Fly Rule,"* 4 J. Contemp. L. 241 (1978); *Aside: The Common Law Origins of the Infield Fly Rule*, 123 U. P. L. Rev. 1474 (1975) [hereinafter *Aside*]. *Cf.* G. Larson, The Far Side (1982).

4. Commissioner of Baseball, Official Baseball Rules (1984). [hereinafter Baseball Rules].

5. *Id.* rules 2.00, 6.05(e). Rule 6.05(e), which provides that a batter is out when he hits an infield fly, is the operative rule. Rule 2.00 defines the term 'infield fly' as "a fair fly ball (not including a line drive nor an attempted bunt) which can be caught by an infielder with ordinary effort, when first and second, or first, second, and third bases are occupied, before two are out." *Id.* rule 2.00.

6. 26 U.S.C. §§ 267, 482 (1982).

determine the extent to which the national pastime[7] mirrors other human endeavors.

The infield fly rule can best be understood by considering its purpose: "[t]o prevent the defense from making a double play by subterfuge, at a time when the offense is helpless to prevent it, rather than by skill and speed."[8] For example, assume that the team at bat has runners on first and second with one out. The batter pops up to the third baseman. Thinking the third baseman will catch the pop up, the base runners do not advance.[9] The third baseman, however, allows the ball to fall to the ground, picks it up, touches third base to force out the runner from second, and throws the ball to the second baseman, who touches second base to force out the runner from first. Thus, a routine pop up has been converted into a double play.

The infield fly rule prevents this type of manipulation. In the situation described, the batter would be out, regardless of whether the ball was caught. The base runners would be free either to stay on their respective bases or to advance at their own risk.[10]

The rule applies when runners are on base with less than two out and the batter hits a fly ball that, in the umpire's judgment, could be caught with ordinary effort by an infielder.[11] Once the umpire has determined that the ball is catchable and has announced the applicability of the rule, the result is automatic.[12] Absent the infield fly rule, the base runners are faced with a Hobson's choice.[14] If the runners stay on base, the infielder can let the ball drop and force a double play. If they advance, the infielder can

---

7. Origin uncertain.

8. *Aside, supra* note 3, at 1477 (citing 1 H. SEYMOUR, BASEBALL 276 (1960)).

9. BASEBALL RULES, *supra* note 4. Rule 7.08(d) provides that a runner is out if "[h]e fails to retouch his base after a fair or foul ball is legally caught before he, or his base, is tagged by a fielder." *Id.* A base runner who attempts to advance on a pop fly usually can be put out easily if a fielder catches the pop fly.

10. *Id.* Rule 2.00 provides that when the batter hits an infield fly, "the ball is alive and the runners may advance at the risk of the ball being caught, or retouch and advance after the ball is touched, the same as on any fly ball." *Id.* rule 2.00.

11. *See supra* note 5.

12. *Id.*

14. "A choice without an alternative; the thing offered or nothing; so called in allusion to the practice of Thomas Hobson (d. 1631), at Cambridge, England, who let horses, and required every customer to take the horse which stood nearest the door." WEBSTER'S NEW INTERNATIONAL DICTIONARY OF THE ENGLISH LANGUAGE 1185 (2d ed. 1934). [Note: The author

catch the ball and "double off" one or both runners.[15] Thus, the infield fly rule prevents what would otherwise be a virtually automatic double play.

The question then becomes, why *shouldn't* a pop up to the infield with runners on base result in a double play? The answer, presumably, is that the defense would gain an "unfair" advantage.[16] In baseball as in life,[17] fairness is an elusive concept that defies precise definition.[18] In this context, the "unfairness" seems to derive from the infielder's ability to manipulate a situation *without incurring any risk*. Baseball is willing to countenance one easy out when the batter pops up. To allow the infielder to convert one easy out into two easy outs would be contrary to fundamental notions of fair play.[19] In effect, the infielder would be shooting fish in a barrel.

Some commentators have suggested that the infield fly rule would be unnecessary if all players behaved as "gentlemen."[20] The suggestion may be correct, but it involves an unnecessary value judgment. Assuming the object of the game is to win,[21] can one justly vilify the infielder for capitalizing on an opportunity to get two outs instead of one? Some might even call failure to make the easy double play a dereliction of duty.[22]

---

has chosen to follow a time-honored baseball tradition and omit footnote 13 out of superstition.]

15. *See supra* note 9.

16. "Fair" in this context should not be confused with "fair" as distinguished from "foul," which distinction is set out in detail in rule 2.00. BASEBALL RULES, *supra* note 4. Nor should "foul" be confused with "fowl," as discussed in A.L.A. Schechter Poultry Corp. v. United States, 295 U.S. 495 (1935) (the "sick chicken" case). *Compare* "Fair is foul, and foul is fair." W. SHAKESPEARE, *Macbeth*, Act I, Scene I, in IX THE WORKS OF SHAKESPEARE 165 (C. Herford ed. 1903).

17. *See supra* note 1.

18. *See supra* note 16.

19. *Cf.* Duncan v. Louisiana, 391 U.S. 145, 172 (1968) (Harlan, J., dissenting) (construing the due process clause of the fourteenth amendment as requiring fundamental fairness).

20. *Aside, supra* note 3, at 1478-79; *see, e.g.*, Pete Rose; *cf.* Kirby, *The Year They Fixed the World Series*, A.B.A.J., Feb. 1, 1988, at 64 (describing the scandal surrounding the alleged "fixing" of the 1919 World Series by the Chicago White Sox).

21. With respect to football, Vince Lombardi said, "Winning isn't everything, it's the only thing." J. BARTLETT, FAMILIAR QUOTATIONS 925 (15th ed. 1980). Leo Durocher said that in baseball, "[n]ice guys finish last." *Id.* at 867.

22. Such a dereliction would not be ruled an error, however. Generally, failure to make a defensive play that could have been accomplished with reasonable effort constitutes an er-

Without accusing the infielder of "unethical conduct,"[23] the observation that at least some players will take advantage of the opportunity to engage in risk-free manipulation should suffice to explain the rule's existence. For purposes of this discussion, whether this tendency is attributable to a lack of ethics or an abundance of zeal is irrelevant.

The existence of the infield fly rule demonstrates three principles. First, in certain situations, infielders are presented with the opportunity to engage in risk-free manipulation. Second, absent a rule preventing such manipulation, at least some infielders would take advantage of this opportunity. Finally, baseball perceives such manipulation as "unfair" and thus has endeavored to prevent it. At least two of these principles support the premise that baseball imitates life, and vice versa. First, life is full of opportunities for risk-free manipulation. Second, at least some people can be expected to take advantage of those opportunties.[24] To determine whether the third principle reflects a similarity between baseball and life, however, one must consider examples of society's response to risk-free manipulation.

One of the more blatant real world examples of the "manipulation without risk" phenomenon can be found in the realm of federal taxation. Like the astute infielder who sees the opportunity to convert a pop up into a double play, the taxpayer who engages in a financial transaction with a related party confronts an almost irresistible temptation to manipulate the situation. For example, assume that Owner is about to sell a property to Ownerco, a corporation. Owner owns all the stock of Ownerco. If Owner sells the property for its true value, she will realize a gain, which will increase her federal income tax liability.[25] If Owner sells the property

---

ror, but for this purpose the assumption is never that the double play could be made with reasonable effort. Whether a transgression is an error is of no significance to the outcome of the game; it is relevant solely for statistical purposes.

23. *Aside, supra* note 3, at 1478.

24. *See* "playing both sides against the middle," "taking candy from a baby," "having one's cake and eating it, too," and "stacking the deck"; *cf.* "hedging one's bet," which connotes minimizing risk rather than eliminating it.

25. Generally, a taxpayer selling property will recognize a gain to the extent that the sales proceeds (the "amount realized") exceed the amount the taxpayer paid for the property (its "basis"). I.R.C. § 1001 (CCH 1988).

to Ownerco for less than its full value, she will recognize less gain or perhaps even a loss.[26]

Whether Ownerco pays full value for the property is immaterial to Owner because she owns the stock of Ownerco. To the extent that Ownerco pays less than full value, the value of Owner's stock will increase correspondingly because the corporation will have parted with less cash and acquired more property. Consequently, like the infielder who lets the pop fly drop in order to make a double play, Owner can manipulate the situation to her advantage without incurring any real cost.[27]

Federal tax law, like the rules of baseball, recognizes and responds to the "manipulation without risk" phenomenon. In Owner's case, section 267 of the Internal Revenue Code deals with the situation by denying a deduction for any loss on a sale by Owner to Ownerco.[28] As with the infield fly rule, the result under section 267 is automatic.[29] Any loss incurred on a sale to a related party is disallowed. Unlike the infield fly rule, however, section 267 is automatic in application as well as in result. The Commissioner[30] is granted no discretion in determining when the statute applies. If one of the statutorily specified relationships[31] exists, the loss is disallowed. In effect, the taxpayer is conclusively presumed to have the ability to manipulate without risk when dealing with a related party.[32] By contrast, the infield fly rule requires the umpire to exercise his or her judgment to determine whether the pop up "can be caught by an infielder with ordinary effort."[33]

---

26. A loss will result if the amount realized is less than the taxpayer's basis. *Id.* The loss will be deductible if it arises out of a transaction entered into for profit, as described in I.R.C. § 165(c)(2) (CCH 1988).

27. *Cf. supra* note 24 and accompanying text.

28. I.R.C. § 267 (CCH 1988). Section 267 provides, in pertinent part, that no deduction shall be allowed in respect of any loss from the sale or exchange of property between certain related persons, including controlling shareholders and their corporations.

29. *See supra* text accompanying note 12.

30. That baseball and federal taxation both function under the supervision of a commissioner demonstrates yet another similarity between the two.

31. The statute covers sales between siblings, spouses, ancestors, or lineal descendants as well as sales between entities and parties having an interest therein. I.R.C. § 267(b).

32. Of course, this presumption is not always justified, but Congress apparently has concluded that the exceptional cases are so rare that a conclusive presumption is acceptable.

33. *See supra* note 5.

A finding that an infielder can catch a pop up with ordinary effort is a justifiable prerequisite to the application of the infield fly rule, because the opportunity for manipulation does not exist unless the infielder can choose between catching the ball and letting it drop. If a pop up would require more than ordinary effort to catch, any resulting double play would be a legitimate product of "skill and speed"[34] rather than the spoils of risk-free manipulation.

By analogy, section 267 arguably should require a determination either that the sale between related parties is an unfair bargain or that the seller has retained an indirect interest in the property. Such a finding is not required, however, probably in order to avoid the litigation that inevitably would follow.[35] The Commissioner's[36] findings of fact, unlike those of the umpire, are reviewable.[37] Thus, the absence of a fact-finding requirement in section 267 promotes efficiency by avoiding litigation of factual questions. In baseball, on the other hand, a factual requisite to the application of a rule is workable because the umpire is the ultimate finder of fact.[38]

The availability of judicial review of factual findings in federal tax matters, and the lack thereof in baseball, reflects a difference in the nature of the respective fact-finding processes, which in turn reflects a difference in the activities themselves. In baseball, the umpire is present for every play and makes a finding of fact with respect to every transaction.[39] This is possible because baseball consists of a series of discrete transactions occurring within clearly marked boundaries. Consequently, each play can be evaluated independently. By contrast, real life is a continuous, evolutionary se-

---

34. *See supra* text accompanying note 8.

35. *But see infra* note 48 and accompanying text, discussing I.R.C. § 482.

36. *See supra* note 30.

37. An umpire's application of a rule may be protested, but factual determinations by the umpire are final. BASEBALL RULES, *supra* note 4, rule 4.19. *But see infra* note 57 regarding the now infamous "pine tar game."

38. BASEBALL RULES, *supra* note 4, rule 4.19.

39. The umpire's omniscience as fact finder is illustrated by the following colloquy, of unknown origin:

Umpire No. One: "I call 'em like I see 'em."

Umpire No. Two: "They ain't anything until I call 'em."

Bill Klem, a former major league umpire, is credited with saying, "I never called one wrong." In view of the finality accorded the unpire's decisions, it is hard to argue with Klem's claim. *Cf.* Brown v. Allen, 344 U.S. 443, 540 (1953) (Jackson, J., concurring) ("We are not final because we are infallible, but we are infallible only because we are final").

ries of events that are related in ways not always readily evident. These events transpire not between chalk lines but in countless boardrooms, back alleys, and business establishments.[40] The Commissioner cannot possibly make factual determinations with respect to more than a small fraction of the transactions that occur.[41] Because the Commissioner makes findings of fact in only a small number of cases, judicial review of those findings is at least feasible.[42] In baseball, in which every play involves a finding of fact by the umpire, review of fact findings would be unworkable. Games would be have to be suspended pending the resolution of factual disputes, or else they would have to be replayed.[43] When a schedule must be completed, a prompt and final determination is as important as a correct determination.[44]

The Commissioner's inability to be present at the time of a taxable transaction, together with the impossibility of investigating more than a small number of tax returns, creates a climate conducive to manipulation.[45] Particularly when related business entities engage in transactions with one another, taxpayers face a great temptation to arrange those transactions, at least superficially, in a manner that yields an advantageous tax result.[46] Section 267, which deals specifically with sales of property, reaches only a narrow segment of the manipulation-without-risk problem inherent in such transactions. In fact, no statute could adequately address all

---

40. *See, e.g.*, Blanche E. Lane, 25 Tax Ct. Mem. Dec. (P-H) ¶ 56,209 (1956) (profits from prostitution are includible in gross income).

41. Overall, less than two percent of tax returns receive a full-scale audit. COMM'R & CHIEF COUNSEL, INTERNAL REVENUE SERV., 1984 ANN. REP. 13.

42. *But see* Tannenwald, *Reflections on the Tax Court*, 36 TAX LAW. 853 (1982-1983) (commenting on the Tax Court's burgeoning caseload).

43. *See infra* note 57. *Cf.* BASEBALL RULES, *supra* note 4, rule 4.19, which provides for games to be continued under protest when a manager claims that an umpire's decision is inconsistent with the rules. Professional football, on the other hand, has begun to experiment with on-the-spot review of referees' *factual* determinations. *See* Taaffe, *It's Super Ref to the Rescue*, Sports Illus. (special ed.), Sept. 3, 1986, at 160. One would hope that baseball will not lower itself to such a level. If baseball imitates football, life cannot be far behind, and when life starts to imitate football, civilization as we know it will cease to exist.

44. *See Aside, supra* note 3, at 1480.

45. "When the cat is away, [t]he mice will play." W. BENHAM, PUTNAM'S DICTIONARY OF THOUGHTS 870b (1930). *See supra* note 24.

46. *See* W. BENHAM, *supra* note 45, at 870b; *supra* note 24.

the possible opportunities for manipulation.[47] Instead of attempting to identify and deal with all such situations, Congress chose to endow the Commissioner with considerable discretion both to identify and to remedy manipulation by related business entities. This grant of discretion appears in section 482, which authorizes the Commissioner[48] to re-allocate gross income, deductions, credits, or allowances among business entities owned or controlled by the same interests if the Commissioner determines that such a re-allocation is necessary "in order to prevent evasion of taxes or clearly to reflect the income" of any businesses.[49]

As with the infield fly rule, a factual determination must precede the application of section 482. This factual determination is less clear cut, however, because the term "controlled" is not defined.[50] Moreover, unlike the umpire, the Commissioner is not required to exercise his or her discretion in any given case. Section 482 also differs from the infield fly rule in result. Rather than an automatic result (that is, the batter is out), section 482 authorizes a discretionary allocation of income, deductions, credits, or allowances among the various commonly controlled businesses.[51]

Because the exercise of discretion invites judicial review, efficiency necessarily is compromised when discretion is granted.[52]

---

47. Virtually any business transaction is potentially susceptible to manipulation. Whenever one entity provides goods or services to a related entity, the tax effect of the transaction can be distorted by charging either more or less than the actual value of the goods or services. If the same financial interests control both entities, the amount charged is immaterial to the overall result. See supra notes 26-27 and accompanying text. Cf. "To rob Peter and pay Paul." The expression "is said to have had its origin in the reign of Edward IV when the lands of St. Peter at Westminster were appropriated to raise money for the repair of St. Paul's in London." J. BARTLETT, supra note 21, at 160 n.2. The phrase "to robbe Peter and paie Poule" appears in JOHN HEYWOOD'S A Dialogue of Proverbs 120 (R. Habenicht ed. 1963).

48. See supra note 30. The Internal Revenue Code actually grants the authority to the Secretary of the Treasury, who delegates it to the Commissioner of Internal Revenue. I.R.C. § 482 (CCH 1988).

49. Id.

50. The regulations provide that "[t]he term 'controlled' includes any kind of control, direct or indirect, whether legally enforceable, and however exercisable or exercised," adding that "[a] presumption of control arises if income or deductions have been arbitrarily shifted." Treas. Reg. § 1.482-1(a)(3) (1987).

51. I.R.C. § 482. The Internal Revenue Code rarely grants discretion comparable to that allowed by section 482.

52. See supra text accompanying note 42.

The type of discretion granted through section 482 is necessary, however, because the Commissioner is not present at the time of the transaction and must make his or her findings after the fact.[53] An absentee fact finder invites the type of manipulation that cannot be undone by the application of fixed rules.[54] In baseball, in which the fact finder is always present, the players' conduct can be monitored more closely.

In any event, a rule giving the umpire discretion comparable to that afforded by section 482 would be unworkable.[55] Just as the umpire's findings of fact must be final, his or her discretion must be minimal.[56] Since the exercise of such discretion would be reviewable, such discretion must be granted sparingly lest the summer schedule degenerate into a litigation docket.[57] In the context

---

53. *See supra* text accompanying notes 40-41.

54. *See supra* notes 45-46 and accompanying text.

55. *See supra* notes 43-44 and accompanying text.

56. *Id.*

57. A now infamous episode involving George Brett of the Kansas City Royals illustrates the potential consequences of a seemingly minor exercise of discretion by an umpire. In a game against the Yankees in New York on July 24, 1983, Brett came to bat with two out in the top of the ninth inning. The Royals were behind 4-3, and one man was on base. Brett hit a home run, putting the Royals ahead 5-4. Yankee Manager Billy Martin pointed out to the umpire that the pine tar on Brett's bat handle extended beyond the allowable limit of 18 inches. The umpire agreed with Martin, disallowed Brett's home run, and called Brett out to end the inning and the game.

Two alternate theories support the umpire's decision. First, under rule 6.06(d), a batter is out when he uses or attempts to use a bat that, *in the umpire's judgment*, has been altered or tampered with to improve the distance factor or cause an unusual reaction to the baseball. OFFICIAL BASEBALL RULES, *supra* note 4, rule 6.06(d) (emphasis added). The alternate theory for calling Brett out is based on rule 1.10(b), which, prior to 1984, provided:

> The bat handle, for not more than 18 inches from the end, may be covered or treated with any material (including pine tar) to improve the grip. Any such material, including pine tar, which extends past the 18 inch limitation, *in the umpire's judgment*, shall cause the bat to be removed from the game. No such material shall improve the reaction or distance factor of the bat.

COMMISSIONER OF BASEBALL, OFFICIAL BASEBALL RULES 1.10(b) (1983) (emphasis added).

Notwithstanding the apparent propriety of the umpire's ruling, four days later, American League President Lee MacPhail overruled the umpire's decision and allowed the home run to stand. MacPhail concluded that the pine tar had been applied to the bat to improve Brett's grip (an allowable alteration) rather than to alter the baseball's reaction to the bat (a prohibited alteration). According to MacPhail, even though the umpire's ruling was "technically defensible," Brett had not violated the "spirit" of the rule.

In light of MacPhail's decision, the game had to be resumed three weeks later. The game began where it had left off—with the Royals at bat with two out in the top of the ninth, leading 5-4. When play resumed, the Yankees alleged that Brett had failed to touch first

of section 482, on the other hand, discretion and the consequent potential for litigation are accepted as necessary evils, because no realistic alternative exists for dealing with the manipulation-without-risk phenomenon.

The finality of the umpire's findings of fact and the application of arbitrary rules instead of case-by-case discretion, when compared with tax law's provisions for judicial review and significant grants of discretion, might lead to the conclusion that baseball prefers efficiency over justice.[58] Such a conclusion, however, overlooks the fact that the participants have willingly submitted to the rules. Baseball is played in a controlled environment and is governed by agreed-on conventions. In short, baseball is a game.

Having reached that unsettling conclusion, does it follow that the original premise of this Even Further Aside is false? This author thinks not. The premise was not that life and baseball are identical, but simply that they imitate each other.[59] The existence of functionally similar manipulation-without-risk rules in baseball and federal taxation indicates that substantial similarities do exist. Baseball, like life, presents opportunities for risk-free manipulation. In baseball, as in life, some people can be expected to take advantage of such opportunities. By attempting to prevent such manipulation through written rules, baseball, like society in general, has indicated a disapproval of risk-free manipulation. The difference in operation between the infield fly rule on the one hand and sections 267 and 482 of the Internal Revenue Code on the other does not necessarily reflect a fundamental difference between

---

base on his home run circuit. Martin's idea was that even if Brett *had* touched first base, the umpiring crew working the resumed game was not the same crew that had worked the original game and thus they could not determine whether Brett had touched first base on the previous play. The umpires had anticipated Martin's gamesmanship, however, and produced a notarized letter from the original umpiring crew indicating that Brett had indeed touched all the bases. The game then proceeded to an anticlimactic finish, with the last batter in the top of the ninth and the first three batters in the bottom of the ninth being retired in order.

The details of the "pine tar game" are set out in Wulf, *Pine-Tarred and Feathered*, Sports Illus., Aug. 29, 1983, at 48. For a more detailed legal analysis, see Commentary, *In re Brett: The Sticky Problem of Statutory Construction*, 52 Fordham L. Rev. 430 (1983). For a criticism of MacPhail's action in overruling the umpire, see McCarthy, *Bad Calls*, The New Republic, Aug. 29, 1983, at 9, 10-11.

58. *See supra* text accompanying note 44.

59. *Cf.* Chadwick, *supra* note 2.

baseball and real life. Rather, this difference is indicative of the fact that baseball is a controlled, condensed version of real life. As one commentator has put it more eloquently: "Baseball is to our everyday experience what poetry often is to common speech—a slightly elevated and concentrated form."[60]

---

60. T. BOSWELL, *supra* note 2, at 6.

## INFIELD FLY RULE

RETHINKING THE APPLICABILITY OF EVIDENTIARY RULES AT SENTENCING:
OF RELEVANT CONDUCT AND HEARSAY
AND THE NEED FOR AN INFIELD FLY RULE

Margaret A. Berger[*]

Although considerable misgivings have been expressed about sentencing practices in the federal courts from constitutional, procedural and policy perspectives,[1] the sentencing guidelines have rarely been critiqued from an evidentiary vantage point.[2] Except for proposals to heighten the burden of proof at sentencing,[3] the interrelationship between the sentencing guidelines and evidentiary doctrine has received little attention. This comment looks at how the guidelines affect evidentiary concerns at trial, probes the premise that evidentiary rules have no role to play at the sentencing phase, and suggests that special rules may be needed at trial and at sentencing in order to further the twin objectives of ensuring the ascertainment of truth and the just determination of proceedings. See Fed. R. Evid. 102.

### The Need for an "Infield Fly Rule"

Although a prosecutor did not have to bring charges based on weak evidence before the guidelines, dropped and uncharged conduct could not automatically increase a defendant's punishment. Now, however, by dropping charges and holding back evidence, the prosecution can aim for the longest possible sentence while avoiding jury scrutiny of the full story and eluding evidentiary limitations at sentencing. This prosecutorial tactic brings to mind outlawed tactics in a game with much less at stake. The infield fly rule was adopted in baseball to preserve the game's underlying spirit of sportsmanship by making it impossible for the fielder to deliberately drop the ball and get the advantage of a double play.[18]

Before the infield fly rule reached its final form, the umpire was relied upon to disallow the double play in egregious circumstances.[19] Under the present sentencing scheme, the court plays a similar role. The court may decide that the prosecution has gone too far when it produces evidence of dropped and uncharged acts at sentencing. But is it wiser to rely on a play-by-play evaluation, or to create a different rule that would not encourage manipulations at odds with notions of fair play?

An evidentiary rule should be adopted that prohibits the prosecution at sentencing from proving facts as relevant conduct that could have been the subject of a separate count. Such a rule would have the advantages of the mature infield fly rule. The rule in its current form provides that the umpire should declare an infield fly immediately when it seems apparent that the batted ball "can be caught by an infielder with ordinary effort"; the batter is then automatically out whether or not the ball is caught.[20] A better sentencing rule would guarantee

adherence to the values underlying the evidentiary rules, and would eliminate issues on appeal. A less radical version could prohibit the prosecution from proving facts at sentencing that it never introduced at trial if those facts are being offered to increase the defendant's base offense level.[21] Such a rule would be consistent with the notion that ascertainment of the truth at trial is furthered by considering all relevant evidence.

### FOOTNOTES

[1] *See* generally Susan Herman, *The Tail That Wagged the Dog: Bifurcated Factfinding Under the Federal Sentencing Guidelines and the Limits of Due Process,* 66 S. Cal. L. Rev. ___ (1992) (in press); Daniel J. Freed, *Federal Sentencing in the Wake of Guidelines: Unacceptable Limits on the Discretion of Sentencers,* 101 Yale L. J. 1681 (1992); Gerald W. Heaney, *The Reality of Sentencing Guidelines: No End to Disparity,* 28 Am. Crim. L. Rev. 161 (1991).

[2] An exception is a recent article that suggests the need to undertake this analysis. *See* Edward R. Becker & Aviva Orenstein, *The Federal Rules of Evidence After Sixteen Years: The Effect of "Plain Meaning" Jurisprudence, the Need for an Advisory Committee on the Rules of Evidence, and Suggestions for Selective Revision of the Rules,* 60 Geo. Wash. L. Rev. 857, 885-891 (1992).

[3] A number of courts and commentators have voiced doubt about evaluating all evidence at sentencing pursuant to a preponderance of the evidence standard, the lowest standard of proof used at trial. A previous issue of FSR dealt with this issue. See 4 Fed. Sent. R. 247 no. 5 (1992).

[18] Aside, *The Common Law Origins of the Infield Fly Rule,* 123 U. Pa. L. Rev. 1474, 1477 (1975) (the infield fly rule "is a technical rule, a legislative response to actions that were previously permissible, though contrary to the spirit of the sport.").

[19] *Id.* at 1477-78.

[20] OFF. R. BASEBALL 2.00 and 6.05 (e). The comment to Rule 2.00 explains: "The infield fly is in no sense to be considered an appeal play." The Aside article, *supra* note 18, at 1480, sets forth the following rationale for the mature version of the Infield Fly Rule: "Strong policy reasons favor this limitation upon the umpire's discretionary power. Because finality of decision is as important as correctness of decision, an action that invites appeal, as broad discretion in the umpire does, is not valued. The umpire must have the status of an unchallengeable finder of fact. Allowing challenges to his authority on matters of rules admits the possibility that he may be wrong, and encourages a new generation of challenges to findings of fact." (citation omitted).

[21] Most of the evidence relating to "relevant conduct" would be admissible at trial regardless of whether a count was added to the indictment. It could be admitted either as "intrinsic" evidence, i.e., evidence inextricably intertwined with the crime charged and, therefore, not within the prohibition of Rule 404, or as other crimes evidence that satisfies Rule 404(b) because it is being used to prove an issue other than defendant's propensity to commit the charged crime.

---

[*] *Professor of Law and Associate Dean for Long Range Planning, Brooklyn Law School.*

# COMMENTARY

## *In re Brett*: The Sticky Problem of Statutory Construction

*George Brett's pine tar almost let the plague of modern life, law-
yers, into the sole redeeming facet of modern life, baseball.* *

*Knowin' all about baseball is just about as profitable
as bein' a good whittler.* **

### INTRODUCTION

On July 24, 1983,[1] at Yankee Stadium[2] in the Bronx,[3] New York,[4]
with two outs in the top of the ninth inning and one man on base,
Kansas City[5] Royal Third Baseman George Brett[6] hit a Goose Gos-
sage[7] pitch into the seats in right field for an apparent home run. New
York Yankees manager Alfred M. Martin[8] ran onto the field and
informed the home-plate umpire that the pine tar on Brett's bat
extended beyond the permissible eighteen-inch limit of the Official
Baseball Rules (Rules).[9] According to the Rules, Martin argued, the
batter should be called out for use of an illegal bat, and the home run
disallowed. The umpires conferred, measured the pine tar and upheld
Martin's protest. The game was over, the Yankees winning 4-3.[10]

The Royals filed a protest with Lee MacPhail, President of the
American League of Professional Baseball Clubs, contending that the

---

* Will, *Such, Such Were the Joys*, Newsweek, Jan. 2, 1984, at 72.
** F. Hubbard, *Saying*, in J. Bartlett, Familiar Quotations 895 (14th ed. 1968).
1. July 24, 1983 occurred on a Sunday. 1983 Julian Calander 7 (Hallmark ed.).
2. The stadium, which opened in 1923, is affectionately known as the "House
that Ruth Built" for the hero of the 1920's, George Herman "Babe" Ruth. 2 D. Voigt,
American Baseball 157 (1970).
3. The borough is "[n]amed for Jonas Bronck, a Dane who settled the region in
1639." 4 Encyclopedia Americana 599 (1968 ed.).
4. "A city that never sleeps." *Hear* F. Ebb & J. Kander, Theme from New York,
New York (F. Sinatra ed. 1980) (Reprise Records no. RPS49233).
5. A city where "[e]v'rythin's up to date . . . ." R. Rogers & O. Hammerstein
2nd, Oklahoma! 6 (1956).
6. Born May 15, 1953. Throws right, bats left. 1983 Topps Baseball Card no.
600.
7. Given name is Richard or "Rich," as is his financial status. Born July 5, 1951.
Throws right, bats infrequently. 1983 New York Yankees Yearbook 70, 76; 1983
Topps Baseball Card no. 240. Signed a contract with the San Diego Padres and now
may occasionally bat right.
8. Also known as Billy Martin. Born Alfred Manuel Pesano, on May 16, 1928.
The Baseball Encyclopedia 1171 (1969).
9. Off. Baseball R. 1.10(b), 6.06(a), (d) (Sporting News 1983); Am. League
Reg. 4.23 (Rules 1.10(b), and 6.06(d) were amended for the 1984 season, see *infra*
note 16).
10. N.Y. Times, July 25, 1983, at A1, col. 2. *But see infra* Conclusion.

umpire's decision was not supported by the Rules. They maintained that the home run should be reinstated and the game continued, the Royals leading 5-4 with two outs in the top of the ninth inning.[11] MacPhail upheld the protest,[12] thus overruling a decision made on the playing field for the first time in his ten-year tenure as League President.[13] In deciding the case, he looked beyond the text of the Rules and relied instead upon the intent of the Rules' drafters, principles of equity, and previous decisions involving pine tar.[14] This Commentary discusses whether the League President's decision was consistent with generally accepted rules of statutory interpretation.[15] While this factual situation will never reoccur, due to a change in the rules,[16] the decision itself is of interest because it may affect the game far beyond the facts[17] of this particular controversy.[18]

---

11. *Id.* at C5, col. 3.

12. Decision Regarding the Protest of the Game of Sunday, July 24, 1983 Kansas City at New York 1 (Press Release, American League, July 28, 1983) [hereinafter cited as *Brett* Decision].

13. Boswell, *Justice is Done with a Sticky Wicket*, Wash. Post, July 29, 1983, at C6, col. 1.

14. *Brett* Decision, *supra* note 12, at 1-2.

15. This Commentary, however, is not in response to Roy Cohn's fantasy that "major sports be governed by rules of law, by rules and regulations with a common sense basis . . . ." Village Voice, Jan. 3, 1984, at 115, col. 6. Mr. Cohn represented the Yankees in the pine tar controversy. *Id.* Rather, this Commentary is in response to some feeling from within.

16. The Official Playing Rules Committee amended Rule 1.10 "so as to provide *only* for the removal of a bat that is not properly treated in accordance with" the pine tar provision. Minutes of the Official Playing Rules Committee, at 2 (Meeting of Winter 1983-1984) (emphasis in original). New Rule 1.10 also contains a note specifically relating to the limit on the remedy for a pine tar infraction. *Id.* at 3. Further, the definition of an illegally batted ball was deleted from Rule 2.00. *Id.* The first part of the definition, relating to balls hit by batters with one or both feet outside of the batters box, was incorporated in Rule 6.06(a), which previously referred to the entire definition in Rule 2.00, *id.*, and the portion referring to Rule 1.10 was omitted, *id.*

This Commentary does not address the merits of the new Rules; however, the author does support the application of the Rules to future incidents involving excess pine tar. This Commentary is limited to an examination of the League President's decision as it relates to the Rules then in effect.

17. Facts lead to trivia, and baseball is filled with facts. For example, since the inception of the Most Valuable Player Award, nine men have won the triple crown (leading the league in batting average, home runs, and runs batted in). Four of these winners did not win the Most Valuable Player Award. Can you name them? See *infra* note 78 (answer).

18. To the extent Mr. MacPhail's decision reflects a reduced acceptance of the sanctity of an umpire's ruling and the use of "clever ploys and gambits," baseball is undermined. See *infra* pt. V.

## I. Textual Analysis of Rules 1.10(b), 6.06(a) and 6.06(d)

In every case involving statutory construction,[19] the relevant language must initially be analyzed.[20] Several rules and regulations are applicable to the pine tar situation.[21] Specifically, Rules 1.10(b),[22] 6.06(a)[23] and 6.06(d)[24] of the Official Rules of Baseball and Regulation 4.23 of the American League Regulations[25] must be considered.

An examination of the rules reveals two possible theories for calling a player out for use of excessive pine tar. The first involves a triad[26] of rules consisting of Rules 6.06(a), 2.00 and 1.10. Rule 6.06(a) states that a player is out when "[h]e hits an illegally batted ball."[27] An illegally batted ball is defined by Rule 2.00 as "one hit with a bat which does not conform to Rule 1.10."[28] Rule 1.10 provides in relevant part that:

> The bat handle, for not more than 18 inches from the end, may be covered or treated with any material (including pine tar) to improve the grip. Any such material, including pine tar, which extends past the 18 inch limitation, in the umpire's judgment, shall cause the bat to be removed from the game. No such material shall improve the reaction or distance factor of the bat.[29]

---

19. A threshold question which may be summarily resolved in the affirmative is whether a baseball rule is a statute. Courts differ in their resolution of similar issues, apparently in response to the nature of the rule involved and the action requested to be taken in regard to it. *Compare* Fund for Constitutional Government v. National Archives, 656 F.2d 856, 867 (D.C. Cir. 1981) (Federal Rule of Civil Procedure is statute) *with* Founding Church of Scientology v. Bell, 603 F.2d 945, 951-52 (D.C. Cir. 1979) (Federal Rule of Civil Procedure not a statute). Because of the nature of the Rules at issue here, see *infra* notes 42-43 and accompanying text, a court of law would certainly hold these rules to be a statute for the limited purpose of construing them.

20. *See* Cannon v. University of Chicago, 441 U.S. 677, 689 (1979); FTC v. Bunte Bros., 312 U.S. 349, 350 (1941); Alabama Power Co. v. Costle, 636 F.2d 323, 379 (D.C. Cir. 1979).

21. Nevertheless, many rules and regulations do not apply to the pine tar incident. *See, e.g.,* Wolfe v. Shelley, 76 Eng. Rep. 206 (1579-1581) (Rule in Shelley's Case); "Can You Top Joey Adams" Contest Official Rules, N.Y. Post, Dec. 23, 1983, at 46, col. 6.

22. Off. Baseball R. 1.10(b) (Sporting News 1983) (amended 1984).

23. *Id.* R. 6.06(a) (amended 1984).

24. *Id.* R. 6.06(d).

25. Am. League Reg. 4.23.

26. As used in this Commentary, "triad" means a group of three. This should not be confused with other meanings of the word triad such as a favorite form of gnomic literature, a trivalent atom, a set of three vectors or a chord of three notes or tones. *See* Webster's International Dictionary 2705 (2d ed. 1957).

27. Off. Baseball R. 6.06(a) (Sporting News 1983) (amended 1984)

28. *Id.* R. 2.00 (amended 1984).

29. *Id.* R. 1.10 (amended 1984).

Together, these three rules imply that a batter should be called out for use of excessive pine tar. Thus, as Mr. MacPhail stated, the umpire's decision was "technically defensible."[30]

The second theory by which a player may be called out involves applying Rule 6.06(d), which concerns the use of "doctored" bats.[31] A violation of this provision results in the batter being called out, ejected from the game, and the imposition of "additional penalties as determined by the League President."[32] League Regulation 4.23, however, specifically addresses the question of whether excessive pine tar constitutes "doctoring" of a bat.[33] The regulation states that the use of pine tar in itself will not be considered to be "doctoring the bat."[34] The regulation apparently takes a pine tar violation out of the coverage of Rule 6.06(d), which penalizes players for using bats that are "doctored." Application of Rule 6.06(a), however, would still result in the batter being called out. This inconsistency in the rules should be settled using various aids to construction.[35] The first step should be to use intrinsic evidence.

## II. INTRINSIC RULES OF INTERPRETATION

### A. *Rule 6.06(d) and Regulation 4.23*

Rule 6.06(d) and Regulation 4.23 present a common problem of interpretation. The drafters of Regulation 4.23 excluded pine tar infractions from only two of the three possible penalties for doctored bats provided by Rule 6.06(d)—suspension and ejection from a game.[36] By failing to exclude the third penalty of calling the batter out, a question is raised whether the drafters intended to retain that provision as a possible penalty for excessive pine tar use.

The rule of interpretation, *expressio unius est exclusio alterius*, states that when specific examples are enumerated, those situations not enumerated are not implied, especially when they are noted elsewhere in the rules.[37] Thus, by specifically removing two of the three

---

30. *Brett* Decision, *supra* note 12, at 1.

31. Off. Baseball R. 6.06(d) (Sporting News 1983). "Doctored" bats are those "which have been altered or tampered with in such a way to improve the distance factor or cause an unusual reaction on the baseball." *Brett* Decision, *supra* note 12, at 2 (emphasis omitted).

32. *Id.* The additional penalty is usually suspension of the player for a number of games.

33. Am. League Reg. 4.23.

34. *Id.*

35. For other construction aids, *see, but do not use* 42 U.S.C. § 5305(a)(2) (Supp. V 1981) (construction aid for public works including neighborhood facilities); *see also* Cal. Civ. Code § 1793.2 (West Supp. 1983) (Lemon-Aid; defective car law).

36. Am. League Reg. 4.23.

37. TVA v. Hill, 437 U.S. 153, 188 (1978); E. Crawford, Construction of Statutes § 195, at 334-37 (1940); *see* Fedorenko v. United States, 449 U.S. 490, 512-13

possible penalties that may be levied when a player uses a bat that is "doctored" with pine tar, the Regulation apparently retains the remedy of calling the player out for such an offense. This analysis seems to indicate that Mr. Brett properly was called out, contrary to the League President's decision. The analysis is not complete, however, until the alternative method of analyzing the pine tar controversy is similarly examined.

### B. *Rules 1.10(b), 2.00 and 6.06(a)*

Application of Rules 1.10(b), 2.00 and 6.06(a) would apparently result in the player being called out for the use of excessive pine tar. A conflict among these rules, however, does exist. Although reading the rules simultaneously implies that a batter should be called out when he uses too much pine tar, Rule 1.10(b) merely seems to provide that the illegal bat should be removed from the game. This conflict was recognized by Mr. MacPhail who stated that "[i]f it was intended that [a pine-tar] infraction should fall under the penalty of the batter's being declared out, it does not seem logical that the rule should specifically specify that the bat should be removed from the game."[38]

The accepted maxim of construction is that the more specific rule will apply when there is a conflict between two rules.[39] Assuming that removal of the bat from the game and calling the player out are considered conflicting remedies, Rule 1.10(b), which specifically provides that a bat with excessive pine tar should be removed from the game, would be applicable in the instant situation. The two remedies, however, may be read consistently as they may apply to different factual situations. Removal of the bat is applicable if the batter has not hit the ball. Calling the player out, on the other hand, is applicable if he has. The two rules may therefore both be valid despite the inclusion of the specific remedy in Rule 1.10(b).

Reinforcing this result is the principle of construction which states that rules should be read so as to give effect to all parts of the statute.[40] If the remedy provided in Rule 1.10(b) is read as being an additional

---

(1981); Note, *Intent, Clear Statements, and the Common Law: Statutory Interpretation in the Supreme Court*, 95 Harv. L. Rev. 892, 895 (1982) (Supreme Court revived this maxim of construction) [hereinafter cited as *Clear Statements*]. *But see* Radin, *Statutory Interpretation*, 43 Harv. L. Rev. 863, 873-74 (1930) (criticism of use of maxim as "direct contradiction to the habits of speech of most persons").

38. *Brett* Decision, *supra* note 12, at 1.

39. Busic v. United States, 446 U.S. 398, 406 (1980); *see* Hill v. Morgan Power Apparatus Corp., 259 F. Supp. 609, 611 (E.D. Ark.), *aff'd*, 368 F.2d 230 (8th Cir. 1966).

40. *See* Noble v. Marshall, 650 F.2d 1058, 1061 (9th Cir. 1981); Citizens to Save Spencer County v. EPA, 600 F.2d 844, 870 (D.C. Cir. 1979).

remedy for a pine tar violation rather than as being in conflict with the remedy provided in Rules 6.06(a) and 2.00, all parts of the Rules are given effect. Both theories, however, lead to the conclusion that Mr. Brett should have been called out for the use of too much pine tar.

## C. *Rule of Lenity*

An additional consideration which must be addressed when analyzing both theories is the rule of lenity. The rule provides that penal statutes are to be strictly construed against the government[41]—in this case the umpires. Thus, any ambiguity in the rule must be decided in favor of the alleged violator—in this case the batter. The baseball rules, while not rules of law or equity,[42] are akin to penal statutes. The rules specify offenses and corresponding punishments.[43] Thus, although the two theories may be harmonized in favor of calling the batter out, the rule of lenity precludes the issue from being definitively resolved. Extrinsic aids to interpretation therefore must be utilized to resolve the conflict between the two sets of rules.

## III. Extrinsic Evidence

To determine the scope of a statute, courts examine legislative history and other extrinsic evidence. This section applies such analysis to the pine tar rule.[44]

## A. *Spirit versus Letter of the Law*

Mr. MacPhail stated that the umpire's decision was within the letter of the Rules, but "not in accord with the intent or spirit of the rules."[45] He noted that Rule 6.06(a), which refers to Rule 1.10, was intended to relate only to "doctored bats." He added that bats with excess pine tar should not be placed in this category.[46] Courts invoke such a rationale, known as equitable interpretation,[47] to remove an act from the scope

---

41. *See* Adamo Wrecking Co. v. United States, 434 U.S. 278, 285 (1978); United States v. Bass, 404 U.S. 336, 348 (1971); United States v. Patterson, 664 F.2d 1346, 1348 (9th Cir. 1982).

42. Aside, *The Common Law Origins of the Infield Fly Rule*, 123 U. Pa. L. Rev. 1474, 1474 (1975).

43. *See* Taylor v. United States, 44 U.S. (3 How.) 197, 210 (1845); E. Crawford, *supra* note 37, § 73, at 105 (1940).

44. See *supra* note 19.

45. *Brett* Decision, *supra* note 12, at 1.

46. *Id.* at 2. Judge Jacob Fuchsberg, recently retired from the New York Court of Appeals, agreed with Mr. MacPhail's ruling. Judge Fuchsberg, however, only referred to Rule 1.10 and not Rule 6.06(a), and based his opinion solely upon the effect of pine tar on hitting the ball. N.Y. Daily News, Aug. 2, 1983, at 29, col. 1.

47. *See* R. Dickerson, The Interpretation and Application of Statutes ch. 11, at 214 (1975); *Clear Statements*, *supra* note 37, at 896; *cf.* Berkow, *The Eternal Pine-*

of a statute.[48] Equitable interpretation may be traced to the writings of Hobbes, who[49] stated that the "[i]ntention of the Legislator is alwayes supposed to be Equity."[50] Aristotle referred to the doctrine as "epieikeia."[51] Under "epieikeia," a judge faced with a difficult case should put himself in the place of the legislator and do what the legislator would have done had he or she known of the present facts. In other words, a judge is obliged to legislate equitably.[52] Recently, however, the Supreme Court has moved away from equitable interpretation and from determining "what statutory words *ought* to mean."[53] Rather, the Court has established that the "law *is* what literal words proclaim it to be."[54] Thus, the League President's reliance upon equitable interpretation is not consistent with present Supreme Court philosophy.

## B. *Legislative Purpose*

A rule's purpose is often the touchstone of statutory construction.[55] "Purpose" is a broader concept than legislative intent.[56] A legislature's "purpose" is the ultimate purpose that the legislature intends the statute to accomplish or help to accomplish. Intent, on the other hand, refers to the immediate goal of the statute.[57] The legislative history of the Rules, therefore, must be examined to determine legislative purpose and intent, thus aiding in the resolution of the conflict between the two sets of Rules.

---

*Tar Case*, N.Y. Times, Aug. 9, 1983, at B9, col. 1 (Professor Halivni of the Jewish Theological Seminary, when discussing the pine tar incident, was reminded of the Talmudic lesson that it is anti-moral to use technical grounds to perpetrate chicanery.).

48. Muniz v. Hoffman, 422 U.S. 454, 469 (1975); *see* Bingler v. Johnson, 394 U.S. 741, 751-52 (1969).

49. Played first base. B. Abbott & L. Costello, *Who's on First*, on Hey Aaa-bott (1978 ed.) (Murray Hill Records no. 899981).

50. T. Hobbes, Leviathan 326 (C.B. MacPherson ed. 1968).

51. Aristotle, Nicomachean Ethics bk. 5, ch. 10, at 141-42 & n.69 (M. Ostwald trans. 1962); Marcin, Epieikeia; *Equitable Lawmaking in the Construction of Statutes*, 10 Conn. L. Rev. 377, 382-84 (1978).

52. Marcin, *supra* note 51, at 393.

53. *Clear Statements*, *supra* note 37, at 896 (emphasis in original).

54. *Id.* An indication whether the Court will continue this trend may be discerned by examining the decision in Washington Post Co. v. United States Dep't of State, 685 F.2d 698 (D.C. Cir. 1982), *cert. granted*, 104 S. Ct. 65 (1983), which involves the literal construction of a statute in apparent contravention of legislative intent and Congress' power under the statement and account clause of the Constitution, U.S. Const. art. I, § 9, cl. 7.

55. R. Dickerson, *supra* note 47, at 87.

56. *Id.* at 88.

57. *Id.*

The legislative history of the Official Baseball Rules is not available for public inspection.[58] The League President's statements and the drafters' public statements regarding their intent, therefore, must be scrutinized. According to Calvin Griffith, a member of the Playing Rules Committee, "[g]uys were slopping that pine tar stuff all over their bats. The balls were all getting discolored. The rule was put into effect to keep the bats from discoloring the balls and having them thrown out."[59] In addition, the accumulation of pine tar was also thought to allow a pitcher to cause the ball to behave erratically when thrown, similar to the outlawed "spit-ball."

The circumstances surrounding the passage of the legislation may also be examined to determine the intent of the drafters.[60] In response to a player being called out for excessive use of pine tar,[61] the rules were amended to provide that "material, including pine tar, which extends past the 18 inch limitation . . . shall cause the bat to be removed from the game."[62] Thus, despite the language of the rules, the drafters apparently intended this to be the exclusive remedy for a pine tar infraction.

Given these legislative purposes, the League President's decision was correct. This conclusion, however, must be viewed in light of the recent judicial trend towards relying upon the express language of a statute rather than ascertaining legislative intent through the use of extrinsic evidence.[63] Under this philosophy of statutory construction, the League President should not have considered the purpose of the drafters. The true purpose of the rule, however, may thus be frustrated. Despite this trend toward literal interpretation, courts usually examine the legislative history of a statute in order to reinforce their decision.[64] Thus, Mr. MacPhail should not be faulted for attempting to ascertain and follow the intent of the drafters. The correctness of his decision nevertheless depends upon the school of interpretation in vogue[65] at the time of the adjudication of the controversy.

---

58. For an irrelevant yet interesting discussion of unpublished opinions see Fenner v. Dependable Trucking Co., 716 F.2d 605, 606 (9th Cir. 1983) (Chambers, J., dissenting) ("Someone here has the horse headed the wrong way between the shafts of the buggy. His head is up against the single tree and the dashboard, and I do not think the first memorandum should be 'depublicized.' ").

59. St. Louis Post Dispatch, July 26, 1983, at 30, col. 1.

60. *See* United States v. Curtis-Nevada Mines, Inc., 611 F.2d 1277, 1280 (9th Cir. 1980).

61. *Brett* Decision, *supra* note 12, at 2.

62. Off. Baseball R. 1.10(b) (Sporting News 1983) (amended 1984).

63. *See Clear Statements, supra* note 37, at 894.

64. *See* Potomac Elec. Power Co. v. Director, OWCP, 449 U.S. 268, 273-80 (1980); Mohasco Corp. v. Silver, 447 U.S. 807, 823, 826 (1980). *But see* Mobil Oil Corp. v. Higginbotham, 436 U.S. 618 (1978) (no discussion of legislative history).

65. *See, e.g., New Ground Rules—Shoes, Stockings and more,* Vogue, July 1983, at 184; *Vogue Patterns: The All-Star Wardrobe, id.* at 240.

## IV. Precedent

*In re Brett* is not the first case involving excess pine tar to come before Mr. MacPhail. At least two players have had hits nullified by an umpire's pine tar call. In 1975, both Thurman Munson[66] of the New York Yankees and Steve Stone[67] of the Chicago Cubs were called out for use of excessive pine tar.[68] Neither of these incidents were protested to the league office. A third incident in which the umpires did not call the batter out is the only case in which a formal protest forced the league to establish precedent.[69] In that case, the California Angels protested a loss to the Kansas City Royals on the ground that John Mayberry,[70] who hit two home runs in the game, had pine tar on his bat beyond the 18 inch limit. The protest was denied.[71] Mr. MacPhail ruled that a ball hit with a bat covered with excess pine tar was not "an illegally batted ball under Rule 6.06(a)."[72] Thus, Mr. MacPhail's decision in *Brett* was consistent with the rationale in *Mayberry*.

## V. Policy Considerations

The pine tar decision may have a significant impact on the game of baseball. By overturning the umpire's decision, Mr. MacPhail has taken away a traditional managerial tactic—to use the rules to your best advantage. "[C]lever ploys and gambits are a part of the essence and history of baseball . . ."[73] and tampering with this tradition erodes part of the game's charm.

---

66. Position: catcher. Batted right, threw right. Batted .318 in 1975, despite being called out for use of excessive pine tar. *See* 1976 Topps Baseball Card no. 650.

67. Position: pitcher. Bats right, throws right. 1976 Topps Baseball Card no. 378. Taking away a base hit from a pitcher is almost cruel and unusual punishment. *See* U.S. Const. amend. VIII.

68. Boswell, *supra* note 13, at C6, col. 1.

69. *Id.*; St. Louis Post Dispatch, July 26, 1983, at 30, col. 1.

70. Position: first base. Bats left, throws left. Had 34 home runs in 1975, due in part to the favorable ruling. 1976 Topps Baseball Card no. 440.

71. Boswell, *supra* note 13, at C6, col. 1; St. Louis Post Dispatch, July 26, 1983, at 30, col. 1.

72. *Brett* Decision, *supra* note 12, at 2.

73. Berkow, *supra* note 47, at B9, col. 3; *see* B. Catton, *The Great American Game*, in The Third Fireside Book of Baseball 90, 91 (C. Einstein ed. 1968) (Baseball has "borrowed nothing from the 'sportsmanship' of more sedate countries . . . . Anything goes; victory is what counts."). *Contra* St. Louis Post Dispatch, July 26, 1983, at 30, col. 3 ("Games are supposed to be decided by skills of players, not technicalities and loopholes.").

Baseball is filled with such artful uses of the rules. Perhaps the most famous is the case of Eddie Gaedel, a midget, being sent to bat for the St. Louis Browns. The act was not favored by the league and the rules were changed to eliminate this possibility from occurring again. *See* B. Veeck & E. Linn, *Veeck—as in Wreck*, in The Third

Moreover, the impact of the pine tar decision may be felt far beyond the immediate controversy. The sanctity of an umpire's ruling is undermined. The pine tar ruling was the first instance during Mr. McPhail's tenure as League President in which an umpire's decision was overruled.[74] This reversal of a technically valid decision may diminish the respect[75] afforded umpires' decisions in the future.[76] It may be argued that the power to overrule a decision made on the field should be reserved for situations in which there is a clear abuse of discretion by an umpire or when there is a clear error in applying the rules.[77] Of course, there will be decisions by the umpires that the

---

Fireside Book of Baseball 479, 479-86 (1968). Perhaps the most consequential use of the rules involved Fred Merkle of the New York Giants in 1908—it cost the Giants the pennant. On September 23, 1908, the Giants were playing against the Chicago Cubs. The score was tied 1-1 as the Giants batted in the bottom of the ninth inning. The Giants put men on first and third with two outs. The next batter singled to center field. The runner on third base crossed home plate with the apparent winning run. The crowd poured onto the field. The runner on first base, Fred Merkle, however, failed to touch second base, instead running for the clubhouse. The Cub's second baseman noticed this and called for the ball. Following a number of mishaps including the ball being thrown into the stands, a substitute ball was thrown to second base. The umpire called Merkle out, and the run did not count. The league office ruled that Merkle was out when he failed to touch second base. Thus, despite the unfairness of the situation, the literal application of the rule was upheld, which disallows any runs scored during a play resulting in the final out of an inning. *See* C. Gregory, H. Kalven & R. Epstein, Cases and Materials on Torts 926-27 (3d ed. 1977); J. Rosenburg, The Story of Baseball 51-58 (1966). Other instances of artful manipulation of the rules include the hidden ball trick, and decoying runners to set up force outs on fly balls. Berkow, *supra* note 47, at B9, col. 3.

74. Boswell, *supra* note 13, at C6, col. 1.

75. For a deeper understanding of respect *hear* O. Redding, *Respect*, on The Soul Years-Atlantic Records 25th Anniversary (A. Franklin ed. 1967) (Atlantic Record no. ST-A-732887 PR); R. Dangerfield *passim*.

76. N.Y. Post, July 29, 1983, at 88, col. 3 (Tim McClelland, home plate umpire during the pine-tar game, stated that "[t]he rulebook is the only thing we have to go by, and if someone wants to make a farce of the rules by saying they're not in the spirit of the game, then we'll have to be men and take it."); *id.* at 82, col. 6 (Richie Phillips, a former umpire and counsel for the Major League Umpires Ass'n stated that the decision "is not going to sit well with our membership. They have a concern about how much support they get from the league offices. . . . [T]his is not going to help.").

77. An example of an umpire clearly misreading the rules occurred in a game between the Boston Red Sox and the Chicago White Sox at Fenway Park on September 3, 1983. Chicago's Jerry Dybzinski came to the plate with none out and runners on first and second. The count was no balls and two strikes when the next pitch hit Dybzinski, who started toward first even though he bunted at the ball, only to be called out by the first-base umpire. While he argued, the two base runners moved up one base. When the "discussions" ebbed, both runners were allowed to remain on second and third base. *See* Boston Globe, Sept. 4, 1983, at 44, col. 2. This is clearly an incorrect result as Rule 6.08(b) states that "[w]hen the batter is touched by a pitched ball which does not entitle him to first base, the ball is dead and no runner

League President will consider to be within the letter of the rules, but not the spirit. Instructing umpires to conform to the spirit of the rules in the future can resolve these inconsistencies.

The umpires' decision in the pine tar controversy could be viewed as a clear abuse of discretion, even though technically defensible, because it was contrary to previous decisions of the League President. This argument, however, assumes that the umpires had a[78] knowledge of the appeals that had been ruled on by the league.[79] An annotated rule book containing the decisions in all appeals may solve this problem. Alternatively, the rules could clearly set out the league policy on various issues and those rules that are in direct conflict with these policies could be eliminated.

## CONCLUSION

Kansas City Royals 5, New York Yankees 4.

*Jared Tobin Finkelstein**

---

may advance." Off. Baseball R. 6.08(b) (Sporting News 1983). In this case, the umpire involved freely admitted that he had made a mistake in allowing both runners to move up a base. Boston Globe, Sept. 4, 1983, at 44, col. 2. This would be an appropriate instance for the league president to overrule an umpire's decision.

78. "A" stands for answer to the trivia question, *supra* note 17. The four Triple Crown winners who were not Most Valuable Players were Chuck Klein, Lou Gehrig, and Ted Williams twice. D. Lally, A Bartender's Guide to Baseball 71, 221 (1981).

79. One commentator notes that the umpires should have known of the *Mayberry* protest and the two other 1975 pine tar incidents and were irresponsible for not following the *Mayberry* ruling. *See* Sports Illustrated, Aug. 8, 1983, at 60.

* The author would like to express his appreciation to Stacey Lane and Stephanie Vardavas for their assistance in the preparation of this Commentary.

# A PINE TAR GLOSS ON QUASI-LEGAL IMAGES

*Christopher H. Clancy\* and Jonathan A. Weiss\*\**

## INTRODUCTION

To understand the adjudication of the pine tar dispute, one must first analyze the decisionmaking model that should be, and often implicitly is, used in the sport of baseball. The thesis of this Article is that there has been an increased use of judicial-type decisionmaking throughout the various organizations that we encounter in our daily lives and in the sports world. Baseball, in particular, provides a framework that is readily adaptable to judicial-type decisionmaking. This is true despite the fact that, in numerous contexts, baseball has been afforded different treatment than other sports. For example, baseball has been provided a unique exception to the antitrust laws. The origin of this treatment can be found in Justice Holmes' opinion[1] in *Federal Baseball Club v. National League of Professional Baseball Clubs.*[2] There the Court held the Sherman Act to be inapplicable

---

* Professor, Seton Hall University School of Law; A.B., 1960, J.D., 1963, University of Maine.

** Director, Legal Services for the Elderly; B.A., 1960, LL.B., 1963, Yale University.

[1] An opinion that must rank with some of his most outrageous. See generally, e.g., Buck v. Bell, 274 U.S. 200, 207 (1927) ("Three generations of imbeciles are enough.").

[2] 259 U.S. 200 (1922). This was the first case in which the Supreme Court considered whether the Sherman Act, ch. 647, 26 Stat. 209 (1890) (current version at 15 U.S.C. §§ 1–7 (1982)), applied to organized baseball. Baltimore's team, the only remaining franchise in the long extinct Federal League, sued the National and American Leagues, alleging that the defendants had conspired to monopolize the baseball business by buying some Federal League teams and inducing others to leave. 259 U.S. at 207. Justice Holmes did not find it necessary to consider the merits of the case because the defendant's conduct was found not to involve commerce among the states, and hence, was not subject to Sherman Act scrutiny. See id. at 209.

It should be recalled that 14 years earlier the Supreme Court had applied the Sherman Act to organized labor. See Loewe v. Lawlor, 208 U.S. 274 (1908). *Loewe,* written by Chief Justice Fuller for a unanimous Court of which Justice Holmes was a member, produced considerable controversy as to whether organized labor was the object of President Roosevelt's trust-busting legislation. Compare A. Mason, Organized Labor and the Law 119–42 (1925) (favoring such application) with E. Berman, Labor and the Sherman Act 51–54 (1930) (rejecting such application). For the definitive study in this area, see Boudin, The Sherman Act and Labor Disputes (pt. 1), 39 Colum. L. Rev. 1283 (1939). In all, the *Loewe* case remained in the courts for 14 years. See W. Merritt, History of the League for Industrial Rights 28 (1925). The final judgment, holding more than 100 individual union members personally liable, was in excess of $250,000. Loewe v. Lawlor, 235 U.S. 522 (1915), aff'g 209 F. 721 (2d Cir. 1913). As one commentator remarked, "[p]robably no case, except the Dred Scott decision, ever caused greater agitation in legal and political circles, and few, if any, have exercised greater influence on our industrial institutions." W. Merritt, supra, at 31; see id. at 22–31.

because the case involved "purely state affairs."[3] Significantly, however, the case has generally been cited for the proposition that baseball is a "sport" and not a business.[4]

Reactions such as this go far to explain how baseball has successfully retained its unique status in situations where boxing,[5] football,[6]
basketball[7] and hockey[8] have failed. Yet, such uniqueness seems unfounded. The pine tar incident provides a fine example of how the
myth of baseball's unique status can be debunked. This Article goes
one step further, demonstrating that the entire decisionmaking process
in baseball can be, and should be, analogized to that of the judicial
system in general, and administrative decision making bodies in particular.

## I. Quasi-Legal Institutions

Administrative agencies issue rules and regulations that serve to
clarify details of the statutory mandates to which the rules and regulations pertain.[9] In administering the statutes and the regulations, agencies also make determinations as to which specific provisions cover

---

[3] 259 U.S. at 208. As Justice Holmes noted: "Of course the scheme [of the National and
American Leagues] requires constantly repeated travelling on the part of the clubs, which is
provided for, controlled and disciplined by the organizations . . . ." Id. According to Justice
Holmes, however, "[t]he business [of] giving exhibitions of base ball [is a] purely state affair[ ],"
id., and "the fact that in order to give the exhibitions the Leagues must induce free persons to
cross state lines, and must arrange and pay for their doing so is not enough to change the
character of the business." Id. at 208–09.

[4] Flood v. Kuhn, 407 U.S. 258, 270 n.10 (1972) (quoting 2 H. Seymour, Baseball 420
(1971)).

[5] See United States v. International Boxing Club, Inc., 348 U.S. 236 (1955).

[6] See Radovich v. National Football League, 352 U.S. 445 (1957). After the Court decided
*Radovich*, Learned Hand wrote Justice Frankfurter: "You and your eight fellow saints at time
push hard upon our insufficient dialectical equipment; for example, to the Lower Orders it
seems difficult to distinguish baseball and football." B. Schwartz, Super Chief 214 (1983)
(quoting letter from Hand to Frankfurter (Feb. 26, 1957)).

[7] See Haywood v. National Basketball Ass'n, 401 U.S. 1204 (1971).

[8] See Philadelphia World Hockey Club, Inc. v. Philadelphia Hockey Club, Inc., 351 F.
Supp. 462 (E.D. Pa. 1972).

[9] One principal advantage of such rulemaking is that it provides clear articulation of
present and past agency policies. The Administrative Procedure Act, 5 U.S.C. §§ 552(c)–(d), 553
(1982), requires that an agency publish its rules and make them readily available to all who are
affected by them. Some agencies publish a plethora of rules and regulations, see, e.g., Treas.
Reg. §§ 1.01 to 55.4981-1 (1982) (regulations issued by the Internal Revenue Service); 29 C.F.R.
§§ 0.735-1 to 2704.310 (1983) (regulations issued by Dept. of Labor), though they are occasionally riddled with inconsistencies. Other agencies, however, virtually ignore the rulemaking
provisions of the Administrative Procedure Act. For example, although the National Labor
Relations Board (NLRB) oversees the labor-management policy for the entire nation, it has *never*
utilized the Act's rulemaking procedures. As a result, the NLRB often has been criticized for

given situations. Decisions of this type arise in a wide variety of settings.[10] To satisfy this demand, administrative agencies allow relatively low level decisionmakers—e.g., intake, contract and hearing officers—to act as impartial adjudicators of disputes. As a result, questions of internal appellate procedure are often of great significance.

Though it seems obvious that the availability of rational appellate review is necessary and desirable, it is not constitutionally mandated. The Supreme Court has held, in other areas, that due process does not necessarily include the right to appellate review,[11] though the

---

directly contravening the Act. See NLRB v. Wyman-Gordon Co., 394 U.S. 759, 765 n.3 (1969); id. at 779 (Douglas, J., dissenting); id. at 781 (Harlan, J., dissenting); NLRB v. Bell Aerospace Co., 416 U.S. 267, 294 (1974) (unequivocally adopting the Court's position in *Wyman-Gordon*). For a more detailed discussion of *Wyman-Gordon*, see Bernstein, The NLRB's Adjudication-Rule Making Dilemma Under the Administrative Procedure Act, 79 Yale L.J. 571, 598–610 (1970); The Supreme Court, 1968 Term, 83 Harv. L. Rev. 62, 220–27, 223 n.15.

[10] See, e.g., 38 U.S.C. § 211 (1976) ("the decisions of the Administrator on any question of law or fact under any law administered by the Veteran's Administration . . . shall be final and exclusive").

[11] Two important Warren Court decisions grappled with both equal protection, as applied to criminal procedure, and due process rationales. See Douglas v. California, 372 U.S. 353 (1963); Griffin v. Illinois, 351 U.S. 12 (1956). In *Griffin*, the Court held that a state's refusal to provide indigent defendants with a free copy of the trial record, thereby preventing defendants from obtaining appellate review, violated the due process and equal protection clauses. Id. at 17–19. Justice Black, writing for a plurality of the Court, stated:

> [A] State is not required by the Federal Constitution to provide appellate courts or a right to appellate review at all. . . . But that is not to say that a state that does grant appellate review can do so in a way that discriminates against some convicted defendants on account of their poverty.
>
> . . . There can be no equal justice where the kind of trial a man gets depends on the amount of money he has. Destitute defendants must be afforded as adequate appellate review as defendants who have money enough to buy transcripts.

Id. at 18–19. Justice Frankfurter concurred separately, while Justices Burton and Minton, joined by Justices Reed and Harlan, dissented.

Justice Black's plurality opinion in *Griffin* should be read together with his earlier procedural due process opinion in Chambers v. Florida, 309 U.S. 227 (1940). In striking down a Florida death sentence imposed on four black tenant farmers, Justice Black commented: "Under our constitutional system, courts stand against any winds that blow as havens of refuge for those who might otherwise suffer because they are helpless, weak, outnumbered, or because they are non-conforming victims of prejudice and public excitement." Id. at 241. Many consider *Chambers* to be a critical point in Justice Black's judicial philosophy. E.g., G. Dunne, Hugo Black and the Judicial Revolution 301 (1977); Reich, Mr. Justice Black and the Living Constitution, 76 Harv. L. Rev. 673, 679 (1963).

*Douglas*, 372 U.S 353, was a companion case to Gideon v. Wainwright, 372 U.S. 335 (1963)—the famous decision that constitutionally mandated the appointment of counsel for indigents in felony cases. Relying heavily on *Griffin*, the *Douglas* Court held that indigent defendants were denied equal protection because the state failed to provide them counsel for the one appeal of right afforded under state law. However, Justice Harlan, joined by Justice Stewart, stated in an emotional dissent:

rationales for such decisions are not entirely clear. Accordingly, in some agencies, no provisions exist for appellate procedures.[12] Among those administrative agencies that do have such provisions, the rules governing hearings often vary from those of judicial proceedings and from agency to agency. For example, rules pertaining to hearsay, introduction of doctors' testimony and admissability of evidence are far more lenient than those applicable in courtroom proceedings.[13]

---

> Laws such as these do not deny equal protection to the less fortunate for one essential reason: the Equal Protection Clause does not impose on the States "an affirmative duty to lift the handicaps flowing from differences in economic circumstances." To so construe it would be to read into the Constitution a philosophy of leveling that would be foreign to many of our basic concepts of the proper relations between government and society. The State may have a moral obligation to eliminate the evils of poverty, but it is not required by the Equal Protection Clause to give to some whatever others can afford.

372 U.S. at 362 (quoting *Griffin*, 351 U.S. at 34 (Harlan, J., dissenting)).

Curiously, Justice Harlan wrote for the majority in the subsequent due process case of Boddie v. Connecticut, 401 U.S. 371 (1971), which allowed indigents access to the state's divorce courts without the payment of court costs. Justices Douglas, id. at 383, 386, and Brennan, id. at 388, concurred with the Court on equal protection grounds under the *Griffin* rationale. Justice Black, however, refused to extend the *Griffin* standard to civil cases, and accordingly, he dissented. Justice Harlan wrote for the Court:

> [B]ecause resort to the state courts is the only avenue to dissolution of their marriages, [plaintiff's plight] is akin to that of defendants faced with exclusion from the only forum effectively empowered to settle their disputes. Resort to the judicial process by these plaintiffs is no more voluntary in a realistic sense than that of the defendant called upon to defend his interests in court. For both groups this process is not only the paramount dispute-settlement technique, but, in fact, the only available one.
>
>     . . . .
>
>     . . . [D]ue process requires, at a minimum, that absent a countervailing state interest of overriding significance, persons forced to settle their claims of right and duty through the judicial process must be given a meaningful opportunity to be heard.

Id. at 376–77. It is interesting to note that, subsequent to Justice Harlan's death and replacement by Justice Rehnquist, two 5-4 decisions came down denying access to the courts. See Ortwein v. Schwab, 410 U.S. 656 (1973) (per curiam) (upholding a $25.00 filing fee imposed by the state of Oregon as a requirement for court review of welfare benefit denials); United States v. Kras, 409 U.S. 434 (1973) (upholding payment of statutory fees as a condition for access to bankruptcy court). The four dissenters, in both cases, were Justices Douglas, Brennan, Stewart and Marshall.

[12] See Gray Panthers v. Schweiker, 652 F. 2d 146, 149 (D.C. Cir. 1980) (no appellate review for Medicare claims involving amounts less than $100).

[13] See, e.g., Richardson v. Perales, 402 U.S. 389 (1971). In *Perales*, a claimant sought Social Security disability benefits because of a severe back injury. According to the only doctor who had both examined the claimant and testified at the district court level, the injury would leave the claimant permanently disabled. Perales v. Secretary of Health, Educ. & Welfare, 288 F. Supp. 313, 314 (W.D. Tex. 1968), aff'd sub nom. Cohen v. Perales, 412 F.2d 44 (5th Cir. 1969), rev'd sub nom. *Richardson v. Perales*, 402 U.S. 389. The Supreme Court concluded that hearsay evidence, in the form of medical reports of five doctors who examined the claimant, could be

The primary problem with administrative procedures, particularly those affecting the poor, is that decisionmakers are not sufficiently accountable. This is predominantly due to the lack of visibility of agency decisionmaking procedures. As a result, of those individuals who come before agencies, few can understand their predicament and many are victimized by the irrationality, arbitrariness or avoidance of appropriate law.[14]

The attempts to rationalize administrative law procedures generally have revolved around issues such as due process, notice and hearing.[15] The essential thrust of such litigation has been that deci-

---

admitted in a disability hearing even though none of the doctors was subject to cross-examination. 402 U.S. at 402.

In pleading his case, the claimant relied heavily on the Supreme Court's holding and rationale in Goldberg v. Kelly, 397 U.S. 254 (1970), particularly emphasing the comment that due process requires notice and " 'an effective opportunity to defend by confronting any adverse witnesses.' " 402 U.S. at 406 (quoting *Goldberg*, 397 U.S. at 268). Both the district court, 288 F. Supp. at 314, and the court of appeals, 412 F.2d 44, agreed with this argument. The Supreme Court, however, reversed, holding that procedural due process was not violated. Justice Blackmun, expressing the views of six members of the Court, wrote for the majority:

> [A]uthority [is] given the Secretary [of Health, Education and Welfare] . . . "to establish procedures" and "to regulate and provide for the nature and extent of the proofs and evidence and the method of taking and furnishing the same in order to establish the right to benefits," and to receive evidence "even though inadmissable under rules of evidence applicable to court procedure."

402 U.S. 409–10 (quoting Social Security Act § 205(a)–(b), 42 U.S.C. § 405(a)–(b) (1976)). According to the majority, "[h]earsay . . . is thus admissible up to the point of relevancy." 402 U.S. at 410.

[14] Weiss, The Law and the Poor, 26 J. Soc. Issues 59, 60–61 (1970). For an interesting short story dealing with this subject, see N. Gogol, The Overcoat, in Diary of a Madman and Other Short Stories (A. MacAndrews trans. 1960).

[15] See Goldberg v. Kelly, 397 U.S. 254 (1970), perhaps the high-water mark of the procedural due process decisions. In *Goldberg*, the Court invalidated a New York State Aid to Families with Dependant Children regulation that failed to require that a recipient be afforded an evidentiary hearing prior to termination of benefits. The Court, per Justice Brennan, required that at least seven procedural necessities be made available to the claimant at a pretermination evidentiary hearing. For example, the Court noted that "[w]ritten submissions are an unrealistic option for most recipients, who lack the educational attainment necessary to write effectively and who cannot obtain professional assistance." Id. at 269. Thus, the Court found that "a recipient must be allowed to state his position orally." Id. Similarly, in finding that "the recipient must be allowed to retain an attorney if he so desires," the Court noted that "[c]ounsel can help delineate the issues, present the factual contentions in an orderly manner, conduct cross-examination, and generally safeguard the interests of the recipient." Id. at 270–71. Other requirements outlined by the Court include timely and adequate notice, an opportunity to confront and cross-examine adverse parties, a statement by the decisionmaker of the evidence relied upon and an impartial decisionmaker. Id. at 267–71.

In Arnett v. Kennedy, 416 U.S. 134 (1974), however, the Court chose to interpret *Goldberg* restrictively. The *Arnett* Court noted that "*Goldberg* held that welfare recipients are entitled under the due process clause of the fifth and fourteenth amendments to an adversary hearing before their benefits are terminated." Id. at 154. The plurality opinion, written by Justice Rehnquist and joined in by Chief Justice Burger and Justice Stewart, rejected the claim, made by an employee discharged for cause, that the statutory hearing procedures were constitutionally

sions must be clear and rational, on the record and subject to rational review.[16] Without such procedures, the advantages sought to be achieved through administrative efficiency are lost, and are replaced by the costly burdens invariably caused by procedural irrationality. For example, in the area of disputes concerning Social Security benefits, it is all too common for cases to go up to federal court only later to be remanded.[17]

In family court, a similar phenomenon exists. Family law was orginially predicated upon the idea that the proper socialization of children in no way necessitated formal judicial proceedings. However, because of the informal procedures in family court, cliches such as "the best interest of the child" were often manipulated in nonjudicial and lawless ways. As a result, it was not rare for children to be brutalized or placed in horrific prison facilities.[18] The essential, and appropriate, response of those concerned with preserving the rights of juveniles was an attempt to implement judicial-type proceedings in family court.[19] Today, to a far greater extent than was true in the past, the procedures of family court adhere to those of more formal tribunals. An example of this can be seen in the area of neglect

---

inadequate. Justice Rehnquist emphasized that the procedural limitations Congress placed on the hearing procedures were part of the same statutory scheme that created the substantive right upon which petitioner based his claim. Id. at 152. The "bitter with the sweet" doctrine was thus created. According to Justice Rehnquist, "[t]he employee's statutorily defined right is not a guarantee against removal without cause in the abstract, but such a guarantee as enforced by the procedures which Congress has designated for the determination of cause." Id. at 152. "[W]here the grant of a substantive right is inextricably intertwined with the limitations on the procedures which are to be employed in determining that right, a litigant in the position of [the discharged employee] must take the bitter with the sweet." Id. at 153–54.

The other six Justices hearing *Kennedy*, although of differing opinions as to the adequacy of the statutory procedures, rejected Justice Renhquist's constitutional analysis and agreed that the due process clause imposed restraints on such procedures. See L. Tribe, American Constitutional Law § 10-12, at 533–34 (1978). In Bishop v. Wood, 426 U.S. 341 (1976), however, the Court effectively adopted Justice Rehnquist's "bitter with the sweet" approach. See id. at 353 n.4 (Brennan, J., dissenting).

[16] See K. Davis, Administrative Law of the Seventies, Supplementing Administrative Law Treatise § 7.00, at 242 (1976).

[17] E.g., Cutler v. Weinberger, 516 F.2d 1282 (2d Cir. 1975); Gold v. Secretary of Health, Educ. & Welfare, 463 F.2d 38 (2d Cir. 1972).

[18] See Weiss, The Poor Kid, 9 Duq. L. Rev. 590 (1971). See generally, F. Allen, The Juvenile Court and the Limits of Juvenile Justice, in The Borderland of Criminal Justice 43, 47 (1964) (juvenile court represents a reaction against the "inhumanity of criminal justice in confronting the problem of the misbehaving child").

[19] Weiss, The Emerging Rights of Minors, 4 U. Tol. L. Rev. 25 (1972); see, e.g., Uniform Juvenile Court Act §§ 1–37, 9A U.L.A. 5–39 (1979).

proceedings, where parents are now afforded counsel as a matter of constitutional right.[20]

Corporations, too, increasingly have been compelled to model their procedures after those encountered in judicial factfinding and appellate review. Workers are given personnel manuals, evaluations and reviews. Decisions regarding pay raises and terminations are supposedly based upon these written records and proceed in a rational manner. This type of structure should prevent the firing of an employee at will.[21] In various types of discrimination suits—for example,

---

[20] *In re* B., 30 N.Y.2d 352, 285 N.E.2d 288, 344 N.Y.S.2d 133 (1972); cf. *In re* Gault, 387 U.S. 1 (1967) (child facing commitment to state institution entitled to court-appointed counsel).

[21] At common law, in the absence of an employment contract, employers and employees have been free to terminate their relationship with or without cause. This rule, during the heyday of substantive due process, temporarily attained constitutional magnitude. See Adair v. United States, 208 U.S. 161 (1908). In *Adair*, the Supreme Court held unconstitutional an act making it illegal for a railroad to prohibit an employee from joining a union. Id. at 172 (declaring Erdmann Act, ch. 370, 30 Stat. 424 (1898), to be "an invasion of the personal liberty, as well as of the right of property, guaranteed by the [Fifth] Amendment"); see also Coppage v. Kansas, 236 U.S. 1, 13–14 (1915) (applying the principles of *Adair* to similar state statutes). As a corollary of the development of legislation, see, e.g., Norris-LaGuardia Act § 3, 29 U.S.C. § 103 (1982); National Labor Relations Act § 1, 29 U.S.C. § 151 (1982), and judicial decisionmaking, see Lincoln Fed. Labor Union v. Northwestern Iron & Metal Co., 335 U.S. 525 (1949) (explicitly rejecting the constitutional principles enunciated in *Adair*); NLRB v. Jones & Laughlin Steel Corp., 301 U.S. 1 (1937).

Employment at will is a common law rule that provides that "an employer, unless otherwise limited by an express term in the employment agreement, [can] discharge an employee for any reason whatsoever without legal liability." Note, A Common Law Action for the Abusively Discharged Employee, 26 Hastings L.J. 1435, 1435 (1975); see also Blades, Employment at Will v. Individual Freedom: On Limiting the Abusive Exercise of Employer Power, 67 Colum. L. Rev. 1404, 1421–27 (1967) (advocating judicial remedy for wrongfully discharged employees based on tort principles). See generally Note, Protecting At Will Employees Against Wrongful Discharge: The Duty to Terminate Only in Good Faith, 93 Harv. L. Rev. 1816, 1844 (1980) (surveying employment at will doctrine and concluding that "courts should imply a contract term allowing only good faith discharges, or create a tort duty that employers discharge only in good faith").

Definitive cases on the employment at will rule and its recent trends include: Pierce v. Ortho Pharmaceutical Corp., 84 N.J. 58, 417 A.2d 505 (1980); Murphy v. American Home Prods. Corp., 58 N.Y.2d 293, 448 N.E.2d 86, 461 N.Y.S.2d 232 (1983); and Weiner v. McGraw-Hill, Inc., 57 N.Y.2d 458, 443 N.E.2d 441, 457 N.Y.S.2d 193 (1982). *Pierce* indicates a willingness on the part of courts to "balance the interests of employee, employer and *the public*." 84 N.J. at 71, 417 A.2d at 511 (emphasis added). This leads the court to conclude that the common law should limit the right of an employer to fire an employee at will. See id. at 72, 417 A.2d at 512 ("Absent legislation, the judiciary must define the cause of action in case-by-case determinations."). In determining whether a discharge was contrary to public policy, the court in *Pierce* directed: "The sources of public policy include legislation; administrative rules, regulations or decisions; and judicial decisions." Id. As a result, "[e]mployees will be secure in knowing that their jobs are safe if they exercise their rights in accordance with a clear mandate of public policy." Id. at 73, 417 A.2d at 512.

those concerning title VII and age discrimination—findings of discrimination are often grounded on the fact that employers have not based employee placement or termination decisions upon job descriptions, evaluations and reviews.[22] Once again, the importance of running programs rationally is clearly recognized. Similarly, union contracts provide mechanisms to handle grievances, adjudications, arbitrations and reviews, and further provide that these should proceed in the manner required by administrative due process.[23] Thus, in a wide variety of areas, due process concerns have been introduced successfully by way of reference to the judicial model.

The world of sports is no stranger to this model of adjudication. Baseball, in particular, has elaborate rules that invite a great deal of discussion regarding their meaning and possible alteration. Weekly

---

In *Murphy*, on the other hand, the court took the opposite tack. Rather than appreciate the need for judicial action in the face of legislative inaction, the court refused to intervene on behalf of the employee without explicit direction from the legislature. See *Murphy*, 58 N.Y.2d at 301, 448 N.E.2d at 89, 461 N.Y.S.2d at 235. As a result of such intentional blindness on the part of courts, employees are left to fend for themselves—a futile endeavor in virtually all employment at will arrangements.

[22] See generally, e.g., Valentino v. United States Postal Serv., 674 F.2d 56 (D.C. Cir. 1982) (no discrimination where employer produced evidence of a legitimate, nondiscriminatory reason for not promoting employee); Melani v. Board of Higher Educ., 561 F. Supp. 769 (S.D.N.Y. 1983) (violation of title VII where salary differential was not linked to objective criteria, e.g., years of service, performance, etc.).

[23] Collective bargaining in the public sector of the labor-management relations area entails dealings between an employer and the bargaining representative of his workers concerning matter such as wages, hours, working conditions and grievance procedures. As one might imagine, the variety of issues that may emerge from such agreements is wide. Prior to the enactment of section 301 of the Taft-Hartley Act, 29 U.S.C. § 185 (1982), the legal status of collective bargaining agreements was unclear. Such agreements had been characterized by some courts as mere gentlemen's agreements, unenforceable at law. See Gregory, The Collective Bargaining Agreement: Its Nature and Scope, 1949 Wash. U.L.Q. 3, 11. Similarly, the Supreme Court had stated that such agreements were merely schedules of terms and commitments and could be "likened to the tariffs established by a carrier." J.I. Case Co. v. NLRB, 321 U.S. 332, 335 (1944). This spawned much confusion as most unions were not incorporated and could not be legal parties to contracts. Since they were not legally recognized parties, they could not act as plaintiffs in lawsuits to enforce collective bargaining agreements. For a detailed discussion and history, see Gregory, supra.

Since the enactment of section 301, the courts have taken a different view towards collective bargaining agreements, often ordering arbitration in accordance with the specific agreements. See United Steelworkers of America v. Enterprise Wheel & Car Corp., 363 U.S. 593 (1960); United Steelworkers of America v. Warrior & Gulf Navigation Co., 363 U.S. 574 (1960); United Steelworkers of America v. American Mfg. Co., 363 U.S. 564 (1960). As Justice Douglas stated in *Warrior & Gulf*, "arbitration of labor disputes . . . is part and parcel of the collective bargaining process itself." 363 U.S. at 578. See generally Comment, Collective Bargaining and the No-Strike Clause: The *Sinclair Refining* Case, 15 Me. L. Rev. 93 (1963) (discussing several decisions enunciating strong policy in favor of resolving labor disputes by arbitration). For more extensive discussions of these three cases—commonly known as "the arbitration trilogy," see Aaron,

columns in publications such as the *Sporting News* deal at length with the proper interpretation of these rules.[24] The *Sporting News* also publishes books that examine extremely difficult questions of interpretation presented by specific situations.[25] In these columns and books, there is rarely equivocation as to whether a rule has been interpreted correctly or incorrectly on a particular occasion. Distinct and definite answers are offered by the authors; answers that are often less equivocal than Supreme Court pronouncements.

What emerges from this brief examination of these diverse institutions—adminstrative agencies, family court, corporations and sports—are several common principles. All these institutions are governed by written rules, and all are administered by reference to those rules. In all these institutions, initial decisions are made upon a rational presentation of evidence and are subject to review upon the record in accordance with rules governing appeals. Underlying all these procedures are concerns with due process, freedom of association and freedom of contract.

Whatever the institutional setting, a dispute may involve one or more of three different elements. First, it may raise what loosely can be called questions of law. For example, when a corporation defines productivity in a certain area, it does so by means of specific quotas. The meaning of these quotas is a question of law. The same situation might also give rise to questions of fact. For instance, whether work was performed properly would raise a question of fact. Finally, a dispute may demand recognition of contractual obligations. When an individual files an application with an adminstrative agency, he states certain facts to which the agency then responds, thereby creating a quasi-contract. Similarly, when an employee enters into an employment relationship with a corporation, and the corporation distributes a personnel manual by which it agrees to be bound, a contractual situation exists.[26] In both situations, issues may be raised as to the extent of the parties' obligations.

---

Arbitration in the Federal Courts: Aftermath of the Trilogy, 9 U.C.L.A. L. Rev. 360 (1962). For further discussion of collective bargaining implications involving enforcement of pension plan agreements, see Preminger & Clancy, Aspects of Federal Jurisdiction Under Sections 302(c)(5) and 302(e) of the Taft-Hartley Act—The "Sole and Exclusive Benefit" Requirement, 4 Tex. S.U. L. Rev. 1, 9–17 (1977).

[24] E.g., the weekly column written by Hal Lebowitz entitled "Ask the Referee."

[25] *The Trivia Book*, published annually by an affiliate of the *Sporting News*, is one such example.

[26] Such was the case in Weiner v. McGraw-Hill, Inc., 57 N.Y.2d 458, 443 N.E.2d 441, 457 N.Y.S.2d 193 (1982); see supra note 21.

To promote fairness and the continuity of games, professional baseball is grounded in agreements to abide by rules. In many non-playing aspects of the game, disputes are handled as they would be in conventional legal settings.[27] Facts are stipulated, legal briefs are submitted, and oral arguments are presented[28]—with all of these culminating in thorough, judicial-type review.

## II. PRINCIPLES OF REVIEW

The basis of appellate procedure is simply this: A review is conducted to determine whether the law has been applied correctly. This may mean one of two things. First, the appellate tribunal may inquire as to whether the applicable law has been correctly *stated*. If the law is clear and the lower decisionmaking entity has misstated that law, there is ground for reversal. The second area for inquiry concerns whether the law has been correctly *applied*. This would be the case where: (a) there had been an accurate finding of fact, but an inappropriate law was applied to those facts; or (b) there had been such an erroneous finding of fact that a seemingly appropriate law was, in effect, inappropriate. When this last possibility occurs, an egregious error of fact *becomes* an error of law.

In the review of administrative agency decisions, the same procedures pertain. The appellate tribunal searches the record to determine whether there are clearly erroneous or arbitrary findings of fact that rise to the level of errors of law. It also reviews the law applied. This standard of review has been set out quite clearly for situations involving contractual disputes.[29] It is equally applicable in the area of Social Security claims.[30] Thus, an appeal properly will lie wherever there is a dispute regarding an agency determination if the dispute is based on mistakes of law or questions of previous deviation from factual correctness.

---

[27] The exclusion of particular spectators and professional athletes from sporting events provides a fine example of the judicial system's use in the context of sports. See infra notes 52–99 and accompanying text.

[28] See, e.g., Progress is Made in Suit by Baseball, N.Y. Times, Jan. 21, 1976, at 49, col. 5 (facts stipulated in preparation for oral arguments in suit involving free agent reserve clause and baseball owners' challenge to power of arbitrator to declare certain players free agents); see also, Yankees Pressed Illegal Agreement with Messersmith, N.Y. Times, Apr. 25, 1976, § 5 (Sports), at 1, col. 3 (Andy Messersmith's contract with Yankees, which contained provisions regarding pitcher's grooming and commercial endorsements, subject of hearing before baseball commissioner in which testimony and written agreement were introduced as evidence).

[29] See United States v. Bethlehem Steel Corp., 315 U.S. 289 (1942).

[30] See Cutler v. Weinberger, 516 F.2d 1282 (2d Cir. 1975).

### III. THE MODEL APPLIED.

#### A. *Dispute Resolution: Questions of Law*

It is clear that the pine tar dispute was fought purely on the rules and their meaning—that is, on a question of law. There was no dispute as to the fact that the pine tar exceeded its prescribed limits.[31] There was little dispute as to the purpose of the pine tar rule.[32] The only question concerned the appropriate sanction to be imposed.[33]

The pine tar incident, while the most recent controversy of its type, is merely one of many. Perhaps the two most dramatic disputes of this sort occurred in 1908 and 1976. In 1908, the New York Giants had only two utility fielders—Fred Merkle and Charley "Buck" Herzog.[34] Herzog, of course, was treated to numerous antisemitic slurs. One commentator actually stated: "The long-nosed rooters are crazy whenever young Herzog does anything noteworthy. Cries of 'Herzog! Herzog! Goot poy, Herzog!' go up regularly, and there would be no let-up even if a million ham sandwiches suddenly fell among these believers in percentages and bargains."[35] As a result, a great deal of attention was focused on Merkle throughout the season. A crucial call on September 4th set the stage for Merkle's fame. In an extra inning game between Pittsburgh and Chicago, Pittsburgh was at bat, with the bases loaded and two men out. On the first pitch, Wilson singled to center, driving in the winning run from third. Thinking the game was over, Gill (the runner on first) never touched second, and Evers (second baseman of Chicago's Tinker to Evers to Chance) tagged the bag.[36] The umpire allowed the run,[37] and Chicago protested the

---

[31] See Official League Ruling, reprinted in N.Y. Times, July 29, 1983, at A16, col. 1 ("portion of the bat covered with pine-tar was measured [by umpires] and found to be well over 18 inches").

[32] American League Rules and Regulations § 1.10(b).

[33] For example, whether the bat simply should have been thrown out of the game.

[34] See G. Fleming, The Unforgettable Season 106 (1981) (quoting N.Y. Herald, June 24, 1908).

[35] Id. at 224 (quoting Vila, Sporting News, Sept. 17, 1908); see id. at 265 (quoting Bagley, N.Y. Evening Mail, Sept. 28, 1908) ("Herzy's nose does stick out a bit . . . . When he slides to a base he must turn on his side. Otherwise he'd be so high off the ground he might as well try to make the bag standing.").

[36] Id. at 206–07 (quoting Sanborn, Chicago Tribune, Sept. 4, 1908).

[37] Exactly why the run was allowed is not perfectly clear. It seems clear that if the umpire had seen the force-out at second, the run would not have counted. Thus, the fact that the umpire had started towards the dressing room, thereby turning his back on the play, could be the only way to rationalize the otherwise incorrect call. Just moments after the game, however, the umpire made it clear that he did not understand the rule. When confronted by the Chicago players, the umpire was quoted as saying: " 'Clarke was over the plate, so his run counted anyway.' " Id. at 207 (quoting Sanborn, Chicago Tribune, Sept. 4, 1908).

game.[38] On September 9th, National League President Harry Pulliam threw out the protest, stating, " 'I think the baseball public prefers to see games settled on the field and not in this office.' "[39]

Then, on September 23rd, with the Cubs facing the Giants at the Polo Grounds, it happened. In the bottom of the ninth, with a man on third and Merkle on first, Bridwell of the Giants hit safely to center, scoring McCormick.[40] Hofman, in center field, threw the ball to Evers,[41] who tagged second, claiming Merkle had not reached it. The umpire—the *same* umpire responsible for the September 4th call—left the field and, after hearing Chicago's claims, declared the game a tie.[42] Merkle claimed that he touched second base on his way to the clubhouse.[43] President Pulliam, however, upheld the umpire's decision.[44] As a result, New York and Chicago ended the regular season in

---

[38] Id. at 207–08 (quoting Pittsburgh Post, Sept. 4, 1908). It is interesting to note that the facts surrounding this controversy were reported widely in Pittsburgh and Chicago, but were merely noted in New York. See id. at 206–68 (quoting various newspapers of New York, Pittsburgh and Chicago); see also id. at 206 (commenting on the lack of New York coverage of the game).

[39] Id. at 213 (quoting N.Y. Globe, Sept. 9, 1908).

[40] Id. at 244 (quoting N.Y. Herald, Sept. 24, 1908).

[41] The path the ball followed to its destination of second base was indirect at best. Hofman fielded the ball in center and threw it in the direction of Evers. However, the throw was wild, ending up in the hands of New York pitcher McGinnity (or perhaps McGinnity ran on the field and cut off the throw). McGinnity immediately ran for the clubhouse (or perhaps he never got the opportunity), but was grabbed initially by Chicago first baseman Chance and then by two more unidentified Chicago players (or perhaps it was not Chance, but rather three unknown players jumping on McGinnity simultaneously). At any rate, by that time the crowd had begun piling onto the field, and McGinnity seized this opportunity by throwing the ball into the mass (or perhaps the ball merely fell from his hand and rolled in that direction). Steinfeldt and Tinker (and maybe Kroh) infiltrated the crowd, Tinker wound up with the ball (or maybe it was Kroh who then passed it to Steinfeldt), and the ball was thrown to Evers on second (no doubt about it). See id. at 244–45 (quoting N.Y. Herald, Sept. 24, 1908); id. at 249 (quoting Dryden, Chicago Tribune, Sept. 24, 1908).

[42] Apparently, the Chicago players (and fans) confronted the umpire on the field. "Those within reach began pounding [the umpire] on all available exposed parts not covered by [his] protector, while the unfortunate attackers on the outskirts began sending messages by way of cushions, newspapers, and other missiles." Id. at 245 (quoting N.Y. Herald, Sept. 24, 1908). The police were then called in, and the umpire was rushed to New York's dugout. Though order was eventually restored, the umpire retired to his dressing room without rendering a decision as to the final play. In fact, it was only after he had dressed that he made a final decision, which was relayed through a sports reporter. Id.

[43] Id. Christy Mathewson supported Merkle's account of the episode. See id. at 251 (quoting N.Y. Evening Mail, Sept. 24, 1908).

[44] Id. at 276–79 (quoting President Pulliam's official decision, quoted in N.Y. American, Oct. 3, 1908).

Because the fans had crowded the field, the game was not continued, but rather was declared a 1-1 tie. This became an additional issue of protest, but was similarly discarded by Pulliam. See id. at 277–78 (quoting the official decision, quoted in N.Y. American, Oct. 3, 1908).

a tie for first place, thereby causing a playoff game. In that game (attended by over 50,000 fans and followed by virtually the entire nation), the Cubs defeated the Giants by a score of 4 to 2[45] and went on to win the World Series. By way of postscript, it should be noted that on July 19th, 1909, President Pulliam committed suicide because of a severe state of depression caused by the turmoil resulting from his decision.[46]

A second significant controversy took place in the third game of the 1975 World Series between the Boston Red Sox and the Cincinnati Reds. In the bottom of the tenth, Armbrister of Cincinnati bunted the ball in front of the plate. As Fisk attempted to throw for a force-out at second, Armbrister got his bat in the way, causing Fisk to throw the ball into right field.[47] The claim of interference was denied,[48] and the game (and probably the Series) was lost as a result.[49] The incorrectness of the call was discussed long thereafter and, as one would imagine, Boston fans have never forgotten.

What these major incidents illustrate can be outlined as follows:

- An individual ruling may affect an entire season.
- Merely upholding an umpire's call causes chaos and a feeling of "we wuz robbed!"
- Precision as to the facts—Did Merkle touch second? Did Armbrister interfere with Fisk?—greatly facilitates resolution of disputes.

---

[45] Id. at 306 (quoting N.Y. Tribune, Oct. 9, 1908). For those interested in baseball history, "Three-Finger" Brown (another Jewish ballplayer) was the winning pitcher for Chicago, while Christy Mathewson was the loser. Id. at 309–310 (quoting Sanborn, Chicago Tribune, Oct. 8, 1908).

Despite the incidents of the 1908 season, Merkle— a nineteen-year-old rookie at the time, see id. at xii—went on to complete a respectable fourteen-year major league career. See C. Mathewson, Pinching In a Pinch 205 (1912). The incident was never lived down, however, and Merkle was forever saddled with the sobriquet "Bonehead." See G. Flemming, supra note 33, at 255 (quoting Bagley, N.Y. Evening Mail, Sept. 25, 1908) ("McGraw had enough of Merkle the day before and called on Tenney for his brains. A one-legged man with a noodle is better than a bonehead.").

[46] Proscript to G. Flemming, supra note 35.

[47] N.Y. Times, Oct. 15, 1975, at A27, col. 3.

[48] Id.

[49] N.Y. Times, Oct. 23, 1975, at 1, col. 1; id., Oct. 16, 1975, at 49, col. 5. John M. Johnson of the Baseball Commissioner's Office backed the umpire's decision. Johnson said the applicable rule was section 7.09(h), which provides that it is interference " 'if in the judgment of the umpire, a batter-runner willfully and deliberately interferes with a batted ball or fielder in the act of fielding a batted ball, with the obvious intent to break up a double play.' " Id. (quoting Off. Baseball R. 7.09(h)). However, as pointed out in the same article, that "subsection was written in to cope with Jackie Robinson, a baserunner who used to let an obvious double-play grounder hit him. That rendered the ball dead and eliminated the double play, although Robinson was out automatically." Id.

- It is highly desirable to have the correct rule applied by the highest authority as soon as possible.

These principles should have been applied in the pine tar case. The case involved the interpretation of rules, and therefore a decision on the merits should have been reached promptly, without attempting to justify the umpire's decision. Fortunately, the Brett incident was not as crucial (in terms of eventual outcome) as the two discussed above.

At their core, all three disputes centered around questions of law. Therefore, all clearly should have been finally adjudicated, as were the Merkle and Brett questions, before appellate tribunals.

## B. *Dispute Resolution: Questions of Fact*

On the other side of the coin, sporting events often raise questions of fact. Every fan has had the experience (sometimes many times in a single game) of watching an instant replay[50] that proves that the determination of the umpire or referee was incorrect. Remembering the significance of appellate review, it becomes clear that such erroneous determinations of fact should also be reviewable. Unlike questions of law, however, initial review could be made by the umpire or referee himself, rather than by an appellate tribunal. Immediate review by the factfinder is made possible by devices that provide instant replays. To discourage unwarranted "litigation," a limit could be put on the number of times during a game that a review could be requested, or a team questioning a call could be fined if its allegations were not borne out by the instant replay. Moreover, additional fines could be levied for appealing a frivolous issue beyond the "umpire" tribunal. Only in cases of clearly erroneous factual determinations would an instant replay be viewed by a league official and used as grounds for reversal. If, for example, an instant replay had shown that Merkle had touched second base, failure to reverse the umpire's call would seem highly unjustified.

It should be noted that it now appears that instant replays will not slow down a game unduly—an obvious concern. In fact, the opposite may be true. When a call is now disputed, arguments may go on for several minutes, almost invariably ending without a reversal.

---

[50] For football fans watching games in which Howard Cosell advertises himself as a broadcaster, it is highly recommended that the viewer turn down the sound on his television and listen to the radio instead. Tex Cobb certainly would agree with this advice. Alluding to the fact that Cosell swore to stop announcing boxing matches after Cobb was pummeled by Larry Holmes in

But the same call could be reviewed by the parties and the officials in a period of several seconds. The officials could then make a prompt and correct determination.* Furthermore, what little delay might result from such a review procedure cannot be deemed intolerable. In a recent New York Jets game, a kickoff was repeated because it had not been seen on television.[51] If a game can be delayed, or a play repeated, simply because of the demands of television, umpires certainly should be allowed to take a quick look at an instant replay. In fact, delays caused by immediate reviews, far less accurate than instant replays, already exist in various sports. In baseball, home plate umpires routinely appeal to first and third base umpires to judge whether a swing has been checked. In football, difficult calls commonly result in a conference of the field officials. Turning around to watch a replay on a television monitor could be highly advantageous and would take little (if any) more time than such procedures.[52]

---

a championship match, Cobb proclaimed: " 'I'd go 15 more rounds with Holmes if I thought it would get Cosell off football broadcasts.' " They Said It, Sports Illustrated, Feb. 8, 1984, at 8.

* As this Article went to press, an example of such a rational use of instant replay technology came to light. On March 13, 1984, in a preliminary round of the NCAA basketball tournament, North Carolina A & T was locked in a 68-68 tie with Morehead State. With 26 seconds remaining on the clock, Earl Harrison of Morehead State was charged with a deliberate foul. The referee saw Harrison pull on an opponent's jersey, but couldn't be sure which opponent had been fouled.

The officials, after a short conference, first agreed that Eric Boyd had been fouled and should shoot. But then, realizing that there was no reason simply to guess, they asked the television commentators at courtside to rerun the play in slow motion on their monitors. The replay showed that it was not Boyd, but James Horace, whose shirt had been pulled. Horace missed one free throw and made the other, giving N.C. A & T a 69-68 lead. Morehead made one more field goal to win the game 70-69.

After the game, the officials issued a joint statement: "We wanted to be sure we had the correct man at the line. We had a conference, were not entirely sure, so we got a clarification from TV and justified our selection." Quoted in Referees Go to the Videotape, Newsday, Mar. 14, 1984, at 102, col. 2.

Here, then, is the sort of rational exploitation of existing technology that is advocated in the text. There was little delay; fans and players felt that a fair determination had been made; and the image of the entire sport was benefited.

[51] N.Y. Times, Sept. 5, 1983, at 11, col. 1.

[52] A recent and somewhat controversial football game offers a possible example. On January 8th, 1984, in the NFC championship game between Washington and San Francisco, a fourth quarter penalty became the subject of some dispute. On Washington's final drive of the game, with the score tied at 21-21, San Francisco defensive back Eric Wright was called for pass interference. As a result, a twenty-seven yard penalty was assessed, putting the Redskins in range for the winning field goal. Pass interference occurs when the defensive player makes contact with the receiver while the pass is in the air (assuming the contact is not merely an incident of the defender's attempt at the ball). However, the call is inappropriate when the intended receiver would not have been able to catch the pass even if he had not been interfered with. The official's

IV. Constitutional Limitations in Sports

### A. Rights of Access

Although sporting contests are controlled by rules promulgated by private organizations, the world of sports remains subject to the mandates of the Constitution. Of particular interest here is the right of participants and spectators to access to sporting events. Disputes concerning the right of access will be considered for two reasons. First, the means by which these disputes are resolved clearly indicate that the courtroom is the proper forum for resolution of off-the-field disputes. Second, and more important, the issue demonstrates the great extent to which the Constitution governs the world of sports.

The access issue implicates two diametrically opposed sets of rights. On the one hand, the owner of a sports facility has a right to exclude undesirable participants (or spectators). On the other, participants (or spectators) have a right of reasonable access to sporting events.

Historically, the fourteenth amendment was interpreted as providing a right of reasonable access to all public places.[53] The current majority American rule, however, has for many years disregarded the right of reasonable access,[54] granting to proprietors of amusement

---

call clearly indicates his belief that the ball was catchable and that sufficient contact was made. After viewing the instant replay, however, the call was not nearly so clear. Art Monk, the Redskins receiver, seemed convinced of the contact: "He really did interfere with me." CBS Postgame Interview with Art Monk (Jan. 8, 1984). Eric Wright, on the other hand, was equally sure that "the ball couldn't have been caught." CBS Postgame Interview with Eric Wright (Jan. 8, 1984). In this case, because of the discretionary nature of the call, the appropriate determination probably should have been made by the official—the factfinder. Use of the instant replay (at the discretion of the official) could have aided in his determination. For as Forty-Niner head coach Bill Walsh indicated, without more, "an official shouldn't . . . make a call that would judge a championship game on something like that." CBS Postgame Interview with Bill Walsh (Jan. 8, 1984).

[53] See, e.g., Ferguson v. Gies, 82 Mich. 358 (1890); Donnell v. State, 48 Miss. 661 (1873).

[54] See Arterburn, The Origin and First Test of Public Callings, 75 U. Pa. L. Rev. 411 (1926); Turner & Kennedy, Exclusion, Ejection, and Segregation of Theater Patrons, 32 Iowa L. Rev. 625 (1947); Wyman, The Law of the Public Callings as a Solution of the Trust Problem, 17 Harv. L. Rev. 156 (1904); Annot., 90 A.L.R.3d 1361 (1979). However, the common law rule that the proprietor of a racetrack may refuse to admit any person to the track has been changed by statute in some jurisdictions. See Greeneberg v. Western Turf Ass'n, 140 Cal. 357, 73 P. 1050 (1903); Orloff v. Hollywood Turf Club, 110 Cal. App. 2d 340, 242 P.2d 660 (1952); Rockwell v. Pennsylvania State Horse Racing Comm'n, 15 Pa. Commw. 348, 327 A.2d 211 (1974); Narragansett Racing Ass'n v. Mazzaro, 116 R.I. 354, 357 A.2d 442 (1976); Burrillville Racing Ass'n v. Garabedian, 113 R.I. 134, 318 A.2d 469 (1974).

places the absolute right to exclude or eject any person arbitrarily.[55] The majority American rule, if not spawned by racial discrimination, owes some of its support to a well-known English case that was implicitly adopted by the United States Supreme Court almost three quarters of a century ago. In the English case, *Wood v. Leadbitter*,[56] the court had occasion to deal, not with exclusion, but with a patron's forcible ejection from the Doncaster race course because of alleged previous malpractices. He later sued in trespass for assault and false imprisonment. In denying the plaintiff recovery, the court took the position that he had no easement or similar property right entitling him to remain on the grounds after having been requested to leave, but only a personal license that could be revoked at any time, leaving him with only a breach of contract claim. In *Marronne v. Washington Jockey Club*,[57] decided sixty-eight years later, the United States Supreme Court implicitly adopted the English rule. The plaintiff, Joseph Marronne, was excluded from the Bennings Race Track on the charge that he had drugged a horse. He brought an action for trespass, alleging that he had been prevented forcibly from entering the track and turned out after dropping his ticket in the box. Mr. Justice Holmes, speaking for the Court, stated: "We see no reason for declining to follow the commonly accepted rule" of *Leadbitter*.[58] The Court failed to discuss any of the pertinent policy considerations regarding reasonable access.[59] Instead, the Court based its decision on archaic

---

[55] Of course, proprietors may not violate civil rights laws. However, denial of reasonable access (following passage of the fourteenth amendment) and creation of a common law right to arbitrarily exclude (following invalidation of segregation statutes) suggest *strongly* that the current majority rule may have less than dignified origins. See, e.g., Hall v. DeCuir, 95 U.S. 485 (1877) (state statute requiring those engaged in transporting passengers to give equal access to *all* persons—regardless of race or color—invalidated as interference with Congress' commerce power).

[56] 153 Eng. Rep. 351 (Ex. Ch. 1845).

[57] 227 U.S. 633 (1913).

[58] Id. at 636.

[59] In fact, a contemporaneous English decision seemingly rejected the holding in *Leadbitter*. Hurst v. Picture Theatres, Ltd., [1915] 1 K.B. 1 (1914). The court in *Hurst* allowed recovery in an assault action where a purchaser of a theatre ticket was forcibly ejected by a proprietor acting on the mistaken belief that the plaintiff had not paid his admission fee. Lord Justice Buckley expressed the view that it would be neither good sense nor good law to hold that a theatre proprietor had the absolute right to eject a patron who had paid for his ticket and was peaceably occupying his assigned seat. Id. at 4–5. The theatre ticket was therefore considered a license bearing an agreement not to revoke that equity would enforce.

The *Hurst* case has been the subject of extensive discussion. Compare Wade, What is a License?, 64 L.Q. Rev. 57 (1948) (approving the court's holding) with Miles, *Hurst v. Picture Theatres, Ltd.*, 31 L.Q. Rev. 217 (1915) (disapproving the court's holding as violative of real property law).

contract and property terms.[60] Thus, owners were given the freedom to exclude any patron for any reason.

Consequently, *Maronne* became the American rule.[61] Amusement place and racetrack owners were given great latitude in ejecting and excluding patrons for whatever reason—illustrating the common American jurisprudential error of importing into constitutional interpretation common law that is at variance with the precepts of the Constitution.[62] Such vast exclusionary power, however, must be lim-

---

[60] Justice Holmes stated, for example:

> The fact that the purchase of the ticket made a contract is not enough. A contract binds the person of the maker but does not create an interest in the property that it may concern . . . . The ticket was not a conveyance of an interest in the race track, . . . because by common understanding it did not purport to have that effect. . . . But if it did not create . . . a right *in rem*, valid against the landowner and third persons, the holder had no right to enforce specific performance by self-help. His only right was to sue upon the contract for the breach.

*Marrone*, 227 U.S. at 636.

[61] Two significant cases help to illustrate the lingering effect of *Leadbitter*. In Shubert v. Nixon Amusement Co., 83 N.J.L. 101, 83 A. 369 (1912), showman Lee Shubert purchased a ticket for a show of his competitor, Florenz Ziegfeld. While peaceably occupying his seat, he was requested to leave. He brought a tort action that was dismissed by the New Jersey Supreme Court. In so holding, the court noted: "[W]hatever views may be entertained as to the natural justice or injustice of ejecting a theatre patron without reason after he has paid for his ticket and taken his seat, we feel constrained to follow [*Leadbitter*] as the settled law." Id. at 106, 83 A. at 106.

In Woollcott v. Shubert, 217 N.Y. 212, 111 N.E. 829 (1916), the court took a similar approach. Alexander Woollcott, the *New York Times* drama critic, had written an adverse review of a production controlled by Lee Shubert and associates. As a result, Woollcott was excluded from a particular theatre and was threatened with exclusion from all Shubert theatres. Woollcott's action for injunctive relief was dismissed in an opinion that stated:

> The acts of the defendants were within their rights at the common law. . . . [A] theatre . . . is in no sense public property or a public enterprise. . . . [The proprietor's] right to and control of it is the same as that of any private citizen in his property and affairs. He has the right to decide who shall be admitted or excluded. His rights at the common law, in the respect of controlling the property, entertainments and audience, have been too recently determined by us to be now questionable.

Id. at 216, 111 N.E. at 830. It is worth noting that although Woollcott lost the case, the *New York Times* was able to exert so much pressure (by excluding Shubert's advertisements and all references to actors in his theatres) that Woollcott quickly regained unrestricted access. As Woollcott recalled: " 'Under this treatment they soon came begging for my return and even ate crow in the form of an open letter asking me to return.' " Conard, The Privilege of Forcibly Ejecting an Amusement Patron, 90 U. Pa. L. Rev. 809, 821 (1942) (quoting letter from Wollcott to Conard (June 5, 1938)).

[62] The *reductio ad absurdum* of this error is illustrated by the importing of "sovereign immunities" into the eleventh amendment to ban retroactive welfare benefit payments. See Edelman v. Jordan, 415 U.S. 651 (1974) (a Rehnquist opinion that is illogical at best).

ited by constitutional principles[63] whenever the agency exercising the franchise is affected with "state action."[64]

The early attempts to link racetracks with "state action" were disposed of quickly. In *Madden v. Queens County Jockey Club, Inc.*,[65] the jockey club excluded Madden from its Aqueduct Race Track in the mistaken belief that he was Frank Costello's book-maker.[66] Because the defendant was licensed to conduct pari-mutuel betting, Madden contended that its license was a franchise to perform a public purpose, demanding treatment as an administrative agency of the state.[67] However, the court found that: (1) the defendant licensee was no more a state administrative agent than was the licensed cab driver, barber or liquor dealer;[68] and (2) the defendant's operation was not under a franchise for the performance of a public function, but was under a license imposed for revenue and the regulation of a private business.[69] In *Greenfeld v. Maryland Jockey Club*,[70] the court noted that racing was "a minutely regulated, heavily taxed business in which private rights and responsibility have not been wholly extinguished."[71] In finding for the track, the court stressed that the racing statute had "confer[red] no personal right on individuals to

---

[63] NAACP v. Alabama *ex rel* Patterson, 357 U.S. 449 (1958) (freedom of association).

[64] Compare Shelley v. Kraemer, 334 U.S. 1, 14, 20 (1948) (state action requirement of fourteenth amendment met where state judicially enforced private discriminatory agreement) and Burton v. Wilmington Parking Auth., 365 U.S. 715, 721-26 (1961) (state found to be joint participant of restaurant that practiced discrimination where restaurant was built and maintained with public funds and operated by state for public purposes) with Moose Lodge No. 107 v. Irvis, 407 U.S. 163, 177 (1972) (state regulatory scheme under which license was granted to club practicing discrimination did not sufficiently implicate state in club's discriminatory practices so as to make those practices state action within the fourteenth amendment) and Jackson v. Metropolitan Edison Co., 419 U.S. 345 (1974) (no state action where an extensively regulated utility, engaged in a business interest and enjoying partial monopoly in its service area, acted to deprive customer of service).

[65] 296 N.Y. 249, 72 N.E.2d 697, cert. denied, 332 U.S. 761 (1947).

[66] Madden sought judicial relief in the form of an entitlement to enter the track upon his payment of the required admission fee. Judge Fuld, writing for the court, cited *Marrone*, 296 N.Y. at 253, 72 N.E.2d at 698, and held that Madden was not entitled to such relief either at common law or under New York's statutory law. Id. at 256, 72 N.E.2d at 700.

[67] Id. at 250, 72 N.E.2d at 697 (argument of plaintiff's counsel).

[68] Id. at 254, 72 N.E.2d at 698-99.

[69] Id. at 255-56, 72 N.E.2d at 699; Salmore v. Empire City Racing Ass'n, 123 N.Y.S.2d 688, 692 (Sup. Ct. 1953) ("law permitting pari-mutuel betting [is] simply a revenue law enacted almost entirely for the purpose of raising money, with the improvement of the breed of horses a mere palliative cloak").

[70] 190 Md. 96, 57 A.2d 335 (1948).

[71] Id. at 104, 57 A.2d at 338.

attend or bet at race meetings,"[72] and that the racing commission (assuming it had power to do so) had never adopted any regulation compelling the licensee "to admit all comers" as spectators and bettors unless excluded for good cause.[73] Unlike *Madden* and *Greenfeld*, which involved spectators,[74] *Martin v. Monmouth Park Jockey Club*[75] concerned a jockey who had been suspended for placing a wager on a horse other than the one he was riding. Although the plaintiff had been reinstated as a jockey, he was notified by the defendant track that he would be unable to ride at its racing meet. The district court, in response to Martin's request for injunctive relief, held that although racing is an intensely regulated industry, the defendant was still a private corporation, having the right to admit to, or exclude from, its property any person it pleased.[76]

More recently, the courts have begun to pay some heed to the state action arguments. Perhaps the pinnacle case is that of *Jacobson v. New York Racing Association*.[77] In apparent retaliation for his labor activities, Howard "Buddy" Jacobson, a licensed owner,[78] was denied stall space at all New York Racing Association (NYRA) tracks, thereby effectively barring him from thoroughbred racing in the state.[79] An appeal by Jacobson had been taken to the appellate division, which appeared willing to reconsider the common law doctrine of *Madden* in light of the 1955 legislation that created the NYRA.[80] More importantly, the court reasoned that the close regulation and supervision of the NYRA by the State Racing Commission, and the NYRA's use of pari-mutuel betting, established sufficient state presence and participation in the challenged activity to invoke the constitutional guarantee of due process of law.[81] On further appeal, the court of appeals held that the arbitrary action of a private association

---

[72] Id. at 105, 57 A.2d at 338.

[73] Id.

[74] See also Watkins v. Oaklawn Jockey Club, 86 F. Supp. 1006 (W.D. Ark. 1949), aff'd, 183 F.2d 440 (8th Cir. 1950). Watkins alleged state action as well as a right to access, but lost on both grounds. 183 F.2d at 443.

[75] 145 F. Supp. 439 (D.N.J. 1956), aff'd, 242 F.2d 334 (3d Cir. 1957).

[76] 145 F. Supp. at 440. Of course, defendant could not refuse access where such refusal was prohibited by New Jersey's civil rights statute. Id.

[77] 33 N.Y.2d 144, 305 N.E.2d 765, 350 N.Y.S.2d 639 (1973).

[78] N.Y. Times, Mar. 9, 1973, at 34, col. 2. At the time of the suit, Jacobson already was a leading trainer on the New York racing circuit. See id.

[79] *Jacobson*, 33 N.Y.2d at 147, 149-50, 305 N.E.2d at 766, 768, 350 N.Y.S.2d at 640, 642.

[80] Jacobson v. New York Racing Ass'n, 41 A.D.2d 87, 89-93, 341 N.Y.S.2d 333, 336-40, modified, 33 N.Y.2d 144, 305 N.E.2d 765, 350 N.Y.S.2d 639 (1973); see 33 N.Y.2d at 148, 305 N.E.2d at 767, 350 N.Y.S.2d at 641.

[81] 41 A.D.2d at 92, 341 N.Y.S.2d at 338; see 33 N.Y.2d at 148, 305 N.E.2d at 767, 350 N.Y.S.2d at 641.

is not immune from judicial scrutiny,[82] thus disagreeing with the appellate division on the state action question.[83] The court, however, cryptically forecast the quagmire of doubt that would follow in state and federal courts: "We note . . . that as a limit on the reach of the Fourteenth Amendment, the 'state action' doctrine is alive and well."[84]

Since *Jacobson*, the state action doctrine has proven its viability in a variety of situations.[85] It thus seems clear that the most effective means by which patrons, jockeys and trainers are likely to succeed under the first and fourteenth amendments is to establish that the actions taken by the various racing commissions constitute state action.

---

[82] According to the court: "[I]t will be plaintiff's heavy burden to prove that the denial of stall space was not a reasonable discretionary business judgement, but was actuated by motives other than those relating to the best interest of racing generally." 33 N.Y.2d at 150, 305 N.E.2d at 768, 350 N.Y.S.2d at 643.

[83] Though the *Jacobson* court found the state action question "interesting," it felt that the issue "need not be reached or decided." Id.

[84] Id. at 150–51, 305 N.E.2d at 768, 350 N.Y.S.2d at 643 (citing Columbia Broadcasting Sys. v. Democratic Nat'l Comm., 412 U.S. 94 (1973); Lloyd Corp. v. Tanner, 407 U.S. 551 (1972); Moose Lodge No. 107 v. Irvis, 407 U.S. 163 (1972)). For an example of the hopeless confusion that now exists, compare Bier v. Fleming, 717 F.2d 308 (6th Cir. 1983) with Fitzgerald v. Mountain Laurel Racing, Inc., 607 F.2d 589 (3d Cir. 1979). In *Bier*, the Court of Appeals for the Sixth Circuit held that the revocation of Bier's racing licence by the Executive Secretary of the Ohio Racing Commission did not constitute state action.

> Although the State regulates the horse racing industry, such extensive regulation does not, in itself, transform otherwise private actions into state action . . . .
>
> We conclude that the conduct of the racing officials was not a sufficient exercise of coercive power or significant encouragement on part of the state to find state action in an otherwise private decision. Accordingly, "[m]ere approval of or acquiescence in the initiatives of a private party is not sufficient to justify holding the State responsible for those initiatives under the terms of the Fourteenth Amendment."

717 F.2d at 311 (citation omitted). But see *Bier*, 538 F. Supp. 437 (N.D. Ohio 1981) (trial court found such revocation to be a violation of state law and an action of the state), rev'd, 717 F.2d 308.

In *Fitzgerald*, on the other hand, the Court of Appeals for the Third Circuit found a sufficiently close nexus between the state and a private harness racing association to trigger state action. See 607 F.2d at 597–99. Furthermore, one should note that while Judge Adams (the dissenter in *Fitzgerald*) apparently would agree with the ultimate holding of *Bier*, his reasoning probably would vary considerably. Unlike the majority in *Bier*, much of Judge Adams' dissent indicates a fear that findings of state action could harm a greater number of employees and jockeys than would be benefitted. Id. at 608 & nn.12–13 (Adams, J., dissenting).

[85] See generally, e.g., Lugar v. Edmonson Oil Co., 457 U.S. 922 (1982) (constitutional requirements of due process applied to garnishment and prejudgment attachment procedures where state oficers act jointly with a private creditor); Robinson v. Price, 553 F.2d 918 (5th Cir. 1977) (due process denied where private non-profit agency, which received federal funds, discharged employee on racial and religious grounds); Ludtke v. Kuhn, 461 F. Supp. 86 (S.D.N.Y. 1978) (state action found where baseball team, which leased stadium from municipality, excluded female reporter from clubhouse); Bonner v. B-W Util., Inc., 452 F. Supp. 1295 (W.D. La. 1978) (actions taken by utlity mortgagee to enforce security interest in collateral deemed state action).

Though the state action doctrine is, at least at present, the argument most likely to persuade a court, a second argument might also be advanced.[86] The basis of this argument is that property can be devoted to public use to such an extent that the rights of a proprietor should be limited by the first amendment rights of others. This theme was developed in *Marsh v. Alabama*,[87] where the Supreme Court held that the first and fourteenth amendments protected the exercise of free speech in a company-owned town that was open to the general public.[88] The characteristic that distinguished this town from all other towns was that title to all property was vested in a private corporation. Justice Black, writing for the majority, reasoned that "[t]he more an owner, for his advantage, opens up his property for use by the public in general, the more do his rights become circumscribed by the statutory and constitutional rights of those who use it."[89] In *Amalgamated Food Employees Union Local 590 v. Logan Valley Plaza, Inc.*,[90] the Supreme Court extended the *Marsh* rationale to provide first amendment protections for union members picketing, on shopping center property, a store with which the union had a labor dispute. Justice Marshall, for the majority, found that the shopping center was "the functional equivalent of a 'business block' and for First Amendment purposes must be treated in substantially the same manner" as the business district in a company town.[91]

Four years later, the Supreme Court began narrowing the scope of *Marsh*. In *Lloyd Corp. v. Tanner*,[92] the Court held that persons in a shopping center who distributed handbills protesting the Vietnam War were not protected by the first and fourteenth amendments.[93] The Court distinguished *Logan Valley* by limiting its application to situations in which (1) the expression sought to be protected is related

---

[86] The fact that the present Supreme Court is reluctant to uphold state action alternatives, such as the "public function doctrine," indicates that such alternatives will not be successful—at least in the near future.

[87] 326 U.S. 501, 506 (1946).

[88] Id. at 510.

[89] Id. at 506.

[90] 391 U.S. 308 (1968).

[91] Id. at 325. Significantly, Justice Black, author of the *Marsh* opinion, dissented. He wrote that "*Marsh* was never intended to apply to this kind of situation. *Marsh* dealt with the very special situation of a company-owned town, complete with streets, alleys, sewers, stores, residences, and everything else that goes to make a town." Id. at 330 (Black J., dissenting).

[92] 407 U.S. 551 (1972); cf. Central Hardware Co. v. NLRB, 407 U.S. 539 (1972) (privately owned parking lot of an employer held not to have acquired the characteristics of a public municipal facility).

[93] 407 U.S. at 567–70.

to the use of the private property and (2) the person claiming protection has no other reasonable opportunity for conveying his message to his intended audience.[94] The restrictive reading of *Marsh* continued in *Hudgens v. NLRB*[95], where the Supreme Court, in an opinion written by Justice Stewart, held that striking warehousemen did not have a first amendment right to enter a private shopping center to picket a retail outlet. The Court, however, did not apply the two elements discussed in *Lloyd*. Instead, it concluded that despite efforts in *Lloyd* to distinguish *Logan Valley*, "the rationale of *Logan Valley* did not survive the Court's decision in the *Lloyd* case."[96] According to the Court in *Hudgens*, the right of free speech is constitutionally guaranteed only against abridgement by the federal or state governments.[97] Thus, the exception of *Marsh* applied solely because the company town was the functional equivalent of a municipality.[98]

Neither *Lloyd* nor *Hudgens* purports to overrule *Marsh*. In fact, they expressly affirm its rationale. However, these decisions make it clear that *Marsh* is to be given a narrow reading. Thus, at present, private property must possess all the attributes of, or be the equivalent of, a state created municipality before it stands in the shoes of the state for first and fourteenth amendment purposes.

Future Supreme Courts may realize that the Constitution calls for a more expansive reading of *Marsh*.[99] Clearly, if a state that allows pari-mutuel wagering and casino gambling decided to provide these services itself, rather than passively reaping the tax benefits, its conduct would be measured against constitutional standards. A state should not be permitted to avoid such constitutional requirements simply by delegating its statutory duty to private associations.[100] Fur-

---

[94] 407 U.S. at 563. The Court described the facts of *Marsh* in the following manner: "In effect, the owner of the company town was performing the full spectrum of municipal powers and stood in the shoes of the State." Id. at 569.

[95] 424 U.S. 507 (1976).

[96] Id. at 518; see also id. at 523-24 (Powell, J., concurring) (Justice Powell's unusual though "mature" apology for his "attenuated" majority opinion in *Lloyd*); PruneYard Shopping Center v. Robins, 447 U.S. 74, 78-79 (1980) (interpreting California constitution as providing right to public enjoyment of private property); State v. Schmid, 84 N.J. 535, 561-63, 423 A.2d 615, 628-29 (1980) (interpreting New Jersey Constitution in a similar fashion).

[97] 424 U.S. at 513.

[98] Id. at 516 (quoting Justice Black's dissenting opinion in *Marsh*).

[99] In time, *Lloyd* and *Hudgens* may prove to be merely two more examples of the Burger-Rehnquist cadre's confused retreat from clear constitutional principles.

[100] See Terry v. Adams, 345 U.S. 461, 469-70 (1953) (state may not deliberately delegate a task to a private entity in order to avoid its constitutional obligations).

thermore, a state's decision to delegate a function to a private association should be scrutinized even when the state has acted for reasons of
convenience and not in bad faith.[101]

The rationale for the state action doctrine is that state authority
may pose threats to constitutional values. A private association vested
with state authority poses those threats just as clearly as a state-created
agency. Thus, *Marsh* well may justify a finding of state action where a
racetrack or casino is open to the public and the appropriate state
agencies license the participants and employees. Mere statutory delegation should not be viewed as converting the nature of a function
from public to private. Rather, the greater the extent that private
property is devoted to public use, the more its owner must accommodate the rights of the general public and the participants who make
that private enterprise profitable to its owners and to the state.
Viewed in this fashion, the common law right to exclude a patron or
discipline a participant would be substantially and appropriately limited by the competing common law right of reasonable access to
public places.[102]

In sports situations, as much as in any others, the applicability of
the Constitution clearly dictates judicial-type review. However, the
extent of the institutions' reach onto the *playing field* is somewhat less
clear. Doctrines such as *Marsh* seem to present strong arguments for
allowing constitutional principles the breadth they deserve. Purely
commercial motivations of sports facility owners should not impinge
on spectators' rights to utilize such facilities, or on participants' rights
to compete. In situations where arguments like that of *Marsh* are
successful, rational review is demanded. Where these arguments fail,
however, the opposite should not be true. For, as demonstrated
above, even where a determination is made that the Constitution is
inapplicable, the greatest merit of the determination may be that it
was reached on a rational basis.

---

[101] See Norwood v. Harrison, 413 U.S. 455, 466 (1973) (state may not induce, encourage or
promote private persons to accomplish what it is constitutionally forbidden to accomplish).

[102] This right to reasonable access would gain further support from the first amendment's
freedom of association. Gambling or attending sporting events, for example, might manifest a
particular life-style, raising first amendment implications. Cf. Weiss & Wizner, Pot, Prayer,
Politics, and Privacy: The Right to Cut Your Own Throat in Your Own Way, 54 Iowa L. Rev.
709 (1969) (discussing drug use as a means of private expression protected by the first amendment).

## B. *Imposition of Fines*

In sports, fines are assessed in three areas. The first of these involves free speech—where participants make comments critical to a league, an umpire or a manager.[103] Under the traditional model of constitutional considerations, such fines seem illegal. The argument in rebuttal, of course, is that these fines are implicitly or explicitly contracted for, and that the contracting away of such constitutional rights is perfectly permissible. Assuming that these constitutional rights can be contracted away, the question becomes whether the assumption of these conditions suggests a contract of adhesion.[104] Some might argue that since players now negotiate huge salaries, we should assume freedom and equality in the bargaining process. But as yet, there appears to be no real negotiation about conditions of freedom. Perhaps the freedom to contract exists for monetary terms, while the same is not entirely clear regarding other matters.[105]

Also in the area of free speech are situations where people arguing calls are thrown out of ballgames or assessed technical fouls.[106] Proceeding pursuant to the judicial model, the proper question appears to be whether contempt has been shown for the decisionmaker.

---

[103] Although not within the scope of this Article, league and team censorship of broadcasts seems to have gotten somewhat out of control. Indeed, at least one exclusively sports-oriented magazine has characterized this as a violation of the first amendment. "This year, the National Hockey League is trying to repeal the first amendment . . . [by providing] guidelines [that] restrict what the play-by-play men and color commentators can say about the way the referee and linesmen are handling the games. NHL: No More Free Speech, Sport, Jan. 1984, at 9.

[104] For a discussion of adhesion contracts, see Kessler, Contracts of Adhesion—Some Thoughts About Freedom of Contract, 43 Colum. L. Rev. 629 (1943); Note, Contract Clauses in Fine Print, 63 Harv. L. Rev. 494 (1950); see also Ricketts v. Pennsylvania R.R., 153 F.2d 757, 760 (2d Cir. 1946) (Frank, J., concurring) (analysis of "actual intent" versus "meeting of the minds" theories of contract formation); Hill v. Marston, 82 F.2d 856, 858 (D.C. Cir. 1936) (no meeting of the minds and hence no contract formed where terms of verbal understanding differed radically from terms of written contract that plaintiff was fraudulently induced to sign); Saylor v. Handley Motor Co., 169 A.2d 683, 685 (D.C. Mun. Ct. App. 1961) ("proposition that one is obligated by his contract, though signed without knowledge of its terms, does not extend to situations where assent to such terms is procured by the proponent's fraud").

[105] See, e.g., Andy Messersmith's contract, which was to have included an illegal side letter dictating his dress and grooming. The contract, which was never signed, was found to have discrepancies with the original negotiations, with Messersmith claiming bad faith on the Yankee's part. Yankees Pressed Illegal Agreement with Messersmith, N.Y. Times, Apr. 25, 1976, § 5 (Sports), at 1, col. 3.

[106] See *In re* Rivera, 467 N.Y.S.2d 698 (App. Div. 1983) (assault of an umpire by an employee in a company softball game was held not to constitute disqualifying conduct for unemployment insurance purposes).

*69*

Contempt is a mechanism for punishing acts committed in front of the court that so diminish the effectiveness of a court, or so tarnish its image, that the procedure cannot be continued effectively. In such a case, the tribunal has the right of summary contempt. The exercise of contempt powers is, of course, subject to the same sort of review as other decisions. Misapplication of law, as well as erroneous findings of fact, are reviewable. In the sports context, rather than allowing inconsistent and varying uses of an official's power (e.g., expulsions versus assessment of technical fouls) from referee to referee, mood to mood, and hometown to hometown, this power could be held in check by making it subject to the same standards of review applicable to a judicial or administrative finding of contempt. Unfortunately, this has not been the case. For example, in *Vasquez v. Van Lindt*,[107] the Second Circuit Court of Appeals upheld a jockey's suspension, pursuant to a hearing held a year prior to the case, on grounds of res judicata of civil rights actions from state to federal court. Thus, the jockey was not afforded judicial-type discovery (or adjudication), and lost a year's income.[108]

Yet another class of fines are assessed for failing to give maximum effort. Such fines seem unjustified unless treated as contractual matters, in which case they should be subject to the same type of arbitrative and grievance review as are other contractual disputes.

The third class of fines are those imposed where rules are broken. These, too, are amenable to a quasi-adminstrative agency process. We live in a time when administrative agencies, such as public housing organizations, cannot impose fines for misconduct without written rules and due process hearings.[109] Surely the same procedural guarantees can be provided in the area of sports.

It would be a mistake to think that the failure to provide constitutionally guaranteed due process and appropriate review in the area of sports fines is an isolated occurrence. For example, a similar failure exists where card counters are excluded from gambling casinos.[110] At

---

[107] No. 83-7723 (2d Cir. Dec. 20, 1983).

[108] Thus, the court confused state and federal actions in such a way that a litigant often will be damned if he does (res judicata) and damned if he doesn't (absention). See Winters v. Lavine, 574 F.2d 46 (2d Cir. 1978) (leaving litigants without guidance and displaying an unwarranted hostility to civil rights cases).

[109] See Escalera v. New York City Pub. Hous. Auth., 425 F.2d 853 (2d Cir. 1970).

[110] The exclusion of persons who can play the licensed games to their advantage seems at variance with the reasonable right to access at common law, and, where provided by statute, unconstitutional as well. Card counters keep track of the playing cards as they are dealt, and adjust their betting patterns as the odds change. When used over a period of time, this method

the root of such exclusions are questions of freedom of association and, perhaps, freedom of contract. Furthermore, the exclusion of winners (besides indicating the rather vicious nature of gambling casinos) involves a denial of access—through a type of eligibility require-ment—without administrative due process. Finally, even if it were argued that such exclusions were permissible through some type of contempt power, casinos should be permitted to exclude only those gamblers who act in such a way as to make the casinos incapable of carrying on their business. In any case, due process and rational review often appear to be given less weight than is merited.

## V. THE PROPER "IMAGE"

A potential argument against affording to sports dispute resolu-tion a treatment similar to judicialized adminstrative agency review is that such treatment adversely would affect the image of the sport. Implicit in this argument is the notion that sports must proceed as if run like an army. Though a football game may at times resemble armed combat, it does not follow that football must be like armed combat in its application of rules. The army presumably operates for speed and efficiency; death and destruction are uncorrectable. Foot-ball, on the other hand, is a game,[111] allowing for replays of downs and corrections of errors. We have no *need*, either in the judicial arena or on the football field, to subject people to the same type of arbitrary powers possessed by army sergeants. Yet, this is precisely what we do by insisting that an umpire's decision is to be supported

---

allegedly insures a profitable encounter with the casino. See Uston v. Hilton Hotels Corp., 448 F. Supp. 116 (D. Nev. 1978); Uston v. Resorts Int'l Hotel, Inc., 89 N.J. 163, 445 A.2d 370 (1982). This power to exclude, whether granted by statute or common law, appears to violate freedom of association. Furthermore, exclusion of those who are able to reap a benefit through their alleged ability to beat the system may diminish public confidence in the fairness and integrity of casino gambling. Card counters are usually excluded from casinos for being defiant trespassers. See the unfortunate tale of David Prinz, Prinz v. Greate Bay Casino Corp., 705 F.2d 692 (3d Cir. 1983) (card counter's guilty plea to the charge of defiant trespass estopped him to contend that he could lawfully remain in the casino). But what criminal act does a card counter commit to become a defiant trespasser? A defiant trespasser can be defined as one who, "knowing that he is not licensed or privileged to do [so,] . . . enters or remains in any place as to which notice against trespass is given." N.J. Stat. Ann. § 2C:18-3(b) (West 1982). If the card counter has a right or privilege to enter, as long as he is peaceful, and to play craps or roulette, why does he become a defiant trespasser when he chooses to play blackjack? Do casinos have a right to bar persons from gambling solely because they are lucky or smart?

[111] Though many coaches—e.g., George Halas and Vince Lombardi—might disagree with the view of football as a game, it is hard to imagine that they would carry their win-or-die-trying enthusiasm to the limit.

blindly whether it is right or wrong. The integrity of sports is effectively diminished until it becomes merely a matter of the exercise of
authority. In a democratic society, there is no reason why this image
of arbitrary authority is superior to an image of individuals following
the laws of the game.

An additional argument against judicial-type review in sports is
that such a process adversely would affect the continuity, and thus the
fans' enjoyment, of the game. But, as noted above,[112] with the availability of instant replay, this argument rings hollow. In a situation
such as the pine tar case, the historical perspective provided by the
"Bonehead" Merkle controversy should point out that a game can
always be replayed from the point at which the error in law was
made. The season in all sports is long (perhaps too long), and findings
of law can be made with reasonable rapidity. Certainly, Fred
Merkle's having touched second base was a condition precedent to a
run scoring, and whether the correct pine tar sanction was to throw
out the bat or to throw out the home run can be adjudicated with
rapidity in this day of electronic communication.

The most difficult area in which to utilize this process, of course,
is the sport of football, because so few games are played. To replay a
game seems an extreme hardship. However, the rules are much more
ambiguous in that sport, and most critical disputes of fact arise at the
very end of the game. Thus, the replaying of a game could be limited
to situations where the dispute proves to the outcome determinative.
Moreover, as an alternative to replaying entire games, the teams could
replay merely the disputed quarter or, where appropriate, the closing
minutes of the game.[113]

---

[112] See supra text accompanying notes 50–52.

[113] The 1984 National Football Conference championship game discussed above, see supra
note 52, provides an example of how such a system might operate. With approximately nine
minutes left in the game, Washington was in a third down and twenty situation from its own
thirteen yard line. At the time, it led San Francisco by a score of 21-14. In an attempt to sustain
their drive, the Redskins sent wide receiver Art Monk long for a pass, which he was unable to
handle. Though Monk protested, there was no penalty called. As a result, the Redskins were
forced to punt, and four plays later, the Forty-Niners scored the tying touchdown. Fortunately
for the Redskins, before the game was over, they were able to convert on a field goal and win the
game. Had that not been the case, this call would have had far greater significance.

The instant replays of this particular play (shot from different cameras at various angles)
quickly revealed that Tim Collier had indeed interfered with Art Monk (as was supported by
CBS sportscasters Pat Summerall and John Madden). The appropriate call would have given
Washington a first down on San Francisco's forty-five yard line (due to the forty-two yard
penalty) and a lead of seven points (21-14). Thus, were it necessary, the game should have been
replayed from that point on.

Finally, it should be noted that judicializing administrative proceedings in sports disputes would actually enhance the role of sport in our democracy. By treating free speech as sacred even in the world of sports, both the importance of free speech and the importance of sports as a democratic institution would be enhanced. Even in the eyes of philosophers, sports are seen as an important American institution.[114] The appearance of honesty in sports therefore is a significant step toward inculcating in individuals a sense of fair play. Since so many people identify with teams and with a game itself, an appearance of dishonesty would seriously diminish not only respect for the game, but for American institutions as well.

The possible rebuttal is that sports are merely entertainment, and therefore should proceed as rapidly as possible, short of blatant dishonesty. Some philosophers, however, might object that sports and games are totally rulebound[115] and therefore should not be considered to be mere entertainment. Sports fans will surely object that sports are not merely entertainment because of their identification with teams, or because crucial events in their lives are identified with sporting events. Certainly, players would not agree, since their careers, statistics, income and self-esteem[116] are all dependent on the outcome of these contests. Those who follow professional sports are generally not entertained by professional wrestling. Boxing has fallen into ill repute because of allegations that fights are fixed. An official fix by nonfeasance is little better than an official fix by malfeasance—it will similarly diminish the popularity of the sport. This is particularly true with the availability of instant replays on one hand and the tremendous number of models of administrative appellate review on the other. Finally, there comes a point where umpires and referees in various sports will gain guidance from the handling of rules in a rational appellate fashion. Just as adminstrative agencies sometimes desire to be sued to see if their rulings were correct, and lower court judges look to appellate court judges, so too, if there is an ambiguous rule (as some maintain the pine tar rule was), appeals—rather than diverse decisions by various umpires at different times—are the preferable means to resolve difficult questions of law.

---

[114] See, e.g., P. Weiss, Sport: A Philosophical Inquiry 142 (1969).

[115] John Madden, an ex-Oakland Raiders coach and current CBS sportscaster, often has commented that the additional penalties assessed against defensive teams in the last few years has detracted from the fundamentals of football.

[116] Virtually all the legendary football coaches—e.g., Vince Lombardi, George Halas, Don Shula and Tom Landry—appear to place enormous emphasis on football as a source of self-esteem.

Conclusion

In the world of sports, as in other areas, there is an increasing awareness of the necessity to refer to "judicialized" proceedings for the adjudication of disputes. Other organizations and institutions that affect American lives—often more vitally than do sports—have found that the delegation of discretion can lead to chaos and disaster. As a result, institutions such as family courts, corporations and adminstrative agencies have judicialized their proceedings so as to ensure accountability, visibility and rationality. The consequence has been that appeals of dispute resolutions are handled by independent arbitrators construing understandable rules. This is precisely what should have occurred in the pine tar case as well as other historical instances.[117]

Further consequences of this recognition should be the changing of the rules for expulsion of individuals from games or amusement places, the recognition of the importance of free speech and better utilization of instant replay technology. American sports can be improved—both as to what they teach our citizens and their entertainment value—by applying to them the types of clear concerns that have been applied to other institutions that affect our daily lives. The rational resolution of disputes can be seen as advantageous to all these institutions, and it is long overdue in the world of sports.

---

[117] Had there been such a final adjudication of the 1908 dispute, Fred Merkle might not be known today as "Bonehead," but rather as an old-time ballplayer who went from first to second and then went on to a distinguished career in the majors. Even more likely, he would not be known at all.

# PART 2

## BASEBALL AND THE ANTITRUST LAWS: THE UNIQUE ANTITRUST STATUS OF BASEBALL

The antitrust laws of the United States were enacted beginning in 1890. These laws prohibit agreements that restrict competition, monopolization, attempted monopolization, and mergers and acquisitions that tend to substantially lessen competition or tend to create a monopoly. The Supreme Court has described the antitrust laws as a charter of economic freedom of nearly constitutional dimension.

Yet these laws do not apply to major league baseball. Major league baseball stands alone among all sports and leisure activities, enjoying a nearly total antitrust immunity [*see Radovich v. National Football League*, 352 U.S. 445, 449-51 (1957)]. Even more curious is the fact that this immunity does not flow from any act of Congress but from a brief decision by the Supreme Court in 1922, *Federal Baseball Club of Baltimore v. National League*, 259 U.S. 200 (1922). Most commentators thought the decision was wrong at the time and now consider it ludicrous as major league baseball has grown into a truly global business with real estate development, corporate finance, merchandising, and broadcasting becoming equally prominent along with the athletic contests presented on the field.

The Supreme Court's decision to exempt baseball probably came as a big surprise to most observers. The earlier baseball cases did not suggest any sweeping immunity and tended to hold that organized baseball's conduct and restrictive rules violated the antitrust laws or the common law.

The decision of the Supreme Court in *Federal Baseball Club of Baltimore v. National League*, 259 U.S. 200 (1922) is often discussed but seldom read. In his simple and simplistic opinion, Justice Holmes did not hold that baseball was immune from the antitrust laws because it was a sport and not a business or because baseball was a sacred national pastime. He instead held baseball was not interstate commerce and, hence, beyond the scope of the

Sherman Act that applied only to interstate or foreign commerce. Justice Holmes managed to undercut whatever logic underlay this breathtaking conclusion the very next year where he held that traveling vaudeville shows *did* constitute interstate commerce [*see Hart v. Keith Vaudeville Exchange*, 262 U.S. 271 (1923)].

As the years have gone by, the Supreme Court has held that virtually everything, from a farmer growing crops for his own consumption, to a real estate brokerage firm, to a physician working in a urban hospital, is interstate commerce. Logic dictates that the business of baseball should be included also.

How then is baseball interstate commerce? Let us count some of the ways, drawing on the type of factors the Supreme Court has identified in other contexts:

1) Teams scout, recruit, train, and employ players and other personnel from all over the United States and the world;

2) Teams purchase equipment and supplies from around the world, including baseballs from Haiti;

3) Teams and players travel most of the fifty states, Canada, and selected other countries in playing and promoting exhibition and league games;

4) Merchandise and souvenirs are advertised and sold throughout the United States and around the world;

5) Fans travel across state and national boundaries to attend games;

6) Cities and states from around the country compete for franchises; and

7) Games are broadcast throughout the world.

There is no one who seriously contends that baseball should continue to be immune from the antitrust laws, at least on the grounds that Holmes enunciated in 1922. In fact, *Federal Baseball* is one of the most heavily criticized decisions and a source of embarrassment for scholars of Holmes and his considerable accomplishments in other areas of the law.[1] However, each time the Supreme Court has revisited this issue, it acts somewhat chagrined, but holds firm to its holding of *Federal Baseball*, reasoning that Congress is aware of the Court's holding in this area for the past seventy years, and that any change in the status quo should come from the legislature.

Congress for its part is content to preserve the status quo in order to maintain its leverage over organized baseball through the threat to remove the antitrust exemption that it played no part in creating. This threat hangs over major league baseball and is trotted out periodically to show Congressional displeasure with the failure to expand to new markets or franchise relocations, such as the decision not to permit the San Francisco Giants to relocate to Saint Petersburg, Florida. Most recently, Congressional displeasure peaked in response to the failure to settle the 1994 players strike in time to save the World Series. The Congressional hearings which occur every decade or two are often educational and occasionally hilarious (see Casey Stengel's testimony on baseball and antitrust), but have never resulted in legislative change, lest the threat of antitrust scrutiny actually be exercised and forever lost as leverage for future years.

Despite this dismal scenario, competitive principles have been leaking into the conduct of the business affairs of baseball since the end of World War II. Baseball increasingly has to compete against other sports and other forms of live and broadcast entertainment for the attendance, viewership, and financial support of its fans. Brave lower courts have nibbled at the lower edges of *Federal Baseball*, distinguishing the holding or the rationale as a way of affording players or owners some relief. Major league baseball typically has wisely settled those cases where it has not prevailed, lest the Supreme Court or Congress change their minds.

The winds of change continue to blow as a district court has recently held that baseball's antitrust immunity only extends to matters pertaining to player contracts [*see Piazza v. Major League Baseball*, 1993 U.S. Dist. LEXIS 10552 (E.D. Pa. 1993)]. Even this immunity may be illusory. Collusion over player contracts and the signing of free agents has been prohibited through collective bargaining, the application of the labor laws, and arbitration decisions that have penalized the owners millions dollars, though not with the full force of the treble damages available to a successful antitrust plaintiff.

The following cases and articles trace the history of this titanic struggle to bring economic competition to the operation of baseball along with the athletic competition on the field. We begin with *Federal Baseball* itself, continue with the cases testing its continuing validity, Congressional testimony and reports that continue to frame this divisive issue, and end with an examination of what would happen if the owners had to operate just like any other business.

## NOTES

1. The critiques of this decision are legion and its fans few. *See* Spencer Weber Waller, "The Antitrust Philosophy of Justice Holmes," 18 *S. Ill. U. L. Rev.* 283 (1993); Jeffrey A. Durney, "Fair or Foul? The Commissioner and Major League Baseball's Disciplinary Process," 41 *Emory L.J.* 581, 617–18 (1992); Thane N. Rosenbaum, "The Antitrust Implications of Professional Sports Leagues Revisited: Emerging Trends in the Modern Era," 41 *U. Miami L. Rev.* 729, 767–68 (1987); Robert G. Berger, "After the Strikes: A Reexamination of Professional Baseball's Exemption from the Antitrust Laws," 45 *U. Pitt. L. Rev.* 209 (1983); Robert C. Berry & William B. Gould, "A Long Deep Drive to Collective Bargaining: Of Players, Owners, Brawls and Strikes," 31 *Case West. L. Rev.* 685, 729–30 & n. 129 (1981); C. Paul Rogers III, "Judicial Reinterpretation of Statutes: The Example of Baseball and the Antitrust Laws," 14 *Hous. L. Rev.* 611, 620 (1977); Jay H. Topkis, "Monopoly in Professional Sports," 58 *Yale L.J.* 691 (1949); John W. Neville, "Baseball and the Antitrust Laws," 16 *Fordham L. Rev.* 208 (1947); Note, Robert W. McClelland, "Flood in the Land of Antitrust: Another Look at Professional Athletics, The Antitrust Laws and the Labor Law Exemption," 7 *Ind. L. Rev.* 541 (1974); Note, Richard B. Blackwell, "Baseball's Antitrust Exemption and the Reserve System: Reappraisal of an Anachronism," 12 *Wm. & Mary L. Rev.* 859, 865 (1971); Note, Barton J. Menitove, "Baseball's Antitrust Exemption: The Limits of Stare Decisis," 12 *B.C. Ind. & Comm. L. Rev.* 737 (1971); Note, James A. Thorpe, "Constitutional Law-Preemption—Baseball's Immunity from State Antitrust Law," 13 *Wayne L. Rev.* 417, 419 (1967); Comment, William K. Atchinson, "The Modern Trend in Antitrust and Professional Sports," 22 *Alb. L. Rev.* 272, 273–4 (1958); Comment, "Monopsony in Manpower: Organized Baseball Meets the Antitrust Laws," 62 *Yale L. J.* 576, 609 (1953); Comment, "Baseball Players and the Antitrust Laws," 53 *Colum. L. Rev.* 242 (1953); Comment, "Organized Baseball is Held to be Commerce Within the Meaning of Anti-Trust Acts," 1 *Syracuse L. Rev.* 148 (1949); Comment, "Interstate Commerce–Restraint of Trade—Professional Baseball May Constitute Interstate Commerce within Antitrust Laws," 62 *Harv. L. Rev.* 1240 (1949); Comment, "Trade Regulation–Sherman Act–Amenability of Organized Baseball," 34 *Iowa L. Rev.* 545 (1949); Note, George N. Kiroff and Carey S. Sheldon, "The Monopoly in Baseball," 18 *U. Cinn. L. Rev.* 203 (1949); Comment, "Constitutional Law-Baseball and the Anti-Trust Laws—A Game or a Conspiracy?," 24 *Notre Dame Law.* 372 (1949).

# FEDERAL BASEBALL CLUB OF BALTIMORE, INC. v. NATIONAL LEAGUE OF PROFESSIONAL BASEBALL CLUBS, ET AL.

ERROR TO THE COURT OF APPEALS OF THE DISTRICT OF COLUMBIA.

No. 204. Argued April 19, 1922.—Decided May 29, 1922.

MR. JUSTICE HOLMES delivered the opinion of the court.

This is a suit for threefold damages brought by the plaintiff in error under the Anti-Trust Acts of July 2, 1890, c. 647, § 7, 26 Stat. 209, 210, and of October 15, 1914, c. 323, § 4, 38 Stat. 730, 731. The defendants are The National League of Professional Base Ball Clubs and The American League of Professional Base Ball Clubs, unincorporated associations, composed respectively of groups of eight incorporated base ball clubs, joined as defendants; the presidents of the two Leagues and a third person, constituting what is known as the National Commission, having considerable powers in carrying out an agreement between the two Leagues; and three other persons having powers in the Federal League of Professional Base Ball Clubs, the relation of which to this case will be explained. It is alleged that these defendants conspired to monopolize the base ball business, the means adopted being set forth with a detail which, in the view that we take, it is unnecessary to repeat.

The plaintiff is a base ball club incorporated in Maryland, and with seven other corporations was a member of the Federal League of Professional Base Ball Clubs, a corporation under the laws of Indiana, that attempted to compete with the combined defendants. It alleges that the defendants destroyed the Federal League by buying up some of the constituent clubs and in one way or another inducing all those clubs except the plaintiff to leave their League, and that the three persons connected with the Federal League and named as defendants, one of them being the President of the League, took part in the conspiracy. Great damage to the plaintiff is alleged. The plaintiff obtained a verdict for $80,000 in the Supreme Court and a judgment for treble the amount was entered, but the Court of Appeals, after an elaborate discussion, held that the defendants were not within the Sherman Act. The appellee, the plaintiff, elected to stand on the record in order to bring the case to this Court at once, and thereupon judgment was ordered for the defendants. 50 App. D. C. 165; 269 Fed. 681, 688. It is not argued that the plaintiff waived any rights by its course. *Thomsen* v. *Cayser*, 243 U. S. 66.

The decision of the Court of Appeals went to the root of the case and if correct makes it unnecessary to consider other serious difficulties in the way of the plaintiff's recovery. A summary statement of the nature of the business involved will be enough to present the point. The clubs composing the Leagues are in different cities and for the most part in different States. The end of the elaborate organizations and sub-organizations that are described in the pleadings and evidence is that these clubs shall play against one another in public exhibitions for money, one or the other club crossing a state line in order to make the meeting possible. When as the result of these contests one club has won the pennant of its League and another club has won the pennant of the other League, there is a final competition for the world's championship between these two. Of course the scheme requires constantly repeated travelling on the part of the clubs, which is provided for, controlled and disciplined by the organizations, and this it is said means commerce among the States. But we are of opinion that the Court of Appeals was right.

The business is giving exhibitions of base ball, which are purely state affairs. It is true that, in order to attain for these exhibitions the great popularity that they have achieved, competitions must be arranged between clubs from different cities and States. But the fact that in order to give the exhibitions the Leagues must induce free persons to cross state lines and must arrange and pay for their doing so is not enough to change the character of the business.   According to the distinction insisted upon in *Hooper* v. *California,* 155 U. S. 648, 655, the transport is a mere incident, not the essential thing.   That to which it is incident, the exhibition, although made for money would not be called trade or commerce in the commonly accepted use of those words.   As it is put by the defendants, personal effort, not related to production, is not a subject of commerce.   That which in its consummation is not commerce does not become commerce among the States because the transportation that we have mentioned takes place.   To repeat the illustrations given by the Court below, a firm of lawyers sending out a member to argue a case, or the Chautauqua lecture bureau sending out lecturers, does not engage in such commerce because the lawyer or lecturer goes to another State.

If we are right the plaintiff's business is to be described in the same way and the restrictions by contract that prevented the plaintiff from getting players to break their bargains and the other conduct charged against the defendants were not an interference with commerce among the States.

*Judgment affirmed.*

es, and that defendants made contracts with radio broadcasting and television companies to send across state lines play-by-play narratives or moving pictures of the games, sufficiently charged that defendants were engaged in "interstate commerce" within Anti-Trust Acts. Sherman Anti-Trust Act, §§ 1–3, as amended, 15 U.S.C.A. §§ 1–3; Clayton Act, §§ 2–4, as amended, 15 U.S.C.A. §§ 13–15.

See Words and Phrases, Permanent Edition, for other judicial constructions and definitions of "Interstate Commerce".

CHASE, Circuit Judge, dissenting.

———————

Appeal from the United States District Court for the Southern District of New York.

Action by Daniel L. Gardella against Albert B. Chandler, individually and as Commissioner of Baseball, and others, for treble damages under the Anti-trust Acts. From judgment dismissing complaint on the merits for lack of jurisdiction, 79 F. Supp. 260, the plaintiff appeals.

Reversed and remanded.

Frederic A. Johnson, of New York City (Frederic A. Johnson, Edward H. Beck, Jr., both of New York City, of counsel), for appellant.

Willkie, Owen, Farr, Gallagher & Walton, of New York City, for appellees.

Baker, Hostetler & Patterson, of Cleveland, Ohio, for appellee William Harridge, individually and as President of The American League of Professional Baseball Clubs, a voluntary unincorporated association.

**GARDELLA v. CHANDLER.**

No. 98, Docket 21133.

United States Court of Appeals
Second Circuit.

Feb. 9, 1949.

**Monopolies** ⊜28(6)

Complaint by baseball player against Commissioner of Baseball and National League and American League and others for treble damages under Anti-trust Acts, which alleged that defendants operated baseball teams which travelled between states for purpose of playing baseball gam-

Hedges, Hoover & Tingley, of Columbus, Ohio, for appellee George M. Trautman, individually and as President of The National Association of Professional Baseball Leagues, described in the complaint herein as "The National Association of Baseball Leagues."

Edgar P. Feeley, of New York City, Raymond Jackson, of Cleveland, Ohio, and Mark F. Hughes, of New York City, for appellee National Exhibition Co.

Before L. HAND, Chief Judge, and CHASE and FRANK, Circuit Judges.

CHASE, Circuit Judge.

The appellant brought this suit to recover treble damages under Secs. 1, 2 and 3 of the Sherman Act, 26 Stat. 209, 15 U.S.C.A. §§ 1, 2 and 3, and under, as stated in the complaint, Secs. 2 and 3 of the Clayton Act, 15 U.S.C.A. §§ 13 and 14. Apparently he relies upon Sec. 4 of the Clayton Act, 38 Stat. 731, 15 U.S.C.A. § 15, and we shall so treat his complaint.

He is a professional baseball player who, while under contract to play exclusively with the ball club popularly called the New York Giants which is owned and operated by one of the appellees, the National Exhibition Company, a New York corporation, violated the terms of the hereafter mentioned reserve clause of that contract by playing professional baseball in Mexico. He was consequently barred for a period of years from playing with baseball clubs in what is known as "organized baseball" in accordance with the provisions of his contract with the National Exhibition Company and thus deprived pro tanto of his means of livelihood. This suit followed and the first issue presented by this appeal is whether the district court had jurisdiction of the cause of action under the Sherman and Clayton Acts. The complaint was dismissed solely on the ground that the court had no such jurisdiction and no other is claimed now. D.C., 79 F.Supp. 260.

The appellant undertook to allege three causes of action against the appellees who are Albert B. Chandler, individually and as the Commissioner of Baseball; Ford C. Frick, individually and as President of the National League of Professional Baseball Clubs, an unincorporated association; William Harridge, individually and as president of the American League of Professional Baseball Clubs, an unincorporated association; George M. Trautman, individually and as president of The National Association of Professional Baseball Leagues, an unincorporated association; and National Exhibition Company, before mentioned.

He alleged generally in support of each cause of action that "organized baseball" comprised two so-called major leagues known respectively as the National and the American and the so-called minor leagues made up of clubs composing leagues of eight grades based upon the respective abilities of the players in the several clubs in each of such leagues. There are eight clubs in each of the major leagues and each club plays during a season games at its home grounds and games at the home grounds of each of the others until each club has played approximately one hundred and fifty games. The winning club in each major league plays a series of games with the winning club in the other at the close of the season for what is called the world championship, and during the season selected players from the clubs in each league perform as a team in playing a similarly selected team in what is called an "all stars" game. The clubs in the National League are located in the following places where each owns or leases a baseball park where games are played. Boston, Mass.; New York, N. Y.; Brooklyn, N. Y.; Philadelphia, Pa.; Pittsburgh, Pa.; Cincinnati, Ohio; Chicago, Ill., and St. Louis, Mo. The clubs of the American League own or lease parks where games are played in the following places. Boston, Mass.; New York, N. Y.; Philadelphia, Pa.; Washington, D. C.; Cleveland, Ohio; Detroit, Mich.; Chicago, Ill.; and St. Louis, Mo. The individual clubs are owned by corporations organized under the laws of the respective states in which their parks are located. The minor leagues are composed of clubs in a similar way and these clubs play games in various cities in this country and Canada.

These leagues and the clubs comprising them have entered into agreements, designed to control the manner in which "organized baseball" shall be conducted, which require players to be bound to their respective clubs by what is known as the standard contract. The so-called major league agreement, among other things, gives to appellee Chandler supervisory and disciplinary power over the major leagues, their clubs and their players. The so-called major-minor league agreement gives him similar powers over the minor leagues, their clubs and their players. The standard player contract includes what is known as a reserve clause which requires a player who is under contract to play with any club to refrain, at the expiration of the period of his employment, from contracting to play for, or playing for, any other club other than the one to which he has been under contract or its assignee. Thus, and in other particulars which need not be presently described, the agreements in "organized baseball" have created a closely knit organization which was intended to, and does, dominate and control to a large extent the playing of professional baseball in this country, Canada, Cuba, Puerto Rico and Mexico.

In playing their games the teams of the various clubs perform in the ball parks already referred to and each game is ended in the park where it is begun. But in order to get to the park where the game is played some or all of the players, managers, coaches, and employees have to travel across state or foreign boundaries; and the equipment necessary for the traveling club, consisting of uniforms, bats, gloves, mitts, masks, chest protectors, shin guards, baseballs and the like is similarly transported.

The club owners charge admission fees for all games played and divide them with the other contesting clubs as agreed. They, or most of them, also sell for valuable consideration the right to broadcast play-by-play descriptions of the games over the radio and thus across state lines, and some of them sell the right to broadcast the games by television. Some of those to whom these broadcast rights are sold get, and use, the opportunity so provided to advertise goods, articles and commodities which are sold and distributed nationally and internationally.

Since my brothers agree that the judgment should be reversed I will now state what are but my own reasons for believing that it should be affirmed; (1) because a controlling decision of the Supreme Court requires it and (2) because, even if that decision is distinguishable, the allegations in the complaint fail to state a cause of action over which the district court had jurisdiction.

The issues here presented are, as the district judge recognized, decidedly not of first impression. This record is with the possible exception of the allegations as to the sale of broadcasting rights for radio and television, not different in any esssential from that before the Supreme Court in Federal Base Ball Club v. National League, 259 U.S. 200, 42 S.Ct. 465, 66 L.Ed. 898, 26 A.L.R. 357 in which it was held that major league ball clubs were not engaged in interstate trade or commerce within the scope of the anti-trust laws. Even the possible exception just mentioned exists only if the sale of these radio and television broadcast rights differs in some material way from the sale of the exclusive right to send "play-by-play" descriptions of the games interstate over telegraph wires, for that feature was present in the previous case before the Supreme Court. In each instance by what is called the sale of rights the appellees made it possible for others to transmit information interstate. The playing of baseball games then created the subject matter concerning which information was sent by symbols carried by telegraph wires and translated into words just as such play now creates the subject matter concerning which information is sent through the air by impulses which are transformed either into words or pictures. So far as I can perceive, the difference in the method of transmission is without significance.

These appellees do not themselves broadcast anything nor do they do anything more by way of production of what is broadcast than was shown to have been done in the former case to "produce" what was described. Since the sellers of the rights to broadcast through the air do only what the sellers of the rights to send descriptions over telegraph wires did in the former case I can find no sound basis on the facts for distinguishing that case from this. It seems to me to have decided the precise question here presented and that it controls our decision.

It has never been expressly overruled, and I do not think it has been overruled by necessary implication by United States v. South-Eastern Underwriters Ass'n, 322 U.S. 533, 64 S.Ct. 1162, 88 L.Ed. 1440, which reflected a trend in decision not apparent in Hooper v. People of State of California, 155 U.S. 648, 15 S.Ct. 207, 39 L.Ed. 297, on which the court relied somewhat in deciding Federal Base Ball Club v. National League, supra. That decisions like Wickard v. Filburn, 317 U.S. 111, 63 S.Ct. 82, 87 L.Ed. 122, and Mandeville Island Farms, Inc. v. American Crystal Sugar Co., 334 U.S. 219, 68 S.Ct. 996 show a wide reach of Congressional power under the Commerce Clause when Congress chooses to exert it cannot be gainsaid. And United States v. South-Eastern Underwriters Ass'n, supra, reiterates that Congress intended to put within the coverage of the Anti-Trust Acts everything which was interstate or foreign trade or commerce. But in none of these decisions mentioned nor in any others of the Supreme Court of which I am aware, save only Federal Base Ball Club v. National League, supra, has there been a definite holding that "organized baseball" is, or is not, trade or commerce within the meaning of those words in the Sherman and Clayton Acts. Moreover, the rule there stated has since been applied by analogy in another field. Hart v. B. F. Keith Vaudeville Exchange, 2 Cir., 12 F.2d 341, certiorari denied, 273 U.S. 704, 47 S.Ct. 98, 71 L.Ed. 849; Neugen v. Associated Chautauqua Co., 10 Cir., 70 F.2d 605. Furthermore, the case was recently cited and distinguished in North American Co. v. S. E. C., 327 U.S. 686, 694, 66 S.Ct. 785, 90 L.Ed. 945. See Sears v. Hassett, 1 Cir., 111 F.2d 961, 965; cf. Perkins v. Endicott Johnson Corp., 2 Cir., 128 F.2d 208, 218.

Under these circumstances it seems to me that our duty as a subordinate court is to follow the Federal Base Ball Club case. I find no necessary implication among the cases to which I have previously alluded or in any others that it has been overruled. All of them relate to activities quite unlike organized baseball and, though general language can be found in the opinions to indicate changes in methods of approach to decision, there is no actual decision so incompatible with that in Federal Base Ball Club v. National League, supra, as to displace the latter by mere weight of its authority. The interpretation of the anti-trust laws has hitherto been ac-

complished in a case by case manner which has given due effect to the particular facts and circumstances shown. I cannot find any authoritative definition of the words "trade or commerce" or "affecting trade or commerce" as used in the cases which is so comprehensive that this method can be dispensed with. The intricate nature of the various questions involved makes it apparently impossible to devise a formula which will automatically, so to speak, put any and all situations either within or without the coverage of the acts.

In dealing with such a unique aggregate as organized baseball and with a decision in respect to it which seems to be directly in point on the facts, we should not be astute in seeking to anticipate that the court which has the power to do so will change that decision. To do so would not only be an unwarranted attempt to usurp the authority of that court but would make its task in general much more difficult since it would lead to a constant alteration in the lower courts of its decisions on specific fact situations in the light of what would appear to be differing rules stated in the course of deciding later cases on different facts. We relied on Federal Base Ball Club v. National League, supra, in our recent decision in Conley v. San Carlo Opera Co., 2 Cir., 163 F.2d 310, and until, and unless, we are advised by competent authority that it is no longer the law we should continue to abide by it.

On the second point, it seems to me that cases which involve more that the regulation of trade and commerce per se, and rest upon the explicit control by Congress in other statutes of the production of goods for commerce or the control of labor relations, furnish but very slippery ground on which to base decision here. What those statutes have in common with the anti-trust acts which is now material, as I see it, is only that all were within the power of Congress to enact under the Commerce Clause. Const. art. 1, § 8. When it is said that Congress has exerted all the power it possessed in the anti-trust acts, Atlantic Cleaners & Dyers v. United States, 286 U.S. 427, 435, 52 S.Ct. 607, 76 L.Ed. 1204, it is meant only that within the field there dealt with Congress meant to act fully, leaving other phases of its power under the Commerce Clause outside their scope.

The field covered was "restraint of trade" which had a well known meaning at common law and the words "or commerce between the several states" were added to put the restraints prohibited within constitutional limitations on Congressional power. The Supreme Court has never, so far as I know, applied the Sherman Act in any case unless it was of the opinion that there was some form of restraint upon commercial competition in the marketing of goods and services in interstate commerce which was within the category of restraints which were illegal at common law, though expressions may be found in opinions which seem to make adherence to this concept somewhat elastic. In any event, as recently as Apex Hosiery Co. v. Leader, 310 U.S. 469, 500, 501, 60 S.Ct. 982, 996, 84 L.Ed. 1311, 128 A.L.R. 1044, Mr. Justice Stone said, in speaking for the majority of the court, "In the cases considered by this Court since the Standard Oil case in 1911 some form of restraint of commercial competition has been the sine qua non to the condemnation of contracts, combinations or conspiracies under the Sherman Act, and in general restraints upon competition have been condemned only when their purpose or effect was to raise or fix the market price.[1] It is in this sense that it is said that the restraint, actual or intended, prohibited by the Sherman Act, are only those which are so substantial as to affect market prices. Restraints on competition or on the course of trade in the merchandising of articles moving in interstate commerce is not enough, unless the restraint is shown to have or is intended to have an effect upon prices in the market or otherwise to deprive purchasers or consumers of the advantages which they derive from free competition. Chicago Board of Trade v. United States, 246 U.S. 231, 238, 38 S.Ct. 242, 243, 62 L.Ed. 683; United States v. United States

Steel Co., 251 U.S. 417, 40 S.Ct. 293, 64 L.Ed. 343, 8 A.L.R. 1121; Cement Manufacturers Protective Ass'n. v. United States, 268 U.S. 588, 45 S.Ct. 586, 69 L.Ed. 1104; United States v. International Harvester Co., 274 U.S. 693, 47 S.Ct. 748, 71 L.Ed. 1302; Appalachian Coals v. United States, 288 U.S. 344, 375 et seq., 53 S.Ct. 471, 479 et seq., 77 L.Ed. 825."

In the Mandeville case, supra, the Court was dealing with a situation which did have a substantial effect upon the prices of goods in the market and did deprive purchasers or consumers of advantages which would have been theirs under free competition. While the test of indirectness of effect was somewhat muted, and perhaps discarded, the substance or the so-called "rule of reason" was not. Whatever the activity and how it may be conducted, it is not within the prohibition of the anti-trust laws unless in some substantial way the prices of goods in interstate commerce are controlled to the detriment of the purchaser or consumer.

The complaint in this case shoots wide of that mark. The wrong alleged as the end result of the monopoly, or conspiracy to create a monopoly, in restraint of trade or commerce is the deprivation of the appellant of the opportunity to play baseball as a means of earning his livelihood. His services, or ability to work, are not subjects of trade or commerce within the anti-trust acts. Indeed, in Sec. 6 of the Clayton Act, 15 U.S.C.A. § 17, it is stated that, "The labor of a human being is not a commodity or article of commerce." Although this, to be sure, was inserted for a purpose not here germane it shows nevertheless that Congress did not intend in the anti-trust acts to cover restraints upon employment. Moreover, Congress has expressly dealt with that subject in other statutes like the National Labor Relations Act, 29 U.S.C.A. § 151 et seq., and the Fair Labor Standards Act, 29 U.S.C.A. § 201 et seq.

Nor are there any allegations as to any monopoly to control, or any conspiracy

---

[1] See e.g. Ethyl Gasoline Corp. v. United States, 309 U.S. 436, 60 S.Ct. 618, 84 L.Ed. 852; United States v. Socony- Vacuum Oil Co., 310 U.S. at page 150, especially Note 59, 60 S.Ct. 811, 84 L. Ed. 1129 and cases cited.

to create one to control, the prices at which the rights to send descriptions of the games, visually or otherwise, are sold; and as much is true as to the advertising by the purchasers of those rights. Nor as to what effect, if any, such by-products of the games have upon the prices at which goods are sold in commerce or upon the purchasers and consumers of those goods. Nor that what is done in respect to broadcasting or telecasting the games has any causal connection with the damage the appellant alleges. See K. & K. Co. v. Special Site Sign Co., 9 Cir., 85 F.2d 742, certiorari denied, 299 U.S. 613, 57 S.Ct. 315, 81 L.Ed. 452.

I would affirm the judgment but as my brothers hold otherwise it is, for the reasons stated in their separate opinions, reversed and the cause is remanded for trial.

L. HAND, Circuit Judge.

The complaint alleges that the defendants make contracts with broadcasting and television companies by which these companies send across state lines play-by-play narratives, or moving pictures, of the games; and, although in Federal Baseball Club v. National League,[1] the record contained evidence that it was the custom to broadcast accounts of the games by telegraph, that was an incident of so little importance that the Court of Appeals merely mentioned it without comment and the Supreme Court did not even allude to it. Besides, the difference between the telegraphing of that time and present-day radio or television, even though it were no more than a difference of degree —which it is not—would be so great as for practical purposes to make a difference in kind. I shall not labor the argument that the transmission of these narratives and moving pictures is itself interstate commerce; the only debatable question is whether the defendants' connection with these activities makes them a part of their business, and enough a part of it to color the whole. As I understand it, they enter into contracts with broadcasting and television companies, by which for large payments they allow the companies to install suitable apparatus in the "ball-parks," by means of which the companies transmit the narratives and pictures to the outside public. It is not necessary to say whether one, who sells goods indifferently to all comers, is pro tanto engaged in interstate commerce, because a part of his customers come from another state and carry their purchases home. In such cases the seller's indifference to the destination of the goods may isolate him from their eventual destination; at least he cannot be said to have joined with the buyers in the interstate part of their purposes. True, the sale is a condition sine qua non of the buyers' ability to carry the goods out of the state; but, if that be enough, there is no apparent reason to end the regression of causes with the sale. Whether every department store is engaged in interstate commerce is a question I shall not undertake to answer; and this I may do, because the defendants' relation to broadcasting and television is quite different. The contracts with the companies are mutual arrangements in which each contributes its share to a common venture; the defendants furnish the spectacle and give the companies leave to enter and set up their apparatus on the grounds, by means of which they transform for transmission the air and light waves, which come from the playing-grounds and the players, or from the narrator who reports the game; and the transformed waves they send abroad either in a form for direct reception or otherwise. This interposition is of course necessary, when the auditory is at a distance; but for our purposes the result seems no different from direct transmission; and the situation appears to me the same as that which would exist at a "ball-park" where a state line ran between the diamond and the grandstand. Nor can the arrangements between the defendants and the companies be set down as merely incidents of the business, as were the interstate features in Federal Baseball Club v. National League, supra.[1] On the contrary, they are part of the business itself, for that consists in

---

[1] 259 U.S. 200, 42 S.Ct. 465, 66 L.Ed. 898, 26 A.L.R. 357.

giving public entertainments; the players are the actors, the radio listeners and the television spectators are the audiences; together they form as indivisible a unit as do actors and spectators in a theatre. I am therefore in accord with my brother Frank that the defendants are pro tanto engaged in interstate commerce.

On the other hand, I cannot go along with his opinion, if I understand it, that these features of the business, no matter how insignificant they may prove, necessarily subject it as a whole to the Anti-Trust Acts. The plaintiff is asking damages for excluding him from his calling; and to succeed he must show that the defendants' conduct, by which he was injured, was itself subject to the law that he invokes. I do not mean that he must show that he was injured by the broadcasting and television; but he must show that those activities together with any other interstate activities mark the business as a whole. Certainly that was implied in Federal Baseball v. National League, supra,[1] itself; nobody questioned that many interstate activities were in fact involved in professional baseball; the Court merely thought them not important enough to fix the business—at large—with an interstate character. I can find nothing in the books since then, which leads me to think otherwise. Mabee v. White Plains Publishing Co.[2] did indeed hold that, quoad those newspapers which crossed a state line, the publisher was engaged in the "production of goods for commerce"; and it may be that employees concerned in the production of even so small a part of a total output are within the Fair Labor Standards Act. However that may be, I cannot believe that that decision was intended to overrule the repeated decisions that the Anti-Trust Acts do not cover all persons who engage to any degree whatever in interstate commerce. If so, we are wasting our time over the Baseball case for it was overruled sub silentio. When the case goes back for trial—assuming that it does so

upon our opinions—it will be necessary, as I view it, to determine whether all the interstate activities of the defendants —those, which were thought insufficient before, in conjunction with broadcasting and television—together form a large enough part of the business to impress upon it an interstate character. I do not know how to put it in more definite terms.

As I understand my brother Chase, he thinks that, even though the defendants' business be in general subject to the Anti-Trust Acts, the "reserve clause" is not in violation of them. For this he relies principally upon Apex Hosiery Co. v. Leader,[3] a case in which the Court found it unnecessary to decide whether labor unions were within the Acts. The Court thought that, although the strike in question might well have had an effect upon the price of stockings which passed into interstate commerce, the purpose of the strikers was not that, and the result, if any, was only an incident. Be that as it may, whatever other conduct the Acts may forbid, they certainly forbid all restraints of trade which were unlawful at common-law, and one of the oldest and best established of these is a contract which unreasonably forbids any one to practice his calling. I do not think that at this stage of the action we should pass upon the "reserve clause"; and therefore I do not join in my brother Frank's present disposition of it, although I do not mean that I dissent from him. All that I wish now to decide is that the complaint avers enough to present an issue upon a trial. I think that the judgment should be reversed and the cause should be remanded for trial.

FRANK, Circuit Judge.

1. No one can treat as frivolous the argument that the Supreme Court's recent decisions have completely destroyed the vitality of Federal Baseball Club v. National League, 259 U.S. 200, 42 S.Ct. 465, 66 L.Ed. 898, 26 A.L.R. 357, decided twenty-seven years ago, and have left that

---

[1] 259 U.S. 200, 42 S.Ct. 465, 66 L. Ed. 898, 26 A.L.R. 357.

[2] 327 U.S. 178, 66 S.Ct. 511, 90 L.Ed. 607.

[3] 310 U.S. 469, 60 S.Ct. 982, 84 L.Ed. 1311, 128 A.L.R. 1044.

case but an impotent zombi. Nevertheless, it seems best that this court should not so hold.[1] However, in Ring v. Spina, 148 F.2d 647, 651, 160 A.L.R. 371, referring to that case and another similar case,[2] this court said that, because of "the steadily expanding content of the phrase 'interstate commerce' in recent years; * * * there is no longer occasion for applying these earlier cases beyond their exact facts." For reasons stated later, I think that, on its facts, we can properly distinguish the suit now before us from the Federal Baseball case.

I think it should be so distinguished, if possible, because (assuming, as we must, at this stage of the litigation, the truth of the statements in the complaint) we have here a monopoly which, in its effect on ball-players like the plaintiff, possesses characteristics shockingly repugnant to moral principles that, at least since the War Between the States, have been basic in America, as shown by the Thirteenth Amendment to the Constitution, condemning "involuntary servitude," and by subsequent Congressional enactments on that subject.[3] For the "reserve clause," as has been observed, results in something resembling peonage of the baseball player. By accepting the "reserve clause"—and all players in organized baseball must "accept" it—a player binds himself not to sign a contract with, or play for, any

---

[1] I reach that conclusion somewhat hesitantly. For, while the Supreme Court has never explicitly overruled the Federal Baseball Club case, it has overruled the precedents upon which that decision was based; and the concept of commerce has changed enough in the last two decades so that, if that case were before the Supreme Court de novo, it seems very likely that the Court would decide the other way. This court cannot, of course, tell the Supreme Court that it was once wrong. But "one should not wait for formal retraction in the face of changes plainly foreshadowed;" this court's duty is "to divine, as best it can, what would be the event of the appeal in the case before it." L. Hand, C. J., dissenting in Spector Motor Service Co. v. Walsh, 2 Cir., 139 F.2d 809, 823. In Perkins v. Endicott Johnson Corp., 2 Cir., 128 F.2d 208, 217, 218, we said: "Legal doctrines, as first enunciated, often prove to be inadequate under the impact of ensuing experience in their practical application. And when a lower court perceives a pronounced new doctrinal trend in Supreme Court decisions, it is its duty, cautiously to be sure, to follow not to resist it." In Picard v. United Aircraft Corp., 2 Cir., 128 F.2d 632, 636, we said per L. Hand, J.: "In this we recognize 'a pronounced new doctrinal trend' which it is our 'duty, cautiously to be sure, to follow not to resist.'"

In Barnette v. West Virginia State Board of Education, D.C., 47 F.Supp. 251, 252, 253 Judge Parker, sitting in a three-judge court, said: "Ordinarily we would feel constrained to follow an unreversed decision of the Supreme Court of the United States, whether we agreed with it or not. * * * The developments with respect to the Gobitis case, [Minersville School Dist. v. Gobitis, 310 U.S. 586, 60

S.Ct. 1010, 84 L.Ed. 1375, 127 A.L.R. 1493], however, are such that we do not feel that it is incumbent upon us to accept it as binding authority. Of the seven justices now members of the Supreme Court who participated in that decision, four have given public expression to the view that it is unsound, the present Chief Justice in his dissenting opinion rendered therein and three other justices in a special dissenting opinion in Jones v. City of Opelika, 316 U.S. 584, 62 S.Ct. 1231, 1251, 86 L.Ed. 1691, [141 A.L.R. 514]. The majority of the court in Jones v. City of Opelika, moreover, thought it worth while to distinguish the decision in the Gobitis case, instead of relying upon it as supporting authority. Under such circumstances and believing, as we do, that the flag salute here required is violative of religious liberty when required of persons holding the religious views of plaintiffs, we feel that we would be recreant to our duty as judges, if through a blind following of a decision which the Supreme Court itself has thus impaired as an authority, we should deny protection to rights which we regard as among the most sacred of those protected by constitutional guaranties."

[2] Hart v. B. F. Keith Vaudeville Exchange, 2 Cir., 12 F.2d 341, 47 A.L.R. 775.

[3] 8 U.S.C.A. § 56 and 18 U.S.C.A. § 1581; see United States v. Reynolds, 235 U.S. 133, 35 S.Ct. 86, 59 L.Ed. 162; Bailey v. Alabama, 219 U.S. 219, 31 S. Ct. 145, 55 L.Ed. 191; Clyatt v. United States, 197 U.S. 207, 25 S.Ct. 429, 49 L. Ed. 726; Taylor v. State of Georgia, 315 U.S. 25, 62 S.Ct. 415, 86 L.Ed. 615; Pollock v. Williams, 322 U.S. 4, 62 S.Ct. 415 86 L.Ed. 615.

172 F.2d—26½

club other than the club which originally employs him or its assignee. Although many courts have refused to enforce the "reserve" clause,[4] yet severe and practically efficacious extra-legal penalties are imposed for violation. The most extreme of these penalties is the blacklisting of the player so that no club in organized baseball will hire him. In effect, this clause prevents a player from ever playing with any team other than his original employer, unless that employer consents. Since the right to play with organized baseball is indispensable to the career of a professional baseball player, violations of the clause by such players are infrequent. The violator may perhaps become a judge (with a less exciting and often less remunerative occupation) or a bartender or a street-sweeper, but his chances of ever again playing baseball are exceedingly slim.

As one court, perhaps a bit exaggeratedly, has put it,[5] "While the services of these baseball players are ostensibly secured by voluntary contracts a study of the system as * * * practiced under the plan of the National Agreement, reveals the involuntary character of the servitude which is imposed upon players by the strength of the combination controlling the labor of practically all of the players in the country. * * * There is no difference in principle between the system of servitude built up by the operation of this National Agreement, which * * * provides for the purchase, sale barter, and exchange of the services of baseball players—skilled laborers—without their consent, and the system of peonage brought into the United States from Mexico and thereafter existing for a time within the territory of New Mexico. * * * The system created by 'organized baseball' in recent years presents the question of the establishment of a scheme by which the personal freedom, the right to contract for their labor wherever they will, of 10,000 skilled laborers, is placed under the dominion of a benevolent despotism through the operation of the monopoly established by the National Agreement." I may add that, if the players be regarded as quasi-peons, it is of no moment that they are well paid; only the totalitarian-minded will believe that high pay excuses virtual slavery.

In what I have said about the nature of the contracts made with the players, I am not to be understood as implying that they violate the Thirteenth Amendment or the statutes enacted pursuant thereto. I mean simply to suggest that those contracts are so opposed to the public policy of the United States [5a] that, if possible, they should be deemed within the prohibitions of the Sherman Act 15 U.S. C.A. §§ 1–7, 15 note.

2. On a motion to dismiss, the complaint must be liberally construed in plaintiff's favor. So construing this complaint, I think that the facts of the instant case significantly differ from those in the Federal Baseball case, because here the defendants have lucratively contracted for the interstate communication, by radio and television, of the playings of the games.[5b] In that earlier case, the Court held that the traveling across state lines was but an incidental means of enabling games to be played locally—i.e., within particular states—and therefore insufficient to constitute interstate commerce.[5c] Here,

---

[4] Allegheny Baseball Club v. Bennett, C.C.W.D.Pa., 14 F. 257; Metropolitan Exhibition Co. v. Ewing, C.C.S.D.N.Y., 42 F. 198, 7 L.R.A. 381; Brooklyn Baseball Club v. McGuire, C.C.E.D.Pa., 116 F. 782; Weeghman v. Killefer, 6 Cir., 215 F. 289, L.R.A.1915A, 820; American League Baseball Club v. Chase, 86 Misc. 441, 149 N.Y.S. 6; Cincinnati Exhibition Co. v. Johnson, 190 Ill.App. 630; Metropolitan Exhibition Co. v. Ward, 9 N. Y.S. 779.

[5] American League Baseball Club v. Chase, 86 Misc. 441, 465, 466, 149 N.Y.S. 6, 19.

[5a] Cf. Hurd v. Hodge, 334 U.S. 24, 34, 68 S.Ct. 847.

[5b] That the defendants' radio contracts are lucrative, see, Pittsburgh Athletic Co. v. KQV Broadcasting Co., D.C., 24 F.Supp. 490; Mutual Broadcasting System, Inc. v. Muzak Corp., 177 Misc. 489, 30 N.Y.S.2d 419.

[5c] In passing, I note that that ruling is difficult to reconcile with the Mann Act cases; Caminetti v. United States, 242 U.S. 470, 37 S.Ct. 192, 61 L.Ed. 442, L.R.A.1917F, 502, Ann.Cas.1917B, 1168; Mortensen v. United States, 322 U.S. 369, 375, 64 S.Ct. 1037, 88 L.Ed. 1331;

although the playing of the games is essential to both defendants' intra-state and interstate activities, the interstate communication by radio and television is in no way a means, incidental or otherwise, of performing the intra-state activities (the local playings of the games).

True, in the Federal Baseball Club case, there was present in the record the fact that the defendants had sold the exclusive right to send "play-by-play" descriptions of the games over interstate telegraph wires. But the brief of the plaintiff filed in the Supreme Court in that case did not contend that that interstate communication was interstate commerce; it merely called attention to the telegraph service as one of several factors tending to show the popularity and national character of "organized Baseball." Moreover, the Supreme Court in its opinion in that case did not note the fact concerning the telegraph service; and it has often been held that a decision is not to be regarded as a precedent concerning a question clearly not considered by the Court, because "to make it so, there must have been an application of the judicial mind to the precise question, * * * " 5d

Accordingly, as the Court in the Federal Baseball case, in deciding that interstate features were absent, discussed nothing but the traveling of the teams and their paraphernalia between states, as a means to the local playing of the games, I think that decision, as above indicated, should be deemed to hold no more than that such traveling does not give rise to interstate commerce for Sherman Act purposes. That such was the ruling appears from the way in which the Supreme Court there dealt with the facts: "A summary statement of the nature of the business involved will be enough to present the point. The clubs composing the Leagues are in different cities and for

the most part in different States. The end of the elaborate organizations and sub-organizations that are described in the pleadings and evidence is that these clubs shall play against one another in public exhibitions for money, one or the other club crossing a state line in order to make the meeting possible. When as the result of these contests one club has won the pennant of its League and another club has won the pennant of the other League, there is a final competition for the World's championship between these two. Of course the scheme requires constantly repeated travelling on the part of the clubs, which is provided for, controlled and disciplined by the organizations, and this it is said means commerce among the States. But we are of opinion that the Court of Appeals was right. The business is giving exhibitions of baseball, which are purely state affairs. It is true that in order to attain for these exhibitions the great popularity that they have achieved, competitions must be arranged between clubs from different cities and States. But the fact that in order to give the exhibitions the Leagues must induce free persons to cross state lines and must arrange and pay for their doing so is not enough to change the character of the business. According to the distinction insisted upon in Hooper v. [People of State of] California, 155 U.S. 648, 655, 15 S.Ct. 207, 39 L.Ed. 297, the transport is a mere incident, not the essential thing."

I think the foregoing will serve alone to distinguish the incidental-means rationale of the Federal Baseball case: There the traveling was but a means to the end of playing games which themselves took place intra-state; here the games themselves, because of the radio and television, are, so to speak, played interstate as well as intra-state.

---

City of Cleveland v. United States, 329 U.S. 14, 19, 20, 67 S.Ct. 13, 91 L.Ed. 12.
5d St. Louis V. & T. H. R. v. Terre Haute R. Co., 145 U.S. 393, 403, 404, 12 S.Ct. 953, 956, 36 L.Ed. 748; Webster v. Fall, 266 U.S. 507, 511, 45 S.Ct. 148, 69 L.Ed. 411; KVOS, Inc. v. Associated Press, 299 U.S. 269, 279, 57 S.Ct. 197, 81 L.Ed. 183; Tefft, Weller & Co. v. Munsuri, 222 U.S. 114, 119, 120, 32

S.Ct. 67, 56 L.Ed. 118; United States v. Mitchell, 271 U.S. 9, 14, 46 S.Ct. 418, 70 L.Ed. 799; United States v. More, 3 Cranch 159, 172, 2 L.Ed. 397; The Edward, 1 Wheat. 261, 275, 276, 4 L.Ed. 86; Mutual Benefit Health & Accident Association v. Bowman, 8 Cir., 99 F.2d 856, 858; United States v. Dunbar, 9 Cir., 154 F.2d 889, 891.

There is, however, another important distinction on which I think we might rely, were another distinction necessary: In that earlier case, persons in other states received, via the telegraph, mere accounts of the games as told by others, while here we have the very substantially different fact of instant and direct interstate transmission, via television, of the games as they are being played, so that audiences in other states have the experience of being virtually present at these games. That degree of difference, known to any one who has ever sat at the receiving end of a television set, is so great as to constitute a difference in kind. To be sure, no one can draw a sharp line between differences of "degree" and "kind." However, to the question whether the difference between a difference of kind and difference of degree is itself a difference of degree or of kind, the sage answer has been given that it is a difference of degree, but a "violent" one.[6] "Courts of justice," said an English judge some sixty years ago, "ought not to be puzzled by such old scholastic questions as to where a horse's tail begins and where it ceases. You are obliged to say, 'This is a horse's tail,' at some time."[7]

In the Federal Baseball case, the Court assigned as a further ground of its decision that the playing of the games, although for profit, involved services, and that services were not "trade or commerce" as those words were used in the Sherman Act. But I think that such a restricted interpretation of those words has been undeniably repudiated in later Supreme Court decisions concerning medical services [7a] and motion pictures.[7b] I believe, therefore, that we will not trespass on the Supreme Court's domain if we hold that the rationale of the Federal Baseball case is now confined to the insufficiency of traveling, when employed as a means of accomplishing local activities, to establish the existence of interstate commerce.[7c]

I conclude, then, that here there is substantial interstate commerce of a sort not considered by the Court in the Federal Baseball case. These questions remain: (a) May Congress constitutionally regulate the interstate portion of such a business as that done by defendants? (b) If so, has Congress in the Sherman Act sufficiently exercised its constitutional power to include that portion of that business? I shall consider those questions in turn.

3. Supreme Court decisions relative to the Fair Labor Standards Act, 29 U.S.C.A. § 201 et seq., leave little doubt that the Constitutional power of Congress, under the commerce clause, extends to such a situation. In Roland Elec. Co. v. Walling

---

6 Williams, Language and The Law, 61 Law.Q.Rev. (1945) 179, 184.

7 Chitty, J., in Lavery v. Pursell (1888) 39 Ch.D. at 517.

Holmes, J., often discussed this matter of line-drawing. Holmes, The Common Law (1881) 68, 110, 127; Holmes, Law in Science—Science in Law, 12 Harv. L.Rev. (1899) 443, reprinted in Holmes, Collected Legal Papers (1920) 210, 232–233; Hudson County Water Co. v. McCarter, 209 U.S. 349, 355, 28 S.Ct. 529, 52 L.Ed. 828, 14 Ann.Cas. 560; Irwin v. Gavit, 268 U.S. 161, 168, 45 S.Ct. 475, 69 L.Ed. 897; Superior Oil Co. v. State of Mississippi, 280 U.S. 390, 50 S.Ct. 169, 74 L.Ed. 504; Empire Trust Co. v. Cahan, 274 U.S. 473, 478, 47 S.Ct. 661, 71 L.Ed. 1158, 57 A.L.R. 921; Haddock v. Haddock, 201 U.S. 562, 631, 732, 26 S.Ct. 525, 50 L.Ed. 867, 5 Ann.Cas. 1; Schlesinger v. State of Wisconsin, 279 U.S. 230, 241, 46 S.Ct. 260, 70 L.Ed. 557, 43 A.L.R. 1224; Louisville Gas & Elec. Co. v. Coleman, 277 U.S. 32, 41, 48 S. Ct. 423, 72 L.Ed. 770; Quaker City Cab Co. v. Commonwealth of Pennsylvania, 277 U.S. 389, 403, 48 S.Ct. 553, 72 L.Ed. 927; Nash v. United States, 229 U.S. 373, 376, 33 S.Ct. 780, 57 L.Ed. 1232; Bullen v. State of Wisconsin, 240 U.S. 625, 630, 631, 36 S.Ct. 473, 60 L.Ed. 830.

7a American Medical Association v. United States, 317 U.S. 519, 63 S.Ct. 326, 87 L.Ed. 434; cf. the reference to that case in United States v. Southeastern Underwriters Association, 322 U.S. 533, 546 and note 25, 64 S.Ct. 1162, 88 L.Ed. 1440.

7b Binderup v. Pathe Exchange, Inc., 263 U.S. 291, 44 S.Ct. 96, 68 L.Ed. 308; Paramount Famous Lasky Corp. v. United States, 282 U.S. 30, 51 S.Ct. 42, 75 L.Ed. 145; United States v. First Natl. Pictures, 282 U.S. 44, 51 S.Ct. 45, 75 L.Ed. 151; Interstate Circuit, Inc. v. United States, 306 U.S. 208, 59 S.Ct. 467, 83 L.Ed. 610; Bigelow v. R. K. O. Radio Pictures, 327 U.S. 251, 66 S.Ct. 574, 90 L.Ed. 652.

7c Cf. North American Co. v. S. E. C., 327 U.S. 686, 694, 66 S.Ct. 785, 90 L.Ed. 945.

326 U.S. 657, 66 S.Ct. 413, 416, 90 L.Ed. 383, an action to enjoin an alleged violation of that Act, the defendant was engaged in commercial and industrial wiring, electrical contracting, and dealing in electrical motors and generators. One of its customers was admittedly engaged in interstate telephony, others in the repair of ships intended for movement in interstate commerce, or in the production of goods for commerce. This the Court said (in an opinion by Justice Burton) brought the defendant within the Act, which "does not require the employee to be directly 'engaged in commerce'" or even "employed * * * in the production of an article which itself becomes the subject of commerce * * *. It is enough that the employee be employed, for example, in an occupation which is necessary to the production of a part of any other 'articles or subjects of commerce of any character' which are produced for trade, commerce or transportation among the several states." Roland Elec. Co. v. Walling was followed in Martino v. Michigan Window Cleaning Co., 327 U.S. 173, 66 S.Ct. 379, 380, 90 L.Ed. 603, where the employer was an independent contractor engaged in washing windows, painting and similar maintenance work entirely within the State of Michigan on premises used in the production of goods for commerce. This the Court said constituted "the production of goods for commerce", under the Fair Labor Standards Act. Several Circuit courts, including this court, have in like manner widely interpreted Congress' constitutional power under the commerce clause. See N.L.R.B. v. Cleveland Cliffs Iron Co., 6 Cir., 133 F.2d 295; Culver v. Bell & Loffland, 9 Cir., 146 F.2d 29; Walling v. Connecticut Co., 2 Cir., 154 F.2d 552; Consumers Power Co. v. N.L.R.B., 6 Cir., 113 F.2d 38; N.L.R.B. v. Gulf Public Service Co., 5 Cir., 116 F.2d 852.

Nor is Congressional exercise of the commerce power barred with respect to a particular business enterprise because its activities in or affecting interstate commerce constitute but a small percentage of its total activities. Thus in Mabee v. White Plains Pub. Co., 327 U.S. 178, 66 S.Ct. 511, 90 L.Ed. 607, the Court held within the Fair Labor Standards Act a publisher of a daily newspaper only ½ of 1% of whose circulation (about 45 daily copies of the paper out of a total of 10,000) was regularly out-of-state. So here: The complaint, liberally construed, imports that the radio and television contracts yield defendants a substantial, not a trifling, sum. On that basis, I think the defendants and the ballplayers are engaged in interstate commerce, regardless of whether or not that sum is but a small percentage of defendants' total earnings.

It seems to me, therefore, that Congress had the Constitutional power to include defendants' interstate business in the Sherman Act. I turn now to the question whether Congress there exercised that power.

4. The Supreme Court has said that (with an exception as to labor unions not relevant here) Congress in the Sherman Act intended to use all the constitutional power conferred on it by the commerce clause. The Court (per Sutherland, J.) so stated for the first time in Atlantic Cleaners & Dyers, Inc. v. United States, 286 U.S. 427, 435, 52 S.Ct. 607, 76 L.Ed. 1204. The Court, per Stone, J., repeated that statement in Apex Hosiery Co. v. Leader, 310 U.S. 469, 496, adding, at page 498, 60 S. Ct. 982, 995, 84 L.Ed. 1311, 128 A.L.R. 1044, that the Sherman Act is aimed at restraints "comparable to restraints deemed illegal at common law, although accomplished by means other than contract and which, for constitutional reasons, are confined to transactions in or which affect interstate commerce." This idea was repeated in United States v. Frankfort Distilleries, 324 U.S. 293, 294, 297, 65 S.Ct. 661, 664, 89 L. Ed. 951: "And with reference to commercial trade restraints such as these, Congress, in passing the Sherman Act, left no area of its constitutional power unoccupied; it 'exercised "all the power it possessed."' "

The most striking statement, however, is in the Southeastern case, 322 U.S. 533, 64 S.Ct. 1162, 1176, 88 L.Ed. 1440, where the argument was pressed that although the Constitutional commerce power empowered it to do so, Congress in the Sherman Act did not intend to cover insurance. The Court found that "all the acceptable evidence points the other way. That Congress wanted to go to the utmost extent of its Constitutional power in restraining trust and monopoly agreements such as the indictment here charges admits of little, if any, doubt. The purpose was to use that power to make of ours, so far as Congress could under our dual system, a competitive business economy."

The comprehensive sweep of the Sherman Act is also shown by the Supreme Court's reliance, in several Sherman Act cases, upon cases construing the National Labor Relations Act and other statutes. For instance, in the Associated Press case, Associated Press v. United States, 326 U.S. 1, 14, 65 S.Ct. 1416, 1421, 89 L.Ed. 2013, the Court disposed, in one sentence, of the argument that that enterprise was not subject to the Sherman Act: "We need not again pass upon the contention that trade in news carried on among the states is not interstate commerce, Associated Press v. Labor Board, 301 U.S. 103, 57 S.Ct. 650, 81 L.Ed. 953". Justice Frankfurter, concurring, agreed, saying, 326 U.S. at page 27, 65 S.Ct. at page 1428, 89 L.Ed. 2013: "Since the Associated Press is an enterprise engaged in interstate commerce, Associated Press v. Labor Board, supra, these plainly are agreements in restraint of that commerce."

In the more recent case of Mandeville Island Farms v. American Crystal Sugar Co., 334 U.S. 219, 236, 68 S.Ct. 996, the Court discussed the scope of the Sherman Act and of the Constitutional commerce power as if they were identical, citing United States v. Darby, 312 U.S. 100, 61 S.Ct. 451, 85 L.Ed. 609, 132 A.L.R. 1430, a Fair Labor Standards Act case, Consolidated Edison Co. v. National Labor Relations Board, 305 U.S. 197, 59 S.Ct. 206, 83 L.Ed. 126, a National Labor Relations Act case, and United States v. Walsh, 331 U.S. 432, 67 S.Ct. 1283, 91 L.Ed. 1585, a Food and Drug Act case. Moreover, the discussion in the Mandeville opinion of the effect of the Shreveport Rate Cases, 234 U.S. 342, 34 S.Ct. 833, 58 L.Ed. 1341, goes to show that, as the Court has come to construe the commerce clause more widely in connection with the coverage of other statutes, such as the Interstate Commerce Act, 49 U.S.C.A. § 1 et seq., it has equivalently interpreted the Sherman Act's coverage.[8] And certainly the Mandeville opinion demonstrates that the Sherman Act covers activities wholly within a state but which affect interstate commerce.

5. In the light of my previous discussion, and having particularly in mind Mabee v. White Plains Pub. Co., 327 U.S. 178, 66 S.Ct. 511, 90 L.Ed. 607, I think we must, for purposes of deciding the applicability of the Sherman Act, consider this case as if the only audiences for whom the games are played consist of those persons who, in other states, see, hear, or hear about, the games via television and radio. The question here is, then, I think, the same as that which we would face if a similar alleged monopoly related to the production of stage-plays in radio and television studios. I believe the producers of such plays would clearly come within the Fair Labor Stand-

---

[8] The Mandeville opinion explains that, in United States v. E. C. Knight Co., 156 U.S. 1, 15 S.Ct. 249, 39 L.Ed. 325; the Court had decided that manufacturing was not commerce; the Sherman Act thereby became a "dead letter," and was not finally reborn until 1911 "with the decisions in Standard Oil Co. v. United States, 221 U.S. 1, 31 S.Ct. 502, 55 L. Ed. 619, 34 L.R.A.,N.S., 834, Ann.Cas. 1912D, 734, and United States v. American Tobacco Co., 221 U.S. 106, 31 S.Ct. 632, 55 L.Ed. 663", 334 U.S. 219, 68 S. Ct. 1003; it was the doctrine of the Shreveport Rate Cases, 234 U.S. 342, 34 S.Ct. 833, 58 L.Ed. 1341, (i.e., that activities within a state may be federally regulated if they affect interstate commerce) as extended by later decisions, which made it no longer necessary "to search for some sharp point or line where interstate commerce ends and intrastate commerce begins * * *." As late as the 1930's (the Court continued in the Mandeville opinion) the old ideas persisted in specific applications, but a growing number of decisions had rejected the idea that manufacturing was purely local simply because that phase of a combination restraining trade was carried on within a single state. It "is the effect upon that commerce, not the moment when its cause arises, which the doctrine [of the Shreveport cases] was fashioned to reach."

ards Acts.[8a] If so, they would be within the Sherman Act. And I would so hold concerning the defendants, if their conduct is as plaintiff describes it.

As the playing of the games is essential both to defendants' interstate and intrastate activities, the players' contracts relate to both. But that, as a consequence, necessary relief with respect to the interstate activities will thus unavoidably affect those which are intrastate does not preclude the granting of such relief.[9] Nor, I venture to repeat, do I think such relief is dependent upon a showing that the illegally monopolized interstate activities, if more than trifling, represent a substantial proportion of defendants' total activities.[9a] See Mabee v. White Plains Pub Co., 327 U.S. 178, 66 S.Ct. 511, 90 L.Ed. 607; cf. Apex Hosiery Co. v. Leader, 310 U.S. 469, 485, 60 S.Ct. 982, 84 L.Ed. 1311, 128 A.L.R. 1044; United States v. Yellow Cab Co., 332 U.S. 218, 225, 67 S.Ct. 1560, 91 L.Ed. 2010.

In United States v. Socony Vacuum Oil Co., 310 U.S. 150, 224 note 59, 60 S.Ct. 811, 845, 84 L.Ed. 1129, the Court said that "the amount of interstate * * * trade involved is not material", citing with approval Montague & Co. v. Lowry, 193 U.S. 38, 24 S.Ct. 307, 48 L.Ed. 608; Steers v. United States, 6 Cir., 192 F. 1, 5; Patterson v. United States, 6 Cir., 222 F. 599, 618, 619. I consider adequate the allegations concerning damages.[10]

6. Defendants suggest that "organized baseball," which supplies millions of Americans with desirable diversion, will be unable to exist without the "reserve clause." Whether that is true, no court can predict. In any event, the answer is that the public's pleasure does not authorize the courts to condone illegality, and that no court should strive ingeniously to legalize a private (even if benevolent) dictatorship.

I think we should reverse and remand.

---

[8a] Cf., as to the National Labor Relations Act, Marcus Loew Booking Agency, Inc., 3 N.L.R.B. 380; Los Angeles Broadcasting Co., 4 N.L.R.B. 443; KMOX Broadcasting Station, 10 N.L.R.B. 479; Louis G. Baltimore, 57 N.L.R.B. 1611; Miami Valley Broadcasting Corp., 70 N.L.R.B. 1015.

In Fisher's Blend Station v. Tax Commission, 297 U.S. 650, 655, 56 S.Ct. 608, 610, 80 L.Ed. 956, the Court said: "By its very nature broadcasting transcends state lines and is national in its scope and importance—characteristics which bring it within the purpose and protection, and subject it to the control, of the commerce clause."

[9] Minnesota Rate Cases, 230 U.S. 352, 399, 33 S.Ct. 729, 57 L.Ed. 1511, 48 L.R.A.,N.S., 1151, Ann.Cas.1916A, 18; Shreveport Rate Cases, 234 U.S. 342, 34 S.Ct. 833, 58 L.Ed. 1341; United States v. New York Central R. Co., 272 U.S. 457, 47 S.Ct. 130, 71 L.Ed. 350; Currin v. Wallace, 306 U.S. 1, 59 S.Ct. 379, 83 L.Ed. 441; Mandeville Farms v. American Crystal Sugar Co., 334 U.S. 219, 236, 68 S.Ct. 996; United States v. Wright-

wood Dairy Co., 315 U.S. 110, 119, 62 S.Ct. 523, 86 L.Ed. 726; Santa Cruz Fruit Packing Co. v. Labor Board, 303 U.S. 453, 466, 58 S.Ct. 656, 82 L.Ed. 954; United States v. Darby, 312 U.S. 100, 118–123, 61 S.Ct. 451, 85 L.Ed. 609, 132 A.L.R. 1430; Wickard v. Filburn, 317 U.S. 111, 122–124, 63 S.Ct. 82, 87 L.Ed. 122.

[9a] If proportions were important, the following would be pertinent: Presumably with little increased expense to the defendants, earnings from the radio and television contracts are something added to what defendants theretofore earned net, so that these added earnings are "velvet" which therefore may (in the Sherman Act context) be regarded as contributing entirely, or almost entirely, to defendants' net profits. Accordingly, in determining proportions, the radio and television net profits should be compared with defendants' other net, not their gross, profits.

[10] Package Closure Corp. v. Sealright, 2 Cir., 141 F.2d 972; Bigelow v. RKO Pictures, 327 U.S. 251, 66 S.Ct. 574, 90 L.Ed. 652.

## TOOLSON *v.* NEW YORK YANKEES, INC. ET AL.

NO. 18. CERTIORARI TO THE UNITED STATES COURT OF
APPEALS FOR THE NINTH CIRCUIT.*

Argued October 13, 1953.—Decided November 9, 1953.

The judgments in these cases are affirmed on the authority of *Federal Baseball Club of Baltimore* v. *National League of Professional Baseball Clubs*, 259 U. S. 200, so far as that decision determines that Congress had no intention of including the business of baseball within the scope of the federal antitrust laws. Pp. 356–357.
200 F. 2d 198, 202 F. 2d 413, 428, affirmed.

*Howard C. Parke* argued the cause for petitioner in No. 18. With him on the brief was *Gene M. Harris.*

*Frederic A. Johnson* argued the cause for petitioner in No. 23 and *Seymour Martinson* argued the cause for petitioners in No. 25. With them on the briefs were *Maurice H. Koodish* and *Edward Martinson.*

*Norman S. Sterry* argued the cause and filed a brief for respondents in No. 18.

*Raymond T. Jackson* argued the cause for respondents in Nos. 23 and 25. With him on the briefs were *Benjamin F. Fiery* and *Louis F. Carroll.*

*Thomas Reed Powell* filed a brief for the Boston American League Base Ball Company in No. 18, as *amicus curiae,* urging affirmance.

PER CURIAM.

In *Federal Baseball Club of Baltimore* v. *National League of Professional Baseball Clubs,* 259 U. S. 200

───────────

*Together with No. 23, *Kowalski* v. *Chandler, Commissioner of Baseball, et al.,* argued October 13–14, 1953, and No. 25, *Corbett et al.* v. *Chandler, Commissioner of Baseball, et al.,* argued October 14, 1953, both on certiorari to the United States Court of Appeals for the Sixth Circuit.

(1922), this Court held that the business of providing public baseball games for profit between clubs of professional baseball players was not within the scope of the federal antitrust laws.   Congress has had the ruling under consideration but has not seen fit to bring such business under these laws by legislation having prospective effect.   The business has thus been left for thirty years to develop, on the understanding that it was not subject to existing antitrust legislation.   The present cases ask us to overrule the prior decision and, with retrospective effect, hold the legislation applicable.   We think that if there are evils in this field which now warrant application to it of the antitrust laws it should be by legislation.   Without re-examination of the underlying issues, the judgments below are affirmed on the authority of *Federal Baseball Club of Baltimore* v. *National League of Professional Baseball Clubs, supra,* so far as that decision determines that Congress had no intention of including the business of baseball within the scope of the federal antitrust laws.

*Affirmed.*

## XIII. Conclusions

Baseball is America's national pastime. It is a game of American origin which has long exemplified the finest traditions of clean, vigorous sportsmanship. Its outstanding record of honesty and integrity, maintained in today's chaotic world conditions, is a symbol to which the people of the United States may justly point with pride.

Professional baseball, however, is not without its problems. Some of these problems have been brought into focus in the course of the antitrust investigation conducted by this subcommittee.

Organized baseball has for years occupied a monopoly position in the business of selling professional baseball exhibitions to the public, and, therefore, has constituted substantially the only market for the services of highly skilled professional baseball players. The keystone of the entire structure of organized professional baseball is the so-called reserve clause, together with its attendant rules and regulations. The subcommittee concludes, on the basis of the evidence reviewed in this report, that professional baseball could not operate successfully and profitably without some form of a reserve clause.

Because the legality of the reserve clause, and of organized baseball's monopoly position has not been successfully challenged for decades, this industry afforded the subcommittee an unusual opportunity to review the basis for our Nation's antitrust policies as applied to a particular case. The basic assumption underlying our antitrust laws is that free competition is the best possible guaranty of an industry's progress and prosperity and that the general public will be best served thereby. To a large extent, that type of economic competition in the baseball industry is foreclosed by a comprehensive and reticulated system of rules and regulations to which all segments of organized baseball subscribe.

Organized baseball is largely a self-regulated industry. The laws of supply and demand are not the inexorable masters of this market place. Competition from other amusement industries, though not without influence, is comparatively ineffective. A more important substitute for regulation by intraindustry competition is afforded by public opinion. Despite the tremendous popular interest in baseball, however, publicity itself does not afford a complete guaranty that the game will always be operated so as to serve the maximum public interest. Public attention is primarily focused on the major leagues, although organized baseball's most serious problems lie in the minor leagues where over 90 percent of its players are employed. The public has little knowledge of the economics of the industry and pays comparatively little heed to the intricacies of baseball law. Moreover, even when the public has recognized the need for important and affirmative changes in industry policies—changes such as a revision of the major league baseball map, which would have taken place long ago if competition were baseball's only master—the men in control of the game have either resisted or been unable to make desirable changes. Examples such as this have reaffirmed the subcommittee's conviction that America's antitrust laws are basically sound because they are built on the principle that free competition best stimulates healthy economic progress.

The subcommittee recognizes, however, that baseball is a unique industry. Of necessity, the several clubs in each league must act as partners as well as competitors. The history of baseball has demonstrated that cooperation in many of the details of the operation of the baseball business is essential to the maintenance of honest and vigorous competition on the playing field. For this reason organized baseball has adopted a system of rules and regulation that would be entirely inappropriate in an ordinary industry.

The legality of these rules and regulations has recently been drawn into question in a series of antitrust treble damage actions. Fearing that these actions might endanger the whole future of our national pastime, friends of baseball asked the Congress for legislation granting professional baseball complete immunity from the antitrust laws. The problem posed by these lawsuits and by the bills which were introduced in the House of Representatives and referred to this subcommittee required careful legislative consideration.

In analyzing this legislative problem the subcommittee soon recognized that five alternative solutions were available. Conceivably the subcommittee could recommend (1) legislation outlawing the reserve clause; (2) favorable consideration of the bills designed to give baseball an unlimited exemption from the antitrust laws; (3) the enactment of a comprehensive baseball code to be enforced by a governmental agency; (4) a limited exemption for the reserve clause; or (5) that no legislation be enacted at this time. These alternatives will be briefly discussed.

*1. Should the reserve clause be outlawed?*

Opponents of the reserve clause criticized it primarily on the ground that it makes possible certain conditions which are inequitable or contrary to the public interest. It was forcefully argued that the unenviable status of the minor league player, the ossification of the major league territorial map, and the tendency of farm systems to enable the richest clubs to engross the player market, are all at least in part the result of the reserve clause. But even assuming that these and other undesirable consequences could not exist without a reserve clause, it does not follow that the clause itself should be abolished. Witnesses who were most bitter in their criticism of the reserve clause recognized that lesser modifications of organized baseball's rules would suffice to correct many of the conditions of which they complained.

On the other hand the overwhelming preponderance of the evidence established baseball's need for some sort of reserve clause. Baseball's history shows that chaotic conditions prevailed when there was no reserve clause. Experience points to no feasible substitute to protect the integrity of the game or to guarantee a comparatively even competitive struggle. The evidence adduced at the hearings would clearly not justify the enactment of legislation flatly condemning the reserve clause.

*2. Should professional baseball be granted a complete immunity from the antitrust laws?*

Four bills have been introduced in the Congress, three in the House, one in the Senate, intending to give baseball and all other professional sports a complete and unlimited immunity from the antitrust laws. The requested exemption would extend to all professional sports enterprises and to all acts in the conduct of such enterprises. The law would no longer require competition in any facet of business activity of any sport enterprise. Thus the sale of radio and television rights, the management of stadia, the purchase and sale of advertising, the concession industry, and many other business activities, as well as the aspects of baseball which are solely related to the promotion of competition on the playing field, would be immune and untouchable. Such a broad exemption could not be granted without substantially repealing the antitrust laws.

Moreover, confining attention to organized baseball, it would seem clear that before recommending a carte blanche immunity, this subcommittee would have to place its stamp of approval on every aspect of the game as now conducted. The subcommittee would thus be approving important practices which representatives of organized baseball have themselves condemned. The restrictions on transfer of baseball franchises, together with the enforcement of those restrictions, have prevented the composition of the major leagues from reflecting the tremendous population shifts which have occurred in the United States since 1903. Immunity for such restrictions would certainly tend to perpetuate the status quo. Similarly, a complete immunity for the reserve clause might sanctify all of the terms of the standard minor league contract and all of the aspects of the farm system which were targets of criticism during the hearings.

If a blanket immunity were granted, all appeal to the courts from a possibly arbitrary decision by the rulers of professional baseball would be foreclosed. In the past the reserve clause has been employed as a "war measure" to fight the development of competing leagues, sometimes at the expense of individual players. Although instances of arbitrary exercise of power have been rare, they have occurred in the past. The possibility, however remote, that power will be misused in the future makes it unwise perpetually to preclude resort to the courts in such cases.

The above considerations are fully recognized by men prominent in baseball. One of the leading major league club owners frankly stated to the subcommittee that he "would not be in favor of baseball being exempt from the antitrust laws." [6] Other representatives of baseball management expressed similar opinions, as did certain players and sports writers. Even the sponsors of the carte blanche legislation conceded, under questioning, that it would be unwise for the Congress to enact their bills into law without any amendment. Accordingly, the subcommittee has decided to report unfavorably H. R. 4229, 4230, and 4231.

*3. Should a Federal agency be created to regulate professional baseball?*

On the assumption that the reserve clause should neither be declared illegal nor completely immunized, it was suggested that a govern-

[6] Hearings, p. 734.

mental code for professional baseball—something akin to the N. R. A. regulatory codes of the 1930's—might be adopted. This subcommittee claims neither the requisite competence nor the desire to draft the intricate code which would be required. Congress cannot properly, nor should it, enact a comprehensive code to govern every detail of baseball's business.

It would be unwise in the extreme to saddle professional baseball with a new governmental bureau to control its destiny. The substantial expense of creating and maintaining such a new Federal agency should not be added to the great burdens which are already being borne by the American taxpayer. But, foremost, the subcommittee is thoroughly convinced that baseball's best interests would not be served by subjecting it to governmental supervision. It will be far better for the industry to work out its own solutions to the problems confronting it.

The subcommittee is opposed to the establishment of a new regulatory agency for professional baseball.

### 4. Should a limited exemption for the reserve clause be enacted?

A statute granting a reasonably limited exemption for the reserve clause would avoid the principal objections to either a blanket immunity or a flat condemnation of organized baseball's reserve rules. For this reason the subcommittee has carefully considered the wisdom of recommending the enactment of broadly phrased legislation intended to accomplish this objective. Such a bill would state in general terms that the antitrust laws shall not apply to reasonable rules and regulations which promote competition among baseball clubs, even though they restrain competition for players' services— as does the reserve clause—provided that such rules guarantee players a reasonable opportunity to advance in their profession and to be paid at a rate commensurate with their ability. This type of legislation would lay down a rule of reason for baseball. It would give no protection to activities designed to thwart geographic realinement of major league franchises, or to arbitrary blacklisting of players in the course of a "war" against an independent league. On the other hand, the reasonable and necessary utilization of the reserve clause would be protected against successful antitrust attack.

There is, however, no need to enact a special rule of reason for baseball unless such a rule is not already applicable to this industry. Organized baseball, represented by eminent counsel, has assured the subcommittee that the legality of the reserve clause will be tested by the rule of reason. Though lawsuits have been filed against organized baseball in recent years, in none of them has the court yet passed on the reasonableness of the reserve clause. The Department of Justice has not disputed baseball's position that the reserve clause is legal under the rule of reason.

It would therefore seem premature to enact general legislation for baseball at this time. Legislation is not necessary until the reasonableness of the reserve rules has been tested by the courts. If those rules are unreasonable in some respects it would be inappropriate to adopt legislation before baseball has had an opportunity to make such modifications as may be necessary. Moreover, the type of general legislation now under consideration would require a series of court actions before the legality of the various reserve rules and regulations could be finally settled. A series of lawsuits under such a new statute might not differ materially from the situation confronting organized baseball today. In either event, the courts may have to differentiate the unreasonable features of baseball's rules and regulations from those which are reasonable and necessary. For these reasons, together with the subcommittee's earnest desire to avoid influencing pending litigation, it is unwise to attempt to anticipate judicial action with legislation.

Accordingly the subcommittee has determined to adopt the fifth of the alternatives stated above, namely, to recommend no legislative action at this time.

EMANUEL CELLER, *Chairman.*
EDWIN E. WILLIS.
BYRON G. ROGERS.
CHAUNCEY W. REED.
KENNETH E. KEATING.
WILLIAM M. McCULLOCH.

O

## STATEMENT OF CASEY STENGEL, MANAGER OF THE NEW YORK YANKEES

Mr. STENGEL. Well, I started in professional ball in 1910. I have been in professional ball, I would say, for 48 years. I have been employed by numerous ball clubs in the majors and in the minor leagues.

I started in the minor leagues with Kansas City. I played as low as class D ball, which was at Shelbyville, Ky., and also class C ball, and class A ball, and I have advanced in baseball as a ballplayer.

I had many years that I was not so successful as a ballplayer, as it is a game of skill. And then I was no doubt discharged by baseball in which I had to go back to the minor leagues as a manager, and after being in the minor leagues as a manager, I became a major league manager in several cities and was discharged, we call it "discharged", because there is no question I had to leave. [Laughter.]

And I returned to the minor leagues at Milwaukee, Kansas City, and Oakland, Calif., and then returned to the major leagues.

In the last 10 years, naturally, in major league baseball with the New York Yankees, the New York Yankees have had tremendous success and while I am not the ballplayer who does the work, I have no doubt worked for a ball club that is very capable in the office.

I must have splendid ownership, I must have very capable men who are in radio and television, which no doubt you know that we have mentioned the three names—you will say they are very great.

We have a wonderful press that follows us. Anybody should in New York City, where you have so many million people.

Our ball club has been successful because we have it, and we have the spirit of 1776.

We put it into the ball field and if you are not capable of becoming a great ballplayer since I have been in as the manager, in 10 years, you are notified that if you don't produce on the ball field, the salary that you receive, we will allow you to be traded to play and give your services to other clubs.

The great proof of that was yesterday. Three of the young men that were stars and picked by the players in the American League to be in the all-star game were Mr. Cerv, who is at Kansas City; Mr. Jensen who was at Boston, and I might say Mr. Triandos that caught for the Baltimore ball club, all three of those players were my members and to show you I was not such a brilliant manager they got away from me and were chosen by the players and I was fortunate enough to have them come back to play where I was successful as a manager.

If I have been in baseball for 48 years there must be some good in it. I was capable and strong enough at one time to do any kind of work but I came back to baseball and I have been in baseball ever since.

I have been up and down the ladder. I know there are some things in baseball, 35 to 50 years ago that are better now than they were in those days. In those days, my goodness, you could not transfer a ball club in the minor leagues, class D, class C ball, class A ball.

How could you transfer a ball club when you did not have a highway? How could you transfer a ball club when the railroads then

29351—58——2

would take you to a town you got off and then you had to wait and
sit up 5 hours to go to another ball club?

How could you run baseball then without night ball?

You had to have night ball to improve the proceeds, to pay larger
salaries and I went to work, the first year I received $135 a month.

I thought that was amazing. I had to put away enough money
to go to dental college. I found out it was not better in dentistry, I
stayed in baseball.

Any other questions you would like to ask me?

I want to let you know that as to the legislative end of baseball you
men will have to consider that what you are here for. I am a bench
manager.

I will speak about anything from the playing end—in the major
or minor leagues—and do anything I can to help you.

Senator KEFAUVER. Mr. Stengel, are you prepared to answer particularly why baseball wants this bill passed?

Mr. STENGEL. Well, I would have to say at the present time, I think
that baseball has advanced in this respect for the player help. That
is an amazing statement for me to make, because you can retire with
an annuity at 50 and what organization in America allows you to
retire at 50 and receive money?

I want to further state that I am not a ballplayer, that is, put into
that pension fund committee. At my age, and I have been in baseball,
well, I will say I am possibly the oldest man who is working in baseball. I would say that when they start an annuity for the ballplayers
to better their conditions, it should have been done, and I think it
has been done.

I think it should be the way they have done it, which is a very
good thing.

The reason they possibly did not take the managers in at that time
was because radio and television or the income to ball clubs was not
large enough that you could have put in a pension plan.

Now I am not a member of the pension plan. You have young
men here who are, who represent the ball clubs.

They represent them as players and since I am not a member and
don't receive pension from a fund which you think, my goodness, he
ought to be declared in that too but I would say that is a great thing
for the ballplayers.

That is one thing I will say for the ballplayers they have an advanced pension fund. I should think it was gained by radio and
television or you could not have enough money to pay anything of
that type.

Now the second thing about baseball that I think is very interesting
to the public or to all of us that it is the owners' own fault if he does
not improve his club, along with the officials in the ball club and the
players.

Now what causes that?

If I am going to go on the road and we are a traveling ball club
and you know the cost of transportation now—we travel sometimes
with three pullman coaches, the New York Yankees and remember I
am just a salaried man and do not own stock in the New York
Yankees, I found out that in traveling with the New York Yankees
on the road and all, that it is the best, and we have broken records in
Washington this year, we have broken them in every city but New

York and we have lost two clubs that have gone out of the city of New York.

Of course we have had some bad weather, I would say that they are mad at us in Chicago, we fill the parks.

They have come out to see good material. I will say they are mad at us in Kansas City, but we broke their attendance record.

Now on the road we only get possibly 27 cents. I am not positive of these figures, as I am not an official.

If you go back 15 years or if I owned stock in the club I would give them to you.

Senator KEFAUVER. Mr. Stengel, I am not sure that I made my question clear. [Laughter.]

Mr. STENGEL. Yes, sir. Well that is all right. I am not sure I am going to answer yours perfectly either. [Laughter.]

Senator KEFAUVER. I was asking you, sir, why it is that baseball wants this bill passed.

Mr. STENGEL. I would say I would not know, but I would say the reason why they would want it passed is to keep baseball going as the highest paid ball sport that has gone into baseball and from the baseball angle, I am not going to speak of any other sport.

I am not in here to argue about other sports, I am in the baseball business. It has been run cleaner than any business that was ever put out in the 100 years at the present time.

I am not speaking about television or I am not speaking about income that comes into the ball parks. You have to take that off. I don't know too much about it. I say the ballplayers have a better advancement at the present time.

Senator KEFAUVER. One further question, and then I will pass to the other Senators.

How many players do the Yankees control, Mr. Stengel?

Mr. STENGEL. Well, I will tell you: I hire the players and if they make good with me I keep them without any criticism from my ownership.

I do not know how many players they own as I am not a scout and I cannot run a ball club during the daytime and be busy at night, and up the next day and find out how many players that the Yankees own.

If you get any official with the Yankees that is here, why he could give you the names.

Senator KEFAUVER. Very well.

Senator Langer?

Senator LANGER. Mr. Stengel?

Mr. STENGEL. Yes, sir.

Senator LANGER. What do you think is the future of baseball? Is it going to be expanded to include more clubs than are in existence at the present time?

Mr. STENGEL. I think every chamber of commerce in the major league cities would not change a franchise, I think they will be delighted because they have a hard time to put in a convention hall or to get people to come to your city and if it is going to be like Milwaukee or Kansas City or Baltimore, I think they would want a major league team.

But if I was a chamber of commerce member and I was in a city I would not want a baseball team to leave the city as too much money is brought into your city even if you have a losing team and great if you have a winning ball team.

Senator LANGER. You look forward then, do you not, to, say, 10 years or 20 years from now this business of baseball is going to grow larger and larger and larger?

Mr. STENGEL. Well, I should think it would.

I should think it would get larger because of the fact we are drawing tremendous crowds, I believe, from overseas programs in television, that is one program I have always stuck up for.

I think every ballplayer and everyone should give out anything that is overseas for the Army, free of cost and so forth.

I think that every hospital should get it. I think that because of the lack of parking in so many cities that you cannot have a great ball park if you don't have parking space.

If you are ancient or 45 or 50 and have acquired enough money to go to a ball game, you cannot drive a car on a highway, which is very hard to do after 45, to drive on any modern highway and if you are going to stay home you need radio and television to go along for receipts for the ball club.

Senator LANGER. That brings us to another question.

Mr. STENGEL. Yes, sir.

Senator LANGER. That is, what do you think of pay-as-you-go television?

Mr. STENGEL. Well, to tell you the truth, if I were starting in it myself I would like to be in that line of business as I did not think they would ever have television and so forth here but they have got it here now. [Laughter.]

Forty years ago you would not have had it around here yourself and you would not have cameras flying around here every 5 minutes but we have got them here and more of them around here than around a ball field, I will give you that little tip.

Senator LANGER. You believe the time is ever going to come when you will have pay-as-you-go in the world series, which would be kept from the public unless they had pay-as-you-go television in their homes?

Mr. STENGEL. I think you have got a good argument there and it is worthy of you to say that.

I am thinking myself of anybody that is hospitalized and anybody who cannot go to a ball park, I should think if they could pass that they should try to pass it.

But I don't think they will be able to do it because they have gone in television so far that they reach so many outside people, you have to have a sponsor for everything else you do, go pay television and that is going to run all the big theaters out of business where you have to use pay television.

All the big theaters and all the big movie companies went broke. We know that. You see that now or you would not have a place to hold a television for pay.

I don't know how they would run that of course. I am not on that side of the fence. I am paid a salary——

Senator LANGER. Just one further question. You do not have to answer it unless you want to. That is, is there any provision made whereby the team owners can keep a racketeer out of the baseball business?

Mr. STENGEL. Well, sir——

Senator LANGER. Can the owners of the New York Yankees, for example, sell out to anyone who may want to buy the club at a big price without the consent of the other owners?

Mr. STENGEL. That is a very good thing that I will have to think about but I will give you an example.

I think that is why they put in as a commissioner Judge Landis, and he said if there is a cloud on baseball I will take it off, and he took the cloud off and they have only had one scandal or if they had it is just one major league city.

How can you be a ballplayer and make 25 ballplayers framed without it being heard?

It is bound to leak, and your play will show it.

I don't think, an owner possibly could do something but he can't play the game for you. It is the most honest profession I think that we have, everything today that is going on outside——

Senator LANGER. Mr. Chairman, my final question. This is the Antimonopoly Committee that is sitting here.

Mr. STENGEL. Yes, sir.

Senator LANGER. I want to know whether you intend to keep on monopolizing the world's championship in New York City.

Mr. STENGEL. Well, I will tell you, I got a little concerned yesterday in the first 3 innings when I say the 3 players I had gotten rid of and I said when I lost 9 what am I going to do and when I had a couple of my players. I thought so great of that did not do so good up to the sixth inning I was more confused but I finally had to go and call on a young man in Baltimore that we don't own and the Yankees don't own him, and he is doing pretty good, and I would actually have to tell you that I think we are more the Greta Garbo type now from success.

We are being hated I mean, from the ownership and all, we are being hated. Every sport that gets too great or one individual—but if we made 27 cents and it pays to have a winner at home why would not you have a good winner in your own park if you were an owner.

That is the result of baseball. An owner gets most of the money at home and it is up to him and his staff to do better or they ought to be discharged.

Senator LANGER. That is all, Mr. Chairman. Thank you.

Senator KEFAUVER. Thank you, Senator Langer.

Senator O'Mahoney?

Senator O'MAHONEY. May I say, Mr. Stengel, that I congratulate you very much for what happened on the field at Baltimore yesterday. I was watching on television when you sent Gil McDougald up to bat for Early Wynn. I noticed with satisfaction that he got a hit, knocking Frank Malzone in with the winning run. That is good management.

Mr. STENGEL. Thank you very much. [Laughter.]

Senator O'MAHONEY. Did I understand you to say, Mr. Stengel, at the beginning of your statement that you have been in baseball for 48 years?

Mr. STENGEL. Yes, sir; the oldest man in the service.

Senator O'MAHONEY. How many major league teams were there in the United States when you entered baseball?

Mr. STENGEL. Well, there was in 1910—there were 16 major league baseball teams.

Senator O'MAHONEY. How many are there now?

Mr. STENGEL. There are 16 major league clubs but there was 1 year that they brought in the Federal League which was brought in by Mr. Ward and Mr. Sinclair and others after a war, and it is a very odd thing to tell you that during tough times it is hard to study baseball. I have been through 2 or 3 depressions in baseball and out of it.

The First World War we had good baseball in August.

The Second World War we kept on and made more money because everybody was around going to the services, the larger the war, the more they come to the ball park, and that was an amazing thing to me.

When you were looking for tough times why it changed for different wars.

Senator O'MAHONEY. How many minor leagues were there in baseball when you began?

Mr. STENGEL. Well, there were not so many at that time because of this fact: Anybody to go into baseball at that time with the educational schools that we had were small, while you were probably thoroughly educated at school, you had to be—we had only small cities that you could put a team in and they would go defunct.

Why, I remember the first year I was at Kankakee, Ill., and a bank offered me $550 if I would let them have a little notice. I left there and took a uniform because they owed me 2 weeks' pay. But I either had to quit but I did not have enough money to go to dental college so I had to go with the manager down to Kentucky.

What happened there was if you got by July, that was the big date. You did not play night ball and you did not play Sundays in half of the cities on account of a Sunday observance, so in those days when things were tough, and all of it was, I mean to say, why they just closed up July 4 and there you were sitting there in the depot.

You could go to work some place else but that was it.

So I got out of Kankakee, Ill., and I just go there for the visit now. [Laughter.]

I think now, do you know how many clubs they have?

Anybody will start a minor league club but it is just like your small cities, the industries have left them and they have gone west to California, and I am a Missourian—Kansas City, Mo.—but I can see all those towns and everybody moving west and I know if you can fly in the air you can see anything from the desert, you can see a big country over there that has got many names.

Well, now why wouldn't baseball prosper out there, with that many million people?

Senator O'MAHONEY. Are the minor leagues suffering now?

Mr. STENGEL. I should say they are.

Senator O'MAHONEY. Why?

Mr. STENGEL. Do you know why?

I will tell you why. I don't think anybody can support minor league ball when they see a great official, it would be just like a great actress or actor had come to town. If Bob Hope had come here or Greta Garbo over there half of them would go to see Greta Garbo and half Bob Hope but if you have a very poor baseball team they are not going to watch you until you become great and the minor leagues now with radio and television will not pay very much attention to minor league ballplayers. Softball is interesting, the parent is interested; he goes around with him. He watches his son and he is more enthusiastic about the boy than some stranger that comes to town and wants to play in a little wooden park and with no facilities to make you be interested. You might rather stay home and see a program.

Senator O'Mahoney. How many baseball players are now engaged in the activity as compared to when you came in?

Mr. Stengel. I would say there are more, many more. Because we did not have as many cities that could support even minor league baseball in those days.

Senator O'Mahoney. How many players did the 16 major league clubs have when you came in?

Mr. Stengel. At that time they did not have as many teams. They did not have near as many teams as below.

Later on Mr. Rickey came in and started what was known as what you would say numerous clubs, you know in which I will try to pick up this college man, I will pick up that college boy or I will pick up some corner lot boy and if you picked up the corner lot boy maybe he became just as successful as the college man, which is true.

He then had a number of players.

Now, too many players is a funny thing, it costs like everything. I said just like I made a talk not long ago and I told them all when they were drinking and they invited me in I said you ought to be home. You men are not making enough money. You cannot drink like that. They said, "This is a holiday for the Shell Oil Co.," and I said "Why is it a holiday?" and they said, "We did something great for 3 years and we are given 2 days off to watch the Yankees play the White Sox," but they were mostly White Sox rooters.

I said, 'You are not doing right.'

I said, "You can't take all those drinks and all even on your holidays. You ought to be home and raising more children because big league clubs now give you a hundred thousand for a bonus to go into baseball." [Laughter.]

And by the way I don't happen to have any children but I wish Mrs. Stengel and I had eight, I would like to put them in on that bonus rule. [Laughter.]

Senator O'Mahoney. What I am trying to find out, Mr. Stengel, is how many players are actively working for the major league teams now as was formerly the case?

How many players do you suppose——

Mr. Stengel. You are right, I would honestly tell you they naturally have more and they are in more competition now.

You have to buck now a university—anyone who wants to be a hockey player——

Senator O'Mahoney. Let's stick to baseball for a minute.

Mr. Stengel. I stay in baseball. I say I can't name them. If you want to know you get any executive, you have got any names, bring any executive with the Yankees that is an official in the ball club and he will tell you how many players the Yankees have.

And there is his jurisdiction—every ball club owner can tell you he is an official, they have enough officials hired with me with a long pencil, too.

Senator O'MAHONEY. I recently saw a statement by a baseball sports writer that there were about 400 active ball players in the major leagues now.

Would you think that is about correct now?

Mr. STENGEL. I would say in the major leagues each club has 25 men which is the player limit.

There are 8 clubs in each league so you might say there are 400 players in the major leagues, you mean outside of it that they own two or three hundred each individual club, isn't that what you have reference to?

Senator O'MAHONEY. I was coming to that, but is that the fact?

Mr. STENGEL. Well, I say that is what you would say [laughter] if you want to find that out you get any of those executives that come in here that keep those books. I am not a bookkeeper for him. But I take the man when he comes to the big league. They can give it to you and each club should.

That does not mean and I would like to ask you, How would you like to pay those men?

That is why they go broke.

Senator O'MAHONEY. I am not in that business.

Mr. STENGEL. I was in that business a short time, too; it is pretty hard to make a living at it.

Senator O'MAHONEY. But the stories that we read in the press——

Mr. STENGEL. That is right.

Senator O'MAHONEY. Are to the effect that the minor leagues are suffering. There are no more major league teams now than there were when you came into baseball, and what I am trying to find out is, What are the prospects for the future growth of baseball and to what extent have the 16 major league teams, through the farm system, obtained, by contract or agreement or understanding, control over the professional lives of the players?

Mr. STENGEL. That is right.

If I was a ballplayer and I was discharged, and I saw within 3 years that I could not become a major league ballplayer I would go into another profession.

That is the history of anything that is in business.

Senator O'MAHONEY. Do you think that the farm system keeps any players in the minor leagues when they ought to be in the majors?

Mr. STENGEL. I should say it would not keep any players behind or I have been telling you a falsehood.

I would say it might keep a few back, but very few.

There is no manager in baseball who wants to be a success without the ability of those great players and if I could pull them up to make money in a gate for my owner and for myself to be a success, I don't believe I would hold him back.

Senator O'MAHONEY. The fact is, is it not, Mr. Stengel, that while the population of the United States has increased tremendously during the period that you have been engaged in professional baseball, the number of major-league teams has not increased; it remains the same as it was then. The number of players actually engaged by the major-league teams is approximately the same as back in 1903, and there is now, through the farm system, a major league control of the professional occupation of baseball playing. Is that a correct summary?

Mr. STENGEL. Well, you have that from the standpoint of what you have been reading. You have got that down very good. [Laughter.]

But if you are a player——

Senator O'MAHONEY. I am trying to get it down from your standpoint as a 48-year man in baseball.

Mr. STENGEL. That is why I stayed in it.

I have been discharged 15 times and rehired; so you get rehired in baseball, and they don't want a good ballplayer leaving, and I always say a high-priced baseball player should get a high salary just like a moving-picture actor.

He should not get the same thing as the 25th man on the ball club who is very fortunate he is sitting on your ball club, and I say it is very hard to have skill in baseball.

Senator O'MAHONEY. You are not changing the subject; are you, sir?

Mr. STENGEL. No. You asked the question and I told you that if you want to find out how minor league baseball is; it is terrible now.

How can you eat on $2.50 a day when up here you can eat on $8 or better than $8?

Now how can you travel in a bus all night and play ball the next night to make a living?

How can you, a major league man, make it so that you can't?

Is he going to fly all of them to each place?

Senator O'MAHONEY. I am not arguing with you, Mr. Stengel.

Mr. STENGEL. I am just saying minor league ball has outgrown itself, like every small town has outgrown itself industrially because they don't put a plant in there to keep the people working so they leave.

Senator O'MAHONEY. Does that mean in your judgment that the major league baseball teams necessarily have to control ball playing?

Mr. STENGEL. I think that they do.

I don't think that if I was a great player and you released me in 4 years, I think it would be a joke if you released a man and he made 1 year for you and then bid for a job and then played the next year, we will say, out of Washington, he played in New York the third year, he would play in Cleveland and put himself up in a stake.

I think they ought to be just as they have been.

A man who walks in and sees you get fair compensation and if you are great be sure you get it because the day you don't report and the day you don't open a season you are hurting the major league and hurting yourself somewhat, but you are not going to be handicapped in life if you are great in baseball.

Every man who goes out has a better home than he had when he went in.

Senator O'MAHONEY. Did I understand you to say that in your own personal activity as manager, you always give a player who is to be traded advance notice?

Mr. STENGEL. I warn him that—I hold a meeting. We have an instructional school, regardless of my English, we have got an instructional school.

Senator O'MAHONEY. Your English is perfect and I can understand what you say, and I think I can even understand what you mean.

Mr. STENGEL. Yes, sir. You have got some very wonderful points in. I would say in an instructional school we try you out for 3 weeks and we clock you, just like—I mean how good are you going to be in the service; before you go out of the service we have got you listed.

We know if you are handicapped in the service and we have got instructors who teach you. They don't have to listen to me if they don't like me.

I have a man like Crosetti, who never has been to a banquet; he never would. He does a big job like Art Fletcher; he teaches that boy and teaches his family; he will be there. I have a man for first base, second base, short; that is why the Yankees are ahead.

We have advanced so much we can take a man over to where he can be a big league player and if he does not, we advance him to where he can play opposition to us.

I am getting concerned about opposition. I am discharging too many good ones.

Senator O'MAHONEY. Mr. Chairman, I think the witness is the best entertainment we have had around here for a long time and it is a great temptation to keep asking him questions but I think I had better desist.

Thank you.

Senator KEFAUVER. Senator Carroll.

Senator CARROLL. Mr. Stengel, I am an old Yankee fan and I come from a city where I think we have hade some contribution to your success—from Denver. I think you have many Yankee players from Denver.

The question Senator Kefauver asked you was what, in your honest opinion, with your 48 years of experience, is the need for this legislation in view of the fact that baseball has not been subject to antitrust laws?

Mr. STENGEL. No.

Senator CARROLL. It is not now subject to the antitrust laws. What do you think the need is for this legislation? I had a conference with one of the attorneys representing not only baseball but all of the sports, and I listened to your explanation to Senator Kefauver. It seemed to me it had some clarity. I asked the attorney this question: What was the need for this legislation? I wonder if you would accept his definition. He said they didn't want to be subjected to the ipse dixit of the Federal Government because they would throw a lot of damage suits on the ad damnum clause. He said, in the first place, the Toolson case was sui generis, it was de minimus non curat lex.

Do you call that a clear expression?

Mr. STENGEL. Well, you are going to get me there for about 2 hours.

Senator CARROLL. I realize these questions which are put to you are all, I suppose, legislative and legal questions. Leaning on your experience as a manager, do you feel the farm system, the draft system, the reserve-clause system, is fair to the players, to the managers, and to the public interest?

Mr. STENGEL. I think the public is taken care of, rich and poor, better at the present time than years ago. I really think that the ownership is a question of ability. I really think that the business manager is a question of ability. Some of those men are supposed to be very brilliant in their line of work, and some of them are not so brilliant, so that they have quite a bit of trouble with it when you run an operation of a club in which the ownership maybe doesn't run the club.

I would say that the players themselves—I told you, I am not in on that fund, it is a good thing. I say I should have been, to tell you the truth. But I think it is a great thing for the players.

Senator CARROLL. I am not talking about that fund.

Mr. STENGEL. Well, I tell you, if you are going to talk about the fund you are going to think about radio and television and pay television.

Senator CARROLL. I do not want to talk about radio and television, but I do want to talk about the draft clause and reserve systems.

Mr. STENGEL. Yes, sir. I would have liked to have been free four times in my life; and later on I have seen men free, and later on they make a big complaint "they wuz robbed," and if you are robbed there is always some club down the road to give you an opportunity.

Senator CARROLL. That was not the question I asked you, and I only asked you on your long experience——

Mr. STENGEL. Yes, sir. I would not be in it 48 years if it was not all right.

Senator CARROLL. I understand that.

Mr. STENGEL. Well, then, why wouldn't it stay that?

Senator CARROLL. In your long experience——

Mr. STENGEL. Yes.

Senator CARROLL. Do you feel—you have had experience through the years——

Mr. STENGEL. That is true.

Senator CARROLL. With the draft system, and the reserve clause in the contracts. Do you think you could still exist under existing law without changing the law?

Mr. STENGEL. I think it is run better than it has even been run in baseball, for every department.

Senator CARROLL. Then I come back to the principal question. This is the real question before this body.

Mr. STENGEL. All right.

Senator CARROLL. Then what is the need for legislation, if they are getting along all right?

Mr. STENGEL. I didn't ask for the legislation. [Laughter.]

Senator CARROLL. Your answer is a very good one, and that is the question Senator Kefauver put to you.

Mr. STENGEL. That is right.

Senator CARROLL. That is the question Senator O'Mahoney put.

Mr. STENGEL. Right.

Senator CARROLL. Are you ready to say there is no need for legislation in this field, then, insofar as baseball is concerned?

Mr. STENGEL. As far as I am concerned, from drawing a salary and from my ups and downs and being discharged, I always found out that there was somebody ready to employ you, if you were on the ball.

Senator CARROLL. Thank you very much, Mr. Stengel.

Senator KEFAUVER. Thank you very much, Mr. Stengel. We appreciate your testimony.

Senator LANGER. May I ask a question?

Senator KEFAUVER. Senator Langer has a question. Just a moment, Mr. Stengel.

Senator Langer. Can you tell this committee what countries have baseball teams besides the United States, Mexico, and Japan?

Mr. Stengel. I made a tour with the New York Yankees several years ago, and it was the most amazing tour I ever saw for a ball club, to go over where you have trouble spots. It wouldn't make any difference whether he was a Republican or Democrat, and so forth.

I know that over there we drew 250,000 to 500,000 people in the streets, in which they stood in front of the automobiles, not on the sidewalks, and those people are trying to play baseball over there with short fingers [laughter], and I say, "Why do you do it?"

But they love it. They are crazy about baseball, and they are not worried at the handicap. And I'll tell you, business industries run baseball over there, and they are now going to build a stadium that is going to be covered over for games where you don't need a tarpaulin if it rains.

South America is all right, and Cuba is all right. But I don't know, I have never been down there except to Cuba, I have never been to South America, and I know that they broadcast games, and I know we have players that are playing from there.

I tell you what, I think baseball has spread, but if we are talking about anything spreading, we would be talking about soccer. You can go over in Italy, and I thought they would know DiMaggio everyplace. And my goodness, you mention soccer, you can draw 50,000 or a hundred thousand people. Over here you have a hard time to get soccer on the field, which is a great sport, no doubt.

Senator Langer. What I want to know, Mr. Stengel, is this: When the American League plays the National League in the world series and it is advertised as the world championship——

Mr. Stengel. Yes, sir.

Senator Langer. I want to know why you do not play Mexico or Japan or some other country and really have a world championship.

Mr. Stengel. Well, I think you have a good argument there. I would say that a couple of clubs that I saw, it was like when I was in the Navy, I thought I couldn't get special unless they played who I wanted to play. So I would look over a team. When they got off a ship I would play them, but if they had been on land too long, my team couldn't play them.

So I would play the teams at sea 6 months, and I would say, "You are the club I would like to play." I would like to play those countries, and I think it should be nationwide and governmentwide, too, if you could possibly get it in.

Senator Langer. Do you think the day is ever going to come, perhaps 5 years from now or 10——

Mr. Stengel. I would say 10 years, not 5.

Senator Langer. When the championship team of the United States would play the championship team of Mexico?

Mr. Stengel. I really think it should be that way, but I don't think you will get it before 10 years, because you have to build stadiums and you have to have an elimination in every country for it, and you have to have weather at the same time, or how could you play unless you would hold a team over?

Senator Langer. Do you not think these owners are going to develop this matter of world championship of another country besides the United States?

Mr. STENGEL. I should think they would do that in time. I really do. I was amazed over in Japan. I couldn't understand why they would want to play baseball with short fingers and used the same size ball, and not a small size, and compete in baseball. And yet that is their great sport, and industries are backing them.

Senator LANGER. In other words, the owners some day, in your opinion, Mr. Stengel, are going to make a lot of money by having the champions of one country play another country and keep on with eliminations until they really have a world championship?

Mr. STENGEL. That is what I say. I think it is not named properly right now unless you can go and play all of them. You would have to do that.

Senator LANGER. That is all, Mr. Chairman.

Senator KEFAUVER. Mr. Stengel, one final question. You spoke of Judge Landis and the fact that he had rather absolute control over baseball. There was a clause in Judge Landis' contract which read:

We, the club owners, pledge ourselves to loyally support the commissioner in his important and difficult task, and we assure him that each of us will acquiesce in his decisions even when we believe they are mistaken, and that we will not discredit the sport by criticism of him or one another.

This same clause was in Mr. Chandler's contract, but we do not understand it to be in Mr. Frick's contract. Do you think the commissioner needs to have this power over the management?

Mr. STENGEL. I would say when there was a cloud over baseball, like any sport, you have to have a man that has the power to change things.

Now when Landis was in, that was the situation with baseball. You were bucking racetracks. We don't have a tote board. We are playing baseball for admission fees.

Now, we don't want a tote board in baseball. Who would? That would be great, if you have that out there, and you could go out there and, you know, use a tote board and say, "Does he get to first or won't he get to first?" and so forth.

Now Landis was an amazing man. I will give you an example of him. It is a good thing you brought him in. I was discharged one year, and I was the president of a ball club at Worcester, Mass., so I discharged myself, and I sent it in to Landis and he O. K.'d it.

Why was I president? Then I could release my player, couldn't I? And I was the player. So I was the only player ever released by the president, and that was in Worcester, Mass., so I got discharged.

Senator KEFAUVER. Do you think the present commissioner ought to have the same power?

Mr. STENGEL. There are 16 men in baseball who own ball clubs. We will say that an individual can hardly make it any more unless he is wealthy. That is how it has grown. I would say the biggest thing in baseball at the present time now, and with the money that is coming in, and so forth, and with an annuity fund for the players, you can't allow the commissioner to just take everything sitting there, and take everything insofar as money is concerned, but I think he should have full jurisdiction over the player and player's habits, and the way the umpires and ball clubs should conduct their business in the daytime and right on up tight up here.

Senator KEFAUVER. Thank you very much, Mr. Stengel. We appreciate your presence here.

The committee is very glad that Senator Mundt is interested and is present.  We will be glad to have any Senators testify or participate in the hearing.

Mr. Mickey Mantle, will you come around?

Mr. Mantel, I am sure all of us saw you play yesterday, either in the sunshine and hot weather in Baltimore, or on television.

Will you very briefly give your baseball experience?  Of course, you are from Oklahoma.

## STATEMENT OF MICKEY MANTLE, NEW YORK YANKEES

Mr. MANTLE. I started playing baseball in 1949 with the Independence, Kans., class D league; and in 1950 I went to Joplin, Mo., a class C league; and in 1951 I came with the Yankees.

Senator KEFAUVER. How many years is that, altogether, that you have been in baseball?

Mr. MANTLE. Well, this would be my 10th year.

Senator KEFAUVER. Mr. Mantle, do you have any observations with reference to the applicability of the antitrust laws to baseball?

Mr. MANTLE. My views are just about the same as Casey's. [Laughter.]

Alexander J. SALERNO and William
Valentine, Plaintiffs-Appellants,

v.

AMERICAN LEAGUE OF PROFESSION-
AL BASEBALL CLUBS, an unincorporated association, Joseph E. Cronin, individually and as President of the
American League of Professional Baseball Clubs, and Paul Porter, Defendants,

Bowie Kuhn, individually and as the Commissioner of Baseball, Defendant-
Appellee.

No. 818, Docket 34653.

United States Court of Appeals,
Second Circuit.

Argued May 26, 1970.

Decided July 13, 1970.

Appeal from order of the United
States District Court for the Southern
District of New York, Thomas F.
Croake, J., 310 F.Supp. 729, dismissing
complaint by two discharged umpires
against professional baseball league,
Commissioner of baseball and others.
The Court of Appeals, Friendly, Circuit
Judge, held that overruling of Supreme
Court holdings that professional baseball
is not subject to antitrust laws is the exclusive privilege of the Supreme Court,
and noted that combining assertion of
general antitrust violation by professional baseball with claim of injury to discharged umpires from breach of contract or tort does not automatically make
the latter a claim under the antitrust
laws.

Affirmed.

1. Courts ⟸284
Combining assertion of general antitrust violation by professional baseball
with claim of injury to discharged umpires from breach of contract or tort does

not automatically make the latter a claim arising under the antitrust laws. Sherman Anti-Trust Act, §§ 1, 2, 15 U. S.C.A. §§ 1, 2; Clayton Act, § 4, 15 U. S.C.A. § 15.

**2. Monopolies** ⊸28(1.1)

Wrongful discharge of employee does not become an antitrust violation simply because the employer is a monopolist; the private right of action is conferred only for an injury by reason of anything forbidden in the antitrust laws. Clayton Act, § 4, 15 U.S.C.A. § 15.

**3. Courts** ⊸96

Possible overruling Supreme Court holdings that professional baseball is not subject to the antitrust laws is the exclusive privilege of that Court. Sherman Anti-Trust Act, §§ 1, 2, 15 U.S.C.A. §§ 1, 2; Clayton Act, § 4, 15 U.S.C.A. § 15.

———◆———

Joseph Kelner, New York City, for plaintiffs-appellants.

George S. Leisure, Jr., New York City (Donovan, Leisure, Newton & Irvine and Paul E. Goodspeed and Paul A. Crotty, New York City, of counsel), for appellee, Bowie Kuhn.

Before WATERMAN, FRIENDLY and HAYS, Circuit Judges.

FRIENDLY, Circuit Judge:

Plaintiffs, former umpires in the American League of Professional Baseball Clubs, were discharged by the president of the League. Although he announced that this was for incompetence, plaintiffs claim "the true and only reason" was their endeavor to organize the American League umpires for collective bargaining. Following an unfair labor practice charge on their part, the National Labor Relations Board issued a complaint under §§ 8(a) (1) and (3) of the Act, Case No. 1–CA–6581, on March 26, 1970, and this has been referred to a Trial Examiner for hearing. See 180 N.L.R.B. No. 30 (Dec. 15, 1969), 38 L. W. 2351.

Before that the plaintiffs had filed a complaint in the District Court for the Southern District of New York. They named as defendants the American League of Professional Baseball Clubs; Joseph E. Cronin, its president; Bowie Kuhn, the Commissioner of Baseball; and Paul Porter, a well-known Washington attorney. Only Kuhn was served. The complaint contained two counts. The first alleged a claim under the Sherman and Clayton Acts, 15 U.S.C. §§ 1, 2 & 15; the second asserted a claim for defamation. When Kuhn moved to dismiss for want of federal jurisdiction, plaintiffs maintained there was both federal question and diversity jurisdiction. Finding neither, the district court granted the motion. Since the diversity claim has now been abandoned, all that is left is the claim under the antitrust laws.

[1, 2] Even if we were sure that professional baseball will be held subject to the antitrust laws, we would entertain serious doubt whether the complaint here stated a claim under them. Combining an assertion of general antitrust violation with a claim of injury from breach of contract or tort does not automatically make the latter a claim arising under the antitrust laws. As Judge Kaufman observed in a rather similar context, Molinas v. National Basketball Ass'n, 190 F.Supp. 241, 243 (S.D.N.Y. 1961), a plaintiff in a civil antitrust action "must establish a clear causal connection between the violation alleged and the injuries allegedly suffered." See also Tepler v. Frick, 204 F.2d 506 (2 Cir. 1953). Wrongful discharge of an employee does not become an antitrust violation simply because the employer is a monopolist; the private right of action is conferred only for an injury "by reason of anything forbidden in the antitrust laws," 15 U.S.C. § 15. Although the complaint has elaborate allegations of conspiracy in restraint of trade, there is nothing to indicate restrictive trade practices directed at umpires. In the nature of things these must be employed —and discharged—by a league rather than by a single club. The only pertinent allegations going beyond discrimi-

natory discharge by the President of the American League are that Kuhn is employed as Commissioner by both the American and the National Leagues, that plaintiffs' discharge was with Kuhn's "knowledge, permission and consent," and that defendants "did, in fact, restrain and monopolize * * * trade and commerce in violation of Sections 1 and 2 of the Sherman Act by means of a group boycott against plaintiffs." Even the requisite liberal interpretation of these allegations does not overcome the great difficulty in finding that a claim was stated under such cases as Klor's, Inc. v. Broadway-Hale Stores, Inc., 359 U.S. 207, 79 S.Ct. 705, 3 L.Ed.2d 741 (1959), and Fashion Originators Guild of America v. FTC, 312 U.S. 457, 61 S. Ct. 703, 85 L.Ed. 949 (1941). Moreover, plaintiffs' real grievance is their alleged discriminatory discharge in violation of the National Labor Relations Act, and this is being considered by the agency appointed for the purpose by Congress. Even assuming this claim somehow also encompasses a violation of the antitrust laws, which is highly doubtful, we would have the further question whether a federal court could consider it once the NLRB has begun proceedings. See Local Union No. 189, Amalgamated Meat Cutters, and Butcher Workmen of No. America, AFL–CIO v. Jewel Tea Co., 381 U.S. 676, 85 S.Ct. 1596, 14 L.Ed.2d 640 (1965); cf. San Diego Bldg. Trades Council v. Garmon, 359 U.S. 236, 79 S. Ct. 773, 3 L.Ed.2d 775 (1959).

[3] Apart from these exceedingly serious obstacles, plaintiffs recognize that they can prevail only if we should be willing to predict the likely overruling of the holdings in Federal Baseball Club of Baltimore, Inc. v. National League of Professional Baseball Clubs, 259 U.S. 200, 42 S.Ct. 465, 66 L.Ed. 898 (1922), and Toolson v. New York Yankees, Inc., 346 U.S. 356, 74 S.Ct. 78, 98 L.Ed. 64 (1953), that professional baseball is not subject to the antitrust laws. Cf. Green v. Board of Elections of City of New York, 380 F.2d 445, 448 (2 Cir. 1967),

and cases there cited. They say that changes in the economics of the sport even since *Toolson,* especially the increasing importance of revenues from interstate television broadcasts, make baseball's immunity from the antitrust laws more anomalous than ever. But the ground upon which *Toolson* rested was that Congress had no intention to bring baseball within the antitrust laws, not that baseball's activities did not sufficiently affect interstate commerce. Cf. Gardella v. Chandler, 172 F.2d 402, 407–408 (2 Cir. 1949). We freely acknowledge our belief that *Federal Baseball* was not one of Mr. Justice Holmes' happiest days, that the rationale of *Toolson* is extremely dubious and that, to use the Supreme Court's own adjectives, the distinction between baseball and other professional sports is "unrealistic," "inconsistent" and "illogical." Radovich v. National Football League, 352 U.S. 445, 452, 77 S.Ct. 390, 1 L.Ed.2d 456 (1957). We add that Boys Mkts., Inc. v. Retail Clerk's Local 770, 398 U.S. 235, 90 S.Ct. 1583, 26 L.Ed.2d 199, decided June 1, 1970, overruling Sinclair Refining Co. v. Atkinson, 370 U.S. 195, 82 S.Ct. 1328, 8 L.Ed.2d 440 (1962), despite Congress' failure to act on invitations to do so, may presage a change from the attitude with respect to such inaction that was expressed in *Toolson,* 346 U.S. at 357, 74 S.Ct. 78, which Mr. Justice Black in dissent invoked to no avail, 398 U.S. at 255, 90 S.Ct. at 1595. However, putting aside instances where factual premises have all but vanished and a different principle might thus obtain, we continue to believe that the Supreme Court should retain the exclusive privilege of overruling its own decisions, save perhaps when opinions already delivered have created a near certainty that only the occasion is needed for pronouncement of the doom. While we should not fall out of our chairs with surprise at the news that *Federal Baseball* and *Toolson* had been overruled, we are not at all certain the Court is ready to give them a happy despatch.

Affirmed.

407 U.S. 258, 32 L.Ed.2d 728

**Curtis C. FLOOD, Petitioner,**

v.

**Bowie K. KUHN et al.**

No. 71-32.

Argued March 20, 1972.

Decided June 19, 1972.

⌐ Mr. Justice BLACKMUN delivered ⌐259 the opinion of the Court.

For the third time in 50 years the Court is asked specifically to rule that professional baseball's reserve system is within the reach of the federal antitrust laws.[1] ⌐ Collateral issues of state law and ⌐260 of federal labor policy are also advanced.

the ability of the club annually to renew the contract unilaterally, subject to a stated salary minimum. Thus

A. Rule 3 of the Major League Rules provides in part:

"(a) UNIFORM CONTRACT. To preserve morale and to produce the similarity of conditions necessary to keen competition, the contracts between all clubs and their players in the Major Leagues shall be in a single form which shall be prescribed by the Major League Executive Council. No club shall make a contract different from the uniform contract or a contract containing a non-reserve clause,

I

The Game

It is a century and a quarter since the New York Nine defeated the Knickerbockers 23 to 1 on Hoboken's Elysian Fields June 19, 1846, with Alexander Jay Cartwright as the instigator and the umpire. The teams were amateur, but the contest marked a significant date in baseball's beginnings. That early game led ultimately to the development of professional baseball and its tightly organized structure.

The Cincinnati Red Stockings came into existence in 1869 upon an outpouring of local pride. With only one Cincinnatian on the payroll, this professional team traveled over 11,000 miles that summer, winning 56 games and tying one. Shortly thereafter, on St. Patrick's Day in 1871, the National Association of Professional Baseball Players was

---

except with the written approval of the Commissioner. . . .

"(g) TAMPERING. To preserve discipline and competition, and to prevent the enticement of players, coaches, managers and umpires, there shall be no negotiations or dealings respecting employment, either present or prospective, between any player, coach or manager and any club other than the club with which he is under contract or acceptance of terms, or by which he is reserved, or which has the player on its Negotiation List, or between any umpire and any league other than the league with which he is under contract or acceptance of terms, unless the club or league with which he is connected shall have, in writing, expressly authorized such negotiations or dealings prior to their commencement."

B. Rule 9 of the Major League Rules provides in part:

"(a) NOTICE. A club may assign to another club an existing contract with a player. The player, upon receipt of written notice of such assignment, is by his contract bound to serve the assignee.

. . . . .

"After the date of such assignment all rights and obligations of the assignor clubs thereunder shall become the rights and obligations of the assignee club . . . ."

C. Rules 3 and 9 of the Professional Baseball Rules contain provisions parallel to those just quoted.

D. The Uniform Player's Contract provides in part:

"4. (a) . . . The Player agrees that, in addition to other remedies, the Club shall be entitled to injunctive and other equitable relief to prevent a breach of this contract by the Player, including, among others, the right to enjoin the Player from playing baseball for any other person or organization during the term of this contract."

"5. (a). The Player agrees that, while under contract, and prior to expiration of the Club's right to renew this contract, he will not play baseball otherwise than for the Club, except that the Player may participate in post-season games under the conditions prescribed in the Major League Rules. . . . "

"6. (a) The Player agrees that this contract may be assigned by the Club (and reassigned by any assignee Club) to any other Club in accordance with the Major League Rules and the Professional Baseball Rules."

"10. (a) On or before January 15 (or if a Sunday, then the next preceding business day) of the year next following the last playing season covered by this contract, the Club may tender to the Player a contract for the term of that year by mailing the same to the Player at his address following his signature hereto, or if none be given, then at his last address of record with the Club. If prior to the March 1 next succeeding said January 15, the Player and the Club have not agreed upon the terms of such contract, then on or before 10 days after said March 1, the Club shall have the right by written notice to the Player at said address to renew this contract for the period of one year on the same terms, except that the amount payable to the Player shall be such as the club shall fix in said notice; provided, however, that said amount, if fixed by a Major League Club, shall be an amount payable at a rate not less than 80% of the rate stipulated for the preceding year.

"(b) The Club's right to renew this contract, as provided in subparagraph (a) of this paragraph 10, and the promise of the Player not to play otherwise than with the Club have been taken into consideration in determining the amount payable under paragraph 2 hereof."

*121*

founded and the professional league was born.

The ensuing colorful days are well known. The ardent follower and the student of baseball know of General Abner Doubleday; the formation of the National League in 1876; Chicago's supremacy in the first year's competition under the leadership of Al Spalding and with Cap Anson at third base; the formation of the American Association and then of the Union Association in the 1880's; the introduction of Sunday baseball; interleague warfare with cut-rate admission prices and player raiding; the development of the reserve "clause"; the emergence in 1885 of the Brotherhood of Professional Ball Players, and in 1890 of the Players League; the appearance of the American League, or "junior circuit," in 1901, rising from the minor Western Association; the first World Series in 1903, disruption in 1904, and the Series' resumption in 1905; the short-lived Federal League on the majors' scene during World War I years; the troublesome and discouraging episode of the 1919 Series; the home run ball; the shifting of franchises; the expansion of the leagues; the installation in 1965 of the major league draft of potential new players; and the formation of the Major League Baseball Players Association in 1966.[2]

Then there are the many names, celebrated for one reason or another, that have sparked the diamond and its environs and that have provided tinder for recaptured thrills, for reminiscence and comparisons, and for conversation and anticipation in-season and off-season: Ty Cobb, Babe Ruth, Tris Speaker, Walter Johnson, Henry Chadwick, Eddie Collins, Lou Gehrig, Grover Cleveland Alexander, Rogers Hornsby, Harry Hooper, Goose Goslin, Jackie Robinson, Honus Wagner, Joe McCarthy, John McGraw, Deacon Phillippe, Rube Marquard, Christy Mathewson, Tommy Leach, Big Ed Delahanty, Davy Jones, Germany Schaefer, King Kelly, Big Dan Brouthers, Wahoo Sam Crawford, Wee Willie Keeler, Big Ed Walsh, Jimmy Austin, Fred Snodgrass, Satchel Paige, Hugh Jennings, Fred Merkle, Iron Man McGinnity, Three-Finger Brown, Harry and Stan Coveleski, Connie Mack, Al Bridwell, Red Ruffing, Amos Rusie, Cy Young, Smokey Joe Wood, Chief Meyers, Chief Bender, Bill Klem, Hans Lobert, Johnny Evers, Joe Tinker, Roy Campanella, Miller Huggins, Rube Bressler, Dazzy Vance, Edd Roush, Bill Wambsganss, Clark Griffith, Branch Rickey, Frank Chance, Cap Anson, Nap Lajoie, Sad Sam Jones, Bob O'Farrell. Lefty O'Doul, Bobby Veach, Willie Kamm, Heinie Groh, Lloyd and Paul Waner, Stuffy McInnis, Charles Comiskey, Roger Bresnahan, Bill Dickey, Zack Wheat, George Sisler, Charlie Gehringer, Eppa Rixey, Harry Heilmann, Fred Clarke, Dizzy Dean, Hank Greenberg, Pie Traynor, Rube Waddell, Bill Terry, Carl Hubbell, Old Hoss Radbourne, Moe Berg, Rabbit Maranville, Jimmie Foxx, Lefty Grove.[3] The list seems endless.

And one recalls the appropriate reference to the "World Serious," attributed to Ring Lardner, Sr.; Ernest L. Thayer's "Casey at the Bat";[4] the ring of

---

2. See generally The Baseball Encyclopedia (1969); L. Ritter, The Glory of Their Times (1966); 1 & 2 H. Seymour, Baseball (1960, 1971); 1 & 2 D. Voigt, American Baseball (1966, 1970).

3. These are names only from earlier years. By mentioning some, one risks unintended omission of others equally celebrated.

4. Millions have known and enjoyed baseball. One writer knowledgeable in the field of sports almost assumed that every-

one did until, one day, he discovered otherwise:
   "I knew a cove who'd never heard of Washington and Lee,
   Of Caesar and Napoleon from the ancient jamboree,
   But, bli'me, there are queerer things than anything like that,
   For here's a cove who never heard of 'Casey at the Bat'!

   .    .    .    .    .

   "Ten million never heard of Keats, or Shelley, Burns or Poe;

⌐264 "Tinker to⌐Evers to Chance"; [5] and all the other happenings, habits, and superstitions about and around baseball that made it the "national pastime" or, depending upon the point of view, "the great American tragedy." [6]

## II

### The Petitioner

The petitioner, Curtis Charles Flood, born in 1938, began his major league career in 1956 when he signed a contract with the Cincinnati Reds for a salary of $4,000 for the season. He had no attorney or agent to advise him on that occasion. He was traded to the St. Louis Cardinals before the 1958 season. Flood rose to fame as a center fielder with the Cardinals during the years 1958–1969. In those 12 seasons he compiled a batting average of .293. His best offensive season was 1967 when he achieved .335. He was .301 or better in six of the 12 St. Louis years. He participated in the 1964, 1967, and 1968 World Series. He played errorless ball in the field in 1966, and once enjoyed 223 consecutive errorless games. Flood has received seven Golden Glove Awards. He was co-captain of his team from 1965–1969. He ranks among the 10 major league outfielders possessing the highest lifetime fielding averages.

⌐265 ⌐Flood's St. Louis compensation for the years shown was:

     1961    $13,500 (including a bonus for signing)
     1962    $16,000

| 1963 | $17,500 |
| 1964 | $23,000 |
| 1965 | $35,000 |
| 1966 | $45,000 |
| 1967 | $50,000 |
| 1968 | $72,500 |
| 1969 | $90,000 |

These figures do not include any so-called fringe benefits or World Series shares.

But at the age of 31, in October 1969, Flood was traded to the Philadelphia Phillies of the National League in a multi-player transaction. He was not consulted about the trade. He was informed by telephone and received formal notice only after the deal had been consummated. In December he complained to the Commissioner of Baseball and asked that he be made a free agent and be placed at liberty to strike his own bargain with any other major league team. His request was denied.

Flood then instituted this antitrust suit [7] in January 1970 in federal court for the Southern District of New York. The defendants (although not all were named in each cause of action) were the Commissioner of Baseball, the presidents of the two major leagues, and the 24 major league clubs. In general, the complaint charged violations of the federal antitrust laws and civil rights statutes, violation of state statutes and the common law, and the imposition of a form of peonage and involuntary⌐servi- ⌐266 tude contrary to the Thirteenth Amend-

5. "These are the saddest of possible words,
    'Tinker to Evers to Chance.'
    Trio of bear cubs, and fleeter than birds,
    'Tinker to Evers to Chance.'
    Ruthlessly pricking our gonfalon bubble,
    Making a Giant hit into a double—
    Words that are weighty with nothing but trouble:
    'Tinker to Evers to Chance.' "
  Franklin Pierce Adams, Baseball's Sad Lexicon.

6. George Bernard Shaw, The Sporting News, May 27, 1943, p. 15, col. 4.

7. Concededly supported by the Major League Baseball Players Association, the players' collective-bargaining representative. Tr. of Oral Arg. 12.

But they know 'the air was shattered by the force of Casey's blow';
They never heard of Shakespeare, nor of Dickens, like as not,
But they know the somber drama from old Mudville's haunted lot.
"He never heard of Casey! Am I dreaming? Is it true?
Is fame but windblown ashes when the summer day is through?
Does greatness fade so quickly and is grandeur doomed to die
That bloomed in early morning, ere the dusk rides down the sky?"
"He Never Heard of Casey" Grantland Rice, The Sportlight, New York Herald Tribune, June 1, 1926, p. 23.

ment and 42 U.S.C. § 1994, 18 U.S.C. § 1581, and 29 U.S.C. §§ 102 and 103. Petitioner sought declaratory and injunctive relief and treble damages.

Flood declined to play for Philadelphia in 1970, despite a $100,000 salary offer, and he sat out the year. After the season was concluded, Philadelphia sold its rights to Flood to the Washington Senators. Washington and the petitioner were able to come to terms for 1971 at a salary of $110,000.[8] Flood started the season but, apparently because he was dissatisfied with his performance, he left the Washington club on April 27, early in the campaign. He has not played baseball since then.

### III

### The Present Litigation

Judge Cooper, in a detailed opinion, first denied a preliminary injunction, 309 F.Supp. 793 (S.D.N.Y.1970), observing on the way:

"Baseball has been the national pastime for over one hundred years and enjoys a unique place in our American heritage. Major league professional baseball is avidly followed by millions of fans, looked upon with fervor and pride and provides a special source of inspiration and competitive team spirit especially for the young.

"Baseball's status in the life of the nation is so pervasive that it would not strain credulity to say the Court can take judicial notice that baseball is everybody's business. To put it mildly and with restraint, it would be unfortunate indeed if a fine sport and profession, which brings surcease from daily travail and an escape from the ordinary to most inhabitants of this land, were to suffer in the least because of undue concentration by any one or any group on commercial and profit considerations. The game is on higher ground; it behooves every one

to keep it there." 309 F.Supp., at 797.

Flood's application for an early trial was granted. The court next deferred until trial its decision on the defendants' motions to dismiss the primary causes of action, but granted a defense motion for summary judgment on an additional cause of action. 312 F.Supp. 404 (S.D. N.Y.1970).

Trial to the court took place in May and June 1970. An extensive record was developed. In an ensuing opinion, 316 F.Supp. 271 (S.D.N.Y.1970), Judge Cooper first noted that:

"Plaintiff's witnesses in the main concede that some form of reserve on players is a necessary element of the organization of baseball as a league sport, but contend that the present all-embracing system is needlessly restrictive and offer various alternatives which in their view might loosen the bonds without sacrifice to the game. . . .

 . . . . .

"Clearly the preponderance of credible proof does not favor elimination of the reserve clause. With the sole exception of plaintiff himself, it shows that even plaintiff's witnesses do not contend that it is wholly undesirable; in fact they regard substantial portions meritorious. . . ." 316 F. Supp., at 275–276.

He then held that Federal Baseball Club v. National League, 259 U.S. 200, 42 S.Ct. 465, 66 L.Ed. 898 (1922), and Toolson v. New York Yankees, Inc., 346 U.S. 356, 74 S.Ct. 78, 98 L.Ed. 64 (1953), were controlling; that it was not necessary to reach the issue whether exemption from the antitrust laws would result because aspects of baseball now are a subject of collective bargaining; that the plaintiff's state-law claims, those based on common law as well as on statute, were to be denied because baseball was not "a matter which admits of diversity of

---

**8.** The parties agreed that Flood's participating in baseball in 1971 would be without prejudice to his case.

treatment," 316 F.Supp., at 280; that the involuntary servitude claim failed because of the absence of "the essential element of this cause of action, a showing of compulsory service," 316 F.Supp., at 281–282; and that judgment was to be entered for the defendants. Judge Cooper included a statement of personal conviction to the effect that "negotiations could produce an accommodation on the reserve system which would be eminently fair and equitable to all concerned" and that "the reserve clause can be fashioned so as to find acceptance by player and club." 316 F.Supp., at 282 and 284.

On appeal, the Second Circuit felt "compelled to affirm." 443 F.2d 264, 265 (1971). It regarded the issue of state law as one of first impression, but concluded that the Commerce Clause precluded its application. Judge Moore added a concurring opinion in which he predicted, with respect to the suggested overruling of *Federal Baseball* and *Toolson*, that "there is no likelihood that such an event will occur." [9] 443 F.2d, at 268, 272.

|269 | We granted certiorari in order to look once again at this troublesome and unusual situation. 404 U.S. 880, 92 S.Ct. 201, 30 L.Ed.2d 160 (1971).

### IV

### The Legal Background

A. Federal Baseball Club v. National League, 259 U.S. 200, 42 S.Ct. 465, 66 L.Ed. 898 (1922), was a suit for treble damages instituted by a member of the Federal League (Baltimore) against the National and American Leagues and others. The plaintiff obtained a verdict in the trial court, but the Court of Appeals reversed. The main brief filed by the plaintiff with this Court discloses that it was strenuously argued, among other things, that the business in which the defendants were engaged was interstate commerce; that the interstate relationship among the several clubs, located as they were in different States, was predominant; that organized baseball represented an investment of colossal wealth; that it was an engagement in moneymaking; that gate receipts were divided by agreement between the home club and the visiting club; and that the business of baseball was to be distinguished from the mere playing of the game as a sport for physical exercise and diversion. See also 259 U.S., at 201–206, 42 S.Ct. 465.

Mr. Justice Holmes, in speaking succinctly for a unanimous Court, said:

"The business is giving exhibitions of base ball, which are purely state affairs. . . . But the fact that in order to give the exhibitions the Leagues must induce free persons to cross state lines and |must arrange and |270 pay for their doing so is not enough to change the character of the business. . . . [T]he transport is a mere incident, not the essential thing. That to which it is incident, the exhibition, although made for money would not be called trade or commerce

---

9. "And properly so. Baseball's welfare and future should not be for politically insulated interpreters of technical antitrust statutes but rather should be for the voters through their elected representatives. If baseball is to be damaged by statutory regulation, let the congressman face his constituents the next November and also face the consequences of his baseball voting record." 443 F.2d, at 272. Cf. Judge Friendly's comments in Salerno v. American League, 429 F.2d 1003, 1005 (CA2 1970), cert. denied, *sub nom.* Salerno v. Kuhn, 400 U.S. 1001, 91 S.Ct. 462, 27 L.Ed.2d 452 (1971):

"We freely acknowledge our belief that *Federal Baseball* was not one of Mr. Justice Holmes' happiest days, that the rationale of *Toolson* is extremely dubious and that, to use the Supreme Court's own adjectives, the distinction between baseball and other professional sports is 'unrealistic,' 'inconsistent' and 'illogical.' . . . While we should not fall out of our chairs with surprise at the news that *Federal Baseball* and *Toolson* had been overruled, we are not at all certain the Court is ready to give them a happy despatch."

in the commonly accepted use of those words. As it is put by the defendant, personal effort, not related to production, is not a subject of commerce. That which in its consummation is not commerce does not become commerce among the States because the transportation that we have mentioned takes place. To repeat the illustrations given by the Court below, a firm of lawyers sending out a member to argue a case, or the Chautauqua lecture bureau sending out lecturers, does not engage in such commerce because the lawyer or lecturer goes to another State.

"If we are right the plaintiff's business is to be described in the same way and the restrictions by contract that prevented the plaintiff from getting players to break their bargains and the other conduct charged against the defendants were not an interference with commerce among the States." 259 U.S., at 208–209, 42 S. Ct., at 466.[10]

⌐271 ⌐The Court thus chose not to be persuaded by opposing examples proffered by the plaintiff, among them (a) Judge Learned Hand's decision on a demurrer to a Sherman Act complaint with respect to vaudeville entertainers traveling a theater circuit covering several States, H. B. Marienelli, Ltd. v. United Booking Offices, 227 F. 165 (S.D.N.Y.1914); (b) the first Mr. Justice Harlan's opinion in International Textbook Co. v. Pigg, 217 U.S. 91, 30 S.Ct. 481, 54 L.Ed. 678

(1910), to the effect that correspondence courses pursued through the mail constituted commerce among the States; and (c) Mr. Justice Holmes' own opinion, for another unanimous Court, on demurrer in a Sherman Act case, relating to cattle shipment, the interstate movement of which was interrupted for the finding of purchasers at the stockyards, Swift & Co. v. United States, 196 U.S. 375, 25 S. Ct. 276, 49 L.Ed. 518 (1905). The only earlier case the parties were able to locate where the question was raised whether organized baseball was within the Sherman Act was American League Baseball Club v. Chase, 86 Misc. 441, 149 N.Y.S. 6 (1914). That court had answered the question in the negative.

B. *Federal Baseball* was cited a year later, and without disfavor, in another opinion by Mr. Justice Holmes for a unanimous Court. The complaint charged antitrust violations with respect to vaudeville bookings. It was held, however, that the claim was not frivolous and that the bill should not have been dismissed. Hart v. B. F. Keith Vaudeville Exchange, 262 U.S. 271, 43 S.Ct. 540, 67 L.Ed. 977 (1923).[11]

It has also been cited, not unfavorably, with respect to the practice of law, United States v. South-Eastern⌐Underwriters Assn., 322 U.S. 533, 573, ⌐272 64 S.Ct. 1162, 1184, 88 L.Ed. 1440 (1944) (Stone, C. J., dissenting); with respect to out-of-state contractors, United States v. Employing Plasterers Assn., 347 U.S. 186, 196–197, 74 S.Ct. 452,

---

10. "What really saved baseball, legally at least, for the next half century was the protective canopy spread over it by the United States Supreme Court's decision in the Baltimore Federal League antitrust suit against Organized Baseball in 1922. In it Justice Holmes, speaking for a unanimous court, ruled that the business of giving baseball exhibitions for profit was not 'trade or commerce in the commonly-accepted use of those words' because 'personal effort, not related to production, is not a subject of commerce'; nor was it interstate, because the movement of ball clubs across state lines was merely 'incidental' to the business. It should be noted that, contrary to what

many believe, Holmes did call baseball a business; time and again those who have not troubled to read the text of the decision have claimed incorrectly that the court said baseball was a sport and not a business." 2 H. Seymour, Baseball 420 (1971).

11. On remand of the *Hart* case the trial court dismissed the complaint at the close of the evidence. The Second Circuit affirmed on the ground that the plaintiff's evidence failed to establish that the interstate transportation was more than incidental. 12 F.2d 341 (1926). This Court denied certiorari, 273 U.S. 703, 47 S.Ct. 97, 71 L.Ed. 849 (1926).

459–460, 98 L.Ed. 618 (1954) (Minton, J., dissenting); and upon a general comparison reference, North American Co. v. SEC, 327 U.S. 686, 694, 66 S.Ct. 785, 791, 90 L.Ed. 945 (1946).

In the years that followed, baseball continued to be subject to intermittent antitrust attack. The courts, however, rejected these challenges on the authority of *Federal Baseball*. In some cases stress was laid, although unsuccessfully, on new factors such as the development of radio and television with their substantial additional revenues to baseball.[12] For the most part, however, the Holmes opinion was generally and necessarily accepted as controlling authority.[13] And in the 1952 Report of the Subcommittee on Study of Monopoly Power of the House Committee on the Judiciary, H. R.Rep.No.2002, 82d Cong., 2d Sess., 229, it was said, in conclusion:

"On the other hand the overwhelming preponderance of the evidence established baseball's need for some sort of reserve clause. Baseball's history shows that chaotic conditions prevailed when there was no reserve clause. Experience points to no feasible substitute to protect the integrity of the game or to guarantee a comparatively even competitive struggle. The evidence adduced at the hearings would clearly not justify the enactment of legislation flatly condemning the reserve clause."

C. The Court granted certiorari, 345 U.S. 963, 73 S.Ct. 948, 949, 97 L.Ed. 1382 (1953), in the *Toolson, Kowalski,* and *Corbett* cases, cited in nn. 12 and 13,

*supra,* and, by a short per curiam (Warren, C. J., and Black, Frankfurter, Douglas, Jackson, Clark, and Minton, JJ.), affirmed the judgments of the respective courts of appeals in those three cases. Toolson v. New York Yankees, Inc., 346 U.S. 356, 74 S.Ct. 78, 98 L.Ed. 64 (1953). *Federal Baseball* was cited as holding "that the business of providing public baseball games for profit between clubs of professional baseball players was not within the scope of the federal antitrust laws," 346 U.S., at 357, 74 S.Ct., at 78, and:

"Congress has had the ruling under consideration but has not seen fit to bring such business under these laws by legislation having prospective effect. The business has thus been left for thirty years to develop, on the understanding that it was not subject to existing antitrust legislation. The present cases ask us to overrule the prior decision and, with retrospective effect, hold the legislation applicable. We think that if there are evils in this field which now warrant application to it of the antitrust laws it should be by legislation. Without re-examination of the underlying issues, the judgments below are affirmed on the authority of Federal Baseball Club of Baltimore v. National League of Professional Baseball Clubs, *supra,* so far as that decision determines that Congress had no intention of including the business of baseball within the scope of the federal antitrust laws." *Ibid.*

This quotation reveals four reasons for the Court's affirmance of *Toolson*

---

12. Toolson v. New York Yankees, Inc., 101 F.Supp. 93 (SD Cal.1951), aff'd, 200 F.2d 198 (CA9 1952); Kowalski v. Chandler, 202 F.2d 413 (CA6 1953). See Salerno v. American League, 429 F.2d 1003 (CA2 1970), cert. denied, *sub nom.* Salerno v. Kuhn, 400 U.S. 1001, 91 S.Ct. 462, 27 L.Ed.2d 452 (1971). But cf. Gardella v. Chandler, 172 F.2d 402 (CA2 1949) (this case, we are advised, was subsequently settled); Martin v. National League Baseball Club, 174 F.2d 917 (CA2 1949).

13. Corbett v. Chandler, 202 F.2d 428 (CA6 1953); Portland Baseball Club, Inc. v. Baltimore Baseball Club, Inc., 282 F.2d 680 (CA9 1960); Niemiec v. Seattle Rainier Baseball Club, Inc., 67 F.Supp. 705 (W.D.Wash.1946). See State v. Milwaukee Braves, Inc., 31 Wis.2d 699, 144 N.W.2d 1, cert. denied, 385 U.S. 990, 87 S.Ct. 598, 17 L.Ed.2d 451 (1966).

and its companion cases: (a) Congressional awareness for three decades of the Court's ⌐274 ruling in *Federal Baseball*, coupled with congressional inaction. (b) The fact that baseball was left alone to develop for that period upon the understanding that the reserve system was not subject to existing federal antitrust laws. (c) A reluctance to overrule *Federal Baseball* with consequent retroactive effect. (d) A professed desire that any needed remedy be provided by legislation rather than by court decree. The emphasis in *Toolson* was on the determination, attributed even to *Federal Baseball*, that Congress had no intention to include baseball within the reach of the federal antitrust laws. Two Justices (Burton and Reed, JJ.) dissented, stressing the factual aspects, revenue sources, and the absence of an express exemption of organized baseball from the Sherman Act. 346 U.S., at 357, 74 S.Ct. 78. The 1952 congressional study was mentioned. *Id.*, at 358, 359, 361, 74 S.Ct., at 79, 80, 81.

It is of interest to note that in *Toolson* the petitioner had argued flatly that *Federal Baseball* "is wrong and must be overruled," Brief for Petitioner, No. 18, O.T.1953, p. 19, and that Thomas Reed Powell, a constitutional scholar of no small stature, urged, as counsel for an *amicus*, that "baseball is a unique enterprise," Brief for Boston American League Base-Ball Co. as Amicus Curiae 2, and that "unbridled competition as applied to baseball would not be in the public interest." *Id.*, at 14.

D.  United States v. Shubert, 348 U. S. 222, 75 S.Ct. 277, 99 L.Ed. 279 (1955), was a civil antitrust action against defendants engaged in the production of legitimate theatrical attractions throughout the United States and in operating theaters for the presentation of such attractions. The District Court had dismissed the complaint on the authority of *Federal Baseball* and *Toolson*, 120 F.Supp. 15 (S.D.N.Y.1953). This Court reversed. Mr. Chief Justice Warren noted the Court's broad conception of "trade or commerce" in the anti-

trust statutes and the types of enterprises already held to be within the reach of that phrase. ⌐ He stated that *Federal* ⌐275 *Baseball* and *Toolson* afforded no basis for a conclusion that businesses built around the performance of local exhibitions are exempt from the antitrust laws. 348 U.S., at 227, 75 S.Ct., at 280. He went on to elucidate the holding in *Toolson* by meticulously spelling out the factors mentioned above:

"In *Federal Base Ball*, the Court, speaking through Mr. Justice Holmes, was dealing with the business of baseball and nothing else. . . . The travel, the Court concluded, was 'a mere incident, not the essential thing.'
. . .

. . . . . .

"In *Toolson*, where the issue was the same as in *Federal Base Ball*, the Court was confronted with a unique combination of circumstances. For over 30 years there had stood a decision of this Court specifically fixing the status of the baseball business under the antitrust laws and more particularly the validity of the so-called 'reserve clause.' During this period, in reliance on the *Federal Base Ball* precedent, the baseball business had grown and developed. . . . And Congress, although it had actively considered the ruling, had not seen fit to reject it by amendatory legislation. Against this background, the Court in *Toolson* was asked to overrule *Federal Base Ball* on the ground that it was out of step with subsequent decisions reflecting present-day concepts of interstate commerce. The Court, in view of the circumstances of the case, declined to do so. But neither did the Court necessarily reaffirm all that was said in *Federal Base Ball*. Instead, '[w]ithout re-examination of the underlying issues,' the Court adhered to *Federal Base Ball* 'so far as that decision determines that Congress had no intention of including the business of baseball within the scope of the federal antitrust laws.' [346 U.S. 356, 74 S.Ct. 79.] In short, ⌐276

*Toolson* was a narrow application of the rule of *stare decisis.*

" . . . If the *Toolson* holding is to be expanded—or contracted—the appropriate remedy lies with Congress." 348 U.S., at 228–230, 75 S.Ct., at 281.

E. United States v. International Boxing Club, 348 U.S. 236, 75 S.Ct. 259, 99 L.Ed. 290 (1955), was a companion to *Shubert* and was decided the same day. This was a civil antitrust action against defendants engaged in the business of promoting professional championship boxing contests. Here again the District Court had dismissed the complaint in reliance upon *Federal Baseball* and *Toolson*. The Chief Justice observed that "if it were not for *Federal Baseball* and *Toolson*, we think that it would be too clear for dispute that the Government's allegations bring the defendants within the scope of the Act." 348 U.S., at 240–241, 75 S.Ct., at 261. He pointed out that the defendants relied on the two baseball cases but also would have been content with a more restrictive interpretation of them than the *Shubert* defendants, for the boxing defendants argued that the cases immunized only businesses that involve exhibitions of an athletic nature. The Court accepted neither argument. It again noted, 348 U.S., at 242, 75 S.Ct., at 262, that *"Toolson* neither overruled *Federal Baseball* nor necessarily reaffirmed all that was said in *Federal Baseball.*" It stated:

"The controlling consideration in *Federal Baseball* and *Hart* was, instead, a very practical one—the degree of interstate activity involved in the particular business under review. It follows that *stare decisis* cannot help the defendants here; for, contrary to their argument, *Federal Baseball* did not hold that all businesses based on professional sports were outside the scope of the antitrust laws. The issue confronting us is, therefore, not whether a previously granted exemption should continue, but whether an exemption should be granted in the first instance.

And that issue is for Congress to resolve, not this Court." 348 U.S., at 243, 75 S.Ct., at 262.

The Court noted the presence then in Congress of various bills forbidding the application of the antitrust laws to "organized professional sports enterprises"; the holding of extensive hearings on some of these; subcommittee opposition; a postponement recommendation as to baseball; and the fact that "Congress thus left intact the then-existing coverage of the antitrust laws." 348 U.S., at 243–244, 75 S.Ct., at 263.

Mr. Justice Frankfurter, joined by Mr. Justice Minton, dissented. "It would baffle the subtlest ingenuity," he said, "to find a single differentiating factor between other sporting exhibitions . . . and baseball insofar as the conduct of the sport is relevant to the criteria or considerations by which the Sherman Law becomes applicable to a 'trade or commerce.' " 348 U.S., at 248, 75 S.Ct., at 265. He went on:

"The Court decided as it did in the *Toolson* case as an application of the doctrine of *stare decisis*. That doctrine is not, to be sure, an imprisonment of reason. But neither is it a whimsy. It can hardly be that this Court gave a preferred position to baseball because it is the great American sport. . . . If *stare decisis* be one aspect of law, as it is, to disregard it in identic situations is mere caprice.

"Congress, on the other hand, may yield to sentiment and be capricious, subject only to due process. . . .

"Between them, this case and *Shubert* illustrate that nice but rational distinctions are inevitable in adjudication. I agree with the Court's opinion in *Shubert* for precisely the reason that constrains me to dissent in this case." 348 U.S., at 249–250, 75 S.Ct., at 266.

Mr. Justice Minton also separately dissented on the ground that boxing is not trade or commerce. He added the comment that "Congress has not attempted" to control baseball and boxing. 348 U. S., at 251, 253, 75 S.Ct., at 267. The two dissenting Justices, thus, did not call for the overruling of *Federal Baseball* and *Toolson*; they merely felt that boxing should be under the same umbrella of freedom as was baseball and, as Mr. Justice Frankfurter said, 348 U.S., at 250, 75 S.Ct., at 266, they could not exempt baseball "to the exclusion of every other sport different not one legal jot or tittle from it." [14]

F. The parade marched on. Radovich v. National Football League, 352 U. S. 445, 77 S.Ct. 390, 1 L.Ed.2d 456 (1957), was a civil Clayton Act case testing the application of the antitrust laws to professional football. The District Court dismissed. The Ninth Circuit affirmed in part on the basis of *Federal Baseball* and *Toolson*. The court did not hesitate to "confess that the strength of the pull" of the baseball cases and of *International Boxing* "is about equal," but then observed that "[f]ootball is a team sport" and boxing an individual one. 9 Cir., 231 F.2d 620, 622.

This Court reversed with an opinion by Mr. Justice Clark. He said that the Court made its ruling in *Toolson* "because it was concluded that more harm would be done in overruling *Federal Base Ball* than in upholding a ruling which at best was of dubious validity." 352 U.S., at 450, 77 S.Ct., at 393. He noted that Congress had not acted. He then said:

"All this, combined with the flood of litigation that would follow its repudiation, the harassment that would ensue, and the retroactive effect of such a decision, led the Court to the practical result that it should sustain the unequivocal line of authority reaching over many years.

"[S]ince *Toolson* and *Federal Base Ball* are still cited as controlling authority in antitrust actions involving

other fields of business, we now specifically limit the rule there established to the facts there involved, *i. e.*, the business of organized professional baseball. As long as the Congress continues to acquiesce we should adhere to—but not extend—the interpretation of the Act made in those cases. . . .

"If this ruling is unrealistic, inconsistent, or illogical, it is sufficient to answer, aside from the distinctions between the businesses, that were we considering the question of baseball for the first time upon a clean slate we would have no doubts. But *Federal Base Ball* held the business of baseball outside the scope of the Act. No other business claiming the coverage of those cases has such an adjudication. We therefore, conclude that the orderly way to eliminate error or discrimination, if any there be, is by legislation and not by court decision. Congressional processes are more accommodative, affording the whole industry hearings and an opportunity to assist in the formulation of new legislation. The resulting product is therefore more likely to protect the industry and the public alike. The whole scope of congressional action would be known long in advance and effective dates for the legislation could be set in the future without the injustices of retroactivity and surprise which might follow court action." 352 U.S., at 450–452, 77 S.Ct., at 393 (footnote omitted).

Mr. Justice Frankfurter dissented essentially for the reasons stated in his dissent in *International Boxing*, 352 U. S., at 455, 77 S.Ct., at 396. Mr. Justice Harlan, joined by Mr. Justice Brennan, also dissented because he, too, was "unable to distinguish football from baseball." 352 U.S., at 456, 77 S.Ct., at 396. Here again the dissenting Justices did not call for the overruling of the baseball decisions. They merely could not

14. The case's final chapter is International Boxing Club v. United States, 358 U.S. 242, 79 S.Ct. 245, 3 L.Ed.2d 270 (1959).

distinguish the two sports and, out of respect for *stare decisis*, voted to affirm.

G. Finally, in Haywood v. National Basketball Assn., 401 U.S. 1204, 91 S.Ct. 672, 28 L.Ed.2d 206 (1971), Mr. Justice Douglas, in his capacity as Circuit Justice, reinstated a District Court's injunction *pendente lite* in favor of a professional basketball player and said, "Basketball . . . does not enjoy exemption from the antitrust laws." 401 U.S., at 1205, 91 S.Ct., at 673.[15]

H. This series of decisions understandably spawned extensive commentary,[16] some of it mildly critical and much of it not; nearly all of it

looked to Congress for any remedy that might be deemed essential.

I. Legislative proposals have been numerous and persistent. Since *Toolson* more than 50 bills have been introduced in Congress relative to the applicability or nonapplicability of the antitrust laws to baseball.[17] A few of these passed one house or the other. Those that did would have expanded, not restricted, the reserve system's exemption to other professional league sports. And the Act of Sept. 30, 1961, Pub.L. 87–331, 75 Stat. 732, and the merger addition thereto effected by the Act of Nov. 8, 1966, Pub. L. 89–800, § 6(b), 80 Stat. 1515, 15 U.S.C. §§ 1291–1295, were also expansive rather than restrictive as to antitrust exemption.[18]

---

15. See also Denver Rockets v. All-Pro Management, Inc., 325 F.Supp. 1049, 1060 (C.D.Cal.1971); Washington Professional Basketball Corp. v. National Basketball Assn., 147 F.Supp. 154 (S.D. N.Y.1956).

16. Neville, Baseball and the Antitrust Laws, 16 Fordham L.Rev. 208 (1947); Eckler, Baseball—Sport or Commerce?, 17 U.Chi.L.Rev. 56 (1949); Comment, Monopsony in Manpower: Organized Baseball Meets the Antitrust Laws, 62 Yale L.J. 576 (1953); P. Gregory, The Baseball Player, An Economic Study, c. 19 (1956); Note, The Super Bowl and the Sherman Act: Professional Team Sports and the Antitrust Laws, 81 Harv.L.Rev. 418 (1967); The Supreme Court, 1953 Term, 68 Harv.L.Rev. 105, 136–138 (1954); The Supreme Court, 1956 Term, 71 Harv.L.Rev. 94, 170–173 (1957); Note, 32 Va.L.Rev. 1164 (1946); Note, 24 Notre Dame Law. 372 (1949); Note, 53 Col.L.Rev. 242 (1953); Note, 22 U. Kan. City L.Rev. 173 (1954); Note, 25 Miss.L.J. 270 (1954); Note, 29 N. Y.U.L.Rev. 213 (1954); Note, 105 U. Pa.L.Rev. 110 (1956); Note, 32 Texas L.Rev. 890 (1954); Note, 35 B.U.L.Rev. 447 (1955); Note, 57 Col.L.Rev. 725 (1957); Note, 23 Geo.Wash.L.Rev. 606 (1955); Note, 1 How.L.J. 281 (1955); Note, 26 Miss.L.J. 271 (1955); Note, 9 Sw.L.J. 369 (1955); Note, 29 Temple L.Q. 103 (1955); Note, 29 Tul. L.Rev. 793 (1955); Note, 62 Dick.L.Rev. 96 (1957); Note, 11 Sw.L.J. 516 (1957); Note, 36 N.C.L.Rev. 315 (1958); Note, 35 Fordham L.Rev. 350 (1966); Note, 8 B. C.Ind. & Com.L.Rev. 341 (1967); Note,

13 Wayne L.Rev. 417 (1967); Note, 2 Rutgers-Camden L.J. 302 (1970); Note, 8 San Diego L.Rev. 92 (1970); Note, 12 B.C.Ind. & Com.L.Rev. 737 (1971); Note, 12 Wm. & Mary L.Rev. 859 (1971).

17. Hearings on H.R. 5307 et al. before the Antitrust Subcommittee of the House Committee on the Judiciary, 85th Cong., 1st Sess. (1957); Hearings on H.R. 10378 and S. 4070 before the Subcommittee on Antitrust and Monopoly of the Senate Committee on the Judiciary, 85th Cong., 2d Sess. (1958); Hearings on H.R. 2370 et al. before the Antitrust Subcommittee of the House Committee on the Judiciary, 86th Cong., 1st Sess. (1959) (not printed); Hearings on S. 616 and S. 886 before the Subcommittee on Antitrust and Monopoly of the Senate Committee on the Judiciary, 86th Cong., 1st Sess. (1959); Hearings on S. 3483 before the Subcommittee on Antitrust and Monopoly of the Senate Committee on the Judiciary, 86th Cong., 2d Sess. (1960); Hearings on S. 2391 before the Subcommittee on Antitrust and Monopoly of the Senate Committee on the Judiciary, 88th Cong., 2d Sess. (1964); S.Rep.No.1303, 88th Cong., 2d Sess. (1964); Hearings on S. 950 before the Subcommittee on Antitrust and Monopoly of the Senate Committee on the Judiciary, 89th Cong., 1st Sess. (1965); S.Rep.No. 462, 89th Cong., 1st Sess. (1965). Bills introduced in the 92d Cong., 1st Sess., and bearing on the subject are S. 2599, S. 2616, H.R. 2305, H.R. 11033, and H.R. 10825.

18. Title 15 U.S.C. § 1294 reads:
"Nothing contained in this chapter shall be deemed to change, determine, or

V

In view of all this, it seems appropriate now to say that:

1. Professional baseball is a business and it is engaged in interstate commerce.

2. With its reserve system enjoying exemption from the federal antitrust laws, baseball is, in a very distinct sense, an exception and an anomaly. *Federal Baseball* and *Toolson* have become an aberration confined to baseball.

3. Even though others might regard this as "unrealistic, inconsistent, or illogical," see *Radovich*, 352 U.S., at 452, 77 S.Ct., at 394, the aberration is an established one, and one that has been recognized not only in *Federal Baseball* and *Toolson*, but in *Shubert*, *International Boxing*, and *Radovich*, as well, a total of five consecutive cases in this Court. It is an aberration that has been with us now for half a century, one heretofore deemed fully entitled to the benefit of *stare decisis*, and one that has survived the Court's expanding concept of interstate commerce. It rests on a recognition and an acceptance of baseball's unique characteristics and needs.

4. Other professional sports operating interstate—football, boxing, basketball, and, presumably, hockey [19] and golf [20]—are not so exempt.

5. The advent of radio and television, with their consequent increased coverage and additional revenues, has not occasioned an overruling of *Federal Baseball* and *Toolson*.

6. The Court has emphasized that since 1922 baseball, with full and continuing congressional awareness, has been allowed to develop and to expand unhindered by federal legislative action. Remedial legislation has been introduced repeatedly in Congress but none has ever been enacted. The Court, accordingly, has concluded that Congress as yet has had no intention to subject baseball's reserve system to the reach of the antitrust statutes. This, obviously, has been deemed to be something other than mere congressional silence and passivity. Cf. Boys Markets, Inc. v. Retail Clerk's Union, 398 U.S. 235, 241–242, 90 S.Ct. 1583, 1587–1588, 26 L.Ed.2d 199 (1970).

7. The Court has expressed concern about the confusion and the retroactivity problems that inevitably would result with a judicial overturning of *Federal Baseball*. It has voiced a preference that if any change is to be made, it come by legislative action that, by its nature, is only prospective in operation.

8. The Court noted in *Radovich*, 352 U.S., at 452, 77 S.Ct., at 394, that the slate with respect to baseball is not clean. Indeed, it has not been clean for half a century.

This emphasis and this concern are still with us. We continue to be loath, 50 years after *Federal Baseball* and almost two decades after *Toolson*, to overturn those cases judicially when Congress, by its positive inaction, has allowed those decisions to stand for so long and, far beyond mere inference and implication, has clearly evinced a desire not to disapprove them legislatively.

Accordingly, we adhere once again to *Federal Baseball* and *Toolson* and to their application to professional baseball. We adhere also to *International Boxing* and *Radovich* and to their respective applications to professional boxing and professional football. If there

---

otherwise affect the *applicability* or *non-applicability* of the antitrust laws to any act, contract, agreement, rule, course of conduct, or other activity by, between, or among persons engaging in, conducting, or participating in the organized professional team sports of football, baseball, basketball, or hockey, except the agreements to which section 1291 of this title shall apply." (Emphasis supplied.)

19. Peto v. Madison Square Garden Corp., 1958 Trade Cases, ¶ 69,106 (SDNY 1958).

20. Deesen v. Professional Golfers' Assn., 358 F.2d 165 (CA9), cert. denied, 385 U.S. 846, 87 S.Ct. 72, 17 L.Ed.2d 76 (1966).

is any inconsistency or illogic in all this, it is an inconsistency and illogic of long standing that is to be remedied by the Congress and not by this Court. If we were to act otherwise, we would be withdrawing from the conclusion as to congressional intent made in *Toolson* and from the concerns as to retrospectivity therein expressed. Under these circumstances, there is merit in consistency even though some might claim that beneath that consistency is a layer of inconsistency.

The petitioner's argument as to the application of state antitrust laws deserves a word. Judge Cooper rejected the state law claims because state antitrust regulation would conflict with federal policy and because national "uniformity [is required] in any regulation of baseball and its reserve system." 316 F.Supp., at 280. The Court of Appeals, in affirming, stated, "[A]s the burden on interstate commerce outweighs the states' interests in regulating baseball's reserve system, the Commerce Clause precludes the application here of state antitrust law." 443 F.2d, at 268. As applied to organized baseball, and in the light of this Court's observations and holdings in *Federal Baseball*, in *Toolson*, in *Shubert*, in *International Boxing*, and in *Radovich*, and despite baseball's allegedly inconsistent position taken in the past with respect to the application of state law,[21] these statements adequately dispose of the state law claims.

The conclusion we have reached makes it unnecessary for us to consider the respondents' additional argument that the reserve system is a mandatory subject of collective bargaining and that federal labor policy therefore exempts the reserve system from the operation of federal antitrust laws.[22]

We repeat for this case what was said in *Toolson*:

"Without re-examination of the underlying issues, the [judgment] below [is] affirmed on the authority of Federal Baseball Club of Baltimore v. National League of Professional Baseball Clubs, *supra*, so far as that decision determines that Congress had no intention of including the business of baseball within the scope of the federal antitrust laws." 346 U.S., at 357, 74 S.Ct., at 79.

And what the Court said in *Federal Baseball* in 1922 and what it said in *Toolson* in 1953, we say again here in 1972: the remedy, if any is indicated, is for congressional, and not judicial, action.

The judgment of the Court of Appeals is affirmed.

Judgment affirmed.

Mr. Justice WHITE joins in the judgment of the Court, and in all but Part I of the Court's opinion.

Mr. Justice POWELL took no part in the consideration or decision of this case.

Mr. Chief Justice BURGER, concurring.

I concur in all but Part I of the Court's opinion but, like Mr. Justice DOUGLAS, I have grave reservations as to the correctness of Toolson v. New York Yankees, Inc., 346 U.S. 356, 74 S.Ct. 78, 98 L.Ed. 64 (1953); as he notes in his dissent, he joined that holding but has "lived to regret it." The error, if such it be, is one on which the affairs of a great many people have rested for a long time. Courts are not the forum in which this tangled web ought to be un-

---

21. See Brief for Respondent in *Federal Baseball*, No. 204, O.T.1921, p. 67, and Brief for Respondent in *Toolson*, No. 18, O.T.1953, p. 30. See also State v. Milwaukee Braves, Inc., 31 Wis.2d 699, 144 N.W.2d 1 (1966), cert. denied, 385 U.S. 990, 87 S.Ct. 598, 17 L.Ed.2d 451 (1966).

22. See Jacobs & Winter, Antitrust Principles and Collective Bargaining by Athletes: Of Superstars in Peonage, 81 Yale L.J. 1 (1971), suggesting present-day irrelevancy of the antitrust issue.

snarled. I agree with Mr. Justice DOUGLAS that congressional inaction is not a solid base, but the least undesirable course now is to let the matter rest with Congress; it is time the Congress acted to solve this problem.

Mr. Justice DOUGLAS, with whom Mr. Justice BRENNAN concurs, dissenting.

This Court's decision in Federal Baseball Club v. National League, 259 U.S. 200, 42 S.Ct. 465, 66 L.Ed. 898, made in 1922, is a derelict in the stream of the law that we, its creator, should remove. Only a romantic view [1] of a rather dismal business account over the last 50 years would keep that derelict in midstream.

In 1922 the Court had a narrow, parochial view of commerce. With the demise of the old landmarks of that era, particularly United States v. E. C. Knight Co., 156 U.S. 1, 15 S.Ct. 249, 39 L.Ed. 325, Hammer v. Dagenhart, 247 U.S. 251, 38 S.Ct. 529, 62 L.Ed. 1101, and Paul v. Virginia, 8 Wall. 168, 19 L. Ed. 357, the whole concept of commerce has changed.

Under the modern decisions such as Mandeville Island Farms v. American Crystal Sugar Co., 334 U.S. 219, 68 S.Ct. 996, 92 L.Ed. 1328; United States v. Darby, 312 U.S. 100, 61 S.Ct. 451, 85 L. Ed. 609; Wickard v. Filburn, 317 U.S. 111, 63 S.Ct. 82, 87 L.Ed. 122; United States v. South-Eastern Underwriters Assn., 322 U.S. 533, 64 S.Ct. 1162, 88 L. Ed. 1440, the power of Congress was recognized as broad enough to reach all phases of the vast operations of our national industrial system.⌐ An industry so ⌐[287] dependent on radio and television as is baseball and gleaning vast interstate revenues (see H.R.Rep.No.2002, 82d Cong., 2d Sess., 4, 5 (1952)) would be hard put today to say with the Court in the *Federal Baseball Club* case that baseball was only a local exhibition, not trade or commerce.

Baseball is today big business that is packaged with beer, with broadcasting, and with other industries. The beneficiaries of the *Federal Baseball Club* decision are not the Babe Ruths, Ty Cobbs, and Lou Gehrigs.

The owners, whose records many say reveal a proclivity for predatory practices, do not come to us with equities. The equities are with the victims of the reserve clause. I use the word "victims" in the Sherman Act sense, since a contract which forbids anyone to practice his calling is commonly called an unreasonable restraint of trade.[2] Gardella v. Chandler, 172 F.2d 402 (CA2). And see Haywood v. National Basketball Assn., 401 U.S. 1204, 91 S.Ct. 672, 28 L.Ed.2d 206 (Douglas, J., in chambers).

If congressional inaction is our guide, we should rely upon the fact that Congress has refused to enact bills broadly exempting professional sports from antitrust regulation.[3]   H.R.Rep.No.2002,

---

1. While I joined the Court's opinion in Toolson v. New York Yankees, Inc., 346 U.S. 356, 74 S.Ct. 78, 98 L.Ed. 64, I have lived to regret it; and I would now correct what I believe to be its fundamental error.

2. Had this same group boycott occurred in another industry, Klor's, Inc. v. Broadway-Hale Stores, Inc., 359 U.S. 207, 79 S.Ct. 705, 3 L.Ed.2d 741; United States v. Shubert, 348 U.S. 222, 75 S.Ct. 277, 99 L.Ed. 279; or even in another sport, Haywood v. National Basketball Assn., 401 U.S. 1204, 91 S.Ct. 672, 28 L.Ed.2d 206 (Douglas, J., in chambers); Radovich v. National Football League, 352 U.S. 445, 77 S.Ct. 390, 1 L.Ed.2d 456; United

States v. International Boxing Club, 348 U.S. 236, 75 S.Ct. 259, 99 L.Ed. 290; we would have no difficulty in sustaining petioner's claim.

3. The Court's reliance upon congressional inaction disregards the wisdom of Helvering v. Hallock, 309 U.S. 106, 119–121, 60 S.Ct. 444, 451, 84 L.Ed. 604, where we said:

"Nor does want of specific Congressional repudiations . . . serve as an implied instruction by Congress to us not to reconsider, in the light of new experience . . . those decisions . . . . It would require very persuasive circumstances enveloping Congressional silence to debar this Court from

⌊288 82nd Cong., 2d Sess.⌋(1952). The only statutory exemption granted by Congress to professional sports concerns broadcasting rights. 15 U.S.C. §§ 1291–1295. I would not ascribe a broader exemption through inaction than Congress has seen fit to grant explicitly.

There can be no doubt "that were we considering the question of baseball for the first time upon a clean slate" [4] we would hold it to be subject to federal antitrust regulation. Radovich v. National Football League, 352 U.S. 445, 452, 77 S.Ct. 390, 1 L.Ed.2d 456. The unbroken silence of Congress should not prevent us from correcting our own mistakes.

Mr. Justice MARSHALL, with whom Mr. Justice BRENNAN joins, dissenting.

Petitioner was a major league baseball player from 1956, when he signed a contract with the Cincinnati Reds, until 1969, when his 12-year career with the St. Louis Cardinals, which had obtained him from the Reds, ended and he was traded to the Philadelphia Phillies. He had no notice that the Cardinals were contemplating a trade, no opportunity to indicate the teams with which he would prefer playing, and no desire to go to Philadelphia. After receiving formal notification of the trade, petitioner wrote to the Commissioner of Baseball protesting that he was not⌈"a piece of ⌋289 property to be bought and sold irrespective of my wishes," [1] and urging that he had the right to consider offers from other teams than the Phillies. He requested that the Commissioner inform all of the major league teams that he was available for the 1970 season. His request was denied, and petitioner was informed that he had no choice but to play for Philadelphia or not to play at all.

To non-athletes it might appear that petitioner was virtually enslaved by the owners of major league baseball clubs who bartered among themselves for his services. But, athletes know that it was not servitude that bound petitioner to the club owners; it was the reserve system. The essence of that system is that a player is bound to the club with which he first signs a contract for the rest of his playing days.[2] He cannot escape from the club except by retiring, and he cannot prevent the club from assigning his contract to any other club.

Petitioner brought this action in the United States District Court for the Southern District of New York. He alleged, among other things, that the reserve system was an unreasonable restraint of trade in violation of ⌈federal ⌋290 antitrust laws.[3] The District Court

re-examining its own doctrines. . . . Various considerations of parliamentary tactics and strategy might be suggested as reasons for the inaction of . . . Congress, but they would only be sufficient to indicate that we walk on quick-sand when we try to find in the absence of corrective legislation a controlling legal principle."
And see United States v. South-Eastern Underwriters Assn., 322 U.S. 533, 556–561, 64 S.Ct. 1162, 1175–1178, 88 L.Ed. 1440.

4. This case gives us for the first time a full record showing the reserve clause in actual operation.

1. Letter from Curt Flood to Bowie K. Kuhn, Dec. 24, 1969, App. 37.

2. As Mr. Justice BLACKMUN points out, the reserve system is not novel. It has

been employed since 1887. See Metropolitan Exhibition Co. v. Ewing, 42 F. 198, 202–204 (C.C.S.D.N.Y.1890). The club owners assert that it is necessary to preserve effective competition and to retain fan interest. The players do not agree and argue that the reserve system is overly restrictive. Before this lawsuit was instituted, the players refused to agree that the reserve system should be a part of the collective-bargaining contract. Instead, the owners and players agreed that the reserve system would temporarily remain in effect while they jointly investigated possible changes. Their activity along these lines has halted pending the outcome of this suit.

3. Petitioner also alleged a violation of state antitrust laws, state civil rights laws, and of the common law, and claimed that he was forced into peonage and in-

thought itself bound by prior decisions of this Court and found for the respondents after a full trial. 309 F.Supp. 793 (1970). The United States Court of Appeals for the Second Circuit affirmed. 443 F.2d 264 (1971). We granted certiorari on October 19, 1971, 404 U.S. 880, 92 S.Ct. 201, 30 L.Ed.2d 160, in order to take a further look at the precedents relied upon by the lower courts.

This is a difficult case because we are torn between the principle of *stare decisis* and the knowledge that the decisions in Federal Baseball Club v. National League, 259 U.S. 200, 42 S.Ct. 465, 66 L.Ed. 898 (1922), and Toolson v. New York Yankees, Inc., 346 U.S. 356, 74 S.Ct. 78, 98 L.Ed. 64 (1953), are totally at odds with more recent and better reasoned cases.

In *Federal Baseball Club,* a team in the Federal League brought an antitrust action against the National and American Leagues and others. In his opinion for a unanimous Court, Mr. Justice Holmes wrote that the business being considered was "giving exhibitions of base ball, which are purely state affairs." 259 U.S., at 208, 42 S.Ct., at 466. Hence, the Court held that baseball was not within the purview of the antitrust laws. Thirty-one years later, the Court reaffirmed this decision, without re-examining it, in *Toolson,* a one-paragraph *per curiam* opinion. Like this case, *Toolson* involved an attack on the reserve system. The Court said:

> "The business has . . . been left for thirty years to develop, on the understanding that it was not subject to existing antitrust legislation. The present cases ask us to overrule the prior decision and, with retrospective effect, hold the legislation applicable. We think that if there are evils in this field which now warrant applica-

|291

tion to it of the antitrust laws it should be by legislation." *Id.,* at 357, 74 S.Ct., at 78.

Much more time has passed since *Toolson* and Congress has not acted. We must now decide whether to adhere to the reasoning of *Toolson*—i. e., to refuse to re-examine the underlying basis of *Federal Baseball Club*—or to proceed with a re-examination and let the chips fall where they may.

In his answer to petitioner's complaint, the Commissioner of Baseball "admits that under present concepts of interstate commerce defendants are engaged therein." App. 40. There can be no doubt that the admission is warranted by today's reality. Since baseball is interstate commerce, if we re-examine baseball's antitrust exemption, the Court's decisions in United States v. Shubert, 348 U.S. 222, 75 S.Ct. 277, 99 L.Ed. 279 (1955), United States v. International Boxing Club, 348 U.S. 236, 75 S.Ct. 259, 99 L.Ed. 290 (1955), and Radovich v. National Football League, 352 U.S. 445, 77 S.Ct. 390, 1 L.Ed.2d 456 (1957), require that we bring baseball within the coverage of the antitrust laws. See also, Haywood v. National Basketball Assn., 401 U.S. 1204, 91 S.Ct. 672, 28 L.Ed.2d 206 (Douglas, J., in chambers).

We have only recently had occasion to comment that:

> "Antitrust laws in general, and the Sherman Act in particular, are the Magna Charta of free enterprise. They are as important to the preservation of economic freedom and our free-enterprise system as the Bill of Rights is to the protection of our fundamental personal freedoms. . . . Implicit in such freedom is the notion that it cannot be foreclosed with respect to one sector of the economy because certain private citizens or groups believe that such foreclosure

|292

---

voluntary servitude in violation of the Thirteenth Amendment to the United States Constitution. Because I believe that federal antitrust laws govern baseball, I find that state law has been pre-

empted in this area. Like the lower courts, I do not believe that there has been a violation of the Thirteenth Amendment.

might promote greater competition in a more important sector of the economy." United States v. Topco Associates, Inc., 405 U.S. 596, 610, 92 S.Ct. 1126, 1135, 31 L.Ed.2d 515 (1972).

The importance of the antitrust laws to every citizen must not be minimized. They are as important to baseball players as they are to football players, lawyers, doctors, or members of any other class of workers. Baseball players cannot be denied the benefits of competition merely because club owners view other economic interests as being more important, unless Congress says so.

Has Congress acquiesced in our decisions in *Federal Baseball Club* and *Toolson*? I think not. Had the Court been consistent and treated all sports in the same way baseball was treated, Congress might have become concerned enough to take action. But, the Court was inconsistent, and baseball was isolated and distinguished from all other sports. In *Toolson* the Court refused to act because Congress had been silent. But the Court may have read too much into this legislative inaction.

Americans love baseball as they love all sports. Perhaps we become so enamored of athletics that we assume that they are foremost in the minds of legislators as well as fans. We must not forget, however, that there are only some 600 major league baseball players. Whatever muscle they might have been able to muster by combining forces with other athletes has been greatly impaired by the manner in which this Court has isolated them. It is this Court that has made them impotent, and this Court should correct its error.

We do not lightly overrule our prior constructions of federal statutes, but when our errors deny substantial federal rights, like the right to compete freely and effectively to the best of one's ability as guaranteed by the antitrust laws, |293 we must admit our error and correct it. We have done so before and we should do so again here. See, *e. g.,* Blonder-Tongue Laboratories, Inc. v. University of Illinois Foundation, 402 U.S. 313, 91 S.Ct. 1434, 28 L.Ed.2d 788 (1971); Boys Markets, Inc. v. Retail Clerks Union, 398 U.S. 235, 241, 90 S.Ct. 1583, 1587, 26 L. Ed.2d 199 (1970).[4]

To the extent that there is concern over any reliance interests that club owners may assert, they can be satisfied by making our decision prospective only. Baseball should be covered by the antitrust laws beginning with this case and henceforth, unless Congress decides otherwise.[5]

Accordingly, I would overrule *Federal Baseball Club* and *Toolson* and reverse the decision of the Court of Appeals.[6]

This does not mean that petitioner would necessarily prevail, however. Lurking in the background is a hurdle of recent vintage that petitioner still must overcome. | In 1966, the Major League |294

---

4. In the past this Court has not hesitated to change its view as to what constitutes interstate commerce. Compare United States v. E. C. Knight Co., 156 U.S. 1, 15 S.Ct. 249, 39 L.Ed. 325 (1895), with Mandeville Island Farms v. American Crystal Sugar Co., 334 U.S. 219, 68 S.Ct. 996, 92 L.Ed. 1328 (1948), and United States v. Darby, 312 U.S. 100, 61 S.Ct. 451, 85 L.Ed. 609 (1941).

"The jurist concerned with 'public confidence in, and acceptance of the judicial system' might well consider that, however admirable its resolute adherence to the law as it was, a decision contrary to the public sense of justice as it is, operate, so far as it is known, to diminish respect for the courts and for law itself."

Szanton, Stare Decisis; A Dissenting View, 10 Hastings L.J. 394, 397 (1959).

5. We said recently that "[i]n rare cases, decisions construing federal statutes might be denied full retroactive effect, as for instance where this Court overrules its own construction of a statute . . ." United States v. Estate of Donnelly, 397 U.S. 286, 295, 90 S.Ct. 1033, 1038, 25 L.Ed.2d 312 (1970). Cf. Simpson v. Union Oil Co. of California, 377 U.S. 13, 25, 84 S.Ct. 1051, 1058, 12 L.Ed.2d 98 (1964).

6. The lower courts did not reach the question of whether, assuming the antitrust laws apply, they have been violated. This should be considered on remand.

Players Association was formed. It is the collective-bargaining representative for all major league baseball players. Respondents argue that the reserve system is now part and parcel of the collective-bargaining agreement and that because it is a mandatory subject of bargaining, the federal labor statutes are applicable, not the federal antitrust laws.[7] The lower courts did not rule on this argument, having decided the case solely on the basis of the antitrust exemption.

This Court has faced the interrelationship between the antitrust laws and the labor laws before. The decisions make several things clear. First, "benefits to organized labor cannot be utilized as a cat's-paw to pull employers' chestnuts out of the antitrust fires." United States v. Women's Sportswear Manufacturers Assn., 336 U.S. 460, 464, 69 S.Ct. 714 (1949). See also Allen Bradley Co. v. Local Union No. 3, 325 U.S. 797, 65 S.Ct. 1533, 89 L.Ed. 1939 (1945). Second, the very nature of a collective-bargaining agreement mandates that the parties be able to "restrain" trade to a greater degree than management could do unilaterally. United States v. Hutcheson, 312 U.S. 219, 61 S.Ct. 463, 85 L.Ed. 788 (1941); United Mine Workers v. Pennington, 381 U.S. 657, 85 S.Ct. 1585, 14 L.Ed.2d 626 (1965); Amalgamated Meat Cutters v. Jewel Tea, 381 U.S. 676, 85 S.Ct. 1596, 14 L.Ed.2d 640 (1965); cf., Local 24, etc., Teamsters, etc., of America v. Oliver, 358 U.S. 283, 79 S.Ct. 297, 3 L.Ed.2d 312 (1959). Finally, it is clear that some cases can be resolved only by examining the purposes and the competing interests of the labor and antitrust statutes and by striking a balance.

It is apparent that none of the prior cases is precisely in point. They involve union-management agreements that work to the detriment of management's competitors. In this case, petitioner

urges that the reserve system works to the detriment of labor.

While there was evidence at trial concerning the collective-bargaining relationship of the parties, the issues surrounding that relationship have not been fully explored. As one commentary has suggested, this case "has been litigated with the implications for the institution of collective bargaining only dimly perceived. The labor law issues have been in the corners of the case—the courts below, for example, did not reach them —moving in and out of the shadows like an uninvited guest at a party whom one can't decide either to embrace or expel." [8]

It is true that in Radovich v. National Football League, *supra*, the Court rejected a claim that federal labor statutes governed the relationship between a professional athlete and the professional sport. But, an examination of the briefs and record in that case indicates that the issue was not squarely faced. The issue is once again before this Court without being clearly focused. It should, therefore, be the subject of further inquiry in the District Court.

There is a surface appeal to respondents' argument that petitioner's sole remedy lies in filing a claim with the National Labor Relations Board, but this argument is premised on the notion that management and labor have agreed to accept the reserve clause. This notion is contradicted, in part, by the record in this case. Petitioner suggests that the reserve system was thrust upon the players by the owners and that the recently formed players' union has not had time to modify or eradicate it. If this is true, the question arises as to whether there would then be any exemption from the antitrust laws in this case. Petitioner also suggests that there are limits to the antitrust violations to which labor and management can agree. These limits should also be explored.

---

7. Cf. United States v. Hutcheson, 312 U.S. 219, 61 S.Ct. 463, 85 L.Ed. 788 (1941).

8. Jacobs & Winter, Antitrust Principles and Collective Bargaining by Athletes: Of Superstars in Peonage, 81 Yale L.J. 1, 22 (1971).

In light of these considerations, I would remand this case to the District Court for consideration of whether petitioner can state a claim under the antitrust laws despite the collective-bargaining agreement, and, if so, for a determination of whether there has been an antitrust violation in this case.

CHARLES O. FINLEY & CO., INC.,
Plaintiff-Appellant,

v.

Bowie K. KUHN et al.,
Defendants-Appellees.*

No. 77–2008.

United States Court of Appeals,
Seventh Circuit.

Argued Feb. 23, 1978.

Decided April 7, 1978.

Before FAIRCHILD, Chief Judge,
SPRECHER and TONE, Circuit Judges.

SPRECHER, Circuit Judge.

The two important questions raised by this appeal are whether the Commissioner of baseball is contractually authorized to disapprove player assignments which he finds to be "not in the best interests of baseball" where neither moral turpitude nor violation of a Major League Rule is involved, and whether the provision in the Major League Agreement whereby the parties agree to waive recourse to the courts is valid and enforceable.

I

The plaintiff, Charles O. Finley & Co., Inc., an Illinois corporation, is the owner of the Oakland Athletics baseball club, a member of the American League of Professional Baseball Clubs (Oakland). Joe Rudi, Rollie Fingers and Vida Blue were members of the active playing roster of the Oakland baseball club and were contractually bound to play for Oakland through the end of the 1976 baseball season. On or about June 15, 1976, Oakland and Blue entered a contract whereby Blue would play for Oakland through the 1979 season, but Rudi and Fingers had not at that time signed contracts for the period beyond the 1976 season.

If Rudi and Fingers had not signed contracts to play with Oakland by the conclusion of the 1976 season, they would at that time have become free agents eligible thereafter to negotiate with any major league club,[1] subject to certain limitations on their right to do so that were then being negotiated by the major league clubs with the Players Association.[2]

On June 14 and 15, 1976, Oakland negotiated tentative agreements to sell the club's contract rights for the services of Rudi and Fingers to the Boston Red Sox for $2 million and for the services of Blue to the New York Yankees for $1.5 million. The agreements were negotiated shortly before the expiration of baseball's trading deadline at midnight on June 15, after which time Oakland could not have sold the contracts of these players to other clubs without first offering the players to all other American League teams, in inverse order of their standing, at the stipulated waiver price of $20,000.

The defendant Bowie K. Kuhn is the Commissioner of baseball (Commissioner), having held that position since 1969. On June 18, 1976, the Commissioner disapproved the assignments of the contracts of Rudi, Fingers and Blue to the Red Sox and Yankees "as inconsistent with the best interests of baseball, the integrity of the game and the maintenance of public confidence in it." The Commissioner expressed his concern for (1) the debilitation of the Oakland club, (2) the lessening of the competitive balance of professional baseball through the buying of success by the more affluent clubs, and (3) "the present unsettled circumstances of baseball's reserve system."

Thereafter on June 25, 1976, Oakland instituted this suit principally challenging, as beyond the scope of the Commissioner's authority and, in any event, as arbitrary and capricious, the Commissioner's disapproval of the Rudi, Fingers and Blue assignments. The complaint set forth seven causes of action: (I) that the Commissioner breached his employment contract with Oakland by acting arbitrarily, discriminatorily and unreasonably; (II) that the Commissioner, acting in concert with others, conspired to eliminate Oakland from baseball in violation of federal antitrust laws; (III) that Oakland's constitutional rights of due process and equal protection were violated; (IV) that Oakland's constitutional rights were violated by the first disapproval of a player assignment where no major league rule was violated; (V) that the defendants (the Commissioner, the National and American Leagues and the Major League Executive Council) induced the breach of Oakland's contracts with Boston and New York; (VI) that the Commissioner did not have the authority to disapprove Oakland's assignments "in the best interests of baseball"; and (VII) that Oakland have specific performance of its contracts of assignment with Boston and New York.

On September 7, 1976, the district court granted the Commissioner's motion for summary judgment as to Counts II, III and IV. Count II was dismissed on the ground that the business of baseball is not subject to the federal antitrust laws. Counts III and IV were dismissed on the ground that Oakland did not allege sufficient nexus between the state and the complained of activity to constitute state action.

A bench trial took place as a result of which judgment on the remaining four counts of the complaint was entered in favor of the Commissioner on March 17, 1977.

1. On December 23, 1975, an arbitration panel under the 1973 collective bargaining agreement between the baseball club owners and the Players Association had held that players Andy Messersmith and Dave McNally were free agents able to negotiate with clubs other than those to which they had previously been contractually bound. On February 11, 1976, the district court ordered the award of the arbitra-

tion panel enforced in *Kansas City Royals Baseball Corp. v. Major League Baseball Players Ass'n*, 409 F.Supp. 233 (W.D.Mo.). On March 9, 1976, the Court of Appeals for the Eighth Circuit affirmed the district court in 532 F.2d 615.

2. Finding of Fact 9. *See also* footnote 26 *infra*.

On August 29, 1977, the district court granted the Commissioner's counterclaim for a declaratory judgment that the covenant not to sue in the Major League Agreement is valid and enforceable. The court had not relied on that covenant in reaching its two earlier decisions.

Oakland appealed from the judgments of September 7, 1976, March 17, 1977, and August 29, 1977, arguing (1) that the court's failure to issue a finding on the question of procedural fairness constituted error; (2) that the exclusion of evidence of the Commissioner's malice toward the Oakland club constituted error; (3) that other errors were committed during trial; (4) that the antitrust count was not barred by baseball's exemption from federal antitrust law; and (5) that baseball's blanket waiver of recourse to the courts is not enforceable.

II

Basic to the underlying suit brought by Oakland and to this appeal is whether the Commissioner of baseball is vested by contract with the authority to disapprove player assignments which he finds to be "not in the best interests of baseball." In assessing the measure and extent of the Commissioner's power and authority, consideration must be given to the circumstances attending the creation of the office of Commissioner, the language employed by the parties in drafting their contractual understanding, changes and amendments adopted from time to time, and the interpretation given by the parties to their contractual language throughout the period of its existence.

Prior to 1921, professional baseball was governed by a three-man National Commission formed in 1903 which consisted of the presidents of the National and American Leagues and a third member, usually one of the club owners, selected by the presidents of the two leagues.[3] Between 1915 and 1921, a series of events and controversies contributed to a growing dissatisfaction with the National Commission on the part of players, owners and the public, and a demand developed for the establishment of a single, independent Commissioner of baseball.[4]

On September 28, 1920, an indictment issued charging that an effort had been made to "fix" the 1919 World Series by several Chicago White Sox players. Popularly known as the "Black Sox Scandal," this event rocked the game of professional baseball and proved the catalyst that brought about the establishment of a single, neutral Commissioner of baseball.[5]

In November, 1920, the major league club owners unanimously elected federal Judge Kenesaw Mountain Landis as the sole Commissioner of baseball and appointed a committee of owners to draft a charter setting forth the Commissioner's authority. In one of the drafting sessions an attempt was made to place limitations on the Commissioner's authority. Judge Landis responded by refusing to accept the office of Commissioner.[6]

On January 12, 1921, Landis told a meeting of club owners that he had agreed to accept the position upon the clear understanding that the owners had sought "an authority  .  .  .  outside of your own business, and that a part of that authority would be a control over whatever and whoever had to do with baseball."[7] Thereupon, the owners voted unanimously to reject the proposed limitation upon the Commissioner's authority,[8] they all signed what they

---

3. Finding of Fact 13. *See* 2 Seymour, Baseball: The Golden Age (1971) 9–18.

4. Finding of Fact 13. *See also* 2 Seymour, *supra* footnote 3, at 18, 259–273.

5. Finding of Fact 14. *See* Asinof, Eight Men Out: The Black Sox and the 1919 World Series (1963).

6. Findings of Fact 17, 18.

7. Finding of Fact 18.

8. Finding of Fact 19. In Spink, Judge Landis and Twenty-Five Years of Baseball (1947) 72, the author says that "Landis agreed to accept if he was given absolute control over baseball."

called the Major League Agreement, and Judge Landis assumed the position of Commissioner. Oakland has been a signatory to the Major League Agreement continuously since 1960.[9] The agreement, a contract between the constituent clubs of the National and American Leagues, is the basic charter under which major league baseball operates.[10]

The Major League Agreement provides that "[t]he functions of the Commissioner shall be  .  .  . to investigate  .  .  . any act, transaction or practice  .  .  . not in the best interests of the national game of Baseball" and "to determine  .  . what preventive, remedial or punitive action is appropriate in the premises, and to

take such action  .  .  .  ." Art. I, Sec. 2(a) and (b).[11]

The Major League Rules, which govern many aspects of the game of baseball, are promulgated by vote of major league club owners.[12] Major League Rule 12(a) provides that "no  .  .  . [assignment of players] shall be recognized as valid unless  .  .  . approved by the Commissioner." [13]

The Major Leagues and their constituent clubs severally agreed to be bound by the decisions of the Commissioner and by the discipline imposed by him. They further agreed to "waive such right of recourse to the courts as would otherwise have existed in their favor." Major League Agreement, Art. VII, Sec. 2.[14]

9. Finding of Fact 3. *See also* Finding of Fact 29.

10. Finding of Fact 5.

11. Art. I, Sec. 2 provides in part:
    The functions of the Commissioner shall be as follows:
    (a) TO INVESTIGATE, either upon complaint or upon his own initiative, any act, transaction or practice charged, alleged or suspected to be not in the best interests of the national game of Baseball, with authority to summon persons and to order the production of documents, and, in case of refusal to appeal or produce, to impose such penalties as are hereinafter provided.
    (b) TO DETERMINE, after investigation, what preventive, remedial or punitive action is appropriate in the premises, and to take such action either against Major Leagues, Major League Clubs or individuals, as the case may be.
    This language is identical to Art. I, Sec. 2(a) and (b) as originally executed on January 12, 1921, with the exception that the words in present paragraph (a) "not in the best interests of the national game of Baseball" were originally "detrimental to the best interests of the national game of baseball." The change was made in 1964. The district court implied that the change broadened the Commissioner's powers when it found that "previously the Commissioner had to find conduct 'detrimental' to the best interests of baseball in order to take remedial or preventive action  .  .  .  ." Finding of Fact 28.

12. Finding of Fact 7.

13. Finding of Fact 39. A rule of this nature was in effect at least as early as 1931. In *Milwaukee American Ass'n v. Landis,* 49 F.2d 298, 302 (N.D.Ill.1931), the court noted that "[w]hether there is given to the commissioner the power in so many words to declare Bennett a free agent is immaterial, since the agreements and rules grant to the commissioner jurisdiction to refuse to approve Bennett's assignment by St. Louis to Milwaukee, and to declare him absolved from the burdens of the same and of his contract with St. Louis."
    A federal district judge in another case has expressed his opinion that the present case was correctly decided by the district court on the sole ground that the Commissioner was given specific authority under Major League Rule 12(a) to disapprove contracts and therefore render players free agents. *Atlanta National League Baseball Club, Inc. v. Kuhn,* 432 F.Supp. 1213, 1224 (fn. 8), 1225 (N.D.Ga.1977).

14. Art. VII, Sec. 2 provides:
    The Major Leagues and their constituent clubs, severally agree to be bound by the decisions of the Commissioner, and the discipline imposed by him under the provisions of this Agreement, and severally waive such right of recourse to the courts as would otherwise have existed in their favor.
    This language is identical to Art. VII, Sec. 1 in the original 1921 agreement. Also, on the same day, January 12, 1921, that the Major League Agreement was signed on behalf of the two major leagues and sixteen baseball clubs, the league presidents and club presidents individually signed the following "Pledge to Support the Commissioner":
    We, the undersigned, earnestly desirous of insuring to the public wholesome and high-

Upon Judge Landis' death in 1944, the Major League Agreement was amended in two respects to limit the Commissioner's authority. First, the parties deleted the provision by which they had agreed to waive their right of recourse to the courts to challenge actions of the Commissioner.[15] Second, the parties added the following language to Article I, Section 3:

> No Major League Rule or other joint action of the two Major Leagues, and no action or procedure taken in compliance with any such Major League Rule or joint action of the two Major Leagues shall be considered or construed to be detrimental to Baseball.

The district court found that this addition had the effect of precluding the Commissioner from finding an act that complied with the Major League Rules to be detrimental to the best interests of baseball.[16]

The two 1944 amendments to the Major League Agreement remained in effect during the terms of the next two Commissioners, A. B. "Happy" Chandler and Ford Frick.[17] Upon Frick's retirement in 1964 and in accordance with his recommendation, the parties adopted three amendments to the Major League Agreement: (1) the language added in 1944 preventing the Commissioner from finding any act or practice "taken in compliance" with a Major League Rule to be "detrimental to baseball" was removed;[18] (2) the provision deleted in 1944 waiving any rights of recourse to the courts

to challenge a Commissioner's decision was restored;[19] and (3) in places where the language "detrimental to the best interests of the national game of baseball" or "detrimental to baseball" appeared those words were changed to "not in the best interests of the national game of Baseball" or "not in the best interests of Baseball."[20]

The nature of the power lodged in the Commissioner by the Major League Agreement is further exemplified "[i]n the case of conduct by organizations not parties to this Agreement, or by individuals not connected with any of the parties hereto, which is deemed by the Commissioner not to be in the best interests of Baseball" whereupon "the Commissioner may pursue appropriate legal remedies, advocate remedial legislation and take such other steps as he may deem necessary and proper in the interests of the morale of the players and the honor of the game." Art. I, Sec. 4.[21]

The Commissioner has been given broad power in unambiguous language to investigate any act, transaction or practice not in the best interests of baseball, to determine what preventive, remedial or punitive action is appropriate in the premises, and to take that action. He has also been given the express power to approve or disapprove the assignments of players. In regard to nonparties to the agreement, he may take such other steps as he deems necessary and proper in the interests of the morale of the players and the honor of the game. Fur-

---

class baseball, and believing that we ourselves should set for the players an example of the sportsmanship which accepts the umpire's decision without complaint, hereby pledge ourselves loyally to support the Commissioner in his important and difficult task; and we assure him that each of us will acquiesce in his decisions even when we believe them mistaken, and that we will not discredit the sport by public criticism of him or of one another.

**15.** The last part of Art. VII, Sec. 2. Footnote 14 *supra*. The parties retained the first part of the section wherein they agreed to be bound by the decisions of the Commissioner and the discipline imposed by him.

**16.** Finding of Fact 22.

**17.** Finding of Fact 23.

**18.** Finding of Fact 26.

**19.** Finding of Fact 27.

**20.** Finding of Fact 28. *See* footnote 11 *supra.*

**21.** The original 1921 agreement contained substantially the same language except it included the words "conduct detrimental to baseball" instead of "not to be in the best interests of Baseball." *See* footnote 11 *supra*. There is a reference to Article I, Section 4 in *Milwaukee American Ass'n v. Landis*, 49 F.2d 298, 299 (N.D.Ill.1931).

ther, indicative of the nature of the Commissioner's authority is the provision whereby the parties agree to be bound by his decisions and discipline imposed and to waive recourse to the courts.

The Major League Agreement also provides that "[i]n the case of conduct by Major Leagues, Major League Clubs, officers, employees or players which is deemed by the Commissioner not to be in the best interests of Baseball, action by the Commissioner for each offense *may include* " a reprimand, deprivation of a club of representation at joint meetings, suspension or removal of non-players, temporary or permanent ineligibility of players, and a fine not to exceed $5,000 in the case of a league or club and not to exceed $500 in the case of an individual. Art. I, Sec. 3.[22]

The district court considered the plaintiff's argument that the enumeration in Article I, Section 3[23] of the sanctions which the Commissioner may impose places a limit on his authority inasmuch as the power to disapprove assignments of players is not included. The court concluded that the enumeration does not purport to be exclusive and provides that the Commissioner *may* act in one of the listed ways without expressly limiting him to those ways.

The court further concluded that the principles of construction that the specific controls the general, or that the expression of some kinds of authority operates to ex-

clude unexpressed kinds, do not apply since the Commissioner is empowered to determine what preventive, remedial or punitive action is appropriate in a particular case and the listed sanctions are punitive only.[24] In fact, from 1921 until 1964, Article I, Section 3, expressly described the enumerated sanctions as "punitive action." [25]

[1] In view of the broad authority expressly given by the Major League Agreement to the Commissioner, particularly in Section 2 of Article I, we agree with the district court that Section 3 does not purport to limit that authority.

### III

Despite the Commissioner's broad authority to prevent any act, transaction or practice not in the best interests of baseball, Oakland has attacked the Commissioner's disapproval of the Rudi-Fingers-Blue transactions on a variety of theories which seem to express a similar thrust in differing language.

The complaint alleged that the "action of Kuhn was arbitrary, capricious, unreasonable, discriminatory, directly contrary to historical precedent, baseball tradition, and prior rulings and actions of the Commissioner." In pre-trial answers to interrogatories, Oakland acknowledged that the Commissioner could set aside a proposed assignment of a player's contract "in an appropriate case of violation of [Major

---

22. Art. I, Sec. 3 provides:

In the case of conduct by Major League Clubs, officers, employees or players which is deemed by the Commissioner not to be in the best interests of Baseball, action by the Commissioner for each offense may include any one or more of the following: (a) a reprimand; (b) deprivation of a Major League Club of representation in joint meetings; (c) suspension or removal of any officer or employee of a Major League Club; (d) temporary or permanent ineligibility of a player; and (e) a fine, not to exceed Five Thousand Dollars ($5,000.00) in the case of a Major League or a Major League Club and not to exceed Five Hundred Dollars ($500.00) in the case of any officer, employee or player.

The original 1921 agreement was substantially the same except that until 1964(1) it used the

phrase "in the case of conduct detrimental to baseball," see footnote 11 *supra*; (2) it described the enumerated forms of action as "punitive action"; and (3) the possibility of assessing a fine against an individual of up to $500 did not appear in the agreement until 1964.

23. *See* footnote 22 *supra*.

24. The district court said in its judgment order of March 17, 1977: "Nowhere in the Agreement is there a comparable list of the 'preventative' or 'remedial' actions he is empowered to take. Obviously such a list would be impossible to draw in the face of the unpredictability of the problems which arise."

25. *See* footnote 22 *supra*.

League] Rules or immoral or unethical conduct."

It is clear from reading the findings of fact that the district court determined through the course of the trial that Oakland was contending that the Commissioner could set aside assignments only if the assignments involved a Rules violation or moral turpitude.

In its briefs on appeal, Oakland summarized this branch of its argument by stating that the Commissioner's "disapproval of the assignments . . . exceeded [his] authority under the Major League Agreement and Rules; was irrational and unreasonable; and was procedurally unfair." The nub of this diffuse attack seems best expressed in a subsequent heading in the brief that the Commissioner's "abrupt departure from well-established assignment practice and his retroactive application of this change of policy to disapprove [Oakland's] assignments was made without reasonable notice and was therefore procedurally unfair."

The plaintiff has argued that it is a fundamental rule of law that the decisions of the head of a private association must be procedurally fair. Plaintiff then argued that it was "procedurally unfair" for the Commissioner to fail to warn the plaintiff that he would "disapprove large cash assignments of star players even if they complied with the Major League Rules."

In the first place it must be recalled that prior to the assignments involved here drastic changes had commenced to occur in the reserve system and in the creation of free agents.[26] In his opinion disapproving the Rudi, Fingers and Blue assignments, the Commissioner said that "while I am of course aware that there have been cash sales of player contracts in the past, there has been no instance in my judgment which had the potential for harm to our game as do these assignments, particularly in the present unsettled circumstances of baseball's reserve system and in the highly competitive circumstances we find in today's sports and entertainment world."

Absent the radical changes in the reserve system, the Commissioner's action would have postponed Oakland's realization of value for these players.[27] Given those changes, the relative fortunes of all major league clubs became subject to a host of intangible speculations. No one could predict then or now with certainty that Oak-

---

26. The following description of the changes in the reserve system appears in *Atlanta National League Baseball Club, Inc. v. Kuhn*, 432 F.Supp. 1213, 1215 (N.D.Ga.1977):

This system, which essentially bound a player to a team perpetually unless traded or released, was known as the reserve system. In 1975, the Players Association filed grievances on behalf of two players, Andy Messersmith and Dave McNally, challenging this system. An arbitration panel considered the grievances and concluded that players who had completed their last year of a contract with a particular club would be obligated, at the option of the club, to play only one additional year for that club. Unless the player and club signed a new agreement during this option year, the player became a free agent, with the right to negotiate contract terms with other major league clubs at the end of the option year season. The decision of the arbitration panel was upheld by the Court of Appeals for the Eighth Circuit in *Kansas City Royals Baseball Corp. v. Major League Baseball Players Ass'n*, 532 F.2d 615 (8th Cir. 1976).

In an effort to implement the *Kansas City Royals* decision, the representatives of the Players Association and the club owners met to hammer out a new collective bargaining agreement. An agreement was reached in July, 1976 which established a special reentry draft to be conducted in November of each year for those players who had become free agents at the end of a baseball season. Procedures were established for the November draft whereby negotiation rights with each free agent could be drafted by up to twelve teams, each of which were then given negotiation rights for that player. Between the end of the season and three days prior to the draft, however, only the club of record, the team for which the prospective free agent was playing out his option, had negotiation rights with that player.

27. This realization of value could come in the form of subsequent player transactions involving less cash but some returning-player value, or in box office profits attributable to these players, or possibly in the aggregate value of the club if and when eventually sold as a franchise and team.

land would fare better or worse relative to other clubs through the vagaries of the revised reserve system occurring entirely apart from any action by the Commissioner.

In the second place, baseball cannot be analogized to any other business or even to any other sport or entertainment. Baseball's relation to the federal antitrust laws has been characterized by the Supreme Court as an "exception," an "anomaly" and an "aberration."[28] Baseball's management through a commissioner is equally an exception, anomaly and aberration, as outlined in Part II hereof. In no other sport or business is there quite the same system, created for quite the same reasons and with quite the same underlying policies. Standards such as the best interests of baseball,[29] the interests of the morale of the players and the honor of the game,[30] or "sportsmanship which accepts the umpire's decision without complaint,"[31] are not necessarily familiar to courts and obviously require some expertise in their application. While it is true that professional baseball selected as its first Commissioner a federal judge,[32] it intended only him and not the judiciary as a whole to be its umpire and governor.

[2] As we have seen in Part II, the Commissioner was vested with broad authority and that authority was not to be limited in its exercise to situations where Major League Rules or moral turpitude was involved. When professional baseball in-

tended to place limitations upon the Commissioner's powers, it knew how to do so. In fact, it did so during the 20-year period from 1944 to 1964.

The district court found and concluded that the Rudi-Fingers-Blue transactions were not, as Oakland had alleged in its complaint, "directly contrary to historical precedent, baseball tradition, and prior rulings." During his almost 25 years as Commissioner, Judge Landis found many acts, transactions and practices to be detrimental to the best interests of baseball in situations whether neither moral turpitude nor a Major League Rule violation was involved, and he disapproved several player assignments.[33]

On numerous occasions since he became Commissioner of baseball in February 1969, Kuhn has exercised broad authority under the best interests clause of the Major League Agreement. Many of the actions taken by him have been in response to acts, transactions or practices that involved neither the violation of a Major League Rule nor any gambling, game-throwing or other conduct associated with moral turpitude. Moreover, on several occasions Commissioner Kuhn has taken broad preventive or remedial action with respect to assignments of player contracts.[34]

On several occasions Charles O. Finley, the principal owner of the plaintiff corporation and the general manager of the Oakland baseball club, has himself espoused

28. *Flood v. Kuhn,* 407 U.S. 258, 282, 92 S.Ct. 2099, 32 L.Ed.2d 728 (1972).

29. Major League Agreement, Article I, Sections 2(a), 3, 4.

30. Major League Agreement, Article I, Section 4.

31. The original "Pledge to Support the Commissioner," *see* footnote 14 *supra.*

32. Judge Kenesaw Mountain Landis was 38 years old when President Theodore Roosevelt appointed him to the United States District Court for the Northern District of Illinois in 1905. When he accepted the office of Commissioner of baseball in November 1920, he continued in his judicial post which provoked heavy

criticism from Congress, the American Bar Association and the press. Landis finally sent his judicial resignation to President Harding in February 1922, to become effective March 1, after having held both positions for more than 15 months. He served as baseball Commissioner for almost 25 years until his death on November 25, 1944. 2 Voight, American Baseball (1970) 141–150; 2 Seymour Baseball: The Golden Age (1971) 367–372; Asinof, Eight Men Out: The Black Sox and the 1919 World Series (1963) 223–224; MacKenzie, The Appearance of Justice (1974) 180–182.

33. Finding of Fact 21.

34. Finding of Fact 30. For examples of such actions, see Findings of Fact 31, 32, 33, 34, 35, 36.

that the Commissioner has the authority to exercise broad powers pursuant to the best interests clause, even where there is no violation of the Major League Rules and no moral turpitude is involved.[35]

Twenty-one of the 25 parties to the current Major League Agreement who appeared as witnesses in the district court testified that they intended and they presently understand that the Commissioner of baseball can review and disapprove an assignment of a player contract which he finds to be not in the best interests of baseball, even if the assignment does not violate the Major League Rules and does not involve moral turpitude.[36] Oakland contended that the district court erred in admitting this testimony since parties are bound "only by their objective manifestations and their subjective intent is immaterial." In this bench trial where Oakland was contending that it was not put on notice that transactions alleged to otherwise conform to the Major League Rules might be invalidated, the court could certainly consider what most of the current parties to the agreement believed they were put on notice of when they became signatories.

Oakland relied upon Major League Rule 21, which deals, in Oakland's characterization of it, with "(a) throwing or soliciting the throwing of ball games, (b) bribery by or of players or persons connected with clubs or (c) umpires, (d) betting on ball games, and (e) physical violence and other unsportsmanlike conduct" as indicating the limits of what is "not in the best interests of baseball." However, Rule 21(f) expressly states:

> Nothing herein contained shall be construed as exclusively defining or other-

wise limiting acts, transactions, practices or conduct not to be in the best interests of Baseball; and any and all other acts, transactions, practices or conduct not to be in the best interests of Baseball are prohibited, and shall be subject to such penalties including permanent ineligibility, as the facts in the particular case may warrant.

Oakland also took issue with language in the district court's judgment order of March 17, 1977, which relied upon *Milwaukee American Ass'n v. Landis,* 49 F.2d 298 (N.D.Ill.1931).[37] Oakland contended that the *Landis* case was distinguishable inasmuch as it involved the violation of a certain rule. In that case Judge Lindley held that the Commissioner "acted clearly within his authority" when he disapproved a player assignment after several assignments of the same player to and from different clubs owned by a single individual. The court said in 49 F.2d at 302:[38]

> Though there is nothing in the rules to prohibit an individual owning control of a Major League club from likewise owning control of Minor League clubs, the intent of the code is such that common ownership is not to be made use of as to give one individual, controlling all of the clubs mentioned, the absolute right, independent of other clubs, to control indefinitely a player acquired and switched about by apparent outright purchases.

[3] We conclude that the evidence fully supports, and we agree with, the district court's finding that "[t]he history of the adoption of the Major League Agreement in 1921 and the operation of baseball for more than 50 years under it, including: the

---

**35.** Finding of Fact 43. For examples of such occasions, see Findings of Fact 44, 45, 46.

**36.** Finding of Fact 37.

**37.** The district court said: "Many years ago, in the case of *Milwaukee American Association v. Landis,* . . . the court determined this same issue in this same manner. From that date to this, if the signatories to the Major League Agreement had wished to bar the Commissioner from their property rights in players'

contracts, it has always been and still remains within their power to do so. They have not."

**38.** The *Landis* court also said at 301: "The parties endowed the commissioner with wide power and discretion . . . of his own initiative to observe, investigate and take such action as necessary to secure observance of the provisions of the agreements and rules, promotion of the expressed ideals of, and prevention of conduct detrimental to baseball."

circumstances preceding and precipitating the adoption of the Agreement; the numerous exercises of broad authority under the best interests clause by Judge Landis and . . . Commissioner Kuhn; the amendments to the Agreement in 1964 restoring and broadening the authority of the Commissioner; . . . and most important the express language of the Agreement itself—are all to the effect that the Commissioner has the authority to determine whether *any* act, transaction or practice is 'not in the best interests of baseball,' and upon such determination, to take whatever preventive or remedial action he deems appropriate, whether or not the act, transaction or practice complies with the Major League Rules or involves moral turpitude." [39] Any other conclusion would involve the courts in not only interpreting often complex rules of baseball to determine if they were violated but also, as noted in the *Landis* case, the "intent of the [baseball] code," an even more complicated and subjective task.

The Rudi-Fingers-Blue transactions had been negotiated on June 14 and 15, 1976. On June 16, the Commissioner sent a teletype to the Oakland, Boston and New York clubs and to the Players' Association expressing his "concern for possible consequences to the integrity of baseball and public confidence in the game" and setting a hearing for June 17. Present at the hearing were 17 persons representing those notified. At the outset of the hearing the Commissioner stated that he was concerned that the assignments would be harmful to the competitive capacity of Oakland; that they reflected an effort by Boston and New York to purchase star players and "bypass the usual methods of player development and acquisition which have been traditionally used in professional baseball"; and that the question to be resolved was whether the transactions "are consistent with the best interests of baseball's integrity and maintenance of public confidence in the game." He warned that it was possible that he might determine that the assignments not be approved. Mr. Finley and representatives of the Red Sox and Yankees made statements on the record.

No one at the hearing, including Mr. Finley, claimed that the Commissioner lacked the authority to disapprove the assignments, or objected to the holding of the hearing, or to any of the procedures followed at the hearing. [40]

On June 18, the Commissioner concluded that the attempted assignments should be disapproved as not in the best interests of baseball. In his written decision, the Commissioner stated his reasons which we have summarized in Part I. The decision was sent to all parties by teletype. [41]

The Commissioner recognized "that there have been cash sales of player contracts in the past," but concluded that "these transactions were unparalleled in the history of the game" because there was "never anything on this scale or falling at this time of the year, or which threatened so seriously to unbalance the competitive balance of baseball." [42] The district court concluded that the attempted assignments of Rudi, Fingers and Blue "were at a time and under circumstances making them unique in the history of baseball." [43]

[4, 5] We conclude that the evidence fully supports, and we agree with, the district court's finding and conclusion that the Commissioner "acted in good faith, after investigation, consultation and deliberation, in a manner which he determined to be in the best interests of baseball" and that "[w]hether he was right or wrong is beyond the competence and the jurisdiction of this court to decide." [44]

39. Finding of Fact 47.

40. Finding of Fact 49.

41. Finding of Fact 50.

42. Finding of Fact 51; Tr. 1867.

43. Finding of Fact 52.

44. Finding of Fact 55. *See also* Finding of Fact 53:

It is beyond the province of this court to consider the wisdom of the Commissioner's reasons for disapproving the assignments of Rudi, Blue and Fingers. There is insufficient evidence, however, to support plaintiff's alle-

[6, 7] We must then conclude that anyone becoming a signatory to the Major League Agreement was put on ample notice that the action ultimately taken by the Commissioner was not only possible but probable. The action was neither an "abrupt departure" nor a "change of policy" in view of the contemporaneous developments taking place in the reserve system, over which the Commissioner had little or no control,[45] and in any event the broad authority given to the Commissioner by the Major League Agreement placed any party to it on notice that such authority could be used.

[8] Oakland has argued that the district court erred in not finding on the issue of procedural fairness. To the extent that Oakland made this an issue during the course of the trial, the court responded with adequate findings, many of which we have discussed in this Part III.

[9] Finally, Oakland has also argued that the court excluded evidence which tended to show the Commissioner's malice toward Mr. Finley. Finley's own testimony on this subject, as well as the Commissioner's deposition covering the subject, were admitted as part of the record. When counsel for the Commissioner attempted to cross-examine Finley in regard to the same subject, Oakland's counsel objected on the

ground of relevancy and the court sustained the objection on the ground that the Commissioner's motivation was not a serious issue in the case.[46] When the Commissioner was being cross-examined the same objection was sustained. However, since the subject had not been covered in direct examination, the court in its discretion could restrict the cross-examination to the scope of the direct; and since the subject of malice and motivation had been covered in Finley's testimony and in the Commissioner's deposition, the court could exclude it as cumulative regardless of its relevancy. The court made an express finding that the Commissioner had not been motivated by malice.[47]

## IV

The district court granted the defendant's motion for summary judgment as to Count II of the complaint, which sought to establish a violation of the Sherman Antitrust Act. The court said that "Baseball, anomaly of the antitrust law, is not subject to the provisions of that Act." The plaintiff on appeal has argued that any exemption which professional baseball might enjoy from federal antitrust laws applies only to the reserve system.[48]

The reserve system "centers in the uniformity of player contracts; the confine-

---

gation that the Commissioner's action was arbitrary or capricious, or motivated by malice, ill will or anything other than the Commissioner's good faith judgment that these attempted assignments were not in the best interests of baseball. The great majority of persons involved in baseball who testified on this point shared Commissioner Kuhn's view.

45. Oakland has not expressly argued that the Commissioner's notice of hearing, the hearing itself, or his written decision with express reasons were procedurally unfair, but only that Oakland was not put on notice of a changed policy and that the Commissioner bore malice toward Finley.

46. Tr. 811:
The Court: Well, it [motivation of the Commissioner] is one [allegation of the complaint] that the testimony thus far has not really supported and I don't think it is a serious allegation. I don't take it seriously.

I am not interested in whether the Commissioner likes Mr. Finley or whether he doesn't. If he had the authority to do what he did, we have a legal issue, and that is the only one I am going to look at, so I will sustain the objection.

47. Finding of Fact 53. See footnote 44 supra.

48. The plaintiff relies principally upon two quotations from Mr. Justice Blackmun's opinion for the Supreme Court in Flood v. Kuhn, 407 U.S. 258, 92 S.Ct. 2099, 32 L.Ed.2d 728 (1972):
For the third time in 50 years the Court is asked specifically to rule that professional baseball's reserve system is within the reach of the federal antitrust laws.
Id. at 259, 92 S.Ct. at 2100.
With its reserve system enjoying exemption from the federal antitrust laws, baseball is, in a very distinct sense, an exception and an anomaly.
Id. at 282, 92 S.Ct. at 2112.

ment of the player to the club that has him under the contract; the assignability of the player's contract; and the ability of the club annually to renew the contract unilaterally, subject to a stated salary minimum." [49]

The Supreme Court has held three times that "the business of baseball" is exempt from the federal antitrust laws.

In *Federal Baseball Club of Baltimore v. National League,* 259 U.S. 200, 208, 42 S.Ct. 465, 466, 66 L.Ed. 898 (1922), Mr. Justice Holmes said that "[t]he business is giving exhibitions of base ball, which are purely state affairs."

In *Toolson v. New York Yankees,* 346 U.S. 356, 356–57, 74 S.Ct. 78, 98 L.Ed. 64 (1953), the Court said in a short per curiam opinion:

In *Federal Baseball Club of Baltimore v. National League of Professional Baseball Clubs,* . . . this Court held that *the business of providing public baseball games for profit between clubs of professional baseball players* was not within the scope of the federal antitrust laws. Congress has had the ruling under consideration but has not seen fit to bring *such business* under these laws by legislation having prospective effect. *The business* has thus been left for thirty years to develop, on the understanding that it was not subject to existing antitrust legislation. The present cases ask us to overrule the prior decision and, with retrospective effect, hold the legislation applicable. We think that if there are evils in this field which now warrant application to it of the antitrust laws it should be by legislation. Without re-examination of the underlying issues, the judgments below are affirmed on the authority of *Fed-*

*eral Baseball Club of Baltimore v. National League of Professional Baseball Clubs, supra,* so far as that decision determines that Congress had no intention of including *the business of baseball* within the scope of the federal antitrust laws. (Emphasis added).

In *Flood v. Kuhn,* 407 U.S. 258, 282, 284, 92 S.Ct. 2099, 2112, 32 L.Ed.2d 728 (1972), the Court said that "Professional baseball is a business and it is engaged in interstate commerce" and "we adhere once again to *Federal Baseball* and *Toolson* and to their application to professional baseball."

Finally, in holding that the antitrust laws do apply to "the business of professional football," the Supreme Court, speaking through Mr. Justice Clark, made a substantive pronouncement regarding the baseball cases in *Radovich v. National Football League,* 352 U.S. 445, 451, 77 S.Ct. 390, 394, 1 L.Ed.2d 456 (1957):

. . . [S]ince *Toolson* and *Federal Baseball* are still cited as controlling authority in antitrust actions involving other fields of business, we now specifically limit the rule there established to the facts there involved, *i. e.,* the business of organized professional baseball.

[10, 11] Despite the two references in the *Flood* case to the reserve system,[50] it appears clear from the entire opinions in the three baseball cases, as well as from *Radovich,* that the Supreme Court intended to exempt the business of baseball, not any particular facet of that business, from the federal antitrust laws.[51]

---

49. *Flood v. Kuhn,* 407 U.S. 258, 259, fn. 1, 92 S.Ct. 2099, 2100, 32 L.Ed.2d 728 (1972). *See also* footnote 26 *supra.*

50. *See* footnote 48 *supra.*

51. We recognize that this exemption does not apply wholesale to all cases which may have

some attenuated relation to the business of baseball. *See, e. g., Twin City Sportservice, Inc. v. Charles O. Finley & Co.,* 365 F.Supp. 235 (N.D.Cal.1972), *rev'd on other grounds,* 512 F.2d 1264 (9th Cir. 1975).

Preserving Baseball's Antitrust Exemption:

# Interview with Professor Gary Roberts

**Editor's note:** *For the first time since the late 1950s, Congress appears to be seriously considering legislation that would subject baseball to the antitrust laws. The issues raised by such legislation are complex; and the way general antitrust policy interacts with widespread popular concerns about our National Pastime is of particular interest to antitrust specialists.*

*Our interviewee, who opposes the pending legislation, is an acknowledged expert on the subject. Professor Gary Roberts, the Vice-Dean of Tulane University's law school, teaches both antitrust and sports law and is the co-author of a forthcoming casebook on sports law. Roberts began his career in sports law as an associate at Covington & Burling in Washington, where he assisted partner (now NFL Commissioner) Paul Tagliabue in representing the National Football League.*

*Contributing Editor Stephen F. Ross conducted the interview for* ANTITRUST, *as is customary. Because Ross (who is Professor of Law at the University of Illinois) is a leading advocate of eliminating baseball's antitrust exemption, we took advantage of this natural opportunity for a clash of views. What emerged is more of a free-wheeling dialogue between two advocates for opposing positions than is typical in the Interview.*

*Both Professors Roberts and Ross testified on March 31, 1993, before the House Antitrust Subcommittee. This interview was conducted just before that testimony.*

**Q:** Why doesn't it follow, then, that Congress should pass legislation overturning baseball's exemption?

**A:** Since the exemption is the status quo, it would seem to me that there ought to be an affirmative reason to change the current legal standards by which baseball has been judged and on which it has relied in structuring its relationships over the years.

**Q:** As you know, I have suggested that the current structure of baseball does harm the public in a number of ways. First, owners limit the number of teams, then use the existence of viable markets without teams to exploit taxpayer subsidies for stadiums by threatening relocation. Second, there is no competitive pressure to keep games on free media, rather than pay or cable. And owners establish player mobility rules that pro-

My problem is that applying the antitrust laws to baseball is not likely to make things any better, and it could make some things worse.

**ROSS:** In 1972, the Supreme Court in *Flood v. Kuhn* held that, although baseball's antitrust exemption was anomalous, it was still justified because of the Court's view of baseball's "unique characteristics and needs." Do you agree that baseball's characteristics still justify a exemption from the antitrust law?

**ROBERTS:** I don't see that baseball is significantly different from the other sports in any meaningful way, except perhaps for the existence of the minor leagues in their structure. However, I wouldn't pose the question that Congress has to decide in that way. Still, there is nothing particularly unique about baseball that would entitle it to a special exemption that any other industry would not be entitled to.

tect inefficient management from competition. Do you agree that these harms are real and warrant legislation subjecting baseball to the antitrust laws?

**A:** I generally agree that these things you've listed harm the public interest, and they are all things that would be in the interest of the public to correct. I do not believe, however, that any one of them would be significantly improved by repealing the baseball exemption. Each of those harms can also be attributed to the National Football League, the National Basketball Association, and the National Hockey League—and the antitrust laws apply to them.

There are no more football franchises with the antitrust laws being applied to it than there are baseball franchises without it. I see no reason to assume that the federal courts are somehow going to use antitrust laws to increase the number of franchises or to change labor relations.

Although the Sherman Act might arguably have some impact on telecasting patterns, it would not necessarily be for the benefit of the public. I don't maintain that baseball is wonderfully structured and the public should just sit back and enjoy it without any complaints. My problem is that applying the antitrust laws to baseball is not likely to make things any better, and it could make some things worse.

Q: Let's walk through some of these specific areas of concern. If baseball were subject to antitrust laws, don't you think a court would hold that the American League and the National League are not allowed to consult or agree with each other as to where they expand or where they relocate franchises?

A: I doubt that, although I am willing to say up front that it is possible that a court would say almost anything! This is one of my problems with applying antitrust laws, particularly Section 1, to sports leagues—the way in which the law is applied is so unclear that you just can never predict what judges are going to say. It certainly is a possibility that a court might prevent interleague franchising discussions; even so it is not necessarily certain that it would result in an increase in the number of franchises.

Q: To use one familiar example, consider the St. Petersburg-Tampa Bay area. If the National League owners were not permitted to consult the American League owners, and were not permitted to share any expansion fee with American League owners, don't you think each league would be rushing to expand into Tampa? In fact, wouldn't both leagues be competing against each other to secure a lease in the Suncoast Dome?

A: Not necessarily. I can easily imagine each league's owners believing that they would have to expand by two teams at a time, and that having to provide two full team rosters, diluting player quality, and having to share national television revenues two more ways would make expansion unattractive, even into a potentially lucrative market like Tampa/St. Pete. But even if I couldn't envision that scenario,

professional sports owners frequently do things that I can't imagine them doing. I just think that your optimistic prediction requires too much speculation as to what is going to happen if we repeal the antitrust exemption—that a judge will find these two leagues to be illegally joined in some way, and that if the leagues are then forced to operate separately they will therefore behave in a particular fashion.

Q: Let's move to television for a moment and the National Basketball Association's attempt to limit superstation Chicago Bulls games shown on WGN, which was found to be a violation of the antitrust laws by the Seventh Circuit. Commissioner Vincent, prior to his resignation, indicated a concern with the proliferation of baseball games that are being shown on superstations. However, baseball could impose these restrictions without threat of antitrust suit. Isn't this an example of a situation where fans would benefit by more games if the antitrust laws are available to prevent league rules that might limit games on superstations?

A: Perhaps. First of all, Judge Easterbrook hinted strongly that he might have found the National Basketball Association to be a single entity and that the only reason he didn't was because the NBA didn't raise the point. Furthermore, the Seventh Circuit didn't find the NBA's limitation on superstation telecasts to violate Section 1; the *district court* made that finding based on several other factual findings, and the Seventh Circuit simply affirmed the judgment on the ground that it was supported by substantial evidence. So it is not at all clear that federal courts would necessarily reach the same result in other cases involving these kinds of television restrictions. Moreover, the decision in the Bulls' case does not necessarily result in a benefit to the consumer. It might create incentives for the leagues to restructure themselves in some way or to create telecasting patterns that are less efficient and even less advantageous for the public. For example, what if instead of allowing the individual clubs to sell their own telecasts, the leagues had all games broadcast pursuant to league-negotiated contracts, which might enjoy the exemption of Sec-

tion 1291 (The 1961 Sports Broadcasting Act)? You might actually have fewer games on television than you do now.

Q: As a practical matter, do you really believe owners would agree to let the league have rights to *every* game? As a legal matter, doesn't the legislative history of the Sports Broadcasting Act show that the Act's exemption does not apply to pay or cable?

A: First of all, the clubs might very well decide to continue owning their own television rights but appoint the commissioner to act as their agent and negotiate their individual contracts "in the best interests of the league." Such an arrangement may itself have antitrust problems, but it might not—underscoring the unitary nature of a league's business enterprise. Only if the clubs transferred their rights to the league would the application of the Sports Broadcasting Act's protection become relevant. As to whether that Act protects pay or cable contracts by a league, the Act only applies to "sponsored telecasting." There are, however, some kinds of cable that might very well qualify—for example, ESPN is sponsored, there are commercials, and an argument could be made for that type of cable channel being covered. Much of the legislative history that people have used to argue that the Act does not cover any kind of cable under any circumstances consists of comments made by various people in congressional hearings *since* 1961. So perhaps owners will not agree to league-wide sales; perhaps the courts will interpret the Act the way you would like it interpreted. The point is that we are engaging in a lot of speculation about what the courts might do with the interpretation of these laws.

Q: Let's talk about the minor leagues for a moment. Recently some baseball officials who have been seeking to defend the exemption have suggested that the baseball exemption protects the continued financial success and vibrancy of minor league franchises. But as you know, baseball has used a vertically integrated system of player development—the Farm System—only since the 1950s. Prior to that time, minor league baseball clubs flourished and prospered by signing young players and then selling the rights to those players once the prospect proved to be sufficiently attractive to a major league team. Isn't it more likely that a repeal of the antitrust exemption would allow the formation of different means to develop players and would permit a more efficient system of player development to flourish?

A: Again, I hesitate to make any statements about what I think is likely to happen if the exemption is repealed because it requires more soothsaying skill and knowledge than I have. That is one of my problems with changing the status quo in this way and with repealing the exemption. I really don't know how the courts are going to interpret the law or how people are going to react to those interpretations. But it does seem to me that one very plausible scenario if the exemption were repealed is that the courts might find the current minor league arrangements to be illegal, and major league clubs would find it no longer to their advantage to continue to subsidize or deal with single A or rookie league clubs. I understand your theory, and I also think it is plausible. However, the potential for generating revenues in the minor leagues is not the same as it was back before 1950 when television didn't bring major league baseball into every small community and the local minor league team was the only exposure to professional baseball the fans got. Today, without the major league subsidy, I fear that a majority of the existing minor league teams would disappear and many communities would be without baseball. Whether that's good or bad is another question, but I think it's a reality that will cause many congressmen from these areas to oppose repealing the exemption.

Q: You mentioned that in the *Bulls* case, Judge Easterbrook alluded to a theory that you certainly have been associated with, that sports leagues are single entities and therefore not subject to the restrictions of Section 1 of the Sherman Act. Why isn't a sports league a joint venture of owners who agree to a limited economic integration, with separate profits and losses, just like many joint ventures in other industries?

A: That is a tough question in this format, because the answer is very complicated. I'm not sure a short answer will

be persuasive; for a more lengthy discussion, I can only urge people to read the various law review articles I have written on the subject. But the short answer is that baseball clubs have virtually no economic value other than as part of a league. In other industries, wholly independent and autonomous business entities that are capable of producing useful products on their own can come together in a joint venture to facilitate some joint operation in a way that is more efficient than if they did it separately. In professional sports, teams are not viable in any sense on their own, and so the product that they produce is inherently wholly integrated. The product depends on the express or implicit cooperation and agreement of each of the members with respect to every aspect of the operation, so that each game is inherently the joint product of every team in the league. It only stands to reason, then, that every team in the league should have the inherent right to some input into the operations of each other club in their "joint venture." Another way of looking at it would be to say that leagues are partnerships—it is only natural that each one should expect all of the others not to do anything that might injure the interests of any of them. There is a fiduciary duty not to do so.

Q: How do you differentiate baseball, which is only marketed effectively at its current level in this integrated form, from the blanket licenses sold by Broadcast Music, Inc. and ASCAP?

A: I think you probably could argue that BMI should be considered a single entity. When that case was litigated, that was not even an issue. There are some obvious distinctions, though, between a blanket license, which is the aggregation of separately produced units of output, and a sports league where the units of output are necessarily jointly produced.

Q: My problem with your analogy to a partnership is that in a partnership, the owners are expected, effectively, to act in the best interests of the whole business. That is certainly an admirable goal, and many commissioners and league officials would like to see that happen. But the reality of sports is precisely the opposite—owners act in the best interests of

their own individual clubs, which makes their joint activity more like a cartel than a partnership. Books like *The League* chronicled the great success of Commissioner Rozelle in trying to get owners to act as a league as a whole—he used a phrase "Leaguethink." The book also demonstrated that those efforts were not always successful.

A: A joint venture *is* a partnership—it's just a type of partnership, but one that is governed by the same legal rules as any other partnership. All partners in any business are going to act in their own individual best interests when they vote or carry out their duties if the partnership rules let them do so. And any partnership can choose to structure itself or create governing rules that in a given situation will allow and create incentives for the partners to act in their own interests instead of in the interests of the partnership. Most partnerships in other industries don't permit such self-serving behavior by their partners, but the law doesn't prohibit them from doing so. What is interesting about a sports league partnership is that the unique athletically competitive nature of its product requires a highly decentralized kind of operation. Thus, leagues generally have many rules that allow the member partners (the clubs) to vote or act in their individual best interests in many situations—because allowing such individualism is in the larger picture what is in the long term best interests of the league. But because a league's rules now allow for such short term self-interested behavior on a particular issue does not mean that antitrust law should require the league to allow it forever. Thus, a sports league's partners should always be allowed to change its governing rules—for example, the National Football League could vote tomorrow to share every dime of revenue generated by National Football League operations, which would dramatically change the incentives that guide the individual NFL club owners in their deliberations on specific issues. If you see owners voting or making operating decisions in their own interests, it is only because the league has, for efficiency reasons, chosen to structure itself in a highly decentralized way that permits and creates the incentives for them to operate in that fashion. But that is not inconsistent with the fundamental nature of a partnership.

**Q:** I guess where we disagree is that, for me, there is a huge difference between a league where all revenue is pooled, and the situation in the major sports leagues in North America where individual club profits and losses vary considerably. The key to me is whether the venture's incentives will be for partners to adopt rules that are not efficient for the partnership.

You and I seem to have differing views of what is an "ancillary" and thereby legal, restraint. Your view of what constitutes a legitimate ancillary restraint in a joint venture seems to underlie your view about sports league rules—which, I take it, you believe are always ancillary.

**A:** First I should note that whether a league chooses to pool most or all of its revenues or chooses to share profits and/or losses in different proportions is a voluntary choice about what structure is optimally efficient. The Supreme Court in *Copperweld* made clear, correctly I believe, that whether a business is a single entity or not hinges on inherent economic realities, not on voluntary structural choices made in the pursuit of efficiency. As for the point about ancillarity, in my view in order to qualify as ancillary, the defendants should have to prove that the restriction is reasonably related to enhancing the efficiency of the overall operation. You could not have several of the NFL owners who also happen to own oil companies fix oil prices and claim that is ancillary to their NFL joint venture simply because it is in the NFL constitution. However, once you have established the ancillarity of the restrictions, then I believe the restraints should be per se legal, if the joint venture is in its inception lawful. Because the rules that have been typically challenged in suits against sports leagues are always reasonably related to league operations, they should be per se legal.

**Q:** The common law origins of the ancillary restraints doctrine suggest that courts have traditionally struck down restraints that are related to lawful agreements, if the restraints are overbroad. This is true whether the agreement involves a dentist who sells her business and accepts a noncompetition covenant that is found to be too long to reasonably recoup good will, or whether the restraint is a sports league agreement that restricts

superstation broadcasts in a way that is overly restrictive of the need to promote local marketing of the team. You seem to reject any inquiry into overbreadth or less restrictive alternatives as proper for a court.

**A:** This gets pretty tricky. If a buyer imposes a noncompetition restriction on the seller of the business that goes beyond any reasonable need of the buyer to be protected, then in my mind it is no longer ancillary. However, courts have mistakenly used the less restrictive alternative doctrine over the years to say that even though a restriction enhances the efficiency of the overall business—that is to say it's truly ancillary, it is still illegal because it does not enhance it enough to overcome what the court thinks is its restrictive nature. It seems to me that once you start getting into that sort of balancing you are allowing juries to micromanage every business in America that is not clearly a single entity. Parenthetically, I might add that I think this is precisely the scheme Congress envisioned in 1890 when in Section 1 it proscribed "*every*" agreement in restraint of trade—that is to say it outlawed all agreements that were not reasonably related to an underlying lawful joint enterprise, but it permitted all restraints that were truly ancillary to an underlying joint business. This is the only way you can explain Congress' choice of the word "every" at the beginning of Section 1, which the courts since *Standard Oil* in 1911 have simply ignored.

**Q:** Consider the *Bulls* case again: it could have significant relevance to baseball, should the exemption be eliminated, in light of a growing hostility to superstation broadcasts of the Cubs, Braves, Mets, and others. The NBA argued that restricting the Bulls was necessary to enhance marketing of its product on a nationwide basis. Yet the multiyear nationwide contracts with NBC and TNT had already been signed before the restriction was put into effect. How was the rule ancillary, then? Why wasn't it appropriate for the court to evaluate the NBA rule as it would a noncompetition covenant ancillary to a sale of a business, that is, determine whether the restriction was agreed to in order to accomplish selling some new product or otherwise to en-

hance the efficient marketing of the NBA product?

**A:** Because you are looking at the efficiency question at the wrong level. The question in the *Bulls* case is whether or not it is reasonable for a league whose product is inherently jointly produced by all the members of the league to prevent individual members from acting in ways that the rest of the league feels is detrimental to their overall joint business. Allowing each club to market itself any way it wants creates the kind of environment in which partnerships cannot thrive. If you allow antitrust juries to second-guess every single business decision that a joint venture makes, to determine whether that *specific* decision was in fact correct from an efficiency standpoint (we're back to my micromanaging point again), you are simply allowing federal courts to take over the management of every business in America that is not a single entity. That is what I am saying is crazy. You need to look at the restraint in a more generic sense. Is this the type of internal business decision that a joint venture should be allowed to make in its own judgment about its own best interests?

**Q:** What you seem to be saying is that a league is a single entity even if the league members agree to function like a cartel.

**A:** Yes, exactly. Although I would not use the word "cartel" in this context. The league members have not chosen to function as a cartel (which implies an entity unlawful in its inception), but rather as a highly decentralized lawful entity. As I mentioned a couple of minutes ago, I think this goes back to the *Copperweld* case. The majority opinion expressly held that whether or not defendants are a single entity for antitrust purposes should not turn on the voluntary decisions of the members of that entity to structure itself in a more efficient fashion. It seems to me that whether or not something is a single entity should turn on the fundamental inherent economic realities of where the sources of economic power lie rather than the voluntary way in which the members have chosen to structure the entity in the pursuit of greater efficiency.

**Q:** Then, to sum up, you seem to concede that the monopolistic structure of Major League Baseball allows owners to cause a variety of harm to consumers. Your predictions are that, were the antitrust laws applied to baseball, things might get better and they might get worse, but we are not sure. Because we know there is a clear harm out there now, why are you unpersuaded that we ought to take the chance and go forward with a repeal and see what happens?

A: Because I do not believe the courts can or will intelligently apply Section 1 of the Sherman Act, which deals with conspiracies among independent businesses, to a wholly integrated sports league in a fashion that will result in a benefit to the public interest. Rather, sports leagues are natural monopolies that need to be regulated in some fashion. But to apply a statute in a way that was never intended and does not make sense is not to me the solution to problems, any more than to say that because IBM had a monopoly in the mainframe computer market, we should therefore apply Section 1 of the Sherman Act to require the various vice presidents of IBM to compete with one another. It doesn't make sense.

It is not so much that the courts are incompetent in applying Section 1; Section 1 is simply not meant to apply to single entities like sports leagues. When you start applying a statute that is not meant for the purpose you are applying it, you end up with some stupid results that in the long run hurt the consumer and hurt the public interest.

What I would ideally like to see, frankly, if I could dream, is that we would extend an exemption from Section 1 of the Sherman Act to all sports leagues on the condition that we regulate them in some fashion. Perhaps the commissioner of these sports leagues could be jointly selected by the owners, the union, and a congressional committee, so that we would be sure that the commissioner of every league is going to be looking out for all of the relevant constituents who are interested in the sport. He would truly be a protector of the public interest. There are many creative ways to use an exemption from Section 1 to really bring about an improvement in the public interest. But simply applying Section 1 to baseball will not, in my judgment, likely do anything to help the public. •

# Run Baseball Just Like Any Other Business? That's the Last Thing the Owners Should Want.

By Spencer Weber Waller and Neil B. Cohen

The owners of the major league baseball teams envision the next baseball commissioner as a chief executive officer, reporting to a board of directors consisting of the twenty-eight owners—just as the chief executive reports to the board of directors in any other business. The owners apparently believe this would be beneficial to their interests.

If baseball is just another business, however, the underpinning from baseball's exemption from the antitrust laws disappears. This exemption, which dates back to 1922, only exists as a result of a near-sighted opinion of Justice Holmes to the effect that baseball is a sport, not commerce. As football owners were recently reminded, no other sport enjoys this irrational exception from the laws that govern other businesses. Indeed, the actions of professional basketball and hockey teams, as well as those of football teams, have been subjected to antitrust scrutiny.

What would being subject to antitrust laws mean for baseball? Generally speaking, the antitrust laws prohibit agreements that restrain trade. As is well known, the baseball owners were found to have engaged in collusion to minimize the market for free agent players for three consecutive seasons in the late 1980s. Indeed, Commissioner Vincent publicly admitted as much, contributing in no small measure to his unpopularity among the owners. If baseball were not exempt from the antitrust laws, the owners would have to be worried about more than arbitrators' decisions and damages; they would also face criminal charges. Violation of the Sherman Act is a felony punishable by up to three years in prison, with some prison time virtually mandated by the sentencing guidelines followed by federal courts. Colluding owners might find their only involvement in sports to be on the tennis courts of a minimum security federal prison. Indeed, if each act of collusion were construed as a separate crime, the owners could find themselves condemned to sentences longer than Nolan Ryan's career.

Other joint practices of the owners, such as trading deadlines, waiver rules, and the amateur draft could also be challenged under the antitrust laws. Finally, attempts to prevent the formation or continued existence of rival leagues, the subject of Justice Holmes's misguided opinion, might be construed as illegal acts of monopolization. It is probably not coincidental that the only sport exempt from the antitrust laws is also the only sport not to be the subject of a serious challenge from a rival league in over a generation.

If the owners tried to escape antitrust scrutiny by claiming that they are not twenty-eight competitors but, rather, one integrated enterprise seeking to maximize profits, they would fail. This argument has

10

been raised unsuccessfully by owners in other sports. Even if this argument prevailed, however, the owners would do themselves no favor. Taking the owners at their word, they see themselves as a board of directors to whom the chief executive officer (a.k.a. the commissioner) reports. Under the law of virtually every jurisdiction, directors have a fiduciary duty to the enterprise they direct—a duty to act in the best interests of the enterprise. In particular, these laws are very strict in conflict of interest situations, preventing directors from voting or otherwise acting to serve their selfish interests rather than those of the joint enterprise. Does the Tribune Company, the owner of, among other things, the Chicago Cubs, WGN (the superstation that transmits Cubs telecasts nationwide), and the local stations that broadcast the games of several other teams really want to be bound to a duty to vote in the best interests of baseball generally, even if that interest would harm the bottom line of the Tribune Company? We doubt it.

Thus, it can be seen that treating baseball like a business would be far from an unalloyed blessing for the owners. There might be some benefits, however. For example, once baseball lost its antitrust exemption, it would no longer be the sub-ject of extortionate political demands backed up by veiled threats to repeal that protection. As Justice Thurgood Marshall observed, the problem with a sword of Damocles, after, all, is that it hangs, not that it falls.

It must be noted that the owners have available to them a simple means of avoiding antitrust problems. All they have to do is resolve the issues involved through good faith negotiations with the players' union. The public pronouncements of many owners, however, suggest that collective bargaining is seen by them as the problem, not the solution.

In short, the result of the owners' expressed desire to run baseball like a business may be to snatch defeat from the jaws of victory. Perhaps, instead of preparing for war against the players, the owners should take a lesson from one of their highly-paid star relievers and focus on saving victories, not giving them away.

—EFQ

 SPENCER WEBER WALLER and NEIL B. COHEN are professors at Brooklyn Law School. Among their future projects will be "Taking Pop-Ups Seriously: The Jurisprudence of the Infield Fly Rule."

# PART 3

## ORGANIZED LABOR AND ORGANIZED BASEBALL: THE IMPACT OF THE LABOR LAWS

What major league baseball players have been unable to achieve through the antitrust laws, they largely have been able to achieve through the labor laws. In the nineteenth century and early twentieth century, players achieved a measure of freedom through the common law of contracts as the courts prevented the owners from enforcing contractual provisions against players seeking to change teams or leagues. These victories quickly paled as the major leagues were able to fend off the challenge of rival leagues through behavior that may well have violated the antitrust laws had organized baseball not enjoyed its peculiar antitrust exemption. As rival leagues were killed off, the reserve clause became a more potent weapon since a recalcitrant player had no choice other than to stay with his present team or remain unemployed as a professional baseball player.

The antidote proved to be the power of organized labor—unionization. But the struggle was not easy. The first players' union was organized in the nineteenth century by John Montgomery Ward, a fine player and a lawyer by training. This and other attempts in the first half of the twentieth century all were unsuccessful in creating a lasting structure for the players to bargain with the owners over pay, conditions of employment, and free agency.

The present players' association dates back to 1956. At its creation, it was by no means clear that the players had formed a union in the traditional sense of the term. Since that time, the players' association's legal status and power have been confirmed many times through collective bargaining agreements that have gained the players unparalleled wealth compared to the rest of the population, and even in excess of that gained by most other professional athletes. The power of the strike has been used to great effect, even at the risk of alienating fans. Due process now rules the disciplining of players by owners and the league. The right to free agency has been achieved. Owner collusion to subvert that right has been punished.

It would be a great irony if the crowning achievement of the American labor movement proved to be the creation of the million-aire baseball player. Whether the players will be able to preserve the fruits of their victories over time will depend on whether players will be able to transfer ever increasing labor costs to owners, who in turn are able to pass those costs off to others, either in form of escalating broadcasting rights payments from the media or higher ticket prices and concessions from the fans.

The materials which follow trace the evolution of the enormous power currently wielded by the players through the major league baseball players' association. We begin with the early contract cases but focus on the history and operation of the players' union and its charismatic early leader Marvin Miller, a labor leader every bit as powerful and influential as Samuel Gompers and Walter Reuther in the more traditional industrial labor unions. The fruits of the players' many, but belated, victories are only partially reflected in the standard form player contract. The many clauses set forth in the contract for the National League (virtually identical to the standard American League agreement) are far less important than the blank spaces in which the owners fill in the salary for the player, now averaging well over one million dollars per year.

THE AMERICAN LEAGUE BASEBALL CLUB OF CHICAGO, Plaintiff, *v.* HAROLD H. CHASE, Defendant.

(Supreme Court, Erie Special Term, July, 1914.)

Equity — will not aid in maintaining monopoly — interference with personal liberty — right to labor.
Specific performance — when not decreed — injunctions — violation of contract for personal services when not restrained.
Contracts — of professional baseball clubs for services — when injunction pendente lite granted — when injunction vacated.

Equity will not lend its aid to enforce an agreement which is part of a general plan having for its object the maintenance of a monopoly and interference with the personal liberty of a citizen and the control of his free right to labor wherever and for whom he pleases.

Specific performance of a contract for personal services will not be decreed, nor a violation thereof be restrained by injunction, except where the services contracted for are of a special, unique and extraordinary character and a substitute for the employee who will substantially answer the purposes of the contract cannot readily be obtained.

Where a contract, drawn as prescribed for the American League of Professional Baseball Clubs by the national commission, for the services of defendant, the foremost first baseman in professional baseball, was terminable by plaintiff, which was a party to the baseball monopoly, on a ten days' notice, but defendant was bound not only for the coming playing season of six months but also for another season if the plaintiff should choose to exercise its option, and if it insisted upon the requirement of an option clause in each succeeding contract defendant could be held for a term of years, his only alternative being an abandonment of his vocation, the absolute lack of mutuality both of obligation and of remedy in the contract prevents a court of equity from making it the basis of equitable relief by injunction or otherwise.

An injunction *pendente lite* granted in an action brought to restrain defendant from playing baseball for any one other than plaintiff during the period of defendant's contract with plaintiff will be vacated on motion.

Motion by defendant to dissolve temporary injunction.

Dirnberger & Augspurger (Keene H. Addington, Edward E. Gates, M. F. Dirnberger, Jr., and Owen B. Augspurger, of counsel), for defendant and motion.

Moot, Sprague, Brownell & Marcy (Ellis G. Kinkead, Adelbert Moot, Wm. L. Marcy, John W. Ryan and Helen Z. M. Rodgers, of counsel), for plaintiff, opposed.

Bissell, J.  The defendant moves for an order dissolving the temporary injunction, *pendente lite,* heretofore and on the 25th day of June, 1914, granted in this action, which has been brought by the plaintiff to restrain the defendant from playing baseball for anyone other than the plaintiff during the period of defendant's contract with the plaintiff.

The determination of the questions raised on the motion involves a careful analysis, not only of the player's contract, the breach whereof by the defendant is admitted, but also of the so-called national agreement and the rules of the national commission, adopted pursuant to the national agreement, which are connected with the player's contract, and evidence the general plan or scheme under which the defendant was employed by the plaintiff.

The game of baseball, which began as an athletic sport of youthful players attending the schools and colleges throughout the country, has continued as the favorite athletic sport of America during the past half century; and has been commercialized and organized as professional baseball and developed into a big business conducted for profit under the name of "Organized Baseball."

The national agreement for the government of professional baseball, together with the rules of the national commission, present to the court the scheme of co-operation and management of baseball leagues and baseball clubs and the control of baseball players.

The defendant, Chase, signed with the plaintiff the "player's contract," as prescribed for the American League of Professional Baseball Clubs by the national commission; and on the 15th day of June, 1914, gave notice in writing to the plaintiff of his intention to avoid, cancel and annul the agreement entered into by him with the plaintiff on the 26th day of March, 1914. Thereafter and on the 20th day of June, 1914, he entered into a contract to play baseball for a rival club, to wit, the Buffalo Club of the Federal League.

It is a well established general rule that equity will not specifically enforce a contract of service, either directly by means of a decree directing the defendant to perform it, or by an injunction restraining the defendant from violating it, except in cases where services contracted for are of a special, unique and extraordinary character, and a substitute for the employee cannot readily be obtained, who will substantially answer the purpose of the contract.

Injunctions in behalf of an employer against an employee to restrain the latter from violating an implied or expressed covenant that he will not work for another, upon the ground that the employee's services are of a unique and unusual character, have frequently been granted since the leading case of *Lumley* v. *Wagner,* 1 De G., M. & G. 604, and the fundamental rules governing their issuance may be said to be well settled. 3 Prom. Eq. Juris., § 1343; *Star Co.* v. *Press Pub. Co.,* 162 App. Div. 486.

The rule has been frequently applied to actors, or stars in the theatrical profession, of special and attractive talents. In *Metropolitan Ex. Co.* v. *Ward,* 24 Abb. N. C. 393, 9 N. Y. Supp. 779, the court said: "Between an actor of great histrionic ability and a professional baseball player, of peculiar fitness and skill to fill a particular position, no substantial distinction in applying the rule laid down in the cases cited, can be made. Each is sought for his particular and peculiar fitness; each performs in public for compensation, and each possesses for the manager a means of attracting an audience. The refusal of either to perform according to contract must result in loss to the manager, which is increased in cases where such services are rendered to a rival."

It is shown by the affidavits read on the hearing of this motion that the defendant, Chase, is reputed to possess special, unique and extraordinary characteristics as a baseball player; and is generally regarded as the foremost first baseman in professional baseball. His reputation for these characteristics was recently advertised in a souvenir of "Hal Chase Day" by the Buffalo Federal League Club for which he recently contracted to play.

The jurisdiction of equity, therefore, is clear in this

case and its power should be exercised by injunction enforcing the negative covenant of the defendant's contract, providing the contract does not lack mutuality and is not a part of an illegal scheme or combination.

The first question, therefore, to be determined is whether the contract between the plaintiff and the defendant is a mutual contract which furnishes a consideration for the negative covenant sought to be enforced in this action. The player's contract, which was signed by the parties, provides: " 7. The Club may, at any time after the beginning and prior to the completion of the period of this contract, *give the player ten days' written notice to end and determine all its liabilities and obligations hereunder;* in which event the liabilities and obligations undertaken by the Club shall cease and determine at the expiration of said ten days. The player, at the expiration of said ten days, shall be freed and discharged from all obligations to render service to the club." It thus appears that the defendant could rely upon only ten days of compensated service with the plaintiff under the contract.

For the purpose of determining to what extent, and for how long a period, the defendant is bound by this contract, as affected by the national agreement and the rules of the national commission, it will be necessary for us to consider analytically what the whole transaction represented by the three instruments, namely, the player's contract, the national agreement, and the rules and regulations of the national commission, undertakes to accomplish, and, in practice, actually does accomplish, as shown by the papers read on this motion.

Section I, article II, of the national agreement provides as follows:

## "Article II.

" Section 1. Each party to this agreement retains the right to conduct its affairs and govern its players according to its constitution and by-laws, *not in conflict with this Agreement.*"

Section 1, article VIII, is in part as follows:

## "Article VIII.

" Section 1. All contracts between clubs and players in the Major Leagues shall be *in form prescribed by the Commission.* All contracts between clubs and players in the National Association shall be in form prescribed by that Association, provided, however, that no *non-reserve* contract shall be entered into by any club operating under the National Agreement, until permission to do so has been first obtained from the Commission when such contract concerns a Major League player, or from the National Board of Arbitration of the National Association when such contract concerns a player of that organization."

Section 1, article IV, is in part as follows:

## "Article IV.

" Section 1. A commission of three members, to be known as the National Commission, is hereby created *with power to construe and carry out the terms and provisions of this Agreement,* excepting when it pertains solely to the internal affairs of a party to this Agreement. One member shall be the President of the National League and one the President of the American League. These two members shall  *  *  * elect by a majority vote a suitable person as the third member."

It thus clearly appears that the player's contract, together with the national agreement and the rules of the national commission adopted pursuant to that agreement, must in law be considered as evidencing the general agreement or plan regulating the employment and conduct of the defendant as a national agreement player. The player's contract further provides as follows:

" 1. The Club agrees to pay the player for the season of 1914 beginning on or about the 14th day of April, 1914, and ending on or about the 15th day of October, 1914, a salary at the rate of $4,500 for such season; and an additional sum at the rate of $1,500 for such season, said additional sum being *the consideration of the option herein reserved to the Club* in clause 10 hereto; said additional sum to be paid whether said option is exercised or not, making the total compensation to the player for the season herein contracted for $6,000.

" 8. The player agrees to perform for no other party during the period of this contract (unless with the written consent of the club)  * * *

" 9. The player will not, either during the playing season or before the commencement or after the close thereof, participate in an exhibition baseball game unless the written consent of the Club has first been given to him.

" 10. The player will, at the option of the Club, *enter into a contract for the succeeding season upon all the terms and conditions of this contract,* save as to Clauses 1 and 10, and the salary to be paid the player in the event of such renewal shall be the same as the total compensation provided for the player in Clause 1 hereto, unless it be increased or decreased by mutual agreement."

Section 3, article VI, of the national agreement provides:

" The right and *title of a major league club to its players shall be absolute* and can be terminated only by release, neglect to comply with requirements under this Agreement for reservations, or failure to fulfill its contractual obligations. *When a major league club serves notice of release on a player,* not secured within that or the preceding year from a minor league club by it or another major league club, *he shall be ineligible to contract with a club of another league,* if, during 10 days after service of such notice of release, a club of the league in which he is at the time playing shall demand his services."

Paragraph II of the player's contract is as follows:

" II. The club shall not *transfer* the services of the player to any other club without furnishing the player in writing all of the conditions under which said transfer is made and showing what team has claim to his services and what that claim is."

Section 9 of article VI of the national agreement provides in this connection:

"A Major League Club *shall not be permitted to sell the release* of a selected player until he has been actually in its service *before the close of the season in which he was drafted* or during the following training or regular season, and then *only after waivers* to him have been obtained from all other Major League Clubs and notice has been received from the Secretary of the National Board that no National Association club has claimed him *at the draft price.*"

It appears that originally the defendant was a " selected " player; but whether he was a selected player at the time he entered the service of the plaintiff is immaterial. Had he come from the vacant lots of the cities, or the fields of the country, or from the college campus, and therefore been "a free agent," at the time he made his entry into "organized baseball," the result would have been the same. If a sale or trade is to be made by one major league club to another, section 3 of article VI governs, and "The right and title of a major league club to its players shall be absolute."

If a sale or trade is to be made by a major league club to a minor league club, section 9 of article VI governs, and the sale or trade is not absolute until waivers have been obtained from the other major league clubs.

Thus a player in the highest league, without the exercise of any individual choice, may be required to take service with a club of a lower league where smaller salaries are paid, and where *both the aggregate of the salary list and the salary of each individual player* are subject to strict limitation under the terms of the national agreement. No opportunity is afforded the player to solicit employment upon his own account. No right is afforded to enable him to resist an unjust limitation upon his power to earn. No consideration is afforded either himself or his family with respect to choosing a home. In short, he is placed where he must at all times while playing in "organized baseball," consider that his home is only the place in which his services are for the time-being controlled.

The baseball player, even though about to be discharged, is still a thing of value to the club owner. The termination of the obligations by the club owner pursuant to the ten days' provision is not accomplished by him without securing some return. If the player goes to another major league club, it is either in exchange for some other more desired player or players,

29

or for the waiver price; and the same is true if the discharged player is sent to a league of lower grade.

It seems that the promotion of the ball player is also hedged about with such limitations as to make the property in him absolute whether he will accept terms or not, and to make those terms when arrived at only liberal enough to prevent the player from seeking other means of earning his livelihood.

Section 6 of article VI is in part as follows:

" Section 6. *The right of a Minor League Club to its players under this agreement shall be absolute* except that from September 15th to September 20th of each year each Major League Club shall have the privilege of selecting players from the National Association Clubs for the following season upon payment of the following sums:

" $2,500 for players selected from Class **AA.**

" $1,500 for players selected from Class A.

" $1,200 for players selected from Class B.

" $ 750 for players selected from Class C.

" $ 500 for players selected from Class D."

This section also provides for the selection or drafting of players by the different minor leagues in the order of their baseball classification. It provides that if there be conflicting drafts the conflict is to be determined by lot. The player is not given the right of choice. If such an opportunity were given him he could perhaps obtain a consideration for the exercise of his choice either in the form of a cash bonus or a larger salary.

" Organized Baseball " as conducted under the terms of the national agreement further seeks to enforce and perpetuate its title to and control of its players as follows:

Section 1, article VI, of the national agreement provides:

" Section 1. *All parties to this agreement pledge themselves to recognize the right of reservation and respect contracts between players and clubs under its protection.* No club operating under this agreement shall at any time *negotiate for the purchase or lease of the property of another club* without first securing the consent of such club."

Section 2 of article VI is as follows:

" Section 2. *Any club or league which harbors a player who refuses to observe his contract with a club member of any party to this agreement, or to abide by its reservation, shall be considered an outlaw organization, and its claim to contractual and territorial rights ignored.*"

Thus the baseball player is made a chattel; the title of the club to the player, if he be a player of a major league, is made absolute; if he be a player of a minor league, its title is absolute, except in so far as the draft provisions are concerned. (Art. VI, § 6.)

Section 2 of article VI recognizes the property of the club in the player as existing under two conditions. *First,* under a contract; and *second,* under reserve without a contract.

Section 1, article VII, provides the manner in which the reservation is to be made, and the effect thereof, and is as follows:

"ARTICLE VII.

" Section 1. On or before the 1st day of October in each year, the Secretary of each party to this Agreement shall transmit to the Secretary of the Commission a list of all players under contract to each of its club members on that date or at the close of the championship the following season, *together with those secured for future service by purchase or draft, or while free agents, and those under suspension or insubordination or other cause, as well as those ineligible for refusal to respect reservation by, or contract with, such club, for that or a preceding season.* The Secretary of the commission shall thereupon promulgate all of such lists which conform to the limitations of the reservation privileges of clubs according to rank and classification as shown in Section 3 of Article VI, and *no player thus promulgated as reserved shall be eligible to contract* or play with any National Agreement club other than that on whose list his name appears as a reserved player until he is regularly released by the reserving club."

If the club has not been able to obtain the player's consent to the salary which has been offered him for the ensuing season, section 2, article VII, accomplishes his release as follows:

" Section 2. No club shall be permitted to reserve a player while in arrears of salary to him; and the *failure of a club to tender a reserved player a contract for the ensuing season by February 1st,* shall be construed as a revocation of its reservation and shall operate as his unconditional release."

If the player has ideas of his own, which fail to accord with those of the club, the national agreement enables the club to enforce its own terms, leaving the player the option to enter some other trade, calling or profession, if he is not satisfied.

The scheme of the national agreement to perpetuate control over a player by means of contracts, apparently legal, is interesting and pertinent. Each term contract, as appears by section 1 of article VIII, must obtain a reserve clause or option to renew, and this article of the national agreement is further enforced by section A, rule 17, of the national commission, which is as follows:

"A non-reserve clause in the contract of a major league player without the approval of the Commission or of a minor league player without the approval of the National Board shall not be valid."

So that each new contract of the player must contain a reserve clause, and so by a series of contracts " Organized Baseball " is able to perpetuate its control over the services of the player. But if, upon the other hand, a contract is at any time unobtainable, or even in fact not in good faith sought to be obtained, as the club owner might offer an immoderately low salary, then the provisions for reservation and the respecting thereof, apply and safeguard the " absolute title " of the club.

But why should a player enter into a contract when his liberty of conduct, and of contract, is thus curtailed? The answer is that he has no recourse. He must either take the contract under the provisions of the national agreement whose organization controls practically all of the good ball players of the country or resort to some other occupation.

Section 2 of article VIII is as follows:

## "ARTICLE VIII.

" Section 2. Any agreement between club and player for service, evidenced by written acceptance, whether by letter or telegram, or receipt from player for money advanced to him to bind such agreement, shall be construed to be a contract and held to be binding, provided the player declines to enter into a formal contract; *but his refusal to sign such formal contract shall render him ineligible to play with the contracting club for more than a period of ten days, or to enter the service of a club of any party to this Agreement unless released."*

And this provision of the national agreement is further enforced by rule 23 of the national commission, which is as follows:

"A fine of $25 shall be imposed on any National Agreement Club that permits a player to play on its team for a longer period than that prescribed in section 2, Article VIII, of the Agreement, without a formal contract, *and the right to reserve such player will not be recognized."*

Rule 19 of the national commission provides for blacklisting players as follows:

"A National Agreement player, adjudged to have violated his contract, *shall be declared and promulgated to be ineligible* to play with or against any club in organized baseball until reinstated on his application by the Commission, if he be a Major League player, or by the National Board if he be a Minor League player. If, after full investigation, the tribunal having jurisdiction finds that such violation of contract was premeditated and without palliating circumstances, the application of the offender for reinstatement will not be considered until the player has given satisfactory assurance that he will not repeat the offense, and will not be granted without the imposition of an adequate penalty."

And also by rule 20:

"A player who fails to report to or deserts the club having title to his services *shall be declared and promulgated to be disqualified* as a National Agreement player until restored to good standing on his application by the Commission, if a Major League player, or by the National Board, if a Minor League player. In all cases of failure to report or desertion the offender may be reinstated with or without a fine, in the discretion of the tribunal having jurisdiction, provided, however, that if the player shall have joined an outlaw team his application for the removal of his disability shall not be acted on within three years after the commission of the offense.''

There are other provisions of the national agreement indicating its purpose. Section 1, article VIII, provides that a drafted major league player's salary shall not be over 25 per cent. in excess of that paid him by the minor league club from which he was secured, the amount to be established by affidavits from him and the president of the club from which he was obtained. All salaries of minor league players are limited; not alone the individual salary of the player, but the aggregate salaries of all the players. Art. VI, § 5. The territory of each club is made inviolate. Art. VI, § 1.

This somewhat extended analysis shows to what extent the contract between the plaintiff and the defendant presents reciprocal and mutual, enforceable obligations. The plaintiff can terminate the contract at any time on ten days' notice. The defendant is bound to many obligations under the remarkable provisions of the national agreement. The player's contract, executed in accordance with its terms, binds him not only for the playing season of six months from April fourteenth to October fourteenth, but also for another season, if the plaintiff chooses to exercise its option, and if it insists upon the requirement of an option clause in each succeeding contract the defendant can be held for a term of years. His only alternative is to abandon his vocation. Can it fairly be claimed that there is mutuality in such a contract? The absolute lack of mutuality, both of obligation and of remedy, in this contract, would prevent a court of equity from making it the basis of equitable relief by injunction or otherwise. The negative covenant, under such circumstances, is without a consideration to support it, and is unenforceable by injunction.

The authorities in the state of New York, with possibly one exception (*Hoyt* v. *Fuller,* 19 N. Y. Supp. 962, decided at the Special Term of the Superior Court of the City of New York in 1892), uniformly sustain the rule that an injunction to restrain a defendant from violating the negative stipulation in his contract and to render his services for another, where the facts in the case otherwise bring him within the rule as to services of a special, unique or extraordinary character, will not lie, where the contract provides that the person seeking to secure the injunction may terminate or revoke the contract on notice. The reasons among others given for this rule are as follows:

*First.* That no court can with reason be called upon to do a vain and useless thing, for, if the court issues the injunction, the person in whose favor the injunction may issue might render nugatory the action of the court by terminating the contract; and,

*Second.* That the contract, being unilateral, lacks mutuality in that the employer having the right to terminate the contract, the employee is remediless when such right is exercised. He can neither secure specific performance of the contract in an action against the employer in a court of equity, nor damages in an action at law; hence, he is remediless, and, therefore, while a court of equity will enjoin the breach of a negative covenant in contracts which contain no clause permitting a termination of the contract upon notice, they will not intervene by injunction where contracts contain such a clause. *Metropolitan Ex. Co.* v. *Ward,* 24 Abb. N. C. 393, 9 N. Y. Supp. 779; *Lawrence* v. *Dixey,* 119 App. Div. 295; *Dockstader* v. *Reed,* 121 App. Div. 846; *Levin* v. *Dietz,* 194 N. Y. 376, 381; *Star Co.* v. *Press Pub. Co., supra.; Arena Athletic Club* v. *McPartland,* 41 App. Div. 352; *Wadick* v. *Mace,* 191 N. Y. 5; *Ide* v. *Brown,* 178 id. 26; *Palmer* v. *Gould,* 144 id. 671.

The case of *Duff* v. *Russell,* 14 N. Y. Supp. 134, cited by the plaintiff, is not an authority upon the question involved in the present case. We are not now dealing with a case like *McCall Co.* v. *Wright,* 198 N. Y. 143, also cited by the plaintiff, in which an employee, after severance of his relations with his employer, endeavors to make merchandise of the latter's secrets which he has learned in the course of his employment; nor with a case in which a person who has sold his business and the good will thereof and received the consideration therefor, has agreed, as a part of the consideration which he has given for the price paid him, not to compete with his vendee. Such cases rest upon quite different principles from those which govern the present case.

The New York rule followed in this case has been uniformly held in other jurisdictions. *Rutland Marble Co.* v. *Ripley,* 10 Wall 339; *Ulrey* v. *Keith,* 237 Ill. 284, and cases there cited; *Hunt* v. *Conrad,* 47 Mich. 557; *Watford Oil & Gas Co.* v. *Shipman,* 233 Ill. 9; *Lee* v. *Chicago League Ball Club,* 169 Ill. App. 525; *Sturgis* v. *Galindo,* 59 Cal. 28; *Marion County Oil & Gas Co.* v. *Dykstra,* 165 Ill. App. 390; *Brooklyn Baseball Club* v. *McGuire,* 116 Fed. Repr. 782; *Weeghman* v. *Killifer,* U. S. Dist. Court W. Dist. of Mich. Southern Div. Opinion Sessions, J. decided April, 1914; *Duff* v. *Hopkins,* 33 Fed. Rep. 599; *Shields* v. *Trammell,* 19

Ark. 51; *Taussig* v. *Corbin,* 73 C. C. A. 656, 142 Fed. Repr. 660; *Giles* v. *Dunbar,* 181 Mass. 22.

The case of *Philadelphia Ball Club* v. *Lajoie,* 202 Penn. 210, cited with *McCaull* v. *Braham,* by the plaintiff in favor of a contrary rule was decided prior to the case of *Brooklyn Baseball Club* v. *McGuire,* 116 Fed. Repr. 782, and other cases constituting the weight of authority, which sustain the rule now followed by this court. In *McCaull* v. *Braham,* 16 Fed. Repr. 37, the question of the lack of mutuality of the contract of personal service was not involved. Since the argument of the present case the Appellate Court of the state of Illinois on June 16, 1914, reversed the decision rendered by Judge Foell June 3, 1914, in the Supreme Court of that state in *Cincinnati Ex. Co.* v. *Johnson.*

Mr. Justice Baker, delivering the opinion of the court, says: '' In the opinion of the majority of the Court, the provision in the contract by which the club by giving notice, could end and determine all the liabilities undertaken by the Club under the contract, is a fatal objection to the right of the Club to enforce by injunction the performance by Johnson of his negative covenant not to play or perform for any other than the Club.''

In *Cincinnati Ex. Co.* v. *Marsans,* U. S. Dist. Court. Dist. of Mo., an examination of the short bench opinion filed July 1, 1914, by Judge Sanborn, for whose learning this court has great respect, discloses no discussion of the question of the mutuality of the contract, and no citation of authorities in support of the court's conclusions.

The question has also been raised on this motion as to whether the national agreement (so-called), and the rules and regulations adopted pursuant thereto, violate the Sherman Act. The novel argument is presented with much earnestness by the learned counsel for the defendant that the combination formed by the operation of the national agreement and the rules and regulations of the national commission thereunder, with which the defendant is connected through his contract with the plaintiff, is in direct violation of " an act to protect trade and commerce against unlawful restraints and monopolies," in force July 2, 1890, and popularly known as " The Sherman Anti-Trust Law." It is apparent from the analysis already set forth of the agreement and rules forming the combination of the baseball business, referred to as " organized baseball," that a monopoly of baseball as a business has been ingeniously devised and created in so far as a monopoly can be created among free men; but I cannot agree to the proposition that the business of baseball for profit is interstate trade or commerce, and therefore subject to the provisions of the Sherman Act. An examination of the cases cited by the defendant confirms rather than changes my conclusion.

Commerce is defined by the Century Dictionary as an " interchange of goods; merchandise or property of any kind; trade; traffic; used more especially of trade on a large scale carried on by transportation of merchandise between different countries, or between different parts of the same country, distinguished as foreign commerce and internal commerce."

The defendant urges that under the national agreement baseball players are bought and sold and dealt in among the several states, and are thus reduced and commercialized into commodities. A commodity is defined as " that which is useful; anything that is useful or serviceable; particularly an article of merchandise; anything movable that is a subject of trade or of acquisition.'' We are not dealing with the bodies of the players as commodities or articles of merchandise, but with their services as retained or transferred by contract. The foundation of the national agreement is the game of baseball conducted as a profitable business and if this game were a commodity or an article of merchandise and transported from state to state, then, the argument of the defendant's counsel might be applicable. Judge Grosscup in *United States* v. *Swift & Co.*, 122 Fed. Repr. 531, said: '' Commerce, briefly stated, is the sale or exchange of commodities. But that which the law looks upon as the body of commerce is not restricted to specific act of sale or exchange. It includes the intercourse — all the initiatory and intervening acts, instrumentalities and dealings — that directly bring about the sale or exchange.''

In *United States* v. *Knight Co.*, 156 U. S. 13, it is said: '' Contracts to buy, sell or exchange goods transported among the several States, the transportation and its instrumentalities, and articles bought, sold, or exchanged for the purposes of such transit among the States, or put in the way of transit, may be regulated, but this is because they form part of interstate trade or commerce.'' Baseball is an amusement, a sport, a game that comes clearly within the civil and criminal law of the state, and it is not a commodity or an article of merchandise subject to the regulation of congress on the theory that it is interstate commerce.

Another question to be determined upon this motion is whether so-called '' organized baseball,'' operating under the provisions of the national agreement and the rules and contracts subsidiary thereto, is an illegal combination or monopoly in contravention of the common law. The affidavits read on the hearing of this motion show that a combination of forty leagues, major and minor, has been formed under the terms of the national agreement controlling for profit the services of 10,000 players of professional baseball, practically all of the good or skillful players in the country. The analysis of the national agreement and the rules of the commission, controlling the services of these skilled laborers, and providing for their purchase, sale, exchange, draft, reduction, discharge and blacklisting would seem to establish a species of *quasi* peonage unlawfully controlling and interfering with the personal freedom of the men employed. It appears that there is only one league of any importance operating independently of the national commission and that is the newly organized Federal League which comprises eight clubs in eight cities. '' Organized baseball '' is now as complete a monopoly of the baseball business for profit as any monopoly can be made. It is in contravention of the common law in that it invades the right to labor as a property right; in that it invades the right to contract as a property right; and in that it is a combination to restrain and control the exercise of a profession or calling.

'' The right to labor is a property right, entitled to the same protection as capital, and it is said that labor is the poor man's capital.'' 3 Elliott Cont. 13, p. 863, § 2698. '' The right of a workman to freely use his hands and to use them for just whom he pleases, is his property, and so in no less degree is a man's business in which he has invested his capital. The right of each — employer and employee — is an absolute one, inherent and indefeasible, of which neither can be deprived, not even by the legislature itself. The protection of it, though as old as the common law, has been re-guaranteed in our bill of rights. 'All men are born equally free and independent, and have certain inherent and indefeasible rights, among which are those of enjoying and defending life and liberty, of acquiring, possessing and protecting property and reputation, and of pursuing their own happiness.' (Const. Art. 1, Sec. 1). ' The principle upon which the cases, English and American, proceed, is, that every man has the right to employ his talents, industry and capital as he pleases, free from the dictation of others; and if two or more persons combine to coerce his choice in this behalf, it is a criminal conspiracy. The labor and skill of the workman, be it of high or low degree, the plant of the manufacturer, the equipment of the farmer, the investments of commerce are all, in equal sense, property.' '' *Purvis* v. *United Brotherhood of Carpenters & Joiners,* 214 Pa. St. 348 (1906); *State* v. *Cadigan,* 73 Vt. 245, 251; *Erdman* v. *Mitchell,* 207 Pa. 79.

In Clark on Employment of Labor (1911) the author on page 5 says: '' Every man has the right to earn his living, or to pursue his trade or business, without undue interference, a right of absolute freedom to employ or to be employed, to make contracts with reference to service, whether as employer or employee, or to refrain from making them, for any reason or no reason, and such a right is both a liberty and property right, within the guarantees of the federal Constitution.'' Citing *Jersey City Printing Co.* v. *Cassidy,* 63 N. J. Eq. 759; *Adair* v. *United States,* 208 U. S. 161; *N. Y. C. & St. L. R. Co.* v. *Schoffer,* 65 Ohio St. 414; *State* v. *Missouri Tie & Timber Co.,* 181 Mo 536; *Jones* v. *Leslie* (Wash.), 112 Pac. Rep. 81.

Again the same author, on pages 315–316, says: '' The right to choose one's calling is an essential part of the liberty which it is the object of the government to protect; and a calling when chosen is one's property and right. The occupation by means of which a man earns a livelihood and supports those dependent upon him is property within the meaning of the law, and entitled to protection as such." Citing *Slaughter House Cases,* 16 Wall (83 U. S.), 36; *Gray* v. *Building Trades Council,* 91 Minn. 171; *Beck* v. *Railway Teamsters' Prot. Union,* 118 Mich. 497.

In Black on Constitutional Law (3d ed.), page 574, section 217, the author says: " Everything which the law recognizes as property is within the protection of the Constitution. Thus the liberty of making contracts is property or at least a property right, and labor is property."

" The relation of master and servant is purely voluntary, resting upon the contract of the parties, and as a general proposition it must ever remain voluntary. The relation ordinarily cannot rest upon compulsion. Every man has a natural right to hire his services to any one he pleases, or refrain from such hiring; and so, likewise, it is the right of everyone to determine whose services he will hire. ' It is a part of every man's civil rights,' says Mr. Cooley, ' that he be left at liberty to refuse business relations with any person whomsoever, whether the refusal rest upon reason, or as the result of whim, caprice, prejudice or malice. With his reasons neither the public nor third person have any legal concern." 2 Tied. State & Fed. Control of Persons & Property (1900) pp. 938, 939, § 204. See also *Gillespie* v. *People,* 188 Ill. 176 (1900); *State* v. *Julow,* 129 Mo. 163.

Under the heading of " Combinations of Capital for (a) unlawful purposes, and for (b) oppressive purposes," Eddy on Combinations (§ 559) says: " The right to employ his labor and capital as he pleases for any lawful purpose is an essential part of the personal liberty guaranteed each man by free institutions. A combination of two or more persons to interfere with this freedom, and by oppression, coercion or intimidation to restrict this right, is a conspiracy. It is a criminal conspiracy if any of the means used or objects in view are of a criminal character; if no criminal element enters into the means or the objects, then it is a civil conspiracy.'' So also *Gleason* v. *Thaw,* 185 Fed. Repr. 345; *Butchers' Union Co.* v. *Crescent City Co.,* 111 U. S. 746; *Hitchman Coal & Coke Co.* v. *Mitchell,* 202 Fed. Repr. 512, 528, 546–547, 551; *Goldfield Consol. Mines Co.* v. *Goldfield Miners' Union No. 220,* 159 id. 500; *State* v. *Stewart,* 59 Vt. 273 (1887).

In *Metropolitan Exhibition Co.* v. *Ewing,* 42 Fed. Repr. 198, 24 Abb. N. C. 419, the national agreement here under consideration was in the earlier years of its operation considered and condemned. The court (Wallace, J.) said: '' Inasmuch as the parties to the national agreement comprise all, or substantially all, of the clubs in the country which employ professional players, this national agreement, by indirection, but practically, affects every professional player, and subordinates his privilege of engaging as he chooses, to the option of the club by which he is under reservation. * * * As a coercive condition which places the player practically, or at least measurably, in a situation where he must contract with the club that has reserved him, or face the probabilities of losing any engagement for the ensuing season, it is operative and valuable to the club. * * * The players were not in a position to act independently and if they refused to consent to the terms proposed by the clubs, they would have done so at the peril of losing any engagement.''

If a baseball player like the defendant, who has made baseball playing his profession and means of earning a livelihood, desires to be employed at the work for which he is qualified and is entitled to earn his best compensation, he must submit to dominion over his personal freedom and the control of his services by sale, transfer or exchange, without his consent, or abandon his vocation and seek employment at some other kind of labor.  While the services of these base-ball players are ostensibly secured by voluntary con-tracts a study of the system as hereinabove set forth, and as practiced under the plan of the national agree-ment, reveals the involuntary character of the servi-tude which is imposed upon players by the strength of the combination controlling the labor of practically all of the players in the country.  This is so great as to make it necessary for the player either to take the contract prescribed by the commission or abandon baseball as a profession and seek some other mode of earning a livelihood.  There is no difference in principle between the system of servitude built up by the operation of this national agreement, which, as has been shown, provides for the purchase, sale, barter and exchange of the services of baseball players— skilled laborers — without their consent, and the system of peonage brought into the United States from Mexico and thereafter existing for a time within the territory of New Mexico.  The *quasi* peonage of baseball players under the operations of this plan and agreement is contrary to the spirit of American insti-tutions, and is contrary to the spirit of the Constitu-tion of the United States.  It is time to heed the warn-ing of that great jurist, the former chief judge of the Court of Appeals, Judge Cullen, who thought it ad-visable to take for the subject of his annual address

30

Supreme Court, July, 1914. [Vol. 86.

at the last meeting of the New York State Bar Association " The decline of personal liberty in America," as evidenced by recent legislation and judicial decisions. The sanction by the courts of the system here outlined would indeed be further evidence of the " The Decline of Personal Liberty."

The system created by " organized baseball " in recent years presents the question of the establishment of a scheme by which the personal freedom, the right to contract for their labor wherever they will, of 10,000 skilled laborers, is placed under the dominion of a benevolent despotism through the operation of the monopoly established by the national agreement. This case does not present the simple question of a laborer who has entered into a fair contract for his personal services.

While the question of the dissolution of this combination on the ground of its illegality is not before this court for decision, it has nevertheless been thought necessary for the purpose of ascertaining whether or not this plaintiff comes into a court of equity with clean hands to inquire into the organization and operations of the combination to which the plaintiff is a party. A court of equity insisting that " he who comes into equity must come with clean hands " will not lend its aid to promote an unconscionable transaction of the character which the plaintiff is endeavoring to maintain and strengthen by its application for this injunction. The court will not assist in enforcing an agreement which is a part of a general plan having for its object the maintenance of a monopoly, interference with the personal liberty of a citizen and the control of his free right to labor wherever and for whom he pleases; and will not extend its aid to further the purposes and practices of an unlawful combination, by restraining the defendant from working for any one but the plaintiff. The motion to vacate the preliminary injunction, *pendente lite,* is, therefore, granted, with $10 costs to the defendant.

Motion granted, with costs.

## Philadelphia Ball Club, Limited, Appellant, *v.* Lajoie.

*Richard C. Dale,* with him *William J. Turner,* for appellee.—
The decree should be affirmed because the contract between
the appellant and the appellee Napoleon Lajoie, which is the
foundation of this suit, is so lacking in mutuality as not to be
enforceable by injunction: Wilson v. Clarke, 1 W. & S. 554;
Martinsburg Bank v. Central Pa. Telephone, etc., Co., 150 Pa.
26; Crane v. Crane, 105 Fed. Repr. 869; Bickford v. Davis,
11 Fed. Repr. 549; Harrisburg Base Ball Club v. Athletic
Assn., 8 Pa. C. C. Rep. 337; Philadelphia Base Ball Club v.
Hallman, 20 Phila. 276; Metropolitan Exhibition Co. v. Ward,
9 N. Y. Supp. 779; Rust v. Conrad, 47 Mich. 449; Patton v. Develin, 2 Phila. 103; Dornan's Est., 2 W. N. C.
522; Philips v. Mining & Mfg. Company, 7 Phila. 619; Bodine v. Glading, 21 Pa. 50; Meason v. Kaine, 63 Pa. 335; Harrisburg Base Ball Club v. Athletic Assn., 8 Pa. C. C. Rep.
337.

The decree should be affirmed because the services of a baseball player are not unique, extraordinary, or of such a personal
or intellectual character that their loss could not be substantially supplied by the similar services of some other baseball
player: Lumley v. Wagner, 1 DeG. M. & G. 603; McCaull v.
Braham, 16 Fed. Repr. 37; Daly v. Smith, 49 Howard's Pr. 150;
Ford v. Jermon, 6 Phila. 6.

The decree of the lower court should be affirmed because
even if the services of a baseball player might, under certain
circumstances, be so unique, personal and extraordinary as to
admit of the remedy by injunction, yet it does not appear that
the place of the appellee Lajoie in this case cannot be, at least
substantially, supplied by other baseball players, or that the
appellant has suffered any irreparable injury: American Assn.
Base Ball Club v. Pickett, 20 Phila. 298; Philadelphia Base
Ball Club v. Hallman, 20 Phila. 276; Metropolitan Exhibition
Co. v. Ward, 9 N. Y. Supp. 779; Metropolitan Exhibition
Company v. Ewing, 42 Fed. Repr. 198; Carter v. Ferguson,

12 N. Y. Supp. 580 ; Rogers Mfg. Co. v. Rogers, 58 Conn. 356 ; 20 Atl. Repr. 467 ; Jaccard Jewelry Co. v. O'Brien, 70 Mo. App. 432 ; Burney v. Ryle & Co., 91 Ga. 701 ; 17 S. E. Repr. 986.

The appellant's bill as a whole discloses no cause for equitable interference, because the injunction prayed for, if granted, would simply work a hardship to the appellees, without any particular benefit to the appellant : Oil Creek R. R. Co. v. Atlantic, etc., R. R. Co., 57 Pa. 72.

The decree in this case should be affirmed because the subject-matter of the controversy between the parties is passed and ended, and could not be affected by a reversal of the decree of the court below : Harper v. Roberts, 22 Pa. 194 ; Singer Mfg. Co. v. Wright, 141 U. S. 696 ; 12 Sup. Ct. Repr. 103.

The decree of the lower court should be affirmed because the fifth paragraph of the contract between appellant and appellee Lajoie does not preclude the said appellee from setting up or the court from considering the defense of nonmutuality, or any other of the above-stated defenses to this proceeding : Pope Mfg. Co. v. Gormully, 144 U. S. 224 ; 12 Sup. Ct. Repr. 632.

Opinion by Mr. Justice Potter, April 21, 1902:

The defendant in this case contracted to serve the plaintiff as a baseball player for a stipulated time. During that period he was not to play for any other club. He violated his agreement, however, during the term of his engagement, and in disregard of his contract, arranged to play for another and a rival organization.

The plaintiff by means of this bill, sought to restrain him, during the period covered by the contract.

The court below refused an injunction, holding that to warrant the interference prayed for, " The defendant's services must be unique, extraordinary, and of such a character as to render it impossible to replace him ; so that his breach of contract would result in irreparable loss to the plaintiff." In the view of the court, the defendant's qualifications did not measure up to this high standard. The trial court was also of opinion that the contract was lacking in mutuality ; for the reason that it gave plaintiff an option to discharge defendant on ten days' notice, without a reciprocal right on the part of defendant.

The learned judge who filed the opinion in the court below, with great industry and painstaking care, collected and reviewed the English and American decisions bearing upon the question involved, and makes apparent the wide divergence of opinion which has prevailed.

We think, however, that in refusing relief unless the defendant's services were shown to be of such a character as to render it impossible to replace him, he has taken extreme ground.

It seems to us that a more just and equitable rule is laid down in Pomeroy on Specific Performance, page 31, where the principle is thus declared : " Where one person agrees to render personal services to another, which require and presuppose a special knowledge, skill and ability in the employee, so that in case of a default the same service could not easily be obtained from others, although the affirmative specific performance of the contract is beyond the power of the court, its performance will be negatively enforced by enjoining its breach. . . . The damages for breach of such contract cannot be estimated with any certainty, and the employer cannot, by means of any damages, purchase the same service in the labor market."

We have not found any case going to the length of requiring as a condition of relief, proof of the impossibility of obtaining equivalent service. It is true that the injury must be irreparable, but as observed by Mr. Justice LOWRIE, in Commonwealth v. Pittsburg, etc., Railroad Company, 24 Pa. 160, " The argument that there is no 'irreparable damage' would not be so often used by wrongdoers if they would take the trouble to discover that the word 'irreparable' is a very unhappily chosen one, used in expressing the rule that an injunction may issue to prevent wrongs of a repeated and continuing character, or which occasion damages which are estimated only by conjecture, and not by any accurate standard."

We are therefore within the term whenever it is shown that no certain pecuniary standard exists for the measurement of the damages. This principle is applied in Vail v. Osburn, 174 Pa. 580. That case is authority for the proposition that a court of equity will act where nothing can answer the justice of the case but the performance of the contract in specie ; and this even where the subject of the contract is what under ordinary circumstances would be only an article of merchandise. In such a case, when owing to special features, the contract involves peculiar convenience or advantage, or where the loss would be a matter of uncertainty, then the breach may be deemed to cause irreparable injury.

The court below finds from the testimony that "the defendant is an expert baseball player in any position; that he has a great reputation as a second baseman; that his place would be hard to fill with as good a player; that his withdrawal from the team would weaken it, as would the withdrawal of any good player, and would probably make a difference in the size of the audiences attending the game."

We think that in thus stating it, he puts it very mildly, and that the evidence would warrant a stronger finding as to the ability of the defendant as an expert ball player. He has been for several years in the service of the plaintiff club, and has been re-engaged from season to season at a constantly increasing salary. He has become thoroughly familiar with the action and methods of the other players in the club, and his own work is peculiarly meritorious as an integral part of the team work which is so essential. In addition to these features which render his services of peculiar and special value to the plaintiff, and not easily replaced, Lajoie is well known, and has great reputation among the patrons of the sport, for ability in the position which he filled, and was thus a most attractive drawing card for the public. He may not be the sun in the baseball firmament, but he is certainly a bright, particular star.

We feel therefore that the evidence in this case justifies the conclusion that the services of the defendant are of such a unique character, and display such a special knowledge, skill and ability as renders them of peculiar value to the plaintiff, and so difficult of substitution, that their loss will produce irreparable injury, in the legal significance of that term, to the plaintiff. The action of the defendant in violating his contract is a breach of good faith, for which there would be no adequate redress at law, and the case therefore properly calls for the aid of equity, in negatively enforcing the performance of the contract, by enjoining against its breach.

But the court below was also of the opinion that the contract was lacking in mutuality of remedy, and considered that as a controlling reason for the refusal of an injunction. The opinion quotes the nineteenth paragraph of the contract, which gives to the plaintiff a right of renewal for the period of six months beginning April 15, 1901, and for a similar period in two successive years thereafter. The seventeenth paragraph also provides for the termination of the contract upon ten days' notice by the plaintiff. But the eighteenth paragraph is also of importance, and should not be overlooked. It provides as follows: "18. In consideration of the faithful performance of the conditions, covenants, undertakings and promises herein by the said party of the second part, inclusive of the concession of the options of release and renewals prescribed in the seventeenth and nineteenth paragraphs, the said party of the first part, for itself and its assigns, hereby agrees to pay to him for his services for said term the sum of $2,400, payable as follows," etc.

And turning to the fifth paragraph, we find that it provides expressly for proceedings, either in law or equity, " to enforce the specific performance by the said party of the second part, or to enjoin said party of the second part from performing services for any other person or organization during the period of service herein contracted for. And nothing herein contained shall be construed to prevent such remedy in the courts in case of any breach of this agreement by said party of the second part, as said party of the first part, or its assigns, may elect to invoke."

We have then at the outset, the fact that the paragraphs now criticised and relied upon in defense, were deliberately accepted by the defendant, and that such acceptance was made part of the inducement for the plaintiff to enter into the contract. We have the further fact that the contract has been partially executed by services rendered, and payment made therefor; so that the situation is not now the same as when the contract was wholly executory. The relation between the parties has been so far changed, as to give to the plaintiff an equity arising out of the part performance, to insist upon the completion of the agreement according to its terms by the defendant. This equity may be distinguished from the original right under the contract itself, and it might well be questioned whether the court would not be justified in giving effect to it by injunction, without regard to the mutuality or nonmutuality in the original contract. The plaintiff has so far performed its part of the contract in entire good faith, in every detail; and it would, therefore, be inequitable to permit the defendant to withdraw from the agreement at this late day.

The term mutuality, or lack of mutuality, does not always convey a clear and definite meaning. As was said in Grove v. Hodges, 55 Pa. 516, " The legal principle that contracts must be mutual, does not mean that in every case each party must have the same remedy for a breach by the other."

In the contract now before us, the defendant agreed to furnish his skilled professional services to the plaintiff for a period which might be extended over three years by proper notice given before the close of each current year. Upon the other hand, the plaintiff retained the right to terminate the contract upon ten days' notice, and the payment of salary for that time, and the expenses of defendant in getting to his home. But the fact of this concession to the plaintiff is distinctly pointed out as part of the consideration for the large salary paid to the defendant, and is emphasized as such. And owing to the peculiar nature of the services demanded by the business, and the high degree of efficiency which must be maintained, the stipulation is not unreasonable. Particularly is this true when it is remembered that the plaintiff has played for years under substantially the same regulations.

We are not persuaded that the terms of this contract manifest any lack of mutuality in remedy. Each party has the possibility of enforcing all the rights stipulated for in the agreement. It is true that the terms make it possible for the plaintiff to put an end to the contract in a space of time much less than the period during which the defendant has agreed to supply his personal services; but mere difference in the rights stipulated for, does not destroy mutuality of remedy. Freedom of contract covers a wide range of obligation and duty as between the parties, and it may not be impaired, so long as the bounds of reasonableness and fairness are not transgressed.

If the doctrine laid down in Rust v. Conrad, 47 Mich. 449, quoted in the opinion, is to prevail, it would seem that the power of the plaintiff to terminate the contract upon short notice, destroys the mutuality of the remedy. But we are not satisfied with the reasoning intended to support that conclusion. We cannot agree that mutuality of remedy requires that each party should have precisely the same remedy, either in form, effect or extent. In a fair and reasonable contract, it ought to be sufficient that each party has the possibility of compelling the performance of the promises which were mutually agreed upon.

It is true also that the case of Rutland Marble Co. v. Ripley, 10 Wall. 339, also quoted in the opinion, while not turning exclusively upon that point, seems to hold that a contract in which the plaintiff has an option to terminate it in a year, cannot be enforced in equity on account of lack of mutuality; but in Singer Sewing Machine Co. v. Union Buttonhole, etc., Co., Holmes' Reports, 253, Judge LOWELL says, with reference to that case: " I cannot think that the court intended to announce any general proposition that they would never enforce a contract which one party had a right to put an end to in a year. Everything must depend upon the nature and circumstances of the business."

This judgment seems to be borne out, for in a later case, that of Franklin Telegraph Co. v. Harrison, 145 U. S. 459; 12 Sup. Ct. Repr. 900, where the plaintiff had a right to terminate the contract for telegraphic service at the end of any year, while the defendant's obligation continued as long as the plaintiff chose to pay the yearly price for the services, the doctrine that such conditions constituted lack of mutuality does not seem to have been recognized.

In Singer Co. v. Union Co., supra, which was a case where an injunction was allowed against the defendant, although the plaintiff had the right to terminate the contract, Judge LOWELL in the course of a strongly reasoned opinion says, page 260, " In many of the cases that I have cited, the plaintiff had it in his power to end the contract. It is certainly competent to the parties to make a contract which will be equitable and reasonable, and in which their rights ought to be protected while they last, though it may be terminable by various circumstances, and though one party may have the sole right to terminate it, provided their stipulation is not one that makes the whole contract inequitable."

On page 258, he says: "I think the fair result of the later cases may be thus expressed. If the case is one in which a negative remedy of injunction will do substantial justice between the parties, by obliging the defendant either to carry out his contract or lose all benefit of the breach, and the remedy at law is inadequate, and there is no reason of policy against it, the court will interfere to restrain conduct which is contrary to the contract, although it may be unable to enforce a specific performance of it."

The case now before us comes easily within the rule as above stated. The defendant sold to the plaintiff for a valuable consideration the exclusive right to his professional services for a stipulated period, unless sooner surrendered by the plaintiff; which could only be, after due and reasonable notice and payment of salary and expenses until the expiration. Why should not a court of equity protect such an agreement until it is terminated? The court cannot compel the defendant to play for the plaintiff, but it can restrain him from playing for another club in violation of his agreement. No reason is given why this should not be done, except that presented by the argument that the right given to the plaintiff to terminate the contract upon ten days' notice destroys the mutuality of the remedy. But to this it may be answered, that as already stated, the defendant has the possibility of enforcing all the rights for which he stipulated in the agreement, which is all that he can reasonably ask; furthermore, owing to the peculiar nature and circumstances of the business, the reservation upon the part of the plaintiff to terminate upon short notice, does not make the whole contract inequitable.

In this connection another observation may be made, which is that the plaintiff by the act of bringing this suit, has disavowed any intention of exercising the right to terminate the contract on its own part. This is a necessary inference from its action in asking the court to exercise its equity power to enforce the agreement made by the defendant not to give his services to any other club. Besides, the remedy by injunction is elastic and adaptable, and is wholly within the control of the court. If granted now, it can be easily dissolved whenever a change in the circumstances or in the attitude of the plaintiff should seem to require it. The granting or refusal of an injunction or its continuance is never a matter of strict right, but is always a question of discretion to be determined by the court in view of the particular circumstances.

Upon a careful consideration of the whole case, we are of opinion that the provisions of the contract are reasonable, and that the consideration is fully adequate. The evidence shows no indications of any attempt at overreaching or unfairness. Substantial justice between the parties requires that the court should restrain the defendant from playing for any other club during the term of his contract with the plaintiff.

The bill as filed contemplated only the services of defendant for the season of 1901, but it is stated in the argument of counsel, that since the hearing in the court below, and prior to the argument in this court, the plaintiff by due notice renewed the current contract for the season of 1902.

The specifications of error are sustained, and the decree of the court below is reversed, and the bill is reinstated. And it is ordered that the record be remitted to the court below for further proceedings in accordance with this opinion.

---

## METROPOLITAN EXHIBITION COMPANY *v.* WARD.

*N. Y. Supreme Court, First District, Chambers; January,* 1890.

O'BRIEN, J.—This is a suit brought in equity to restrain the defendant from playing the game of base ball or rendering services of any kind until October 31st, 1890, for or in behalf of any person or corporation except the plaintiff. It is sought by this motion to enjoin the defendant until the trial can be had.

The plaintiff bases its right to the relief sought upon an agreement between the New York Base Ball Club and the defendant, dated April 23d, 1889. This agreement provided that the defendant was to engage in the exhibition of the game of base ball for the said club for the period of seven months between April 1st, 1889, and October 31st, 1889. It also contained a provision which will be hereafter more fully set forth and discussed, by which it gave to the plaintiff the right "to reserve the defendant for the season of 1890."

One of the principal questions discussed upon the argument was as to the meaning of this word " reserve," as used in the contract.

Upon the part of the plaintiff it is claimed that the meaning of this word is clear and unambiguous, requiring no explanation, being used in its ordinary sense of—" to hold, to keep for future use." The defendant, on the other hand, claims that this word, which was not a new one to the parties, has a history, and with that history both parties to the contract were well acquainted—that it had always been used in a particular sense, and in order to ascertain that meaning reference must be had to the history of the word.

That if resort is had to such history it will result in a construction to be given to the contract which shall determine that when the defendant accorded the right to reserve his services, that it was not thereby meant that he was absolutely pledged, or bound to plaintiff, but that his services were reserved to the exclusion of any other member of the league of ball clubs. In other words the word " reserve," defendant contends, referred only to the right and practice of reservation previously exercised under the national agreement, and did not prohibit a player from contracting with or playing for any club outside the purview of the national agreement.

It is not necessary to go over the history of the word or mention the agreements subsequent to the one entered into at the meeting of the National League of Base Ball Clubs in September, 1879, when this word "reserve" appears to have been first used in a contract, since it is sufficient to say that whether we have regard to the history of the word as used in the various contracts, or give it its ordinary and well accepted meaning, we shall arrive at the same conclusion as to the meaning of the word adverse to defendant's contention, and in favor of the meaning given to it by the plaintiff. It means exactly what the defendant himself said it meant, when in the supplementary contract of 1889, he employed the word " held " as synonymous with the word " reserve," as used in the original contract. Therefore, it will be seen that I have adopted as the meaning of the word " reserve," the one contended for by plaintiff.

Nor do I agree with the defendant's statement of law, wherein he asserts that the general rule is that an injunction will not be granted in aid of a contract for personal services. Whatever doubt may have existed in the past, it is now the settled law of England and America, that where a person has entered into a definite contract to render services to another of such a nature as not to be easily replaced, and the loss of his services to the employer will be a loss not to be compensated for in damages, a breach or a threatened breach of such contract may be restrained by injunction.

While a distinction is observed between affirmative and negative covenants in such an agreement, and while the court does not possess the power to compel a person to render services which he has agreed to perform, yet when he has stipu-

Metropolitan Exhibition Co. *v.* Ward.

lated not to work for another the court can and will in a proper case prevent his doing so. In England, since the decision in 1852 of the case of Lumley *v.* Wagner (1 *De Gex*), such has been the law. In this country endless citations of authorities might be resorted to to show that a similar principle of law prevails. In this State one of the leading cases is that of Daly *v.* Smith (38 *Super. Ct.* 158 ; 49 *How. Pr.* 150). In that case one Fanny Morant Smith had agreed to act during the season of 1874, 1875 and 1876. She broke this contract. A preliminary injunction was granted. A motion was made to continue it pendente lite. The learned justice, in delivering the opinion in that case, after an exhaustive examination of authorities which were ably collated and reviewed in his opinion, says :

" The question whether or not a court of equity will interfere by injunction to prevent a breach of a contract for personal services, or whether the complainant must look to his damages at law as his sole redress, has been frequently and on several occasions quite elaborately discussed, both in England and in this country. On a cursory reading, the authorities may seem somewhat conflicting, but a careful perusal of them in the light of the facts before the court on the several occasions, can leave no doubt as to the existence of the power."

In another part of his opinion he says :

" I am of the opinion that actors and actresses, like all other persons, should be held to a true and faithful performance of their engagements, and that whenever a court has not proper jurisdiction to enforce the whole engagement, it should, like in all cases, operate to bind their consciences, at least as far as they can be bound, to a true and faithful performance of their engagements."

Quoting from another case, he continues : " The resort to actions at law for damages for a sudden desertion of the performers in the middle of their season, will in most cases fail to afford adequate compensation ; and it is not only that the manager is deprived of his means of carrying on business, but that his performers, by carrying their services to other establishments, deprive him of the fruits of his diligence and enterprise, increase rivalry against him and cause him irreparable injury."

Between an actor of great histrionic ability and a professional base ball player, of peculiar fitness and skill to fill a particular position, no substantial distinction in applying the rule laid down in the cases cited, can be made. Each is sought for his particular and peculiar fitness ; each performs in public for compensation, and each possesses for the manager a means of attracting an audience. The refusal of either to perform according to contract must result in loss to the manager, which is increased in cases where such services are rendered to a rival.

While, therefore, in a proper case, the defendant is amenable to this rule of law, and the court has the power and right to prevent his breaking any covenant made not to give his services to another, it remains to be seen whether upon the facts and proofs as they exist here a case is presented for the intervention and exercise of the court's power during the pendency of the action, and before the rights of the parties are determined by the more deliberate proceeding of a trial.

To quote from the opinion in Murray *v.* Knapp (42 *How. Pr.* 462): "A plaintiff on an *ex parte* application at the beginning of the action has too often obtained a remedy which he should not have until the hearing of both parties on the trial, and which he might then have been found not to be entitled to."

" In many cases of this kind the plaintiff practically has obtained his judgment at the outset, and a continuance of the action has been only a struggle by the defendant to relieve himself from an *ex parte* decision." In the case of Mapleson *v.* Del Puente (13 *Abb. N. C.* 144), which was brought by plaintiff, who was a manager of an operatic company, to restrain defendant, who was an operatic singer, the judge, in denying the application, says: "The granting of an injunction pendente lite is always in the discretion of the court, and should be ordered with caution and even with some reluctance, and only where the rights of the plaintiff on the law and the facts are clear, and the necessity for that form of equitable relief is manifest in order to prevent a failure of justice."

It will thus be seen that a court of equity is extremely loth in cases of this kind to not only practically decide and give judgment, but also to execute it, by enjoining the defendant before any trial upon the merits has been had. A preliminary injunction will not be granted except in cases where there is the strongest probability that the court will ultimately decide that plaintiff is entitled to the relief which it demands in its complaint (Hamilton v. Accessory Transit Co., 3 *Abb. Pr.* 255).

These cases and many more that might be cited, hold that the granting of this extraordinary relief by way of preliminary injunction rests in the sound discretion of the court, and should not be granted except upon proof of facts and circumstances showing that a contract exists which is reasonably definite and certain, and that for a breach thereof no adequate remedy exists at law, and the probability of plaintiff's finally succeeding in the action is free from all reasonable doubt.

It is insisted here, however, by the plaintiff, that there exists a definite and reasonable contract, and that the probability of its succeeding finally is of the strongest and most certain kind.

In examining into the claims thus made by plaintiff and into the facts of this case, we must keep constantly in mind the distinction which exists between an action at law and suit in equity. As before said this is a suit in equity wherein the court has no power to enforce the affirmative covenant claimed to exist, which would compel the defendant to play ball with plaintiff; but the court is asked in effect to decree the specific performance of a negative covenant claimed to have been made by the defendant that he should not play ball with others.

Metropolitan Exhibition Co. *v.* Ward.

To determine whether or not the probability of its success in a final suit is of the strongest and most certain kind, certain questions must be determined.

Is there such a definite contract existing between the parties that it can be enforced?

If sufficiently definite, is it entirely conscionable, wanting neither in fairness or mutuality? That a court of equity will not make a contract which the parties themselves have not made, and that it will not enforce an indefinite one, are elementary propositions that need no citation of authorities to support them. In the contract sued on, wherein defendant agrees to give his services for the ball season terminating October, 1889, we find the provision upon which it is admitted all plaintiff's right to succeed in this action depends. It reads as follows: " Eighteenth. It is further understood and agreed that the said party of the first part shall have the right 'to reserve' said party of the second part for the next season ensuing, the term mentioned in paragraph 2 herein provided; and said right or privilege is hereby accorded the said party of the first part upon the following conditions, which are to be taken and construed as conditions precedent to the exercise of such extraordinary right or privilege, namely: First, That the said party of the second part shall not be reserved at a salary less than that mentioned in the 20th paragraph herein, except by consent of the party of the second part.

" Second, That the said party of the second part, if he be reserved by the said party of the first part for the next ensuing season, shall be one of not more than fourteen players then under contract."

The only other provision bearing on this subject is that contained in the supplementary agreement dated April 23, 1889, which reads as follows: " The New York Base Ball Club agrees that John M. Ward, who this day signs a contract to play with it for the season of 1889, shall not be held by the New York Club for the season of 1890, at a salary of

Metropolitan Exhibition Co. *v.* Ward.

less than $3,000. This supplemental contract is hereby made a part of the main contract."

These provisions of the main and supplemental contract quoted, are all and the only ones relied upon by plaintiff to enforce which this action is brought.

Do these provisions constitute a definite contract between the parties, or do they do more than reserve the services of defendant, subject to the making of a contract thereafter with definite terms and conditions?

It must be noticed that these provisions standing alone fail to disclose what are to be the terms and conditions of the agreement between the parties in the event that plaintiff shall exercise its option, which is accorded, to reserve defendant for the ball season of 1890.

What are the terms and conditions of the alleged agreement for the season of 1890 now sought to be enforced?

What does the defendant Ward agree to do?

What salary is to be paid him?

Not only are there no terms and conditions fixed, but I do not think it is entirely clear that Ward agrees to do anything further than to accord the right to reserve him upon terms thereafter to be fixed. He does not covenant to make a contract for 1890 at the same salary, nor upon the same terms and conditions as during the season of 1889.

The provision relied upon as constituting the contract between the parties merely reserves Ward for 1890, at a salary of not less than $3,000. But how much more is he to receive?

And in case of a dispute between the parties, how is the amount of salary to be determined? It is nowhere provided that the terms and conditions for 1890 are to be the same as those for 1889. As stated in *Fry on Specific Performance* (p. 165, § 229): "It will be obvious that an amount of certainty must be required in the specific performance of a contract in equity greater than that demanded in an action for damages at law. For to sustain the latter proceeding the proposition required is the negative one that defendant has not performed the contract, a conclusion which may be often arrived at without any exact consideration of the terms of the contract; whilst in equity it must appear not only that the contract has not been performed, but what is the contract which is to be performed?

The learned author, in a note to the section quoted, cites a number of cases which hold that where the terms of a contract are indefinite or uncertain, specific performance will not be decreed. But it may be urged that the court should infer that it was the intent of the party that the terms and conditions should be the same. It is extremely doubtful if a court of equity would resort to any such inference or presumption for the purpose of first making a contract for the parties and thereafter enforcing it. But assuming that the court would indulge in such an inference or presumption, what contract would the court require the defendant to perform?

Will it be one under which he is to receive the same salary and containing all the provisions including the reserve clause, *verbatim et literatim*, as in the contract of 1889? And upon the defendant's refusal in 1891, will it under the reserve clause make a similar contract and enforce it for that year, and thereafter from year to year as long as plaintiff elects to hold defendant?

The failure in the existing contract to expressly provide the terms and conditions of the contract to be made for 1890, either renders the latter indefinite and uncertain, or we must infer that the same terms and conditions are to be incorporated in the one to be now enforced, which necessarily includes the reserve clause, for no good reason can be suggested, if all the others are to be included, why this should be omitted. Upon the latter assumption the want of fairness and of mutuality, which are fatal to its enforcement in equity, are apparent, as will be seen when we consider to what extent under such circumstances each of the parties is bound. Every player who signs such a contract is bound for the current playing season and also for the ensuing

Metropolitan Exhibition Co. *v.* Ward.

playing season, and is obliged at the close of the first season to make another contract with the same terms and conditions binding him as before for the then approaching season, and reserving him for the second season, and so on as long as plaintiff elects, the player being always bound one year in advance.

On the other hand, this contract, after having provided, at paragraph 15, that the club might terminate the contract at any time because of a violation of the agreement by the player, it further provides at paragraph 17, that the club may " at any time, by giving the party of the second part ten days' notice of its option and its intention so to do, end and determine all its liabilities and obligations under this contract, in which event, upon the expiration of said ten days, all liabilities and obligations undertaken by said party of the first part to this contract shall at once cease and determine, and said party of the second part shall thereupon be also free from his obligation thereunder, and shall have no claim for wages for any period after said ten days." So that the club may at any time, at the beginning, in the middle or at the end of the playing season, when the player is in New York or San Francisco or anywhere else, and without the assignment of any cause whatever, " determine all its liabilities and obligations under said contract," leaving the player to make his way home as best he can.

In thus considering the obligations which, under the plaintiff's construction of the contract each has assumed, we have the spectacle presented of a contract which binds one party for a series of years and the other party for ten days, and of the party who is itself bound for ten days coming into a court of equity to enforce its claims against the party bound for years.

In leases of property and in similar contracts clauses are frequently inserted giving options which can be enforced, but the distinction between such optional clauses in leases which have been upheld as fair and binding upon the parties to the covenant, and the one here sought to be enforced, is apparent when we remember that in the former instance mentioned upon exercising the option a new and binding agreement is created, while in this case there is no obligation after the option is exercised, except for a period of ten days. There is no obligation on the part of the club to pay the player any salary whatever for the second playing season. True, it is stated that he shall not be reserved at less than a certain salary. But the reserving club may easily dispose of this. It may wait until just before the second playing season opens, and after every chance for a profitable engagement has passed by, then give the player ten days' notice of its election to end and determine all its liabilities and obligations under the contract, and as the playing season has not opened, the club would not even be obliged to pay the ten days' salary.

As stated by *Fry on Specific Performance* (New ed. § 286), "A contract, to be specifically enforced by the court, must be mutual; that is to say, such that it might at the time that it was entered into have been enforced by either of the parties against the other of them. Whenever, therefore, whether from personal incapacity, the nature of the contract, or any other cause, the contract is incapable of being enforced against one party, that party is equally incapable of enforcing it against the other." And, again, " A contract that is sought to be specifically enforced must be mutual both as to the remedy and the obligation. A party not bound by the agreement itself has no right to call upon a court of equity to enforce specific performance against the other contracting party by expressing his willingness in his bill to perform his part of the engagement. His right to the aid of the court does not depend upon his subsequent offer to perform the contract on his part, but upon its original obligatory character."

The application of these principles are well exemplified in the case of Marble Company *v.* Ripley (10 *Wall.* 339). That

Metropolitan Exhibition Co. *v.* Ward.

was a case of a contract in the nature of a partnership, by which the grantee of a marble quarry agreed to furnish all the marble the other party should require. In case of default by the grantee, the other party might enter and take out sufficient marble. The grantor or marble company was bound for all time. The right was reserved to grantee to terminate the contract at any time on one year's notice. The marble company asked for an injunction restraining Ripley (who denied there had been a default in furnishing marble) from entering and cutting out marble, and second for a cancellation of the contract. Ripley on his side asked for the specific performance of the contract. In disposing of Ripley's prayer for specific performance the United States supreme court said, "Another reason why specific performance should not be decreed in this case is found in the want of mutuality. Such performance by Ripley could not be decreed or enforced at the suit of the marble company, for the contract expressly stipulates that he may relinquish the business and abandon the contract at any time, on giving one year's notice. It is a general principle that when from personal incapacity, the nature of a contract, or any other cause, a contract is incapable of being enforced against one party, that party is equally incapable of enforcing it specifically against the other" (see also Gorman *v.* Machin, 6 *Paige, Ch.* 288, and Woodward *v.* Harris, 2 *Barb.* 429).

It will thus be seen that I do not fully concur in the claims made by plaintiff that the probability of finally succeeding is of the strongest and most certain kind. Upon either one or both of the grounds considered, but principally upon the ground that the contract is indefinite and uncertain, does there arise a serious doubt as to plaintiff being accorded upon the trial the relief asked for.

However that may be, what was said by the learned judge in Mapleson *v.* Del Puente (*supra*), in denying a motion for a preliminary injunction, is applicable here : " This action is now at issue on the complaint and answer, and there is no reason why it should not be speedily tried, and the various questions of law and fact which arise in it be deliberately and finally disposed of."

The plaintiff seeks by injunction to restrain the defendant from playing for other clubs during the season of 1890. The playing season of 1890 does not open until the middle of April. Before that time this action can be tried at the Special Term and final judgment rendered. A final judgment before the playing season opens will secure every possible right of plaintiff.

Thus plaintiff may have final judgment, if entitled thereto, at least one month before the act sought to be enjoined can be done.

In denying, therefore, the motion for a preliminary injunction, it is entirely appropriate to quote from the language of the learned judge in Van Vechten *v.* Howland (12 *Abb. N. S.* 461), wherein he says : " There is a distinction between a preliminary and a final injunction. . . . Looking back at settled rules of equity we shall find that while final injunctions are matters of right, preliminary injunctions are matters of discretion. Their object is to prevent such acts during the litigation as would preclude the court from giving the plaintiff his remedy at the end. When the plaintiff shows that he is entitled to a final injunction, it does not necessarily follow that he is entitled to a preliminary injunction. Such an injunction should not be granted or sustained unless without it the court could not by its final judgment do justice between the parties. Where the preliminary injunction restrains the defendant from doing the very acts to restrain which the final judgment is sought, then the plaintiff has practically succeeded without a trial, and at the very beginning of his case."

While, therefore, I think that this is not a case in which a preliminary injunction should be granted, it is proper that the rights of the parties should be determined by a trial before the ball season begins, and to that end, on application made, I shall assist in securing a speedy trial, upon which a final and deliberate judgment upon the rights of the parties can be pronounced.*

---

* The trial of the issues resulted in a dismissal of the complaint, the following memorandum being filed (March 31, 1890).

LAWRENCE J.—As I am informed by counsel for the plaintiff that they do not intend to submit a brief in this case, and as I am of the opinion that the contract referred to in the complaint is one which a court of equity will not enforce, judgment will be granted dismissing the complaint with costs.

METROPOLITAN EXHIBITION CO. *v.* EWING.

*(Circuit Court, S. D. New York.* March 25, 1890.)

CONTRACT—INTERPRETATION—INJUNCTION.

The contract with defendant for his services as a base-ball player gave plaintiff, a base-ball association, the "right to reserve" him for the next season on condition that he should not be reserved at a salary less than for the current season without his consent, and that he should be one of not more than 14 reserved. *Held,* (1) the term "right to reserve" is ambiguous, and does not imply a contract by the player to devote his services exclusively to the association during the ensuing season, without the aid of extrinsic evidence to show that it has a recognized meaning in the nomenclature of the business to which the contract relates; (2) that, in order to ascertain the meaning of such a term, it is competent to do so by reference to other parts of the contract, and to other contracts made by the parties in respect to the same subject-matter on previous occasions; (3) that interpreting the contract by resorting to the proper sources of explanation the term is meant to give a prior and exclusive right in favor of one base-ball association as against other base-ball associations to contract with a player for his services for another season, and the contract is merely an exclusive right to make a contract upon terms to be agreed upon by the parties; (4) that although courts of equity will prevent by injunction the breach of contracts for professional services in some cases in which they will not decree specific performance, they will not undertake to make contracts for parties, or to enforce in any way those as to the terms of which the parties have not arrived at a definite understanding; (5) although preliminary relief will not be granted in a case in which it is doubtful whether the plaintiff will be finally successful, yet, where the questions are such that they can be as fully considered and as safely decided upon a motion for a preliminary injunction as at the final hearing, it is the duty of the court to decide them upon such a motion when such an injunction is essential to the protection of the plaintiff.

In Equity.  On bill for injunction.
*Joseph F. Choate* and *George F. Duysters*, for plaintiff.
*Henry Bacon*, for defendant.

WALLACE, J.  This action is brought to restrain a threatened breach of contract for the performance of personal services which require special aptitude, skill, and experience.  It is a case in which an action at law would not afford the plaintiff an adequate remedy for the breach, and in which the power of the court should be exercised by preventive interposition, if it is found that the contract is such as the plaintiff claims it to be.  The circumstances are such that, unless a preliminary injunction is granted, the plaintiff will obtain no effectual remedy, because, before the cause can be brought to final hearing, the time will have passed within which the relief sought would be practically useful, and, if it be then adjudged that the plaintiff is entitled to a permanent injunction, the judgment will be declaratory merely.  Although preliminary relief is not to be granted in a case in which it is doubtful whether the plaintiff will be finally successful, yet, where the questions are such that they can be fully considered and as safely decided upon a motion for a preliminary injunction as at final hearing, it is the duty of the court to consider and determine them, and not defer the party invoking its assistance to a time when a decree, if awarded, would be too late.

The contract upon which the plaintiff founds its claim for relief is in form between the New York Base-Ball Club as party of the first part, and the defendant as party of the second part; but there is no reason to doubt that the New York Base-Ball Club was the agent of the plaintiff in entering into the contract, that the plaintiff is the real principal, that the contract was intended to inure for the benefit of the plaintiff, and that the plaintiff is entitled to enforce it against the defendant to the extent that the New York Base-Ball Club could do so.  The doctrine is now generally recognized that, while a court of equity will not ordinarily attempt to enforce contracts which cannot be carried out by the machinery of a court, like that involved in the present case, it may nevertheless practically accomplish the same end by enjoining the breach of a negative promise, and this power will be exercised whenever the contract is one of which the court would direct specific performance, if it could practically compel its observance by the party refusing to perform through a decree for specific performance.  It is indispensable, where the contract does not relate to realty, that it be one for the breach of which damages would not afford an adequate compensation to the plaintiff.  It must be one in which the plaintiff comes into court with clean hands, and which is not so oppressive as to render it unjust to the defendant to enforce it.  It must be one in which there are mutual promises, or which is founded on a sufficient consideration.  It must be one the terms of which are certain, and in respect to which the minds of the parties have distinctly met, so that there can be no misunderstanding of their rights and obligations.

The contract is executed as of the date of April 29, 1889.  It is a formal document, consisting of 20 articles, by which the New York Base-Ball Club employs the defendant, and the defendant undertakes to perform professional services as a base-ball player for the club for the season (specified in article 2) beginning April 1, 1889, and ending October 31, 1889. Article 20 provides that the salary to be paid the defendant shall be $2,000, payable semi-monthly. Among other things, the contract provides by different articles that the club may at any time terminate the contract on 10 days' notice to the defendant, whereupon the obligations of both parties are to cease; that the club shall provide the defendant while "abroad" with proper board and lodging, and pay all necessary traveling expenses; that if the defendant, during the term of his employment, be guilty of any excessive indulgence in liquor, or of gambling, or of insubordination, he shall be liable to certain specified penal-. ties; and that, if the club ceases to be a member of the National League of Professional Base-Ball Clubs, either compulsorily or voluntarily, the "defendant shall, if the right of reservation be transferred" by the club to any other club, receive from that club at least the same amount in salary that he receives by the present contract. It contains, also, the following provision:

"Article 18. It is further understood and agreed that the party of the first part shall have the right to 'reserve' the said party of the second part for the season next ensuing the term mentioned in paragraph 2, herein provided, and that said right and privilege is hereby accorded to said party of the first part upon the following conditions, which are to be taken and construed as conditions precedent to the exercise of such extraordinary rights or privileges, viz.: (1) That the said party of the second part shall not be reserved at a salary less than that mentioned in the 20th paragraph herein, except by the consent of the party of the second part; (2) that the said party of the second part, if he be reserved by the said party of the first part for the next ensuing season, shall not be one of more than 14 players then under contract,—that is, that the right of reservation shall be limited to that number of players, and no more."

The plaintiff alleges that the defendant was one of 14 players, and no more, so reserved under said contract; that on the 22d day of October, 1889, plaintiff exercised its option to reserve the defendant for the season of 1890 by giving the defendant due and timely notice, in writing, of its intention to do so; and that, notwithstanding the exercise of this option, the defendant has engaged his services for the season of 1890 to another organization, to act for it as a base-ball player during that season. The plaintiff insists that, by the terms of the contract, it is entitled to the services of the defendant as a base-ball player for the season of 1890 upon the terms and conditions of the contract for the season of 1889, except the condition giving a right to reserve him for a subsequent season.

The case turns upon the meaning and effect of the clause and contract which gives the club the right to reserve the defendant for the season next ensuing. It is plain enough that the option is a right of reservation for the next ensuing season only,—the season ensuing the term mentioned in article 2,—and does not extend beyond the term from April 1,

1890, to October 31, 1890. It is equally plain that the salary for the ensuing season is to be the same as that for the season of 1889, unless the parties mutually consent to a change. But what is the character of the option which the plaintiff is permitted to exercise? What is the right to "reserve" the defendant? If it is the right to retain and have his services as a base-ball player for the season of 1890, when is the right of election to be manifested, and upon what terms are these services to be rendered? Can the club wait until April 1, 1890, before it manifests its intention to exercise the option? Is the club to pay the defendant's board and lodging while he is "abroad," serving the club, during the season of 1890? Can the club discharge him at any time during that season on 10 days' notice? Are the penalties for intoxication, gambling, or insubordination enforceable during the season of 1890? In short, does the contract embody the definite understanding of the parties to it in respect to their reciprocal rights and obligations after the season of 1889 shall have ended? If the term, "the right to reserve," has no defined meaning, and there were no extrinsic sources by which to ascertain the sense in which it is used by the parties, it would be an ambiguous phrase. As applied to a contract for personal services, the right to reserve would convey a very unintelligible conception of the conditions and incidents of the service to be rendered or enjoyed. A contract by which one party agrees, for an equivalent, to reserve himself for another for a stated period, or to reserve himself as a lawyer or doctor or artist or laborer for a specified term, would very inadequately express a promise to devote his professional or manual services exclusively to the other during that period; and the promise of a base-ball player to reserve himself for a particular club for a given season would hardly, without more, convey any definite meaning of the understanding of the parties. It certainly would not bind him to submit to any special rules or regulations respecting the performance of his services not expressly consented to, or not to be necessarily implied from the nature of the employment and the situation of the contracting parties. If it had been the meaning of the contract to allow the club to renew the engagement of the defendant for a second season upon the same conditions as those for the first season, that intention could have been easily and unequivocally expressed. As it is, it is left wholly to implication, unless the "right to reserve" is a term having a defined and specific signification. This ambiguity suggests such grave doubt as to the meaning of the clause that in two adjudged cases, in which it has been considered by the courts, the judges have thought it too indefinite to be enforceable. In *Exhibition Co.* v. *Ward*, 9 N. Y. Supp. 779, (in the supreme court of this state,) Mr. Justice O'BRIEN was of the opinion that the failure to provide for the terms and conditions of the contract for the second season rendered the clause so indefinite and uncertain that it could not be the basis of equitable relief, or that it meant that every player is bound for the ensuing season upon the same terms and conditions as those of the first season, including the signing of a new contract containing the option to reserve. In *Philadelphia Ball Club* v. *Hallman*, in the court of common pleas of Philadelphia, Judge THAYER

was of the opinion that the failure to designate the terms and conditions
of the new engagement under which the player is to be reserved rendered
the contract of reservation wholly uncertain, and therefore incapable of
enforcement.

Where the terms employed to express some particular condition of a
contract are ambiguous, and cannot be satisfactorily explained by reference to other parts of the contract, and the parties have made other contracts in respect to the same subject-matter, and apparently in pursuance
of the same general purpose, it is always permissible to examine all of
them together in aid of the interpretation of the particular condition;
and, if it is found that the ambiguous term has a plain meaning by a
comparison of the several contracts and an examination of their provisions, that meaning should be attributed to it in the particular condition.
So, also, if it appears that the term used has an established meaning
among those engaged in the business to which the contract has reference,
and, unless it is given that meaning, is indefinite and equivocal, it should
be treated, in interpreting the contract, as used according to that understanding; and in construing a contract the court is always at liberty to look
at the surrounding and antecedent circumstances, and avail itself of the
light of any extrinsic facts which will enable it to view the contract from
the stand-point of the parties at the time when it was made.    In the
present case, it will satisfactorily appear, by resort to these sources of interpretation, that the term "right to reserve" is used in the contract in
the sense that obtains in base-ball nomenclature, and that it is intended to
signify an option, the character of which was well understood by baseball clubs and professional players when the present contract was made.
Obviously, the right to reserve given by the eighteenth clause of the
contract is the same thing as the right of reservation mentioned in that
part of the contract which provides that the present club may disband,
and transfer its right of reservation to some other club.    The agreement
is in a form common to all contracts between base-ball clubs organized
under what is known as the "national agreement" and professional players, a form which is prescribed by the national agreement.    The national
agreement is a compact between the various base-ball associations constituting the National League Base-Ball Clubs and the American Association of Base-Ball Clubs, made with a view to regulate the rights and obligations of the members as respects one another.    One of its paramount
features consists of provisions regulating the privilege of clubs to reserve
a stated number of players.    The provisions are framed to prevent any
club of the National League or the American Association from engaging
a player already reserved by another, and to render the player so reserved
ineligible for employment by any other club.    They require each club,
on the 10th day of October in each year, to transmit to all the other
clubs a reserved list of players, not exceeding 14 in number, then under
contract, and of such players reserved in any prior list who have refused
to contract for another year, and declare such players ineligible to contract with any other club.    Inasmuch as the parties to the national
agreement comprise all, or substantially all, the clubs in the country

which employ professional players, this national agreement, by indirection, but practically, affects every professional player, and subordinates his privilege of engaging as he chooses to the option of the club by which he is under reservation. As is stated in a recent publication edited by a prominent professional player:

"The most important feature of the national agreement, unquestionably, is the provision according to the club members the privilege of reserving a stated number of players. No other club of any association under the agreement dare engage any player so reserved. To this rule, more than any other thing, does base-ball, as a business, owe its present substantial standing. By preserving intact the strength of the team from year to year, it places the business of base-ball on a permanent basis, and thus offers security to the investment of capital. The reserve rule itself is a usurpation of the player's rights; but it is, perhaps, made necessary by the peculiar nature of the ball business, and the player is indirectly compensated by the improved standing of the game. The reserve rule takes a manager by the throat, and compels him to keep his hands off his neighbor's enterprise."

In the contracts between clubs and players as framed prior to November, 1887, there was no provision by which the player consented to the option for reserve on the part of the club. But the contracts did contain a condition that the player should conform to, and be governed by, the constitution and provisions of the national agreement; and the player thereby assented to become ineligible for engagement by any other club of the league during the season of his engagement by a particular club, or while the option of re-engaging him for an ensuing year on the part of that club remained in force. Changes were made from time to time in various features of the national agreement. The players were obliged to inform themselves of the latest changes, in order to understand the precise terms of their contract with the clubs. They became unwilling to consent to a form of contract by which they were to be subjected to conditions not mentioned in the contract itself. In November, 1887, a committee representing the professional players met a committee representing the parties to the national agreement for the purpose of agreeing upon certain changes to be made in the form of the contract. The committees finally agreed that the obnoxious clause in the contract should be omitted, and the clause now found in the eighteenth article should be inserted. This was the origin of the clause giving to the club, by the contract itself, the option of reserve. The clause was manifestly inserted in order to give, by an express condition, the right of reservation to the clubs which theretofore the players had only given by agreeing to be bound by the terms of the national agreement. By ascertaining what that right of reservation was, it can be plainly seen what the parties had in mind in using the term in the present contract. If, when the contract was made, the term had a well-understood definition, there was no necessity to particularize in the contract the conditions or characteristics of the option.

Reference has already been made to the provision of the national agreement requiring each club, on the 10th day of October in each year, to transmit to all the other clubs a reserved list of players, and declaring such players ineligible to contract with any other club. This provision is to be read in connection with another provision of the national agreement, which prescribes that no contract shall be made "for the services of any player by any club for a longer period than seven months, beginning April 1st and terminating October 31st, and no such contract for services to be rendered after the expiration of the current year shall be made prior to the 20th day of October of such year." The two provisions, read together, allow a period of 10 days to intervene between the time when a club can exercise the privilege of placing a player upon its reserved list and the time when it can make a contract with him for services to be rendered in an ensuing year, thus emphasizing a distinction between the right to treat the player as reserved and the contract which is to fix the terms upon which the reservation is to be complete. The effect of these provisions is that, when the club has exercised its privilege of reservation, no other club is permitted to negotiate with the player; but the club which has placed him upon the reserved list, and no other, is then at liberty to enter into a contract with him to obtain his services for an ensuing year. Consequently the right of reservation is nothing more or less than a prior and exclusive right, as against the other clubs, to enter into a contract securing the player's services for another season. Until the contract is made which fixes the compensation of the player and the other conditions of his service, there is no definite or complete obligation upon his part to engage with the club. He agrees that he will not negotiate with any other club, but enjoys the privilege of engaging with the reserving club or not, as he sees fit. Read with this understanding, the clause in question by which the privilege of reserving the defendant is given to the club expresses definitely the terms of the option. If the club exercises the right of reservation, it agrees in advance that the player shall receive at least as large a salary as he has received during the current year, and leaves it open to him to contract on that basis for the next season, or to insist on a larger salary. All the other terms of the engagement are matters of negotiation between the club and the player. The law implies that the option of reservation is to be exercised within a reasonable time; but when this has been done the right to reserve the player becomes the privilege, and the exclusive privilege, as between the reserving club and the other clubs, to obtain his services for another year if the parties can agree upon the terms. As a coercive condition which places the player practically, or at least measurably, in a situation where he must contract with the club that has reserved him, or face the probability of losing any engagement for the ensuing season, it is operative and valuable to the club. But, as the basis for an action for damages if the player fails to contract, or for an action to enforce specific performance, it is wholly nugatory. In a legal sense, it is merely a contract to make a contract if the parties can agree. It may be that heretofore the clubs have generally insisted upon treating the option to reserve as a contract by which they were entitled to have the services of the player for the next season upon the terms and conditions of the first season, and even requiring him to enter into a new contract containing the option for reservation; and it may be that the play-ers have generally acquiesced in the claims of the clubs. However this may be, the players were not in a position to act independently; and, if they had refused to consent to the terms proposed by the clubs, they would have done so at the peril of losing any engagement. The facts, therefore, are not such as to permit any weight to be given to the acts of the parties as evincing their own construction of the contract.

It follows that the act of the defendant in refusing to negotiate with the club for an engagement for the season of 1890, while a breach of contract, is not the breach of one which the plaintiff can enforce. The motion for an injunction is denied.

----

# NOTES

### Baseball and the Law—Yesterday and Today

The activities of Mr. Robert Murphy [1] and Señor Jorges Pasquel [2] in the baseball world this season have resulted in unprecedented moves on the part of Baseball's government and its club owners to soothe their player-employees and to convince them that the present organization and system of self-government are best suited to their welfare. In addition to representation on the newly organized Executive Council, second in power only to the Commissioner, the players now have a guaranteed minimum wage, a pension fund, a maximum limit on salary cuts in any one year, a longer "notice of release" period, and other security benefits,[3] all in keeping with the liberal labor policies of the day. Whether or not these counter-moves will be successful is yet to be determined, but it emphasizes the fact that Baseball depends almost entirely on its own powers in settling its problems. Through the years organized baseball has had to handle its own difficulties with very little assistance from the courts; and it has been able to do this only because of its tight-knit, monopolistic [4] structure which makes exclusion of dissenters the means of enforcing its decisions and edicts. But the evolution from Baseball's humble beginning to the high and apparently invulnerable position it holds today has not been easy.[5] The game has overcome a great many obstacles, not the least of which have been its struggles with dissatisfied players and envious rival leagues, singly and combined. Therefore, it is necessary to review briefly the troubled existence it has had in order to understand its actions in the current situation.

1. Robert Murphy is the Labor Relations Director of the American Baseball Guild, a labor union which this year attempted to organize several major league clubs. The high-water mark of its activities, after an abortive strike attempt on June 5, was its success in having the Pennsylvania Labor Relations Board order an election to determine whether or not the players of the Pittsburgh Athletic Company (Pirates) wanted the Guild as their collective bargaining agent. The Guild was rejected on August 20 by a 15-3 vote.

2. Jorges Pasquel, President of the Mexican Baseball League, has attempted to persuade several prominent baseball players in the United States to sign contracts with him to play in Mexico. He has offered large salaries, payment of expenses, and large bonuses for signing—in utter disregard of the fact that all players contacted were subject to the "reserve clause" and some had even signed contracts for the current season. For instance, Mickey Owen signed a contract calling for a bonus of $12,500.00 for signing and $15,000.00 annually for five years commencing on April 2, 1946. In addition Mr. Owen was to receive transportation to and from Mexico and have all his living expenses paid while there.

3. Chicago Daily Tribune, Aug. 29, 1946, p. 25, col. 1. The new contracts containing the pertinent provisions are expected to be ready about November 1.

4. See American League Baseball Club of Chicago v. Chase, 86 Misc. 441, 459, 149 N. Y. Supp. 6, 16 (Sup. Ct. 1914); Gilbert, *Enforcement of Negative Covenants* (1916) 4 CALIF. L. REV. 114.

5. There are few comprehensive studies. See MORELAND, BALLDOM (1914), and Stayton, *Baseball Jurisprudence* (1910) 44 AM. L. REV. 374.

### History of Baseball

Although Abner Doubleday originated our game of baseball as far back as 1839,[6] it wasn't until 1857 and 1858 that interest became general enough to warrant a national organization and uniform rules. Over this two year span two national conventions met, formed the National Association of Baseball Players,[7] and adopted the first generally recognized, official baseball rule book.[8]

At this stage the game was played on a strictly amateur basis, but in the succeeding years professionalism crept in and gradually became the dominant influence in the national organization.[9] However, there were a few sincere amateurs who couldn't acquiesce in this trend; so they withdrew, making way in 1871 for the National Association of *Professional* Baseball Players.[10] The new association was a league as we understand that term today, with member teams in nine cities and a regular schedule of games. It operated until 1875 when, in order to combat bribery, dishonest playing, and pool room manipulations, the National League of Baseball Clubs, our present National League, was founded.[11] Even so, it became necessary within two years to take additional action to control the corrupt element; and accordingly Baseball, without resort to the courts, banned for life four players who had been guilty of throwing games.[12]

Meanwhile, contract-breaking and player desertions had become more and more troublesome, and in 1879 the "reserve clause"[13]

---

**6.** Moreland, Balldom (1914) 5.

**7.** 3 Encyclopedia Americana (1942) 5.

**8.** Prior to this time each club had its own version of the rules to be followed. These new official ones were simply an adaptation of the New York *Knickerbockers'* rules of 1845. The only major change was that under the new set the game was won by the team having the most runs at the end of nine innings instead of the team that first scored twenty-one "aces."

**9.** Originally a prospective player had to be not only an amateur but also a member of his club for thirty days before he could participate. "Money, place or emolument" was *supposed* to be an absolute bar to participation, but the subsidization of the better players, plus the charging of admission fees in which the players soon shared, paved the way for professionalism which became open and aboveboard when A. J. Reach left his amateur standing with a Brooklyn club and played in Philadelphia for a fee. In 1868 Cincinnati assembled the first completely salaried team (with annual wages running from $800.00 to $1400.00), and total professionalism was a foregone conclusion when this team won all its games except one in its two-year existence. The one loss was to a Brooklyn club whose fans came out of the stands and held the Cincinnati outfielders until the winning runs crossed the plate.

**10.** 3 Encyclopedia Britannica (1939) 161.

**11.** Moreland, Balldom (1914) 17.

**12.** *Id.* at 18. Louisville was leading the league until it made its last eastern swing when it lost seven straight games. An investigation revealed that four players had been paid to lose the games, and they were expelled for life.

**13.** The so-called "reserve clause" is a contractual clause which permits a club to have the exclusive rights to a player's services for the succeeding baseball season. While a player is so "reserved," no other club can offer him a position, nor can he offer to play for someone else. The evils of player desertion (or club "jumping") were brought to a climax when four members

made its first appearance—in the form of a secret agreement between the owners of the National League clubs.[14]  With only minor
changes it has remained a foundation stone of baseball ever since.[15]

The American Association, formed in 1882, was the first major
organization to challenge the National League's exclusive field; but
by an agreement [16] made the following year a harmonious compromise was effected.[17]  Next, the Union Association [18] attempted to
force itself into the national baseball picture, criticizing the National
(Tripartite) Agreement and the "reserve clause" (which had been
incorporated into it) in an effort to persuade players to "jump" to
the new league.  However, the players' major grievance seemed to
be that the "reserve clause" was in the National Agreement rather
than in their individual contracts, so the Union Association, unable
to arouse any great player interest, met with defeat—after which a
joint player-management committee made the desired change.[19]

In 1890 the Players' League was organized, immediately placed
rival clubs in major league cities, and attempted to take under contract some of organized baseball's most talented players.  Baseball,
however, relying on public support and the firm grip it had on its
players, elected to fight it out; and by scheduling as many conflicting games as possible, it broke the "wildcat" league within a year.[20]
Thereupon all players who had been "emancipated" were ordered
back to the clubs from which they had "jumped"; but because of a
mix-up which resulted in the American Association losing two of
its players, that body withdrew from the National Agreement and
attempted to compete as an independent.  Absorption of the Association by the well-established National League was the result.[21]

In ten years two other groups felt that the National League's
monopoly on major league ball could be broken; so the second Players' Brotherhood and our present American League were formed.
The former lasted only two years, but the latter, composed of several former National League clubs and a few new ones, succeeded

---

of Boston's championship team of 1875 signed for the next season with a
rival club, leaving Boston to replace its stars as best it could.

**14.** ENCYCLOPEDIA BRITANNICA (1939) 161.  Originally each team was permitted to reserve only five players for the ensuing season.  Currently the
number is forty.

**15.** MAJOR LEAGUE RULES, Rule 4.

**16.** The Tripartite Agreement signed by the National League, the American Association, and the Northwestern League.

**17.** SPALDING-REACH OFFICIAL BASEBALL GUIDE (1941) 455.

**18.** The Union Association was a league which played for only one year.
After its demise the players who had "jumped" signed contracts were fined
$1,000.00—those who had violated "reserve clauses," $500.00.

**19.** The committee met in 1877.  See Metropolitan Exhibition Co. v. Ewing, 42 Fed. 198, 203 (C. C. S. D. N. Y. 1890).

**20.** MORELAND, BALLDOM (1914) 23, 276.

**21.** *Id.* at 107.  Two American Association players who had "jumped" to
the Players' League were inadvertently left off the American Association's
reserve list when the League disbanded.  They were immediately signed by
two National League clubs, and a Board of Arbitration decided against the
Association.  The Pittsburgh *Pirates*, who got one of the players involved,
received their nickname because of this incident.

in forcing recognition by 1903.[22]  The new National Agreement signed that year provided for the establishment of a National Commission of three members with authority to handle Baseball's major problems, and the signatories included for the first time a vast majority of the professional minor league baseball clubs.[23]

The succeeding eleven years were uneventful from a legal standpoint except for the organization in 1912 of the Baseball Players' Fraternity, a labor union in fact if not in name.  However, in 1914 this peaceful era was suddenly terminated when the Fraternity proved itself powerful enough to force on the National Commission eleven of seventeen demands [24] and almost powerful enough to succeed in its call for a general strike of all major league ball players.[25]

The evident general dissatisfaction paved the way for the organization of the Federal League in 1914,[26] and a great number of players took advantage of the opportunity to "jump."  But in spite of adverse judicial action on Baseball's standard players' contracts, financial defeat for the Federal League coupled with the prolonged civil action against the major leagues for violation of the Sherman Anti-Trust Act [27] (which terminated in a finding that baseball was neither interstate commerce nor even commerce at all) [28] spelled the end of major "wildcat" league attempts in this country.

In 1916 the Baseball Players' Fraternity made further demands for concessions to players; but after considerable bargaining, the owners determined to abrogate their agreement with that group.[29] Unfortunately, perhaps, from a legal viewpoint, World War I prevented a final determination of the issues.

After the war general dissatisfaction with the National Commission and the wave of public disapproval over the notorious Black Sox scandal [30] resulted in a new National Agreement and the election of Judge Kenesaw Mountain Landis to the newly created office of Commissioner of Baseball.[31]  The new commissioner's rulings were at times difficult for management to accept, but from the time of Judge Landis' election until his death Baseball enjoyed a growing prestige that was the envy of all sportsdom.  And although he was often more severe than a court of justice would ever have been, his authority was sustained by a federal district court on the gen-

**22.** Spalding-Reach Official Baseball Guide (1941) 456.
**23.** *Id.* at 457; Moreland, Balldom (1914) 26.  The Commission was composed of the President of the National League, the President of the American League, and a third member selected by the first two.
**24.** Spalding-Reach Official Baseball Guide (1941) 457.
**25.** *Ibid.*
**26.** *Ibid.*
**27.** 26 Stat. 209 (1890), 15 U. S. C. §§ 1 *et seq.* (1940).
**28.** Federal Baseball Club of Baltimore v. National League of Professional Baseball Clubs, 259 U. S. 200, 66 L. Ed. 898, 42 Sup. Ct. 465 (1922).
**29.** Spalding-Reach Official Baseball Guide (1941) 458.
**30.** Another case of intentionally losing ball games, similar to the Louisville affair.  See n. 12 *supra.*
**31.** 3 Encyclopedia Britannica (1939) 162.  One of Judge Landis' first official acts was to bar from baseball for life those players embroiled in the Black Sox scandal.

eral grounds that an arbitrator's decisions based on sufficient evidence are binding.[32]

Early in 1945 a new National Agreement,[33] to be effective until 1970, was signed by the major and minor leagues, and a few months later Senator A. B. Chandler of Kentucky was named the second Commissioner of Baseball.[34]

This year the attempted unionization of the major leagues and the "raiding" by Señor Pasquel have resulted in Baseball taking affirmative action in its own behalf. This has taken the form of player-appeasement, as was previously suggested, and a five-year suspension for each player who has "jumped." Currently, the counter-moves seem to be working because there has been no further "jumping." Moreover, several "jumpers" have expressed dissatisfaction with the Mexican League, and at least one has returned to seek reinstatement.[35] But the situation is still quite fluid, and anything can happen.

## BASEBALL CONTRACTS

### I

"While courts have frequently declined to enforce such contracts for clubs, close organization among club owners has now relieved them of the necessity of resorting to the courts." [36]

From professional baseball's beginning the owners of the clubs have been faced with a dilemma in their players' contracts. On the one hand there is the desirableness, bordering on necessity, of being able to retain players as long as they are needed by the team, and on the other the financial necessity of being able to release them when they are no longer of value. Obviously these are two conflicting needs, and under such circumstances a binding contract has been fairly difficult to formulate. In fact, on strict principles of contract law, it is highly questionable that Baseball has ever had one. In particular the so-called "reserve and release clauses," which have attempted to meet the owners' requirements, have been stumbling blocks when the contracts were subjected to judicial scrutiny.

These contracts were initially tested in 1890 when the first Players' League succeeded in persuading several players under contract to "jump" to the new league. At that time the pertinent clauses read as follows:

"17. It is further understood and agreed that the party of the first part (owner) expressly reserves the right, at any time prior to the completion of the period when this contract, by its terms, is to end, by giving the party of the second part (player) ten

---

32. Milwaukee American Association Baseball Club v. Landis, 49 F. (2d) 298 (N. D. Ill. 1931).

33. BASEBALL BLUE BOOK (1945) 199.

34. 1946 BRITANNICA BOOK OF THE YEAR (1946) 199.

35. Mickey Owen, formerly of the Brooklyn Dodgers. Señor Pasquel promptly filed suit for $127,000.00.

36. Note (1937) 46 YALE L. J. 1386, 1387.

days' notice of its option and intention so to do, to end and determine all its liabilities and obligations under this contract, in which event, upon the expiration of said ten days, all liabilities and obligations undertaken by said party of the first part in this contract shall at once cease and determine, and said party of the second part shall thereupon be also freed from his obligation hereunder, and shall have no claim for wages for any period after said ten days. * * *

"18. It is further understood and agreed that the said party of the first part shall have the right to 'reserve' the said party of the second part for the season next ensuing the term mentioned in paragraph 2 herein provided, and said right and privilege is hereby accorded the said party of the first part upon the following conditions, which are to be taken and construed as conditions precedent to the exercise of such extraordinary right or privilege, viz.:

> I. That the said party of the second part shall not be reserved at a salary less than that mentioned in the 20th paragraph herein except by consent of the party of the second part;

> II. That the said party of the second part, if he be reserved by the said party of the first part for the next ensuing season, shall be one of not more than fourteen players then under contract; that is, the right of reservation shall be limited to that number of players and no more." [37]

Unfortunately for Baseball, in the few cases that were tried not a single court held that the contracts were valid and enforceable.[38] Many reasons were given as dicta, but most of them centered around "lack of mutuality." In an action for specific performance of a negative covenant a Philadelphia court said:

> "While the defendant (player) has sold himself for life to the plaintiffs (owners) * * *, if they choose to hold him for that length of time, he has no hold upon them for any period longer than ten days. * * * it is perfectly apparent that such a contract is so wanting in mutuality that no court of equity would lend its aid to compel compliance with it." [39]

> "A contract that is sought to be specifically enforced must be mutual both as to the remedy and the obligation. A party not bound by the agreement itself has no right to call upon a court of equity to enforce specific performance against the other contracting party by expressing his willingness in his bill to perform his part of the agreement. His right to the aid of the court does not depend upon his subsequent offer to perform the

---

37. These clauses are from the contract between the Metropolitan Exhibition Co. and John M. Ward, signed April 23, 1889.
38. *E. g.*, Metropolitan Exhibition Co. v. Ward, 24 Abb. N. Cas. 393 (1890).
39. See Philadelphia Ball Club, Ltd. v. Hallman, 8 Pa. C. C. 57, 62 (1890).

And in the opinion of a New York court:

contract on his part, but upon its original obligatory character." [40]

But the absolute necessity for the "reserve clause" was recognized by Judge Wallace of the United States Circuit Court for the Southern District of New York when he observed:

"To this rule (the reserve rule) more than any other thing does baseball, as a business, owe its present substantial standing; by preserving intact the strength of the team from year to year, it places the business of baseball on a permanent basis, and this offers security to the investment of the capital. The reserve rule itself is a usurpation of the players' rights, but it is perhaps made necessary by the peculiar nature of the ball business, and the player is indirectly compensated by the improved standing of the game. The reserve rule takes a manager by the throat and compels him to keep his hands off his neighbor's enterprise." [41]

As unfortunate as these decisions were for Baseball, the demise of the Players' League made it unnecessary either to fight them in the appellate courts or amend the contracts substantially. So long as there was no competition, a player could either accept the standard contract, or he simply didn't play major league ball. Moreover, any tendency to change the contracts was deterred by a 1902 decision in which the standard contract (slightly modified) was declared valid.

"We are not persuaded," said the court, "that the terms of this contract manifest any lack of mutuality in remedy. Each party has the possibility of enforcing all the rights stipulated for in the agreement. It is true that the terms make it possible for the plaintiff to put an end to the contract in a space of time much less than the period during which the defendant has agreed to supply his personal services; but mere difference in the rights stipulated for does not destroy mutuality of remedy. * * * Upon a careful consideration of the whole case, we are of opinion that the provisions of the contract are reasonable, and that the consideration is adequate." [42]

But a few months later a Missouri court, with the record of *Philadelphia Ball Club, Ltd.* v. *Lajoie* [43] before it held "the contract (was) lacking in mutuality."

"Defendant (player) is bound as with bands of steel for the entire contractual period, while * * * (plaintiff has) the right to end and determine all its rights and obligations * * *

---

40. See Metropolitan Exhibition Co. v. Ward, 24 Abb. N. Cas. 393, 416 (1890).
41. See Metropolitan Exhibition Co. v. Ewing, 42 Fed. 198, 203 (C. C. S. D. N. Y. 1890).
42. See Philadelphia Ball Club, Ltd. v. Lajoie, 202 Pa. 210, 219, 51 Atl. 973, 975 (1902).
43. 202 Pa. 210, 51 Atl. 973 (1902).

by simply giving the defendant ten days' notice of its intention to do so."[44]

A decade later the activities of the Federal League brought about another series of test cases on the standard contract, and again the decisions were adverse. Although some of the contracts by this time called for a definite percentage of the salary involved to be paid and accepted in consideration for the "reserve clause,"[45] still the courts considered the contracts lacked mutuality and were, therefore, unenforceable, primarily because one party was, in effect, bound for life—the other for ten days. Typical of the judges' reactions are these excerpts:

> "The plaintiff (club) can terminate the contract at any time on ten days' notice. * * * The player's contract binds him not only for the playing season * * * but also for another season, if the plaintiff chooses to exercise its option, and if it insists upon the requirement of an option clause in each succeeding contract, the defendant can be held for a term of years. His only alternative is to abandon his vocation. Can it fairly be claimed that there is mutuality in such a contract?"[46]

And:

> "It (the standard contract) lacks mutuality, because the Philadelphia Club may terminate it at any time upon ten days' notice while the other party has no such option and is bound during the entire contract period. * * * the courts are helpless either to enforce its performance or to award damages for its breach."[47]

But again, the dissolution of opposition to organized ball made it unnecessary to find a legal solution, and it has been unnecessary since. Wise administration and lack of effective competition have combined to keep Baseball's contracts out of the courts.

Were the problem to come before a court of law or equity today it is predictable that the same general results would be reached. The contracts have changed considerably in form since 1914, but very little in actual content.[48] The fact that Baseball has not taken its

---

**44.** See American Baseball and Athletic Exhibition Co. v. Harper (unreported), noted (1902) 54 CENT. L. J. 449, 450.

**45.** "The compensation of the party of the second part (player) stipulated in this contract shall be apportioned as follows: 75% thereof for services rendered and 25% thereof for and in consideration of the player's covenant to sanction and abide by his reservation by the party of the first part (owner) for the season of 1914 * * *."

**46.** See American League Baseball Club of Chicago v. Chase, 86 Misc. 441, 455, 149 N. Y. Supp. 6, 14 (Sup. Ct. 1914).

**47.** See Weegham v. Killifer, 215 Fed. 168, 170 (W. D. Mich. 1914).

**48.** "5. (b) This contract may be terminated at any time by the Club or by any assignee upon ten days' written notice to the Player.

"8. (a) * * * the Club or any assignee hereof may renew this contract for the term of that year (succeeding year) except that the salary shall be such as the parties may then agree upon, or in default of agreement

"jumping" players to court in the present period indicates, perhaps, that its legal counsel is of the same opinion. Too, the general doctrine concerning lack of mutuality has the support of the highest court of our land which held that the right of one of the parties to terminate an agreement on notice while the other continues bound and has no such option of revocation is so wanting in mutuality as to be unenforceable in equity.[49]

## II

But assuming for the moment that the standard baseball contract is valid (which it apparently is not [50]) and is not lacking in mutuality, the question of enforcement arises. Of course it is obvious that under such assumed circumstances the party who breached would be subject to a suit for damages; but in a contract for personal services, it is the services that are wanted, not damages. Moreover, in most cases the damages would be so speculative as to be incapable of ascertainment, leaving specific performance the only adequate relief. But unfortunately for employers, courts of equity have consistently refused to decree specific performance in these personal service cases, primarily because the courts are unable to oversee performance.[51] But, generally speaking, ever since the decision in *Lumley* v. *Wagner*,[52] negative covenant clauses [53] in contracts for personal services have been specifically enforced where the services in question were special, unique, and extraordinary.[54] Within thirty years the English rule as laid down in *Lumley* v. *Wagner* was paralleled in our law by *McCaull* v. *Braham*.[55] In this case Lillian Russell, the defendant, had signed a contract with the plaintiff to sing under his management for an entire season, and she had further covenanted that she would sing for no one else. When she signed to perform for another during the time her contract with plaintiff was still in effect, a decree issued, not ordering her to sing for McCaull,

---

the Player will accept such salary rate as the Club may fix, or else will not play baseball otherwise than for the Club or for an assignee hereof.

"(b) The Club's right of reservation of the Player, and of renewal of this contract as aforesaid, and the promise of the Player not to play otherwise than with the Club or an assignee hereof, have been taken into consideration in determining the salary specified herein and the undertaking by the Club to pay said salary is the consideration for both said reservation, renewal option and promise, and the Player's service" (from a 1946 contract).

**49.** See Rutland Marble Co. v. Ripley, 10 Wall. 339, 359, 19 L. Ed. 955, 961 (U. S. 1870).

**50.** "It is doubtful if it should be sustained even in a court of law." Annotation in (1902) 54 Cent. L. J. 449, 453.

**51.** *E. g.*, Rutland Marble Co. v. Ripley, 10 Wall. 339, 358, 19 L. Ed. 955, 961 (U. S. 1870).

**52.** 1 DeG. M. & G. 604, 42 Eng. Rep. 687 (Ch. 1852); see *The Doctrine of Lumley v. Wagner* (1897) 13 Law Q. Rev. 306.

**53.** "The player agrees to perform for no other party during the period of this contract * * *."

**54.** The services must be difficult of replacement; otherwise, there is no damage.

**55.** 16 Fed. 37 (C. C. S. D. N. Y. 1883).

but restraining her from performing for any one else for the duration of plaintiff's contract with her.

In 1890 this doctrine was carried over into the field of baseball by dicta in several cases,[56] but at the same time the general rule was limited by requiring that the services contracted for be difficult of replacement, unique, extraordinary, etc.[57] In *Carter* v. *Ferguson*[58] a request for an injunction to restrain an actor under contract from performing for someone else was refused on the grounds that his artistic abilities were not "extraordinary and pre-eminent," and to the same effect was *Columbus Baseball Club* v. *Reilly*.[59] Furthermore, as recently as 1931 the rule was applied to athletes when an injunction to enforce a negative covenant was refused on the grounds that the boxers concerned were mediocre and capable of replacement.[60]

After the *Lajoie* case,[61] in which an injunction issued, the few decisions that were handed down recognized that an injunction would issue where there were negative covenants, if the contracts were valid and if the players' services were unique, pre-eminent, etc.[62]

"It is safe to say (then) that in the case of a clear and definite contract by a ball player, which is fair and valid, an injunction will issue to prevent him from playing with another club in violation of his agreement."[63]    But as a practical matter it makes little difference. A player can't compel a team to hire and play him, and so, if he has no other league in which he can play, he must accept Baseball's terms or quit—which sounds like monopoly.

## BASEBALL AS A MONOPOLY

In its most extensive meaning the word "monopoly" signifies the sole power of dealing in any article or doing a specific thing, either generally or in a particular place,[64] and it embraces any combination the tendency of which is to prevent competition in its broad and general sense.[65]    By definition, then, it seems a fairly reasonable conclusion that Baseball is a monopoly since there is, for all practical purposes, no competition outside the organization.    But being a mo-

---

**56.** *E. g.,* Philadelphia Ball Club, Ltd. v. Hallman, 8 Pa. C. C. 57, 58 (1890).

**57.** See American Association Baseball Club of Kansas City, Mo. v. Pickett, 8 Pa. C. C. 232 (1890).

**58.** 58 Hun 569, 12 N. Y. Supp. 580 (Sup. Ct. 1890).

**59.** 11 Ohio Dec. 272 (1891).

**60.** Safro v. Lakofsky, 184 Minn. 336, 238 N. W. 641 (1931).

**61.** Philadelphia Ball Club, Ltd. v. Lajoie, 202 Pa. 210, 51 Atl. 973 (1902).

**62.** *E. g.,* Cincinnati Exhibition Co. v. Johnson, 190 Ill. App. 630 (1914); American League Baseball Club of Chicago v. Chase, 86 Misc. 441, 149 N. Y. Supp. 6 (Sup. Ct. 1914).

**63.** Note, *Baseball Law* (1914) 17 LAW NOTES 207.

**64.** 36 AM. JUR., MONOPOLIES (1941) § 2.

**65.** See Love v. Kozy Theatre Co., 193 Ky. 336, 339, 236 S. W. 243, 245 (1922).

nopoly and being an *illegal* monopoly are obviously two different things.[66]

At common law personal services could not be the subject of a technical monopoly, a monopoly being predicated only of rights or interests in property.[67] And most of the anti-trust statutes in the states where major league clubs are operated specify that the monopoly to be illegal must be one of manufacture, production, transportation, sale, mining, etc., of articles or commodities.[68] New York, moreover, specifically provides that the "labor of human beings shall not be deemed or held to be a commodity or article of commerce," [69] thus clearly indicating that monopolies of personnel would not be illegal.

The federal anti-trust act [70] is a bit broader, providing that

"every contract, combination in the form of trust or otherwise, or conspiracy, in restraint of trade or commerce among the several states or with foreign nations is hereby declared to be illegal." [71]

But like the New York statute [72] its effect on personnel is restricted.

"The labor of human beings is not a commodity or article of commerce." [73]

In the only test to date of Baseball's status under the federal monopoly laws, Justice Holmes, speaking for an unanimous court, held that it did not violate the federal anti-trust law because it wasn't interstate commerce or even commerce at all.[74]

Although there has been agitation for prosecution under the act since then, there has been no direct action, the Attorney General ruling in 1937 that an investigation by the Justice Department was precluded by the 1922 decision in *Federal Baseball Club of Baltimore* v. *National League of Professional Baseball Clubs*.[75]

And as recently as this year the National Labor Relations Board refused to take jurisdiction of the Pittsburgh Ball Club labor dispute on the grounds that interstate commerce was not involved.[76]

Prior to the decision in the *Federal Baseball* case, some state judges recognized that Baseball was not a violation of the Sherman Act, yet

---

66. 36 Am. Jur., Monopolies (1941) § 5.
67. *Id.* § 109.
68. *E. g.*, Ill. Ann. Stat. (Smith-Hurd, 1934) c. 38, § 569; Mass. Ann. Laws (Michie, 1933) c. 93, § 2; Mo. Rev. Stat. (1939) § 8301; Ohio Gen. Code Ann. (Page, Supp. 1945) § 6391.
69. N. Y. Gen. Bus. Law § 340.
70. 26 Stat. 209 (1890), 15 U. S. C. §§ 1 *et seq.* (1940).
71. 26 Stat. 209 (1890), 50 Stat. 693 (1937), 15 U. S. C. § 1 (1940).
72. N. Y. Gen. Bus. Law § 340.
73. 38 Stat. 731 (1914), 15 U. S. C. § 17 (1940).
74. Federal Baseball Club of Baltimore v. National League of Professional Baseball Clubs, 259 U. S. 200, 66 L. Ed. 898, 42 Sup. Ct. 465 (1922).
75. N. Y. Times, April 15, 1937, p. 25, col. 2.
76. Brief on the subject of jurisdiction, case no. 83, year of 1946, before Pennsylvania Labor Relations Board.

felt that it was a common law conspiracy.[77]  However, as things stand today it is improbable that Baseball could be convicted either under federal or state anti-trust laws.  The Supreme Court's unanimous opinion and the absolute lack of any prosecutions under monopoly statutes which have been on the books for years indicate this.

But there is always the possibility that the present liberal court might reverse the 1922 decision or that the Congress might attempt to regulate Baseball by redefining "commerce" so as to include athletics and athletes or entertainments and entertainers.  If the latter should happen, it is almost certain that the Supreme Court would accept the definition.  The trend of decisions in the last few years has been to permit Congress to define for itself its powers under the commerce clause,[78] and if it felt Baseball needed regulation, there is little reason to suppose the Court wouldn't go along.

## Labor and Baseball

The Supreme Court has said many times that the right of self-organization and collective bargaining is a "fundamental right," [79] and this has been emphasized by positive legislation on the subject both by the Congress [80] and by various state legislatures.[81]  Yet with all this legislative and judicial protection, it has so far been impossible to organize baseball players effectively, although, as has been pointed out, there have been numerous attempts to do so.

It might be argued that ball players are not "working men" and "employees" in the sense that those words are used in the labor statutes,[82] but Baseball has never denied that its players have the right to organize.  On the contrary it has attempted to meet all reasonable demands made by players or groups of players, and accordingly collective bargaining has been unnecessary.[83]

In the current labor dispute the Pittsburgh Baseball Club, while not denying the right of self-organization and collective bargaining, has vigorously contested the jurisdiction of the Pennsylvania Labor Relations Board.[84]  The Club's contention has been that the act which created the Board was aimed at industrial disputes and not at Baseball, relying on *Rector of Church of the Holy Trinity* v. *United States*.[85]  But, although there has been no decision as yet, it is sug-

---

**77.** American League Baseball Club of Chicago v. Chase, 86 Misc. 441, 149 N. Y. Supp. 6 (Sup. Ct. 1914).

**78.** Dowling, *Constitutional Developments in Five War Years* (1946) 32 Va. L. Rev. 461, 469.

**79.** See Amalgamated Utilities Workers v. Consolidated Edison Co., 309 U. S. 261, 263, 84 L. Ed. 738, 741, 60 Sup. Ct. 561, 562 (1940) ; N. L. R. B. v. Jones & Laughlin Steel Corp., 301 U. S. 1, 33, 81 L. Ed. 893, 909, 57 Sup. Ct. 615, 622 (1936).

**80.** National Labor Relations Act, 49 Stat. 449-457 (1935), 29 U. S. C. §§ 151-166 (1940).

**81.** *E. g.*, N. Y. Labor Law §§ 700-716; Pa. Stat. Ann. (Purdon, 1941) tit. 43, §§ 211.1-211.39.

**82.** 31 Am. Jur., Labor (1940) § 2.

**83.** See historical section, *supra*.

**84.** See n. 76 *supra*.

**85.** 143 U. S. 457, 36 L. Ed. 226, 12 Sup. Ct. 511 (1892).

gested that the state board's jurisdiction will be sustained. The act says "employers" and "employees," [86] and it takes no great effort to construe "owners" and "players" to fit into these categories.

But even before a decision has been reached, the player-management dispute is apparently at an end. The American Baseball Guild claims that the formation of the joint Player-Management Committee was an unfair labor practice,[87] and perhaps it was—in the eyes of the ultra-liberals. But the practice of employers and employees getting together to settle their differences without the aid of a third party appears to be an adequate solution—and one which might well be used to advantage in other fields.

## CONCLUSION

Perhaps Baseball has impaired some of its players' rights by enforcing contracts that the law will not enforce, and perhaps it is improper to freeze out competition in this field. But the two "evils" have resulted in an undeniably "honest" sport and the type of competition which is so highly cherished by Americans everywhere. The general public, the players, and management seem to be satisfied now—certainly the current season has left nothing to be desired by any of the three groups.

Sincere legal theorists and "professional" labor executives may deplore the situation; but so long as the government of Baseball is benevolent and the public receives the quality of sport it wants, there is no compelling reason to alter the situation.

If the time ever comes when Baseball cannot or will not control itself to the satisfaction of all concerned, quick action by the Congress in declaring it interstate commerce and subsequent prosecutions under the Sherman Act will soon remedy the difficulties. And the possibility of such action will be an ever-present deterrent should management contemplate abandoning the course it now follows.

*M. L. C.*

EDITOR'S NOTE—Since the writing of this Note, a new Uniform Player's Contract has been published. Some of its more interesting provisions follow:

"2. * * * If the rate of payment stipulated * * * is less than $5,000.00 per year, the player, nevertheless, shall be paid at the rate of $5,000.00 per year for each day of his service as a player on a Major League team.

"4. (a) The Player represents and agrees that he has exceptional and unique skill and ability as a baseball player; that his services to be rendered hereunder are of a special, unusual and extraordinary character which gives them peculiar value which cannot be reasonably or adequately compensated for in damages at law, and that the Player's breach of this contract will cause the Club great and irreparable injury and damage. The Player agrees that, in addition to other remedies, the Club shall be entitled to injunctive and other equitable relief to prevent a breach of this contract by the Player, including

---

86. PA. STAT. ANN. (Purdon, 1941) tit. 43, §§ 211.5-211.6.
87. Pennsylvania Labor Relations Board v. Pittsburgh Athletic Co., Case No. 104, year of 1946, before Pennsylvania Labor Relations Board.

among others, the right to enjoin the Player from playing baseball for any other person or organization during the term of this contract.

"7. (e) If this contract is terminated by the Club (for listed reasons) * * * the Player shall be entitled to an additional amount (of salary) equal to thirty (30) days payment at the rate stipulated * * *.

"10. (a) On or before February 1st * * * of the year next following the last playing season covered by this contract, the Club may tender to the Player a contract for the term of that year * * *. If prior to the March 1 next succeeding said February 1, .the Player and the Club have not agreed upon the terms of such contract, then on or before 10 days after said March 1, the Club shall have the right by written notice to the Player * * * to renew this contract for the period of one year on the same terms, except that the amount payable to the Player shall be such as the Club shall fix in said notice; provided, however, that said amount, if fixed by a Major League Club, shall be an amount payable at a rate not less than 75% of the rate stipulated for the preceding year."

# Baseball's Third Strike: The Triumph of Collective Bargaining in Professional Baseball

*Robert A. McCormick\**

*Since the inception of professional baseball, team owners have imposed limits on the freedom of players to negotiate contract terms. In this article Professor McCormick traces the history of attempts by professional baseball players to obtain contractual freedoms through the use of the antitrust and labor relations laws, attempts that culminated with the players' strike of 1981. Although players in other team sports successfully have utilized antitrust laws to increase player bargaining power, Professor McCormick argues that labor law has provided baseball players the only effective means to gain increased contractual freedoms. Professor McCormick concludes that player-owner disputes over the reserve system in baseball today fall within the labor exemption to the antitrust laws and, therefore, that players and owners will resolve future conflicts solely within the structure of labor relations law.*

## I. INTRODUCTION

For countless followers of professional baseball, as well as team owners, players, and numerous dependent businesses, the 1981 baseball season will be remembered more for the off-the-field strife than for the games themselves. Players engaged in a seven week work stoppage, which brought play to a halt in the middle of the championship season. After charges of bad faith bargaining,[1] an action in federal district court seeking to postpone the strike,[2] testimony before the National Labor Relations Board,[3] the involvement of the Federal Mediation and Conciliation Service,[4] and

---

\* Associate Professor of Law, Detroit College of Law. B.A., 1969, Michigan State University; J.D., 1973, University of Michigan. The author wishes to thank Edwin Fisher and James McNally, class of 1982, Detroit College of Law, for their considerable assistance in the preparation of this Article.

1. *See infra* note 16.
2. *See infra* note 17.
3. N.Y. Times, July 8, 1981, at A19, col. 1; *id.*, July 6, 1981, at C6, col. 3.
4. The Federal Mediation and Conciliation Service, created by the Labor-Management Relations Act of 1947, makes available "government facilities for conciliation, mediation and

the Secretary of Labor,[5] management and labor ultimately negotiated a resolution to their dispute. The agreement was the product of collective bargaining and the economic sanctions which accompany that system.

The 1981 strike was an outgrowth of the historic conflict between the reserve system[6] and the players' desire for full freedom of contract. This conflict is virtually as old as professional baseball itself. Although the 1981 strike was unprecedented in its duration and timing, it was merely a new manifestation of the struggle between players, their unions, and team owners to resolve the conflict. For more than a century professional baseball players were subject to the reserve system; employment terms that, in effect, prevented players from seeking employment with other teams even after the expiration of their contracts. Throughout the history of baseball players had sought freedom from the reserve system and the resulting incapacity to contract freely. Players attempted to organize or play for teams in new leagues that arose in competition with established leagues.[7] Players brought numerous law suits, contending that the reserve system was an unlawful restraint on trade.[8] In addition, players and others who were concerned about the perceived imbalance of power in the employment relationship in professional baseball called for congressional action to outlaw or modify the reserve system.[9] These efforts failed to alter the system significantly.

During the 1970's players in all other major professional sports succeeded in effectuating major modifications in their reserve systems, primarily through successful antitrust challenges.[10] The Supreme Court, however, had ruled in 1922 that the professional

---

voluntary arbitration to aid and encourage employers and the representatives of their employees to reach and maintain agreements concerning rates of pay, hours and working conditions." 29 U.S.C. § 171(b) (1976). "The Service may proffer its services in any labor dispute in any industry affecting commerce, either upon its own motion or upon the request of one or more of the parties to the dispute . . . . " *Id.*

For information on the involvement of the Federal Mediation and Conciliation Service in the baseball negotiations of 1981, see N.Y. Times, July 17, 1981, at A15, col. 5; *id.*, July 10, 1981, § A at 15, col. 4.

5.  N.Y. Times, July 18, 1981, at 17, col. 3; *id.*, July 17, 1981, at A15, col. 5.

6.  For an explanation of reserve system restraints, see *infra* notes 26-34 and accompanying text.

7.  *See infra* notes 43-83 and accompanying text.

8.  *See infra* notes 84-111 and accompanying text.

9.  *See infra* notes 191-98 and accompanying text.

10.  *See infra* note 215 and accompanying text.

baseball industry was exempt from the antitrust laws.[11] In 1972 the Court reaffirmed this exemption in the celebrated Curt Flood case,[12] leaving baseball alone among the professional sports beyond the reach of the antitrust laws. As a result of this case, the law could not impose sanctions upon the owners for collectively fixing the terms and conditions of employment for players. Despite the owners' success in maintaining monopoly power, baseball players, like players in other sports, succeeded in making major inroads upon the reserve system in the 1970's. Unlike athletes in the other sports, however, baseball players gained concessions through the development of the Professional Baseball Players' Association. In 1976 an arbitrator's award gave impetus to the emerging organization and overcame a century of baseball history—effectively disestablishing the reserve system. As a result of this decision and the development of the Players' Association into a representative labor union, management and labor in baseball have engaged in protracted and bitter negotiations over the reserve system, culminating in the 1981 strike.

The specific issue that gave rise to the 1981 players' strike was the amount of compensation paid to a team that "loses" a free agent player.[13] Team owners took the position that when a player's contract with one team terminated and the player signed to play for another team, his new team should compensate the former team for its loss by awarding the former team a major league player.[14] The Players' Association was willing to accept the premise

---

11.   Federal Baseball Club of Baltimore, Inc. v. National League of Professional Baseball Clubs, 259 U.S. 200 (1922); *see infra* notes 84-92 and accompanying text.

12.   Flood v. Kuhn, 407 U.S. 258 (1972). *See infra* notes 103-08 and accompanying text.

13.   A free agent player in professional team sports is a player who has completed the term of his contractual obligation with one club and, therefore, is available for hire by other clubs pursuant to league rules. These league rules may continue to limit a player's freedom to choose a new team. For example, a team may possess a right of first refusal on any offer that the player receives from another club. Moreover, if a free agent signs with another club, the former club may be entitled to compensation from the acquiring team. Finally, a draft, which allocates among teams the right to negotiate with available free agent players, may limit the selection of a free agent. *See* J. WEISTART & C. LOWELL, THE LAW OF SPORTS 523 (1979).

14.   Free agent compensation or indemnity systems have been a regular part of intraleague rules in sports leagues in which players may sign with teams other than their original teams. League bylaws usually provided that if the player's original team and the team acquiring the player's services could not agree on the type or amount of compensation the former team should receive, the determination would be made by the league commissioner, who was empowered by league rules to award either future draft rights or a current player. In essence, the compensation is a forced trade. *See* J. WEISTART & C. LOWELL, *supra*

that the teams losing a player should be afforded some form of compensation. It argued, however, that the owners' formula would discourage team owners from offering more lucrative contracts to players who had completed their contractual obligations with other teams.[15] Team owners would fear losing a valuable member of their roster in return. The Players' Association further charged that the owners had failed to bargain in good faith in this dispute.[16] The National Labor Relations Board first sought injunctive relief upon the claim,[17] and then commenced unfair labor practice proceedings against the owners.[18]

Although negotiations took place, the two sides seemed to grow further apart. When owners purchased strike insurance,[19] players claimed that the owners' tactics and intransigence showed their intention to "bust" the union.[20] After weeks of stalemate, the

---

note 13, at 502-03. These schemes have produced much litigation. For a further discussion of free agent compensation plans in various team sports, see Mackey v. National Football League, 407 F. Supp. 1000 (D. Minn. 1975), *modified,* 543 F.2d 606 (8th Cir. 1976); Robertson v. National Basketball Ass'n, 389 F. Supp. 867 (S.D.N.Y. 1975); Kapp v. National Football League, 390 F. Supp. 73 (N.D. Cal. 1974).

15.  Players in all sports that utilize free agent compensation systems have contended that the system operates as a restraint on player mobility. Some courts have agreed. *See, e.g.,* Mackey v. National Football League, 407 F. Supp. 1000 (D. Minn. 1975). Prospective employers face the prospect of relinquishing valuable present or future players if later they wish to sign an available free agent. Several economists have noted that, as a result, owners become less willing to hire available free agents than they would be if the "forced trade" system were not in effect. *See, e.g.,* H. DEMMERT, THE ECONOMICS OF PROFESSIONAL TEAM SPORTS 38 (1973); J. QUIRK & M. EL HODIRI, *The Economic Theory of a Professional Sports League,* in GOVERNMENT AND THE SPORTS BUSINESS 34 (R. Noll ed. 1974).

16.  The Players' Association alleged that the owners had claimed an inability to withstand the players' free agency demands financially, but that the owners had refused at the same time to open their books to substantiate this claim. NAT'L L.J., May 20, 1981, at 13. This charge, if established, could have constituted a violation of § 8(a)(5) of the National Labor Relations Act, 29 U.S.C. § 158(a)(5) (1976). NLRB v. Truitt Mfg. Co., 351 U.S. 149 (1956). The allegation presented the first impression issue of whether conduct away from the bargaining table by persons not directly involved in negotiations could constitute a *Truitt* type of violation.

17.  *Judge Puts Off Baseball Decision,* N.Y. Times, June 5, 1981, at A19, col. 2; *Baseball Strike Off as Players, Owners Extend Deadline,* N.Y. Times, May 29, 1981, at A17, col. 1; *Labor Board Starts Legal Moves Aimed at Postponing Strike,* N.Y. Times, May 28, 1981, at B11, col. 5. On June 10, 1981, U.S. District Judge Henry F. Werker denied the injunction, saying "there is no reasonable cause to believe that an unfair labor practice has been committed." *Baseball Poised for Strike as Judge Denies Injunction,* N.Y. Times, June 11, 1981, at D21, col. 4.

18.  *Baseball Impasse: Many Sides to Story,* N.Y. Times, May 25, 1981, at C4, col. 1.

19.  The owners were insured against potential losses up to $50 million. Under the policy the owners received $100,000 per game after a 153 game deductible amount. *Id.*

20.  New York Yankees player Reggie Jackson stated at the time: "I think the owners realize they can't break the union—at least, I hope they realize that." Anderson, *The Baseball Strike Situation,* N.Y. Times, June 11, 1981, at D21, col. 4. A Baltimore player repre-

parties moved negotiations from New York to Washington at the behest of the Secretary of Labor,[21] who pressured the parties to reach a settlement and salvage the season. Numerous formulae for resolving the dispute were proposed and rejected.[22] Ultimately, the parties reached a compromise, creating a complex free agent compensation scheme[23] and resolving other contract issues.[24] Thus, the events of the 1981 strike had the elements of a full scale labor dispute with sophisticated and resolute principals who engaged in protracted negotiations, endured an enormously costly work stoppage,[25] and finally reached a complicated agreement that was satisfactory, for the present, to all of the parties to the negotiations. This strike, like most strikes, had effects beyond the costs incurred by the parties engaged in the collective bargaining process. The

---

sentative said: "The owners apparently thought it was their last chance to break the union." Kaplan, *Let the Games Begin,* SPORTS ILLUSTRATED, Aug. 10, 1981, at 14, 18.

21.   *Talks Resume in Washington,* N.Y. Times, July 21, 1981, at C11, col. 5.

22.   Originally the owners had wanted to rank half of all major league players by position. Depending upon where the player stood on the ranking list, the team signing the free agent could protect either 15 or 18 players. The team losing the player would have the right to select any unprotected player. The Players' Association was willing initially to rank only five percent of all players. *The Issue, id.,* May 25, 1981, at C4, col. 2. In July the Association proposed sending the free agent compensation question to binding arbitration; the owners rejected the proposal. *Chronology of the Baseball Strike, id.,* Aug. 1, 1981, at 18, col. 4.

23.   Under the agreement teams may protect 24 players each if they sign a ranking free agent and 26 if they do not. All other players go into a "compensation pool." "Type A" ranking free agents are those who fall within the top 20% of all players at each playing position based on statistics of the players' two most recent seasons. "Type B" ranking free agents are the players rated in the 20-30% category in their positions. A team that loses a Type A player may select an unprotected player from the pool. A team that loses a Type B player receives a draft choice from the signing team. A team losing an unranked player receives no compensation. *Baseball Strike Issues,* N.Y. Times, Aug. 1, 1981, at 18, col. 1; Kaplan, *supra* note 20, at 14, 18. For a further discussion of the several proposals, see Kaplan, *No Games Today,* SPORTS ILLUSTRATED, June 22, 1981, at 17.

24.   Under the agreement players received credit toward free agent status for the strike period. The contract extended the duration of the basic agreement for one year, to December 31, 1984. Kaplan, *supra* note 20, at 17-18.

25.   The strike cost the players an estimated $28 million in salaries. The clubs' losses for the 713 unplayed games were approximately $116 million. The owners' insurance policy paid $44 million, leaving a net loss of $72 million. Kaplan, *supra* note 20, at 17; *Strike Over, Baseball Resumes Aug. 9,* N.Y. Times, Aug. 1, 1981, at 1, col. 1. Dave Winfield of the Yankees lost approximately $338,500 in salary. *Strike Losses Heavy and Widespread,* N.Y. Times, Aug. 1, 1981, at 17, col. 3. The major league cities also suffered considerable losses. The Philadelphia Chamber of Commerce reported losses of $75,000 to $100,000 for each home game that the Phillies failed to play. Each game missed at Boston's Fenway Park cost the city $18,000 in taxes and $650,000 that fans ordinarily would have spent in and around the stadium. The Mayor of Cincinnati said: "Our local estimate is that for each game not played the community loses $900,000 in money not spent." *Id.* New York City's comptroller estimated that the strike cost the city at least $8,400,000 in lost business and wages. *City's Loss Put at $8.4 Million,* N.Y. Times, Aug. 1, 1981, at 19, col. 2.

willingness of both owners and players to incur those pressures attests to the difficulty of resolving the ancient conflict at issue.

The free agent compensation controversy is only one aspect of the genuine issue that has separated players from owners. For more than a century, baseball's reserve system has bound professional baseball players. The reserve system in the past included several components that limited both the ability of owners to negotiate for players and the right of players to contract freely. Team owners by agreement circumscribed their own capacity to trade in players through the draft,[26] the no-tampering rule,[27] and blacklisting sanctions.[28] The assignment clause,[29] the compensation rule,[30]

---

26. Under the draft owners allocate available players among teams, usually in reverse order of the team's previous year's performance record. Once a team drafts a player, the drafting team holds the exclusive right to contract with that player. Leavell & Millard, *Trade Regulation and Professional Sports*, 26 MERCER L. REV. 603, 610-11 (1975); Pierce, *Organized Professional Team Sports and The Antitrust Laws*, 43 CORNELL L.Q. 566, 603 (1958); Note, *The Battle of the Superstars: Player Restraints in Professional Team Sports*, 32 U. FLA. L. REV. 669, 670 (1980) [hereinafter cited as Note, *Player Restraints*].

27. Professional sports leagues commonly have prohibited member clubs from "tampering" with players on other teams. League bylaws typically prohibit a team from negotiating or making an offer to a player who is under contract with another team. The penalties for violating the rule may include loss of a draft choice and a fine. The justification usually advanced for the rule is that if an athlete is negotiating with another team, he might have a disincentive to play aggressively for his present team. Courts and commentators have disagreed over the validity of this justification. *See* Kapp v. National Football League, 390 F. Supp. 73, 82 (N.D. Cal. 1974); H. DEMMERT, *supra* note 15, at 92.

The Bylaws of the National Basketball Association provide:

(g) Any person who, directly or indirectly, entices, induces, persuades or attempts to entice, induce, or persuade any player, coach, trainer, general manager or any other person who is under contract to any other member of the Association to enter into negotiations for or relating to his services or negotiates or contracts for such services shall, on being charged with such tampering, be given an opportunity to answer such charges after due notice and the Commissioner shall have the power to decide whether or not the charges have been sustained; in the event his decision is that the charges have been sustained, then the Commissioner shall have the power to suspend such person for a definite or indefinite period, or to impose a fine not exceeding $5,000, or inflict both such suspension and fine upon any such person.

For a further discussion of the no-tampering rules, see J. WEISTART & C. LOWELL, *supra* note 13, at 506; Rottenberg, *The Baseball Players' Labor Market*, 64 J. POL. ECON. 242, 245 (1956).

28. Under a blacklisting agreement teams agree not to negotiate with players who are under contract with another team. *See* Rottenberg, *supra* note 27, at 245.

29. An assignment provision permits a team to assign a player's contract to another team without the player's consent. J. WEISTART & C. LOWELL, *supra* note 13, at 292.

30. The compensation rule provides that any club which hires a player who has fulfilled his contractual obligation to his former club must compensate the former employer in the form of cash, a player, or a draft choice. Goldstein, *Out of Bounds Under the Sherman Act? Player Restraints in Professional Team Sports*, 4 PEPPERDINE L. REV. 285, 291 (1977).

and the reserve clause[31] have been parts of the uniform player contracts that owners have required all players to sign. Professor Sobel describes the consequences of the restraints of the reserve system:

> The total effect of these contract provisions and league rules was this. Once a player signed his first professional baseball employment contract, he became the property of his team. His contract could be renewed by the team, year after year, without his consent and at salaries he never agreed to accept. His only options were to play or to retire from professional baseball, because no other team would even consider hiring him as long as he was under contract. Further, he could be traded from team to team, with or without his consent. If he was traded, he was as bound to the new team as he had been to the former team, because the new team had the right to reserve him perpetually.[32]

Since the implementation of the first reserve system over a century ago, players, courts,[33] and commentators[34] have criticized the servitude associated with the system.

The justification for the reserve system advanced most often is the maintenance of team competition. Team owners and commentators postulate that the opportunity for players to move freely from team to team would destroy competition and exciting play among teams within a league.[35] According to this theory, the own-

---

31.  A reserve clause is a contractual provision that binds a player in perpetuity to the club holding his contract. Allison, *Professional Sports and the Antitrust Laws: Status of the Reserve System*, 25 BAYLOR L. REV. 1, 18 (1973); Note, *Baseball's Antitrust Exemption and the Reserve System: Reappraisal of an Anachronism*, 12 WM. & MARY L. REV. 859, 860-62 (1971).

32.  L. SOBEL, PROFESSIONAL SPORTS & THE LAW 91 (1977).

33.  *See, e.g.,* Gardella v. Chandler, 172 F.2d 402 (2d Cir. 1949). For a discussion of *Gardella,* see *infra* text accompanying note 96. In Smith v. Pro-Football, 420 F. Supp. 738, 744-45 (D.D.C. 1976), the court characterized the National Football League player draft as "a group boycott in its classic and most pernicious form." The court found the draft to be a naked restraint on trade with no purpose except stifling of competition. *Id.*

34.  A January 31, 1899, editorial in the *Cleveland Plain Dealer* called baseball "the most grasping and most absolutely selfish and soulless monopoly in existence." HOUSE SUB-COMM. ON STUDY OF MONOPOLY POWER, H.R. DOC. No. 2002, 82d Cong., 2d Sess. 38 (1952) [hereinafter cited as HOUSE REPORT ON ORGANIZED BASEBALL]. Representative Gallagher of Illinois introduced a resolution calling for a federal investigation of organized baseball as a "predaceous [sic] and mendacious trust." *Id.* at 49.

35.  *See* J. WEISTART & C. LOWELL, *supra* note 13, at 596; Morris, *In the Wake of the Flood,* 38 LAW & CONTEMP. PROB. 86, 87-90 (1973); Note, *The Legality of the Rozelle Rule and Related Practices in the National Football League,* 4 FORD. URBAN L.J. 582, 587-89 (1976); Note, *The Super Bowl and the Sherman Act: Professional Team Sports and the Antitrust Laws,* 81 HARV. L. REV. 418, 424-26 (1967) [hereinafter cited as Note, *The Super Bowl and the Sherman Act*]; Comment, *Player Control Mechanisms in Professional Team Sports,* 34 U. PITT. L. REV. 645, 666-70 (1973).

The assumptions about the stabilizing influence of player restraints have been debated. The district court in Mackey v. National Football League, 407 F. Supp. 1000, 1008 (D.

ers' ability and willingness to pay, and, to a lesser extent, the location of the team, would determine team quality in the absence of an effective reserve system. Certain teams would dominate play and alter the competitive balance, with the result that followers easily could predict the outcome of many games. Fan interest would wane and the industry itself ultimately would fail.[36] Because of the imperative that teams be competitive, many have argued that traditional employee contractual freedom cannot exist within the sports industry.[37]

This Article analyzes the history of player-owner relations in professional baseball. Part II of the Article describes attempts by players since the inception of organized baseball to alter the reserve system—the same issue that gave rise to the 1981 strike. Part III of the Article discusses the development of collective bargaining in professional baseball and the rise of the Players' Association. Part IV of the Article analyzes the utility of antitrust laws to challenge player restraints and examines various congressional proposals to bring baseball under the rubric of the antitrust laws. After describing the application of the labor exemption to the negotiated reserve system, the Article concludes that collective bargaining and not antitrust law must shape the contours of baseball's reserve system in the future.

---

Minn. 1975) said, "the existence of the Rozelle Rule and the other restrictive devices on players have not had any material effect on competitive balance in the National Football League." Professor Noll comments,

> A central issue in the debate about the extent to which restrictive practices are necessary in sports centers on the issue of competitive balance. . . . In any systematic analysis of the competitive balance of leagues . . . there is absolutely no evidence that competitive balance is accomplished by the mechanism for dealing with players.

American Enter. Inst. for Pub. Policy Research, Pro Sports: Should Government Intervene? (February 22, 1977). *See* H. DEMMERT, *supra* note 15, at 31-39; J. WEISTART & C. LOWELL, *supra* note 13, at 623-24.

36. *See* Note, *The Super Bowl and the Sherman Act, supra* note 35, at 421; Note, *Flood in the Land of Antitrust: Another Look at Professional Athletics, the Antitrust Laws, and the Labor Exemption,* 7 IND. L. REV. 541, 572-73 (1974) [hereinafter cited as Note, *Flood in the Land of Antitrust*]; Comment, *Monopsony in Manpower: Organized Baseball Meets the Antitrust Laws,* 62 YALE L.J. 576, 585 (1953).

"[M]ost commentators, including those otherwise unsympathetic to the player restraints, have recognized that the success of a league's sports venture depends upon the unpredictability of the outcome of on-the-field competition between clubs." J. WEISTART & C. LOWELL, *supra* note 13, at 595; *see* authorities cited *id.*

37. Krasnow & Levy, *Unionization and Professional Sports,* 51 GEO. L.J. 749, 751 & n.8 (1963); Note, *The Balance of Power in Professional Sports,* 22 ME. L. REV. 459, 471 (1970).

III.  Collective Bargaining Comes of Age

A.  *Early History of the Players' Association: Strike One*

The absence of redress under the antitrust laws for players subject to the restraints of the reserve system led many commentators to urge the use of concerted activity and collective bargaining as a countervailing force to the power of the owners:

> Since the professional athlete has been able to do little when faced with the monopolistic activities of the owners which have resulted in harsh contract provisions and sub-standard working conditions, it would appear that the logical course of action is to experiment with collective action as the possible answer to the professional athlete's problems.[112]

Other commentators viewed the imbalance of bargaining power between the owners and the individual player as an evil that "must be eliminated if the professional sports world is to avoid a total breakdown in labor-management relations."[113] These observers suggested that the players' associations affiliate with national labor organizations to gain expertise and wider influence.[114]

The difficulties, however, of organizing professional athletes appeared to make unionization impracticable, and most observers were doubtful of the success of a unionizing effort.[115] Employment in the industry, some commentators argued, depended entirely upon individual ability.[116] Athletes as a class tended to be individualistic and motivated by rewards other than monetary gain.[117] Other critics noted that "[b]all playing is a calling brief in duration, migratory and seasonal in character."[118] Organizing and collective bargaining, therefore, would be unusually difficult. Public opinion, according to some observers, opposed the unionization of

---

112.  Krasnow & Levy, *supra* note 37, at 759.

113.  *See, e.g.,* Note, *supra* note 37, at 459.

114.  *See, e.g.,* Krasnow & Levy, *supra* note 37, at 774-76; Note, *supra* note 37, at 479-80.

115.  *See* Keith, *Developments in the Application of Antitrust Laws to Professional Team Sports,* 10 Hastings L.J. 119, 136 (1958); Topkis, *Monopoly in Professional Sports,* 58 Yale L.J. 691, 711-12 (1949); Note, *Baseball and the Law—Yesterday and Today,* 32 Va. L. Rev. 1164, 1175 (1946); Comment, *supra* note 36, at 635.

116.  *See* Krasnow & Levy, *supra* note 37, at 759-60; Note, *supra* note 37, at 474; Comment, *supra* note 36, at 635.

117.  *See* Krasnow & Levy, *supra* note 37, at 760.

118.  Comment, *supra* note 36, at 635.

professional athletes.[119] Resort to a work stoppage not only would alienate the public but, because of the seasonal nature of the industry, also would hurt financially weak teams.[120] Indeed, players considered and rejected affiliation with a national union out of fear of damaging their public image or antagonizing owners.[121] Although organizations of players existed in professional team sports, none was a bona fide labor organization engaging in collective bargaining.[122] Skeptics cited the American Baseball Guild fiasco[123] as an example of the futility of organizational efforts.[124]

In response to the threat of unionization in 1946, team owners had implemented a representation plan.[125] Owners, however, limited representation to providing a means for communicating players' suggestions and complaints.[126] Players would "then await whatever action the club owners are willing to take."[127] The Major League Players' Association, which had formed in 1954, operated solely as this kind of conduit for information, without even a full time executive officer for more than a decade. During its early years the Players' Association was neither a union nor a collective bargaining agent.[128] Indeed, the Players' Association itself denied any intention to establish a union.[129] Commentators criticized the inadequacy of the representative system: "In short, the representative system in baseball is a form of company unionism in which the player representatives are afforded an opportunity to air their grievances on a league-wide basis. . . . Unfortunately, reliance on

---

119.  *See id.* at 635-36.

120.  *See id.*

121.  *See* Note, *supra* note 37, at 479; Comment, *supra* note 36, at 628.

122.  L. SOBEL, *supra* note 32, at 267-72; Krasnow & Levy, *supra* note 37, at 762, 771.

123.  *See* notes 96-97 and accompanying text.

124.  *See* Krasnow & Levy, *supra* note 37, at 762; Note, *Arbitration of Grievance and Salary Disputes in Professional Baseball: Evolution of a System of Private Law*, 60 CORNELL L. REV. 1049, 1053 (1975).

125.  *See* L. SOBEL, *supra* note 32, at 272; Maher, *Player's Ass'n: A United Front . . . To Face Owners*, L.A. Times, Feb. 12, 1973, § 3, at 8, col. 1.

126.  HOUSE REPORT ON ORGANIZED BASEBALL, *supra* note 34, at 176; *see* L. SOBEL, *supra* note 32, at 272-73.

127.  HOUSE REPORT ON ORGANIZED BASEBALL, *supra* note 34, at 176.

128.  Krasnow & Levy, *supra* note 37, at 771. The relationship between owners and players was characterized as "paternalistic." Shulman & Baum, *Collective Bargaining in Professional Athletics—The NFL Money Bowl*, 50 CHI. BAR REC. 173 (1969).

129.  *Hearings before the House Subcommittee on Antitrust and Monopoly of the House Comm. on the Judiciary*, 89th Cong., 1st Sess. 104 (1964); Krasnow & Levy, *supra* note 37, at 771. Professional athletes, like many other professional, managerial, and technical employees, often prefer not to be identified as trade union members. *See* Berry & Gould, *A Long Deep Drive to Collective Bargaining: Of Players, Owners, Brawls & Strikes*, 31 CASE W. RES. L. REV. 685, 687 & n.2, 688 & n.3 (1981).

owner benevolence is a rather tenuous solution to the long-range problems in the area."[130]

The Players' Association gradually evolved from its earlier status as an information exchange group to a bona fide labor organization. In 1966 the Association named Marvin Miller, former chief economic advisor and assistant to the President of the United Steelworkers of America, as the executive director of the Association.[131] Early concerted union activity occurred in 1969 when players and managment could not reach agreement on the funding of the players' pension plan. Most players boycotted spring training camps.[132] Labor and management exchanged charges and threats of economic sanctions[133] before the commissioner of baseball intervened to settle the controversy.[134]

The Association's position as a representative organization received further impetus in December 1969 when the National Labor Relations Board indirectly approved the organization's collective bargaining status. The NLRB in *American League of Professional Baseball Clubs and Association of National Baseball League Umpires*[135] reversed the position it had taken in 1946 and held that professional baseball was an industry "in or affecting interstate commerce."[136] Remarkably, the NLRB decision occurred three years before the Supreme Court in *Flood* found that baseball was an industry that affected interstate commerce. This decision subjected the principals of professional baseball to the protections and requirements of the National Labor Relations Act (NLRA).[137] Among its mandates the NLRA requires labor and management to

---

130.  Krasnow & Levy, *supra* note 37, at 772.
131.  L. SOBEL, *supra* note 32, at 273; Note, *supra* note 124, at 1053; Maher, *supra* note 125, at 8. Many commentators have recognized the appointment of Miller as a signal event in the development of the organization as a viable collective bargaining organization. *See Professional Sports, supra* note 52, at 306.
132.  *Players Seek Owners' Compromise on Baseball Pension*, N.Y. Times, Feb. 7, 1969, at 41, col. 1.
133.  J. WEISTART & C. LOWELL, *supra* note 13, at 780. The players charged that the owners caused the delay to test the resolve of the players. The owners said that, if necessary, they would play the exhibition season as well as the regular season with minor league players. *Id.*
134.  *Id.*
135.  180 N.L.R.B. 190 (1969).
136.  *Id.* at 191.
137.  29 U.S.C. §§ 151-69 (1976). The NLRA provides in pertinent part that employees have the "right to self-organization, to form, join, or assist labor organizations, to bargain collectively through representatives of their own choosing, and to engage in other concerted activities for the purpose of collective bargaining or other mutual aid or protection." 29 U.S.C. § 157 (1976).

bargain in good faith over terms and conditions of employment.[138] For professional baseball players the reserve system unquestionably was a mandatory subject of bargaining.[139] In 1972 the Players' Association confronted the owners in the first test of the organization's strength and the owners' resolve. Several months before the Supreme Court's decision in *Flood,* players undertook the first industry-wide strike, demanding an increase in pensions.[140] After a thirteen day work stoppage,[141] players and team owners reached an accord that raised the pension contribution of team owners by approximately $500,000.[142]

The Supreme Court's decision that year in *Flood,* however, left the reserve system wholly intact. The uniform player contract provided that if the player and the owner did not reach agreement prior to the commencement of a season, the team had the right unilaterally to renew the contract and to cut the player's salary by twenty percent.[143] The contract further provided that the player could not play for another team while under contract and that the team could enjoin the player's contract breach.[144] Major league rules continued to prohibit any league member from negotiating with a reserved player,[145] and the player agreed that his team

---

138.  *Id.* § 158(a)(5).

139.  Jacobs and Winter observed: "We find it difficult to construct even a hypothetical argument that a contractual provision so intimately connected with determining the team for which an athlete will play and what salary and other benefits he may extract through bargaining is not a term and condition of employment." Jacobs & Winter, *Antitrust Principles and Collective Bargaining by Athletes: Of Superstars in Peonage,* 81 Yale L.J. 1, 10-11 (1971). *See* Flood v. Kuhn, 316 F. Supp. 271, 283 (S.D.N.Y. 1970), *aff'd,* 443 F.2d 264 (2d Cir. 1971), *aff'd,* 407 U.S. 258 (1972).

140.  J. WEISTART & C. LOWELL, *supra* note 13, at 781.

141.  The players contended that the owners' purpose was to punish the players by making them "eat dirt" and "bend down and kiss the shoes of the owners." *Players' Offer Is Rejected; Long Strike Seems Likely,* N.Y. Times, Apr. 4, 1972, at 49, col. 6. Players also alleged that the owners had terminated several players because of their union activity. *Baseball Owners Reject an Offer, id.,* Apr. 8, 1972, at 19, col. 5. Some commentators argued that the strike was to preserve the "dignity" of the players. J. WEISTART & C. LOWELL, *supra* note 13, at 781 n.39.

142.  *Baseball Strike is Settled; Season to Open Tomorrow,* N.Y. Times, Apr. 14, 1972, at 1, col. 6.

143.  Uniform Player's Contract, clause 10(a), *reprinted in* Flood v. Kuhn, 407 U.S. 258, 259-61 n.1 (1972). The Uniform Player's Contract further provided that Player could be assigned by Club to any other club, *id.* clause 6(a), and that Club would be entitled to injunctive relief to prevent Player from playing baseball for any other organization, *id.* clause 4(a). *See Flood in the Land of Antitrust, supra* note 36, at 543-44.

144.  Uniform Player's Contract, clauses 4(a) & 5(a), *reprinted in* Flood v. Kuhn, 407 U.S. at 259-61 n.1.

145.  Rule 3(g) of the Major League Rules provided:

(g) TAMPERING. To preserve discipline and competition, and to prevent the entice-

could assign him to another team without his consent.[146] Moreover, although the NLRA obligated team owners to bargain with the Players' Association[147] over the reserve system, the duty to bargain does not require the parties to reach an agreement. The duty to bargain dictates only that parties "enter into negotiations with an open and fair mind and with a sincere desire to reach a mutual basis for agreement."[148] Therefore, the owners lawfully could continue to bargain to an impasse over the reserve system without modifying their position.

Although the owners had no legal duty to change the system, by October 1973 the players had sufficient bargaining strength to force the team owners to agree finally to some alterations of the reserve system. As part of a new three year accord between the owners and the Players' Association, the owners agreed to submit their salary disputes with the players to binding arbitration.[149] This aspect of the agreement marked "the end of management's powerful authority to determine salaries unilaterally, leaving a dissatisfied player only two options: accept the offer or quit the game."[150] Moreover, although the Supreme Court in *Flood* had held that the antitrust laws did not prohibit owners from assigning a player's contract without his consent, the owners, nevertheless, acceded to an Association proposal giving a player the right to refuse to be traded under certain circumstances.[151] In announcing the new agreement, a spokesperson for the owners said that the new arbitration system "effectively answers . . . [the] most effective argument against the reserve clause by achieving a balance of

---

ment of players, coaches, managers and umpires, there shall be no negotiations or dealings respecting employment, either present or prospective, between any player, coach or manager and any club other than the club with which he is under contract or acceptance of terms, or by which he is reserved, or which has the player on its Negotiation List, or between any umpire and any league other than the league with which he is under contract . . . unless the club or league with which he is connected shall have, in writing, expressly authorized such negotiations or dealings prior to their commencement.

*Flood in the Land of Antitrust, supra* note 36, at 543 n.9.

146. Uniform Player's Contract, clause 6(a), *reprinted in* Flood v. Kuhn, 407 U.S. at 259-61 n.1.

147. *See supra* notes 137-38 and accompanying text.

148. NLRB v. Truitt Mfg. Co., 351 U.S. 149 (1956); H.J. Heinz Co. v. NLRB, 311 U.S. 514 (1941). *See supra* note 16.

149. *See* L. SOBEL, *supra* note 32, at 91-93; Note, *supra* note 124, at 1067; Bernstein, *Baseball Adopts Plan to Eliminate Holdouts,* L.A. Times, Oct. 11, 1973, § 3, at 1.

150. Bernstein, *supra* note 149, at § 3, at 1.

151. The veto power applied to players with ten or more years of service and five years with one club. L. SOBEL, *supra* note 32, at 95-96; Bernstein, *supra* note 149, at § 3, at 1.

power between player and club."[152] The Players' Association, however, disagreed with this assessment. The Association argued that the reserve system continued to restrain player mobility, and it vowed to lobby Congress to eliminate the reserve system.[153] Forthcoming events, however, would shift the balance of power between player and club and make congressional action unnecessary.

## B.  The Messersmith Arbitration

The reserve clause historically contained a "renewal year" provision, which gave team owners the option to renew a player's contract under the terms of the previous contract if the owner and the player failed to reach agreement on a new contract.[154] Andy Messersmith, a pitcher for the Los Angeles Dodgers, played during the 1975 season under the renewal year provision of his contract. Upon completion of the 1975 season, Messersmith attempted to open negotiations with other teams. When no club bid for his services, Messersmith filed a grievance with the Players' Association, and the union took his complaint through the grievance procedure.[155] The Players' Association alleged before the arbitrator that the baseball clubs had "conspired to deny Mr. Messersmith [his right to contract] and [had] maintained the position that the Los Angeles Club is still exclusively entitled to his services."[156] The renewal clause, according to the Players' Association, gave the Dodgers the right to renew the contract for one additional year only. The Dodgers and the leagues argued that when a team renewed a player's contract "on the same terms" as the previous contract, the re-

---

152.  Bernstein, *supra* note 149, at 10, col. 3 (quoting John J. Gaherin, head of the Player Relations Committee for the Major Leagues of Professional Baseball Clubs).

153.  *Id.*, at § 3, at 1.

154.  The Uniform Player's Contract provided:
"If [prior to the beginning of the season] the Player and the Club have not agreed upon the terms of [a] contract, . . . the Club shall have the right . . . to renew this contract for the period of one year on the same terms . . . .

The Club's right to renew this contract . . . and the promise of the Player not to play otherwise than with the Club have been taken into consideration in determining [the Player's compensation].
Uniform Player's Contract, clauses 10(a) & (b), *reprinted in* Flood v. Kuhn, 407 U.S. at 259-61 n.1.

155.  Article X of the Collective Bargaining Contract contained the grievance procedure. This procedure defined "grievance" as "a complaint which involves the interpretation of, or compliance with, the provisions of any agreement between the Association and the Clubs . . . or any agreement between a Player and a Club . . . ." The grievances consisted of the reserve clauses in the Uniform Player Contracts between the clubs and the grievants. *In re* the Twelve Clubs, 66 LAB. ARB. (BNA) 101, 109 n.20 (1975).

156.  *Id.* at 101.

newed contract contained the right of renewal clause.[157] Thus, in the owners' view the right of renewal was perpetual. In an opinion that revolutionized baseball the arbitrator concluded that the renewal clause gave a club the right to renew the contract for one additional year only and did not create a contract with another renewal clause.[158] The arbitrator noted that although contract law does not prevent parties from entering into perpetual contracts, the intent to make this type of contract must be express and will not be implied, particularly when the contract is for personal services.[159] Accordingly, the arbitrator concluded that "Messersmith was not under contract when his renewal year came to an end" and was free to negotiate with any team he chose.[160]

Many commentators have written about the Messersmith decision and its revolutionary consequence.[161] The propriety of the arbitrator's decision, however, is questionable. An arbitrator's role in contract interpretation is, among other things, to determine the intent of the parties when they executed the contract.

> The rule primarily to be observed in the construction of written agreements is that the interpreter must, if possible, ascertain and give effect to the mutual intent of the parties. . . .
> In determining the intent of the parties, inquiry is made as to what the language meant to the parties when the agreement was written. It is this meaning that governs, not the meaning that can be possibly read into the language.[162]

When Messersmith contracted with the Dodgers, both parties certainly believed that the language in question embodied the reserve system as it had always operated.

> Since the issue before [the arbitrator] was purely one of contract interpretation, one might ask why the arbitrator did not give greater weight to the fact that it has historically been assumed that baseball's right to renew was perpetual in nature. It is generally accepted that particular terms of a contract are to be interpreted consistent with the customs and usages which the parties have developed under it.[163]

---

157.  *Id.* at 112-13.
158.  *Id.* at 114.
159.  *Id.* at 113.
160.  *Id.* at 114.
161.  *See* Comment, *Nearly a Century in Reserve: Organized Baseball, Collective Bargaining and the Antitrust Exemption Enter the 80's,* 8 PEPPERDINE L. REV. 313, 338 (1981). "The result [of the decision and free agency] was an unprecedented increase in salaries. In 1976 . . . the average salary was $52,300. By 1980 it had risen to $143,756 . . . ." Kaplan, *supra* note 23, at 17, 18.
162.  F. ELKOURI & E. ELKOURI, HOW ARBITRATION WORKS 202-03 (3d ed. 1973).
163.  J. WEISTART & C. LOWELL, *supra* note 13, at 518-19 (footnotes omitted); *see* A. CORBIN, CORBIN ON CONTRACTS §§ 544-45 & 556-58 (1951). Moreover, the Restatement (Sec-

The reserve system had bound the players to teams in perpetuity since the early years of baseball. Moreover, the arbitrator noted that when the contract was executed in 1973, the Players' Association had acquiesced to the renewal year provision "reluctantly."[164] If the parties had believed only one year after the *Flood* decision that the contract eliminated the reserve system and thereafter would bind the players only for one additional year, the Players' Association assent would not have been "reluctant." Indeed, such a contract would have achieved the goal of player contractual freedom that the players had sought for nearly a century through court action,[165] the creation of new leagues,[166] and strikes.[167] Notwithstanding these years of conflict, the arbitrator concluded that the parties did not *intend* to bind the players in perpetuity.[168] The decision thus reversed a century of baseball history and fundamentally changed the relationship between the owner and the player. By limiting the reserve period to one year, the decision greatly diminished the owners' overwhelming contractual advantage. The pendulum, for the first time, had swung to the players.

---

ond) of Contracts sets forth the following standards for contract interpretation:

§ 201. WHOSE MEANING PREVAILS

. . . .

(2) Where the parties have attached different meanings to a promise or agreement or a term thereof, it is interpreted in accordance with the meaning attached by one of them if at the time the agreement was made

(a) that party did not know of any different meaning attached by . . . the first party; or

(b) that party had no reason to know of any different meaning attached by the other, and the other had reason to know the meaning attached by the first party.

RESTATEMENT (SECOND) OF CONTRACTS § 201 (1979).

164.   *In re* the Twelve Clubs, 66 LAB. ARB. (BNA) 101, 107 (1975).

165.   *See supra* text accompanying notes 84-111.

166.   *See supra* text accompanying notes 43-83.

167.   *See supra* text accompanying notes 140-42; *infra* text accompanying notes 172-80.

168.   The arbitrator protested too much when he wrote:

It deserves emphasis that this decision strikes no blow emancipating players from claimed serfdom or involuntary servitude such as was alleged in the Flood case. It does not condemn the Reserve System presently in force on constitutional or moral grounds. It does not counsel or require that the System be changed to suit the predilections or preferences of an arbitrator acting as a Philosopher-King intent upon imposing his own personal brand of industrial justice on the parties. It does no more than seek to interpret and apply provisions that are in the agreements of the parties . . . . To go beyond this would be an act of quasi-judicial arrogance!

*In re* the Twelve Clubs, 66 LAB. ARB. (BNA) 101, 112 (1975).

## C.   Strike Two

What antitrust attacks on the reserve system restraints had done for the players in the other major professional sports, the *Messersmith* arbitration decision did for baseball players: it provided a major boost to their union's efforts and "forced the owners to engage in good faith, arms-length negotiations . . . concerning these restraints and all other aspects of player-management relations."[169] In the first contract negotiated after *Messersmith,* the owners for the first time found themselves attempting to persuade the players of the need for some form of reserve system. The Players' Association and the owners agreed to a new system under which a player would be bound to a team for six years instead of becoming a free agent after only one year.[170] During each year of the last three years of that period the player and the owner would negotiate compensation terms. If the parties were unable to agree, the player could take his claim to an arbitrator, who would determine whether the owner's proposal or the player's demand more closely represented the player's relative value. After the six-year contract period had elapsed the player would become a free agent and any team desiring his services and willing to enter the bidding could select him. This new system still would require the team that acquired the player to give up a draft choice to the player's former team.[171] Nevertheless, the new contract replaced the historic reserve system and gave the players freedom of movement for the first time in nearly a century.

The 1976 collective bargaining contract expired on December 31, 1979. During negotiations for a new contract the owners proposed that the club losing a free agent should receive greater compensation than simply a draft choice. Under the owners' proposal the club that a free agent left would have a limited right to select a player from the team that signed the free agent. A team could exempt fifteen players from selection, leaving ten players eligible for

---

169. Note, *supra* note 26, at 670; *see* Comment, *supra* note 161, at 340.

170. 1976 Baseball Basic Agreement, Art. XVII, B(2), *reprinted in* Comment, *supra* note 161, at 358; *see* Berry & Gould, *supra* note 129, at 777; Kaplan, *supra* note 23, at 18.

171. 1976 Baseball Basic Agreement, Art. XVII C(2)(c), *reprinted in* Comment, *supra* note 161, at 362; *see* Berry & Gould, *supra* note 129, at 778; Kaplan, *supra* note 23, at 18. Commentators noted the significance of the contract: "Baseball's owners and players reached agreement today on a four-year pact that for the first time gives the players freedom of movement. . . . The agreement . . . replaces the so-called reserve system which throughout the baseball history has restricted a player to one club traded, sold or released him." *New Baseball Contract Limits Reserve System,* N.Y. Times, July 13, 1976, at 1, col. 1.

selection by the club that the free agent had left.[172] Negotiations over this issue stalled, and on April 1, 1980, the players struck for the second time in a decade. The players walked out of spring training camps, forcing cancellation of the final eight days and ninety-two games of the exhibition season.[173] The players agreed to return for the commencement of the season, but voted to strike on May 23, 1980, unless they reached agreement with the owners.[174] On May 23 the parties reached an accord on all issues except free agent compensation,[175] which they referred to a player-management committee for further study.[176] Under the May 23 agreement the owners reserved the right to implement unilaterally their final version of the compensation scheme if the parties were unable to agree on the free agent compensation issue.[177] Similarly, the players reserved the right to strike over the issue.

The team owners implemented their free agent compensation plan on February 19, 1981, after the player-management committee failed to reach a compromise.[178] On February 25, 1981, the Players' Association executive board approved a May 29, 1981, strike date.[179] Subsequently, the NLRB attempted to enjoin the implementation of the owners' compensation scheme.[180] Finally, on June 12, 1981, the players struck for the third time in nine years. The third strike was truly a watershed event in baseball labor-management relations. The 1981 strike and the negotiated settlement completed the transformation of dispute resolution in baseball—particularly over the reserve system issue—to collective bargaining.

---

172. Comment, *supra* note 161, at 350.

173. Note, *supra* note 26, at 681; Kaplan, *supra* note 23, at 17-21.

174. *Chronology of the Baseball Strike, supra* note 22, at 18, col. 4.

175. *Id.; see* Comment, *supra* note 161 at 351.

176. *Chronology of the Baseball Strike,* N.Y. Times, Aug. 1, 1981, at 18, col. 4.

177. This element of the agreement actually gained no more for the owners than the law already permitted. Under the NLRA management may implement its last best offer if the parties reach an impasse during collective bargaining negotiations. Taft Broadcasting Co., 163 N.L.R.B. 475, 478 (1967), *enforced sub nom.* AFTRA v. NLRB, 395 F.2d 622 (D.C. Cir. 1968); Bi-Rite Foods, Inc., 147 N.L.R.B. 59, 64-65 (1964). *See* R. GORMAN, BASIC TEXT ON LABOR LAW UNIONIZATION AND COLLECTIVE BARGAINING 445-46 (1976).

178. *Chronology of the Baseball Strike, supra* note 22, at 18, col. 4.

179. *Id.*

180. N.Y. Times, June 11, 1981, at D21, col. 4. Judge Henry F. Werker ruled that "there is no reasonable cause to believe that an unfair labor practice has been committed." *Id.; see supra* note 5.

## IV. The Irrelevancy of Antitrust

Baseball's antitrust exemption, created in *Federal Baseball*[181] and reaffirmed in *Toolson* and *Flood*,[182] permits baseball—alone among professional sports—to operate freely as a monopoly. Courts,[183] commentators,[184] members of Congress,[185] and players[186] have criticized the reserve system restraints. Moreover, commentators have criticized *Flood* on both legal and policy grounds.[187] Widespread recognition existed that the reserve system restraints clearly would violate the antitrust laws but for the baseball exemption. Antitrust challenges in all other major professional team sports were responsible for fundamental restructuring of player restraint systems during the 1970's. Invalidation of player restraint systems in case after case under the Sherman Act in other professional sports[188] forced owners to engage in good faith collective bargaining with the associations that represent their players.[189] As a result, major changes in the player restraint systems in football, basketball, and hockey occurred during the 1970's. Nevertheless, antitrust law, not collective bargaining, provided the impetus for

---

181. *See supra* notes 84-92 and accompanying text.

182. *See supra* notes 101-08 and accompanying text.

183. *See* Gardella v. Chandler, 172 F.2d 402 (2d Cir. 1949); *supra* notes 95-100 and accompanying text. One court said: "The *quasi* peonage of baseball players under the operations [sic] of this plan and agreement is contrary to the spirit of American institutions and is contrary to the spirit of the Constitution. . . . " American League Baseball Club v. Chase, 86 Misc. 441, 465, 149 N.Y.S. 6, 19 (1914) (emphasis in original).

184. *See supra* note 34.

185. *See, e.g., Professional Baseball: Hearings on S.2373 Before the Subcomm. on Antitrust and Monopoly of the Senate Comm. on the Judiciary,* 92d Cong., 1st Sess. 12 (1971) (remarks of Sen. Ervin).

186. *See, e.g.,* C. Flood, The Way It Is (1971).

187. *See* L. Sobel, *supra* note 32, at 66-72 (calling the decision a misapplication of stare decisis and an inappropriate reliance on testimony that owners would not have invested in teams but for the exemption); Comment, *Baseball's Antitrust Exemption: The Limits of Stare Decisis,* 12 B.C. Ind. & Comm. L. Rev. 737 (1971) (emphasizing that although Congress has refused to enact legislation bringing baseball within the antitrust laws, it has also refused specifically to sanction the exemption); Comment, *Antitrust Law—Baseball Reserve System—Concerted Conspiracy—Stare Decisis—Congressional Inaction—Professional Baseball Remains Exempt from State and Federal Antitrust Statutes,* 48 Notre Dame Law. 460 (1972) (criticizing the Court for accepting the owners' competitive balance theory while rejecting it in *Radovich*); *see also* Allison, *supra* note 31; Note, *Applicability of Antitrust Laws to Baseball,* 2 Mem. St. U.L. Rev. 299 (1972); *see generally* Berry & Gould, *supra* note 129, at 729 & n.129 (discussing criticism of the courts' reliance on stare decisis as the basis of baseball's exemption from the antitrust laws).

188. *See, e.g.,* Philadelphia World Hockey Club, Inc. v. Philadelphia Hockey Club, Inc., 351 F. Supp. 462 (E.D. Pa. 1972) (hockey); Peto v. Madison Square Garden Corp., 1958 Trade Cas. (CCH) ¶ 69,106 (S.D.N.Y.) (hockey).

189. *See* Note, *supra* note 26, at 670.

the restructuring of the player restraint systems in these sports. One commentator observed, "[C]ollective bargaining on the restraints themselves was a joke. There never would have been a discussion about the draft, the reserve clause, or the Rozelle rule, between the leagues and the players had it not been for the antitrust laws, period, exclamation point."[190] Baseball players, however, could not use antitrust law to relax player restraints because of the *Flood* decision. Without the antitrust option players faced a closely knit monopoly of employers who were free to fix conditions of employment. Thus, baseball's exemption from the antitrust laws left collective action as the players' only recourse.

## A.  Congressional Inaction

Congress has considered bills that addressed the role of antitrust law in professional sports on many occasions. Between 1951 and 1965 members of Congress introduced more than sixty bills on this issue.[191] Some bills would have exempted all professional sports from the antitrust laws;[192] other proposals would have included baseball within the antitrust laws.[193] Finally, some bills embraced compromise approaches.[194] One bill, for example, subjected professional sports to coverage of the antitrust statutes but exempted certain practices that legislators considered essential to the successful operation of professional sports.[195] Another legislative approach subjected professional sports to the antitrust laws, but empowered courts to permit certain practices under a rule of reason.[196]

Congress did not adopt any of these proposals. This refusal to extend the coverage of the antitrust laws to professional sports in part reflected a consensus that some form of restraint on player

---

190.  *Professional Sports, supra* note 52, at 307.

191.  Hoffman, *supra* note 93, at 241.

192.  *See, e.g.,* H.R. 5383, 85th Cong., 1st Sess. (1957); H.R. 4229, H.R. 4230, H.R. 4231, 82d Cong., 2d Sess. (1952).

193.  *See, e.g.,* H.R. 5307, H.R. 5319, 85th Cong., 1st Sess. (1957).

194.  *See* H.R. 6876, H.R. 6877, H.R. 8023, H.R. 8124, 85th Cong., 1st Sess. (1957).

195.  H.R. Res. 10378, introduced by Congressman Celler, expressly exempted activities that were "reasonably necessary" to equalize competitive playing strengths, to grant exclusive franchise territories, and to preserve public confidence in the integrity of professional sports. *See Organized Professional Team Sports: Hearings on S. 616 and S. 886 Before the Subcomm. on Antitrust and Monopoly of the Senate Comm. on the Judiciary,* 86th Cong., 1st Sess. 5 (1959).

196.  *See Hearings on H.R. 5307, H.R. 5319, H.R. 5383, H.R. 6876, H.R. 8023, and H.R. 8124 Before the Antitrust Subcomm. of the House Comm. on the Judiciary,* 85th Cong., 1st Sess. 2 (1957); L. SOBEL, *supra* note 32, at 38.

mobility was essential to the survival of league sports.[197] Moreover, the reticence of Congress to tamper with the internal regulation of sports, and particularly baseball, unquestionably reflected the sacrosanct position that baseball holds in the United States. Throughout the debates on these measures members of Congress demonstrated a marked preference for intrasport dispute resolution:

> Constant intervention in their affairs by paternalistic do-gooders will lead to nothing but trouble for all concerned. In our view, the policy decisions of sports should be made by people in sports—the owners and players alike. They should not be made by men in black robes who may never have been to a ball park.[198]

The 1981 strike and negotiated settlement only can amplify this congressional reluctance to interfere in the internal workings of the baseball industry. Both labor and management, having attained relative parity in bargaining power, appear fully capable of protecting the interests of employees and the owners without the need for antitrust measures to alter the rules of employment.

### B.  The Labor Exemption and its Application to the Negotiated Reserve System

The 1981 strike and negotiated resolution effectively ends debate over whether the antitrust laws should apply to baseball's reserve system. The reserve system now has been subjected to rigorous collective bargaining. As a result, even if Congress or the courts removed baseball's exemption from the antitrust laws, the labor exemption to the antitrust laws would foreclose an antitrust challenge now brought by a player dissatisfied by the restraints of the reserve system.[199]

The labor exemption represents an attempt to reconcile two important national policies that under some circumstances are inherently at odds. The purpose of antitrust legislation is to foster competition in the marketplace.[200] National labor policy, however,

---

197.  *See, e.g.*, Pierce, *supra* note 26, at 580.

198.  H.R. REP. No. 1720, 85th Cong., 2d Sess. 12 (1958).

199.  Congressional efforts to remove baseball's exemption have continued. During the summer of 1981, broadcaster Howard Cosell and baseball team owner Ted Turner among others testified before a congressional committee that no justifications existed for the continued exemption. *See* L.A. Times, July 17, 1981, § III at 4, col. 1; *id.*, July 16, 1981, § III at 4, col. 1; *id.*, July 15, 1981, § III at 5, col. 1.

200.  Northern Pac. Ry. v. United States, 356 U.S. 1, 4-5 (1958) ("The Sherman Act was designed to be a comprehensive charter of economic liberty aimed at preserving free and unfettered competition as the rule of trade."); Allen Bradley Co. v. Local Union No. 3, IBEW, 325 U.S. 797, 806 (1945) ("[Antitrust policy] . . . seeks to preserve a competitive business economy."); L. SULLIVAN, HANDBOOK OF THE LAW OF ANTITRUST 14 (1977) ("The

reflects a congressional assessment that individual bargaining with employers creates an inequality of bargaining power that "prevent[s] the stabilization of competitive wage rates and working conditions between industries."[201] The preamble to the NLRA sets forth the intention of Congress to protect unions and to encourage collective bargaining:

> It is declared to be the policy of the United States to eliminate the causes of certain substantial obstructions to the free flow of commerce . . . by encouraging the practice and procedure of collective bargaining and by protecting the exercise by working of full freedom of association, self-organization, and designation of representatives of their own choosing, for the purpose of negotiating the terms and conditions of their employment or other mutual aid or protection.[202]

As a result, unions, in pursuit of improved terms and conditions of employment for employees, have negotiated and struck for contracts establishing uniform wages, hours, and working conditions. One effect of the uniform provisions is that competition in the labor market is eliminated.[203] In addition, union activity has restricted competition in the product market to the extent that labor costs determine product prices.[204] Thus, unions and their legitimate goals are, by their nature, anticompetitive.[205]

The Supreme Court in *Allen Bradley Co. v. Local Union No. 3, IBEW*[206] succinctly stated the conflict that the courts face when attempting to fashion an accomodation between labor and antitrust policies:

> [W]e have two declared congresssional policies which it is our responsibility to try to reconcile. The one seeks to preserve a competitive business economy; the other to preserve the rights of labor to organize to better its conditions through the agency of collective bargaining. We must determine here how far Congress intended activities under one of these policies to neutralize the results envisioned by the other.[207]

---

purpose of the antitrust laws is to promote competition and to inhibit monopoly and restraints upon freedom of trade in all sectors of the economy to which these laws apply."). *See* Fried & Crabtree, *Labor*, 33 ANTITRUST L.J. 38 (1967).

    201.   National Labor Relations Act § 1, 29 U.S.C. § 151 (1976).

    202.   *Id.*

    203.   Cox, *Labor and the Antitrust Laws: Pennington and Jewel Tea*, 46 B.U.L. REV. 317, 317-18 (1966).

    204.   A. COX, D. BOK, & R. GORMAN, CASES AND MATERIALS ON LABOR LAW 872 (9th ed. 1981).

    205.   "In short, unionization, collective bargaining and standardization of wages and working conditions are inherently inconsistent with many of the assumptions at the heart of anti-trust policy." *Id.* at 872.

    206.   325 U.S. 797 (1945).

    207.   *Id.* at 806.

Courts created the labor exemption to the antitrust laws to harmonize these conflicting policies. Under the labor exemption doctrine courts, in certain circumstances, will not subject agreements about wages, hours, and conditions of employment that employers and unions have reached through collective bargaining to antitrust scrutiny.[208]

Commentators first advocated application of the labor exemption to immunize collectively bargained player restraint systems from the antitrust laws at the time *Flood* was pending before the Supreme Court. Michael Jacobs and Professor Winter in a seminal article argued that the Supreme Court had granted certiorari improvidently in *Flood*.[209] Since the team owners and the Players' Association had engaged in collective bargaining regarding a mandatory term or condition of employment—in this case the reserve system—as required by the labor laws, Jacobs and Winter opined that antitrust policy should be subordinate to labor policy favoring collective bargaining.[210] To conclude otherwise, they argued, would threaten two fundamental tenets of labor law: "the exclusive power of the bargaining agent and freedom of contract between employer and union."[211] Supreme Court precedent had held clearly that the courts should invoke the antitrust laws only when employers conspired to utilize their collective bargaining relationship as a sword to injure competitors.[212] A conspiracy of this

---

208. The labor exemption to the antitrust laws is a subject that has engaged many of the nation's leading labor and antitrust scholars. The focus of the treatment in this Article is solely upon the application of the doctrine to player restraint systems in professional team sports. A partial list of important writings on the labor exemption to the antitrust laws includes: Boudin, *The Sherman Act and Labor Disputes* (pts. 1 & 2), 39 COLUM. L. REV. 1283 (1939), 40 COLUM. L. REV. 14 (1940); Cox, *Labor and Antitrust Laws—A Preliminary Analysis*, 104 U. PA. L. REV. 252 (1955); Handler & Zifchak, *Collective Bargaining and the Antitrust Laws: The Emasculation of the Labor Exemption*, 81 COLUM. L. REV. 459 (1981); Meltzer, *Labor Unions, Collective Bargaining, and the Antitrust Laws*, 32 U. CHI. L. REV. 659 (1965); St. Antoine, Connell: *Antitrust Law at the Expense of Labor Law*, 62 VA. L. REV. 603 (1976); Sovern, *Some Ruminations on Labor, the Antitrust Laws and* Allen Bradley, 13 LAB. L.J. 957 (1962); Winter, *Collective Bargaining and Competition: The Application of Antitrust Standards to Union Activities*, 73 Yale L.J. 14 (1963).

209. Jacobs & Winter, *supra* note 139, at 29. For a discussion of Flood v. Kuhn, see *supra* notes 103-08 and accompanying text.

210. Jacobs & Winter, *supra* note 139, at 29.

211. *Id.* at 6.

212. *Id.* at 26 (citing Local Union No. 189, Amalgamated Meat Cutters v. Jewel Tea, 381 U.S. 676 (1965); UMW v. Pennington, 381 U.S. 657 (1965); Allen Bradley Co. v. Local Union No. 3, IBEW, 325 U.S. 797 (1945)). Subsequently, the Court in Connell Constr. Co. v. Plumbers & Steamfitters Local Union No. 100, 421 U.S. 616 (1975), proved this conclusion unfounded. In *Connell Construction* the union pressured the employer to agree to subcontract certain work only to firms who were signatory to collective bargaining contracts with

type, Jacobs and Winter argued, was not present in *Flood,* which concerned the reserve clause—"strictly a labor market issue."[213]

The Supreme Court's adherence to *Federal Baseball* and *Toolson* in *Flood* made any consideration of the labor exemption unnecessary. Justice Marshall, however, referred to the labor exemption in his dissent in *Flood,* finding it inapposite to that case:

> There is a surface appeal to respondents' argument that petitioner's sole remedy lies in filing a claim with the National Labor Relations Board, but this argument is premised on the notion that management and labor have agreed to accept the reserve clause. This notion is contradicted, in part, by the record in this case. Petitioner suggests that the reserve system was thrust upon the players by the owners and that the recently formed players' union has not had time to modify or eradicate it. If this is true, the question arises as to whether there would then be any exemption from the antitrust laws in this case.[214]

Although the Supreme Court did not rely on the labor exemption doctrine in *Flood,* the other professional sports leagues utilized the defense in subsequent player challenges to their reserve systems. During the 1970's the players in other professional team sports repeatedly challenged player restraint systems.[215] In each of these actions the leagues invoked the labor exemption to preserve the player restraint systems. For example, in *Mackey v. National Football League*[216] present and former players challenged the free agent compensation structure of the National Football League. The free agent provision, commonly known as the Rozelle Rule, permitted the commissioner of the National Football League to designate the compensation to be awarded to a team losing a free agent from the team hiring that athlete.[217] "The case developed

---

the union. Simultaneously, it disavowed any interest in representing the employer's employees. The Supreme Court held the agreement outside of the labor exemption notwithstanding that the employer had made no effort to utilize its collective bargaining relationship to restrain competition in the product market.

213.   Jacobs & Winter, *supra* note 139, at 27.

214.   Flood v. Kuhn, 407 U.S. at 295 (Marshall, J., dissenting).

215.   Smith v. Pro-Football, 420 F. Supp. 738 (D.D.C. 1976) (football); Mackey v. National Football League, 407 F. Supp. 1000 (D. Minn. 1975), *remanded,* 543 F.2d 606 (8th Cir. 1976) (football); Robertson v. National Basketball Ass'n, 389 F. Supp. 867 (S.D.N.Y. 1975) (basketball); Kapp v. National Football League, 390 F. Supp. 73 (N.D. Cal. 1974) (football); Philadelphia World Hockey Club, Inc. v. Philadelphia Hockey Club, Inc., 351 F. Supp. 462 (E.D. Pa. 1972) (hockey); Boston Professional Hockey Ass'n v. Cheevers, 348 F. Supp. 261 (D. Mass.), *remanded,* 472 F.2d 127 (1st Cir. 1972) (hockey).

216.   543 F.2d 606 (8th Cir. 1976).

217.   The Rozelle Rule stated:

> Any player, whose contract with a League club has expired, shall thereupon become a free agent and shall no longer be considered a member of the team of that club following the expiration date of such contract. Whenever a player, becoming a free

into a major test for the labor exemption question. Unlike the . . . prior sports cases in which the exemption question was decided in preliminary proceedings, the district court opinion in *Mackey* followed a full evidentiary trial on the antitrust issues."[218] The district court found that the Rozelle Rule constituted an unreasonable restraint on trade.[219] On appeal, the Eighth Circuit set forth a three-pronged test to determine the applicability of the labor exemption in the context of antitrust challenges to player restraints:

> First, the labor policy favoring collective bargaining may potentially be given pre-eminence over the antitrust laws where the restraint on trade primarily affects only the parties to the collective bargaining relationship. Second, federal labor policy is implicated sufficiently to prevail only where the agreement sought to be exempted concerns a mandatory subject of collective bargaining. Finally, the policy favoring collective bargaining is furthered to the degree necessary to override the antitrust laws only where the agreement sought to be exempted is the product of bona fide arm's-length bargaining.[220]

The court found that the Rozelle Rule had no appreciable impact outside the bargaining unit and that it affected "only the parties to the agreements sought to be exempted."[221] Moreover, team compensation for the loss of a free agent fell within the definition of wages, hours, and working conditions and, therefore, was a mandatory subject of bargaining.[222] The League's claim of immunity under the labor exemption, however, failed the third prong of the court's test because the Rozelle Rule had not been the subject

---

agent in such manner, thereafter signs a contract with a different club in the League, then, unless mutually satisfactory arrangements have been concluded between the two League clubs, the Commissioner may name and then award to the former club one or more players, from the Active, Reserve, or Selection List (including future selection choices) of the acquiring club as the Commissioner in his sole discretion deems fair and equitable; any such decision by the Commissioner shall be final and conclusive. CONSTITUTION AND BY-LAWS FOR THE NATIONAL FOOTBALL LEAGUE, art. 12.1(H), *reprinted in* J. WEISTART & C. LOWELL, *supra* note 13, at 502-03, n. 167.

218. J. WEISTART & C. LOWELL, *supra* note 13, § 5.06, at 575.

219. The district court held the Rozelle Rule to be a per se violation of the Sherman Act as well as impermissable under the rule of reason test. Mackey v. National Football League, 407 F. Supp. at 1007-08. The court found that the Rozelle Rule effectively deterred clubs from signing free agents, *id.* at 1006-07, and thus, was "substantially identical" to a perpetual reserve system, *id.* at 1006. Under the rule of reason analysis the district court found the rule (1) unreasonably broad because it affected all players, not merely those whose movement might upset competitive balance; (2) unreasonable in its failure to provide procedures to inform players of negotiations for his services and to protect against a current employer's unreasonable actions which might discourage trades; (3) unreasonable in its duration; and (4) unreasonable in conjunction with other anticompetitive practices of defendants. *Id.* at 1007-08.

220. Mackey v. National Football League, 543 F.2d at 614 (citations omitted).

221. *Id.* at 615.

222. *Id.*

of bona fide arm's-length bargaining.[223] Thus, the exemption from coverage of the antitrust laws would not promote collective bargaining under the circumstances of *Mackey*.[224]

After the *Mackey* decision the League and the Players' Association negotiated an agreement over the free agent compensation issue.[225] In a subsequent challenge to this agreement, the Eighth Circuit again considered the application of the labor exemption to player restraints.

> We emphasize today, as we did in *Mackey* . . . that the subject of player movement restrictions is a proper one for resolution in the collective bargaining context. When so resolved, as it appears to have been in the current collective bargaining agreement, the labor exemption to antitrust attack applies, and the merits of the bargaining agreement are not an issue for court determination.[226]

The Sixth Circuit in *McCourt v. California Sports, Inc.*[227] recently addressed the application of the labor exemption to negotiated player restraints. In 1976 the National Hockey League and the Hockey Players' Association negotiated a collective bargaining agreement that provided for an "equalization payment" or free agent compensation rule. In *McCourt* the league assigned plaintiff player to a new team as compensation against his wishes, and plaintiff challenged the equalization payment rule as violative of the antitrust laws. The National Hockey League argued that the labor exemption immunized the provision from antitrust scrutiny.[228] The trial court found that the equalization payment rule had been imposed unilaterally upon the Players' Association and, therefore, failed the third prong of the *Mackey* test.[229] On appeal the Sixth Circuit reversed the district court and held that the labor exemption was applicable to the equalization payment provision.[230] The court agreed that *Mackey* sets forth the proper standard to determine whether the labor exemption is applicable in a given case.[231] The court, however, concluded that the equalization pay-

---

223.  *Id.* at 615-16.

224.  *Id.*

225.  Reynolds v. National Football League, 584 F.2d 280, 282 (8th Cir. 1978).

226.  *Id.* at 289. In this case fifteen active and one inactive NFL players objected to the settlement agreement between the NFL and the National Football League Players' Association following the *Mackey* decision.

227.  600 F.2d 1193 (6th Cir. 1979).

228.  McCourt v. California Sports, Inc., 460 F. Supp. 904, 910 (E.D. Mich. 1978), *rev'd*, 600 F.2d 1193 (6th Cir. 1979).

229.  *Id.* For the *Mackey* test, see text accompanying note 220.

230.  McCourt v. California Sports, Inc., 600 F.2d at 1203.

231.  *Id.* at 1198.

ment provision was the product of collective bargaining:

> [T]he trial court failed to recognize the well established principle that nothing in the labor law compels either party negotiating over mandatory subjects of collective bargaining to yield on its initial bargaining position. Good faith bargaining is all that is required. That the position of one party on an issue prevails unchanged does not mandate the conclusion that there was no collective bargaining over the issue.[232]

The court found that the equalization payment provision was the product of arm's length bargaining and, therefore, that it was immune from antitrust interdiction under the labor exemption doctrine.

The *Mackey-McCourt* standard for the application of the labor exemption in the context of player restraints represents an accomodation of the collective bargaining process within the antitrust laws. Continued application of this doctrine, however, leads to the conclusion that future action by Congress or the courts to bring the baseball player restraint system within the purview of the antitrust laws is now unnecessary. The reserve system is a mandatory subject of bargaining and primarily affects only the parties to the agreement. Arm's length collective bargaining is shaping the contours of the reserve system in professional baseball. Thus, the negotiated format of the reserve system restraints is appropriately immune from antitrust scrutiny.

## V.  CONCLUSION

The 1981 strike was the third work stoppage in the history of baseball and the first to come in midseason. The strike was costly to the players, the owners, related businesses, the cities, and, of course, the followers of the game. After seven weeks of often bitter negotiations, management and labor finally reached a resolution of the issues. Because of the events of the 1981 strike, collective bargaining will shape the contours of the reserve system, with all of the costs and periodic dislocations that attend this system of dispute resolution. Congressional action, which advocates sought in order to bring baseball within the antitrust laws, is no longer necessary. Moreover, the labor exemption from the antitrust laws clearly would foreclose attack by dissatisfied players even if the courts or Congress revoked the historic exemption. The application of the antitrust laws to the reserve system "is an issue whose time

---

232.  *Id.* at 1200.

has come and gone."[233] Collective bargaining has come of age in the United States' national pastime. In that arena alone players and management will carry on the historic conflict over the reserve system.

---

233.  Jacobs & Winter, *supra* note 139, at 1.

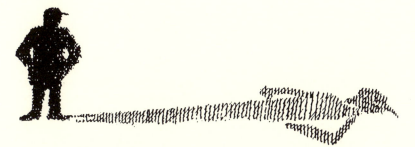

# When the Commissioner was the Law
## *or* When Czardom was in Flower
### Norm Rosenberg

In September of 1987, an arbitrator ruled that major league baseball owners had conspired to break "the law." Specifically, Thomas Roberts decided that club owners had violated Article 18H of the contractual agreement between capital and labor— better known as "the owners" and the "The Major League Baseball Players Association"—by "act[ing] in concert with other clubs" in refusing to bargain with free agents. In simple terms, the owners, obviously encouraged by Commissioner Peter Ueberroth, sought to use their superior economic resources and bargaining power to drive down player salaries. But truth, justice, and the American way triumphed: "The law" stepped in, once again, to remind baseball owners that they could no more make up "the rules" as they went along than could their players on the field.

Robert's decision, along with the subsequent "remedy" that redressed Kirk Gibson in Dodger Blue and left six less-marketable players hanging on the "free agent" rack, joined the burgeoning list of legal precedents that now make up "the law of baseball." Although the Commissioner himself emerged relatively unscathed, the decision underscored, once more, precisely how much baseball law has changed since the days of Commissioner Landis, the white-maned patriarch who, in large measure, *did* make up rules as he went along And in significant contrast with both the pre-Landis era and the recent past, the nation's legal system let baseball's first Commissioner, a former Federal District Court Judge, have broad sway. Truly, during the 1920s and 1930s, baseball's own Czardom was in flower.[1]

Kenesaw Mountain Landis arrived at a critical moment in baseball's history. Surveying their futures, the owners of 1920 could find disturbing portents, many of them legal ones, and these helped Landis to gain immense grants of power from the owners as he bargained over the precise terms under which he would leave the federal bench for baseball's new commissionership.

Some of baseball's legal problems were longstanding ones. Anticipating the labor-capital-contractual battles of more recent times, for example, baseball owners consistently discovered that the nation's law courts invariably looked askance at the "reserve clause," the provision of the stan-

21

dard baseball contract that bound players to a single club year after year. During the Players League revolt at the end of 1890s and again during the Federal League challenge of 1914-16, courts ruled such coercive terms unenforceable.

A 1914 decision by the New York Supreme Court was especially blunt. Ironically, the case at hand concerned Hal Chase, the cagey first baseman who championed legal proprieties in the law courts while simultaneously establishing the record for illegally fixing games on the field. But the New York court was only concerned wth the terms of Chase's public contract which the White Sox unsuccessfully claimed prevented Prince Hal from "jumping" to the Federal League. Seeing baseball's contracts as analogous to the debt-peonage arrangements forced upon Mexican immigrants in the Southwest, the New York Court found the standard contract "contrary to the spirit of American institutions" and "to the spirit of the Constitution of the United States."

Baseball owners also confronted long-term problems within their own legal structure, the so-called "National Commission" system. Created in 1903 after several years of warfare between the National and American Leagues, the three-person Commission, composed of the two league presidents and a third "neutral" party, enjoyed supposedly broad authority to settle baseball's intramural disputes. In fact, Ban Johnson, the American League's strong-willed prexy, had long dominated the body which, giving it benefit of every doubt, merely muddled through a succession of legal difficulties.

By 1920, the time for muddling had passed: Baseball's longstanding legal problems merged with more immediate juridical concerns. Questions about the legality of concerted action by Major League owners, issues analogous to those of the 1970s and 1980s, were headed for the United States Supreme Court when, in the spring of 1919, a lower federal court found "organized" baseball in violation of the country's anti-trust laws. Baseball's magnates confronted the very real possibility that the High Court would, as had the New York Supreme Court n 1914, find baseball's basic system of private self-government, formally supervised by the new commissionership in conflict with the public law of the land, especially various antitrust provisions. Now, however, a decision of the U.S. Supreme Court would not be binding simply upon one player-club contract, but upon the entire legal structure of "organized" baseball.

At the other end of the legal spectrum—in the much-maligned legal system of Cook County, Illinois, target of many of the jokes in the classic farce, *The Front Page*—the fate of baseball, in terms of both public law and popular image, was also held hostage in the public legal order. During late September of 1920, as the American League pennant chase neared its end, grand jurors in Chicago heard Eddie Cicotte, star pitcher of the White Sox, "confess" to having helped fix the 1919 World Series. Later, the grand jury would indict eight members of the Sox, a group of alleged gamblers, and the ubiquitous Hal Chase for conspiring to throw the World Series of 1919 to the Cincinnati Reds. When Cicotte and several other of the "Black Sox" recanted, a long, embarrassing court trial seemed inevitable; baseball's owners found events spiralling out of their control.

In contrast to the famed gambler Arnold Rothstein, who (at least according to legend) escaped indictment by arranging the disappearance of key evidence, baseball's owners seemed unable to devise

22

any methods of self-help, even legal ones. The National Commission, for example, lay in shambles; its "neutral" member, Garry Herrman of the Cincinnati Reds, long considered Ban Johnson's lackey, had resigned, and no replacement had appeared. "The game" desperately needed coherent leadership, since legal problems were only part of the national pastime's difficulties.

The years of the teens, as Bill James has emphasized, had not been good ones for major league baseball. Club owners, for example, experienced a decade of "no-growth" at the turnstiles. It had also been a "decade wrapped in greed," one rife with rumors of fixed games. These trends all seemed to come together in the White Sox. Though Charley Comiskey's Sox had outdrawn every other major league club at the gate, the "old Roman" had one of the stingiest salary scales in the business, a fact that apparently exacerbated tensions between players of working-class and middle-class backgrounds and contributed, in part, to some players' decisions to at least consider earning extra cash from the game betting market.

Taken together, immediate and long-range problems finally forced a unanimous decision from the owners: They offered Judge Landis, who had long coveted the job, a position as baseball's first Commissioner. Arriving with a well-deserved reputation as a judicial hardliner, especially toward militant labor oganizations, Landis used the emergency-crisis atmosphere to wring a grant of broad powers from nervous owners. He even succeeded in obtaining a combination loyalty oath-gag order that required owners "to loyally support the commissioner in his important and difficult task," to "acquiesce in his decisions even when he believed them mistaken" and not to "discredit the sport by criticism of him or one another."

Although sports writers had never formally signed such an agreement with Landis, most quickly joined the Judge's own crusade to use, and then to legitimate, his broad, formal authority. Warming up for possible action against the Black Sox, Landis banished Gene Paulette, a first-sacker for the Phillies, for allegedly associating with gamblers, one of whom had been linked to the Black Sox affair. The game's bible, *The Sporting News*, praised Landis' guilt-by-association style of justice for bringing tough legal standards and a "higher moral tone" to the National Pastime. Robert Edgren of the Chicago *Tribune* called Landis the "right man," the kind of patriarchical judge "who has the habit of saying: 'Six Months – next case!'"

Press puffs for Landis style of private justice, which he demonstrated in April of 1921 by banning Benny Kauff of the Giants, often compared his higher standards with the lax mores of public courts. A one-time Federal League phenom who had garnered something of a Hal Chase image, Kauff had been charged with auto theft. Here, Landis believed that application of the public court maxim innocent until proven guilty ignored the general taint of scandal that had enveloped Kauff. According to *The Sporting News*, Landis' refusal to allow Kauff to accept the Giants invitation to report to spring training provided "refreshing evidence of the new moral consciousness in Organized Baseball." Thus, even before the long delayed "Black Sox" trial ever began, the baseball press had already suggested that, even if the "eight men out" were found innocent, Judge Landis' private judiciary, not the public tribunals of Cook County, would be their court of last resort.

The "Black Sox" trial, which hardly in-

23

·ired confidence in Chicago-style justice and did little to clarify what had actually happened during the 1919 World Series, ended with not guilty verdicts for all the defendants. But, within hours, Judge Landis issued his own decision. "Regardless of the verdict of juries, no player that [sic] throws a ball game; no player that undertakes or promises to throw a ball game; no player that sits in a conference with a bunch of crooked players and gamblers where the ways and means of throwing games are planned and discussed, and does not promptly tell his club about it, will ever play professional baseball." Reiterating the idea that baseball's private system of justice, not the public one, would be determinative, Landis concluded that, "regardless of the verdict of juries, baseball is entirely competent to protect itself against crooks, both inside and outside the game."

Coverage of the trial, and of Judge Landis' response, followed the pro-Commissioner frame that had been developed since Landis' accession to baseball's judicial bench. According to *Literary Digest*, a periodical that surveyed press coverage from across the country, only a handful of papers and periodicals accepted "the legal verdict at face value." Conversely, Judge Landis' "guilty" verdict showed that baseball might provide a corrupt society with *both* moral and legal models worthy of emulation. The New York *Evening World* summarized the dominant media frame.

"The supreme court of baseball is not governed by the same restrictions as a court of law. It is concerned primarily in protecting the game and not the technical rights of players.

There are no two sides to the [Black Sox] case. If the crooks who were acquitted try to show their faces in decent sporting circles they should be boycotted and blackballed."

Although several of the tainted eight could make good cases for clemency, if not for their complete innocence, Landis steadfastly refused to rescind his ban. Moreover, Landis either banished directly or informally excommunicated a number of other major league players – nineteen by Bill James' count – after conducting his own one person brand of diamond justice. Although Landis' legal order subordinated the "technical rights" of players – including freedom to contract, to bargain collectively and even to appeal to the public courts – the judge garnered praise, especially from the popular press, for creating a commissionership that protected "the people" – fans, players, and owners – far more effectively than the public courts or baseball's own pre-Commissiner legal system.

Landis-style justice not only helped refurbish the image of the national pastime but contributed to a continual expansion in the reach of "organized" baseball. While major league baseball was booming in both attendance and offensive fire-power during the 1920s, Landis systematically extended his disciplinary authority. In a celebrated 1921 run-in with Babe Ruth, Landis spanked the "childlike" Sultan of Swat. He suspended the Bambino for the first eight weeks of the 1922 season for having defied the commissioner's ban against playing in one of the hitherto traditional post-World Series tours through the southern states. The Babe's right to negotiate his own contracts gave way to Landis' power to determine what activities, by individual players, were in the "best interests" of "the game."

Moreover, despite the fact that Landis' formally mandated power extended only to "organized" baseball, he managed to enlarge his de facto domain into the realms

24

of amateur, semi-pro, and "outlaw"
baseball during the early 1920s. Judged
from the perspective of the late 1980s,
when hindsight shows how professional
baseball had solidified its economic base
by the end of the roaring twenties, such a
move might seem relatively insignificant.
But the constant jeremiads of 1921-22 in
*The Sporting News* against the evils of
unorganized, "outlaw" baseball suggest a
different tale and tend to support the claims
of contemporary ballplayers, such as my
father who played semi-pro baseball in the
early '20s, that many a talented middle-
westerner preferred the security of a nine-
to-five job and relatively high pay from
weekend stints in "town" and "outlaw" ball
to the risk of financial uncertainty on the
fringes of "organized" baseball. (Similar,
anti-"outlaw" crusades marked other
sports, such as auto-racing, in the post-
WW I years, and the whole subject of the
consolidation of "organized" sport during
the 20s deserves more attention than it has
hitherto received from sports historians.)
In any event Landis himself became embroiled in the affairs of various "outlaw"
teams, especially when they played against
some of the people he had banned from
"organized" ball. Ironically, Landis even
temporarily suspended Dickie Kerr, one of
the "White Sox" of the 1919 series, for
committing the sin of playing against some
of his "Black Sox" while embroiled in a
contract dispute with the still penurious
Chicago club during the mid-twenties.

In addition to bringing law-and-order to
baseball's own domain and refurbishing the
National Pastime's public image, Landis
saw "organized" baseball win a series of
significant legal victories in the 1920s and
1930s, the kind of one-sided triumphs that
had eluded Ban Johnson and continue to
evade Peter Ueberroth. In brief, Landis
won acceptance from the public legal
system of the broad grant of authority he

had received from baseball's owners. In 1922, for example, the United States Supreme Court overturned a lower-court ruling that baseball's business structure did not violate anti-trust laws. Nine years later, Judge Walter Lindley of the Federal district court for the Northern District of Illinois rejected claims, growing out of Landis' efforts to restrain Branch Rickey's machinations with the Cardinals minor league system, that delegation of so much legal authority to a private individual was "contrary to public policy."

Judge Lindley warmly endorsed Landis' authority. Admitting that the Commissioner enjoyed "all the attributes of a benevolent but absolute despot and all the disciplinary powers of the proverbial pater familias," Judge Lindley considered this broad sway essential if baseball's czar were to achieve his goals of bringing rational order to the business of baseball, of fostering "keen, clean competition," and of preserving "discipline and a high standard of morale." Through the power and authority of the Commissioner, in other words, "organized" baseball enjoyed the ability, free from most public legal restraints, to keep its own house in "order."

From the 1920s well into the 1970s, it seems clear, most of baseball's magnates—and the pro-owner sportswriting establishment—continued to view the legal arrangements of the Landis and immediate post-Landis years as "normalcy." In this version of baseball history the ordinary rules of the pubic legal system did *not* apply, save in rare instances, to the National Pastime. Although "organized" baseball's system of private legal ordering survived court challenges growing out of the Mexican league insurgency of the late 1940s and from the Curt Flood case, the last two decades have, from a broad historical view, seen emergence of a much

more complex variation of the pre-Landis situation: the law of baseball exists within a complex mixture of private-and-public legal rules.

The Commissioner, though still a figure of some power and undetermined symbolic authority, hardly reigns supreme. Indeed, for those who still tend to glorify the reign of Czar Landis, especially in the area of labor-management relations, it could seem as if baseball's contemporary, merely mortal, leadership now finds itself enmeshed in the legal barbarism of the National Pastime's own Bolshevik era.

1. I have previously published a different, longer, and footnoted version of the story of baseball's legal history under *the* Commissioner. It appeared as "Here Comes the Judge! The Origins of Baseball's Commissioner System and American Legal Culture," in the *Journal of Popular Culture (1986), pp 129-48.* In addition to sources cited there, this present article has benefited from the insights of *The Bill James Historical Baseball Abstract (1986),* an invaluable history that was still at press when the *Journal of Popular Culture* article appeared.

---

*If you don't think you're out, read the morning paper.*
Bill McGowan, former umpire, to runners who protested they were safe at first.

# ESSAY/BOOK REVIEW

From the Land of Bondage:* The Greening of Major League Baseball Players and The Major League Baseball Players Association

*Michael J. Cozzillio***

Marvin Miller's book, *A Whole Different Ballgame: The Sport and Business of Baseball*, is a breezy, informative and certainly controversial chronicle of the evolution of the Major League Baseball Players Association (MLBPA or Players Association) from an amoebic, ill-defined amalgam of players to a fully-developed specimen of trade unionism in professional sports.[1] Readers who seek to be entertained will find the sports anecdotes and inside information replete with proverbial page-turning excitement and energy. Those who seek to be educated in many of the legal nuances and practical ramifications of collective bargaining, antitrust regulation, individual contract negotiation, and varieties of arbitration in the world of Major League Baseball will find Miller's book illuminating. The book will expand

---

* Arbitrator Peter Seitz, in a letter to the *New York Times*, wrote: " 'In 1982 it developed that [Bowie] Kuhn was departing from his long-held job as commissioner of baseball; and that [Marvin] Miller, the Moses who had led Baseball's Children of Israel out the land of bondage, was resigning his position [as Executive Director of the Major League Baseball Players Association].' " MARVIN MILLER, A WHOLE DIFFERENT BALLGAME: THE SPORT AND BUSINESS OF BASEBALL 331 (1991).

** Associate Professor of Law, Widener University School of Law. B.A., 1970, University of Delaware; J.D., 1973, The Catholic University of America, Columbus School of Law. The author gratefully acknowledges the invaluable assistance of Krista J. Cozzillio and John P. Valente.

1. MARVIN MILLER, A WHOLE DIFFERENT BALLGAME: THE SPORT AND BUSINESS OF BASEBALL: (1991). Marvin Miller served as the first full-time Executive Director of the Major League Baseball Players Association from 1966 until 1983. Prior to his election to this post, he worked with the United Steelworkers of America as their Chief Labor Economist and Assistant to the International President. He also advised the MLBPA in various interim capacities between 1983 and 1985.

The MLBPA was first chartered in 1954. Former Cleveland Indians' pitcher and Hall of Fame member Bob Feller was elected as its first president in 1956. The Players Association was a loosely organized group of players with little concept of their identity, institutional stature and ultimate objectives. *See* JAMES B. DWORKIN, OWNERS VERSUS PLAYERS: BASEBALL AND COLLECTIVE BARGAINING 28 (1981); LEE LOWENFISH & TONY LUPIEN, THE IMPERFECT DIAMOND (1980); *infra* notes 110-13 and accompanying text.

*271*

the reader's knowledge of baseball and its collective bargaining history, without any of the pain and suffering typically associated with the assimilation of this much raw data.

The greatest attribute of Miller's work is the rare glimpse it offers of the Major League Baseball player as an employee. Miller's book reflects his profound understanding of the working class, whether embracing the most unskilled laborers or the most elegantly tooled professional athletes. His vast experience in trade unionism and his unique appreciation of what motivates workers lend considerable authority to his accounts of heated negotiating sessions, early "organizing" efforts rife with internecine debate, and legal strategies in complex antitrust and contract litigation. Although many of these accounts have entertainment value simply due to the "fly on the wall" revelations that only an insider can provide, Miller's reporting of these events rises above that level to instill the reader with a better understanding of the psyches, motivations, and tactics of the various participants.

All is not well, however, with Miller's review of the MLBPA's development. Readers who took the title "The Business of Baseball" literally may be disappointed at the paucity of detail regarding the economic underpinnings of the sport.[2] There is little discussion of the manner in which club revenues are amassed, divided among league members, and infused into minor league programs. We learn virtually nothing about the costs of operating a major league franchise and the various means through which these costs are offset through the myriad marketing schemes and revenue-producing stratagems cultivated by the league and club owners.[3]

Moreover, readers who desire a neatly packaged chronology of the origins of baseball's relationship with its players as a collective body may find themselves confused at various points. Miller frequently places us in one period in time but then shifts to collateral events without sufficient linkage or reference points.[4] For example, although Miller attempts to segregate the various labor disputes by chapter, his analysis of such events is often

---

2. Miller, however, does not totally ignore baseball's economics. For example, he gives considerable attention to baseball card licensing arrangements, *see* MILLER, *supra* note 1, at 92, pension plan funding, *id.* at 75-78, 81, 86-90, 95, and television contracts, *id.* at 98, 105, 338-39, 350-51. Much of his discussion of money matters, however, revolves around the finances or financing of the Players Association and the salary structures affecting the players.

3. *Cf.* DAVID HARRIS, THE LEAGUE: THE RISE AND DECLINE OF THE NFL (1986) (exploring in vivid detail the economics of professional football).

4. *See, e.g.*, MILLER, *supra* note 1, at 320-49. Miller's detailed recounting of the circumstances that led to baseball's work stoppages over the past 20 years, his salient differentiation of lockouts and strikes, and his probing exploration of the underlying motives that prompted the labor strife lost punch due to the somewhat disorganized treatment that these topics received. *See also* James E. Miller, *Labor's Last Heavy Hitter*, N.Y. TIMES, July 14, 1991, at 12.

meandering. Readers who are intimately familiar with Major League Baseball and its player relations developments will have little problem maintaining perspective. Neophytes, however, may find themselves flipping
backward through the pages to ascertain whether perplexity over a chrono-
logical detail is attributable to the author's omission or to the reader's
oversight.

In Miller's defense, the book does not purport to be a primer on collective
bargaining and baseball; anticipating a road map treatment probably is asking too much from a work of this kind. Miller's desultory roaming, particularly in recounting the strikes and lockouts, is partially explainable because
the issues spawning the disputes often overlapped, creating a complex mo-
saic rather than a simple, straight-line chronology. In any event, Miller's
organizational problems do not detract substantially from the broad historical perspective that he provides.

Further, those readers who expect a detached and dispassionate mono-
logue on labor relations in Major League Baseball should abandon the effort
forthwith. Miller makes no mistake about his distaste for dealing with club
owners, his dismay at their frugality (to put it generously), his frustration
with their ignorance of relevant legal constraints or their misguided belief
that they are above such law, and his own view of the monumental contribution that he has made to the players' prosperity. In this sense, one of the
book's virtues is also its vice. Much of the insight and rich detail surrounding the background of the Players Association's development comes directly
from Miller's first-hand experience and observation. Unfortunately, this autobiographical perspective, combined with Miller's hearty ego, detracts from
the account.

The reams of literature[5] addressing the history of the players' struggle
with management in Major League Baseball recognize Miller as one of the
country's most creative, dedicated and successful trade unionists.[6] Yet
Miller's self-indulgence is excessive. Often, in subtle ways, he heaps praise

---

5. *See, e.g.*, LOWENFISH & LUPIEN, *supra* note 1, at 195; *see also* DWORKIN, *supra* note
1, at 37. Professor Dworkin's book provides an outstanding and very readable synopsis of
collective bargaining developments in Major League Baseball, as well as in other professional
sports.

6. Marvin Miller inherited a labor union that was far less than a union, consisting of
players who knew very little of collective bargaining, and who, in fact, were quite resistant to
the notion of any dramatic change. These players were part of their employer's capital and did
not enjoy the most fundamental prerogative of every other employee—the ability to switch
jobs (within the same profession) at the end of their contract term. Moreover, they were
hardly remunerated in proportion to their contribution to the presentation of the owner's
product. MILLER, *supra* note 1, at 95. Add to this scenario the owners' absolute intransigence
and their own deluded view that their actions were immune from all scrutiny, together with
the fans' view that the players were having fun in a "non-business" enterprise.

upon the Players Association, and derivatively himself, perceiving no apparent limits to his own influence upon the players' financial, social, and even intellectual growth.[7] Moreover, Miller misses no opportunity to chastise his many tormentors—defined, by inference, as anyone who opposes, questions, or fails to accord him the lavish praise and deference that he feels is due.[8]

Perhaps, given Miller's contribution to the game of baseball and its most important assets—the players—it would have been difficult for him to recount accurately the events of those turbulent seventeen years without a modicum of self-promotion, however shameless, and antipathy, however strident. It is difficult to conceive that the players would have recognized even a small portion of their substantial gains without Millers' tireless leadership, keen appreciation of labor relations, and uncanny ability to judge the human spirit and tap wells of potential energy.[9]

---

Under these circumstances, it is undeniable that Miller was a giant among labor leaders who left his indelible mark upon Major League Baseball. When he departed in 1985, the MLBPA had secured geometric increases in players salaries (including contractual minimums), had gained players the qualified right to free agency, had enhanced the life style of retired players through the funding of the pension plan, and had become a formidable decision-making component in the development of the game of baseball. *See, e.g., id.* at 87-90, 293, 316-19.

7. See, for example, Miller's references to the numerous prominent players who asked him to be their personal agent, MILLER, *supra* note 1, at 315, his self-assumed patriarchy, *id.* at 335, his condemnation of his immediate successor, Ken Moffett, *id.* at 320-29, his faint praise of current MLBPA Executive Director Don Fehr, *id.* at 334-35, 338-39, 345-46, and his assessment of head-to-head confrontations with Bowie Kuhn and baseball's well-heeled Player Relations Committee, *id.* at 292. Miller's lamentations about baseball players' failure to extend proper appreciation to him, such as the following commentary on former New York Yankee Catfish Hunter's autobiography, are most telling.

> Either Hunter or Armen Keteyian, the writer working with him, or a source supplying Keteyian, would have readers believe that the chief executive of the Association (yours truly) somehow vanished during two of the most important arbitrations in the union's history. A nifty feat, considering that nothing of significance occurred without my direct involvement in the entire seventeen years of my tenure. I was very much a 'hands on' administrator.

*Id.* at 347.

8. While the field of labor relations is not to be occupied by the faint-hearted, and while one can expect industrial combat to yield considerable animosity and hurt feelings, some of Miller's observations are gratuitous, truculent, and ill-conceived. For example, Miller unnecessarily calls the reader's attention to San Francisco Giants' owner Horace Stoneham's drunkenness during one of their informal conversations. *See* MILLER, *supra* note 1, at 50-51. More often than not, Miller's most snide and demeaning comments are directed toward former Commissioner Bowie Kuhn. Although these comments discredit to a degree the credibility of Miller's account, it is difficult to criticize his deprecating air given Kuhn's unctuous, condescending, and disparaging review of Miller and his organization. *See generally* BOWIE KUHN, HARDBALL: THE EDUCATION OF A BASEBALL COMMISSIONER (1987); *see also infra* notes 14, 15, 74-101 and accompanying text.

9. Miller's ability to convert an impotent quasi-trade association into the most proficient labor organization in sports industry is testimony to his ability to coalesce forces of divergent interests, backgrounds, and talents. Indeed, although players seem to have an unrivaled com-

Much of Millers' vitriol can be explained by the fact that he, and the tactics that he employed as Executive Director of the Players Association, had been vilified in accounts that preceded this book.[10] Miller is the repository for the hostile invective of fans, the press, and all elements of the baseball community who misperceive the players as spoiled brats. In fact, Miller became the fall guy largely through the orchestration of the owners and the Commissioner's office,[11] who seemed unwilling to admit that the players had enough intelligence or perseverance to make demands and engage in collective action to secure them. Under the circumstances, some no-holds-barred retaliation should be expected.[12]

As suggested earlier, Miller often employs a stream of consciousness approach in reliving the evolution of the MLBPA. This Essay/Book Review will attempt to provide more traditional structure to Miller's historical musings. Typically, a course in professional sports law examines the nature of a sports league, emphasizing the roles played by commissioners, owners, players, and the players' representatives. Then, by examining the relationships of these individuals and institutions, a sports law class focuses upon critical areas of sports jurisprudence such as contracts, antitrust, and labor law.[13] This Essay/Book Review critiques Miller's book from that perspective, and attempts to provide observations and commentary on the various legal and technical issues that require clarification or elaboration.

---

munity of interest, it must be noted that almost 200 times a year they compete with one another in athletic events that determine, to a large degree, their value and eventual financial compensation.

10. *See, e.g.*, KUHN, *supra* note 8, at 76-84; *see infra* note 15.

11. Bowie Kuhn suggests that Miller was the darling of the sporting press and attributes this kinship to Miller's smooth and ingratiating style. *See, e.g.*, KUHN, *supra* note 8, at 80, 106, 313, 336, 347. In truth, Miller received more than his share of negative press coverage and was frequently the whipping boy for the poisoned pen of columnists such as Dick Young of the *New York Times*. *See* MILLER, *supra* note 1, at 85, 205-06, 215, 218, 262, 284, 292, 297, 300, 307.

12. As I read each page with great curiosity and greater enjoyment, I could not help but think how much more I might have relished the experience had the account been more biographical than autobiographical, and if the book had been written, rather than introduced, by a historian such as Studs Terkel. Doubtless, Terkel would have extolled Miller's virtues much the same as the author did himself. While the result would have been largely the same, it is likely that Terkel's sardonic, yet avuncular, wit would alienate far fewer than Miller's book obviously will, and thereby would greatly increase the universe of those readers who might be receptive to the many relevant and salient points advanced by Miller. *See, e.g.*, STUDS TERKEL, TALKING TO MYSELF: A MEMOIR OF MY TIMES (1973).

13. *See, e.g.*, 1 ROBERT C. BERRY & GLENN M. WONG, LAW AND BUSINESS OF THE SPORTS INDUSTRIES: PROFESSIONAL SPORTS LEAGUES (1986). Miller's book does not follow this basic pattern, but rather visits these areas in random fashion. As discussed at various points herein, his account suffers somewhat from disorganization. Thus, this review has realigned the discussion to facilitate the reader's understanding of the people and events that Miller recollects.

## I. THE OWNERS

Miller makes no secret of his perception of who occupy the hero and villain roles in the world of Major League Baseball. There are few owners whom he likes, and fewer still who have managed to earn his respect.[14] His dismay derives from his perception of the hypocrisy of the owners' relish for the free enterprise, capitalist system when it comes to amassing their own wealth, but their total abhorrence of such a program of economic operation when it is practiced by players who are attempting to profit from their own athletic and entrepreneurial skills.[15] Without listing all of Miller's individual complaints about each owner and about Major League Baseball's collective managerial body, the primary sources of his consternation warrant examination.

Over the years, team owners have grown accustomed to complete and unfettered control over their game and its participants. Miller sees this manic need to control all phases of the sport and the failure to recognize that the players are entitled to some input in the governance of the enterprise as major impediments in the development of meaningful collective bargaining.[16] The observation that sports club owners perceive themselves as feudal lords indenturing their serfs, or chessmasters moving their players around as pawns, is an oft-repeated refrain.[17]

---

14. *See generally* MILLER, *supra* note 1, at 363-92. Miller strains to offer some positive comments about the owners and other managerial officials with whom he waged daily war. Michael Burke, former president of the New York Yankees, is identified as one who maintained an air of grace and objectivity notwithstanding the adversarial relationship. *Id.* at 64, 94, 162. Owners Charles Finley of the Oakland A's, Walter O'Malley of the Los Angeles Dodgers, and George Steinbrenner of the New York Yankees were also found to possess some redemptive qualities. *Id.* at 370, 377, 381.

Miller was particularly fond of the late Bill Veeck, whose innovations and maverick style offended many of baseball's power elite. *Id.* at 364, 367. Veeck was not viewed in the same shining light by Bowie Kuhn. *See* KUHN, *supra* note 8, at 213, 220-21.

15. MILLER, *supra* note 1, at 351-52. Noted journalist Red Smith declared: "Nobody gives more pious lip service to the free-enterprise system than the typical owner of a baseball club. But he does not want it operating in baseball. In spite of a whole series of court rulings, he still believes his players are property . . . ." KUHN, *supra* note 8, at 337.

16. MILLER, *supra* note 1, at 114, 123-24.

17. Noting that baseball's arcane antitrust exemption bestowed a gift of perpetual potential collusion upon the owners, Miller comments:

[C]ollusion had been an everyday part of baseball since 1876. The owners controlled everything from ticket prices to the color of a ballplayer's skin. Take salaries: There had been an unwritten rule for years (a collusive "understanding") that said no player—not Ted Williams, Joe DiMaggio, or Stan Musial—would be paid more than $100,000 a year. The reserve rules system was more of the same. Each club agreed not to talk to any player who *belonged* to another club. . . .

*Id.* at 257; *see also* LOWENFISH & LUPIEN, *supra* note 1, at 39.

Nowhere is the owners' preoccupation with dominance more visible than in the endless debate surrounding the reserve clause and free agency.[18] Miller notes that the owners' persistent complaints about free agency and its deleterious impact upon league balance and competition have been little more than a "smoke screen."[19] As he suggests, the owners' hysterical predictions that the elimination of the reserve system would bring about the ruination of the game arguably is nothing more than a pretext to hide their real concern—the permanent end to their absolute control over the game of baseball.[20]

The players' desire to loosen the bonds of the reserve system, however, was neither a novel nor a subversive notion. As early as 1887, baseball star and innovator John Montgomery Ward declared: " 'Like a fugitive slave law, the reserve rule denies [the player] a harbor or a livelihood, and carries him back, bound and shackled, to the club from which he attempted to es-

---

18. The reserve rule, which in some form or other has been in place for over a century, permits Major League clubs to freeze a certain number of players and to prohibit them from signing with other teams. The original reservation of rights has been modified over the years and is now embraced in the collective bargaining agreement between Major League Baseball and MLBPA. *See* Jeffrey S. Moorad, *Negotiating for the Professional Baseball Player, in* LAW OF PROFESSIONAL AND AMATEUR SPORTS 5-1 app. at 5-62 to 5-71 (Gary A. Uberstine ed., 1991); (providing a copy of Article XX, Reserve System, of the Basic Agreement between The American League of Professional Baseball Clubs and The National League of Professional Baseball Clubs and MLBPA (Effective Jan. 1, 1990)). Free agency generally refers to limitations on the clubs' reservation of rights and the expansion of a player's ability to negotiate with the team of his choice upon expiration of his Uniform Players' Contract. *Id.; see also* Kansas City Royals Baseball Corp. v. Major League Baseball Players Ass'n, 532 F.2d 615 (8th Cir. 1976) (affirming lower court order sustaining Arbitrator Peter Seitz's ruling that the Uniform Player Contract and the Major League rules did not establish permanent control over a player's movement); *see also infra* notes 143-49, 154-55 and accompanying text; DWORKIN, *supra* note 1, at 80-82; Moorad, *supra.*

19. During collective bargaining and work stoppages that succeeded Arbitrator Seitz's decision and the unsuccessful appeals, several owners declared that free agency would sound a death knell for Major League Baseball. MILLER, *supra* note 1, at 275, 287.

20. Miller, whose entry onto the baseball scene was greeted with cries of " 'cataclysmic,' " " 'disastrous,' " and " 'certain bankruptcy,' " clearly has no sympathy for the owners' perpetual "wolf" cries of poverty. MILLER, *supra* note 1, at 85. He notes that in 1990, a "year of record-breaking profits," Charles Bronfman of the Montreal Expos declared that " 'expenses may soon choke many of us' " and that the current salary configuration " 'had to be eliminated.' " *See id.* at 287. Shortly after the players had secured free agency, approximately 10 years earlier, Bronfman stated " 'baseball is not a healthy industry.' " *Id.* More incredibly, Ray Grebey, league negotiator, added that most owners could earn a better living " 'as a waiter at the ballpark.' " *Id.* (footnote omitted).

Miller indicates that one seldom hears owners comment favorably on the game's increasing popularity and prosperity over the last 15 years. Commenting on what he characterizes as the " 'trickle-up' theory" of economic development, Miller explains that the gains of the players resulted in substantial financial advancement for "trainers, coaches, field managers, general managers, league presidents, club officials, umpires, owners, players' agents, and, yes, the commissioner." *Id.* at 287-88.

cape.' "[21]  Borrowing on Ward's characterization, and adopting verbatim some of his thoughts, the Manifesto of the Brotherhood of Professional Baseball Players states: " 'By a combination among themselves, stronger than the strongest trust, the owners were able to enforce the most arbitrary measures, and the player had either to submit or get out of the profession in which he had spent years attaining proficiency.' "[22]

Indeed, many owners portray themselves as a cadre of entrepreneurs who see no bounds to the extent of control that they should be permitted to exercise over all facets of the game,[23] including their erstwhile chattel, the players. Former Oakland A's owner Charlie Finley acknowledged: "We run our club like a pawn shop—we buy, we trade, we sell."[24]  Similarly, George Steinbrenner, former owner of the New York Yankees, offered this comment, perhaps tongue in cheek, but nonetheless demeaning: "I like my horses better because they can't talk to sportswriters."[25]

Miller also seriously questions the character and moral fiber of most of the individual owners. He highlights several of their foibles, including their outright refusals to pay monies owed contractually,[26] their attempts to subvert

---

21. Lowenfish & Lupien, *supra* note 1, at 31. The involuntary servitude theme was echoed in 1949 by United States Court of Appeals Judge Jerome Frank, who dismissed suggestions that the reserve system's legitimacy could be evidenced by the handsome salaries paid to many players. He stated that "only the totalitarian-minded will believe that high pay excuses virtual slavery." Gardella v. Chandler, 172 F.2d 402, 410 (2d Cir. 1949). As recently as 1972, baseball player Curt Flood, plaintiff in the infamous lawsuit challenging baseball's reserve clause and the sport's singular immunity from antitrust scrutiny, analogized himself to a slave. Curt Flood, The Way It Is 14-16 (1971).

22. Lowenfish & Lupien, *supra* note 1, at 27 (quoting Manifesto of the Brotherhood of Professional Baseball Players, Nov. 6, 1889).

23. *See, e.g.*, Kuhn, *supra* note 8, at 66.

24. L.A. Times, June 23, 1977, pt. III, at 2.

25. *They Said It*, Sports Illustrated, Apr. 22, 1985, at 18. Unfortunately, the livestock comparison is not idiosyncratic to Mr. Steinbrenner. Curt Flood, whose autobiography shows him to be a thoughtful and perceptive analyst of baseball and its personages, laments, "in the hierarchy of living things, he [the baseball player] ranks with poultry." Flood, *supra* note 21, at 15.

26. Miller, *supra* note 1, at 224-87; Matter of the Arbitration between American and National Leagues of Professional Baseball Clubs (Oakland Athletics) and Major League Baseball Players Ass'n (James A. Hunter), Doc. No. 23, Grievance Nos. 74-18 and 74-20, Seitz, Impartial Chairman of Panel, Dec. 13, 1974. Miller frowns upon Commissioner Kuhn's reaction to Seitz's decision releasing grievant Catfish Hunter from further contractual obligations due to owner Charles Finley's material breach (repeated failure to pay money due and owing). Kuhn claims that the award was excessive, characterizing the contract forfeiture as " 'giving a life sentence to a pickpocket.' " Miller, *supra* note 1, at 235. Miller correctly points out that the award was nothing more than the remedy ordained by the contract itself. *Id.* at 228. Further, Kuhn, as an experienced lawyer, should have realized that a material breach evincing a breaching party's failure to perform substantially his contractual obligation warrants contract forfeiture. *See* John D. Calamari & Joseph M. Perillo, The Law of Contracts §§ 11-18, at 458-64 (3d ed. 1987).

provisions such as free agency through unlawful collusive efforts,[27] and their overall disingenuousness in dealing with the players, the Players Association, and one another.[28] He wryly notes that owners are plainly cognizant of their own avarice, and have consistently attempted to cajole players into accepting bargaining proposals that protect the owners from themselves.[29]

Miller's myriad problems with the ethics of baseball ownership are hardly unique characterizations. One of baseball's first operators, Ferdinand Able, co-owner of the Brooklyn franchise in the National League, admitted: "Whenever I go to a baseball meeting, I never forget to check my money and valuables at the hotel office before entering the session chamber."[30] Mr. Able's comments portended other self-effacing observations about the financiers of Major League Baseball. Approximately seventy-five years later, Ewing Kauffman, popular and successful owner of the Kansas City Royals, noted with apparent chagrin that "[b]aseball has 24 teams and the owners have inherited wealth, or become wealthy themselves. They are self-confident, egotistical, even egocentric, and need a broad, strong hand in order to keep baseball running smoothly."[31]

Miller's disenchantment also stems from the owners' lack of sophistication in the nuances of the law and their belief that they were beyond its purview and immune from its sanctions, particularly in the area of labor management relations and collective bargaining. Miller suggests that, given baseball's ridiculous insulation from antitrust scrutiny, the owners can hardly be faulted for any misguided belief that whatever they did with their game was above reproach.[32] On more than one occasion, Miller points out that the owners committed unpardonable labor relations sins, notwithstanding the fact that many of them had considerable experience with unions and the collective bargaining process in their other financial endeavors.[33] Perhaps nothing evinces in more glaring fashion the owners' disregard for labor law than the fact that they repeatedly attempted to advise, run, and even finance the Play-

---

27. Matter of the Arbitration between Major League Baseball Players Association and the Twenty-Six Major League Baseball Clubs, Doc. No. —, Grievance No. 86-2, Roberts, Impartial Chairman of Panel, Sept. 21, 1987.

28. *See, e.g.,* MILLER, *supra* note 1, at 68, 309; KUHN, *supra* note 8, at 219-20.

29. MILLER, *supra* note 1, at 82, 296, 309.

30. LOWENFISH & LUPIEN, *supra* note 1, at 57.

31. *Royal's Kauffman Backs Kuhn in Player Suit Filed by Finley,* WASH. POST, Jan. 8, 1977, at B4.

32. *See* Flood v. Kuhn, 407 U.S. 258 (1972); *see also* MILLER, *supra* note 1, at 90-91; *infra* notes 136-41 and accompanying text.

33. MILLER, *supra* note 1, at 107, 124.

ers Association—flagrant unfair labor practices and probably violations of the National Labor Relations Act's anti-racketeering provisions.[34]

Aside from his observations regarding the blatant subversion of federal labor law represented by the owners' virtual dominance of the Players Association, Miller contends that there were numerous other examples of the owners' utter disregard for labor regulation and their overt desire to break the union at any cost.[35] He cites instances in which the owners engaged in bad faith bargaining by: outright refusals to bargain;[36] bypassing the collective bargaining representative;[37] employing dilatory tactics during negotiations;[38] and attempting to take away gains hard-earned through earlier bargaining and arbitrations.[39] Miller also strongly urges that baseball owners repeatedly culled the ranks of player representatives by trading, releasing, or otherwise adversely affecting the working conditions of the most vocal Players Association activists.[40]

Miller is also concerned with the owners' insensitivity to civil rights issues and, at times, their abject bigotry in dealing with minorities. The issue came into full bloom following the ABC television *Nightline* interview in which former Dodger executive Al Campanis responded to Ted Koppel's inquiry regarding whether there was still significant prejudice in baseball and about the absence of blacks in managerial positions by stating: "No, I don't believe it's prejudice. I truly believe that they may not have some of the necessities to be, let's say, a field manager or, perhaps, a general manager."[41]

It is clear that Miller, without recalling the incident specifically, does not view Campanis' comment as aberrational in the baseball community. Rather, Miller's account suggests that these words are all too indicative of

---

34. *Id.* at 87-88. During the first days of Miller's tenure, the owners had tentatively committed to the subsidization of the Players Association with funds derived from the Major League All-Star game. This type of employer contribution was part and parcel of the owners' overall treatment of the Players Association. The MLBPA was viewed as some type of corporate subdivision that had to be subsidized and accommodated, but in no way would it be permitted to interfere substantially with basic management prerogatives or the direction of the business. To his credit, legal counsel Paul Porter eventually acknowledged that federal labor law, 29 U.S.C. §§ 158(a)(2), 186 (1988), rendered any transmission of All-Star game revenue money to support the labor union illegal, "and that he and other baseball attorneys had not 'focused on' the Players Association as a union until 'very recently.'" MILLER, *supra* note 1, at 71. From the time Miller took office, there were no misconceptions about the nature of the MLBPA.

35. *See, e.g.,* MILLER, *supra* note 1, at 203-06.

36. *Id.* at 96. *See generally* 29 U.S.C. § 158(a)(5) (1988).

37. *Id.* at 213, 270.

38. *Id.* at 99, 190.

39. *Id.* at 113-16.

40. *Id.* at 163, 206, 303-04. *See generally* 29 U.S.C. § 158(a)(3) (1988).

41. *Nightline: Prejudice in Baseball* (ABC television broadcast, Apr. 8, 1987).

the mindset of baseball's ruling class vis-à-vis minorities. Miller cites dramatic examples of both owner and public perceptions that indicate considerably less tolerance of the frailties and mistakes of black athletes and greater resentment of their economic advancements.[42] Certainly, the raw statistics, standing alone, speak volumes about baseball's "good old boy" network and the absence of any meaningful upward mobility for blacks, even veteran players.[43]

In sum, Miller expresses unequivocally his view that on several levels baseball's owners have failed to demonstrate a modicum of respect for their players or for each other. In fact, the available evidence lends considerable support for his assertions. Yet, if Miller could have distanced himself somewhat, he may have provided some plausible explanations for the owners' attitudes and conduct beyond greed, megalomania, and ignorance. At no point does he elaborate on the prudence of club ownership as a business venture, the costs of minor league player development, any affirmative action programs to rectify the discrimination problems, or other stratagems that he undoubtedly observed during seventeen years at the bargaining table. It is likely that readers would have heartily endorsed many of Miller's observations about the character and predilections of baseball's owners. Indeed, many of the owners' actions over the past several decades resist any plausible explanation. Still, Miller's points would have had greater impact if the readers had been given more information from which to draw their own conclusions.

## II. The Commissioner

Marvin Miller's dismay with baseball's "brass" is by no means limited to club owners and their operating officers. Most commissioners absorb their fair share of Miller's vituperative comments. At the core of Miller's disenchantment is the commissioners' unwillingness to acknowledge that, though they hold the title, "Commissioner of baseball," they are allied with

---

42. MILLER, *supra* note 1, at 133-34, 308; *see also* FLOOD, *supra* note 21, at 74-76.

43. *See* Jim Meyers, *Pros Make Progress on Race Issue*, USA TODAY, July 10, 1990. For example, between 1947 and 1971, baseball did not hire a single black manager. MILLER, *supra* note 1, at 39-40. Miller is astounded that, at a time when other industries were subject to the strictest scrutiny for failing to promote minority employees, baseball was "as lawless . . . as Dodge City in 1876." *Id.* at 40. Again, Miller sees a perverse logic in the owners' belief that they had no need to defend their hiring practices; in every other legal venue, their conduct seemed to be sacrosanct. Indicative of baseball's unconsciousness in the civil rights area is Minnesota Twins' owner Calvin Griffith's statement that he made the decision to relocate the Washington Senators in Minnesota "when I found you only had 15,000 blacks here." Bob Fowler, *Twins' Players Raging Over Cal's Remarks*, THE SPORTING NEWS, Oct. 14, 1978.

and answerable to only the ownership component of the sport.[44] He concedes that this view is not entirely inaccurate in the sense that, vis-à-vis the players, the commissioners' power is paramount and supreme.[45] Miller points out that in relationships with certain owners, the commissioners also have been able to exert considerable pressure,[46] and that in most instances, the commissioners' exercise of authority in matters pertaining to the business of baseball has not and will not be questioned by courts or arbitrators.[47] Miller, however, contends that the apparently unfettered authority of the commissioner is exclusively a function of the owners' whim. He explains that, even in those cases where the commissioner has wielded his power against an owner (e.g., through fines, suspensions or veto of trades or sales of players), the allegedly recalcitrant owner has been a "new kid[ ] on the block . . . considered expendable by establishment owners."[48] Miller believes that the media's romantic view of baseball and the purity of the commissioner's authority contributes substantially to the public's misperceptions as to where the ultimate power rests: "If Fay Vincent or any other commissioner ever attempted to act 'in the best interests of baseball' *but* against the best interests of a significant group of owners, the press's illusions about the commissioner's power would be quickly shattered."[49]

---

44. *See, e.g.,* MILLER, *supra* note 1, at 110, 293-94.

45. *Id.* at 405.

46. *Id.* at 406.

47. *See, e.g.,* Charles O. Finley & Co. v. Kuhn, 569 F.2d 527 (7th Cir. 1978); Milwaukee American Ass'n v. Landis, 49 F.2d 298 (N.D. Ill. 1931). *But see* Atlanta Nat'l League Baseball Club, Inc. v. Kuhn, 432 F. Supp. 1213 (N.D. Ga. 1977). Recently, limits on the commissioners' broad authority were recognized when former Cincinnati Reds player and manager Pete Rose obtained a Temporary Restraining Order precluding Commissioner Bart Giamatti from conducting a hearing on Rose's alleged gambling in violation of baseball rules. The court concluded that Giamatti's conduct, particularly sending a letter to the United States District Court for the Southern District of Ohio's Chief Judge Carl B. Rubin extolling the virtues of Ron Peters, a convicted drug trafficker awaiting sentencing, manifested pre-judgment bias. Specifically, Giamatti declared that Peters had been a "candid, forthright and truthful" witness in his testimony about Rose's activities. Rose v. Giamatti, No. A8905178, 1989 Ohio Misc. LEXIS 4, at *5 (C.P. June 19, 1989). In fact, Giamatti had never seen or heard Peters testify, and Rose had had no opportunity to cross-examine him. *See id.; infra* notes 88-91, 103-06 and accompanying text.

48. MILLER, *supra* note 1, at 383, 406.

49. *Id.* at 406. The press is certainly a minor actor in the "commissioner as absolute" scenario. Much of the mythology surrounding the evolution of the commissioner's role stems from the early days of Judge Kenesaw "Mountain" Landis' reign. Judge Landis became baseball's first commissioner (baseball previously operated with two league presidents) following the infamous Black Sox scandal of 1919. Given the disarray in Major League Baseball at the time, and the fear that the gambling scandal would have a permanent negative impact upon fan support, the owners were prepared to take drastic measures.

Sensing the need for cohesion and control, Landis agreed to become commissioner on the condition that his power be absolute. Team owners, in no mood to debate the finer points of

According to Miller, all commissioners, in one fashion or another, have succumbed to the notion that they are no longer accountable to any mortal soul. Illustrations of primogenitor Judge Kenesaw Landis' imperious bearing and unbridled arrogance need not be documented here. He successfully rebuked superstars like Babe Ruth[50] and Shoeless Joe Jackson,[51] as well as certain league owners,[52] with scarcely more than a whimper from the opposition.

Landis' successors likewise operated under the assumption that they were beyond sanction, whether it be for violations of the law or transgressions against basic human dignity. Miller claims that Landis' immediate successor, A.B. "Happy" Chandler, portrayed his indifference to law and public opinion by, among other things, spying on the union activities of early player organizer Robert Murphy,[53] suspending Leo Durocher for an entire season,[54] and subverting players' attempts to conduct a peaceful work stoppage.[55] However, Ford Frick, next in Miller's fools' parade, quickly

---

commissioner authority and prompted by a need to convince the public that the sport was not rudderless, agreed to Judge Landis' terms. As Miller correctly points out, it set a precedent in which baseball's commissioner gradually assumed broad authority over all aspects of the game—again, so long as the "good old boy network" remained, for the most part, undisturbed. *Id.* at 107.

50. *See* ROBERT W. CREAMER, BABE 244-52 (1974).

51. MILLER, *supra* note 1, at 215; ELIOT ASINOF, EIGHT MEN OUT 292 (1963).

52. *See* Milwaukee Am. Ass'n v. Landis, 49 F.2d 298 (N.D. Ill. 1931).

53. MILLER, *supra* note 1, at 6. Such surveillance is a violation of section 8(a)(1) of the National Labor Relations Act. 29 U.S.C. § 158(a)(1) (1988).

54. MILLER, *supra* note 1, at 57. Miller depicts Chandler as a somewhat paranoid, devious, and vindictive commissioner. When he was criticized by renowned baseball writer Red Smith as being a pawn for the owners and for the excessiveness of his season-long suspension of Leo Durocher, Chandler accused Smith of conspiratorial activity and of "trying to run him out of baseball . . . Smith replied: 'If I can get paid for thinking Happy Chandler has performed like a clown and a mountebank, then I want all that kind of money I can get. Ordinarily I have to work for mine.'" *Id.*

55. *Id.* at 64. Ironically, in some circles, Chandler is viewed as having been a players' commissioner. In 1946, Commissioner Chandler, who had been appointed less than a year earlier, announced that those players who "'jumped'" to the Mexican league would be barred from Major League Baseball for five years. *Id.* at 176. The word "jump" is clearly a misnomer because the players simply left after their contracts had expired. The only thing they were "jumping" was the outrageous reserve rule and system of perpetual options. One of the players, Danny Gardella, instituted an antitrust action, claiming that the blacklist was a violation of the Sherman Antitrust Act, 15 U.S.C. §§ 1-3 (1988). *See* Gardella v. Chandler, 172 F.2d 402 (2d Cir. 1949). His case was particularly poignant because he had never been subject to the reserve clause; rather, he had simply turned down a $5,000 signing bonus from the New York Giants to play baseball in the United States. With the lawsuit pending, Chandler granted amnesty to all players who had defected to the Mexican League. His purpose allegedly was to temper justice with mercy—thus the designation "players' Commissioner." Miller disputes the title, however, claiming that Chandler was motivated by the pending Second Circuit case

developed a reputation as a " 'do-nothing' "[56] commissioner whose greatest offense was his inactivity rather than his power-mongering.[57] Frick was followed in office by Colonel William "Spike" Eckert, who was commonly viewed as the " 'know-nothing' " counterpart to Frick and someone who, by his own admission, was ill-suited for the position.[58] Eckert lacked sophistication in labor relations and by many accounts was "overmatched by the job."[59]

Miller's most pointed commentary is reserved for Bowie Kuhn and, somewhat surprisingly, the late Bart Giamatti. A perusal of Miller's book in comparison with Kuhn's *Hardball*[60] will convince most readers that there is precious little common ground upon which these adversaries stand. While a litany of the differences between Miller and Kuhn would fill a separate volume, a few brief illustrations on the 1981 strike will make the point.

In recounting the strike, where the gravamen of the impasse centered upon the owners' demand that the acquiring club compensate (e.g., with a roster player) the club losing a player to free agency, Miller recalls: "The 1981 strike was the most principled I've ever been associated with . . . . [I]t

---

and by a desire to forestall any decision in which baseball's reserve clause would be threatened and baseball's antitrust exemption removed. MILLER, *supra* note 1, at 176-80.

56. MILLER, *supra* note 1, at 70.

57. In addition, there were instances in which Frick distinguished himself for his insensitivity to blacks as well as for his commitment to integration. For example, at one point he explained the absence of blacks from baseball by saying, " 'Colored people' . . . 'did not have a chance to play' during slavery, 'and so were late in developing proficiency . . . . Consequently, it was another fifty years before they arrived at the stage where they were important in the organized baseball picture.' " HAROLD SEYMOUR, BASEBALL: THE PEOPLE'S GAME 532 (1972). As National League President, however, Frick responded to threats by some teams that they would strike rather than play against Jackie Robinson. "I do not care if half the league strikes. Those who do will encounter quick retribution. . . . This is the United States of America and one citizen has as much right to play as another." ROGER KAHN, THE BOYS OF SUMMER 45 (1972). In attempting to identify the real Ford Frick, one should be aware that he opposed admitting Negro Leaguers into the Hall of Fame. KUHN, *supra* note 8, at 110. Kuhn noted that as "[w]rong though Frick may have been on this issue, no one could challenge his honesty, genuineness or decency." *Id.* This naivete probably explains Kuhn's wonderment as to why baseball has had a difficult time attracting black fans. "Although blacks are measurably strong baseball fans, there has always been a notable failing on the part of the major leagues to turn them into paying customers. Why this is, I have never been quite sure." *Id.* at 116-17. Perhaps it escapes Kuhn's ken that, until 1947, blacks were excluded from those major leagues.

58. MILLER, *supra* note 1, at 70; *see also* KUHN, *supra* note 8, at 29-30.

59. MILLER, *supra* note 1, at 69-70. Even the hapless Eckert was carried away by his title. When confronted by Miller regarding his decision to bar the Executive Director from a crucial meeting with player representatives, Eckert declared: "The Commissioner decides who will come to these meetings, and the Commissioner has made that decision." He soon relented. *Id.* at 70.

60. *See supra* note 8.

was the Association's finest hour."[61]  Kuhn, on the other hand, comments, "On June 12 the Major League Players Association blundered into a strike that would prove to be the worst in American sports history."[62]

Miller adds that the owners' lamentation about free agency was a subterfuge. In his view, the owners were aware that more teams would have an opportunity to improve themselves, and the game as a whole would prosper as a result of the open bidding.[63]  Kuhn was strongly in favor of a compensation package[64] and frequently expressed his concern that unqualified free agency would cripple the industry.[65]

Finally, Miller characterizes the strike as a players' dispute in which the athletes "[t]op to bottom, star to sub, liberal to conservative . . . stood firm."[66]  He quotes numerous players who endorsed the strike and lauded its accomplishments.[67]  In assessing the aftermath, Miller notes that the players, while losing thirty-four million dollars, secured their future income earning potential—a fact borne out by data that compares player payrolls of 121 million dollars in 1981 to over 388 million dollars in 1990.[68]  Kuhn, conversely, labels the 1981 work stoppage as "Miller's strike,"[69] in which the players were "[l]ed . . . as a trusting light brigade into the valley of death . . . . [T]hey were the major financial losers."[70]

Their direct evaluations of each other round out these dramatically opposite perspectives.  Kuhn, who admits to the existence of "rogues in our business,"[71] opines that Miller "hated management generally and the management of baseball specifically."[72]  Kuhn states that Miller perceived the owners as "scoundrels" and "tyrants," emulating those employers of bygone days "who had suppressed the rightful interests of American labor."[73]  Kuhn would have his readers believe that Miller's perspective is a product of his standing as "an old-fashioned, nineteenth-century trade unionist" who "harbored a suspicion of most institutions" and who "had a deep hatred and suspicion of the American right and of American capitalism."[74]  Yet,

---

61. MILLER, *supra* note 1, at 302.
62. KUHN, *supra* note 8, at 3.
63. MILLER, *supra* note 1, at 118.
64. KUHN, *supra* note 8, at 3.
65. *Id.* at 338; MILLER, *supra* note 1, at 248, 275.
66. MILLER, *supra* note 1, at 302.
67. *Id.* at 303.
68. *Id.* at 318.
69. KUHN, *supra* note 8, at 346.
70. *Id.* at 362.
71. *Id.* at 77.
72. *Id.*
73. *Id.* at 78.
74. *Id.* at 77.

Kuhn's assessment of Miller overstates the point. Rather, Kuhn's observation that professional baseball fits the prototype of what Miller must despise, "with its rich, lordly owners and its players shackled by the reserve system," together with Miller's awareness of the role that he occupies as union leader, offers a more plausible explanation for Miller's perennial distance from baseball's ownership and inherent distrust for many of its actions.[75]

Miller makes clear that he regards Kuhn as a shill for baseball's owners, insensitive to players,[76] and bent on destroying their Association.[77] The fact that Kuhn, an experienced Wall Street lawyer, manifested such a profound lack of sophistication with regard to legal matters,[78] especially in the areas of labor relations[79] and due process, is particularly frustrating to Miller.[80] Miller remembers Kuhn as unreliable,[81] disingenuous,[82] paternalistic,[83] and unrealistic,[84] and he highlights the shameless and repeated distortion of facts and events appearing in Kuhn's autobiography.[85]

At the close of his book, Miller reflects upon those Commissioners who followed his retirement as Executive Director. He finds virtue in both Peter

---

75. *Id.* Nothing contributed to the inability of Miller and Kuhn to find a common ground so much as their own self-perceptions. Miller saw and correctly positioned himself in an adversarial role vis-à-vis baseball's owners. MILLER, *supra* note 1, at 110-11. Indicative of Miller's allegiance to the Players Association and his traditional view of trade unionism is his refusal to accept his salary while the players were on strike. *Id.* at 212. Kuhn, on the other hand, appeared to view himself as a man for all seasons, a moderating influence upon the opposing forces, a servant to the game and, at times, even a players' commissioner. *Id.* at 105-06, 111, 293-94. "I wanted to reach the players. . . . I admired them. . . . I would always be the little kid on the curb watching the parade of stars march by." KUHN, *supra* note 8, at 44. As Curt Flood says, however, "From the players' point of view, he was straight Establishment, a grinder of the owners' ax." FLOOD, *supra* note 21, at 169. Throughout his book, Miller expresses his disdain for what he perceives to be Kuhn's self-delusions.

76. MILLER, *supra* note 1, at 127.

77. *Id.* at 91.

78. *Id.* at 234-35; *see also supra* note 26.

79. MILLER, *supra* note 1, at 96.

80. *Id.* at 130.

81. *Id.* at 93.

82. *Id.* at 119.

83. *Id.* at 202.

84. *Id.* at 294.

85. *Id.* at 300. Miller's synopsis of Kuhn is most damning.

> His moves consistently backfired . . . . His inability to distinguish between reality and his prejudices, his lack of concern for the rights of players, sections of the press, and even of the stray, unpopular owner—all combined to make Kuhn a vital ingredient in the growth and strength of the union. To paraphrase Voltaire on God, if Bowie Kuhn had never existed, we would have had to invent him.

*Id.* at 91.

Ueberroth's[86] and Fay Vincent's[87] tenures, but gives each of them a mixed review. He has few kind words for the late Bart Giamatti, who was lionized as Commissioner and almost canonized since his untimely death.

Miller's principal dispute with Giamatti centers upon the latter's handling of the Pete Rose case[88] and his response to Arbitrators Thomas Robert's and George Nicolau's collusion decisions of 1985, 1986, and 1987.[89] With regard to Rose, Miller contends that Giamatti acted irresponsibly and seriously undermined Rose's due process rights by crediting an adverse witness before he heard the testimony of that witness and without the benefit of any cross-examination.[90] He adds that Giamatti signed an agreement with Rose specifically acknowledging no finding of any baseball-related gambling; yet,

---

86. Miller praises certain aspects of Ueberroth's tenure, including his reversal of Kuhn's banning of Willie Mays and Mickey Mantle from Major League Baseball due to their affiliation with Atlantic City casinos. He was also impressed with Ueberroth's interest in the Players Association's collective bargaining history. MILLER, *supra* note 1, at 386-88. On the negative side of the ledger, Miller calls Ueberroth to task for bypassing the Players Association in a grandstand fashion on the drug testing question. *Id.* at 389-90. Further, he identifies Ueberroth as one of the architects in the infamous collusion cases where the owners were found guilty of conspiring to suppress free agency during the 1985, 1986, and 1987 seasons (with a resultant liability of $280 million in backpay). *Id.* at 390-92; *see also supra* note 33.

87. Miller states that Vincent may be the "best baseball commissioner of the last quarter century." MILLER, *supra* note 1, at 407. He comments favorably on Vincent's intelligence, sense of humor, interest in the game, and lack of self-righteousness. *Id.* at 403. Miller suggests, however, that recent events have caused him to doubt Vincent's stature. In particular, Miller believes that Vincent has joined the "Illusion of the Commissioner Having Real Power Club," *id.* at 406, as evidenced by Vincent's statement that " 'I'm not going to resign. . . . The decision whether I stay or go is mine. . . . That's the way it is.' " *Id.* at 407. Moreover, Miller is troubled by Vincent's contention that disciplining guilty owners for their collusive activity would amount to double jeopardy because the owners had already absorbed a $280 million backpay liability. Miller irrefutably points out: "Imagine that a bank robber was caught red-handed, convicted and forced to return the loot—and then claimed that going to jail constituted double jeopardy!" *Id.* at 400.

88. *Id.* at 393-98, 400-01.

89. *Id.* at 351, 398-99.

90. Many commentators have suggested that allegations of Giamatti's bias and the issuance of a Temporary Restraining Order by Ohio Circuit Court Judge Norbert Nadel violated all precedent and represented a marked and unprovoked departure from judicial deference to private associations and their decision-making procedures. They have even gone so far as to discredit Judge Nadel by suggesting that his decision was politically motivated. A close examination of the facts, however, indicates that Judge Nadel's action and Miller's criticism of Giamatti are perhaps more well-placed than one would think at first blush. No one questions that Rose was entitled to some type of hearing and due process prior to any final determination of his guilt. *See* Major League Agreement, Major League Rules of Procedure, §§ 2, 3; Gibson v. Berryhill, 411 U.S. 564 (1973); Erving v. Virginia Squires Basketball Club, 349 F. Supp. 716, 719 (E.D.N.Y.), *aff'd*, 468 F.2d 1064 (2d Cir. 1972). While the amount of due process to which a litigant is entitled may vary from case to case, *see, e.g.*, Mathews v. Eldridge, 424 U.S. 319 (1976), there is little doubt that an unbiased decision maker is an indispensable component. For that reason, Judge Nadel's decision reflects sound legal analysis and courageous jurisprudence, rather than hometown politics and pandering for reelection.

within a few hours, Giamatti pronounced in a news conference that Rose had indeed bet on baseball games. Miller finds this conduct to be contemptible both in the dictionary and legal sense of that term.[91]

Miller's other dispute with Giamatti concerns the Commissioner's alleged involvement with, or at least tacit approval of, the owners' collusion to stifle the proliferation of free agents in violation of the collective bargaining agreement.[92] Miller finds it unfathomable that Giamatti viewed the collusion case as a non-issue and ignored the overwhelming evidence and legal conclusions of the arbitration panels. More significantly, Miller cannot comprehend Giamatti's argument that, as National League President, he was completely unaware of any collusion in the face of evidence placing him in meetings in which the owners' conspiratorial activities were discussed.[93] Miller concludes that Giamatti lied about his involvement, and intimates that the final arbitration decision in 1990 preserved the late Commissioner's reputation by refraining from any mention of Giamatti's National League presidency coinciding with the years of collusion.[94]

The principal difficulty with Miller's evaluation of the Commissioner's office and his *ad hominem* attack on its various office holders is his failure to present his arguments in an organized fashion. He devotes an entire chapter to Commissioner Kuhn, yet proceeds to lace every other chapter with innuendo and direct criticism of Kuhn's performance. He likewise reserves separate chapter treatment for "Owners and Other Bosses" and "white collar" types after having filled the preceding chapters with observations on many of the same people. While Miller's insights are sharp and clear, the packaging leaves something to be desired.

## III.  PLAYERS AND THE MLBPA

Miller recalls that throughout baseball history players sporadically have attempted to establish a collective body to deal with the owners on the most crucial issues affecting their "employment." From 1885 through 1946, the players established four different unions, each enjoying limited success, but none creating a long-term collective bargaining relationship.[95]

---

91. MILLER, *supra* note 1, at 397.
92. *Id.* at 351, 399.
93. *Id.*
94. *Id.*
95. *Id.* at 6; DWORKIN, *supra* note 1, at 8-21. Before the formation of the MLBPA, the players had "unionized" (in a fashion) four different times: The National Brotherhood of Professional Baseball Players (1885-1890); The League Protective Players Association (1900-1902); The Baseball Players Fraternity (1912-1918); and The American Baseball Guild (1946). *Id.*; *see also* Erwin G. Krasnow & Herman M. Levy, *Unionization and Professional Sports*, 51 GEO. L.J. 749 (1963).

In 1954, the sixteen player representatives, one from each team (chosen by the commissioner), voted to establish the MLBPA.[96] Although there was clearly some intent that this group would air work-related grievances with the owners, the MLBPA described itself as a social or fraternal organization and not as a union.[97] Presumably, some players viewed themselves as something more than employees, akin to independent contractors, existing on a level with the owners. If so, Miller points to their working conditions, especially the reserve system, to show that they were whistling past the graveyard. Between 1954 and 1966 it became apparent that the MLBPA was a toothless consensus—a company union relatively impotent in terms of accommodating the players' growing concerns about salaries, job security, and retirement.[98]

Miller graphically describes the appointment process leading to his directorship of the MLBPA. As part of a strategy to formalize the MLBPA and give it greater credibility, the players decided to create the position of full-time Executive Director and selected a screening committee to consider candidates for the inaugural post. Miller recounts that Robin Roberts, former Philadelphia Phillies' pitcher and member of the committee, contacted Dr. George Taylor, Dean of the University of Pennsylvania's Wharton Business School, and asked for possible suggestions. Taylor, after consulting with Miller, recommended him to Roberts; Miller was asked to interview shortly thereafter.[99] At this initial interview with the players' screening committee, Miller received his first of many shocks regarding the players' naivete about collective bargaining in general and its application to baseball specifically. Miller was told directly that, if elected, his general counsel would be former President Richard Nixon. Miller could think of no one less suitable for the position, and he felt that the mere mention of Nixon's name showed how

---

96. DWORKIN, *supra* note 1, at 27. Subsequent to the formation and quick demise of Robert Murphy's American Baseball Guild in 1946, the owners attempted to forestall future organizing by establishing a two-pronged representation plan whereby sixteen player representatives, one from each club, were selected by the Commissioner for the purpose of airing player grievances, and two additional players, one from each league, were chosen to serve on baseball's Executive Council. *Id.* at 26.

97. *Id.* at 27.

98. Between 1947 and 1966, the minimum salary for a Major League baseball player was increased once, from $5,000 to $6,000. MILLER, *supra* note 1, at 156. The reserve system guaranteed that a player signed to a Uniform Player Contract, encumbered as it was with the repeating option clause, was bound to the signing club in perpetuity. *Id.* at 41-42; *see also* *supra* note 18. Retirement benefits were gossamers, hardly providing any assurances of security or quality of life after the player's career ended. *Id.* at 7, 40, 45. The Uniform Player Contract, in Miller's words, was "one sided," reminding him of a lease "drawn up by an association of landlords and handed to prospective tenants for signature." *Id.* at 41.

99. *Id.* at 3-5.

"little the players knew about labor relations" or about him.[100] At the conclusion of the interview, Miller indicated that he would not work with Nixon and that Nixon was an " 'owners man' " who " 'wouldn't know the difference between a pension plan and a pitcher's mound.' "[101]

After Miller declined the offer, the player representatives awarded the executive directorship to Milwaukee Circuit Judge and perennial owner advocate Robert Cannon. Within a short time, Cannon was dismissed.[102] After Cannon's ouster, Miller received the nomination of the screening committee. In his brief "campaign" to gain membership approval, he met with the players from each club during spring training. Despite setbacks early in his tour, Miller was overwhelming confirmed.[103]

When Miller assumed the position of Executive Director in 1966, two things were readily apparent. First, the players were sorely in need of an outside agent to represent them, notwithstanding the protest of baseball's owners that the players were better served dealing on a one-to-one basis. Second, until some inroads were made into the impenetrable reserve system, players would never be able to assert themselves and secure a proportionate share of the profits to which they contributed so substantially. Miller's book explains the paths taken and strategies employed in approaching these problems.

Miller relates that he immediately set about addressing the first issue through an exhaustive campaign to apprise the players of their organization's potential, and to cultivate the players' confidence in his ability to help effectuate their objectives. The first order of business was the funding of the union and appropriation of his salary. At one point, the owners had represented to the players that their labor organization could be financed with funds deducted from revenues from the annual All Star game. Shortly thereafter, the owners reneged on this promise claiming, among other things, that this type of contribution would violate the National Labor Relations Act.[104]

After some debate, the problem was resolved when Miller convinced the ownership to convert from an employee contribution pension plan to an employer funded program. Under this arrangement, those funds formerly remitted from players' salaries as pension contributions would no longer be

---

100.  *Id.* at 3-4.

101.  *Id.* at 9-10.

102.  *See id.*, at 6. After Miller's initial interview with the Players Association, Cannon became a front-runner for the Executive Director position and was approved by a plurality of the players. *Id.* at 33. Shortly thereafter, Cannon, who had never endorsed a "players' union" and had alienated the player representatives, was fired. *Id.* at 34, 65; *see also,* FLOOD, *supra* note 21, at 153 (stating that Cannon "stopped giving owners a hard time.")

103.  MILLER, *supra* note 1, at 61.

104.  *Id.* at 67-68; *see also supra* note 34 and accompanying text.

required to finance the plan.[105] The amount that had been appropriated for pension plan funding became "employee money" and could be utilized to sustain the Players Association without running afoul of the National Labor Relations Act. The players actually received a modest windfall because the former pension allocation was sufficient to provide the Players Association its requisite financial backing—obviating the fifty dollar monthly union dues that the players had been paying.[106]

Miller recounts that his next hurdle involved negotiation of a more structured pension plan, an issue that had been at the forefront of the players' concerns since Miller's initial meeting with the screening committee.[107] During the early discussions with management concerning this issue, Miller first recognized that the owners were not aware of their full responsibilities in the area of collective bargaining. The pension plan was not due to expire for approximately nine months. The owners, however, were about to announce changes in the plan as a *fait accompli*, without any consultation with the Players Association. Eventually, after Miller's vehement protest and less vehement primer on management's duty to bargain in good faith with the employees' exclusive bargaining representative, negotiations commenced and a settlement was reached. This accord marked a watershed event in sports negotiations—the first collective bargaining agreement of any type.[108]

The 1966 pact was merely the first step, addressing only pension and insurance benefits. Miller immediately turned to the task of reaching a collective bargaining agreement on all wages, hours, and working conditions. Again, after some disagreement as to the role of the MLBPA in the bargaining process, including further manifestations of the commissioner's reluctance to recognize the Association's status, good faith negotiations ensued and a definitive collective bargaining agreement was reached. Miller boasts that its advancements included the incorporation of the Uniform Players Contract (rendering any changes therein subject to collective bargaining), a formal grievance procedure circumscribing, to some extent, the commissioner's role as neutral arbitrator, and an initial agreement to begin reconsideration of the noxious reserve rule.[109]

During the term of the 1968 contract, the first threat of a major work stoppage was presented and averted. Although the agreement did not expire until 1970, the pension and benefit plan of 1966 was due to lapse in the spring of 1969. The owners had made it clear to Miller that they were

---

105. MILLER, *supra* note 1, at 69-72, 92-94.
106. *Id.*
107. *Id.* at 7.
108. *Id.* at 87-89, 95.
109. *Id.* at 95-98.

adopting an aggressive position on the pension program and that they were hoping to roll back some of the current benefits.[110] As a result of the owners' intransigence, the players agreed that no one would sign a 1969 Uniform Player Contract until some type of accord could be reached on the benefit issues.[111] With spring training rapidly approaching, the owners relented. Even Miller, ever the optimist, seemed surprised at the magnitude of the achievements, especially the increases in the owners' contribution to the pension plan from 4.1 million to 6.5 million dollars per year and the reduction of pension eligibility from five to four years (applied retroactively to 1947).[112] Miller acknowledges that Bowie Kuhn promoted the resolution of this dispute, characterizing it as one of Kuhn's "finest hours."[113]

Miller recounts that the next significant development in the Players Association's bargaining history occurred in 1972 when, once again, the dispute arose over pensions (amount and eligibility).[114] Miller notes that although negotiations proceeded slowly, he had not anticipated a strike. In fact, he admits that he had not even mentioned the possibility of major confrontation at his pre-negotiation meetings with the players.[115] It quickly became apparent that Miller had misgauged the owners' position. In Miller's mind, the pension issue constituted the owners' veiled attempt to "destroy the union."[116] On the other side, the owners and many of the members of the press characterized Miller as an extremist, and even questioned whether pensions for baseball players were necessary or appropriate.[117] In just a few years, the roles of each side had become clearly defined and the positions on various issues had begun to crystallize.

Miller explains that, as a result of the pension impasse, the players voted to strike, precipitating a thirteen-day, eighty-six-game work stoppage. Seeking to terminate the first major strike in sports history, the parties quickly reached agreement.[118] The owners acceded to the players' pension demands

---

110. *Id.* at 98-99.

111. *Id.* at 99-100.

112. *Id.* at 104-05.

113. *Id.* at 105.

114. *Id.* at 203-06.

115. *Id.* at 204.

116. *Id.* at 203-06.

117. *Id.* at 213-15.

118. *Id.* at 221-22. This strike marked Miller's earliest realization that the players had truly warmed to the task of supporting his efforts in developing the Players Association as a true trade union. Early on, they demonstrated the solidarity necessary to achieve their desired collective bargaining objectives. At an initial strike poll, the players voted 663-10 to endorse a strike in support of the players' demand regarding the pension plan. Miller, however, was concerned about the strike and the players' inadequate funding to support such a collective action. As a result, he suggested an alternative strategy in which negotiations would continue

while the players forfeited salaries lost for games missed during the strike. The players did not surrender any accumulation of seniority or service benefits. Because Miller had held no realistic hope for recovering lost wages, he considered the settlement a victory and a signal to the owners that the players on the field had now become players in the theater of collective bargaining.[119]

While Miller was well on the way toward establishing the Players Association as a force in Major League Baseball, no meaningful progress had been made on the reserve clause question. Although study groups had gathered to discuss the matter, they had proved to be unproductive. The owners' position appeared to be unyielding.[120] As Miller recalls, at this stage of the players' development, litigation and not negotiation was perceived as the route to free agency.

In 1970, baseball player Curt Flood decided to contest the decision of his team, the Saint Louis Cardinals, to assign his contract—trade him, in common parlance—to the Philadelphia Phillies. He approached Miller to discuss the possibility of initiating an antitrust action to challenge the reserve

---

throughout the season, thereby postponing a strike to the following year when the basic agreement expired. *Id.* at 211. When Miller presented his postponement idea to the player representatives, however, they voted 47-0 (one abstention) in favor of a strike, with the lone abstainer subsequently impeached by his fellow players. *Id.* at 212. This demonstration of the players' resolve, sustaining a strike that cost them approximately $600,000 and the ownership $5.2 million, prompted Miller to comment: " 'All fans should be proud of the players. They showed courage and hung together against terrible odds. They made the owners understand that they must be treated as equals.' " *Id.* at 222. Miller's pride and the esteem that he felt for the players was echoed in the work stoppages that followed in 1976 and, particularly, in 1980-81. *Id.* at 258, 262, 302-03.

Yet, one of the unfortunate aspects of Miller's book is his inability to understand how Major League Baseball players could not immediately grasp the significance of the issues before them and, more importantly, how they could not accord him and the Players Association appropriate recognition for their overall advancement as "employees." Miller's musings are replete with expressions of hurt feelings about incidents which he believed were indicative of the players' lack of appreciation and simpatico. Even players who at one point in the book were praised for their dedication to the Players Association found themselves on the wrong end of Miller's invective for failing, for example, to mention the contributions of the Players Association in their autobiographies. *See id.* at 254-55, 274-75, 348.

119. One of the by-products of this negotiation was an agreement on a salary arbitration program implemented to resolve impasses on questions of players' salaries, which, except for minimums, were not and are not collectively bargained. DWORKIN, *supra* note 1, at 33-34, 136-50. Through salary arbitration, the players received a benefit that permitted them, after a certain number of years of service (it has varied over the years), to submit their claims for arbitration to a neutral arbitrator. Under the system, the player and his club owner each submit final offers, from which the arbitrator must choose. There is no compromise figure that the arbitrator is permitted to reach, thus insuring that each side will present the arbitrator with a realistic figure. *Id.*; *see also* MILLER, *supra* note 1, at 109-110.

120. MILLER, *supra* note 1, at 189-90.

system in a judicial forum. As Miller's vivid account illustrates, his response to Flood was hardly sanguine. Miller carefully explained the history of baseball's arcane antitrust exemption and his cynicism about the possibility of convincing the court to reverse fifty years of *stare decisis*.[121]

Once Flood made it clear that he was prepared to pursue the litigation notwithstanding the limited chance of success, Miller and his general counsel, Dick Moss, took various steps to promote Flood's lawsuit. They met with scores of players explaining the imminence of Flood's litigation and its potential impact, secured the financial backing of the players and selected former Supreme Court Justice Arthur Goldberg to represent Flood.[122]

In recalling the early stages of Flood's lawsuit, Miller underscores Commissioner Kuhn's unwillingness or inability to appreciate the players' concerns. After Flood had sent an obligatory letter to Kuhn protesting the trade, expressing his legal position, and asking for relief, Kuhn paternalistically acknowledged the letter but remonstrated that Flood had not voiced a specific objection. Miller sardonically observes, "[c]lose your eyes and poke your finger at Flood's letter; you will scarcely find a sentence that doesn't 'specify' Curt Flood's 'objection'."[123] Having exhausted his remedies, Flood instituted his action in federal court. Most followers of law or baseball are intimately familiar with the progress of that litigation; baseball's exemption was sustained and the merits of the antitrust challenge to the reserve system were never broached.[124]

In reflecting upon events leading to Flood's defeat, Miller acknowledges that he was responsible for deficiencies in the presentation of the case. For example, he believes that the players did not demonstrate the requisite solidarity through a sufficient courtroom presence. Few players attended the hearings or the Supreme Court oral argument and, in fact, many of them even openly debated whether elimination of the reserve system would be det-

---

121. Flood v. Kuhn, 407 U.S. 258 (1972); Toolson v. New York Yankees, Inc., 346 U.S. 917 (1953); Federal Baseball Club, Inc. v. National League of Prof. Baseball Clubs, 259 U.S. 200 (1922). Given the 50-year history of the mysterious baseball exemption, Miller's cynicism was certainly justified. MILLER, *supra* note 1, at 109-10.

122. MILLER, *supra* note 1, at 182-88. Several factors prompted Miller's recommendation, including Goldberg's considerable experience as Secretary of Labor, Supreme Court Justice, and private practitioner, his sensitivity to the concerns of organized labor, spawned in part by his considerable experience with the Steelworkers' union, and his outrage at the continued existence of the reserve clause. *Id.* at 188-90. The only reservation that Miller experienced centered on the possibility that Goldberg would make a bid in New York's gubernatorial race. When Goldberg made it abundantly clear that he had no intention to run for governor, Miller, Dick Moss, and others decided that he should represent Flood. *Id.* at 198.

123. *Id.* at 192.

124. *See* Flood v. Kuhn, 407 U.S. 258 (1972).

rimental to the game of baseball.[125] Further, Miller questions his own selection of Arthur Goldberg as counsel. Most observers of the Supreme Court oral argument found that Goldberg's performance, while thorough, was uninspired and uninspiring. Miller suggests that Goldberg was distracted by the governor's race in New York (Goldberg had decided to run for governor after assuring Miller prior to the litigation that he had no intention of doing so), contributing to his sub-par performance.[126] In any event, regardless of the mistakes and misapplied strategies, the *Flood* case looms, at best, as an aberration and, at worst, as a proverbial derelict in mainstream antitrust jurisprudence.[127]

Given the owners' absolute refusal to grant any meaningful concessions at the bargaining table, Miller realized after Flood's defeat that the battle for free agency would have to be fought and won in another forum. The avenue of next (and apparently last) resort was the collective bargaining agreement's grievance machinery. The point of attack was the Uniform Player Contract and the owners' persistent contention that the option clause of that contract created a system of perpetual renewal and, thus, permanent reserve.

Miller's recollections of the strategy employed in attacking the reserve system through the collective bargaining agreement are thoughtful and thought provoking. He explains that in 1975 players Dave McNally and Andy Messersmith refused to sign their individual contracts at the conclusion of the option year. Miller recalls that, although the grievants were rightfully concerned about the impact of this litigation upon their careers, they agreed to pursue the matter through arbitration—notwithstanding attempts by the owners to dissuade them.[128] They argued, through the Players Association, that the option clause did not renew with the contract and that they could only be bound for one year after the contract containing the option had expired.

Following the denial of the McNally and Messersmith grievances, the Players Association proceeded through the contractual machinery to submit the matter before the arbitration panel. Arbitrator Peter Seitz, who had decided the controversial Catfish Hunter case, was the neutral arbitrator.[129]

---

125. MILLER, *supra* note 1, at 196-97.

126. *Id.* at 198.

127. *See, e.g.,* Robert G. Berger, *After the Strikes: A Reexamination of Professional Baseball's Exemption from the Antitrust Laws,* 45 U. PITT. L. REV. 209, 210 n.3 (1983); William N. Eskridge, Jr., *Overruling Statutory Precedents,* 76 GEO. L.J. 1361, 1381 (1988); *see* BOB WOODWARD & SCOTT ARMSTRONG, THE BRETHREN 189-92 (1979) (accounting briefly the tragi-comical nature of the machinations surrounding the eventual Flood decision).

128. Miller, *supra* note 1, at 242-45.

129. *Id.* at 245. While typical labor arbitration cases involve a single arbitrator, baseball often employs a three-person panel. In this scenario, each adversarial party chooses its own

At the conclusion of the arbitration, Seitz found that the reserve system constituted a violation of the collective bargaining agreement and the Uniform Player Contract that it embraced.[130] Rejecting the owners' procedural argument that the collective bargaining agreement specifically precluded consideration of the reserve system under the grievance clause, Seitz concluded on the merits that the option clause did not perpetually renew. He further found that the Major League rules establishing a system of reserve were ineffectual in preventing McNally and Messersmith from becoming free agents because the rules depended upon the allegedly insulated player being signatory to a Uniform Player Contract.[131] It cannot be denied that *McNally-Messersmith* is one of the most significant decisions in baseball's mercurial legal history and one that was to have a profound impact on labor negotiations during the succeeding fifteen-year period. Yet, Miller does not characterize the Seitz ruling as a bombshell, suggesting, rather, that the owners had seen it coming since the initiation of the suit.[132]

Miller explains that in 1976 the owners and players again found themselves at impasse. On this occasion, the precipitate was the *McNally-Messersmith* decision and the owners' purposeful goal of eliminating free agency at the bargaining table.[133] Whether the true motive for the owners' intransigence on the free agency question was the fear of escalated salaries, domi-

---

arbitrator/representative and those two individuals select an impartial chairman who represents neither party. MILLER, *supra* note 1, at 250. Commissioner Kuhn and others had vigorously opposed the selection of Seitz to resolve this case, given his earlier decision in the *Hunter* case. *See supra* note 26.

130. 66 Lab. Arb. Rep. (BNA) 101, 118 (1975).

131. *Id.; see also* Kansas City Royals Baseball Corp. v. Major League Baseball Players Ass'n, 532 F.2d 615 (8th Cir. 1976) (affirming 409 F. Supp. 233 (W.D. Mo. 1979)).

132. MILLER, *supra* note 1, at 250. In truth, a close reading of Seitz's decision demonstrates that he had made a diligent effort to limit the reach of this decision and, prior to deciding the case, had encouraged the parties to resolve their differences through collective bargaining prior to deciding the case. *See id.* at 251-52. Some commentators have even suggested that his decision seemed "apologetic," not because he regretted its reasoning or conclusions, but, rather, because he believed that the parties should have been able to compromise on the reserve question. DWORKIN, *supra* note 1, at 80. Notwithstanding these assessments, Kuhn reminisced: "Kindly and well-intentioned, [Seitz] was a prisoner of his own philosophy and would rationalize his way to the destruction of the reserve system." KUHN, *supra* note 8, at 157. Kuhn reminisced further that Seitz's ultimate conclusions were preordained, describing the arbitrator (prior to the hearing) as follows: "Seitz, benign and gracious with visions of the Emancipation Proclamation dancing in his eyes." *Id.* at 158.

133. MILLER, *supra* note 1, at 254-55, 259. One interesting feature of the 1976 dispute is that there may have been a larger area for compromise than the owners realized. Miller himself was concerned that an unqualified, wide-open free agency system would glut the market with available players, thereby increasing supply, reducing demand, and suppressing salary elevation. *See id.* at 259, 267. Only Charlie Finley seemed to appreciate that modification of the *McNally-Messersmith* decision through collective bargaining could ironically provide the Players Association with its most significant long-range gain. *Id.* at 259.

nant franchises, and ruination of competition, or simply surrender of the reserve system and total entrepreneurial control of player movement, the owners were adamant.[134] To rectify the problem, they proposed diluting the absolute free agency decreed by Seitz with a series of qualifiers.

Included among the owners' conditions for the unqualified free agency already captured by the players through *McNally-Messersmith* was a nine-year service requirement (with a tenth-year option year), a "kicker" that the club could preclude free agency by offering the player a contract of $30,000 or more, and a requirement that the club who acquired the free agent would be responsible for a large cash settlement to the jilted team.[135] Miller characterizes these initial proposals as "preposterous" and, given the owners' clear intractability, recalls that the players were prepared for his worst expectations—a lockout.[136]

On March 1, 1976, as expected, the owners closed the doors to spring training and locked the players out. After seventeen days, the owners reopened spring training camps and negotiations resumed, largely through the intervention of Los Angeles Dodgers' owner Walter O'Malley and the action of Commissioner Bowie Kuhn.[137] After various attempts to stimulate a compromise, including the exclusion of attorneys from the bargaining process,[138] negotiations improved and the opportunity for a mid-summer settlement seemed possible.[139] The parties finally reached agreement on July 12, 1976. In addition to a new four-year pension agreement, this settlement in-

---

134. *Id.*

135. *See* MILLER, *supra* note 1, at 256.

136. *Id.* Again, Miller was astounded at some players' continued naivete, as many of them believed that total free agency would destroy baseball and that the owners actually had offered something of value. *Id.* at 258-59. At the same time, Miller was heartened by the sophistication and vocal support of many other players. *Id.* at 263.

Miller takes great pains to explain that the eventual cessation of work in 1976 was a lockout rather than a strike. At various points he was asked why the players would not return to work while efforts were made to resolve the impasse. On each occasion, he emphasized that the players were powerless because the lockout was not a strike and thus could only be ended upon the players' capitulation or the owners' decision to resume play. *Id.* at 262. Although a lockout can assume various forms, including defensive and offensive postures, it is an aggressive move by management to close its doors and suspend salaries as a means of exerting economic pressure upon a union, much the same as a strike and the withholding of the labor supply exerts economic pressure upon management. *See* International Bhd. of Boilermakers Local 88 v. NLRB, 858 F.2d 756, 760 (D.C. Cir. 1988); ABA SEC. LAB. REL. L., THE DEVELOPING LABOR LAW 539-51 (Charles A. Morris ed. 1971).

137. *See id.* at 264.

138. *Id.* at 265. Miller secured the League's permission for Players Association General Counsel Dick Moss to remain at the table. *Id.* at 265-66.

139. *Id.* at 266. Miller gives credit for the "movement" to American League President Lee MacPhail, who acknowledged the inevitability of free agency and encouraged the owners to accept it. " 'We're trying to swim against the social current. We've got to change.' " *Id.*

cluded resolution of the free agency question through a compromise package that contained a complex reentry draft and amateur player compensation system, a six-year length of league service requirement for eligibility, and modifications on management's right to assign or deny reassignment of a player's contract.[140]

It was Miller's belief that the acrimony of the 1976 negotiations would produce peace and order in the years that immediately followed.[141] In fact, that period was rife with tension, debate, and the owners' escalated resolve to recoup the control categorically taken away in the *McNally-Messersmith* decision and partially surrendered in the 1976 agreement.[142] Miller was perplexed with management's position because baseball was enjoying tremendous prosperity and popularity. For example, in 1978, baseball grossed approximately $278 million, of which approximately $68.5 million was attributable to salary expenditures.[143] Miller notes that remaining "expenses did not come close to absorbing" the remaining profit of over $200 million.[144] Again, Miller reiterates that the problem was neither profitability nor competitiveness, but rather the owners' surrender of power and control.[145] If Miller had any doubts about the mood preceding the next stage of the players' collective bargaining saga, a meeting with Commissioner Kuhn in the fall of 1979 removed them. Over drinks, the Commissioner boldly declared: "Marvin, the owners need a victory."[146] Miller construed this comment as a request that he take a dive, and, upon returning to his office, confided to his deputy, Donald Fehr, "We're in for a hell of a fight."[147]

The agreement emerging from the crucible of the 1976 lockout expired on December 31, 1979. When negotiations commenced in 1979, the possibility of a major confrontation quickly became self-evident. The owners posited that salaries had spiraled out of control and that the only way to alleviate the problem was to establish a compensation plan in which the club losing a roster player would be reimbursed with a player from the acquiring club.[148]

---

140. *See* DWORKIN, *supra* note 1, at 82-88; MILLER, *supra* note 1, at 267. Regarding eligibility, the new agreement did not affect any players who had become free agents under the *McNally-Messersmith* ruling; they were able to sign with any club without condition. *Id.* at 266.
141. MILLER, *supra* note 1, at 275.
142. *See id.* at 295. The 1976 agreement, though diluting part of the freedom dictated by *McNally-Messersmith*, represented the owners' first negotiated concession on the reserve system.
143. *Id.* at 285.
144. *Id.*
145. *Id.*
146. *Id.*
147. *Id.*
148. *Id.* at 287, 290.

The owners also proposed terminating salary arbitration and individual contract negotiations, and substituting a fixed salary schedule.[149]

The players vociferously opposed any type of compensation plan resulting in the depletion of the signing club's roster, and likewise refused to accept the elimination of individual salary negotiations—especially now that free agency gave such negotiations meaning. *Boston Globe* writer Bob Ryan tersely expressed the view of the union and most of the players: " 'There is no sense in even dignifying the proposal by analyzing it as a legitimate expression of human thought. It is merely the depraved workings of some reactionary brains.' "[150]

The negotiations that spilled over into 1980 and 1981 were probably the most bitter in the history of professional baseball.[151] In April 1980, a player walkout cancelled the final week of spring training. At that time, the players agreed to begin the season as scheduled, but also voted 967 to 1 (one player objecting for religious reasons) to strike on the highly attended Memorial Day weekend, beginning May 23, 1980.[152] The owners averted this strike at the eleventh hour by agreeing to continue salary arbitration, to reduce eligibility for such arbitration from three years to two years of service, and to increase pension benefits.[153] The parties deferred the free agency/compensation issue and convened a study group to research the question further. As part of this understanding, the Players Association agreed that they would call a strike over the controversial compensation proposal no later than June 1, 1981.[154]

Miller comments that the efforts of the study group produced nothing of value and that the players and the owners found themselves at an impasse. The owners attempted to implement unilaterally the "harshest proposal" yet proffered, one that had been "consistently rejected" by the players.[155] After

---

149. *Id.* at 290, 296.

150. *Id.* at 296.

151. *Id.* at 286. Miller claims that Commissioner Kuhn's remonstration regarding the owners' lack of preparedness for a strike are misleading, given their purchase of a $50 million strike insurance policy from Lloyds' of London and their creation of a $15 million war chest. *Id.* at 294-95.

152. *Id.* at 291.

153. *Id.* at 291-92; *see also* DWORKIN, *supra* note 1, at 92.

154. MILLER, *supra* note 1, at 291-92.

155. *Id.* at 292. It is settled law that, once impasse has been reached, an employer may unilaterally implement changes that are "reasonably comprehended within his pre-impasse proposals." Bridgeman v. National Basketball Ass'n, 675 F. Supp. 960, 966 (D.N.J. 1987) (quoting Taft Broadcasting Company, 163 N.L.R.B. 475, 476 (1967)). Miller mentions that the owners' right to change the free agency system unilaterally was triggered 30 days after the issuance of the study group proposal—but he does not explain if or why that is the impasse date. This type of spotty reporting characterizes Miller's discussion of the 1980-81 strike, which is a treasure trove of insight, but an organizational quagmire.

the season had reached its halfway point, the players called a strike in support of their demands. This work stoppage lasted fifty days and cost the owners over $72 million after insurance payments. The players lost almost $34 million in salary, an average of $52,000 per man.[156] Miller reflects upon the senselessness of this strike, emphasizing that the owners failed to achieve a single additional restraint on the free agency system. Further, Miller proudly asserts that the result of the players' perseverance is a relatively unfettered free agency program that promoted the average pre-strike salary of $186,000 to its current figure of $597,000 per year.[157]

Nowhere is Miller's insight more evident than in the accounts of his initial meetings and confrontations with the union membership, and his subsequent negotiating struggles with league owners. To comprehend the dynamics of labor negotiation, one must fully appreciate the skills, motives, and personalities of the negotiators, as well as the economic power and strength of character of the parties who provide the marching orders. Miller's astute observations will instill the reader with the necessary understanding in this regard. Further, Miller's recollections doubtless will provide baseball historians with valuable nuggets of information that have heretofore escaped their notice. Unfortunately, Miller's disorganization often makes the reader pan for these nuggets much like a prospector who knows their general whereabouts but must patiently sift through the silt. Miller's redemption is that the results are well worth the effort.

## IV.  CONCLUSION: THE MLBPA AFTER MARVIN MILLER

Since Marvin Miller's departure, the MLBPA has continued to represent the players in an able fashion predominantly under the leadership of Execu-

---

156. MILLER, *supra* note 1, at 318.

157. *Id.* When Miller discusses salaries, he also expresses his scorn for many players' agents. While saving praise for certain agents, such as Dick Moss, Miller finds that many agents have reaped the benefits of the players' substantial salary advances with little effort and less expertise. *See, e.g., id.* at 271-74, 277-78. At first blush, it may appear that players' agents and the Players Association share a special relationship as custodians of the players' economic advancement. Oftentimes, nothing could be further from the truth. In fact, the goals of the individual and the objectives of the collective are frequently at odds, particularly where there may be a finite amount of funds available to be distributed among the members of the bargaining unit. *See, e.g.,* Agreement between the National Basketball Ass'n and NBAPA, Art. VII (Salary Cap). Professional sports are unique in the sense that, although the athletes may have an exclusive collective bargaining representative, they retain the right to negotiate salaries on an individual basis. This prerogative is a function of the bargaining representative's waiver, often incorporated into an "special covenants" provision. *See* Basic Agreement between Major League Baseball and the MLBPA, Art. III; Uniform Player Contract, Special Covenants; *see also* J.I. Case Co. v. NLRB, 321 U.S. 332 (1944); Midland Broadcasting Company, 93 N.L.R.B. 455 (1951).

tive Director Donald Fehr. During the period following his resignation, Miller served intermittently as a formal and informal consultant, enabling him to provide first-hand observation of the union's continuing developments. However, in recounting the events of the Moffet-Fehr period,[158] Miller intimates that the leadership shunted him aside, often leaving him in the dark on critical issues.

Miller's assessment of the union's involvement in, and the results of, two major bargaining events post-dating his resignation—the 1985 negotiations, characterized by a two day walkout, and the 1990 lockout—are damning and lukewarm, respectively. He asserts that in 1985, "[f]or the first time in almost twenty years of existence, the Players Association took backward steps."[159] In part, he faults the players for their diminished concern for younger colleagues and their " 'I've got mine' " mentality.[160] He also gives Don Fehr a dubious compliment: "By 1985 the players had lost touch with their own history. This was the union's fault—Don Fehr's fault. Which is not to say that Don didn't negotiate a good agreement."[161]

Regarding the 1990 lockout and the resultant agreement, Miller confesses to "mixed feelings,"[162] particularly regarding the divisions among player ranks. He is most concerned with the fact that the owners' "futile and incompetent" strategy for 1989-90 negotiations signaled that they will never cease their efforts to reverse baseball's growth and the advances of the Players Association.[163]

Plainly, Miller has conflicting emotions regarding his tenure with the MLBPA and the aftermath of those turbulent years. He is rightfully proud of the Players Association's accomplishments and his contribution to the

---

158. Ken Moffet served as Executive Director for a brief period following Miller's resignation. The players had been impressed with his performance as a federal mediator during the 1981 strike. However, Miller severely criticizes Moffet's tenure as head of the Players Association. MILLER, *supra* note 1, at 320-39. Further, Miller notes that the 1985 baseball negotiations were personally unrewarding because he neither made decisions nor initiated strategy, despite rumors that he was "a puppeteer pulling the Association's strings." *Id.* at 335. Further, addressing the lockout of 1990, *id.* at 290, 350-62, Miller scotches rumors that he had secretly been orchestrating the union's negotiating strategy: "[T]he truth is that I sweated out this lockout as any fan would, and often had nothing to go by except what I read in the papers." *Id.* at 358.

159. *Id.* at 335. Apparently, Miller presumes that the MLBPA has only been in existence since he assumed the helm. He later explains that, prior to 1966, the Players Association was not a legitimate union because it had been company-dominated and illegally financed. Yet, Miller's comments are counter-intuitive. In order for him to assert that the MLBPA was "illegally" financed, he must assume that it was a labor organization already.

160. *Id.* at 336.

161. *Id.* at 338.

162. *Id.* at 362.

163. *Id.* at 350.

development and growth of the union. On the other hand, he retains feelings of frustration and unappreciation that, to some degree, impact his analysis of events occurring both during and after his reign as Executive Director. Given the huge salary increases enjoyed by almost everyone connected with the game (except for Miller during his term of office), and given the fact that history may not fairly accord him proper credit for his achievements, his feelings are not altogether unwarranted.

Although some of his accounts were one-sided, they were no more one-sided than the early confrontations between baseball's owners and players. The combination of the arcane insulation from antitrust scrutiny, together with the outrageous reserve system that robbed players of the fundamental prerogative to contract freely with the employer of choice, placed the players at a severe disadvantage. Miller arrived and picked up the gauntlet that had been slapped across the players' collective visage for one hundred years.

Thus, while Miller's account is somewhat imbalanced, overall it is a thorough, insightful review of an exciting period in baseball and labor relations. And, although Miller's recollection's are often meandering, almost to the point of being irritating, they possess a diary-like intrigue that is redeeming. I would highly recommend his work to anyone remotely interested in baseball, baseball players, underdogs, labor relations, antitrust, or any combination thereof.

# COMMENT

# Random Urinalysis: Violating The Athlete's Individual Rights?

## INTRODUCTION

The increasing annual rate of drug consumption indicates that drugs have become an integral part of American culture.[1] Due to unlimited availability, a large segment of the population, regardless of age, class, professional and geographic distinctions, continue to use and abuse illicit drugs. The negative result of such widespread use becomes evident with respect to the individual's physical health and the effect of drugs on family and work. In the employment context, an employer's implementation of objective methods to screen its employees for suspected drug use has been justified on several economic grounds. Drug dependent employees tend to be less productive due to absenteeism from the job, are more likely to file workers' compensation claims, and significantly increase the potential for endangering the public safety.[2]

Although drug abuse is a societal problem, it is important to note that "[w]hatever happens in society is going to happen in the professional ranks—of any profession,"[3] including sports. Athletes use drugs for the same reasons as the general public: peer pressure, insecu-

---

1. A 1985 study by the National Narcotics Intelligence Consumers Committee found that overall consumption of drugs rose eleven percent (+11%) in 1984. Specifically, an increase was seen with respect to dangerous drugs (PCP, hallucinogens) (+15%), a slight decrease in marijuana (−3%) and heroin (−1%), and continued widespread use of cocaine. This information was secured from the New York Drug Enforcement Administration, Public Relations Department (April 21, 1986).

2. *See* Goldsmith, *To Test or Not to Test: Laws Provide Framework for Procedure*, N.Y. Times, Feb. 9, 1986, Section S, at 2, col. 1; Bishop, *Worker Drug Tests Resisted: Coast Cases Are Watched*, N.Y. Times, Nov. 27, 1985, at D1, col. 3; *Level of Tolerance of Illegal Drugs Believed Rising Throughout U.S. Society*, N.Y. Times, March 21, 1983, at B5, col. 4.

3. *Sports and Drug Abuse: Senate Hearings 98-1220 Before the Subcomm. on Alcoholism and Drug Abuse of the Senate Comm. on Labor and Human Resources, 98th Cong., 2d Sess.* 34 (1984) (hereinafter cited as "1984 Hearings") (Statement of Eugene "Mercury" Morris, Former Miami Dolphin). *See also* Beckett, *Use and Abuse of Drugs in Sports*, J. Biosoc. Sci. Supp. 7 (1981): 163, 169 ("It is only correct to consider the drug misuse of sport in the correct perspective of drug misuse in society.").

rity, boredom, and a desire for status.[4] In addition, there are several other factors peculiar to professional athletes. First, the immense pressure to excel[5] tempts athletes to use drugs to enhance their performance and thereby gain a competitive edge.[6] Second, more and more athletes are cutting short their college careers in order to reap the economic benefits of professional salaries. This sudden accession to wealth makes a variety of activities, including drug use, more affordable.[7]

For almost two decades, the issue of drug use in sports has been close to the surface, popping through occasionally to reveal the magnitude of the problem. During the past year and a half, the full extent of the problem was revealed to the public by widespread media coverage of the following events: the implication of cocaine use by baseball players during the Pittsburgh drug trials,[8] the New England Patriots' revelation of drug use by its football players,[9] and the relapse and subsequent permanent disqualification from the NBA of the New Jersey Nets guard Michael Ray Richardson.[10] These events have generated a call from several sources for testing professional athletes. Due to the public display of their athletic abilities and their status as role models for younger individuals,[11] the public demands that athletes conform to

---

4. 1984 Hearings, *supra* note 3, at 44 (Statement of Calvin Hill, former running back for the Dallas Cowboys and Cleveland Browns).

5. *Id.* at 45 (Statement of Nancy Hogshead, Olympic Gold Medalist in Swimming) (pressure from coaches). *See also* Lorge, *A Thoroughly Modern Athlete: Bigger, Better—and on Drugs*, Washington Post, May 27, 1979, at A6, col. 6 (pressure from the public, the sports fans, and sometimes from the local government).

6. Note, *Drugs, Athletes, and the NCAA: A Proposed Rule for Mandatory Drug Testing in College Athletics*, 18 J. Mar. L. Rev. 205 (1984) (hereinafter cited as *"Drugs, Athletes, and the NCAA"*); Oseid, *Doping and Athletics—Prevention and Counseling*, J. Allergy Clin. Immun., 1984 May: 73(5 Part 2) 735; Murray, *The Coercive Power of Drugs in Sports*, Hastings Cent. Rep. 1983 August 13(4): 24 ("At the highest levels of competitive sports, where athletes strain to improve performances already at the limits of human ability, the temptation to use a drug that might provide a competition edge can be powerful."). *See also* Lorge, *Chemical "Edge": A Long History Behind Search*, Washington Post, May 27, 1979, at D4, col. 1 ("Historically, [athletes] have been more willing to experiment with any substance they thought could make them quicker, stronger, tougher or better prepared for the competition at hand."); J. WEISTART & C. LOWELL, THE LAW OF SPORTS, § 1.25 at 90 (1979) (hereinafter cited as "WEISTART & LOWELL").

7. "Cocaine Drain," *see infra* note 163 (Statement of Bob Lanier, past president of National Basketball Players Association.

8. *See infra* notes 97-101 and accompanying text.

9. *See infra* notes 165-67 and accompanying text.

10. *See infra* note 37.

11. Beckett, *Use and Abuse of Drugs in Sport*, J. Biosoc. Sci. Supp. 7 (1981) 163, 165 Table 2 (pragmatic argument for classifying some drugs as doping agents is because of the danger of setting bad examples to young people); 1984 Hearings, *supra* note 3, at 2 (Opening Statement of

higher standards of personal conduct.[12] When conformity is lacking, many believe that this group of drug users should be subjected to objective methods of control.

The owners and management of professional sports teams are a second source concerned about drug use by athletes. Not only could the above-mentioned events adversely affect the public confidence and trust in the respective sport,[13] but it has economic ramifications similar to those of other employers. An athlete's use of drugs is likely to result in irregular attendance at practices and games, in sub-par performance due to impaired reflexes, coordination and endurance, and additional team costs for rehabilitation of players adjudged to be chemically dependent.[14]

A third perspective on the issue of drug testing is presented by the players themselves. The respective players associations and sometimes individual players have objected to testing, especially random testing, of athletes as an invasion of privacy, an insult to player integrity and an ineffective deterrent to drug use.[15] In addition, players have questioned whether the results of urinalysis were always accurate and feared the manner in which such test results might be used by management.[16] Notwithstanding the vocal resistance, most professional sports either presently have adopted or have had agreements governing the drug testing procedures to be used in the respective sport. Tennis provides for mandatory testing of all male players whereas the present agreements of basketball, football and the former agreement of

---

Senator Hawkins) ("When a major sports figure is found to be drug dependent, even though he may be an involuntary role model, he disappoints and hurts [himself] . . . and the young person who idolizes and often emulates him."); *id.* at 39 (Statement of Rev. Roosevelt Grier, former professional football player) ("It is a serious thing when we realize the responsibility that we have for our young people . . . We are their models, we are the examples for our young people."); *id.* at 47 (Statement of Tom McMillen, star forward with Washington Bullets basketball team).

12. Beckett, *Use and Abuse of Drugs in Sports*, J. Biosoc. Sci. Supp. 7 (1981): 163, 169 ("Sport, however, should have higher ideals than those which obtain in society as a whole."); 1984 Hearings, *supra* note 3, (Opening Statement of Senator Hatch).

13. Looney, *A Test With Nothing But Tough Questions*, SPORTS ILLUS., Aug. 9, 1982, at 25 ("owners could claim that without drug testing the public's trust and confidence in the sport could be jeopardized, which would hurt the integrity and thereby the profitability of the game.") *But cf. infra* note 164.

14. *See infra* notes 146-147 and accompanying text.

15. Goodwin, *Should Baseball Have Mandatory Drug Testing?*, N.Y. Times, Issue and Debate, Nov. 13, 1985, at B14, col. 5 (baseball); Looney, *A Test With Nothing But Tough Questions*, SPORTS ILLUS., Aug. 9, 1982, at 24-25 (football).

16. *Id. See also infra* notes 192-194 and accompanying text.

baseball all require "reasonable cause" before imposition of the testing procedures.

As private employers, one does not question the authority of management and the owners to test its athletes-employees for drugs. The crucial legal issue raised is whether testing can be conducted on a random basis without cause. In order to determine the constitutionality of random testing, Section I of this Comment will outline the standard provisions contained in the random testing agreement of tennis and the "reasonable cause" agreements of basketball, football, and the recently revoked agreement of baseball. Section II will then scrutinize these agreements under the Constitution. Individuals who are employed by a state instrumentality can be tested for drugs only upon "reasonable cause," unless unique institutional or security needs require otherwise. On the other hand, private employees, absent statutory or contractual provisions to the contrary, may be tested on a mandatory, random or "reasonable cause" basis. In the unionized context of professional sports, random testing will not violate individual rights if such testing has been mutually agreed upon by the players and management. Finally, Section III will present legal, technical and ethical arguments against subjecting athletes to random testing. Testing without probable cause is an invasion of the player's right to privacy, increases the discretionary nature of the testing procedures used and, due to the large number of players who would be tested, adversely affects the accuracy of the test results obtained. Thus, the only way to eradicate drugs from professional sports is to test the players *and all other interested parties* only upon "reasonable cause."

## D.  Major League Baseball

### 1.  *Former Agreement*

#### (a)  *Background*

In May 1984, the twenty-six Major League Baseball Clubs ("Clubs") and the Major League Baseball Players Association ("MLBPA" or "Players Association") reached a tentative agreement for "reasonable cause" testing in baseball. This Agreement was ratified by both parties on July 13, 1984 and given retroactive effect to the date of May 24, 1984. During the Fall of 1985, in the aftermath of the Pittsburgh drug trials, the Commissioner of Major League Baseball, Peter Ueberroth, began discussing the issue of random testing with the Players Association and encouraged them to negotiate on the issue.[71] The Players Association was unconvinced that wholescale drug testing was necessary and would be an actual deterrent to drug use in baseball, especially since there was no scientific data showing how widespread drug use was among its players. Commissioner Ueberroth, frustrated in his efforts with the MLBPA, bypassed the Players' Association and wrote directly to the six hundred and fifty major league players to encourage their support of mandatory drug testing.[72] The MLBPA responded by filing an unfair labor practice charge on October 29, 1985. A few days before this filing, the owners invoked Section XII and unilaterally terminated the Agreement.[73] Although it was revoked, it is still instructive to examine the relevant provisions of the MLB Agreement. The general purpose of the Agreement was to educate and treat chemical dependence and drug abuse problems in Major League Baseball.[74] Substances covered by this Agreement included

---

71. Commissioner Ueberroth proposed to use tests similar to those he had used at the 1984 Summer Olympics in Los Angeles where he was President of the Olympic Organizing Committee. "Random urine samples would be collected three times a year . . . with the results reported to the players and their clubs. Positive tests would mean confirmation tests, followed by counseling and if necessary, treatment. Punishment would be allowed if the player persisted in using drugs. Confidentiality was promised." Goodwin, *Should Baseball Have Mandatory Drug Testing?*, N.Y. Times, Issue and Debate, Nov. 13, 1985, at B14, col. 4.

72. Chase, *Baseball's Tests For Drugs Stalled*, N.Y. Times, Dec. 1, 1985, Section 5, at 1, col. 5.

73. *See* MLB Agreement, section XII at 16 (Agreement may be terminated by either party upon written notice after December 31, 1984); *Drug Agreement Ended By Owners*, N.Y. Times, Oct. 24, 1985, at B1, col. 1.

74. Specifically, the MLB Agreement had a four-fold purpose: (1) to educate players and other personnel about chemical dependence and the inherent problems of drug abuse; (2) to encourage players with actual or potential drug abuse problems to immediately seek appropriate

cocaine, heroin, barbituates and all other drugs listed on Schedule II of the Federal Controlled Substances Act of 1970 (hereinafter "specified substances").[75]

### (b)  *Substantive Provisions*

### (i)  *Joint Review Council*

Section IV of the MLB Agreement established a Joint Review Council ("JRC") consisting of three members who are mutually agreed upon by both the Clubs and the MLBPA, and who possess special knowledge and experience in the area of drug abuse. The primary functions of the JRC are to make general recommendations regarding implementation and operation of the Agreement, treatment and after-care programs, including testing, and settlement of disputes between a player and his Club.[76] "Costs of the JRC [are] shared jointly by the Players Association and the Player Relations Committee, subject to a budget to be agreed upon by the parties."[77]

Proceedings before the JRC are to be conducted in an informal, nonadversarial manner. When asked to determine whether there is "reason to believe" that a player is using a specified substance, the JRC will evaluate all necessary information, which may include an interview with the player at the latter's option. Both the Club and the player may be represented by anyone of their choosing and have the right to cross-examine witnesses testifying before the JRC. JRC decisions finding "reason to believe" must be unanimous, whereas all other decisions regarding selection of treatment and after-care programs, and settlement of intra-club disputes, require only a two member majority vote.[78] Absent prior written consent of the player, any information supplied by the player to the Club or the JRC, or determinations of the JRC and results of the player's medical evaluation, treatment or aftercare, may not be used against the player in subsequent proceed-

---

professional and medical assistance; (3) to provide confidential diagnostic and treatment services to players who need such assistance; and (4) to establish procedures for the identification and treatment of individuals who are chemically dependent. MLB Agreement, Preamble at 1-2.

75. MLB Agreement, section II at 3.

76. *Id.* section IV.A. at 5. The appointment of any member of the JRC may be terminated by either the Club or MLBPA upon written notice to the other party.

77. *Id.* section IX(b) at 15.

78. *Id.* section IV.A. at 7.

ings regarding contract interpretation or discipline.[79]

### (ii)   *Use Acknowledged by Player*

When a player voluntarily comes forward to his Club and acknowledges his use of a specified substance, the club will assist the player in securing appropriate diagnosis and treatment giving priority consideration to the player's choice of professional and medical treatment.[80]   If the player and Club cannot agree on the proper course of evaluation and treatment, the dispute will be resolved by the JRC.[81] "The costs of treatment under this program over and above that provided by the Major League Baseball Player's Benefit Plan shall be borne by the club holding title to the player's contract."[82]

When a player does not come forward voluntarily but the Club has "reason to believe" that the player is using a specified substance, the Club must meet with the player to inform him of the basis for its belief.   The player must be given at least twenty-four hours advance notice of this meeting so that his agent, counsel, and/or representative of the MLBPA may be present.   After the meeting, if the player either acknowledges his use or denies such use but agrees to evaluation, the procedures for when a "player voluntarily comes forward" will be followed.[83]

### (iii)   *Use Not Acknowledged by Player*

If a Club approaches a player it has "reason to believe" is using a specified substance but the player denies such use and refuses to seek appropriate treatment, the Club has the option of referring the matter to the JRC for a determination of whether the Club has "reason to believe."[84]   If the JRC determines that "reason to believe" does exist, the player and Club will work together to secure appropriate treatment.   Refusal to comply with the JRC's recommended treatment will result in the player's exclusion from the protections of Section IV of

---

79. *Id.* sections IV.I.(1) and (2) at 13-14.

80. *Id.* section IV.B.(1) at 7-8.

81. *Id.* section IV.C. at 8.

82. *Id.* section IX(a) at 15.

83. *Id.* section IV.B.(2). The significance of sections IV.B(1) and (2) is that treatment of a player's acknowledged use of a specified substance does not depend on whether the admission was voluntarily acknowledged or secured through the "reasonable cause" procedure.

84. *Id.* section IV.C. at 8.

the Agreement and thereby will subject the player to discipline and/or dismissal by the Commissioner.[85] If "reason to believe" is lacking, the matter is closed until such time as the Club invokes the procedures based upon subsequent events or additional information.[86]

### (iv)  *Effect on Salary*

A player who undergoes evaluation and/or treatment for a specified substance abuse may continue to receive his salary according to the following schedule. The player will receive full salary for the first thirty days he is on the Rehabilitation List during a Championship Season.[87] During the second thirty-day period he is on such List, the player will receive one-half his salary or the Major League minimum salary, whichever is greater.[88] If the player remains on the List beyond sixty days, he will receive only the then applicable Major League minimum salary.[89]

### (v)  *Actions Outside the Agreement*

The procedures outlined in Section IV of the Agreement are not applicable when the player "is convicted of a criminal charge of possession, use, or distribution[90] of any controlled substance . . . [or] has unlawfully used a controlled substance on the playing field or on the premises of a league stadium."[91]

---

85.  *Id.* section IV.G. at 12-13. *See also* Memorandum from Commissioner Kuhn to All Major League Clubs and Players, "Joint Drug Program & Discipline," (June 28, 1984) (hereinafter cited as "Commissioner Kuhn's Memorandum").

86.  MLB Agreement, section IV.C. at 8.

87.  One day on the Rehabilitation List during Championship Season counts towards one day in the player's thirty-day cumulative basis. However, it requires three days on the List during Spring Training to equal one day of the Championship Season. MLB Agreement, section IV.E.(2)(h) at 12.

88.  *Id.* sections IV.E.(2)(a) and(b) at 10-11. Note that the salary during both thirty-day periods is computed on a cumulative basis during the player's career.

89.  *Id.* section IV.E.(2)(c). Also note that any player who has been on the Rehabilitation List for more than sixty days will be excluded from the protections afforded by Section IV of the Agreement and will be subject to such discipline as the Commissioner finds appropriate. Commissioner Kuhn's Memorandum, *supra* note 85, point 7 at 2.

90.  Any player who is convicted of or pleads guilty to charges of *possession or use* of a controlled substance will be suspended by the Commissioner without pay for one year, Commissioner Kuhn's Memorandum, *supra* note 85, point 4 at 2, whereas a conviction or guilty plea for *distribution* will result in suspension without pay for a minimum of one year up to a maximum of permanent ineligibility, *id.* point 2 at 2.

91.  MLB Agreement, section V at 14. A player who is found to have used drugs in a league

### (vi)  *Effect of the Agreement*

Any player who comes within the provisions of the Agreement cannot be subjected to disciplinary or other action[92] by the Clubs, the League or the Commissioner of Baseball.[93] Section IV is the exclusive procedure by which to determine actual or suspected player abuse of specified substances. In addition, Section IV must be followed when a player involved with a controlled substance not covered by the Agreement voluntarily seeks treatment for such a problem.[94] This Agreement does not "amend, modify or limit the powers or duties of the Commissioner" to impose discipline for activities expressly excluded from coverage of the Agreement.[95]

### (vii)  *Arbitration*

Section XI of the Agreement provides that "[a]ll disputes with respect to the interpretation of, compliance with or application of the provisions of this Agreement shall be submitted to binding arbitration before an impartial arbitrator mutually selected by the parties."[96]

## 2.  *Policy without Agreement*

The former MLB Agreement explicitly provided that "[i]n the event of termination of the Agreement, the rights of the parties shall be what they are in the absence of this Agreement, and this Agreement shall not be used as precedent or to prejudice the rights of the parties."[97] With the Agreement no longer in effect, the Commissioner once again has unfettered discretion to impose upon the players such discipline as he finds appropriate. The uncertainty which has been

---

stadium will be suspended without pay for one year. Commissioner Kuhn's Memorandum, *supra* note 85, point 5 at 2.

92. MLB Agreement, section VI at 14.

93. *Id.* section VII at 14-15; section IV.F. at 12.

94. *Id.* section IV.F. at 12. In such circumstances, the player "will be accorded amnesty and not be subject to discipline [by the Commissioner]. Such players will, however, be subject to appropriate probationary terms which may include testing, aftercare and community service." Commissioner Kuhn's Memorandum, *supra* note 85, point 9 at 2.

95. MLB Agreement, section VII at 14-15. In addition to imposition of discipline, a player may also be put on probation at the Commissioner's discretion. "During this probationary period, the player will be subject to *mandatory, unannounced testing* for the purpose of assuring that the player is no longer involved with a controlled substance." Commissioner Kuhn's Memorandum, *supra* note 85, point 8 at 2 (emphasis added).

96. MLB Agreement, section XI at 16.

97. *Id.* section XII at 16.

present since revocation of the Agreement is no where more apparent than in the aftermath of the Pittsburgh drug trials.

In September 1985, seven non-athlete defendants were charged with distribution of cocaine to baseball players in the Pittsburgh, Pennsylvania area.[98] Five of the defendants pleaded guilty whereas the remaining two were tried and convicted primarily upon incriminating testimony given by present and former baseball players.[99] Although granted immunity by federal prosecutors in exchange for their testimony, this did not immunize the players from Commissioner-imposed discpline.

During January and February of 1986, Commissioner Ueberroth interviewed those players who either had testified at or were implicated by testimony during the Pittsburgh drug trials. On February 28, 1986, he announced that twenty-one players would be suspended from the League for their acknowledged or imputed involvement with cocaine. However, suspensions would be lifted if the players agreed to certain conditions: (1) career drug testing; and (2) donations of time and money to drug abuse-prevention programs for either one or two years.[100] Although not challenged by the disciplined players, the

---

98. *See* United States v. Curtis Strong, No. 85-3559, slip. op. (D. Pa. 1985).

99. Curtis Strong, a Philadelphia caterer, was sentenced to a ten-year prison term; Jeffrey Mosco, an employee at the Pittsburgh club "Michael J's", was sentenced to four years.

100. *See* Goodwin, *Ueberroth Changes Tactics, Gets His Way on Drug Issue,* N.Y. Times, March 3, 1986, at C2, col. 4; Goodwin, *Ueberroth Came to See Users as Deterrent: He Explains His Decision,* N.Y. Times, March 2, 1986, Section S, at 4, col. 1. Commissioner Ueberroth established three categories of offenders and the discipline imposed was as follows:

*Category 1*

*Definition*—First-degree offenders were disciplined on the basis of an admission or other evidence establishing a prolonged pattern of drug use; for facilitating the distribution of drugs in baseball; or for introducing other players to drug dealers or providing dealers access to players. Players faced a possible one-year suspension *or* career drug testing and donation of ten-percent of their 1986 salary and one-hundred hours (two-hundred for Hernandez and Berra) of community service in each of the next two years to a drug abuse-prevention program.

*Players*—Joaquin Andujar (Oakland A's); Dale Berra (N.Y. Yankees); Enos Cabell (L.A. Dodges); Keith Hernandez (N.Y. Mets); Jeff Leonard (S.F. Giants); Dave Parker (Cincinnati Reds); and Lonnie Smith (Kansas City Royals).

*Category 2*

*Definition*—Second-degree offenders were individuals who engaged in more limited use of or involvement with drugs. Players faced a sixty-day suspension *or* career drug testing and donation of five-percent of their 1986 salary and fifty hours of community service to a drug abuse-prevention program for one year.

*Players*—Al Holland (N.Y. Yankees); Lee Lacy (Baltimore Orioles); Lary Sorenson (released); and Claudell Washington (Atlanta Braves).

*Category 3*

MLBPA has filed a grievance before the National Labor Relations Board alleging that the Commissioner had no authority to discipline the players in the above-mentioned fashion. A second grievance was also filed against the Club owners for allegedly revoking the former MLB Agreement on improper grounds in order to presently conduct the random drug testing they were not allowed to do under the terms of the Agreement.[101]

---

*Definition*—Third-degree offenders included players for whom insufficient evidence existed to establish their involvement with drugs. Nonetheless, these players were required solely to submit to career drug testing.

*Players*—Dusty Baker (Oakland A's); Vida Blue (S.F. Giants); Gary Matthews (Chicago Cubs); Dickie Noles (Minor Leagues); Tim Raines (Montreal Expos); Manny Sarmiento (released); Daryl Sconiers (released); Rod Scurry (N.Y. Yankees); Darryl Thomas (released); and Allan Wiggins (Baltimore Orioles).

Telephone Interview with Craig Barbarino, Public Relations Department, Commissioner's Office of Major League Baseball (April 18, 1986).

101. Telephone Interview with Eugene Orza, Associate General Counsel, MLBPA (March 28, 1986). Perhaps Commissioner Ueberroth's greatest flaw is that he "disciplined [the] 21 players without providing any specific plan for other future offenders." Anderson, *Punishment but No Policy*, N.Y. Times, Sports of the Times, March 2, 1986, Section S, at 3, col. 1.

# THE NATIONAL LEAGUE OF
# PROFESSIONAL BASEBALL CLUBS

**Parties**

Between _____ herein called the Club,

and _____

of _____ , herein called the Player.

**Recital**

The Club is a member of The National League of Professional Baseball Clubs, a voluntary association of member Clubs which has subscribed to the Major League Rules with The American League of Professional Baseball Clubs and its constituent Clubs and to The Professional Baseball Rules with that League and the National Association of Baseball Leagues.

**Agreement**

In consideration of the facts above recited and of the promises of each to the other, the parties agree as follows:

**Employment**

1.  The Club hereby employs the Player to render, and the Player agrees to render, skilled services as a baseball player during the year(s) 19____
_____ including the Club's training season, the Club's exhibition games, the Club's playing season, the League Championship Series and the World Series (or any other official series in which the Club may participate and in any receipts of which the Player may be entitled to share).

**Payment**

2.  For performance of the Player's services and promises hereunder the Club will pay the Player the sum of $_____

_____

_____

in semi-monthly installments after the commencement of the championship season(s) covered by this contract except as the schedule of payments may be modified by a special covenant. Payment shall be made on the day the amount becomes due, regardless of whether the Club is "home" or "abroad." If a monthly rate of payment is stipulated above, it shall begin with the commencement of the championship season (or such subsequent date as the Player's services may commence) and end with the termination of the championship season and shall be payable in semi-monthly installments as above provided.

Nothing herein shall interfere with the right of the Club and the Player by special covenant herein to mutually agree upon a method of payment whereby part of the Player's salary for the above year can be deferred to subsequent years.

If the Player is in the service of the Club for part of the championship season only, he shall receive such proportion of the sum above mentioned, as the number of days of his actual employment in the championship season bears to the number of days in the championship season.

Notwithstanding the rate of payment stipulated above, the minimum rate of payment to the Player for each day of service on a Major League Club shall be at the applicable rate set forth in Article VI(B)(1) of the Basic Agreement between the American League of Professional Baseball Clubs and the National League of Professional Baseball Clubs and the Major League Baseball Players Association, effective March 19, 1990 ("Basic Agreement"). The minimum rate of payment for National Association

service for all Players (a) signing a second Major League contract (not covering the same season as any such Player's initial Major League contract) or a subsequent Major League contract, or (b) having at least one day of Major League service, shall be at the applicable rate set forth in Article VI(B)(2) of the Basic Agreement.

Payment to the Player at the rate stipulated above shall be continued throughout any period in which a Player is required to attend a regularly scheduled military encampment of the Reserve of the Armed Forces or of the National Guard during the championship season.

**Loyalty**

3.(a) The Player agrees to perform his services hereunder diligently and faithfully, to keep himself in first-class physical condition and to obey the Club's training rules, and pledges himself to the American public and to the Club to conform to high standards of personal conduct, fair play and good sportsmanship.

### Baseball Promotion

3.(b)  In addition to his services in connection with the actual playing of baseball, the Player agrees to cooperate with the Club and participate in any and all reasonable promotional activities of the Club and its League, which, in the opinion of the Club, will promote the welfare of the Club or professional baseball, and to observe and comply with all reasonable requirements of the Club respecting conduct and service of its team and its players, at all times whether on or off the field.

### Pictures and Public Appearances

3.(c)  The Player agrees that his picture may be taken for still photographs, motion pictures or television at such times as the Club may designate and agrees that all rights in such pictures shall belong to the Club and may be used by the Club for publicity purposes in any manner it desires. The Player further agrees that during the playing season he will not make public appearances, participate in radio or television programs or permit his picture to be taken or write or sponsor newspaper or magazine articles or sponsor commercial products without the written consent of the Club, which shall not be withheld except in the reasonable interests of the Club or professional baseball.

## PLAYER REPRESENTATIONS

### Ability

4.(a)  The Player represents and agrees that he has exceptional and unique skill and ability as a baseball player; that his services to be rendered hereunder are of a special, unusual and extraordinary character which gives them peculiar value which cannot be reasonably or adequately compensated for in damages at law, and that the Player's breach of this contract will cause the Club great and irreparable injury and damage. The Player agrees that, in addition to other remedies, the Club shall be entitled to injunctive and other equitable relief to prevent a breach of this contract by the Player, including, among others, the right to enjoin the Player from playing baseball for any other person or organization during the term of his contract.

### Condition

4.(b)  The Player represents that he has no physical or mental defects known to him and unknown to the appropriate representative of the Club which would prevent or impair performance of his services.

### Interest in Club

4.(c)  The Player represents that he does not, directly or indirectly, own stock or have any financial interest in the ownership or earnings of any Major League Club, except as hereinafter expressly set forth, and covenants that he will not hereafter, while connected with any Major League Club, acquire or hold any such stock or interest except in accordance with Major League Rule 20(e).

### Service

5.(a)  The Player agrees that, while under contract, and prior to expiration of the Club's right to renew this contract, he will not play baseball otherwise than for the Club, except that the Player may participate in post-season games under the conditions prescribed in the Major League Rules. Major League Rule 18(b) is set forth herein.

### Other Sports

5.(b)  The Player and the Club recognize and agree that the Player's participation in certain other sports may impair or destroy his ability and skill as a baseball player. Accordingly, the Player agrees that he will not engage in professional boxing or wrestling; and that, except with the written consent of the Club, he will not engage in skiing, auto racing, motorcycle racing, sky diving, or in any game or exhibition of football, soccer,

professional league basketball, ice hockey or other sport involving a substantial risk of personal injury.

### Assignment

6.(a)  The Player agrees that this contract may be assigned by the Club (and reassigned by any assignee Club) to any other Club in accordance with the Major League Rules and the Professional Baseball Rules. The Club and the Player may, without obtaining special approval, agree by special covenant to limit or eliminate the right of the Club to assign this contract.

### Medical Information

6.(b)  The Player agrees that, should the Club contemplate an assignment of this contract to another Club or Clubs, the Club's physician may furnish to the physicians and officials of such other Club or Clubs all relevant medical information relating to the Player.

### No Salary Reduction

6.(c)  The amount stated in paragraph 2 and in special covenants hereof which is payable to the Player for the period stated in paragraph 1 hereof shall not be diminished by any such assignment, except for failure to report as provided in the next subparagraph (d).

### Reporting

6.(d)  The Player shall report to the assignee Club promptly (as provided in the Regulation) upon receipt of written notice from the Club of the assignment of this contract. If the Player fails to so report, he shall not be entitled to any payment for the period from the date he receives written notice of assignment until he reports to the assignee Club.

### Obligations of Assignor and Assignee Clubs

6.(e)  Upon and after such assignment, all rights and obligations of the assignor Club hereunder shall become the rights and obligations of the assignee Club; provided, however, that

(1)  The assignee Club shall be liable to the Player for payments accruing only from the date of assignment and shall not be liable (but the assignor Club shall remain liable) for payments accrued prior to that date.

(2)  If at any time the assignee is a Major League Club, it shall be liable to pay the Player at the full rate stipulated in paragraph 2 hereof for the remainder of the period stated in paragraph 1 hereof and all prior assignors and assignees shall be relieved of liability for any payment for such period.

(3)  Unless the assignor and assignee Clubs agree otherwise, if the assignee Club is a National Association Club, the assignee Club shall be liable only to pay the Player at the rate usually paid by said assignee Club to other Players of similar skill and ability in its classification and the assignor Club shall be liable to pay the difference for the remainder of the period stated in paragraph 1 hereof between an amount computed at the rate stipulated in paragraph 2 hereof and the amount so payable by the assignee Club.

### Moving Allowances

6.(f)  The Player shall be entitled to moving allowances under the circumstances and in the amounts set forth in Articles VII(F) and VIII of the Basic Agreement.

### "Club"

6.(g)  All references in other paragraphs of this contract to "the Club" shall be deemed to mean and include any assignee of this contract.

## TERMINATION

### By Player

7.(a) The Player may terminate this contract, upon written notice to the Club, if the Club shall default in the payments to the Player provided for in paragraph 2 hereof or shall fail to perform any other obligation agreed to be performed by the Club hereunder and if the Club shall fail to remedy such default within ten (10) days after the receipt by the Club of written notice of such default. The Player may also terminate this contract as provided in subparagraph (d)(4) of this paragraph 7. (See Article XV(H) of the Basic Agreement.)

### By Club

7.(b) The Club may terminate this contract upon written notice to the Player (but only after requesting and obtaining waivers of this contract from all other Major League Clubs) if the Player shall at any time:

(1) fail, refuse or neglect to conform his personal conduct to the standards of good citizenship and good sportsmanship or to keep himself in first-class physical condition or to obey the Club's training rules; or

(2) fail, in the opinion of the Club's management, to exhibit sufficient skill or competitive ability to qualify or continue as a member of the Club's team; or

(3) fail, refuse or neglect to render his services hereunder or in any other manner materially breach this contract.

7.(c) If this contract is terminated by the Club, the Player shall be entitled to termination pay under the circumstances and in the amounts set forth in Article IX of the Basic Agreement. In addition, the Player shall be entitled to receive an amount equal to the reasonable traveling expenses of the Player, including first-class jet air fare and meals en route, to his home city.

### Procedure

7.(d) If the Club proposes to terminate this contract in accordance with subparagraph (b) of this paragraph 7, the procedure shall be as follows:

(1) The Club shall request waivers from all other Major League Clubs. Such waivers shall be good for three (3) business days only. Such waiver request must state that it is for the purpose of terminating this contract and it may not be withdrawn.

(2) Upon receipt of waiver request, any other Major League Club may claim assignment of this contract at a waiver price of $1.00, the priority of claims to be determined in accordance with the Major League Rules.

(3) If this contract is so claimed, the Club shall, promptly and before any assignment, notify the Player that it had requested waivers for the purpose of terminating this contract and that the contract had been claimed.

(4) Within five (5) days after receipt of notice of such claim, the Player shall be entitled, by written notice to the Club, to terminate this contract on the date of his notice of termination. If the Player fails to so notify the Club, this contract shall be assigned to the claiming Club.

(5) If the contract is not claimed, the Club shall promptly deliver written notice of termination to the Player at the expiration of the waiver period.

7.(e) Upon any termination of this contract by the Player, all obligations of both Parties hereunder shall cease on the date of termination, except the obligation of the Club to pay the Player's compensation to said date.

### Regulations

8. The Player accepts as part of this contract the Regulations set forth herein.

### Rules

9.(a) The Club and the Player agree to accept, abide by and comply with all provisions of the Major League Agreement, the Major League Rules, the Rules or Regulations of the League of which the Club is a member, and the Professional Baseball Rules, in effect on the date of this Uniform Player's Contract, which are not inconsistent with the provisions of this contract or the provisions of any agreement between the Major League Clubs and the Major League Baseball Players Association, provided that the Club, together with the other clubs of the American and National Leagues and the National Association, reserves the right to modify, supplement or repeal any provision of said Agreement, Rules and/or Regulations in a manner not inconsistent with this contract or the provisions of any then existing agreement between the Major League Clubs and the Major League Baseball Players Association.

### Disputes

9.(b) All disputes between the Player and the Club which are covered by the Grievance Procedure as set forth in the Basic Agreement shall be resolved in accordance with such Grievance Procedure.

### Publication

9.(c) The Club, the League President and the Commissioner, or any of them, may make public the findings, decision and record of any inquiry, investigation or hearing held or conducted, including in such record all evidence or information, given, received, or obtained in connection therewith.

### Renewal

10.(a) Unless the Player has exercised his right to become a free agent as set forth in the Basic Agreement, the Club may, on or before December 20 (or if a Sunday, then the next preceding business day) in the year of the last playing season covered by this contract, tender to the Player a contract for the term of the next year by mailing the same to the Player at his address following his signature hereto, or if none be given, then at his last address of record with the Club. If prior to the March 1 next succeeding said December 20, the Player and the Club have not agreed upon the terms of such contract, then on or before ten (10) days after said March 1, the Club shall have the right by written notice to the Player at said address to renew this contract for the period of one year on the same terms, except that the amount payable to the Player shall be such as the Club shall fix in said notice; provided, however, that said amount, if fixed by a Major League Club, shall be an amount payable at a rate not less than as specified in Article VI, Section D, of the Basic Agreement. Subject to the Player's rights as set forth in the Basic Agreement, the Club may renew this contract from year to year.

10.(b) The Club's right to renew this contract, as provided in subparagraph (a) of this paragraph 10, and the promise of the Player not to play otherwise than with the Club have been taken into consideration in determining the amount payable under paragraph 2 hereof.

### Governmental Regulation – National Emergency

11. This contract is subject to federal or state legislation, regulations, executive or other official orders or other governmental action, now or hereafter in effect respecting military, naval, air or other governmental service, which may directly or indirectly affect the Player, Club or the League and subject also to the right of the Commissioner to suspend the

operation of this contract during any national emergency during which Major League Baseball is not played.

## Commissioner

12. The term "Commissioner" wherever used in this contract shall be deemed to mean the Commissioner designated under the Major League Agreement, or in the case of a vacancy in the office of Commissioner, the Executive Council or such other body or person or persons as shall be designated in the Major League Agreement to exercise the powers and duties of the Commissioner during such vacancy.

## Supplemental Agreements

The Club and the Player covenant that this contract, the Basic Agreement and the Agreement Re Major League Baseball Players Benefit Plan effective April 1, 1984, and applicable supplements thereto fully set forth all understandings and agreements between them, and agree that no other understandings or agreements, whether heretofore or hereafter made, shall be valid, recognizable, or of any effect whatsoever, unless expressly set forth in a new or supplemental contract executed by the Player and the Club (acting by its President or such other officer as shall have been thereunto duly authorized by the President or Board of Directors as evidenced by a certificate filed of record with the League President and Commissioner) and complying with the Major League Rules and the Professional Baseball Rules.

# REGULATIONS

1. The Club's playing season for each year covered by this contract and all renewals hereof shall be as fixed by The National League of Professional Baseball Clubs, or if this contract shall be assigned to a Club in another League, then by the League of which such assignee is a member.

2. The Player, when requested by the Club, must submit to a complete physical examination at the expense of the Club, and if necessary to treatment by a regular physician or dentist in good standing. Upon refusal of the Player to submit to a complete medical or dental examination the Club may consider such refusal a violation of this regulation and may take such action as it deems advisable under Regulation 5 of this contract. Disability directly resulting from injury sustained in the course and within the scope of his employment under this contract shall not impair the right of the Player to receive his full salary for the period of such disability or for the season in which the injury was sustained (whichever period is shorter), together with the reasonable medical and hospital expenses incurred by reason of the injury and during the term of this contract or for a period of up to two years from the date of initial treatment for such injury, whichever period is longer, but only upon the express prerequisite conditions that (a) written notice of such injury, including the time, place, cause and nature of the injury, is served upon and received by the Club within twenty days of the sustaining of said injury and (b) the Club shall have the right to designate the doctors and hospitals furnishing such medical and hospital services. Failure to give such notice shall not impair the rights of the Player, as herein set forth, if the Club has actual knowledge of such injury. All workmen's compensation payments received by the Player as compensation for loss of income for a specific period during which the Club is paying him in full, shall be paid over by the Player to the Club. Any other disability may be ground for suspending or terminating this contract.

3. The Club will furnish the Player with two complete uniforms, exclusive of shoes, unless the Club requires the Player to wear nonstandard shoes in which case the Club will furnish the shoes. The uniforms will be surrendered by the Player to the Club at the end of the season or upon termination of this contract.

4. The Player shall be entitled to expense allowances under the circumstances and in the amounts set forth in Article VII of the Basic Agreement.

5. For violation by the Player of any regulation or other provision of this contract, the Club may impose a reasonable fine and deduct the amount thereof from the Player's salary or may suspend the Player without salary for a period not exceeding thirty days or both. Written notice of the fine or suspension or both and the reason therefor shall in every case be given to the Player and the Players Association. (See Article XII of the Basic Agreement.)

6. In order to enable the Player to fit himself for his duties under this contract, the Club may require the Player to report for practice at such places as the Club may designate and to participate in such exhibition contests as may be arranged by the Club, without any other compensation than that herein elsewhere provided, for a period beginning not earlier than thirty-three (33) days prior to the start of the championship season, provided, however, that the Club may invite players to report at an earlier date on a voluntary basis in accordance with Article XIV of the Basic Agreement. The Club will pay the necessary traveling expenses, including the first-class jet air fare and meals en route of the Player from his home city to the training place of the Club, whether he be ordered to go there directly or by way of the home city of the Club. In the event of the failure of the Player to report for practice or to participate in the exhibition games, as required and provided for, he shall be required to get into playing condition to the satisfaction of the Club's team manager, and at the Player's own expense, before his salary shall commence.

7. In case of assignment of this contract the Player shall report promptly to the assignee Club within 72 hours from the date he receives written notice from the Club of such assignment, if the Player is then not more than 1,600 miles by most direct available railroad route from the assignee Club, plus an additional 24 hours for each additional 800 miles.

Post-Season Exhibition Games. Major League Rule 18(b) provides:

(b) EXHIBITION GAMES. No player shall participate in any exhibition game during the period between the close of the Major League championship season and the following training season, except that, with the consent of his club and permission of the Commissioner, a player may participate in exhibition games for a period of not less than thirty (30) days, such period to be designated annually by the Commissioner. Players who participate in barnstorming during this period cannot engage in any Winter League activities. Player conduct, on and off the field, in connection with such post-season exhibition games shall be subject to the discipline of the Commissioner. The Commissioner shall not approve of more than three (3) players of any one club on the same team. The Commissioner shall not approve of more than three (3) players from the joint membership of the World Series participants playing in the same game. No player shall participate in any exhibition game with or against any team which, during the current season or within one year, has had any ineligible player or which is or has been during the current season or within one (1) year, managed and controlled by an ineligible player or by any person who has listed an ineligible player under an assumed name or who otherwise has violated, or attempted to violate, any exhibition game contract; or with or against any team which, during said season or within one (1) year, has played against teams containing such ineligible players, or so managed or controlled. Any player violating this Rule shall be fined not less than Fifty Dollars ($50.00) nor more than Five Hundred Dollars ($500.00), except that in no event shall such fine be less than the consideration received by such player for participating in such game.

PRINTED IN U.S.A. G                    Revised as of 6/1/90

Special Covenants

# PART 4

## FRANCHISE RELOCATION: CHANGING CITIES

The loss of a franchise can be devastating to a community both economically and psychologically. Just ask long-time residents of Brooklyn. The legal remedies to halt such a move are limited. Just ask former fans of the Baltimore Colts in the National Football League.

To a large extent, the losses of the industrial Northeast and the Midwest have been the gains of the Sunbelt, California, and Florida. These regions have been net winners in the franchise relocation game as owners have followed demographic and economic development trends to relocate in these desirable markets. The attraction of a professional sports franchise, especially a baseball team with its lengthy season and eighty-one home games, can be a financial bonanza.

However, the opposite financial incentives apply when an existing team seeks or threatens to relocate. Cities will bid for the franchise with precious public resources. Cities with budget crises will find the funds to pay for new stadiums, new infrastructure, and other benefits to tempt a team pondering relocation. The price for victory can be substantial. The price for failure can be even worse. The city elders of St. Petersburg, Florida, and the operators of a domed baseball stadium with no team currently in residence have learned this lesson.

Nor will the incumbent cities go quietly as in the past. Cities like Chicago have paid dearly in response to relocation threats by the White Sox. The owners were rewarded with a new stadium and other significant benefits that were presumably more lucrative than St. Petersburg or the next best offer.

There are also costs when teams are prevented from relocating by the decision of the other owners. In Bill Veeck's autobiography, *Veeck as in Wreck*, the late owner of the Saint Louis Browns (and several other franchises) recounts his unsuccessful efforts to move the Browns. Eventually, he was forced temporarily out of major league baseball, and it was the subsequent owners of the Browns who moved out of the shadow of the St. Louis Cardinals to far greater success and prosperity as the Baltimore Orioles. Although Veeck enjoyed later and greater success upon his return to major league baseball, he felt he had no real recourse against his fellow owners who blocked the relocation of the Browns, in part due to baseball's antitrust exemption.

More recently, baseball fans were treated to the irony of the San Francisco Giant's failed attempt to relocate back to the East. In the late 1950s, it was the New York Giants who followed the Dodgers to California. When the San Francisco Giants appeared poised to relocate to St. Petersburg, citizens in Florida rejoiced and appeared to forgive baseball for jilting them over the White Sox. Then major league baseball owners blocked the sale and transfer of the team and forced the existing owners to accept a lower offer that kept the team in San Francisco. The failed St. Petersburg ownership group fought back with an antitrust suit of their own, bucking the Supreme Court's consistent holdings that baseball will remain exempt from the antitrust laws until such time as Congress chooses to change the law. Not surprisingly, a senator from Florida has introduced legislation to do just that. More surprisingly, a district court has crafted its own narrow version of baseball antitrust immunity to allow the suit involving the Giants to go forward.

The legal and emotional issues over team relocation will recur as long as owners see greener pastures as a result of either market forces or municipal largesse. We present both the "case" that started it all involving the Brooklyn Dodger's move to Los Angeles and the most recent case or controversy involving the Giant's involuntary decision to remain in the West.

[¶ 70,315]   Vincent M. Piazza, et al. v. Major League Baseball, et al.

U.S. District Court, Eastern District of Pennsylvania. Civil Action No. 92-7173. Dated August 4, 1993.

### Sherman Act

**Antitrust Immunity—Federal Government Involvement—Professional Baseball—Judicial Creation, Congressional Inaction—Sale of Franchise.**—Neither the unique judicially created antitrust exemption for professional baseball nor congressional "positive inaction" made the conduct of a professional baseball league and some of its individual representatives in frustrating the attempts of an investor group from purchasing one of the league's franchises attributable to the federal government. The federal government neither coerced the league into behaving as it did nor provided significant encouragement for the league to do so. At best, the government's involvement alleged could be viewed as acquiescence. Claims that the investor group's First and Fifth Amendment rights were violated were dismissed.

See ¶ 1020.

**Restraint of Trade—Monopolization—Relevant Product Market—Purchase of Professional Sports Team—League Interference.**—In an antitrust action arising from frustration of an investor group's attempt to purchase a professional baseball league franchise, the relevant product market consisted of the market for existing teams, rather than the creation of new franchises. The investor group was not seeking to redress injury to an intra-league market made up of major league baseball and that might or might not have included competition among present franchise owners. Rather, the group alleged that it was competing in the team franchise market with other potential investors located primarily outside of professional baseball and that the league interfered directly and substantially with competition in that market.

See ¶ 660, 760.

**Standing to Sue—Partnerships, Partners—Particularized Injuries—Baseball Team Purchase.**—Even though an alleged conspiracy among a professional league and its representatives was intended to, and did, prevent an investment group partnership from purchasing a league franchise, individual partners had standing to seek damages over contentions that the partnership was the more direct victim. While the partners cited injury to the partnership as a consequence of the league's behavior, they did not seek to redress a diminution in the value of their interests in the partnership; rather, they identified unique, particularized injuries to themselves.

See ¶ 9032.

**Injury to Business or Property—Exclusion from Market—Professional Baseball Team Purchase.**—Frustration of an investor group's attempts to purchase a professional baseball team as the result of a conspiracy among the team's league and its representatives would constitute the type of injury that Congress sought to redress through the antitrust laws.

See ¶ 9026.

**Injury to Business or Property—Duplicative Recovery—Complex Apportionment of Damages—Partners.**—In an antitrust action arising from alleged frustration of an investment group partnership's attempt to purchase a professional baseball team as the result of a conspiracy among the team's league and its representatives, there was no danger of duplicative recovery or complex apportionment of damages because the individual partners sought only to redress their own particular injuries rather than those of the partnership.

See ¶ 9026.

**Interstate Commerce—Sports—Baseball—Purchase of Ownership Interests.**—The antitrust exemption for professional baseball created by the U.S. Supreme Court in 1922 was limited in a 1972 decision by the Court to the reserve clause aspect of the business and, therefore, would not apply to the activities of a professional baseball league and its representatives for their parts in a conspiracy to frustrate the purchase of an existing league franchise. Even if a broader "business of baseball" exemption were still applicable, the frustrated purchasers were not targeting anticompetitive activity in the market for the exhibition of baseball games but anticompetitive activity in the market for the sale of ownership interests in baseball teams. Anticompetitive conduct toward those who seek to purchase existing teams had never been considered an essential part of the exhibition of baseball games. However, the exemption might apply if the market for ownership interests were central to the unique characteristics and needs of baseball exhibitions.

See ¶ 675.58, 685.56.

For defendants: Bruce W. Kauffman, of Dilworth, Paxson, Kalish & Kauffman, Philadelphia, Pa., and Arthur Makadon, Philadelphia, Pa.

## Opinion

PADOVA, D.J.: Plaintiffs allege that the organizations of professional major league baseball and an affiliated individual frustrated their efforts to purchase the San Francisco Giants baseball club (the "Giants") and relocate it to Tampa Bay, Florida. Plaintiffs charge these defendants with infringing upon their rights under the United States Constitution and violating federal antitrust laws and several state laws in the process.

Asserting that this Court lacks subject matter jurisdiction over plaintiffs' federal and state claims and that plaintiffs' federal claims fail to state a cause of action, defendants move to dismiss this suit. With regard to plaintiffs' federal antitrust claims, defendants also claim exemption from antitrust liability under *Federal Baseball Club of Baltimore, Inc. v. National League of Professional Baseball Clubs*, 259 U.S. 200 (1922), and its progeny. For the following reasons, I will grant defendants' motion as to plaintiffs' direct claims under the Constitution; but I will deny defendants' motion in all other respects. As to defendants' assertion of exemp-

tion from antitrust liability, I hold that the exemption created by *Federal Baseball* is inapplicable here because it is limited to baseball's "reserve system."

### I. *Background*

#### A. *The Allegations* [1]

Plaintiffs are Vincent M. Piazza and Vincent N. Tirendi, both Pennsylvania residents, and PT Baseball, Inc. ("PTB"), a Pennsylvania corporation wholly owned by Piazza and Tirendi. Pursuant to a written Memorandum of Understanding ("Memorandum") dated August 18, 1992, Piazza and Tirendi agreed with four other individuals, all Florida residents, to organize a limited partnership for the purpose of acquiring the Giants. (The parties to the Memorandum will be referred to collectively as the "Investors".)

The Investors anticipated that they would form individual corporations to serve as general partners of the partnership. Accordingly, on August 26, 1992, PTB entered into a Limited Partnership Agreement (the "Partnership Agreement") with corporations owned by the

---

[1] The following relevant facts were taken either directly or inferentially from plaintiffs' complaint.

**¶ 70,315**

other Investors. This Partnership Agreement implemented the intent of the Memorandum and created a partnership entity known as Tampa Bay Baseball Club, Ltd. (the "Partnership"). PTB agreed to contribute $27 million to the Partnership, making it the single largest contributor of Partnership capital.

Earlier, on August 6, 1992, the Investors had executed a Letter of Intent with Robert Lurie, the owner of the Giants, to purchase the Giants for $115 million. Pursuant to this Letter of Intent, Lurie agreed not to negotiate with other potential buyers of the Giants and to use his best efforts to secure from defendant Major League Baseball[2] approval of the sale of the Giants to the Partnership and transfer of the team to the Suncoast Dome, located in St. Petersburg, Florida.[3]

As required by the rules of Major League Baseball, the Partnership submitted an application to that organization on September 4, 1992 to purchase the Giants and move the team to St. Petersburg. In connection with this application, Major League Baseball and its "Ownership Committee" undertook or purported to undertake a personal background check on the Investors. On September 10, 1992, defendant Ed Kuhlmann, Chairman of the Ownership Committee, stated at a press conference that, among other things, the personal background check on the Investors had raised a "serious question in terms of some of the people who were part of that group" and that "a couple of investors will not be in the group." Complaint at ¶ 53. Kuhlmann elaborated that there was a "background" question about two of the investors rather than a question of financial capability and that something had shown up on a "security check." *Id.* Kuhlmann also stated that the "money" of the two investors "would not have been accepted." *Id.* Immediately following Kuhlmann at the news conference, Jerry Reinsdorf, a member of the Ownership Committee, added that the Ownership Committee's concern related to the "out-of-state" money and that the "Pennsylvania People" had "dropped out." Complaint at ¶ 56.

As the only principals of the Partnership who reside in Pennsylvania, Piazza and Tirendi aver that the clear implication of Kuhlmann's and Reinsdorf's comments, combined with the fact that Piazza and Tirendi are of Italian descent, was that the personal background check had associated them with the Mafia and/or other criminal or organized criminal activity. Piazza and Tirendi further allege that they have never been involved in such activity; nor had they "dropped out" of the Partnership. They also allege that they were never apprised by Baseball or anyone else of the charges against them nor given an opportunity to be heard.

On September 11, 1992, plaintiffs' counsel sent letters to Major League Baseball, Kuhlmann, and Reinsdorf requesting immediate correction of these statements and their implications. Plaintiffs' counsel never received a response to these letters, but on September 12, 1992, defendant Kuhlmann admitted to some members of the media that "there was no problem with the security check." Complaint at ¶ 63.

On the same day that the Partnership submitted its application to purchase and relocate the franchise, Kuhlmann directed Lurie to consider other offers to purchase the Giants, in knowing violation of Lurie's exclusive agreement with the Partnership. On September 9, 1992, Bill White, President of the National League, invited George Shinn, a North Carolina resident, to make an alternative bid to purchase the Giants in order to keep the team in San Francisco. An alternative offer was ultimately made by other investors to keep the Giants in San Francisco. Even though this offer was $15 million less than the $115 million offer made by the Partnership, Major League Baseball formally rejected the proposal to relocate the Giants to the Tampa Bay area on November 10, 1992.

Plaintiffs allege that Baseball never intended to permit the Giants to relocate to Florida and failed to evaluate fairly and in good faith their application to do so. They claim that to avoid relocation of the Giants, Baseball set out to "destroy the financial capability of the Partner-

---

[2] Plaintiffs describe defendant Major League Baseball as an unincorporated association comprised of two professional leagues, the American League and the National League, and their 28 professional baseball teams.

In addition to Major League Baseball, plaintiffs have named the following as defendants: American League of Professional Baseball Clubs; National League of Professional Baseball Clubs; Office of the Commissioner of Major League Baseball; Ed Kuhlmann; The Orioles, Inc.; The Boston Red Sox Baseball Club; Golden West Baseball Co.; Chicago White Sox, Ltd.; Cleveland Indians Co.; John E. Fetzer, Inc.; Kansas City Royals Baseball Corp.; Milwaukee Brewers Baseball Club; Minnesota Twins; New York Yankees Partnership; The Oakland Athletics Baseball Co.; Seattle Baseball, L.P.; B.R. Rangers Associates, Ltd.; To-

ronto Blue Jays Baseball Club; Atlanta National Baseball Club, Inc.; Chicago National League Ball Club, Inc.; The Cincinnati Reds; Houston Sports Association, Inc.; Los Angeles Dodgers, Inc.; Montreal Baseball, Ltd.; Sterling Doubleday Enterprises, L.P.; The Phillies; Pittsburgh Associates; St. Louis National Baseball Club, Inc.; San Diego Padres Baseball Partnership; San Francisco Giants; Florida Marlins, Inc.; and Colorado Rockies Baseball.

All defendants will be referred to collectively as "Baseball."

[3] On August 28, 1992, the Partnership entered into an agreement with the City of St. Petersburg, Florida for management and use of the Florida Suncoast Dome.

---

ship by vilifying plaintiffs." Complaint at ¶ 65. And in addition to preventing plaintiffs' purchase and relocation of the Giants, plaintiffs allege that Baseball's allegedly defamatory statements cost them the loss of a significant contract in connection with one of their other businesses, which depends upon "impeccable personal reputations." Complaint at ¶ 69.

### B. *The Claims*

#### 1. *Federal claims*

Plaintiffs first claim that the above actions of Baseball violated the First and Fifth Amendments to the United States Constitution by (1) depriving them of their liberty and property interests and privileges without due process of law, (2) denying them equal protection of the laws, and (3) impairing their freedom of contract and association. In this connection, plaintiffs claim that Baseball's actions should be attributed to the federal government, to which the constraints of the U.S. Constitution apply, because the federal government has granted Baseball a unique exemption from the federal antitrust laws.

Plaintiffs next assert a claim under 42 U.S.C.A. § 1983 (West 1981),[4] alleging that Baseball acted under color of state law in unlawfully depriving them of the rights, privileges, immunities, freedoms, and liberties secured by Article IV, Section 2 of the U.S. Constitution, as well as the First, Fifth and Fourteenth Amendments. Plaintiffs claim that Baseball's actions took place under color of state law because (a) Baseball is exempt from liability under state antitrust laws; (b) there is a close nexus and symbiotic relationship between Baseball and state and local governments; and (c) Baseball acted in concert with the City of San Francisco to prevent the Giants from being relocated.

Plaintiffs' final federal claim asserts violations of sections 1 and 2 of the Sherman Anti-Trust Act, 15 U.S.C.A. § § 1 and 2 (West 1973 & Supp. 1993).[5] Plaintiffs claim that Baseball has monopolized the market for Major League Baseball teams and that Baseball has placed direct and indirect restraints on the purchase, sale, transfer, relocation of, and competition for such

teams. Plaintiffs allege that these actions have unlawfully restrained and impeded plaintiffs' opportunities to engage in the business of Major League Baseball.

---

[4] Every person who, under color of any statute, ordinance, regulation, custom, or usage, of any State or Territory ... subjects, or causes to be subjected, any citizen of the United States or other person within the jurisdiction thereof to the deprivation of any rights, privileges or immunities secured by the Constitution and laws, shall be liable to the party injured in an action at law, suit in equity, or other proper proceeding for redress. ...

42 U.S.C.A. § 1983

[5] Section 1 of the Sherman Act provides, in pertinent part, that "[e]very contract, combination in the form of

### 3. *Exemption from Antitrust Liability*

I now turn to the heart of Baseball's motion to dismiss plaintiffs' Sherman Act claim—that in *Federal Baseball Club of Baltimore, Inc. v. National League of Professional Baseball Clubs, Inc.*, 259 U.S. 200 (1922); *Toolson v. New York Yankees* [1953 TRADE CASES ¶ 67,602], 346 U.S. 356 (1953); and *Flood v. Kuhn* [1972 TRADE CASES ¶ 74,041], 407 U.S. 258 (1972), the United States Supreme Court exempted Baseball from liability under the federal antitrust laws. Plaintiffs do not deny that these cases recognize some form of exemption from antitrust liability related to the game of baseball, but argue alternatively that the exemption either does not apply in this case, cannot be applied as a matter of law to the facts of this case, or should no longer be recognized at all.

### a. *Evolution of the exemption*

Writing for a unanimous Supreme Court over seventy years ago, Justice Holmes affirmed a judgment of the Court of Appeals of the District of Columbia and held that the business of giving exhibitions of baseball games for profit does not constitute trade or commerce within the meaning of the Sherman Act, and thus the Act does not apply to that business. See *Federal Baseball*, 259 U.S. at 208-09, and the underlying decision of the Court of Appeals, *National League of Professional Baseball Clubs v. Federal Baseball Club of Baltimore, Inc.*, 269 F. 681 (C.C.D.C. 1920) ("*D.C. Opinion*"). The plaintiff in that case, Federal Baseball of Baltimore, Inc. ("Federal Baseball"), owned a franchise in the Federal League of Professional Baseball Clubs until dissolution of that league in 1915 pursuant to an agreement with the National League and American League of Professional Baseball Clubs. *D.C. Opinion*, 269 F. at 682. With the demise of the Federal League, Federal Baseball was left without an organization within which to compete, and subsequently brought suit against the National and American Leagues, among others, for violation of the Sherman Act. *Id.* A jury found in favor of Federal Baseball, awarding it $240,000 in treble damages, costs, and attorneys fees.

The gravamen of Federal Baseball's case was the alleged anticompetitive impact of what is known as the "reserve clause" in the yearly contracts of players in the National and American Leagues. *Id.* at 687-88. The reserve clause bound a player to either enter a new contract with the same team in the succeeding year of the player's contract or be considered ineligible by the National and American Leagues to serve any baseball club. *Id.* at 687. Because of this restrictive provision, the Federal League and its constituent clubs were unable to obtain players who had contracts with the National and American Leagues, the effect of which, as found by the

jury, was to damage Federal Baseball. *Id.* at 682, 687.

The Court of Appeals reversed the jury's verdict and remanded, making four significant findings. First, and quite simply, the court found that the business in which the defendants were engaged was the business of giving exhibitions of the game of baseball. *Id.* at 684.

Second, the court found that "[a] game of baseball is not susceptible of being transferred, . . . [and] [t]he transportation in interstate commerce of the players and the paraphernalia used . . . was but an incident to the main purpose of the [defendants], namely, the production of the game." *Id.* at 684-85. Thus, the court reasoned, a baseball exhibition could not be considered interstate commerce, and the business of giving such an exhibition could not be subject to the Sherman Act. *Id.*

The third finding of the Court of Appeals was that, despite the fact that the giving of an exhibition was not interstate commerce, there were interstate components of Federal Baseball's business, the direct interference with which was redressable under the Sherman Act. *Id.* at 686. These interstate features included such things as the movement of players and their paraphernalia from place to place across state lines. *Id.* The court found that if unlawful anticompetitive activity directly interfered with the business of moving the players or their equipment, as opposed to the exhibition of the game itself, the Sherman Act would apply. *Id.*

Finally, the Court of Appeals found that the reserve clause only indirectly, if at all, affected the interstate aspects of Federal Baseball's business (the business of moving players and their equipment), which was not sufficient to give rise to a Sherman act violation. *Id.* at 687-88.

These four findings can be condensed into two reasons why the Court of Appeals found that the reserve clause did not offend the Sherman Act. First, the anticompetitive impact of the reserve clause on the business of giving a baseball exhibition was not redressable as a matter of law under the Sherman Act, such business found not to be interstate commerce. Second, the reserve clause had, at best, only an incidental impact on the portion of Federal Baseball's business that was considered interstate commerce.

The Supreme Court affirmed. The Court agreed that the defendants' exhibitions of baseball games "are purely state affairs," lacking the character of interstate commerce. *Federal Baseball*, 259 U.S. at 208. From this, the Court reasoned, "[i]f we are right the plaintiff's business is to be described the same way and the restrictions by contract that prevented the plaintiff from getting players to break their bargains [the reserve clause] and the other con-

**¶ 70,315**

duct charged against the defendants [buying up Federal League clubs] were not an interference with commerce among the States." *Id.* at 209.

The Supreme Court next addressed the exemption in *Toolson v. New York Yankees, Inc.* [1953 TRADE CASES ¶ 67,602], 346 U.S. 356 (1953), a *per curiam* opinion affirming decisions of the Sixth and Ninth Circuits.[18] The plaintiffs in the underlying cases were professional baseball players who brought suit under the federal antitrust laws alleging harm by virtue, again, of the reserve clause. *Id.* at 362 (Burton, J. dissenting). Seeking to avoid *Federal Baseball*, the plaintiffs stressed, among other things, the obsolescence of that decision in light of the increased revenue generated by baseball due to interstate radio and television broadcasts. See *Toolson v. New York Yankees* [1950-1951 TRADE CASES ¶ 62,939], 101 F. Supp. 93. Unpersuaded by this position, the district courts dismissed the claims and the Courts of Appeals affirmed. The plaintiffs then petitioned the Supreme Court to overturn *Federal Baseball*. In a terse opinion, the Court refused, upholding *Federal Baseball* "so far as that decision determines that Congress had no intention of including the business of baseball within the scope of the federal antitrust laws." *Toolson*, 347 U.S. at 357 (*per curiam*).

Following *Toolson*, several attempts were made to extend its reasoning and that of *Federal Baseball* beyond the context of baseball. See, e.g., *United States v. Shubert* [1955 TRADE CASES ¶ 67,942], 348 U.S. 222 (1955) (theater); *United States v. International Boxing Club* [1955 TRADE CASES ¶ 67,941], 348 U.S. 236 (1955) (boxing); *Radovich v. National Football League* [1957 TRADE CASES ¶ 68,628], 352 U.S. 445 (1957) (football). In each of these cases, however, the Court declined the invitation. Moreover, to head off any further attempted extensions of those decisions, the Court stated in *Radovich* with crystal clarity that "we now specifically limit the rule ... established [in *Federal Baseball* and *Toolson*] to the facts there involved, i.e., the business of organized professional baseball." *Radovich*, 352 U.S. at 451.

The next and most recent time the Supreme Court directly considered the exemption was in *Flood v. Kuhn* [1972 TRADE CASES ¶ 74,041], 407 U.S. 258 (1972). Like *Toolson*, the plaintiff in *Flood* was a professional baseball player dissatisfied with the reserve clause in his contract and the "reserve system" generally.[19] After an extensive analysis of the history of the exemption, Justice Blackmun, who delivered the opinion of the Court, produced a list of statements

that can be made regarding the exemption and its circumstances:

1. Professional baseball is a business and it is engaged in interstate commerce.

2. With its reserve system enjoying exemption from the federal antitrust laws, baseball is, in a very distinct sense, an exception and an anomaly. *Federal Baseball* and *Toolson* have become an aberration confined to baseball.

3. Even though others might regard this as "unrealistic, inconsistent, or illogical," the aberration is an established one ..., heretofore deemed fully entitled to the benefit of *stare decisis*, and one that has survived the Court's expanding concept of interstate commerce. . . .

4. Other professional sports operating interstate—football, boxing, basketball, and, presumably, hockey and golf—are not so exempt.

5. The Court has emphasized that since 1922 baseball, with full and continuing congressional awareness, has been allowed to develop and to expand unhindered by federal legislative action. ... The Court accordingly has concluded that Congress as yet had no intention to subject baseball's reserve system to the reach of the antitrust statutes. ...

*Id.* at 282-84 (footnotes and citations omitted).

b. *Discussion*

(i) *Scope of the exemption*

In each of the three cases in which the Supreme Court directly addressed the exemption, the factual context involved the reserve clause. Plaintiffs argue that the exemption is confined to that circumstance, which is not presented here. Baseball, on the other hand, argues that the exemption applies to the "business of baseball" generally, not to one particular facet of the game.

Between 1922 and 1972, Baseball's expansive view may have been correct. Although *Federal Baseball* involved the reserve clause, that decision was based upon the proposition that the business of exhibiting baseball games, as opposed to the business of moving players and their equipment, was not interstate commerce and thus not subject to the Sherman Act. *Toolson*, also a reserve clause case, spoke in terms of the "business of baseball" enjoying the exemption. *Toolson*, 346 U.S. at 357. Likewise, *Radovich*, a 1957 decision concerning football, recognized the exemption as extending to the

---

[18] See *Toolson v. New York Yankees, Inc.* [1950-1951 TRADE CASES ¶ 62,939], 101 F Supp 93 (S.D. Cal. 1951), aff'd without opinion, 200 F.2d 198 (9th Cir. 1952); *Kowalski v. Chandler*, 202 F.2d 413 (6th Cir. 1953), *Corbett v. Chandler*, 202 F.2d 428 (6th Cir. 1953).

[19] The "reserve system" includes the reserve clause and Major League Baseball rules designed to complement the clause in confining the player to the club that has him under contract and otherwise providing contract uniformity. See *Flood*, 407 U.S. at 259 n.1

Trade Regulation Reports                                      **¶ 70,315**

"business of organized professional baseball." *Radovich*, 352 U.S. 450-53.

In 1972, however, the Court in *Flood v. Kuhn* stripped from *Federal Baseball* and *Toolson* any precedential value those cases may have had beyond the particular facts there involved, *i.e.,* the reserve clause. The *Flood* Court employed a two-prong approach in doing so. First, the Court examined the analytical underpinnings of *Federal Baseball*—that the business of exhibiting baseball games is not interstate commerce. In the clearest possible terms, the Court rejected this reasoning, removing any doubt that "[p]rofessional baseball is a business ... engaged in interstate commerce." *Flood*, 407 U.S. at 282.

Having entirely undercut the precedential value of the *reasoning* of *Federal Baseball*, the Court next set out to justify the continued precedential value of the *result* of that decision. To do this, the Court first looked back to *Toolson* and uncovered the following four reasons why the Court there had followed *Federal Baseball:*

(a) Congressional awareness for three decades of the Court's ruling in *Federal Baseball*, coupled with congressional inaction. (b) *The fact that baseball was left alone to develop for that period upon the understanding that the reserve system was not subject to existing antitrust laws.* (c) A reluctance to overrule *Federal Baseball* with consequent retroactive effect. (d) A professed desire that any needed remedy be provided by legislation rather than court decree.

*Id.* at 273-74 (emphasis added). The emphasized text indicates that the *Flood* Court viewed the *disposition* in *Federal Baseball* and *Toolson* as being limited to the reserve system, for baseball developed between 1922 and 1953 with the understanding that its *reserve system*, not the game generally, was exempt from the antitrust laws. This reading of *Flood* is buttressed by (1) the reaffirmation in *Flood* of a prior statement of the Court that " '*Toolson* was a narrow application of the doctrine of *stare decisis*,' " *id.* at 276 (quoting *Shubert*, 348 U.S. at 228-30); and (2) the *Flood* Court's own characterization, in the *first sentence* of its opinion, of the *Federal Baseball*, *Toolson*, and *Flood* decisions: "For the third time in 50 years the Court is asked *specifically* to rule that professional baseball's *reserve system* is within the reach of the antitrust laws." *Id.* at 259 (emphasis added) (footnote omitted).

Viewing the dispositions in *Federal Baseball* and *Toolson* as limited to the reserve clause, the *Flood* Court then turned to the reasons why, even though analytically vitiated, the precise results in *Federal Baseball* and *Toolson* were to be accorded the continuing benefit of *stare decisis*. Like *Toolson*, the *Flood* Court laid its emphasis on continued positive congressional inaction and concerns over retroactivity. *Id.* at 283-84. In particular, the *Flood* Court "concluded that Congress as yet has had no intention to subject baseball's *reserve system* to the reach of the antitrust statutes." *Id.* at 283 (emphasis added). Finally, the Court acknowledged that "[w]ith its *reserve system* enjoying exemption from the federal antitrust laws, baseball is, in a very distinct sense, an exception and an anomaly. *Federal Baseball* and *Toolson* have become an aberration confined to baseball." *Id.* at 282 (emphasis added). Thus in 1972, the Supreme Court made clear that the *Federal Baseball* exemption is limited to the reserve clause.

Relying primarily upon *Charles O. Finley & Co. v. Kuhn* [1978-1 TRADE CASES ¶ 61,978], 569 F.2d 527 (7th Cir. 1978), cert. denied, 439 U.S. 876 (1978), defendant Baseball offers a different reading of *Flood*. The plaintiff in that case, Charles O. Finley & Co. ("Finley"), owned the Oakland Athletics ("Oakland") baseball club. *Finley*, 569 F.2d at 530. In June of 1976, Oakland negotiated tentative agreements to sell Oakland's contract rights in three players to other teams. *Id.* at 531. Defendant Commissioner of Baseball Bowie Kuhn disapproved of the sale, and Finley subsequently brought suit, claiming, among other things, that the Commissioner conspired with others in violation of the antitrust laws. *Id.* Finding the Commissioner exempt from the antitrust laws under *Federal Baseball*, the district court granted summary judgment in favor of the Commissioner, and Finley appealed.

Like plaintiffs here, Finley argued on appeal that the exemption applies only to the reserve system. The Seventh Circuit disagreed, finding that "[d]espite the *two* references in the *Flood* case to the reserve system, it appears clear from the entire opinions in the three baseball cases, as well as from *Radovich*, that the Supreme Court intended to exempt the business of baseball, not any particular facet of that business, from the federal antitrust laws." *Id.* at 541 (emphasis added) (footnotes omitted).

In reaching this conclusion, the Seventh Circuit looked back to *Federal Baseball*, *Toolson*, and *Radovich*, as I have done here, and concluded that the Court had focused in those cases upon the business of baseball, not just the reserve clause. Then the court discussed *Flood:*

In *Flood v. Kuhn*, the Court said that "Professional baseball is engaged in interstate commerce" and "we adhere once again to *Federal Baseball* and *Toolson* and to their application to professional baseball."

*Id.* (citation omitted). This single paragraph represents the Seventh Circuit's entire substantive discussion of *Flood*—the Supreme Court's most recent and most thorough explanation of the *Federal Baseball* exemption. The court discounted two references in *Flood* to the reserve clause[20] and made no mention of the fact that *Flood* refers to the reserve clause at least *four* times, the two not discussed by the court indicating that (1) the Supreme Court reads *Federal Baseball* and *Toolson* as reserve clause cases, *Flood*, 407 U.S. at 273-74; and (2) the Court continues to follow the precise disposition of those decisions because Congress continues to express no intention of subjecting the *reserve clause* to the antitrust laws, *id.* at 283.

But there is an even more significant flaw in the Seventh Circuit's analysis of *Flood* than in failing to note the extent to which that decision turned upon the reserve clause: Application of the doctrine of *stare decisis* simply permits no other way to read *Flood* than as confining the precedential value of *Federal Baseball* and *Toolson* to the precise facts there involved. To understand why this is so, one must fully understand the doctrine of *stare decisis* and its application by lower courts to Supreme Court decisions. The Third Circuit recently offered the following explanation:

> [Supreme Court] . . . opinions usually include two major aspects. First, the Court provides the legal standard or test that is applicable to laws implicating a particular . . . provision. This is part of the reasoning of the decision, the *ratio decidendi*. Second, the Court applies that standard or test to the particular facts of the case that the Court is confronting—in other words, it reaches a specific result using the standard or test.

> As a lower court, we are bound by both the Supreme Court's choice of legal standard or test and by the result it reaches under the standard or test. As Justice Kennedy has stated, courts are bound to adhere not only to results of cases, but also "to their explications of the governing rules of law." Our system of precedent or *stare decisis* is thus based on adherence to both the reasoning and result of a case, and not simply to the result alone. This distinguishes the American system of precedent, sometimes called "rule stare deci-

sis," from the English system, which historically has been limited to following the results or disposition based on the facts of a case and thus referred to as "result stare decisis."

> Like lower courts, the Supreme Court applies principles of *stare decisis* and recognizes an obligation to respect both the standard announced and the result reached in its prior cases. Unlike lower courts, the Supreme Court is free to change the standard or result from one of its earlier cases when it finds it to be "unsound in principle [or] unworkable in practice."

*Planned Parenthood of Southeastern Pa. v. Casey*, 947 F.2d 682, 691-92 (3d Cir. 1991) (citations omitted), aff'd in part and rev'd in part on other grounds. — U.S. —, 112 S. Ct. 2791 (1992).

Applying these principles of *stare decisis* here, it becomes clear that, before *Flood*, lower courts were bound by both the *rule* of *Federal Baseball* and *Toolson* (that the business of baseball is not interstate commerce and thus not within the Sherman Act)[21] and the *result* of those decisions (that baseball's reserve system is exempt from the antitrust laws). The Court's decision in *Flood*, however, effectively created the circumstance referred to by the Third Circuit as "result stare decisis," from the English system. In *Flood*, the Supreme Court exercised its discretion to invalidate the *rule* of *Federal Baseball* and *Toolson*. Thus no rule from those cases binds the lower courts as a matter of *stare decisis*. The only aspect of *Federal Baseball* and *Toolson* that remains to be followed is the result or disposition based upon the facts there involved, which the Court in *Flood* determined to be the exemption of the reserve system from the antitrust laws.

Neither *Finley* nor any other case cited by Baseball in support of its view of the exemption has undertaken such an analysis of the Supreme Court's baseball trilogy.[22] And as none of these decisions is binding upon this Court, I will not follow them.[23] It is well settled that exemptions from the antitrust laws are to be narrowly construed. See *Group Life & Health Ins. Co. v.*

---

[20] The *Finley* court identified the following two references to the reserve clause in *Flood:*

"For the third time in 50 years the Court is asked specifically to rule that professional baseball's reserve system is within the reach of the federal antitrust laws."

*Finley*, 569 F.2d at 540 n.48 (quoting *Flood*, 407 U.S. at 259).

"With its reserve system enjoying exemption from the federal antitrust laws, baseball is, in a very distinct sense, an exception and an anomaly."

*Id.* (quoting *Flood*, 407 U.S. at 282)

[21] *Radovich* later made clear that this rule applied only to the business of organized baseball, prohibiting its applica-

tion to other professional sports. See *Radovich*, 352 U.S. at 450

[22] Baseball cites the following decisions, among others, in support of its view: *Professional Baseball Schools & Clubs, Inc. v. Kuhn* [1982-83 TRADE CASES ¶ 65,089], 693 F.2d 1085 (11th Cir. 1982); *Triple-A Baseball Club Associates v. Northeastern Baseball, Inc.*, 832 F.2d 214 (1st Cir. 1987), cert. denied, 485 U.S. 935 (1988), *Portland Baseball Club, Inc. v. Kuhn* [1974-1 TRADE CASES ¶ 75,092], 491 F.2d 1101 (9th Cir. 1974); *Salerno v. American League of Professional Baseball Clubs* [1970 TRADE CASES ¶ 73,276], 429 F.2d 1003 (2d Cir. 1970), cert. denied. 400 U.S. 1007 (1971)

[23] I note that the Third Circuit has neither analyzed *Flood* nor construed the contours of the *Federal Baseball*

---

**¶ 70,315**

*Royal Drug Co.* [1979-1 TRADE CASES ¶ 62,479], 440 U.S. 205, 231 (1979). Application of this principle is particularly appropriate, if not absolutely critical, in this case because the exemption at issue has been characterized by its own creator as an "anomaly" and an "aberration." *Flood,* 407 U.S. at 282; see also *id.* at 286 (*Federal Baseball* is a "derelict in the stream of the law." (Douglas, J. dissenting)). For these reasons, I conclude that the antitrust exemption created by *Federal Baseball* is limited to baseball's reserve system, and because the parties agree that the reserve system is not at issue in this case, I reject Baseball's argument that it is exempt from antitrust liability in this case.

### (ii) *Nature of the exemption*

Although it would be appropriate to end here my discussion of the *Federal Baseball* exemption, for the purpose of providing a complete record of decision in the event of certification for immediate appeal under 28 U.S.C.A. § 1292(b) (West Supp. 1993), I will press on to consider the implications of applying "rule stare decisis" to *Federal Baseball* and plaintiffs' complaint.

Assuming, as Baseball would have it, that *Finley* is correct and the exemption extends beyond the reserve system, I must determine exactly how far the exemption reaches. I find that stating, as did the *Finley* court, that the exemption covers the "business of baseball" does little to delineate the contours of the exemption.

As mentioned above, to state a claim under the Sherman Act, plaintiffs must allege injury to competition in a relevant product market. See *Mid-South Grizzlies,* 720 F.2d at 785. Although the Supreme Court has not couched its explanation of the exemption in these terms, I believe that the only arguably surviving rule to be gleaned from the Court's baseball trilogy is that if the relevant product market involved is the market defined as the "business of baseball," injury to competition in that market may not be redressed under the Sherman Act.[24] Cf. *Henderson Broadcasting Corp. v. Houston Sports Ass'n* [1982-2 TRADE CASES ¶ 64,966], 541 F. Supp. 263 (S.D. Tx. 1982) (exemption does not apply to market for broadcast of baseball games). *Federal Baseball* itself made this clear. The focus in that case was upon competition in two different businesses or markets. The first was defined as the business of "giving exhibitions of base ball

[sic]." *Federal Baseball,* 259 U.S. at 208. The second was defined as the business of "moving players and their paraphernalia from place to place." *D.C. Opinion,* 269 F. at 686. The Sherman Act was held not to apply to restraints in the first market because that market did not implicate interstate commerce. *Federal Baseball,* 259 U.S. at 208-09. Restraints in the second market, however, were redressable under the Sherman Act because that market did implicate interstate commerce. *D.C. Opinion,* 269 F. at 687-88. Thus, assuming the validity of *Finley,* the *Federal Baseball* exemption is one related to a particular market—the market comprised of the exhibition of baseball games—not a particular type of restraint (such as the reserve clause) or a particular entity (such as Major League Baseball).

It follows from having expressed the exemption as relating to a particular market that the next question is whether the plaintiffs in this case seek relief for restraints in that market or some other market. If Baseball's allegedly unlawful conduct merely restrained competition in the market comprised of baseball exhibitions, Baseball is immune from liability under the Act. If some other market was involved, however, even the expansive version of the *Federal Baseball* exemption would not apply.

A "market" may be defined as "any grouping of sales whose sellers, if unified by a hypothetical cartel or merger, could raise prices significantly above the competitive level." Philip E. Areeda & Herbert Hovenkamp, *Antitrust Law* ¶ 518.1b (Supp. 1991) (footnote omitted). As stated above, plaintiffs allege that the relevant product market in this case is the market for ownership of existing major league professional baseball teams. Reduced to its essentials, one can infer at this stage of the proceedings that this market has the following components: (1) the product being sold is an ownership interest in professional baseball teams; (2) the sellers are team owners; and (3) the buyers are those who would like to become team owners. Viewing the complaint in the light most favorable to plaintiffs, it would not be unreasonable also to infer that if the team owners combined, they could increase the price of teams considerably and control the conditions of sale.[25]

The market to which the expansive version of the *Federal Baseball* exemption applies, on the

(Footnote Continued)

exemption. I am bound, however, to follow the approach to *stare decisis* set forth by the Third Circuit in *Planned Parenthood.*

[24] In light of *Flood,* I do not believe, nor do I understand Baseball to argue, that *Federal Baseball's* interstate commerce reasoning remains vital.

[25] One might also view the relevant market more narrowly as the market for the purchase and transfer of the

Giants only, where there was but one seller, Robert Lurie, constituting a monopoly, with the buyer group including only those interested in the Giants, as opposed to other professional baseball teams. On a motion to dismiss, I must view the relevant market in the manner most favorable to plaintiffs.

other hand. has the following components: (1) the product is the exhibition of baseball games; (2) the sellers, as with the market defined by plaintiffs, are team owners; and (3) the buyers are fans and, perhaps, the broadcast industry. Thus the two markets have different products—baseball teams versus baseball games—and different consumers.

Although not expressed in market terms, the Court of Appeals in *Federal Baseball* attributed great weight to such differences. The court distinguished for Sherman Act purposes between the business that encompassed the exhibition of baseball games (the "game exhibition market") and the business that involved the movement of players and their paraphernalia (the "player transportation market"). *D.C. Opinion*, 269 F. at 686. The focus of the exemption was on the exhibition of games only, which Justice Holmes characterized in affirming the Court of Appeals as "purely state affairs." *Federal Baseball*, 259 U.S. at 208. Other aspects of a baseball team's business—interstate aspects distinguishable from but nonetheless related to the games such as the movement of players and equipment—were not part of the exemption. Thus the anticompetitive nature of the reserve clause in the game exhibition market was found not to violate the Sherman Act, but could have given rise to a claim under the Act had it directly affected other markets. A similar distinction may be made here. The plaintiffs in this case target not anticompetitive activity in the market for the exhibition of baseball *games*; but anticompetitive activity in market for the sale of ownership interests in baseball *teams*—a market seemingly as distinguishable from the game exhibition market as the player transportation market.

Recent courts construing the expansive version of the exemption, although not focusing upon the distinction made by the Court of Appeals in *Federal Baseball*, have defined the exempted market (characterized as the "business of baseball") as that which is central to the " 'unique characteristics and needs' " of baseball. *Postema v. National League of Professional Baseball Clubs*, 799 F. Supp. 1475, 1488 (S.D.N.Y. 1992) (quoting *Flood*, 407 U.S. at 282), rev'd on other grounds, — F.2d —, 1993 WL 240824 (2d Cir. July 6, 1993); [26] *Henderson*, 541 F. Supp. at 268-69, 271 (*Federal Baseball* exemption not applicable to market for broadcast of baseball games). There seems to be agreement among these courts and others that, defined in this way, the exempted market includes (1) the reserve system and (2) matters of

league structure. See, e.g., *Professional Baseball Schools and Clubs. Inc. v. Kuhn* [1982-83 TRADE CASES ¶ 65,089], 693 F.2d 1085 (11th Cir. 1982); *Postema*, 799 F. Supp. at 1489; *Henderson*, 541 F. Supp. at 269; *State v. Milwaukee Braves, Inc.* [1966 TRADE CASES ¶ 71,843], 31 Wis.2d 699. 144 N.W.2d 1, 15 (1966), cert. denied, 385 U.S. 990 (1966).

I do not view these decisions as conflicting with the analysis of the Court of Appeals in *Federal Baseball*. Applying their logic, the Court of Appeals can be understood as essentially viewing the movement of players and their equipment from game to game as a market activity not central to the unique characteristics and needs of exhibiting baseball games. Thus, when these decisions are considered together, the following list of activities or markets that are *not* within the exempted market can be generated: (1) the movement of players and their equipment from game to game; (2) the broadcast of baseball games; and, perhaps, (3) employment relations between organized professional baseball and non-players.

No court, however, has analyzed or applied the expansive view of the *Federal Baseball* exemption to the market for ownership interests in existing baseball teams. Thus I must determine whether this market is central to the unique characteristics and needs of baseball exhibitions. I conclude that such a determination is not possible without a factual record, and that, viewing plaintiffs' complaint in their favor, plaintiffs may be able to demonstrate that team ownership is not central to baseball's unique characteristics.

Plaintiffs plead that they were attempting to acquire an interest in a business owned by Robert Lurie engaged in the exhibition of baseball games—the San Francisco Giants. As stated above, the products being sold in this market (teams) are different from those being sold in the exempted market (games). And acquiring an ownership interest in a team may very well be no more unique to the exhibition of baseball games than is moving players and their equipment from game to game. Although players and their equipment are, beyond doubt, uniquely necessary to a baseball game, the Court of Appeals in *Federal Baseball* found, on a trial record, that their movement—which essentially involves the transportation of men and equipment—was not. Likewise, although teams, as business entities engaged in exhibiting baseball games, are undoubtedly a unique necessity to

---

[26] *Postema* held that the *Federal Baseball* exemption does not apply to baseball's employment relationships with non-players such as umpires because such relationships "are not a unique characteristic or need of the game." *Id.* at 1489. But see *Salerno v. American League of Professional Baseball Clubs* [1970 TRADE CASES ¶ 73,276], 429 F.2d 1003 (2d Cir.

1970) (holding that employment relations with umpires are within the exemption), cert. denied, 400 U.S. 1001 (1971). *Postema* chose not to follow *Salerno* because it was decided before "*Flood's* apparent endorsement of a limited view of the exemption." *Postema*, 799 F. Supp. at 1475.

the game, the transfer of ownership interests in such entities may not be so unique. Moreover, anticompetitive conduct toward those who seek to purchase existing teams has never been considered by any court to be an essential part of the exhibition of baseball games.

On the other hand, it is conceivable that, although the precise products in plaintiffs' market and the exempted market are different, these markets nonetheless overlap to such an extent that they should be treated identically for purposes of the expansive view of *Federal Baseball.* In other words, the acquisition of a business that is engaged in baseball exhibitions may be central in some way not apparent on the face of the complaint to the unique characteristics of baseball exhibitions. Without a factual record, I would be engaged in mere speculation in deciding now whether it is or is not.

Accordingly, I conclude that if "rule stare decisis" and the *Finley* expansive view were applied, this case would not be ripe for determination of whether the *Federal Baseball* exemption applies. Thus, even under this analysis, Baseball's motion would be denied. One additional observation bears mentioning. I have considered plaintiffs' complaint in the light most favorable to plaintiffs and have accepted their definition of the relevant market as the market

for team *ownership.* But the gravamen of plaintiffs' case may be Baseball's interference with plaintiffs' efforts to acquire and *relocate* the Giants to Florida. As stated earlier, matters of league structure have been viewed by other courts as being unique to baseball. The physical relocation of a team and Baseball's decisions regarding such a relocation could implicate matters of league structure, and thus be covered by the exemption. If, therefore, the expansive view of *Federal Baseball* were applied and a factual record were developed showing that this case concerns only restraints on the market for ownership *and* relocation of the Giants as inseparable activities, "rule stare decisis" could require application of the exemption.

### III. *Conclusion*

Baseball's motion to dismiss is granted in part and denied in part. Plaintiffs' direct claims under the U.S. Constitution are dismissed. In all other respects the motion is denied. Because I have not dismissed all of plaintiffs' claims over which this Court has original jurisdiction, I will continue to exercise supplemental jurisdiction over plaintiffs' state law claims. See 28 U.S.C.A. § 1367 (West Supp. 1993).

An appropriate order follows.

# BOOK REVIEW

## WHEN THE LAWYERS SLEPT: THE UNMAKING OF THE
## BROOKLYN DODGERS

*Robert M. Jarvis†*

## I
## INTRODUCTION

Since World War II, the movement of franchises from one city to another has become a regular part of professional sports;[1] in recent years, relocations have reached unprecedented levels.[2] Yet de-

---

† Assistant Professor of Law, Nova University; B.A., Northwestern University; J.D., University of Pennsylvania; LL.M., New York University.

[1] The first modern professional sports team relocation probably occurred in 1903, when the National League Baltimore Orioles moved to the American League and became the New York Highlanders. The atrocious Highlanders eventually renamed themselves the Yankees, acquired Babe Ruth from the Boston Red Sox, and went on to become one of the most famous teams in professional sports history. After this shift only a handful of relocations occurred before World War II, mostly in the National Football League. Beginning in 1950, however, franchise shifts became increasingly popular, and nearly seventy modern took place during the next thirty years. Johnson, *Municipal Administration and the Sports Franchise Relocation Issue*, 43 PUB. ADMIN. REV. 519, 520 (1983).

[2] During the last decade, numerous sports teams have relocated. In the National Basketball Association, poor attendance forced the New Orleans Jazz to become the Utah Jazz, the New York Nets to move to New Jersey, the Kansas City Kings to switch to Sacramento, and the San Diego Clippers to regroup in Los Angeles. In the National Football League, more attractive stadiums lured the Oakland Raiders to Los Angeles, the Baltimore Colts to Indianapolis, the St. Louis Cardinals to Phoenix, and the New York Giants and New York Jets to New Jersey. In the National Hockey League, a combination of problems led the Atlanta Flames to Calgary and the Colorado Rockies to New Jersey, where they became the Devils. In addition to actual franchise shifts, there have been a number of threatened shifts. In Major League Baseball, the Chicago Cubs threatened to move to the suburbs if the city of Chicago refused to install lights in Wrigley Field. The Chicago White Sox held negotiations designed to bring them to a new stadium in St. Petersburg, thereby escaping from their crumbling stadium on the rundown South Side of Chicago. The San Francisco Giants have considered a number of new homes due to sagging attendance and the poor playing conditions at Candlestick Park. Meanwhile, the Cleveland Indians, Pittsburgh Pirates, and Seattle Mariners have all at one time or another suggested that they might move. In the National Football League, the Houston Oilers looked into moving to Jacksonville prior to deciding to stay in the Astrodome. The New Orleans Saints considered leaving Louisiana until the state granted millions of dollars of tax concessions. In the National Hockey League, the St. Louis Blues came very close to relocating to Saskatoon; only last minute intervention by league officials kept the team in St. Louis.

The current rash of attempted and successful relocations has produced a strong backlash among both fans and owners, the introduction of anti-relocation legislation in Congress, and a number of lawsuits. The wealth of literature which has grown up around the subject reviews these matters at length. *See, e.g.*, Eisen, *Franchise Relocation in*

spite dozens of shifts and threatened shifts, no relocation has generated the level of passion, study, and controversy as the decision of the Brooklyn Dodgers to move to Los Angeles after the 1957 season. For many older Brooklynites, even those who have since moved away from the borough, the loss of the Dodgers is still a staple of conversation.[3]

Over the years, conventional wisdom has taught that the Dodgers moved to Los Angeles because of the greed of their owner, Walter O'Malley, who was dissatisfied with the team's revenues in Brooklyn and saw a chance to make greater profits on the West Coast. As a result, O'Malley's status as a traitor to the people of Brooklyn has become legendary.[4] But in a new work entitled *The Dodgers Move West*,[5] Neil J. Sullivan has gone back in time in an attempt to ferret out the truth about O'Malley's decision to move the Dodgers. The results of his painstaking research[6] are startling.

According to Professor Sullivan, O'Malley initially opposed moving the Dodgers to Los Angeles, and eventually did so only with great reluctance. In Professor Sullivan's view, O'Malley would have kept the Dodgers in Brooklyn if he could have built a new stadium to replace the aging Ebbets Field.[7]

The author believes that the Dodgers ultimately moved to Los Angeles because O'Malley lacked sufficient funds to buy the land

---

*Major League Baseball*, 4 ENT. & SP. L.J. 19 (1987); Glick, *Professional Sports Franchise Movements and the Sherman Act: When and Where Teams Should be Able to Move*, 23 SANTA CLARA L. REV. 55 (1983); Lazaroff, *The Antitrust Implications of Franchise Relocation Restrictions in Professional Sports*, 53 FORDHAM L. REV. 157 (1984); Quirk, *An Economic Analysis of Team Movements in Professional Sports*, 38 LAW & CONTEMP. PROBS. 42 (1973); Roberts, *The Single Entity Status of Sports Leagues Under Section 1 of the Sherman Act: An Alternative View*, 60 TUL. L. REV. 562 (1986); Shropshire, *Opportunistic Sports Franchise Relocations: Can Punitive Damages in Actions Based Upon Contract Strike a Balance?*, 22 LOY. L.A.L. REV. 569 (1989); Weistart, *League Control of Market Opportunities: A Perspective on Competition and Cooperation in the Sports Industry*, 1984 DUKE L.J. 1013; Comment, *Keeping the Home Team at Home*, 74 CALIF. L. REV. 1329 (1986); Note, *The Professional Sports Community Protection Act: Congress' Best Response to Raiders?*, 38 HASTINGS L.J. 345 (1987).

    3    For a time, Brooklynites talked of bringing the Dodgers back to Brooklyn. Still later, some Dodger fans came to accept the New York Mets, a National League expansion team, as their team. Today, talk focuses on establishing a minor league team on Coney Island and naming it the Brooklyn Dodgers. Rangel, *State Proposes Baseball Stadium for Coney I.*, N.Y. Times, Dec. 5, 1986, at A1, col. 3.

    4    *See, e.g.*, P. GOLENBOCK, BUMS—ORAL HISTORY OF THE BROOKLYN DODGERS (1984); R. KAHN, THE BOYS OF SUMMER (1971); D. RICE, SEASONS PAST (1976).

    5    N. SULLIVAN, THE DODGERS MOVE WEST (1987).

    6    Although Walter O'Malley had died by the time the book was begun, Professor Sullivan was able to speak at length with O'Malley's son, Peter, who took over the club from his father. *Id.* at xi, 192. In addition, Professor Sullivan spoke with a number of Walter O'Malley's contemporaries, including Vin Scully, the team's long-time announcer; former New York City Mayor Robert Wagner; former Los Angeles Councilwoman Rosalind Wyman; and Congressman Edward Roybal. *Id.* at xi.

    7    *Id.* at ix.

needed for the stadium. When O'Malley turned to New York City for help in acquiring the land through eminent domain proceedings, master builder Robert Moses, who was at the height of his power, rebuffed him. With no hope of building a new stadium in Brooklyn, and opposed to the idea of accepting a stadium built with public funds, O'Malley had no choice but to leave for Los Angeles, where the city fathers were willing to provide him with a large tract of land known as Chavez Ravine.[8]

## II
### THE BIRTH OF THE BROOKLYN DODGERS AND THE BUILDING OF EBBETS FIELD

Professional baseball first came to Brooklyn in 1884, when the American Association admitted a team from Brooklyn.[9] Then just three years old, the American Association was attempting to compete with the more powerful National League which had been formed as the nation's first professional baseball league in 1876. The new Brooklyn team, known as the Trolley Dodgers, prospered, and in 1889 became the champions of the American Association.[10] In the next year, the team switched leagues, joining the National League as the Brooklyn Bridegrooms.[11]

In 1898, Charles Ebbets assumed the presidency of the Bridegrooms.[12] During the next few years the Bridegrooms, subsequently known as the Superbas, enjoyed great success, but after 1902 many of their star players retired and the team foundered.[13] After nearly ten years of futility, however, Ebbets began to rebuild the team both on and off the field. He hired Wilbert Robinson away from the cross-town rival Giants and began cultivating a battery of future star players.[14] More importantly, he began construction of a new stadium.

The plan to build a new stadium in Brooklyn first began to take shape in 1908.[15] After much searching, he selected a desolate part of the borough known at various times as Pigtown, Goatville, Tin Can Alley and Crow Hill.[16] The decision to build a new stadium in so bleak a place was a masterful piece of planning, for Pigtown had plenty of empty land which could support a new stadium.

---

8   *Id.* at viii.
9   *Id.* at 5.
10  *Id.*
11  *Id.*
12  *Id.* at 6.
13  *Id.*
14  *Id.* at 7.
15  *Id.* at 56.
16  *Id.* at 4.

During the next three years, Ebbets busied himself with the task of acquiring the parcels for his new stadium. This proved much harder to do than expected, for forty different owners held the land which Ebbets needed.[17] In order to disguise his true purpose and thereby avoid a ruinous jump in land prices, Ebbets formed a dummy corporation to buy the needed parcels.[18] Although the entire task was not completed until the end of 1911, Ebbets managed to keep the news of what he was doing away from much of the public and the press.[19] As a result, the purchases, although time-consuming, went smoothly and without substantial price gouging.

With the land now in hand, Ebbets set about to build his stadium. Within a year, and after the expenditure of $750,000 (at the time a remarkable sum of money), the stadium was ready.[20] When Ebbets Field opened on April 4, 1913, sports writers and fans heralded it as a magnificent stadium.[21]

## III
### THE NEED FOR A NEW STADIUM

During the next four decades, Ebbets Field served as the faithful home of the team now called the Brooklyn Dodgers. Dodger fans affectionately nicknamed their team the Bums, and in 1955 the Dodgers beat the New York Yankees to win their only World Series.[22] But neither the success of the team nor the faithfulness of its fans could conceal the fact that time had taken its toll on the stadium.[23]

By now, the team was under the control of Walter O'Malley, a hard-nosed businessman.[24] He realized that the stadium's small size, cramped conditions, and inhospitable surroundings made a new stadium imperative if the team were to continue its success.[25]

---

17    *Id.* at 56.
18    *Id.*
19    *Id.*
20    *Id.* at 4.
21    *Id.*
22    *Id.* at 7-17, 58-67.
23    *Id.* at 38-41.
24    *Id.* at 29-32. O'Malley also was a lawyer. After graduating from the University of Pennsylvania, O'Malley obtained a law degree from Fordham Law School and then opened a corporate practice in Manhattan. *Id.* at 29. In 1941, the Dodgers appointed him club attorney. In 1944, O'Malley, together with Branch Rickey and John Smith, purchased a 75% interest in the club. *Id.* After years of bickering, O'Malley bought out Rickey in 1950 for the then astronomical sum of $1,050,000 and thereby secured total ownership of the Dodgers. *Id.* at 30.
25    *Id.* at 38-44. When Ebbets decided to build his stadium in Pigtown, the area was virtually uninhabited. In the years which followed, however, urban development converted Pigtown into Crown Heights, a fashionable neighborhood. Following World War II, Crown Heights began to suffer from urban blight and the flight of its middle class

Thus, O'Malley began the search for a suitable new home.

Because by this time others had developed the land around Ebbets Field to its full capacity, O'Malley rejected renovating Ebbets Field.[26] Instead, his attention turned to a plot of land at the Brooklyn terminal of the Long Island Rail Road at the corner of Atlantic and Flatbush Avenues, about a mile from Ebbets Field. The new site was accessible to fans via the Long Island Rail Road and two subway lines.[27]

O'Malley liked the idea of building a new stadium at this new location and already had the necessary money. What he lacked was easy access to the land.[28] Recalling the difficulties that Ebbets encountered in acquiring land in Pigtown, O'Malley concluded that only the government, exercising its eminent domain powers,[29] could in a single stroke collect the necessary parcels of land and sell them to the Dodgers at a price that made economic sense.[30]

---

inhabitants. By the 1950's, Crown Heights had become "an uninviting place in an increasingly unfamiliar neighborhood, and many former Brooklyn residents stopped attending games." *Id.* at 39.

[26] *Id.* at 41. Whether O'Malley ever considered seriously the idea of refurbishing Ebbets Field is an open question. As Professor Sullivan notes, "[p]erhaps O'Malley thought a serious upgrading of Ebbets Field would preclude the support he needed for a new stadium." *Id.* at 41. Professor Sullivan, however, is convinced that a new stadium was a necessity. In 1938, Larry MacPhail, then president of the Brooklyn Dodgers, renovated Ebbets Field at a cost of $100,000. "The stadium was repainted, given new seats, renovated dugouts and clubhouses, and the field was groomed to eliminate rocks and divots that had plagued infielders for years." *Id.* at 11. A similar renovation, according to Professor Sullivan, would not work in the 1950's. Although other parks built at the same time as Ebbets Field, including Comiskey Park, Wrigley Field, Fenway Park, and Tiger Stadium, remain in use, see Berkow, *Baseball's Palaces of the Mind*, N.Y. Times, July 11, 1988, at 35, col. 1, Ebbets Field was, in Professor Sullivan's opinion, "beyond repair." N. SULLIVAN, *supra* note 5, at 41. "By the 1950s, . . . the old preserve had become obsolete. The most compelling evidence of that obsolescence is the fact that despite its small size and the perpetual drama of the pennant races of those years the park was hardly ever filled to capacity." *Id.* at 40.

[27] *Id.* at 44, 54.

[28] *Id.* at 44 ("[w]hat O'Malley needed from New York City officials was not money for the stadium but access to the site."). While O'Malley was willing to pay for the land, he needed "help from the city to acquire the necessary land at a reasonable price." *Id.* at 54.

[29] Eminent domain, of course, is the power of the state to acquire private land without first obtaining the owner's consent. In the United States, two checks on this power exist. First, the government may not take property except for a public purpose or use. Second, the owner must receive reasonable compensation. *See generally* J. SACKMAN, NICHOLS' THE LAW OF EMINENT DOMAIN (rev. 3d ed. 1973 & Supp. 1988).

[30] N. SULLIVAN, *supra* note 5, at 55-57:

> The chances that in the 1950s Walter O'Malley could have formed a secret corporation and purchased land for a new stadium without the media and then the public finding out are too remote to be entertained seriously. Such a scenario would have brought a real estate boom to the Atlantic-Flatbush area.

*Id.* at 56.

On August 10, 1955 O'Malley wrote to the city to request that it condemn specific parcels under a postwar law known as the Housing Act of 1949.[31] Title I of the law encouraged local governments to clear slums and reverse urban blight by providing them federal funds to help finance such projects.[32] In order for the private sector to be eligible for federal funding for participating in the renewal, the projects had to have a "public purpose."[33] Accordingly, O'Malley proposed that in addition to building a new stadium for the Dodgers, he would have the area around Atlantic and Flatbush Avenues cleaned up, a new meat market built, and the old Long Island Rail Road terminal torn down and a new station erected.[34]

O'Malley's proposal went to Robert Moses, the architect of many of New York City's present highways, tunnels, bridges, beaches, and parks and, at that time, the New York City administrator of Title I.[35] Within days, Moses rejected O'Malley's proposal and wrote: "I can only repeat what we have told you verbally and in writing, namely, that a new ball field for the Dodgers cannot be dressed up as a Title I project."[36]

## IV
### THE LEGAL EFFECT OF TITLE I AND THE CORPORATION COUNSEL'S ALTERNATIVE PLAN

Robert Moses was wrong that New York City's condemnation and subsequent sale of land to the Dodgers would not fit within the strictures of Title I; moreover, he knew he was wrong.[37] Moses opposed building a new stadium at Atlantic and Flatbush Avenues be-

---

[31] Pub. L. No. 81-171, 63 Stat. 413 (codified in scattered sections of 12 U.S.C. & 42 U.S.C.). President Truman pushed through the Act on July 15, 1949 as part of his "Fair Deal" legislation. The Act's goal was to stimulate residential housing construction in order to alleviate the post-war shortage of affordable housing for lower and middle-income families. In order to accomplish this goal, the Act provided federal assistance for local public housing, slum clearance, and farm housing projects. The Act's passage and purposes are discussed at length in Robinson & Robinson, *A New Era in Public Housing*, 1949 WIS. L. REV. 695, and in Comment, *The Housing Act of 1949—A Federal Program for Public Housing and Slum Clearance*, 44 ILL. L. REV. 685 (1949). For a discussion of the Act's role in national housing policy in the forty years since its passage, see McDougall, *Affordable Housing for the 1990's*, 20 U. MICH. J.L. REF. 727 (1987).

[32] Ch. 338, §§ 101-10, 63 Stat. 413, 414-21. Title I officially was entitled, "Slum Clearance and Community Development and Redevelopment."

[33] N. SULLIVAN, *supra* note 5, at 47-48.

[34] *Id.* at 48.

[35] *Id.* at 49-51. Moses' life is the subject of a now famous biography. *See* R. CARO, THE POWER BROKER (1975).

[36] N. SULLIVAN, *supra* note 5, at 48.

[37] As Professor Sullivan states, "[w]hen Moses told Walter O'Malley that Title I of the Federal Housing Act would not permit the use of land for the construction of a baseball stadium, what he meant was that he did not wish the land used in that way." *Id.* at 50.

cause it conflicted with his plans to see New York City emerge as a modern metropolis connected by an intricate series of highways built around numerous public parks and beaches.[38] As a result, Moses instead suggested that New York build a new publicly financed and publicly owned stadium as part of a grand plan to develop Flushing Meadows.[39] O'Malley refused the offer of a public stadium.[40]

From 1955 through 1957, Moses and O'Malley remained locked in constant battle, with Moses continuing to argue, in the face of numerous proposals, that the legal constraints of Title I made it impossible for the Dodgers to acquire the needed land through city efforts.[41] No one challenged Moses' view,[42] despite extensive media coverage[43] and the existence of seemingly adequate legal precedent.[44] Finally, New York City Corporation Counsel Pe-

---

[38] Moses was against the Atlantic-Flatbush proposal for three additional reasons. First, Moses was not overly concerned with Brooklyn. Second, Moses favored participatory recreation over spectatorship. Third, the renovation of the Atlantic-Flatbush area would have meant an improvement in the Long Island Rail Road's Atlantic Avenue depot. Any movement away from the automobile and towards mass transportation threatened Moses' own power resulting from his control over the city's highways, tunnels, and bridges as the head of the Triborough Commission and numerous other public authorities. Therefore, Moses needed to keep the Atlantic Avenue area in decay. *Id.* at 50-51.

[39] *Id.* at 110-11. The idea of developing Flushing Meadows, a large and ugly expanse of land located in the geographic center of New York City, had long fired Moses' imagination. *Id.* Moses' plan to develop Flushing Meadows on a grand scale eventually did come to pass. In 1964-65, the World's Fair was held in Flushing Meadows. *Id.* at 111. At the same time, the expansion New York Mets moved to the very site which Moses had offered to O'Malley. *Id.* at 116. *See further infra* notes 46 and 52.

[40] O'Malley said he did not "want to be a tenant in a political ball park," but rather wanted to "own my own ball park and run it the way I think it should be run." *Id.* at 127. A strong argument can be made that O'Malley's refusal to accept a long-term lease in a public stadium was a product of greed, stubbornness, or both. The last stadium built with private funds had been Yankee Stadium in 1923. *Id.* at 44. In the meantime, the Milwaukee Braves and Baltimore Orioles had both moved from private to public stadiums (in 1953 and 1954, respectively). *Id.* Moreover, public financing was about to become an accepted way of building professional sports arenas. *See infra* note 50. Ultimately, even the New York Yankees joined the move to public funding. In the early 1970's, over $100 million of public funds were used to finance the renovation of Yankee Stadium. N. SULLIVAN, *supra* note 5, at 213.

[41] *Id.* at 51-57, 130-32.

[42] Professor Sullivan does not account for why lawyers did not challenge Moses' view, although he does point out that Moses was at the height of his power at this time and beyond the control of normal political forces. *Id.* at 49. Professor Sullivan also does not explain why O'Malley, himself a lawyer, did not seek to bring the issue to a judicial resolution. While discussing another aspect of the move, however, Professor Sullivan does suggest that O'Malley's legal foresight was less than may have been expected of a successful executive. *Id.* at 138-39.

[43] As Professor Sullivan points out, however, the media may have been biased against O'Malley, and frequently reported his side of the story incorrectly. *Id.* at 115, 131-32.

[44] Several years before O'Malley first asked New York City to help the Dodgers by

ter Brown issued a legal opinion on September 11, 1957 offering a

---

invoking Title I, a law review article studied in great detail all legal challenges to public slum clearance and low-recent housing projects. Hill, *Recent Slum Clearance and Urban Redevelopment Laws*, 9 WASH. & LEE L. REV. 173 (1952). After noting that the overwhelming number of these challenges had failed, the author concluded that:

> The *unanimity* of judicial decisions on these questions clearly establishes the validity of this approach to the slum clearance problem. The exercise of the power of eminent domain and the expenditure of public funds to acquire and clear slum areas is proper as being for a public purpose and use.

*Id.* at 185-86 (emphasis added). The article further stated that "[a]lthough the program described in Title I of the Housing Act of 1949 has not yet been similarly tested under the Federal Constitution, there appears to be no distinction in principle, purpose or approach as to warrant a different result." *Id.* at 183.

Shortly after the appearance of Hill's article, but still before O'Malley sent his proposal to Moses, the United States Supreme Court decided Berman v. Parker, 348 U.S. 26 (1954). In *Berman*, the Court adopted a broad definition of the phrase "public use" for eminent domain proceedings. The Court stated that land could be given to private individuals. Because "[t]he concept of public welfare is broad and inclusive," *id.* at 33, Congress could condemn property on a whole-sale basis, whether for the purpose of erecting schools and churches, or even "shopping centers." *Id.* at 35. The final definition of public use and welfare would rest with the legislature, not the courts. *Id.* at 35-36. Thus, virtually any use which would bestow an advantage on the public would justify a taking by the government.

Also prior to O'Malley's letter, Congress expanded the scope of its housing program by enlarging the reach of Title I. Under the amendments, individuals could now apply slum prevention programs not only to deteriorating areas but also to areas in danger of deterioration. Housing Act of 1954, Pub. L. No. 83-560, tit. III, § 311, 68 Stat. 590, 626, *repealed by* Housing and Community Development Act of 1974, Pub. L. No. 93-383, tit. I, § 116, 88 Stat. 633, 652 (codified at 42 U.S.C. § 5316 (1982)). The impact of the amendments was immediate and significant. Just four years after the amendments became law, Yale Law Professor Quintin Johnstone noted that:

> Despite Congressional indications that improvement of housing is the primary objective of the urban renewal program, many important projects have as their primary purpose the revival of business districts that have been declining due to suburban or outlying business competition. Project area improvements to fulfill this purpose are new store and office buildings; hotels; markets; parking facilities; traffic patterns; and, adjacent to the business districts, new high income apartments to add retail sales volume.

Johnstone, *The Federal Urban Renewal Program*, 25 U. CHI. L. REV. 301, 321-22 (1958).

Despite these precedents, Professor Sullivan concludes (without explaining why) that it was unclear whether adequate precedents existed in 1957 which would have allowed the Dodgers to invoke Title I. N. SULLIVAN, *supra* note 5, at 120. Yet O'Malley's Atlantic-Flatbush proposal had all the characteristics which Professor Johnstone described and which federal and local officials previously approved. As Professor Sullivan explains, the site O'Malley wanted:

> was part of a proposed redevelopment project, . . . [of which a] new stadium for the Dodgers was only one item proposed to the Board Estimate. Also mentioned were the need for commercial and residential redevelopment of substandard and unsanitary dwellings, the problem of traffic congestion, a possible new terminal for the Long Island Rail Road, and relocation of the Fort Greene Meat Market.

*Id.* at 54-55. O'Malley stressed these aspect of the project while testifying to the Antitrust Subcommittee of the House Judiciary Committee in June 1957, just months before he announced his decision to relocate to Los Angeles. *Id.* at 124.

way around Moses' position.[45]

Unfortunately, Brown's suggestion came too late. After years of attempting to get New York City to assist him, O'Malley on October 8, 1957, announced that he had decided to move the Dodgers to Los Angeles.[46] The Los Angeles city fathers had been working for some time to put together an attractive package for O'Malley and in the end had placed a large plot of land known as Chavez Ravine at O'Malley's disposal.[47] Thus, in the winter of 1958, the Dodgers moved to Los Angeles, and for the next four seasons played in the oversized and ill-equipped Los Angeles Coliseum while construction proceeded on their new stadium.[48] On April 10, 1962, the

---

[45] As reported by *The New York Times*, Brown believed that New York City could acquire the necessary land and resell it to the Dodgers "if the city Planning Commission determined that the area was substandard and unsanitary." *Id.* at 134. Doing so would avoid Title I and circumvent Robert Moses' power as the Title I Administrator. Deputy Mayor John Theobald eagerly announced that this proposal would be studied by the New York City Board of Estimate at its forthcoming meeting on September 19, 1957. *Id.*

[46] *Id.* at 3. The manner of O'Malley's announcement is worth recounting. As Professor Sullivan tells it:

> [D]uring a World Series game between the Yankees and Braves, the Dodgers announced they would move to Los Angeles for the 1958 season. The manner of the announcement showed little consideration for the Brooklyn fans being left behind. A publicist for the Dodgers read the . . . statement to those in the press room at the Waldorf-Astoria Hotel. . . . Walter O'Malley was not in attendance for the announcement, nor was Brooklyn invited to bid its team farewell.

*Id.* at 135-36.

O'Malley decided to leave New York just a few months after Horace Stoneham, the owner of the New York Giants, decided to move to San Francisco due to sagging attendance at the ancient Polo Grounds. *Id.* at 133. Although many commentators argued that Stoneham's decision absolutely was necessary if the team were to survive, Professor Sullivan suggests that this was not true. If the Giants had stayed in New York, they would have had the lucrative New York broadcast market to themselves. *Id.* at 116. Moreover, it is likely that Moses would have proposed a new stadium in Flushing Meadows for the Giants, just as he had done for the Dodgers and would do for the New York Mets in the early 1960's. *Id. See further infra* note 52. The Mets "have prospered [in Flushing Meadows], while the Giants, meanwhile, have battled to survive in San Francisco." *Id.* For a history of the Giants in New York, see N. HYND, THE GIANTS OF THE POLO GROUNDS (1988). The final chapter of Hynd's book recalls Stoneham's decision to move the Giants to San Francisco. *Id.* at 378-82.

[47] N. SULLIVAN, *supra* note 5, at 83-106.

[48] *Id.* at 137-89. During this period, numerous legal challenges were brought to halt the building of Dodger Stadium. At the core of these challenges was the argument which Robert Moses had raised in New York, namely, that the government could not turn public land over to a private baseball club for the erection of a private stadium. When this issue finally reached the California Supreme Court, the court held that a public purpose was present. *See* City of Los Angeles v. Superior Court of the County of Los Angeles, 51 Cal.2d 423, 333 P.2d 745 (1959). As part of the contract with Los Angeles under which it obtained Chavez Ravine, the Dodgers agreed to convert a portion of the land into public recreational facilities and maintain them as such for at least twenty years. In addition, the Dodgers agreed to turn over to the city a minor league ballpark which the team had acquired while it was still in Brooklyn. Taken together, the land and the minor league ballpark were enough to convince the court that Los Angeles met the

Dodgers moved into the private Dodger Stadium, and have played there ever since.[49]

### CONCLUSION

Today, sports team owners expect to have their stadiums paid for through public funds,[50] and it is quite rare for them to use their own funds to build a new stadium.[51] Thus, Walter O'Malley's strug-

---

public purpose requirement. N. SULLIVAN, *supra* note 5, at 173. Professor Sullivan reproduces a copy of the agreement between the Dodgers and the City of Los Angeles towards the end of his book. *Id.* at 220-27. In the years that followed, numerous other courts confronted the same issue that had faced the California Supreme Court. All employed similar reasoning to find that the municipal action was proper. *See, e.g.*, Ginsberg v. City & County of Denver, 164 Colo. 572, 436 P.2d 685 (1968); New Jersey Sports & Exposition Auth. v. McCrane, 119 N.J. Super. 457, 292 A.2d 580 (Super. Ct. Law Div. 1971); Conrad v. City of Pittsburgh, 421 Pa. 492, 218 A.2d 906 (1966); Martin v. City of Philadelphia, 420 Pa. 14, 215 A.2d 894 (1966).

49   N. SULLIVAN, *supra* note 5, at 190-211.

50   *Id.* at 213-15. *See generally* Wilkerson, *What Taxpayers and Their Teams Do for Each Other*, N.Y. Times, July 24, 1988, at E26, col. 1 (nat'l ed.). *See also supra* note 2. *But see Jersey Officials See Defeat on Stadium Bond Issue*, N.Y. Times, Oct. 30, 1987, at 12, col. 1 (nat'l ed.) (reporting on the failure of a $185 million bond issue designed to lure a professional baseball team to the Meadowlands). Without a doubt, however, the master of stadium shopping is Al Davis, the owner of the National Football League Raiders. Davis has raised shopping for stadium concessions and improvements from local municipalities to an art form. After he became dissatisfied with the Oakland Coliseum, he moved his team to Los Angeles in the early 1980's. This move led to the filing of numerous lawsuits. *See* Koppett, *Raider Colors Match Judges' Robes*, N.Y. Times, July 13, 1988, at 49, col. 1; *see also* Comment, *City of Oakland v. Oakland Raiders: Defining the Parameters of Limitless Power*, 1983 UTAH L. REV. 397; Comment, *Taking the Oakland Raiders: A Theoretical Reconsideration of the Concepts of Public Use and Just Compensation*, 32 EMORY L.J. 857 (1983); Note, *Public Use in Eminent Domain: Are There Limits After Oakland Raiders and Poletown?*, 20 CAL. W.L. REV. 82 (1983); Note, *Eminent Domain Exercise—Stare Decisis or a Warning: City of Oakland v. Oakland Raiders*, 4 PACE L. REV. 169 (1983); Note, *Eminent Domain and the Commerce Clause Defense: City of Oakland v. Oakland Raiders*, 41 U. MIAMI L. REV. 1184 (1987). When Irwindale, a nearby suburb, subsequently made a better offer in August 1987, Davis announced that he again would move the team. *See* Cummings, *From Rocks to Riches: Tiny Suburb That Landed a Pro Team*, N.Y. Times, Sept. 12, 1987, at 6, col. 1. Since then, however, Irwindale has expressed doubt over its ability to finance the promised stadium. *See Raider Stadium Facing Problems*, N.Y. Times, May 28, 1988, at 32, col. 1. Davis, however, already has received a non-refundable advance of $10 million from Irwindale. *Raider Move is Set Back*, N.Y. Times, Sept. 18, 1987, at 50, col. 1. Moreover, there have been reports that Davis has been negotiating with Oakland officials to return the team to the Oakland Coliseum. *See* Heisler & Reich, *Oakland Says it Awaits Raiders—Irwindale Failure*, L.A. Times, May 19, 1989, pt. 2, at 3, col. 1.

51   A notable exception is Joe Robbie, the owner of the National Football League Miami Dolphins. Turning his back on Miami after years of pleading with it to repair the aging, decaying Orange Bowl, Robbie built a new stadium by raising more than $100 million in private funds. In doing so, however, Robbie encountered problems similar to those faced by O'Malley:

> On March 5, 1984, he announced plans to build a stadium in time for the 1987 season, when he would no longer be bound by his Orange Bowl lease. He said that after 1986, the Dolphins would never play another game in the city-owned stadium, which was built in 1937 by the Works Project Administration.

gle to build a new stadium using his own money is in many ways now nothing more than a quaint idea of a bygone era. Nevertheless, there is an important lesson for lawyers to learn in the decision of the Brooklyn Dodgers to move West. Had the bar challenged Robert Moses' reading of the Housing Act of 1949, or had Peter Brown made his alternative suggestion sooner, the Dodgers probably would still be playing in Brooklyn. The fact that they are not is living testimony to a collective failure not of law, but of lawyers.[52]

---

. . . Robbie had to hock the Dolphins, right down to their last jersey and pair of cleats, to keep construction going, . . . .

Robbie leases the property from Dade County for $1 a year on a 99-year lease. The site was donated to the county by the property owners, Lawrence and Emil Morton of Miami, with an understanding that it would be used as a stadium site. The Mortons still own 270 acres adjacent to the stadium and plan to develop the land with hotels, restaurants, offices, shops and condominiums.

The plan did not please everyone, however. As was Walter O'Malley's takeover of Chavez Ravine for the Dodgers in 1958, Robbie's was met with resistance by residents of neighboring tracts.

Glick, *Miracle of Miami: They Said Joe Robbie Could Not Do It, But his Stadium is Proof he Could—and Did*, L.A. Times, Aug. 16, 1987, pt. 3, at 3, col. 2.

[52] Following the defection of the Dodgers, the New York bar, led by William A. Shea, a partner in a Manhatten law firm, redeemed itself to an extent by persuading the National League to award New York City an expansion team. Dubbed the New York Mets, the team quickly was installed in a city-built stadium in Flushing Meadows named Shea Stadium. N. SULLIVAN, *supra* note 5, at 119.

# PART 5

## INTELLECTUAL PROPERTY: IMAGES OF BASEBALL

Most fans know by heart the mantra chanted at least once during any baseball game on television or radio. It goes something like this: "This broadcast is the property of Major League Baseball and the X Baseball Club and is being presented for the private noncommercial use of our audience only. Any reproduction, re-transmission, or other use of this broadcast without the express written consent of Major League Baseball and the X Baseball Club is strictly prohibited." This carefully crafted phrase is but part of the overall attempt to protect the valuable intellectual property rights associated with major league baseball. Major league base-ball owns some of the most valuable trademarks and copyrights in the entertainment industry. Without the exploitation of such rights, no team would be profitable in relying on ticket revenues alone. The broadcast rights alone supported the massive increase in player salaries in the 1980s while still permitting substantial profits, at least for the teams in larger media markets. The decrease in the value of such broadcasting rights in the 1990s has been an equally significant factor pushing owners toward realign-ment, more playoff games, revenue sharing, and seeking a salary cap from the players association.

Broadcast rights are only one of the lucrative revenue streams not directly related to the playing of the game on the field that are exploited by major league baseball. Probably the most important decision by the Colorado Rockies and the Florida Marlins was the design of the team logos, uniforms, and caps which were available for sale long before either team played its first game. The licensing of merchandise for all teams is big business and must be zealously guarded through legal means against infringers and outright counterfeiters. In addition to the current logos and designs, major league baseball has fed the insatiable hunger of collectors by producing reproductions of historical caps and uniforms and other paraphernalia for existing teams and long-dead franchises.

Players participate in these revenue streams both indirectly and directly. Players indirectly benefit through the growth of salaries and bonuses. Players benefit more directly through licensing of their likeness and celebrity both during their career and long afterwards. Current players can add to their salaries through fees from the production of baseball cards, a booming and lucrative market made possible by the end of the former exclusive arrangement between Topps and major league baseball. Other revenue streams for players include sporting goods companies, shoe endorsements, television and radio commercials, celebrity restaurants, and part-time or full-time careers in sports broadcasting. All of these opportunities have great value because of the protections of the intellectual property laws. Even the relatively new phenomenon of the routine commercial sale of autographs and other signed merchandise may qualify for common law protection against passing off and other unfair trade practices designed to infringe the image of the athlete. Most of these income sources may be more important than the player's salary, especially for those star players who retired prior to the era of millionaire reserve infielders. Only empirical research will reveal whether more people know Joe DiMaggio as the "Yankee Clipper" or as the spokesperson for Mr. Coffee. Undoubtedly, he was better paid for the commercials.

We present for you three items regarding this critical connection between the worlds of law and baseball. We can assure you that each piece is presented with the express written consent of the authors or copyright owners. Any unauthorized reproduction is strictly prohibited.

# Indiana Law Journal

*Vol. 59, No. 2*
*1984*

## Sports Broadcasting and the Law†

ROBERT ALAN GARRETT*
PHILIP R. HOCHBERG**

Nearly forty-five years ago, on May 17, 1939, the Columbia and Princeton baseball teams squared off to battle for fourth place in the Ivy League. The game would have been as unremarkable as the issue it decided,[1] but for the fact that it became the first sports event ever televised in America. By today's standards, the telecast was of exceptionally poor quality. The celebrated Bill Stern, who announced the telecast, reportedly "prayed for all the batters to strike out" because that "was the one thing [he] knew the camera could record."[2] Even less clear than the picture itself was the future that lay ahead for televised sports. Orrin E. Dunlap, Jr., who did *The New York Times'* coverage of radio in those days, perhaps best expressed the skeptical view:

> [S]eeing baseball by television is too confining . . . . To see the fresh green of the field as The Mighty Casey advances to the bat, and the dust fly as he defiantly digs in, is a thrill to the eye that cannot be electrified and flashed through space . . . . What would Christy Mathewson, Smokey

---

* B.A. 1970, J.D. 1973, Northwestern University. Mr. Garrett is a partner in the law firm of Arnold & Porter, Washington, D.C., which represents Major League Baseball.

** B.A. 1961, Syracuse University; LL.B. 1965, George Washington University; M.A. 1974, American University. Mr. Hochberg is a partner in the law firm of Baraff, Koerner, Olender and Hochberg, Washington, D.C., which represents the National Basketball Association, National Hockey League, North American Soccer League, Major Indoor Soccer League, and College Football Association.

The authors have been involved directly in many of the matters which are discussed in the Article. The views expressed in the Article are those of the authors alone—although they may have been influenced somewhat by the authors' membership in the Emil Verban Memorial Society, a group of long-suffering Chicago Cubs fans dedicated to the principles of patience, humility and everlasting hope, and proud of the fact that their team has not lost a World Series in nearly forty years. This Article was prepared for the Center for Law and Sports, Indiana University School of Law, Bloomington, Indiana. The research in this Article is current as of April 1, 1984.

1. Diehard Princeton fans may recall that the Tigers won, in extra innings, by the lackluster score of 2-1.

2. Quoted in W. JOHNSON, SUPER SPECTATOR AND THE ELECTRIC LILLIPUTIANS 36 (1971).

Joe Wood, Home Run Baker, Eddie Collins, Frank Chance, Tris Speaker, Ty Cobb, Rube Marquard and those old-timers think of such a turn of affairs—*baseball from a sofa*! Television is too safe. There is no ducking the foul ball . . . .[3]

However safe and confining, "sports from a sofa" has now become entrenched in the American way of life. Billions of dollars have been invested with the conviction that people not only will sit at home to watch sports on television; they will even *pay* to do so. As a consequence, the economic well-being of the sports industry has become inextricably intertwined with television. In the words of former Baseball Commissioner Ford Frick "[T]he advent of television [has] really turned the economics of the game topsy-turvy."[4]

Often overlooked is the role that the law has played in this process. Quite simply, there would be no broadcast revenues if the law had not recognized certain property rights in the accounts and descriptions of sports events; the size of these revenues is itself a function of the way in which the law has defined and restricted such property rights. As this Article will illustrate, the relationship between sports and television has been, and will continue to be, defined in large measure by a multitude of judicial, legislative and administrative pronouncements.[5]

---

3. *Id.* at 39.

4. F. Frick, Games, Asterisks and People 110 (1973).

5. This Article is not limited to questions arising under the normal patterns of television distribution which the sports industry has employed for decades—that is, the sale of rights to local over-the-air television stations and to conventional broadcast networks. The evolution in communications technology during the late 1970's and early 1980's has spawned many of the issues addressed in this article. Some of the forms of distribution used in recent years and examples of these include—

Nationwide distribution of local television stations through cable television distant signal importation (*e.g.*, Atlanta Braves on the "superstation" WTBS);

Basic local cable service, provided at no additional charge to cable subscribers, primarily as an inducement to subscribe (*e.g.*, Buffalo Sabres on International Cable);

Basic national cable service, provided at little or no additional charge to cable subscribers (*e.g.*, the National Hockey League on USA Network);

Per-channel pay cable service with flat rate payment per month (*e.g.*, Philadelphia Phillies, Flyers, and 76ers on PRISM);

Per-program pay cable service with separate charge per event (*e.g.*, Leonard-Hearns fight);

Over-the-air pay television (Subscription Television or STV) package with flat rate per month requiring special television set attachment (*e.g.*, SportsVision in Chicago) (*see* Over-the-Air Subscription Television Operations, 47 C.F.R. §§ 73.641-.644 (1982));

Multipoint Distribution Service (MDS) with flat rate per month requiring special antenna (*e.g.*, Phoenix Suns) (*see* Multipoint Distribution Service, 47 C.F.R. §§ 21.900-.908 (1982));

Closed circuit distribution for arenas and theatres (*e.g.*, Portland Trailblazers);

Direct Broadcast Satellite-to-home (DBS), providing five program services for a flat monthly charge, including NCAA events on Entertainment and Sports Programming Network (ESPN) (*see* Docket Report and Order in Gen. Docket No. 80-603, 90 F.C.C.2d 676 (1982)).

Still other forms of distribution which may be in the offing include: Low Power Television (*see*

## I.  Establishing The Property Right

The law of sports broadcasting had its origin some five years before the Princeton-Columbia matchup when a Mr. A.E. Newton, who operated radio station WOCL from the basement of his Jamestown, New York home, decided to go into the sports broadcasting business. Since 1921, Major League Baseball had entered into contracts authorizing the broadcast of World Series games by various radio stations. Newton, however, conceived of a way to broadcast the 1934 World Series between the Cardinals and Tigers without negotiating (*i.e.*, paying) for the right to do so. He simply provided his audience with "running accounts" of the games based upon information that he had received while listening to authorized radio broadcasts.

Newton's "play-by-play" subsequently formed the basis of a challenge to his license renewal before the Federal Communications Commission (FCC). The claim was that such conduct violated section 325(a) of the Communications Act of 1934, which prohibits one station from rebroadcasting, without consent, another station's programming.[6] The FCC considered Newton's conduct to be "inconsistent with fair dealing," "dishonest in nature," "unfair utilization of the results of another's labor," "deceptive to the public upon the whole, and contrary to the interests thereof"—but not violative of section 325.[7] Emphasizing that he had confined his sportscasting career to the 1934 World Series, the Commission renewed Newton's license.[8]

---

Report and Order in BC Docket No. 78-253, 47 Fed. Reg. 21,468 (1982), *as corrected,* 47 Fed. Reg. 30,495 (1982) (to be codified at 47 C.F.R. pts 73, 74, 76 & 78)), and Multi-Channel MDS (*see* Report and Order in Gen. Docket No. 80-112, 48 Fed. Reg. 33,873 (1983) (to be codified at 47 C.F.R. pts 2, 21 & 74)). For an examination of some of these methods of transmission, see Hochberg, *The Four Horsemen Ride Again: Cable Communications and Collegiate Athletics,* 5 J.C. & U.L. 43 (1977).

6. 47 U.S.C. § 325(a) (1976) provides in part: "[N]or shall any broadcasting station rebroadcast the program or any part thereof of another broadcasting station without the express authority of the originating station."

7. *In re* A.E. Newton, 2 F.C.C. 281, 284 (1936).

8. *Id.* at 285. The FCC dealt with a case similar to Newton's nearly twenty years later when the New York Yankees, Brooklyn Dodgers, and St. Louis Cardinals challenged the license renewal of radio station KELP (El Paso, Texas). *In re* Trinity Broadcasting Corp., 18 F.C.C. 501 (1954). Station KELP broadcast "recreations" of the games of these clubs, without their consent, based upon information received from authorized broadcasts. (*See infra* note 14.) The clubs argued that KELP's actions involved an unlawful misappropriation of private property rights, as well as violations of § 303 of the Communications Act (prohibiting "false or deceptive" transmissions) and § 325(a). 18 F.C.C. at 501. The Commission observed that a number of courts had held conduct such as KELP's to be unlawful. *Id.* at 503. However, one court in Texas, where KELP was located, had ruled to the contrary. (*See infra* note 17.) Noting that there may "well be difference of opinion with respect to the correctness of the legal doctrine adopted by the [Texas] court," the FCC nevertheless dismissed the challenge to KELP's license renewal. 18 F.C.C. at 503.

In a 1953 report the Senate Commerce Committee suggested that the FCC should "take into consideration" any unauthorized sports broadcasts when deciding whether to renew a station's license. S. Rep. No. 387, 83d Cong., 1st Sess. 10-12 (1953). The Committee further noted that these broadcasts are typically "inaccurate and misleading," "deceptive of the public" and

Newton's was the first in a series of reported decisions involving the right of sports clubs to control the dissemination of the accounts of their games. The forum, however, soon shifted from the FCC to the state and federal courts, where the sports clubs were more effective than they had been before the Commission. Those who sought to follow in Newton's footsteps argued that the accounts of sports events constituted news in the public domain and that any person had the right to disseminate the news. The courts took a different view.

The leading case is *Pittsburgh Athletic Co. v. KQV Broadcasting Co.*[9] The defendant in that case was a Pittsburgh radio station, KQV, which had broadcast play-by-play descriptions of the Pirates' baseball games without the consent of the Pirates. The KQV announcers obtained their information about the games from station employees positioned at vantage points outside the Pirates' Forbes Field. The Pirates, who had licensed their radio rights to NBC, sued to enjoin the unauthorized KQV broadcasts.

The 1938 Pirates had the rare distinction of losing the National League pennant to the Chicago Cubs.[10] But they were victorious against station KQV. The court enjoined KQV's activities, concluding that the ball club "by reason of its creation of the game, its control of the park, and its restriction of the dissemination of news therefrom, has a property right in such news, and the right to control the use thereof for a reasonable time following the games."[11] The court held that KQV had misappropriated the property rights of the Pirates in the "news, reports, descriptions or accounts" of the Pirates' games; that such misappropriation resulted in KQV's "unjust enrichment" to the detriment of the Pirates; and that KQV's actions constituted "unfair competition," a "fraud on the public" and a violation of unspecified provisions of the Communications Act.[12]

A similar result obtained some seventeen years later in *National Exhibition*

---

"injurious to the property rights of the baseball clubs and the authorized broadcasters of their games." *Id.* at 10. According to the Committee:

> The plays which make up baseball games and the sequence of those plays constitute original and unique performances which are of great interest to the public and of commercial value to the clubs as the creators and exhibitors of the games and as licensors of rights to broadcast and telecast descriptions and reproductions of the games. The clubs employ extensive capital, expense and labor in exhibiting the games and are entitled to protection against misappropriation by others of the fruits of the clubs' efforts. Your committee understands that these property rights are supported by well-established principles of law, including principles of common law copyright and the principles of equitable protection against unfair competition.

*Id.* at 11.

9. 24 F. Supp. 490 (W.D. Pa. 1938).

10. Only once in the succeeding forty-five years could any team say it lost the pennant to the Cubs.

It might be noted that the Cubs went on to lose four straight to the Yankees in the 1938 World Series. As Jim Enright observes in his book *The Chicago Cubs*: "One miracle was all they had in them in 1938."

11. 24 F. Supp. at 492.

12. *Id.* at 494.

*Co. v. Fass*.[13] The defendant in that case, an "independent newsgatherer" named Martin Fass, listened to authorized radio and television broadcasts of the 1953 and 1954 New York Giants. Without securing the Giants' consent, Fass simultaneously teletyped reports of their games to radio stations across the country for immediate rebroadcast.[14] The Giants made it to the World Series in 1954; Fass did not. Some three months before Willie Mays turned his back on the celebrated Vic Wertz fly ball, the court enjoined Fass' activities and awarded the Giants damages, concluding:

> Plaintiff is the owner of the professional baseball exhibitions which it produces; and its property rights, as owner of such exhibitions, include the proprietary right to sell to others, who desire to purchase and to whom plaintiff desires to sell, licenses or rights under which the purchasers are authorized to [broadcast the games] in such geographical area or areas as may be agreed upon between plaintiff and such purchasers. . . .
> . . . In creating the games, the competing clubs not only create an exhibition for the spectators at the game but also create, as the game unfolds, a drama consisting of the sequence of plays, which is valuable program material for radio and television stations and for which licensees have paid and are paying plaintiff substantial sums.[15]

Other courts likewise have protected the sports clubs' property rights in the accounts and descriptions of their games, and have prevented the unauthorized exploitation of these rights.[16] There appear to be only two cases

---

13. 133 N.Y.S.2d 379 (Sup. Ct.) (preliminary injunction), *aff'd without opinion*, 136 N.Y.S.2d 358 (App. Div. 1954), 143 N.Y.S.2d 767 (Sup. Ct. 1955) (final judgment).

14. These stations presented what had been known as "recreations," perhaps the most celebrated of which were those done by Gordon McLendon:

> Saving the expense of pickups from baseball parks, entrepreneur Gordon McLendon staged hair-raising play-by-play descriptions in a Dallas studio from information on a news-agency ticker while an engineer, like an organist selecting stops, faded sound-effects records in and out: quiet crowds, restless crowds, hysterical crowds. His selections stimulated the announcer, who invented reasons for any sudden crowd excitement: a fan had made an unbelievable one-hand catch of a foul, or a peanut vender had fallen downstairs. McLendon was scholarly too: he had tape recordings of "The Star-Spangled Banner" as played at each ball park. The McLendon broadcasts were often more exciting than the ball games.

2 E. BARNOUW, THE GOLDEN WEB: A HISTORY OF BROADCASTING IN THE UNITED STATES·289 (1968).

15. 143 N.Y.S.2d at 770.

16. *E.g.*, Madison Square Garden Corp. v. Universal Pictures Co., 255 A.D. 459, 7 N.Y.S.2d 845 (N.Y. App. Div. 1938) (owner of New York Rangers stated a cause of action against defendants who had incorporated film of the Rangers' hockey game in a motion picture; defendants had been authorized to use the film in newsreels only); Mutual Broadcasting Sys., Inc. v. Muzak Corp., 177 Misc. 489, 30 N.Y.S.2d 419 (1941) (defendant enjoined from retransmitting to paying customers plaintiff's broadcasts of the 1941 World Series); Twentieth Century Sporting Club, Inc. v. Transradio Press Serv., Inc., 165 Misc. 71, 300 N.Y.S. 159 (1937) (defendant enjoined from supplying radio station with "up to the minute" "ringside descriptions" of the Louis-Farr fight in Yankee Stadium); Southwestern Broadcasting Co. v. Oil Center Broadcasting Co., 210 S.W.2d 230 (Tex. Civ. App. 1947) (defendant enjoined from broadcasting high school football games, the broadcast rights to which had been licensed to the plaintiff). *See also* Johnson-Kennedy Radio Corp. v. Chicago Bears Football Club, Inc., 97 F.2d 223 (7th Cir. 1938) (radio station enjoined from broadcasting a professional football game, the rights to which had previously been granted to another station); Liberty Broadcasting Sys. v. National League Club of Boston, Inc., 1952 Trade Cas. (CCH) ¶ 67,278 (N.D. Ill. 1952) (concluding that each baseball club has

in which courts refused to do so[17]—although it is unlikely that either of these decisions would be followed today.[18]

The sports property right concept was strengthened by the Supreme Court in *Zacchini v. Scripps-Howard Broadcasting Co.*[19] There, an Ohio television station broadcast a fifteen-second tape of the celebrated "Flying" Zacchini's "human cannonball" performance without obtaining his consent. In response to Zacchini's claim that the station had unlawfully misappropriated his professional property, the station responded that its broadcast was protected free speech. A five to four majority of the United States Supreme Court sided with the Flying Zacchini. Citing the *Pittsburgh Athletic* decision and other authority, the Court concluded:

> Wherever the line in particular situations is to be drawn between media reports that are protected and those that are not, we are quite sure that the First and Fourteenth Amendments do not immunize the media when they broadcast a performer's entire act without his consent. *The Constitution no more prevents a State from requiring respondent to compensate petitioner for broadcasting his act on television than it would privilege respondent to film and broadcast* a copyrighted dramatic work without liability to the copyright owner . . . a *prize fight . . . or a baseball game*, where the promoters or the participants had other plans for publicizing the event.[20]

---

a property right in its games and the "news, reports, descriptions and accounts thereof," and the "sole right" to disseminate these accounts).

17. Loeb v. Turner, 257 S.W.2d 800 (Tex. Civ. App. 1953); National Exhibition Co. v. Teleflash, Inc., 24 F. Supp. 488 (S.D.N.Y. 1936).

18. The court in *Pittsburgh Athletic* specifically rejected the *Teleflash* decision, characterizing it as an "incorrect" interpretation of the law. 24 F. Supp. at 493. Moreover, on several subsequent occasions, the New York state courts rendered decisions at odds with *Teleflash*. *See* authority cited *supra* note 16. The decision in *Loeb v. Turner* appears to be inconsistent with a sister court's decision in Southwestern Broadcasting Co. v. Oil Center Broadcasting Co., 210 S.W.2d 230, which was not even mentioned in *Loeb v. Turner*.

In any event, the courts in *Teleflash* and *Loeb v. Turner* suggest that one could prevent persons located *within* the stadium from disseminating accounts of the sports event by conditioning admittance on this ground. *See* 24 F. Supp. at 488-89; 257 S.W.2d at 802. Many tickets and Working Press Passes have such a condition:

> This pass is issued subject to the condition and by use of this pass each person admitted hereunder agrees that he will not transmit or aid in transmitting any report, description, account or reproduction of the baseball game, except . . . to the newspaper or press association represented by him . . . .

1983 Baltimore Orioles Working Press Pass.

> This working credential is issued to an organization for the sole purpose of providing stadium access to an accredited individual who has a legitimate working function (media or game service) in connection with this game. It is non-transferable. Any unauthorized use of this credential subjects the bearer to ejection from the stadium and prosecution for criminal trespass.

1983 Washington Redskin Working Press Credentials Conditions.

19. 433 U.S. 562 (1977). *See generally* Samuelson, *Reviving Zacchini: Analyzing First Amendment Defenses in Right of Publicity and Copyright Cases,* 57 TULANE L. REV. 836 (1983).

20. 433 U.S. at 574-75 (emphasis added) (citations omitted). *See also* Post Newsweek Stations-Conn., Inc. v. Travelers Ins. Co., 510 F. Supp. 81 (D. Conn. 1981), where the court ruled that a television station does not have "a constitutional right of special access" to a skating competition being held in a civic arena. The court upheld the defendants' right to deny access to the station unless the station agreed not to broadcast footage of the event before the ABC television

Congress added a new dimension to the sports property right concept when it enacted the Copyright Act of 1976.[21] At the urging of the professional sports leagues,[22] Congress extended federal copyright protection to live sports broadcasts, thereby vesting the owners of these telecasts with the exclusive right to "perform" them "publicly."[23] To be eligible for copyright protection, the broadcast must be "fixed" (*i.e.*, recorded) simultaneously with its transmission.[24] The remedies afforded by the Copyright Act are particularly valuable because they permit the copyright owner to recover statutory damages of between $250 and $50,000 for each act of infringement without regard to actual damages suffered.[25]

---

network (to whom defendants had licensed the television rights) concluded its coverage. The court noted:

> It is clear that the [International Skating Union] has a legitimate commercial stake in this event, and they, like *Zacchini*, are entitled to contract regarding the distribution of this entertainment product. . . . It is established . . . that the press has no constitutional right of special access to an event such as these skating championships.
>
> . . . .
>
> . . . [T]he entertainment here is the exposition of an athletic exercise. As such, it is on the periphery of protected speech (for purposes of a balancing of conflicting interests), as opposed, for example, to political speech, which is at the core of first amendment protection.

510 F. Supp. at 84-85, 86.

A similar case arose again in mid-1982, when Home Box Office and ABC had contracted to show delayed the Holmes-Cooney heavyweight championship fight in its entirety, but NBC News showed excerpts taken from the pay-television transmission. *See infra* note 112.

*See also* USA Today, Feb. 17, 1984, at 1-D (ABC, the purchaser of broadcast rights to the 1984 Winter Olympics, complained about NBC's unauthorized broadcast of highlights of an award ceremony and threatened to bar NBC from access to certain highlight film).

21. 17 U.S.C. §§ 101-801 (Supp. V 1982).

22. The sports leagues originally sought federal copyright protection as a means of controlling the unauthorized retransmission of their broadcasts by cable television systems. *See, e.g., Hearings on S. 1006 Before the Subcomm. on Patents, Trademarks and Copyrights of the Senate Comm. on the Judiciary*, 89th Cong., 2d Sess. 162-63 (1965); *Hearings on H.R. 4347 Before Subcomm. No. 3 of the House Comm. on the Judiciary*, 89th Cong. 1st Sess. 1825-26, 1842-43, 1848 (1965) [hereinafter cited as *1965 House Hearings*]; *Hearings on S. 1006 Before the Subcomm. on Patents, Trademarks, and Copyrights of the Senate Comm. on the Judiciary*, 89th Cong., 2d Sess. 6 (1966) (statement of Abraham Kaminstein, Register of Copyrights).

23. 17 U.S.C. § 106(4) (Supp. V 1982).

24. H.R. REP. No. 1476, 94th Cong., 2d Sess. 52-53, *reprinted in* 1976 U.S. CODE CONG. & AD. NEWS 5659, 5665-67 [hereinafter cited as H.R. REP. No. 94-1476]. *See* 43 Fed. Reg. 40,225 (1978) (Copyright Royalty Tribunal noted that the baseball recording procedures are "suitable" to "establish proof of fixation.").

Once fixed, the live sports telecast qualifies for copyright protection as a "motion picture" which is a form of "audiovisual works." *See* 17 U.S.C. § 101 (definitions of "motion picture" and "audiovisual works"); 17 U.S.C. § 102(a)(6) (including "motion pictures and other audiovisual works" among the forms of copyrightable subject matter); 37 C.F.R. § 202.20(c)(2)(ii) & 202.21(g) (1983) (Copyright Office regulation concerning registration of copyrighted "television transmission programs").

It has been noted that many sports fans will be shocked to learn that since 1976 virtually every televised sports event has been "fixed." *See* Hochberg, *Second and Goal to Go: The Legislative Attack in the 92d Congress on Sports Broadcasting Practices*, 18 N.Y.L.F. 841, 863 n.97 (1973).

25. 17 U.S.C. § 504(c) (Supp. V 1982). Such damages, however, may not be available unless the sports club complies with the notice and registration provisions of 17 U.S.C. § 411(b) (1982). *See* 17 U.S.C. § 412; Pacific & S., Inc. v. Duncan, No. C81-1106 (N.D. Ga. filed Oct. 13, 1983), discussed *infra* note 111.

MAJOR LEAGUE BASEBALL PROP-
ERTIES, INC. and Los Angeles
Dodgers, Inc., Plaintiffs,

v.

SED NON OLET DENARIUS, LTD., d/b/a
The Brooklyn Dodger Sports Bar & Restaurant, Bums, Inc., d/b/a The Brooklyn
Dodger, David Senatore, Richard Picardi
and Kevin Boyle, Defendants.

No. 90 CIV 2170 (CBM).

United States District Court,
S.D. New York.

April 6, 1993.

OPINION

MOTLEY, District Judge.

FINDINGS OF FACT AND
CONCLUSIONS OF
LAW

I.  INTRODUCTION

Plaintiffs, Major League Baseball Properties, Inc. ("Properties") and Los Angeles
Dodgers, Inc. ("Los Angeles"), allege in their
Amended Complaint[1] that the conduct of the
three corporate defendants, Sed Non Olet
Denarius, Ltd., d/b/a The Brooklyn Dodger
Sports Bar and Restaurant ("SNOD"),
BUMS, Inc., d/b/a The Brooklyn Dodger
Sports Bar and Restaurant ("BUMS"), and
9506, Inc., d/b/a The Brooklyn Dodger
("9506") (hereinafter collectively "The Brooklyn Dodger"), and the conduct of the three
individual defendants, David Senatore, Richard Picardi and Kevin Boyle, constitute: a)
an infringement upon the rights of plaintiffs'
trademarks in violation of 15 U.S.C. §§ 1114
and 1117;  b) a wrongful appropriation of
plaintiffs' trademarks in violation of 15
U.S.C. § 1125 c) a violation of plaintiffs' common law trademark and property rights; d) a
violation of plaintiffs' rights under the New
York General Business Law § 368–d;  e) unfair competition;  and f) the intentional use
by defendants of a counterfeit mark in violation of 15 U.S.C. § 1117(b).

Each of these six causes of action is alleged to flow from defendants' use of the
words "The Brooklyn Dodger" as the name
and servicemark of the restaurants which
defendants have operated in Brooklyn, New
York, beginning in March 1988.  Plaintiffs
initially sought permanent injunctive relief,
an accounting of profits, the destruction of
physical items containing the allegedly infringing marks, monetary damages, and attorneys' fees.

By their Answer and Amended Answer
defendants denied any infringement of plaintiffs' alleged right to use a "Brooklyn Dodger" trademark.  Defendants also pleaded the
defenses of abandonment by plaintiffs of any

"Brooklyn Dodgers" mark which plaintiffs may have owned at one time, as well as *laches.* The abandonment defense was premised upon the plaintiffs' failure to make any commercial or trademark use of the "Brooklyn Dodgers" name for at least 25 years after Los Angeles left Brooklyn in 1958. The *laches* defense was premised upon the fact that plaintiffs waited for more than a year and a half after learning of defendants' use of the allegedly infringing trademark before advising defendants of any alleged infringement. During this period defendants expended substantial resources and monies in establishing their restaurants in Brooklyn, New York. Defendants further pleaded the defense of unclean hands.

Finally, in their Amended Answer, defendants counterclaimed for the cancellation of various trademark registrations for "Brooklyn Dodgers" filed by plaintiffs after defendants' application to register the "Brooklyn Dodger" servicemark was filed on April 28, 1988.[2] These cancellations are sought on the ground that plaintiffs' registrations: a) falsely and deceptively suggest and imply a connection between plaintiffs and the Borough of Brooklyn which has not existed since 1958; b) inherently and directly misrepresent the origin of plaintiffs' goods and services as Brooklyn, New York when in fact this is untrue, in violation of 15 U.S.C. § 1052; and c) plaintiffs' use of a "Brooklyn Dodgers" mark suggests an association with defendants which does not exist, in violation of 15 U.S.C. § 1125(a).

On July 29, 1991, plaintiffs filed a motion for a preliminary injunction seeking to enjoin the use of the "Dodger" and "Brooklyn Dodger" name and defendants' logo in connection with the Canarsie establishment. (Tr. of 3/31/92 Hearing at 72; Tr. 707)

On March 31, 1992, the Honorable Kimba M. Wood of this court, to whom this case was then assigned, conducted a hearing. The parties submitted memoranda of law and affidavits in connection with the motion for a preliminary injunction. The court granted plaintiffs' motion for a preliminary injunction

and enjoined defendants from using the mark the "Brooklyn Dodger" and the word "Dodger" written in standard athletic script as now used by defendants in connection with their third restaurant. (Tr. of 3/31/92 Hearing 69)

However, the court denied plaintiffs' application for summary judgment. Plaintiffs withdrew all claims for legal damages set forth in paragraph 4 of their Prayer for Relief, leaving only their equitable claims for injunctive relief (Prayer for Relief ¶ 1) and the destruction of all physical objects which make use of the "Brooklyn Dodger" mark (Prayer for Relief ¶ 3) and an accounting on their Lanham Act and common law claims. (*See* correspondence between counsel dated April 14, 16 and 17, 1992) (Tr. 2) Plaintiffs also seek an award of their attorneys' fees under the Lanham Act and common law. Following a preliminary hearing, a bench trial commenced on May 18, 1992 and continued until May 21, 1992. At the close of the trial the court reserved decision on all issues presented and requested that the parties submit proposed Findings of Fact and Conclusions of Law not later than July 17, 1992.

## II.  FINDINGS OF FACTS

After hearing the evidence and weighing the testimony and exhibits received in evidence, as well as the credibility of the witnesses, the court makes the following findings of fact:

### A.  *The Parties*

Plaintiff Properties is a corporation with offices and its principal place of business in New York, New York. It is the official trademark licensing, publishing, and marketing arm of the 26 Major League Baseball Clubs (the "Major League Clubs"). Properties is also charged with the responsibility of protecting the trademarks of these teams. (Trial Transcript "Tr." at 41)

Plaintiff Los Angeles is a corporation with offices and its principal place of business in Los Angeles, California. It is the owner of the Los Angeles Dodgers, a professional

---

**2.** In 1989, after this action had commenced, plaintiffs filed registrations for three different "Brooklyn Dodgers" marks. On July 7, 1992 plaintiffs filed to register a "Brooklyn" mark in athletic script.

baseball team which, since 1958, has played baseball in Los Angeles, California under the name the "Los Angeles Dodgers." (Plaintiffs' Exhibit "PX" 17) Prior to 1958 the same professional baseball team played baseball in Brooklyn, New York and were known as the "Brooklyn Dodgers" or the "Dodgers."

In 1958, the team moved the site of its home games from Brooklyn to Los Angeles. (Tr. 252–53) At that time, the corporation was known as the Brooklyn National League Baseball Club, Inc. which owned the Brooklyn Dodgers or the Dodgers. It pointedly changed its name to Los Angeles Dodgers, Inc. (Tr. 259–60) Since then the team known as the "Los Angeles Dodgers" has never played baseball in Brooklyn, New York. (Tr. 332).

By agreement with the Major League Clubs, Properties has been granted the exclusive right to market, license, publish, publicize, promote nationally, and protect the trademarks owned by the Major League Clubs, including those owned by the Los Angeles Dodgers. (Tr. 41, 52–53, 116–17)

Properties' licensing activities on behalf of the Major League Clubs have evolved and expanded over time. In the early 1980s, the Major League Clubs were responsible for licensing on their own, with some additional baseball-wide licensing provided by Properties. In the mid–1980s, by agreement with the Major League Clubs, all of the retail licensing activities of the Major League Clubs were consolidated within Properties. (Tr. 41–42)

Over 400 licensed manufacturers sell more than 2,500 different Major League Baseball licensed products. (Tr. 57) The range of products includes apparel, such as caps and T-shirts, trading cards, games, electronic items, novelties and accessories, and youth "Little League" merchandise.

In 1986, retail sales of licensed Major League Baseball merchandise were approximately $200 million. (PX 16 at 11) By 1991, retail sales of licensed Major League Baseball merchandise were in excess of $2 billion. (Tr. 55–56) Properties, however, receives only a royalty payment on the wholesale price of these products. (Tr. 55) After trial,

in response to the court's request for information concerning the amount of sales attributable to commercial use of the "Brooklyn Dodgers" mark after 1981, plaintiffs responded that precise figures could not be provided. Specifically, plaintiffs stated:

... Properties' records from the 1980s regrettably do not permit a precise breakdown of sales of goods bearing a specific trademark. As a result, figures representing sales of goods bearing the Dodgers' marks incorporating the word Brooklyn were, in most instances, subsumed within overall sales figures of merchandise bearing the Dodgers' marks, and not separately itemized. Recently, however, we have been accumulating more accurate records regarding sales of goods bearing individual Club trademarks. Based on this information and our general knowledge of our products, it is our best estimate that approximately $9 million worth of goods bearing the Dodgers' marks incorporating the word Brooklyn were sold in 1991.... we have contacted many of Properties' licensees, but unfortunately their records also do not permit us to obtain a more precise determination of annual retail sales during the 1980s of good bearing specifically the mark "Brooklyn Dodgers," separate and apart from retail sales of goods bearing the Dodgers' trademarks as a group.

(*See* Affidavit of Richard E. White, sworn Sept. 11, 1992 at 5–6)

In addition to its licensing and marketing efforts, Properties seeks to prevent infringement of the trademarks of the Major League Clubs. (Tr. 71–72)

Properties seeks to protect the Major League Clubs and retailers from unfair competition by counterfeiters, to ensure that consumers are not confused as to which products are authorized by the Major League Clubs, and to ensure that only safe, quality products reach consumers. (Tr. 73–74)

To enforce the trademark rights of the Major League Clubs, Properties relies on counsel, relies on the Clubs, polices and investigates the market itself, and relies on licensees. (Tr. 75) At times, Properties commences litigation to prevent infringement at substantial expense. (Tr. 75–76)

Defendant SNOD is a corporation organized and existing under the laws of the State of New York and has its office and principal place of business at 7509 Third Avenue, Brooklyn, New York. (Tr. 480) On March 17, 1988 SNOD began doing business as a restaurant under the name "The Brooklyn Dodger Sports Bar and Restaurant." (Tr. 480)

Defendant BUMS was a corporation organized and existing under the laws of the State of New York and had an office and principal place of business at 360 Coney Island Avenue, Brooklyn, New York. On February 6, 1989 BUMS began doing business as a restaurant under the name "The Brooklyn Dodger Sports Bar and Restaurant." (Tr. 646) In November 1990, for reasons wholly unrelated to this litigation, BUMS ceased doing business as "The Brooklyn Dodger Sports Bar and Restaurant."

Defendant 9506 is a corporation organized and existing under the laws of the State of New York and has its office and principal place of business at 9505 Avenue L, Brooklyn, New York. (Tr. 384) On July 1, 1991, to replace the restaurant previously operated by BUMS, 9506 began doing business as a restaurant under the name "The Brooklyn Dodger Sports Bar and Restaurant."

All three corporate defendants, at various times during this litigation, have been engaged in providing restaurant and tavern services to the consuming public in Brooklyn, New York. This is the only business in which the defendants are engaged. (Tr. 383)

Defendant David Senatore is an owner of all three corporate defendants and assisted in forming the businesses. (Tr. 383) Defendant Richard Picardi is a resident of New York, New York, an owner of all three corporate defendants and assisted in forming the businesses. (Tr. 383) Defendant Kevin Boyle is a resident of Brooklyn, New York, an owner of BUMS and 9506 and assisted in forming all three businesses. (Tr. 383) These businesses were to be the livelihood of Senatore, Picardi, and Boyle. (Tr. 521, 623, 706)

B. *The Brooklyn Dodger Restaurants*

In 1987, the individual defendants, together with Brian Boyle, defendant Kevin Boyle's brother, decided to open a restaurant in Brooklyn, New York. (Tr. 483, 516–517, 599–600, 740).

It was the individual defendants' decision that their restaurants would emphasize the multiple themes of fun, sports and Brooklyn. Their intention was to create a nostalgic setting where Brooklynites could relax and reminisce about times gone by. (Tr. 526, 534, 607, 742; DX C)

They initially chose to name their establishment "Ebbets Field" after the former baseball park located in Brooklyn, New York in which a baseball team know as the "Brooklyn Dodgers" played baseball until October, 1957. (Tr. 499, 518, 601, 740–41)

To assure themselves that the use of this name would not conflict with any other person's use of it, the individual defendants commissioned a trademark search for the name "Ebbets Field" in April, 1987. (Tr. 518, 522, 602, 741; DX U) Although this search established that no trademark registration for "Ebbets Field" had been filed, the individual defendants learned that a small restaurant, not unlike the one they hoped to open in Brooklyn, was operating in Hicksville, New York. (Tr. 524, 604–605, 741–64)

In light of this fact, and in an attempt to avoid any possible legal entanglements, the individual defendants chose not to use the name "Ebbets Field" and continued their search for another name. (Tr. 520, 525–26, 561, 607, 646–47, 765)

The individual defendants were aware that there once was a baseball team known as the "Brooklyn Dodgers" which had once played in Brooklyn, New York. Defendants also knew that in 1958 that team left Brooklyn and relocated to Los Angeles, California.

The defendants knew that the departure of the "Brooklyn Dodgers" in 1958 had been accompanied by monumental hard feelings in the Borough of Brooklyn. In fact the relocation was one of the most notorious abandonments in the history of sports. (Tr. 527, 563) At the time defendants selected their logo, they were aware that Los Angeles owned federal trademark registrations for the word "Dodgers." (Tr. 492, 562, 659, 735–36) However, at no time during their consideration of the "Brooklyn Dodger" name did the individual defendants have any reason to believe that "The Brooklyn Dodger" mark was being used by Los Angeles, and certainly not for restaurant or tavern services. (Tr. 526–27) When considering the use of the "Brooklyn Dodger" mark, at no time was there any discussion among the individual defendants and Brian Boyle about trading on the goodwill of Los Angeles in Brooklyn. (Tr. 528) Indeed, non-party witness Brian Boyle, a lifelong Brooklyn resident, testified that, given the acrimonious abandonment of Brooklyn by Los Angeles, the idea of trading on Los Angeles' "goodwill" in Brooklyn is almost "laughable." (Tr. 529)

Nevertheless, acting in good faith, the individual defendants, again desirous of avoiding any legal entanglements, commissioned yet a second trademark search, this one for the name "Brooklyn Dodger" in October, 1987. (Tr. 489, 609–11, 621–22, 744; PX 28) While defendants were aware at the time they selected their logo that Los Angeles owned federal trademark registrations for the word "Dodgers,"[3] their second trademark search established that no registration of any "Brooklyn Dodger" mark had ever been filed. (Tr. 492, 532, 562, 659, 735–36; PX 28)

Accordingly, in October, 1987 the individual defendants formed the corporate defendant SNOD for the purpose of operating a restaurant. SNOD began doing business with the public on March 17, 1988 as "The Brooklyn Dodger Sports Bar and Restaurant." (Tr. 480)

Having invested the time, money, and effort in founding this restaurant and having exercised all reasonable diligence to satisfy

themselves that no one was using a "Brooklyn Dodger" trademark for restaurant and tavern services, and that no one had filed a registration for this trademark for use in any other field, the principals of SNOD sought to protect their interests in their new name. (Tr. 571) Accordingly, on April 28, 1988, an application to register a composite design mark incorporating the term "The Brooklyn Dodger" as a servicemark for restaurant and tavern services was filed with the United States Patent and Trademark Office in Washington, D.C. (Tr. 571, 630, 637, 728; PX 37)

### C. Defendants' Use of the Trademark

In connection with each of defendants' "The Brooklyn Dodger" restaurants, defendants make and/or made prominent use of the "Dodger" name and the "Brooklyn Dodger" name, with the word "Dodger" in stylized script, in the color blue, and in blue script. (PX 40 at 1, 27, 31–37, 41–44)

The defendants' composite design mark consisted of three words: "The," "Brooklyn" and "Dodger" are entwined with one another and with an impish character, designed by Lincoln Peirce, which was styled after the Charles Dickens' character, the "Artful Dodger" from the novel *Oliver Twist*, leaning against the "r" in "Dodger." (Tr. 165; PX 37, 38) Defendants, however, make significant use of their logo without the cartoon character to promote their business, including on merchandise such as apparel, in advertisements, on their letterhead and as part of their servicemark. (PX 32, 33 at 1, 34, 35; DX V; Tr. 674–79)

Defendants' logo is similar to Los Angeles' trademarks. The name "Brooklyn Dodgers" is similar to the name "Brooklyn Dodgers" as

---

3. No fewer than eleven Dodgers' trademarks are presently federally registered with the United States Patent and Trademark Office. (PX 2) While some of these marks were registered within the last three years, the mark Dodgers and the mark Dodgers in the distinctive Dodgers script were initially federally registered as early as 1967. (PX 2 at 23)

   Los Angeles ranks consistently among the top Major League Clubs in terms of retail sales of licensed merchandise bearing their trademarks. In 1991 alone, Properties *estimates* that $100

million worth of goods bearing Los Angeles' trademarks were sold. (Tr. 77–78, 90–91) Defendants' own expert testified that "[w]e don't dispute as far as I understand, certainly I don't dispute that Los Angeles Dodgers is a well-know name. Brooklyn Dodger is probably still to some degree a well-known name." (Tr. 421) Defendants' counsel similarly represented during trial that defendants "certainly have never contested and concede the popularity of the Los Angeles Dodgers baseball team." (Tr. 254)

used by plaintiffs. The script used by the defendants in their logo is similar to that used in Los Angeles' trademarks. The color blue used by defendants is similar to the color blue used by and associated with Los Angeles' sports club in Brooklyn. The swash or tail of the word "Dodger" used by defendants is similar to that used in Los Angeles' trademarks in terms of style and length. (PX 2, 3, 58 at 2, 53 at 69; Tr. 227, 319, 430, 673–74, 682, 759)

The similarity of the parties' marks is further evidenced and emphasized by the fact that defendants use their logo in a sports-oriented atmosphere containing numerous references to baseball and the Brooklyn Dodgers. (*See* PX 40)

The similarity of defendants' logo to Los Angeles' trademarks as used prior to 1958 is further evidenced and emphasized by the fact that defendants, in selecting their name and creating their logo, intended to allude to the Brooklyn Dodgers baseball club and to track the script used by the Brooklyn Dodgers. (Tr. 486–89) Indeed, virtually every witness at trial, including the artist who designed defendants' logo and defendants' expert witness, testified to the similarity of the marks. (Tr. 115, 148–58, 167, 319, 430–31, 486–87, 569, 667–68, 684, 759; PX 53 at 69)

In selecting their logo, defendants intentionally sought to reproduce the Brooklyn Dodgers' trademarks. Indeed, the script for the defendants' logo was intentionally chosen by defendants to track the script used by the Brooklyn Dodgers. As one of defendants' former principals testified:

Q: ... The script for the Dodger restaurant, the Brooklyn Dodger restaurant, the script, that tracks that of the Brooklyn Dodger baseball team, doesn't it?

A: Yes.

Q: And that was intentional, wasn't it?

A: I imagine so ... We wanted a reference to the Brooklyn Dodgers baseball team, yes. (Tr. 569)

Defendants' cartoon character was intentionally selected to allude in part to the famous "Brooklyn Bum" character associated with the Brooklyn Dodgers. (Tr. 487–89; *compare* PX 40 at 6 (The Brooklyn Dodger bum)

*with* PX 11 at 6 (the Brooklyn Dodgers bum)) In selecting their name, logo and cartoon character, defendants were intentionally alluding to the Brooklyn Dodgers. (Tr. 486–89, 569, 688) However, rather than tracing the allegedly infringing mark "Dodger" from any exemplar, Peirce testified quite clearly that "I drew it freehand. I drew it, I outlined it in a pen, a felt-tipped pen, and I think I colored it in." (Tr. 165) Peirce was paid $100.00 for his services. (Tr. 165, 684–86; DX J)

The exteriors of defendants' bars have signs and awnings bearing the Brooklyn Dodger logo. The "Dodger" portion of the sign outside of the Bay Ridge Brooklyn restaurant is in blue script with the "r" in the word "Dodger" continuing in a "swash" or tail which underlines the word "Dodger." (PX 40 at 1; Tr. 384)

Defendants and their employees wear or have worn shirts with defendants' "Brooklyn Dodger" logo or with "Dodger Staff" printed on them, the "Dodger" portion being in stylized script similar to Los Angeles' trademark for the mark Dodgers in cursive script. Defendants had these shirts designed and manufactured for their restaurants. (PX 31, 53 at 87, 54 at 94; Tr. 384–85) Defendants' sell and have sold or distributed apparel, including T-shirts and caps, bearing the name "Brooklyn Dodger." (PX 40 at 9; Tr. 386) Defendants have also sold or given to patrons bumper stickers and gift certificates bearing the "Brooklyn Dodger" logo. (Tr. 387)

Defendants have used the word "Dodger" alone without the word "Brooklyn" on merchandise, such as apparel bearing the logo "Dodger Staff," and on food products to promote their business, such as "Dodger Blue" Cheese, "Deep Dish Dodger" pizza, "Dodger Seafood Chowder," ribs with "Dodger Sauce," "Dodger Pee–Wee" pasta, and "The Duke" and "The Furillo" hamburgers (references to former Dodgers Pee Wee Reese, Duke Snider, and Carl Furillo). (PX 14, 31, 53 at 87, 54 at 94; Tr. 311, 385, 482, 654) Defendants also sell food products referring to the "bum" character associated with the Brooklyn Dodgers, such as "Bum's House Salad." (PX 14)

There is a replica of a Brooklyn Dodgers jersey and cap displayed inside defendants' restaurant. (PX 40 at 4) A baseball bat used by Brooklyn Dodgers player Jackie Robinson and baseballs autographed by Brooklyn Dodgers players are also displayed in defendants' restaurant. (PX 40 at 5; Tr. 386) A wall-sized mural of Ebbets Field, the Brooklyn ballpark of the Brooklyn Dodgers, dominates one wall in defendants' restaurant. (PX 40 at 5; Tr. 386) Photographs of Los Angeles and Brooklyn Dodgers players and newspaper articles referring to the Brooklyn Dodgers are displayed throughout defendants' restaurant. (PX 40) Defendants decorate their restaurant with cartoons depicting the "bum" character associated with the Brooklyn Dodgers. (PX 40 at 4, 6)

Defendants' menus and placemats reference the names of Brooklyn Dodgers players and the word "Dodger." (PX 14; Tr. 311, 385, 482, 654) Defendants have disseminated to the public corporate checks identifying the drawer as "The Brooklyn Dodgers" (with the "s"). (PX 45 at 4; Tr. 387, 389, 652-53)

Defendants have caused to be published a newspaper advertisement referring to their establishments as "The Brooklyn Dodgers" (with the "s"). (PX 34)

In February 1989, the individual defendants, through a second corporate defendant, BUMS, Inc., opened a second "The Brooklyn Dodger Sports Bar and Restaurant" on Coney Island Avenue, not far from defendants' initial establishment. The same logo and servicemark were used with respect to this restaurant.[4]

### D. *Plaintiffs' Use of the Trademark*

Upon relocating its franchise to Los Angeles, California, plaintiff Los Angeles changed its corporate name from the "Brooklyn National Baseball Club, Inc." to "Los Angeles Dodgers, Inc." and began playing baseball under the same name. Of the 26 baseball

teams currently playing baseball, no team plays under the name the "Brooklyn Dodgers." The only Dodger team currently playing baseball is the "Los Angeles Dodgers" (PX 17) which is the name the team has played under since its departure from Brooklyn in 1958. (Tr. 563)

Plaintiffs' use of the "Brooklyn Dodgers" mark was based upon its physical location, until October 1957, in Brooklyn, New York. However, in 1959, Los Angeles made prominent commercial use and reference to their Brooklyn heritage and trademarks in connection with the promotion of Roy Campanella Night, honoring the former Brooklyn Dodgers player and present employee. (Tr. 94-96, 266-67; PX 1 at 2, 22) Los Angeles made prominent use of their trademarks incorporating the word "Brooklyn" at their annual oldtimers games. (PX 1 at 37, 40; Tr. 270) Oldtimers games are commercial baseball exhibitions at which former players are honored and perform so that older fans can recall the past and younger fans can learn about the history of the Club. (Tr. 267-68)

In 1966, Los Angeles sent a cease and desist letter to a member of the Continental Football League to prevent it from infringing Los Angeles' trademark by calling itself the Brooklyn Dodgers. (PX 8; Tr. 287-89)

Since approximately 1967, Los Angeles has licensed manufacturers of hot dogs to sell a hot dog known as the Dodger Dog using the Los Angeles' trademarks (without the "s"). (PX 12, 13; Tr. 305-08) The wrapper for the Dodger Dog bears the word "Dodger" in blue script and is underlined. (PX 13A; Tr. 308) Other uses of the "Dodger" trademark by Los Angeles include the authorization of Aloma, Inc. to use Los Angeles' trademarks in the operation of the Dodger Pines Golf and Country Club, including its restaurant facilities. (PX 10, 11; Tr. 298) Displayed in that restaurant are an array of sports photographs and memorabilia referring to the Los Angeles Dodgers, including their Brooklyn

---

4. In November 1990, for reasons unrelated to this litigation, defendants closed the restaurant operated by BUMS, Inc. In June 1991 the individual defendants, after consulting with trademark counsel (Tr. 660, 729), through defendant 9506, opened a restaurant on Avenue L in Brooklyn under the name "The Brooklyn Dodger

Sports Bar and Restaurant" to replace BUMS' establishment. By Order of the court (Wood, J.) dated March 31, 1992 defendants were preliminarily enjoined from the use of the "Brooklyn Dodger" mark at 9506's restaurant, although not at SNOD's, pending this court's decision.

history, such as a photograph of Ebbets Field and a pennant depicting the "bum" associated with the Brooklyn Dodgers. (Tr. 302–03; PX 11)

Los Angeles authorizes the Dodgertown Conference Center, located at the Los Angeles Dodgers' Spring training facility in Vero Beach, Florida, to use Los Angeles' trademarks to decorate a cafeteria and lounge. (PX 11; Tr. 298) Displayed in those facilities are sports photographs and memorabilia referring to the Los Angeles Dodgers, including their Brooklyn history. (PX 11; Tr. 302–03) Los Angeles has authorized the concessionaire at Dodger Stadium to decorate a restaurant, bar, and meeting facility called The Stadium Club at Dodger Stadium with photographs and/or paintings of Brooklyn Dodgers players. (Tr. 297) A restaurant owned by Bobby Valentine, manager of the Texas Rangers baseball club, is also authorized to use the trademarks of certain Major League Clubs. (Tr. 108)

One document which covered calendar year 1977, established that there was a licensing agreement between Major League Baseball Promotion Company, the predecessor to Properties, and a third party which was licensed to use the names, symbols, and logos of all major league baseball teams including "Los Angeles Dodgers." (DX F) No reference to the "Brooklyn Dodgers" is made in this agreement. However, on April 6, 1981, this licensing agreement was amended to include the name, symbols, logos, etc. of The "Brooklyn Dodgers" as well. (PX 19) Despite voluminous discovery in this case, at trial this document was the earliest licensing use of the "Brooklyn Dodger" name, following Los Angeles' departure from Brooklyn.

While plaintiffs have from time to time made use of their former "Brooklyn Dodgers" mark occasionally and sporadically for historical retrospective such as "Old Timer's Day" festivities, the documentary proof establishes that, following its departure from Brooklyn, Los Angeles' earliest licensing of the "Brooklyn Dodgers" mark occurred on April 6, 1981. (PX 19)

Between 1981 and March 17, 1988, the date of defendants' first use of their mark for restaurant and tavern services, plaintiffs

used their "Brooklyn Dodgers" mark for a variety of purposes. Those uses were almost exclusively in the context of T-shirts, jackets, sportswear, sports paraphernalia and on various types of novelty items (i.e. on drinking mugs, cigarette lighters, pens, Christmas tree ornaments, wristbands, etc.). (PX 2, 16) However, none of these uses competes with defendants' use of the mark for restaurant and tavern services.

In 1981, plaintiffs licensed Eastport manufacturing Co. to merchandise T-shirts bearing, *inter alia*, the Brooklyn Dodger named and logo. (PX 19; Tr. 79–81)

In 1984, Los Angeles agreed to permit Martin Dorf to use photographs of the Brooklyn Dodgers as wall decorations in a restaurant in New Jersey called Burger Boys of Brooklyn. (PX 4; Tr. 78–79)

In 1985, Los Angeles authorized United Airlines to broadcast radio commercials which referred to the Brooklyn Dodgers. (PX 6; Tr. 282)

In 1986, Los Angeles agreed to license the Bank of New England to run an advertisement using the Los Angeles' trademarks incorporating the word "Brooklyn." (PX 5; Tr. 281) In 1986, Los Angeles entered into an agreement with Oxford University Press to permit them to use Los Angeles' trademarks incorporating the word "Brooklyn" in connection with a book. (PX 7; Tr. 283) In 1986, plaintiffs authorized Trench Manufacturing Co. to sell various items of merchandise bearing, *inter alia*, the Los Angeles' trademarks incorporating the word "Brooklyn." (PX 20; Tr. 82)

In March 1987, plaintiffs and Roman Art Embroidery Corp. entered into a licensing agreement to manufacture and sell caps bearing, *inter alia*, Los Angeles' trademarks incorporating the word "Brooklyn." (PX 21; Tr. 83–84)

In approximately 1986, Properties began promoting Los Angeles' trademarks incorporating the word "Brooklyn" together with other "oldtimer" trademarks of Major League Clubs (that is, trademarks that had not been worn on the playing field for at least five years) under the name "the Cooperstown Collection." (Tr. 83–86; *see also* PX 18)

Los Angeles licensed the use of their marks incorporating the word "Brooklyn" in connection with the television series "Brooklyn Bridge." (Tr. 296–97) Los Angeles licensed the Brooklyn Dodgers Hall of Fame, located in Brooklyn, to use Los Angeles' trademarks incorporating the word "Brooklyn." (Tr. 296–97)

Defendants did not select the name "The Brooklyn Dodger" for their restaurant until sometime after October 14, 1987, and did not open their first bar and restaurant using their "Brooklyn Dodger" logo until March 1988. (Tr. 383, 480, 490–91, 541, 621)

While plaintiffs placed in evidence various uses of the "Brooklyn Dodgers" mark, such as photo permissions in 1984 (PX 4, 5), a permission for use on United Airlines Radio Commercials (PX 6) and a permission to use the Brooklyn "B" in conjunction with a written history of the Brooklyn Dodgers baseball team (PX 7), such uses, granted, for minimal or no compensation, do not constitute trademark uses as is discussed more fully in the court's Conclusions of Law. Similarly plaintiffs attempt to prevent a third party from using the "Brooklyn Dodgers" mark in 1966 (PX 8) is not a trademark use; neither did these uses involve restaurant and tavern services.

With respect to restaurant and tavern services, the evidence established that while the "Brooklyn Dodgers" were playing baseball in Brooklyn, there existed, also in Brooklyn, a restaurant and tavern which used the name "Dodgers Cafe." (DX K) The logo of this establishment was the word "Dodgers," in script, with the figure of a swinging baseball batter. (DX L) The evidence shows that the "Dodgers Cafe" began operating with a State Liquor Authority license in 1942 and continued to operate until 1968, long after Los Angeles had left Brooklyn. Plaintiffs conceded that they took no step whatsoever while they were playing baseball in Brooklyn, or after they had relocated to Los Angeles, to cause the "Dodgers Cafe" to cease using the name as its servicemark for its restaurant.

### E. *Timing of the Litigation*

In September, 1987 at approximately the same time that the trademark search for the name "The Brooklyn Dodger" was being conducted, defendant Boyle wrote a letter to Peter O'Malley, the President and part owner of Los Angeles, seeking O'Malley's best wishes "for the new business" which Boyle advised O'Malley he was about to open in Brooklyn. (Tr. 609–11)

In July 1988, plaintiff Los Angeles discovered defendants' use of the Brooklyn Dodger logo when plaintiff received a copy of the menu of defendant SNOD bearing the allegedly infringing mark. (Tr. 310; PX 14) This menu was sent to Los Angeles by defendant Boyle. (Tr. 631–32, 643) Although finding the allegedly infringing mark to be "a serious concern" (Tr. 345–46), on July 20, 1988 Los Angeles sent the menu bearing the allegedly infringing mark to Properties for further action, asking Properties to investigate the potential infringement of Los Angeles' trademarks but asking Properties to consider, before taking any enforcement action, the potential for negative publicity to the Los Angeles Dodgers. (Tr. 115–16, 346; PX 55; *see* Tr. 114, 319) Los Angeles took this action pursuant to the agreement between the Major League Clubs and Properties. Neither plaintiff Los Angeles nor plaintiff Properties chose to do anything further about the alleged infringement until April 24, 1989. (Tr. 361; PX 15)

As defendants' success in their new venture grew, they sought to take additional legal steps to protect their mark. Accordingly, on August 9, 1988 the composite design mark at issue, containing the term "The Brooklyn Dodger" was registered as a servicemark with the Secretary of State of the State of New York, yet again giving notice of defendants' interest in the name. (Tr. 555–56, 643; DX V)

In approximately February 1989, notice of defendants' attempt to register their logo with the United States Patent and Trademark Office was first officially published. (Tr. 494)

On April 24, 1989, fully nine (9) months after receipt by plaintiff Los Angeles of the menu sent by Boyle, plaintiffs wrote to defendants and claimed for the first time that the defendants' conduct was allegedly infringing their trademark and demanding that they cease and desist from any acts of infringement. (Tr. 318, 383, 646; PX 15 at 1–2)

From April 1989 to March 1990, there were periodic conversations during which the parties attempted unsuccessfully to resolve the dispute. (Tr. 319) When those efforts failed, plaintiffs filed their complaint in March 1990.

In June 1991, while this litigation was pending, counsel for plaintiffs learned during discovery that defendants had formed 9506 to open yet another establishment calling itself "The Brooklyn Dodger Sports Bar and Restaurant" in a new neighborhood in Brooklyn. Within days of that discovery, counsel for plaintiffs delivered to counsel for defendants a letter demanding that defendant cease and desist. (PX 15 at 3; Tr. 383) Defendants nevertheless chose to open another establishment in the Canarsie section of Brooklyn. (Tr. 704–06)

In July 1991 plaintiffs field their amended complaint. In March 1992 Judge Wood granted plaintiffs' motion for preliminary injunction concerning the Canarsie establishment but denied plaintiffs application for summary judgment. This court concluded trial of this matter in May 1992.

## III. CONCLUSIONS OF LAW

### A. *Jurisdiction*

This court has jurisdiction over the subject matter of each of the plaintiffs' causes action pursuant to 28 U.S.C. §§ 1331, 1338 and 15 U.S.C. § 1121 and principles of pendant jurisdiction, and consequently also has jurisdiction over the parties and over defendants' pleaded defenses and counterclaims.

### B. *Plaintiffs' Federal and Common Law Causes of Action*

[1, 2] In order to obtain relief for common law trademark infringement or violations of the Federal Trademark Act ("the Lanham Act") for trademark infringement,[5] or for false representation of goods, or false designation of origin, and wrongful appropriation of plaintiffs' trademarks,[6] plaintiffs were required to prove by a fair preponderance of the credible evidence either actual confusion or a likelihood of confusion.[7]

---

5. 15 U.S.C. § 1114 provides in pertinent part:
   Any person who shall, without the consent of the registrant, ... (a) use in commerce any reproduction, counterfeit, copy, or colorable imitation of a registered mark in connection with the sale, offering for sale, distribution, or advertising of any goods or services on or in connection with which such use is likely to cause confusion, or to cause mistake, or to deceive ... shall be liable in a civil action by the registrant for the remedies hereinafter provided.
   15 U.S.C. § 1117 provides in pertinent part: When a violation of any right of the registrant of a mark registered in the Patent and Trademark Office, or a violation under section 1125(a) of this title, shall have been established in any civil action arising under this chapter, the plaintiff shall be entitled, subject to the provisions of sections 1111 and 1114 of this title, and subject to the principles of equity, to recover (1) defendant's profits, (2) any damages sustained by the plaintiff, and (3) the costs of the action.....
   Plaintiffs withdrew their claim, under Paragraph 4 of their Prayer for Relief for an Order, pursuant to 15 U.S.C. § 1117, concerning damages, including treble damages together with a reasonable attorneys' fee, in an amount presently

not determinable, as well as the costs, fees and disbursements of the action.

6. 15 U.S.C. § 1125 provides in pertinent part:
   Any person who shall affix, apply, or annex, or use in connection with any goods or services, or any container or containers for goods, a false designation of origin, or any false description or representation, including words or other symbols tending falsely to describe or represent the same ... shall be liable to a civil action by ... any person who believes that [he or she] is or is likely to be damaged by the use of any false description or representation.

7. As part of their remedy, plaintiffs seek the destruction of all physical objects which make use of the "Brooklyn Dodgers" mark. 15 U.S.C. § 1118 provides:
   In any action arising under this chapter, in which a violation of any right of the registrant of a mark registered in the Patent and Trademark Office shall have been established, the court may order that all labels, signs, prints, packages, wrappers, receptacles, and advertisements in the possession of the defendant, bearing the registered mark or any reproduction, counterfeit copy, or colorable imitation

W.W.W. Pharmaceutical Co. v. Gillette Co., 984 F.2d 567, 571 (2d Cir.1993). In order to secure injunctive relief or other equitable relief, plaintiffs were required to prove a likelihood of confusion. Had plaintiffs sought to secure damages, they would have been required to prove actual confusion. See W.W.W. Pharmaceutical Co., Inc. v. Gillette Co., 808 F.Supp. 1013, 1020–21 (S.D.N.Y. 1992), aff'd, 984 F.2d 567 (2d Cir.1993). Thus, as to the likelihood of confusion, Los Angeles and Properties must show that "an appreciable number of ordinarily prudent purchasers are likely to be misled, or indeed simply confused, as to the source" of the services provided by the defendants because of their use of the words "The Brooklyn Dodger" in conjunction with their restaurants in Brooklyn. W.W.W. Pharmaceutical, 984 F.2d at 571 (quoting Mushroom Makers, Inc. v. R.G. Barry Corp., 580 F.2d 44, 47 (2d Cir.1978) (per curiam), cert. denied, 439 U.S. 1116, 99 S.Ct. 1022, 59 L.Ed.2d 75 (1979) quoted in McGregor–Doniger Inc. v. Drizzle Inc., 599 F.2d 1126, 1130 (2d Cir.1979)).

[3] This court finds and concludes that plaintiffs have failed to prove either actual confusion or likelihood of confusion stemming from defendants' trademark "The Brooklyn Dodger" even though it is similar to the "Brooklyn Dodgers" trademark that plaintiffs held as a sports club in Brooklyn.

[4] In determining whether a plaintiff has proven likelihood of confusion, the courts of this Circuit follow and apply to the evidence the factors set forth in Polaroid Corp. v. Polarad Electronics Corp., 287 F.2d 492, 495 (2d Cir.1961), cert. denied, 368 U.S. 820, 82 S.Ct. 36, 7 L.Ed.2d 25 (1961). "The [Polaroid ] factors are designed to help grapple with the 'vexing' problem of resolving the likelihood of confusion issue." W.W.W. Pharmaceutical, 984 F.2d at 572 (quoting Lois Sportswear, U.S.A., Inc. v. Levi Strauss & Co., 799 F.2d 867, 872 (2d Cir.1986) (citation omitted)). These factors are:

a) strength of plaintiff's trademark,

thereof, and all plates, molds, matrices, and other means of making the same, shall be

b) similarity between the trademark used by the parties,

c) proximity of the products,

d) the likelihood that plaintiffs will "bridge the gap,"

e) actual confusion,

f) good faith or intent of the defendant,

g) quality of defendants' services,

h) sophistication of purchasers.

This court finds only factors a) and b) in favor of plaintiffs. However, "[t]his list of factors does not exhaust the possibilities— the court may have to take still other variables into account. American Law Institute, Restatement of Torts §§ 729, 730, 731." W.W.W. Pharmaceutical, 984 F.2d at 572 (quoting Polaroid Corp., 287 F.2d at 495).

1. Strength of the Mark

[5, 6] The strength of the mark is determined by "the distinctiveness of the mark, or more precisely, its tendency to identify the goods sold under the mark as emanating from a particular, although possibly anonymous source." W.W.W. Pharmaceutical, 984 F.2d at 572 (quoting McGregor–Doniger, 599 F.2d at 1131). A mark's strength, which turns on its " 'origin-indicating' quality in the eyes of the purchasing public," W.W.W. Pharmaceutical, 984 F.2d at 572 (quoting McGregor–Doniger, 599 F.2d at 1131), is determined by two factors: "(1) the degree to which it is inherently distinctive; and (2) the degree to which it is distinctive in the marketplace." W.W.W. Pharmaceutical, 984 F.2d at 572 (quoting McGregor–Doniger, 599 F.2d at 1131–33).

Courts have used four categories in measuring the distinctiveness of a mark: generic, descriptive, suggestive, and arbitrary or fanciful. Abercrombie & Fitch Co. v. Hunting World, Inc., 537 F.2d 4, 9 (2d Cir.1976). "A generic mark is generally a common description of goods and is ineligible for trademark protection. A descriptive mark describes a product's features, qualities or ingredients in ordinary language, and may be protected only if secondary meaning is established. A

delivered up and destroyed.

suggestive mark employs terms which do not describe but merely suggest the features of the product, requiring the purchaser to use 'imagination, thought and perception to reach a conclusion as to the nature of the goods....' Fanciful or arbitrary marks are eligible for protection without proof of secondary meaning and 'with ease of establishing infringement.'" *W.W.W. Pharmaceutical,* 984 F.2d at 572 (citations omitted).

[7, 8] In assessing the strength of a mark outside its field, "coined" marks, such as "Xerox" or "Kodak," are considered the strongest marks and are accorded the highest degree of trademark protection. *See Landers, Frary and Clark v. Universal Cooler Corp.,* 85 F.2d 46, 48 (2d Cir.1936). Marks incorporating words of common English usage are not accorded the same degree of protection as "coined" terms. The Court of Appeals for the First Circuit has explained the basis for this generally-accepted legal maxim:

> We do not think a trader can pluck a word with favorable connotations [Esquire] for his goods or services out of the general vocabulary and appropriate it to his exclusive use no matter how much effort and money he may expend in the attempt.

*Esquire Inc. v. Esquire Slipper Manufacturing Co.,* 243 F.2d 540, 543 (1st Cir.1957)

Unlike the case with "coined" or arbitrary words, the courts have consistently held the common English words, even if used arbitrarily in application to a user's services, are of weak trademark significance outside their field of operations. *See, e.g., Sun Banks of Florida v. Sun Federal Savings and Loan,* 651 F.2d 311, 316 (5th Cir.1981) ("sun" of weak trademark significance).

[9] Even if there was a greater proximity of the parties' service lines, the name "Dodgers" would still not receive the protection plaintiffs here seek. The courts have demonstrated a reluctance to grant a user or holder of a mark which consists of a word of common English usage, even a word less commonly used than "dodgers," a monopoly on that term outside its field. *See e.g., Mead Data Central, Inc. v. Toyota Motor Sales, U.S.A., Inc.,* 875 F.2d 1026, 1027 (2d Cir. 817 F.Supp.–26

1989) (court declined to find "Lexis" a strong mark outside its field due to its common use in the English language).

While the "Brooklyn Dodgers" mark, used by Los Angeles before it left Brooklyn, is not arbitrary or fanciful, its strength as the name of a nationally known sports team was more than just generic or descriptive. With respect to the precise issue presented here— the strength of the trademarks of a sports franchise—the Fifth Circuit Court of Appeals has noted: "Nearly everyone is familiar with the artistic symbols which designate the individual teams in various professional sports." *Boston Professional Hockey Ass'n v. Dallas Cap & Emblem Mfg., Inc.,* 510 F.2d 1004, 1008 (5th cir.), *cert. denied,* 423 U.S. 868, 96 S.Ct. 132, 46 L.Ed.2d 98 (1975). *See National Football League Properties, Inc. v. New Jersey Giants, Inc.,* 637 F.Supp. 507, 517 (D.N.J.1986) ("the NFL Marks ... are extremely strong, ... and, accordingly, are entitled to a wide range of protection").

Los Angeles' mark was suggestive, the strength of the mark and the suggestiveness of the mark derived from the use of two common English words together. *See W.W.W. Pharmaceutical,* 984 F.2d at 572. The words "Brooklyn" and "Dodgers" together "make up a composite more distinctive than the sum of its parts." *W.W.W. Pharmaceutical,* 984 F.2d at 572. As opposed to considering the word "Brooklyn" or the word "Dodgers" alone, the imaginative mind could consider "Brooklyn Dodgers" as connotative of a sports club in Brooklyn, as is required of suggestive marks.

The public undoubtedly identified the mark "Brooklyn Dodgers" with the Brooklyn-based baseball team. To that extent, the mark was strong and deserving protection.

2. Similarity Between the Trademarks Used by the Parties

[10] In determining the similarity of the mark, the test is "whether the similarity of the marks is likely to provoke confusion among potential customers." *W.W.W. Pharmaceutical,* 984 F.2d at 573; *McGregor–Doniger,* 599 F.2d at 1133. For this factor, the court looks to "the general impression created by the marks, keeping in mind all factors

which the buying public will likely perceive and remember." *W.W.W. Pharmaceutical,* 984 F.2d at 573; *McGregor–Doniger,* 599 F.2d at 1133.

The defendants' "The Brooklyn Dodger" mark is clearly similar to the "Brooklyn Dodgers" mark used by Los Angeles as a Brooklyn sports club. The blue color of the mark is similar. The script is similar. That defendants' mark is singular as opposed to Los Angeles' plural mark is insignificant. *E.g., Mushroom Makers, Inc. v. R.G. Barry Corp.,* 580 F.2d 44, 47–48 (2d Cir.1978) (per curiam), *cert. denied,* 439 U.S. 1116, 99 S.Ct. 1022, 59 L.Ed.2d 75 (1979) ("it is difficult to conceive of any reason to distinguish" between trademarks that, among other things, "are merely the singular and plural forms of the same word").

[11] The periodic use by defendants of a cartoon figure in their logo also does not make the logo dissimilar from Los Angeles' "Brooklyn Dodgers" trademark. The addition of a cartoon figure to a mark is insufficient to prevent a likelihood of consumer confusion. *See also James Burrough Ltd. v. Sign of the Beefeater, Inc.,* 540 F.2d 266, 275 (7th Cir.1976) (mark comprising phrase "Sign of the Beefeater" in combination with a cartoon depiction of a fat hungry man infringed plaintiff's "Beefeater" mark); *Coherent, Inc. v. Coherent Tech., Inc.,* 736 F.Supp. 1055, 1064 (D.Colo.1990) (inclusion of a bug character does not differentiate parties' marks), *aff'd,* 935 F.2d 1122 (10th Cir.1991). Even if the presence of a cartoon character could make two trademarks dissimilar, it does not have that effect here, where the cartoon is omitted from significant uses of defendants' logo, and where defendants concede that their cartoon figure is at least in part an allusion to "the famous 'Brooklyn Bum'" character associated with the "Brooklyn Dodgers." In fact, defendants' witness concedes that the entire mark was designed to allude to the mark used by Los Angeles when it was a Brooklyn-based baseball club. (Tr. 486–89, 569, 688)

Defendants' mark is similar to plaintiffs' "Brooklyn Dodgers" mark used by Los Angeles as a Brooklyn sports club.

3. Proximity of the Products

[12] The third prong of the *Polaroid* test considers whether the products compete with each other. *Lang v. Retirement Living Pub. Co.,* 949 F.2d 576, 582 (2d Cir.1991). "To the extent goods (or trade names) serve the same purpose, fall within the same general class, or are used together, the use of similar designations is more likely to cause confusion." *Lang,* 949 F.2d at 582. Thus, in determining proximity of the products, the court considers content, geographic distribution, market position, and audience appeal. *W.W.W. Pharmaceutical,* 984 F.2d at 573 (*citing C.L.A.S.S. Promotions, Inc. v. D.S. Magazines, Inc.,* 753 F.2d 14, 18 (2d Cir. 1985)).

[13] Competitive proximity "addresses whether, due to the commercial proximity of the competitive products, consumers may be confused as to their source." *Hasbro, Inc. v. Lanard Toys, Ltd.,* 858 F.2d 70, 77 (2d Cir. 1988). Confusion is more likely when the parties compete in the same market.

[14] In determining competitive proximity a court will compare such factors as advertising orientation, function of the services, geographical and cultural audiences, style, price, marketing channels and competitor. *See, e.g., McGregor–Doniger,* 599 F.2d at 1134 (upholding district court finding of significant difference in products); *C.L.A.S.S. Promotions,* 753 F.2d at 18 (no proximity though both magazines directed to Black audiences due to difference in appearance, size, content, geographical distribution and audience appeal); *Transamerica Corp. v. Trans-America Abstract Service,* 698 F.Supp. 1067, 1074 (E.D.N.Y 1988) (no proximity though both sell title insurance because different geographical markets targeted). The evidence presented at trial indicated the diversity between the parties' goods and services, their advertising orientation, the function of their services, their geographical markets and their marketing channels and competitors.

Plaintiffs' primary services involve the giving of baseball exhibitions, principally in Los Angeles, sometimes in New York State, never in Brooklyn. Defendants, on the other hand, provide restaurant and tavern services exclusively in Brooklyn. These services share no common functions, are not competitive, share no salient attributes and are not inherently comparable. Also there is no commonality with respect to the parties' marketing functions, advertising orientation, geographical audiences, etc.[8] In sum, the court finds that the parties do not use the same name and are not in the same business; they cater to different markets 3,000 miles apart. The law, as applied to the facts proven at trial, makes clear that plaintiffs have failed to establish a likelihood of confusion based on this factor.

4. Likelihood that Plaintiffs will "Bridge the Gap" Between the Two Markets

[15] The "bridging the gap" factor is intended to protect the senior user's ability to bridge the gap; that is, the senior user's "interest in being able to enter a related field at some future time...." *W.W.W. Pharmaceutical*, 984 F.2d at 574 (*citing Scarves by Vera, Inc. v. Todo Imports Ltd.*, 544 F.2d 1167, 1172 (2d Cir.1976)). While some allowance is made for the senior user to preserve future expansion possibilities (*see Centaur Communications Ltd. v. A/S/M Communications, Inc.*, 830 F.2d 1217, 1227 (2d Cir.1987); *Lever Bros. v. American Bakeries Co.*, 693 F.2d 251, 258 (2d Cir.1982), there must be some credible evidence of the plaintiff's present intent to enter defendants' field.

Plaintiff Los Angeles claims to have existed for more than 100 years. Major League Baseball has existed for over 100 years. "Sports bars" have existed for almost as long. Over all this period Major League Baseball has never operated a sports bar and restaurant nor indicated a desire to do so. The selling of food stuffs such as hot dogs (Dodger Dogs) and the licensing of a single third party in New Jersey to hang photographs is not equivalent to use of a name for a restaurant in Brooklyn or sufficient to indicate a likelihood of bridging the gap. While the court is aware of the evidence presented

at trial that at least one restaurant has used the name of a major league baseball team ("The San Diego Padres") no such evidence was presented with respect to plaintiff Los Angeles. Since plaintiffs have not "bridged the gap" in 100 years, there has been no proof that they will "bridge the gap" in the future.

5. Actual Confusion

"The Lanham Act seeks to prevent consumer confusion that enables a seller to pass off [the seller's] goods as the goods of another." *W.W.W. Pharmaceutical*, 984 F.2d at 574 (citation omitted).

[16] In order to recover damages under the Lanham Act, "the Second Circuit requires proof of real and precise actual confusion." *W.W.W. Pharmaceutical v. Gillette Co.*, 808 F.Supp. 1013, 1020 (S.D.N.Y.1992), *aff'd*, 984 F.2d 567 (2d Cir.1993) (*citing Coach Leatherware Co. v. AnnTaylor, Inc.*, 933 F.2d 162 (2d Cir.1991); *Getty Petroleum Corp. v. Island Transportation Corp.*, 878 F.2d 650 (2d Cir.1989); *PPX Enterprises, Inc. v. Audiofidelity Enterprises, Inc.*, 818 F.2d 266 (2d Cir.1987); *Shen Mfg. Co. v. Suncrest Mills, Inc.*, 673 F.Supp. 1199 (S.D.N.Y.1987)).

[17, 18] As discussed above,[9] plaintiffs have dropped their claims for monetary damages and are now seeking only injunctive relief which requires proof of a likelihood of confusion, rather than actual confusion. *See W.W.W. Pharmaceutical v. Gillette Co.*, 808 F.Supp. 1013, 1021 (S.D.N.Y.1992), *aff'd*, 984 F.2d 567 (2d Cir.1993). While actual confusion is not required for injunctive relief, *W.W.W. Pharmaceutical v. Gillette Co.*, 808 F.Supp. 1013, 1024 (S.D.N.Y.1992), *aff'd*, 984 F.2d 567 (2d Cir.1993), it is one of the *Polaroid* factors used in this Circuit in determining likelihood of confusion.

[19] While the plaintiff in an infringement action need not prove actual confusion, it is proper for the court to infer from the

---

8. The court notes that at various times since opening their restaurants, defendants have offered T–shirts and caps to the public. However, the court finds that this was a minuscule portion of defendants' business as such items were offered principally as promotional items. (Tr. 650, 755)

9. See *supra* p. 1109.

absence of actual confusion, particularly after defendants' operation for a lengthy period of time, that there is no likelihood of confusion. *See also Universal City Studios v. T–Shirt Gallery, Ltd.,* 634 F.Supp. 1468, 1478 (S.D.N.Y.1986); *W.W.W. Pharmaceutical v. Gillette Co.,* 808 F.Supp. 1013, 1024 (S.D.N.Y. 1992), *aff'd,* 984 F.2d 567 (2d Cir.1993) ("absence of evidence of actual confusion over a period of several years is 'a strong indicator that the likelihood of confusion is minimal'") (*citing Plus Products v. Plus Discount Foods, Inc.,* 722 F.2d 999, 1006 (2d Cir. 1983)).

[20] Plaintiffs presented evidence that certain of defendant SNOD's cancelled checks contained the legend "The Brooklyn Dodgers," alleging that some of defendants' business associates may have confused defendants' singular name with the plural name that plaintiffs held while in Brooklyn. The court concludes that this evidence constitutes typographical errors. Moreover, cancelled checks are no proof of actual consumer confusion of the restaurant with the baseball organization.

[21] Plaintiffs also submitted survey evidence which, if credible and not fatally flawed by its structure or content, might have been probative on this factor. *See Universal City Studios,* 634 F.Supp. at 1478. This evidence consists of two (2) consumer surveys. The first survey claims that "46% of relevant consumers believe that the ['Brooklyn Dodger'] restaurant had to obtain authorization from the Los Angeles Dodgers baseball team, or from Major League Baseball, to use this name." (PX 24) In response, defendants retained an expert, Dr. Michael Rappeport, who after his review of plaintiffs' survey, rendered a critique of plaintiffs' first survey which concluded that, for a number of reasons the survey was fatally flawed. Dr. Rappeport identified four substantive or "content" questions that were asked in plaintiffs' survey in addition to a number of screening and/or background questions which

were used to define the sample and/or to separate the respondents into subgroups for analysis purposes. (DX BB at 1) The first two questions—questions 4a and 4b concerned, according to Dr. Rappeport, the issue of association.[10] The court concludes that Dr. Rappeport's criticism of the significance of the associational questions is valid. In other words, the issue here is not whether defendants' name brings to mind any other name; defendants' admit that part of their goal is to promote nostalgia or association with part of Brooklyn's cultural history. Rather, the issue here is one of actual confusion. Plaintiffs' survey questions regarding association are irrelevant to the issue of actual confusion.

The second two questions—questions 5a and 5b concerned the issue of sponsorship. (*See* DX BB at 1–2) The second pair of questions read as follows:

> 5a   Do you believe that the restaurant had to get authorization, that is, permission to use the name, "The Brooklyn Dodger?"
>
> 5b   From whom did they have to get authorization, that is permission?

According to Dr. Rappeport, the second two questions were intended to determine:

> 1) That applicable consumers will be confused as to the actual ownership of The Brooklyn Dodger restaurant, i.e. that they will think the restaurant is owned by the owners of the Los Angeles Dodgers baseball team.
>
> 2) That applicable consumers will believe that The Brooklyn Dodger restaurant is sponsored/authorized by the people who now own the Los Angeles Dodgers baseball team.

(DX BB at 1–2) Dr. Rappeport found, however, that questions 5a and 5b failed to effectively address the intended issues of confusion regarding actual ownership and authorization and that the questions were "fatally flawed" such that the "questions (and thus

---

10. The first pair of questions read as follows:
4a   Do you associate this name with anyone or anything or do you think that it's just the name of the restaurant without any other association, or don't you know?"

4b   IF YES: What or who do you associate that name with?

the [plaintiffs'] survey as a whole) do not yield *any meaningful evidence* with regard to the remaining issue of likelihood of sponsorship or authorization." (DX BB at 2) (emphasis in original) Dr. Rappeport explained that questions 5a and 5b were "inherently highly likely to lead respondents in a direction favorable to the plaintiffs." (DX BB at 2)[11]

The court concludes that these questions were leading, causing the survey to be fatally flawed.[12] Moreover, the court concludes that these questions were indistinguishably similar to the questions in *WUV's International v. Love's Enterprises,* 208 USPQ (BNA) 736 (D.Colo.1980) which were also held to be invalid. In *WUV's,* the court concluded that the following question was "open-ended" and "valid":

> 4. What company or person do you believe owns or operates this restaurant?

However, the court concluded that a subsequent question,

> 6. Do you believe that this restaurant is connected with or related to any other restaurant?

was "leading and unnecessarily suggestive." 208 USPQ (BNA) 736. Both plaintiffs' questions, 5a and 5b, are leading and suggestive in the same fashion as questions 6 in *WUV's.*

In addition to the leading nature of questions 5a and 5b, Dr. Rappeport criticized what he described at trial as the "central problem" in plaintiffs' survey which was that the survey provided for no controls. Dr.

Rappeport provided in juxtaposition some examples of control questions that plaintiffs might have used.[13] (DX BB at 4) Dr. Rappeport concluded:

> Because [plaintiffs' survey] failed to use any controls, they have no measure of what percentage of respondents are reacting to the particular stimuli and what [percentage] would be confused no matter what they were asked. Thus the interpretation of their data is impossible, and any conclusions drawn from their data must be seen as meaningless.

(DX BB at 4)

As to the entire survey Dr. Rappeport concluded, "in my opinion the results of this survey should be considered to have no value in demonstrating that the applicable public believes that 'The Brooklyn Dodger' restaurant is authorized by or got permission from Major League Baseball Properties, Inc. or the Los Angeles Dodgers, Inc." (DX BB at 5)

In the face of defendants' criticism, plaintiffs commissioned a "Supplemental Consumer Survey" in an attempt to address the criticisms of Dr. Rappeport, defendants' expert. (PX 26) Dr. Rappeport reviewed the "Supplemental Consumer Survey" and testified at trial that while plaintiffs' "Supplemental Consumer Survey" addressed a number of his criticisms, it "never touched, never dealt at all with the fourth and by far the most important of the critiques," concerning lack of controls.[14] (Tr. 428)

---

11. In criticizing the leading nature of plaintiffs' survey, Dr. Rappeport drew proof from an inconsistency in the survey itself. Dr. Rappeport pointed out that 38% of those who did not associate the name with something else (according to question 4a) still said authorization was needed. Dr. Rappeport explained the inconsistency of this result in the following manner:

> The obvious question is "Why would people who did not associate The Brooklyn Dodger restaurant with anything else, let alone baseball, suddenly decide the restaurant needed permission from baseball to operate?" From our experience, by far the most reasonable answer is that the message sent to respondents who said "no association" in answer to 4a was that their initial response was incorrect. Thus, when they are asked about whether anyone gave permission, the natural tendency for many people is to assume that someone must

have given permission and the "test" is to figure out who.
(DX BB at 3)

12. In addition to criticizing the leading nature of plaintiffs' questions, Dr. Rappeport criticized the absence of a "Don't Know" option in plaintiffs' survey. (DX BB at 4)

13. Dr. Rappeport suggested:
> The Brooklyn Bridge restaurant (perhaps one needs permission from New York City)
> The Brooklyn Yankees restaurant (alluding to the New York Yankees baseball team)
> The Brooklyn Eagles restaurant (named after a defunct newspaper)
(DX BB at 4)

14. Plaintiffs argue that the survey was controlled by not changing the question structure—that is, using the same questions that Dr. Rappeport

The court concludes that plaintiffs' surveys are flawed, that both surveys contain a complete lack of controls rendering the data meaningless and having no evidentiary value. Therefore, the court concludes that there is no proof of actual confusion.

6.  Good Faith or Intent of the Defendant

[22–24] This factor looks to "whether the defendant adopted its mark with the intention of capitalizing on plaintiff's reputation and goodwill and any confusion between [defendant's] and the senior user's product." *W.W.W. Pharmaceutical,* 984 F.2d at 575 (*quoting Lang,* 949 F.2d at 583 (citation omitted)). Even if a junior user has notice of a senior mark, this is not an indication of bad faith. *Edison Bros. Store, Inc. v. Cosmair, Inc.,* 651 F.Supp. 1547, 1560 (S.D.N.Y.1987). Indeed, even if a mark is registered, the presumption of an exclusive right to use it extends only as far as the goods or services noted in the registration certificate. *Mushroom Makers,* 580 F.2d at 48.

The proof at trial clearly establishes that at every turn defendants acted in good faith in electing, adopting, and using their mark. They made no effort to use their mark in such a way as to trade upon the reputation of plaintiff Los Angeles, but rather to elicit memories of the "Brooklyn Dodgers," a historical concept. Indeed, the trial testimony establishes that, given the notoriety of Los Angeles's departure from Brooklyn and the ill will that flows from that event even to this day (PX 31), trading upon Los Angeles' "good will" in Brooklyn would have been fatal to defendants because many Brooklynites despise the "Los Angeles Dodgers." (Tr. 529, 608–09)

The testimony given in this matter establishes that it was defendants' intention that

their proposed sports bar would have a strong Brooklyn identity. They first considered the name "Ebbets Field" and commissioned a trademark search for that name. While the search uncovered no current uses of that name, defendants were informed that a small bar in Hicksville, New York was using it. Ironically, wishing to avoid any possible legal entanglements, defendants then did a trademark search of "The Brooklyn Dodger" name. Finding no registration for "Brooklyn Dodgers," and aware that the "Brooklyn Dodgers" had not existed for more than 30 years, Boyle wrote to Peter O'Malley, the owner and president of Los Angeles in the latter part of 1987 and told him that the Boyle restaurant would be called "The Brooklyn Dodger."

On April 28, 1988 defendants filed an application to register "The Brooklyn Dodger" as part of the previously described composite design and mark with the U.S. Patent and Trademark Office and also registered it as a servicemark with the New York State Secretary of State on August 9, 1988. The evidence leaves no doubt but that defendants only took these steps after assuring themselves that no one else was using this mark and after writing to the owner of the Los Angeles Dodgers and advising him of their intent to use "The Brooklyn Dodger" as the name of their restaurant. Such conduct weighs heavily on a court seeking to do equity.[15]

7.  Quality of Defendants' Services

Plaintiffs merely assert that defendants' products are inferior. This court finds no evidence that defendants' products or services are inferior. Moreover, the trial evidence indicates that the parties' respective products

---

criticized and comparing the variations, if any. The court concludes that this "control" was insufficient and produced two flawed surveys rather than one sufficient set of surveys.

15.  The court is cognizant of the fact that trademark rights flow from use, and not from registration, of the mark. Nevertheless, plaintiffs chose to file a registration for its "Dodgers" mark in 1976. They failed to register any "Brooklyn Dodgers" mark until after defendants' application was filed. Then, in 1989 plaintiffs filed

registrations for three different "Brooklyn Dodgers" marks. (PX 2 at 04293, 04303, 04304). This court finds it inescapable that, given the good faith demonstrated by defendants in their having conducted trademark searches on each of the marks they considered, this entire controversy and litigation might have been avoided if plaintiffs had undertaken the simple task of filing an application to register a "Brooklyn Dodgers" trademark as notice to potential users.

and services simply do not compete in any market.

### 8. Sophistication of the Likely Purchasers

"Likelihood of confusion must be assessed by examining the level of sophistication of the relevant purchasers." *W.W.W. Pharmaceutical*, 984 F.2d at 575; *McGregor–Doniger*, 599 F.2d at 1137.

Defendants' patrons are drawn from the general public and to some extent cannot be said to have unique qualities or sophistication. On the other hand, defendants established at trial that a significant number of the customers who patronize defendants' restaurants in Brooklyn are sophisticated concerning the issue before this court—the difference between plaintiffs' goods and services and defendants' services and the likelihood of confusion. Defendants testified that many of the patrons who frequent "The Brooklyn Dodger" are well aware of Los Angeles' now infamous abandonment of the Borough of Brooklyn and—to the third generation since then—remain bitter about it. (Tr. 563, 608–09) In Brooklyn, the "Los Angeles Dodgers" and the "Brooklyn Dodgers" are seen as two separate entities which have been wholly unrelated for more than 30 years. (Tr. 547; 648 *et seq.*) It is unlikely that Los Angeles' now infamous departure from Brooklyn and its attendant negative notoriety could be ignored by actual or would-be patrons of defendants' restaurants. Given the entirety of facts, therefore, there is virtually no likelihood of confusion by these sophisticated consumers that plaintiffs have somehow authorized defendants to do business under "The Brooklyn Dodger" name—a name plaintiffs abandoned when they became the "Los Angeles Dodgers."

### 9. The Centaur Factors

[25] In addition to the analysis under *Polaroid* which is required in this Circuit, the Court of Appeals has added three more factors which, when applied, similarly assist the factfinder in determining the core question in any trademark litigation—whether defendants' use of the plaintiffs' mark is likely to cause an appreciable number of reasonably prudent purchasers to believe that services offered by the defendants are from the same source as the goods and services that they know are sold under the plaintiffs' trademark. *See Centaur Communication v. A/S/M Communications*, 830 F.2d 1217, 1228 n. 2 (2d Cir.1987). These so-called *Centaur* factors are: a) the nature of the senior user's priority; b) its delay in asserting its claim and c) the balance of harm and benefit that would result from granting an injunction against the junior user's use of the mark. *Centaur Communication*, 830 F.2d at 1228 n. 2.

The nature of the senior user's priority is particularly germane in this litigation. The evidence at trial established that in October 1958 plaintiffs' goodwill nexus to the Borough of Brooklyn was irretrievably shattered. Following Los Angeles' departure from Brooklyn, no commercial use was made by plaintiffs of any "Brooklyn Dodgers" mark until 1981. However it is likewise clear that in 1981 plaintiffs did resume commercial use of the "Brooklyn Dodgers" mark. While plaintiffs' resumed use was dramatically reduced relative to its use as the name of a major league baseball team, geared primarily toward novelty items and token remembrances, this resumed use occurred prior to defendants' first use of the mark for their restaurants in Brooklyn in 1988. Therefore, plaintiffs have priority to the extent of their use as of 1981.

The second *Centaur* factor, plaintiffs' failure to move in a timely fashion. Plaintiffs claim that they did not learn of defendants' use of "The Brooklyn Dodger" mark until July 1988. The parties agree the plaintiffs' first "cease and desist" request was not made until April 24, 1989 when plaintiffs' counsel sent a letter to Kevin Boyle. (PX 15) Given that defendants' took significant steps in establishing their Brooklyn restaurant business in that interim, plaintiffs' failure to act was somewhat prejudicial.

Finally, on the issue of balancing the harm and benefit which would result from granting an injunction. The balancing of these equities favors defendants. The equities show that prior to its move from Brooklyn, Los Angeles held rights in a strong mark which is very similar to defendants' mark and that plaintiffs still have priority in use of the mark. However, what the equities also show is a small neighborhood restaurant which has acted in good faith and which has been dogged by this massive litigation brought by plaintiffs who, by their own admission, generated retail sales in excess of $1.5 billion in 1990 and, for reasons never made clear at trial, chose not to file an application to register any "Brooklyn Dodgers" trademark until one year after defendants' application despite plaintiffs' alleged ownership of the mark for almost a century.

This court might have thought that in the execution of its crucial purpose of protecting and preserving the sanctity of major league baseball teams' mark, plaintiff Properties might have found a way, between 1958 and 1989, of taking the simple and expedient step of filing an application for trademark registration of the "Brooklyn Dodgers" name as it plainly did for each of the twenty-six (26) other names in its collection. Having moved away from Brooklyn in 1957, having failed to put the "Brooklyn Dodger" mark to a trademark use of at least two decades and having failed to file an application to register the "Brooklyn Dodger" mark until 1989—a step defendants took in April 1988 for its "The Brooklyn Dodger" mark—the court concludes that the equities lie in defendants' favor. If plaintiffs were still located in Brooklyn and if they had continued to use the mark through the present, then the equities would be different.

When the trial evidence is weighed in the balance this court concludes that, under the *Polaroid* factors, as expanded by the *Centaur* factors, plaintiffs have failed to prove, by a fair preponderance of the credible evidence, actual confusion or a likelihood of confusion between plaintiffs' "Brooklyn Dodgers" mark as used by them in Brooklyn and defendants' "The Brooklyn Dodger" mark.

### C. *Defendants' Affirmative Defenses*

#### 1. Abandonment

[26] Under the Lanham Act a federally registered trademark is considered abandoned if its "use has been discontinued with

intent not to resume." *Cerveceria Centroamericana, S.A. v. Cerveceria India, Inc.,* 892 F.2d 1021, 1023 (Fed.Cir.1989) (*quoting* Lanham Act, 15 U.S.C. § 1127 (1988)).

Abandonment is defined in the Lanham Act: "A mark shall be deemed 'abandoned'—(a) When its use has been discontinued with intent not to resume. Intent to resume may be inferred from circumstances." 15 U.S.C. § 1127 (1988).

[27–29] Rights in a trademark are acquired and maintained through use. *See United Drug Co. v. Theodore Rectanus Co.,* 248 U.S. 90, 97, 39 S.Ct. 48, 50, 63 L.Ed. 141 (1918) ("The law of trademarks is but a part of the broader law of unfair competition; the right to a particular mark grows out of its use, not its mere adoption"). *See also D.V.L. Mastrullo, Trademark Parody Litigation and the Lanham Act: Fitting a Square Peg in a Round Hole,* 54 U.CIN.L.REV. 1311, 1324 (1986) ("Rights to a trademark are acquired only through deliberate and continuous use of the trademark, and thus rights to a trademark can be lost where the mark is abandoned or so widely used that it no longer functions as a distinctive representation of the single source of the product"). "A federal registration of a trademark may be cancelled if the mark is abandoned." *Cerveceria India,* 892 F.2d at 1023. *See also Societe de Developments et D'Innovations des Marches Agricoles et Alimentaires–Sodima–Union de Cooperatives Agricoles ("Sodima") v. International Yogurt Co., Inc.,* 662 F.Supp. 839, 843 (D.Or.1987) (Lanham Act permits cancellation at any time where registered mark has been abandoned). Therefore abandonment is an affirmative defense to trademark infringement. *See Roulo v. Russ Berrie & Co.,* 886 F.2d 931, 935 (7th Cir.1989), *cert. denied,* 493 U.S. 1075, 110 S.Ct. 1124, 107 L.Ed.2d 1030 (1990) (abandonment is affirmative defense). The burden of proving abandonment falls upon the party seeking cancellation of a registered mark because a certificate of registration is " 'prima facie evidence of the validity of the registration' and continued use." *Cerveceria India,* 892 F.2d at 1023 (*quoting J.C. Hall Co. v. Hallmark Cards, Inc.,* 340 F.2d 960, 962–63 (CCPA 1965)); *Exxon Corp. v. Humble Exploration Co.,* 695 F.2d 96, 99

(5th Cir.), *reh'g denied*, 701 F.2d 173 (5th Cir.1983) (citation omitted). The party seeking cancellation must establish abandonment by a preponderance of the evidence. *See Cerveceria India*, 892 F.2d at 1023–24.

[30] The Lanham Act provides that "[n]onuse for two consecutive years shall be prima facie abandonment." 15 U.S.C. § 1127. *Stetson v. Howard D. Wolf & Assoc.*, 955 F.2d 847, 850 (2d Cir.1992) (prima facie abandonment exists where there has been nonuse for two consecutive years); *Saratoga Vichy Spring Co. v. Lehman*, 625 F.2d 1037, 1043 (2d Cir.1980) (same). *See also Cerveceria India*, 892 F.2d at 1023 ("nonuse for two consecutive years constitutes 'prima facie abandonment'") (*quoting* Lanham Act, 15 U.S.C. § 1127); *Sterling Brewers, Inc. v. Schenley Industries, Inc.*, 441 F.2d 675, 679 (CCPA 1971) (nonuse for over two years constitutes prima facie abandonment). Prima facie abandonment establishes a rebuttable presumption of abandonment. *Lehman*, 625 F.2d at 1044. *See also Star-Kist Foods, Inc. v. P.J. Rhodes & Co.*, 769 F.2d 1393, 1396 (9th Cir.1985) (prima facie abandonment creates presumption that may be rebutted); *Roulo*, 886 F.2d at 935 (prima facie abandonment shifts burden of production to trademark owner to explain nonuse or establish existence of intent to resume). *See, e.g., Lipton Industries, Inc. v. Ralston Purina Co.*, 670 F.2d 1024, 1031 (CCPA 1982) ("board properly required appellant to put

forth at least some evidence to explain its nonuse which, in conjunction with the presumption of validity [due to trademark registration], might have defeated appellee's case") (citation omitted).[16]

[31] The evidence presented at trial established that between 1958 and 1981 plaintiffs made no commercial trademark use[17] whatsoever of any "Brooklyn Dodgers" mark.[18] Minor changes in a trademark that do not affect the overall commercial impression of the mark do not constitute abandonment. *See Sands, Taylor & Wood Co. v. Quaker Oats Co.*, 978 F.2d 947, 955 (7th Cir.), *reh'g en banc denied* (*quoting* 1 J. Thomas McCarthy, *Trademarks and Unfair Competition*, § 17:10, at 787 (2d ed.1984)). However, Los Angeles' change, in this case, from "Brooklyn Dodgers" to "Los Angeles Dodgers" was not minor; it involved an essential element affecting the public's perception of the mark and the team.[19] *Compare Quaker Oats*, 978 F.2d at 955 (change from THIRST–AID, FIRST AID FOR YOUR THIRST to THIRST–AID not abandonment) *and Puritan Sportswear Corp. v. Shure*, 307 F.Supp. 377 (W.D.Pa.1969) (change from PURITAN SPORTSWEAR, THE CHOICE OF ALL AMERICANS to PURITAN not abandonment).

Moreover, plaintiffs in this case did not simply adopt a second name, "Los Angeles Dodgers," in addition to their first name,

---

16. While the Second Circuit has determined that prima facie abandonment establishes only a rebuttable presumption of abandonment that plaintiffs may counter by satisfying a burden of producing evidence of intent to resume, *Lehman*, 625 F.2d at 1044, other circuits have held that the burden of persuasion shifts to the trademark owner to show intent to resume. *See Stanley A. Bowker, Jr., The Song is Over But the Melody Lingers On: Persistence of Goodwill and the Intent Factor in Trademark Abandonment*, 56 FORDHAM L.REV. 1003, 1021 (1988) (discussing differences among circuits in allocating evidence burden).

17. That is, they sold no goods or services under the mark and did not license its use to third parties in the ordinary course of trade.

18. In fact, plaintiffs did not even attempt to register a "Brooklyn Dodgers" mark or a "Brooklyn" mark until well after this action had been filed.

19. While Los Angeles ceased commercial use of the trademark because of its relocation from Brooklyn to Los Angeles, its motive, justifiable or not, is irrelevant. *Stetson*, 955 F.2d at 851. Nevertheless, Los Angeles' nonuse in this case was voluntary. Courts have been more reluctant to find an absence of intent to resume where the trademark owner had an excusable reason for nonuse—that is, where nonuse was involuntary. *See, e.g., Defiance Button Machine Co. v. C & C Metal Products Corp.*, 759 F.2d 1053, 1059 (2d Cir.), *cert. denied*, 474 U.S. 844, 106 S.Ct. 131, 88 L.Ed.2d 108 (1985) (no abandonment where cessation of business was involuntary); *American International Group, Inc. v. American International Airways, Inc.*, 726 F.Supp. 1470 (E.D.Pa. 1989) (where airline declared bankruptcy, remaining goodwill and lack of intent to abandon precluded finding abandonment).

"Brooklyn Dodgers," as did plaintiff in *Guiding Eyes For the Blind, Inc. v. Guide Dog Foundation For the Blind, Inc.*, 384 F.2d 1016 (CCPA 1967). In *Guiding Eyes*, appellee adopted a second trademark, "Second Sight," for use in addition to its original trademark "Guiding Eyes." The court held that because appellee had continued to use the original mark after and along with its use of the second mark, there was no abandonment of the original mark. In this case, however, plaintiffs did not use the "Los Angeles Dodgers" mark along with the "Brooklyn Dodgers" mark; plaintiffs used the "Los Angeles Dodgers" mark instead of the "Brooklyn Dodgers" mark as the name of the sports team.

Plaintiffs argue that their "Dodgers" mark without a geographical reference—that is, "Dodgers" alone—is a protected use infringed by defendants actions. However, in this context, "Brooklyn" is more than a geographic designation or appendage to the word "Dodgers." The *"Brooklyn Dodgers"* was a non-transportable cultural institution separate from the "Los Angeles Dodgers" or the "Dodgers" who play in Los Angeles. It is not simply the "Dodgers," (and certainly not the "Los Angeles Dodgers"), that defendants seek to invoke in their restaurant; rather defendants specifically seek to recall the nostalgia of the cultural institution that was the "Brooklyn Dodgers." It was the *"Brooklyn Dodgers"* name that had acquired secondary meaning in New York in the early part of this century, prior to 1958. It was that cultural institution that Los Angeles abandoned.

Nevertheless, assuming arguendo, that the relevant mark is "Dodgers" which plaintiffs claim to have used continuously for the past fifty years for sports and entertainment purposes, the parties uses are sufficiently distinct to permit defendants' use. Plaintiffs did not register the "Dodgers" mark (without "Brooklyn") for commercial use until 1967, almost a decade after their abandonment. (PX 2) Plaintiffs, even after using the "Dodger" mark for fifty years, have never used the name for a nostalgic sports restaurant as defendants have. Defendants in operating their restaurant did not register the "Dodger" mark (without "Brooklyn") and have not used the "Dodger" mark in any form outside of New York. However, this court concludes that "Brooklyn Dodgers" rather than "Dodgers" is the trademark that acquired secondary meaning as a cultural institution in New York, and it is "Brooklyn Dodgers" rather than "Dodgers" that is at issue in this litigation.

[32–34] A determination of the issue of abandonment requires an analysis of the trademark holder's occupation or business to determine what constitutes use of the mark. *Stetson*, 955 F.2d at 851. In this case, in order to maintain use of the mark, Los Angeles would have had to continue to use "Brooklyn Dodgers" as the name of its baseball team. Only in this way would the public continue to identify the team with the team. *Defiance Button Mach. Co. v. C & C Metal Products Corp.*, 759 F.2d 1053, 1059 (2d Cir.), *cert. denied*, 474 U.S. 844, 106 S.Ct. 131, 88 L.Ed.2d 108 (1985) (if owner abandons mark through nonuse with intent not to resume, "others are no longer restrained from using it since it ceases to be associated in the public's mind with the owner's goods or services") (*citing Manhattan Industries, Inc. v. Sweater Bee by Banff, Ltd.*, 627 F.2d 628, 630 (2d Cir.1980)).[20] *See, e.g., Stetson*, 955 F.2d

---

20. The outcome in *Defiance*, finding no abandonment, is distinguishable from the case at hand because the court in *Defiance* held that the continued goodwill toward the button company after it stopped producing goods and the fact that the company intended to retain its trademark for some commercial use precluded a finding of abandonment. Similarly, the court in *Schenley Industries*, 441 F.2d 675 held that continued goodwill and lack of intent to abandon precluded finding of abandonment.

In the unique facts of this case, however, plaintiffs have not succeeded in demonstrating that much goodwill in Brooklyn survived Los Angeles' move in 1957. But more importantly, while plaintiff in *Defiance* was at least able to demonstrate an intent not to abandon, plaintiffs here have not even demonstrated an intent not to abandon, much less the statutory requirement of intent to resume. A mark retains "residual" goodwill "if the proponent of a mark stops using it but demonstrates an intent to keep the mark alive for use in resumed business." *Pan American World Airways, Inc. v. Panamerican School of Travel, Inc.*, 648 F.Supp. 1026, 1031 (S.D.N.Y.), *aff'd without op.*, 810 F.2d 1160 (2d Cir.1986)

at 851 (use must be sufficient to maintain public's identification of mark with proprietor).

[35] Evidence was presented at trial that Los Angeles occasionally gave written permission, for little or no compensation, to use the "Brooklyn Dodgers" name. In 1959, Los Angeles made prominent commercial use of and reference to their Brooklyn heritage and trademarks in connection with the promotion of Roy Campanella Night, honoring the former Brooklyn Dodgers player and present employee. (Tr. 94–96, 266–67; PX 1 at 2) Los Angeles made prominent use of their trademarks incorporating the word Brooklyn at their annual oldtimers games. (PX 1 at 37, 40; Tr. 270) Oldtimers games are commercial baseball exhibitions at which former players are honored and perform so that older fans can recall the past and younger fans can learn about the history of the Club. (Tr. 267–68)

[36] The case law is clear that such uses do not constitute trademark uses of the "Brooklyn Dodgers" name. Amended Section 45 of the Lanham Act defines "use in commerce" as "the bona fide use of a mark in the ordinary course of trade, and not made merely to reserve a right in the mark." 15 U.S.C. § 1127.[21] Neither " 'challenging infringing uses' nor 'sporadic licensing' for noncommercial activities constitutes use." *Stetson*, 955 F.2d at 851 (*quoting Silverman v. CBS, Inc.*, 870 F.2d 40, 47 (2d Cir.), *cert. denied*, 492 U.S. 907, 109 S.Ct. 3219, 106 L.Ed.2d 569 (1989)); *La Societe Anonyme des Parfums Le Galion v. Jean Patou, Inc.*, 495 F.2d 1265, 1271 (2d Cir.1974) (*citing* 3 Callmann, Unfair Competition, Trademarks & Monopolies § 76.2(d) (1969)) ("To prove bona fide usage, the proponent of the trade-

mark must demonstrate that [its] use of the mark has been deliberate and continuous, not sporadic, casual or transitory").

[37] Rather than using the "Brooklyn Dodgers" mark in the ordinary course of trade, a more accurate description of Los Angeles' use of the mark, at least between 1958 and 1981, was given by its General Counsel in a 1985 letter to someone seeking to use it on a novelty item:

> Since the Dodgers moved to Los Angeles in 1958 the name 'Brooklyn Dodgers' has been reserved strictly for use in conjunction with items of historical interest. (PX 9)

Under the law, such warehousing is not permitted. *See Jean Patou*, 495 F.2d at 1272 (citation omitted) ("where no present intent has been found to market the trademarked product, minimal sales have been held insufficient to establish trademark rights"). *See also Exxon*, 695 F.2d at 101 ("The Act does not allow the preservation of a mark solely to prevent its use by others"). Instead, trademarks must be used as trademarks to retain enforceable property rights in them. *Stetson*, 955 F.2d at 851 (*quoting Silverman*, 870 F.2d at 48) (use must be "sufficient to maintain 'the public's identification of the mark to the proprietor' "). Rights in a trademark are lost when trademarks are "warehoused" as plaintiffs attempted to "warehouse" the "Brooklyn Dodgers" mark for more than two (2) decades. *See Stetson*, 955 F.2d at 851 ("trademark must be used or lost to another economic actor more willing to promote the mark in commerce"). Plaintiffs' failure to use the "Brooklyn Dodgers" trademark between 1958, when Los Angeles left Brooklyn, and 1981 constitutes abandonment of the trademark.[22]

---

(citing *Defiance, supra*). The claim to residual goodwill will not preclude a finding of abandonment where, as in this case, the owner unequivocally declares its intention to discontinue use. SIEGRUN D. KANE, TRADEMARK LAW: A PRACTITIONER'S GUIDE 167 (1987).

21. *See also S. Bowker, supra*, at 1022 (Lanham Act, as interpreted by Fifth Circuit in *Exxon Corp. v. Humble Exploration Co.*, 695 F.2d 96 (5th Cir.), *reh'g denied*, 701 F.2d 173 (5th Cir. 1983), requires "not just use, but active commercial use").

22. *See also Susan Naresh, Incontestability and Rights in Descriptive Trademarks*, 53 U.CHI. L.REV. 953, 981 n. 120 (1986) (distinguishing between intentional and unintentional abandonment). " 'Unintentional abandonment' contrasts with 'intentional abandonment': the latter occurs when use of the mark has been discontinued with intent not to resume it, and the former when the registrant's conduct causes the mark to lose its significance as a indication of origin." *S.Naresh, supra*, at 981 n. 120 (*citing* Lanham Act, 15 U.S.C. § 1127(a), (b)). Plaintiffs' abandonment in this case fits both definitions, to

In this Circuit the law of trademark abandonment is set forth in *Silverman v. CBS, Inc.*, 870 F.2d 40 (2d Cir.1989). *See also Stetson*, 955 F.2d at 850–51 (district court should use *Silverman* criteria). In *Silverman* a dispute arose over the use of the characters from the "Amos & Andy" radio and television programs. Although CBS held the trademark and copyrights from the original airings, it had discontinued its broadcasts in 1966 due to criticism as to the programs' negative stereotyping of African–Americans. In 1981 Silverman wrote a script for a Broadway musical based on the "Amos & Andy" characters and sought a license from CBS to use them. When CBS refused, Silverman brought an action seeking, *inter alia*, a declaratory judgment that CBS no longer had any rights in these marks. Silverman argued that CBS' failure to broadcast the programs or to make commercial use of the characters led to an abandonment of the marks. CBS countered that its discontinuance of the program broadcasts was done for "worthy motives." In addition, CBS claimed, not unlike plaintiffs here, that it had licensed the program for non-commercial use, had challenged infringing uses of the name brought to its attention, and periodically considered whether to resume use of the programs. 870 F.2d at 47. The court in *Silverman* found no merit in CBS's claims and found all of its "Amos & Andy" property rights to have been abandoned.

[38] This court concludes that the *Silverman* rationale applies here and that plaintiffs abandoned the "Brooklyn Dodgers" trademark. Plaintiffs plainly had not used the term "Brooklyn Dodgers" for trademark purposes for at least 23 years following their departure from Brooklyn. Their occasional licensing and using the name for historical retrospective and matters of historical interest did not constitute trademark uses of the mark but were non-commercial activities and certainly not more than sporadic. Defendants, therefore, have proven nonuse by plaintiffs sufficient for their claim of abandonment.

[39] Abandonment under the Lanham Act, however, requires both nonuse and intent not to resume use. *Stetson*, 955 F.2d at 850 (citation omitted); *Lehman*, 625 F.2d at 1043 (abandonment requires nonuse and intent not to resume). *See also Loctite Corp. v. National Starch and Chemical Corp.*, 516 F.Supp. 190, 218 (S.D.N.Y.1981) (*citing Lehman*, 625 F.2d at 1043) (same); *Sodima*, 662 F.Supp. at 843 (statute contains elements of intent and nonuse, and intent not to use may be "inferred from actual non-use which has lasted for two years").

[40, 41] Once prima facie abandonment has been proven, the trademark registrants—in this case plaintiffs—must carry their burden of producing evidence that there was an intent to resume use of the trademark. *Cerveceria India*, 892 F.2d at 1025–26. *See also Sodima*, 662 F.Supp. at 844–45, 848–49; *Schenley Industries*, 441 F.2d at 679. While the trademark registrant has the burden of production as to intent to resume, the ultimate burden of persuasion remains with the party claiming abandonment. *Quaker Oats*, 978 F.2d at 956.

[42] Rather than merely proving that it did not intend to abandon its trademark, the trademark registrant must demonstrate that it intended to use or resume use. *See Exxon*, 695 F.2d at 99, 102–103 ("Stopping at an 'intent not to abandon' [rather than 'intent to resume'] tolerates an owner's protecting a mark with neither commercial use nor plans to resume commercial use. Such a license is not permitted by the Lanham Act"); *Roulo*, 886 F.2d at 938 (discussing differences among circuits in requiring intent to resume versus intent not to abandon and holding that proper test is intent to resume); *Ambrit, Inc. v. Kraft, Inc.*, 812 F.2d 1531, 1550 (11th Cir.1986) (inquiry is intent to resume rather than intent not to abandon). *See also Sodima*, 662 F.Supp. at 849 (same). Lack of intent to resume use may be inferred from the circumstances surrounding the nonuse of the mark. *Vitaline Corp. v. General Mills*,

---

some extent. On one hand, plaintiffs' discontinued use of the "Brooklyn Dodgers" mark for over 20 years with no intent to resume use. On the other hand, plaintiffs' moved from Brooklyn to Los Angeles and adopted the "Los Angeles Dodgers" trademark, causing the "Brooklyn Dodgers" mark to lose its significance as a name of an existing sports club.

*Inc.*, 891 F.2d 273, 275 (Fed.Cir.1989) ("Although abandonment requires both non-use and intent not to resume use of the mark, the element of intent can be established inferentially by the same facts that establish nonuse"). *See also Anvil Brand, Inc. v. Consolidated Foods Corp.*, 464 F.Supp. 474, 481 (S.D.N.Y.1978) (inference of intent not to resume use may be drawn from proof of nonuse for two years). For Los Angeles to have had an "intent to resume" it must have had plans to resume commercial use of the mark within two years at the time that it left Brooklyn in 1958. *See Exxon*, 695 F.2d at 102; *Imperial Tobacco, Ltd. v. Philip Morris, Inc.*, 899 F.2d 1575, 1580 (Fed.Cir.1990) ("where there is use, followed by a period of nonuse, the question is whether the registrant 'discontinued' use with an 'intent not to resume'" (no citation)). *See, e.g. E. Remy Martin & Co., S.A. v. Shaw–Ross International Imports, Inc.*, 756 F.2d 1525, 1532 (11th Cir.), *reh'g denied, enbanc*, 765 F.2d 154 (11th Cir.1985) (party that discontinues use must show plans to resume commercial use).

[43] Plaintiffs have in no way demonstrated their intent to resume commercial use of the "Brooklyn Dodgers" mark within two years after Los Angeles left Brooklyn in 1958 or at anytime within the ensuing quarter century. In *Ambrit*, the court ruled that registration of a mark during a period of abandonment is insufficient to prove intent to resume. Plaintiffs changed their name from "Brooklyn Dodgers" to "Los Angeles Dodgers" immediately after arriving in Los Angeles. They registered their new name "Los Angeles Dodgers" in 1958. They did not register simply as the "Dodgers" which plaintiffs claim is their true trademark until 1967. Here, plaintiffs neither registered the "*Brooklyn* Dodgers" mark prior to their resumed use of the mark in 1981 nor did they produce any other evidence indicating that they had plans to resume use of the "Brooklyn Dodgers" mark when they intentionally abandoned it and Brooklyn in 1958.

2. Resumption

Having determined that plaintiffs abandoned the "Brooklyn Dodgers" mark, the next inquiry is to determine the effect of that abandonment, given that plaintiffs have recently resumed limited use of the trademark.

Plaintiffs resumed use of the "Brooklyn Dodgers" mark in 1981 following an abandonment of almost a quarter of a century. In 1981, plaintiffs licensed Eastport Manufacturing Co. to merchandise T-shirts bearing, *inter alia*, the "Brooklyn Dodgers" name and logo. (PX 19; Tr. 79–81) In 1984, Los Angeles agreed to permit Martin Dorf to use photographs of the "Brooklyn Dodgers" as wall decorations in a restaurant in New Jersey called Burger Boys of Brooklyn. (PX 4; Tr. 278–79) In 1985, Los Angeles authorized United Airlines to broadcast radio commercials which referred to the "Brooklyn Dodgers." (PX 6; Tr. 282) In 1986, Los Angeles agreed to license the Bank of New England to run an advertisement using Los Angeles' trademarks incorporating the word Brooklyn. (PX 5; Tr. 281) In 1986, Los Angeles entered into an agreement with Oxford University Press to permit them to use the "Brooklyn Dodgers" mark in connection with a book. (PX 7; Tr. 283) In 1986, plaintiffs authorized Trench Manufacturing Co. to sell various items of merchandise bearing, *inter alia*, the "Brooklyn Dodgers" mark. (PX 20; Tr. 82) In approximately 1986, plaintiff Properties began promoting Los Angeles' trademarks incorporating the word Brooklyn, together with other "oldtimer" trademarks of Major League Clubs (that is, trademarks that had not been worn on the playing field for at least five years) under the name "The Cooperstown Collection." (Tr. 83–86; *see also* PX 18) In March 1987, plaintiffs and Roman Art Embroidery Corporation entered into a licensing agreement to manufacture and sell caps bearing, *inter alia*, the "Brooklyn Dodgers" mark. (PX 21; Tr. 83–84) Los Angeles licensed the use of their marks incorporating the word "Brooklyn" in connection with the television series "Brooklyn Bridge." Los Angeles licensed the Brooklyn Dodgers Hall of Fame, located in Brooklyn, to use Los Angeles' trademarks incorporating the word "Brooklyn." (Tr. 294) These were all sporadic licensings of the use of the words "Brooklyn Dodgers"; none was for continuous commercial use of the words "Brooklyn Dodgers" by plaintiffs themselves prior to 1986 when Properties entered the name in the Cooperstown Collection.

Defendants did not select the name "The Brooklyn Dodger" for their restaurant until sometime after October 14, 1987, and did not open their first bar and restaurant using their "Brooklyn Dodger" logo until March 1988. (Tr. 383, 480, 490–91, 541, 621) Plaintiffs, on the other hand, resumed use of the Brooklyn Dodgers mark, as indicated above, a relatively short time prior to the opening of defendants' restaurant.

While no case law in this Circuit has been found precisely on point, the Eleventh Circuit has addressed this issue and held that an abandonment, once established, is not cured by a resumption of use and that upon resumption of use of the mark the holder's rights flow from the date it resumes use. *Ambrit, Inc. v. Kraft, Inc.*, 812 F.2d 1531 (11th Cir.1986). In *Ambrit*, plaintiff sought to cancel Kraft's "Polar B'ar" trademark due to abandonment pursuant to Section 45 of the Lanham Act. What was novel about *Ambrit* was the fact that at the time plaintiff sought cancellation of the mark, Kraft had resumed extensive use of it. The Eleventh Circuit held:

> [Plaintiff] does not argue that Kraft's current use of the mark is insignificant and, indeed it is beyond dispute that abandonment would be out of the question had Kraft used the mark continuously from 1932 to 1980 in the same manner that it is now using the mark. Rather [plaintiff] contends that Kraft's non-use between 1932 and 1980 caused the mark to be void. [Plaintiff] asserts that Kraft's subsequent use beginning in 1980 does not retroactively cure its past abandonment. We agree.

*Ambrit*, 812 F.2d at 1550.

[44] The court rejected Kraft's argument that its resumption of the use of the mark in 1980 made a cancellation of the registration in 1986 inappropriate. The court found that once abandoned, a mark may be cancelled even after its holder resumes commercial use of the mark. *Id.* at 1551. As applied to this case, then, once plaintiffs abandoned the "Brooklyn Dodgers" mark, they forfeited the right to exclude defendants from using the mark. *Defiance Button Machine Co. v. C &*

*C Metal Products Corp.*, 759 F.2d 1053, 1059 (2d Cir.1985) (when owner abandons mark, "others are no longer restrained from using it ...."). Even though plaintiffs resumed use of the mark before defendants began using the mark, plaintiffs' abandonment critically alters their rights to the mark. *Ambrit*, 812 F.2d at 1551 ("the competitor's right to cancel the registration flows not from the competitor's use of the mark but from the holder's abandonment"); *First Nat. Bank v. Autoteller Systems Service Corp.*, 9 U.S.P.Q.2d 1740 (BNA) (Trademark Trial & App.Bd. 1988) (Abandonment cannot be reversed by subsequent re-adoption of a mark"); *Parfums Nautee Ltd. v. American International Industries*, 22 U.S.P.Q.2d (BNA) 1306 (Trademark Trial & App.Bd.1992) (same). *See also Sodima*, 662 F.Supp. at 850 (citation omitted) ("Once a mark is abandoned, subsequent use does not retroactively cure its past abandonment. A court may cancel a mark because of abandonment even after the registrant has resumed use"). Therefore, in 1988 defendants' in this case had rights equal to plaintiffs' rights in using the mark and acquiring the mark. *Cerveceria India*, 892 F.2d at 1027 (*citing Mission Dry Corp. v. Seven-up Co.*, 193 F.2d 201, 203 (CCPA 1951) ("Once a trademark is abandoned, its registration may be cancelled even if the registrant resumes use").

[45, 46] This analysis of the effect of the abandonment of a trademark comports with the view expressed by one highly regarded commentator in this area who observes:

> Once a mark has been abandoned, "any other person has the right to seize upon it immediately ... and thus acquire a right superior not only to the right of the original user but of all the world ... Even though a mark has been intentionally abandoned, if there is no intervening right thereto, it would be illogical to deny its former owner the same right to appropriate it as any other party would have ... *Appropriation after abandonment is a new phase in the history of the mark*, and it should be considered without reference to the abandonment, whether appropriated by a stranger or reused by its prior owner. *Priority, however, goes back only to the*

*time the first owner reappropriated the mark.*

Callmann, *The Law of Unfair Competition, Trademarks, and Monopolies § 19.67* at 515 (1989) (emphasis added).

These legal principles, when applied to the facts at bar, make plain that if plaintiffs have any interest in a "Brooklyn Dodgers" mark, that interest arose in 1981 when commercial use of the mark resumed after a twenty-three (23) year hiatus. Plaintiffs' preemptive rights in the "Brooklyn Dodgers" mark would extend only to the precise goods on or in connection with which the trademark was used since its resumption (i.e. clothing, jewelry, novelty items). (*See* the various uses listed at PX 2)

In other words, the fact that plaintiffs resumed use prior to defendants' use does not mean that plaintiffs may preclude defendants' use of the mark in their restaurant business in Brooklyn. *See Manhattan Industries, Inc. v. Sweater Bee by Banff, Ltd.,* 627 F.2d 628, 630 (2d Cir.1980) (where plaintiff began using abandoned mark slightly prior to defendant, significant use by defendant precluded plaintiffs' exclusivity; "concept of priority in the law of trademarks is applied 'not in its calendar sense' but on the basis of 'the equities involved,'" *quoting Chandon Champagne Corp. v. San Marino Wine Corp.,* 335 F.2d 531, 534 (2d Cir.1964)). The Supreme Court discussed the common law allocation of trademark rights in *Hanover Star Milling Co. v. Metcalf,* 240 U.S. 403, 36 S.Ct. 357, 60 L.Ed. 713 (1916). In setting forth an exception to the blanket application of the "prior use" rule, the Court stated:

In the ordinary case of parties competing under the same mark in the same market, it is correct to say that prior appropriation settles the question. But where two parties independently are employing the same mark upon goods of the same class, but in separate markets wholly remote from one another, the question of prior appropriation is legally insignificant, unless at least it appear [sic] that the second adopter has selected the mark with some design inimical to the interest of the first user ...

*Hanover,* 240 U.S. at 415, 36 S.Ct. at 361. *See also Sweetarts v. Sunline, Inc.,* 380 F.2d

923, 928 (8th Cir.1967) (prior trademark user has valid common law trademark within area developed by it). *See, e.g., Li'l Red Barn, Inc. v. Red Barn System, Inc.,* 322 F.Supp. 98, 109 (N.D.Ind.), *aff'd,* 174 U.S.P.Q. (BNA) 193 (7th Cir.1972) (restaurant use of mark did not infringe with convenience store use of mark).

The court concludes that plaintiffs' interest, which is a new phase in the history of this mark, is only in the fields in which the mark has been used since plaintiffs chose to resume its use. *See, e.g., Conwood Corp. v. Loew's Theatres, Inc.,* 173 U.S.P.Q. (BNA) 829 (Trademark Trial & App.Bd.1972) (where trademark holder resumed use after competitor began using mark, trademark holder's use was new). The evidence makes clear that the uses to which the plaintiffs put their marks were generally sportswear and novelty items which are in no way related to defendants' restaurant and tavern services in the limited geographic area of New York City known as Brooklyn.

In addition to using the "Brooklyn Dodgers" mark for different purposes than defendants, plaintiffs presented no evidence that their commercial uses since 1981 (as opposed to their uses as the Brooklyn Dodgers baseball team prior to 1958) extend into defendants' geographical area of use. "[I]f the use of the marks by the registrant and the unauthorized user are confined to two sufficiently distinct and geographically separate markets, with no likelihood that the registrant will expand his use into defendant's market, so that no public confusion is possible, then the registrant is not entitled to enjoin the junior user's use of the mark." *Dawn Donut Co. v. Hart's Food Stores, Inc.,* 267 F.2d 358, 364 (2d Cir.1959). *See also Tally-Ho, Inc. v. Coast Community College Dist.,* 889 F.2d 1018, 1023 (11th Cir.1989) (subsequent use may establish common law rights to same mark for similar products as long as there is no competitive overlap with prior user); *Comidas Exquisitos, Inc. v. O'Malley & McGee's Inc.,* 775 F.2d 260, 262 (8th Cir. 1985) (use in geographically separate and distinct areas with no real competition or likelihood of expansion presents no cause for relief); *Cotton Ginny, Ltd. v. Cotton Gin,*

*Inc.,* 691 F.Supp. 1347, 1352 (S.D.Fla.1988) (despite plaintiff's prior use, "trademark is acquired only within those markets where the mark has been used and its meaning become known") (*citing Hanover,* 240 U.S. at 415–16, 36 S.Ct. at 361 *and Spartan Food Systems, Inc. v. HFS Corp.,* 813 F.2d 1279, 1282–84 (4th Cir.1987)). *See, e.g., Wiener King, Inc. v. The Wiener King Corp.,* 546 F.2d 421 (3rd Cir.1976), *published at,* 192 U.S.P.Q. 353 ("Absent proof that plaintiff's 'advertising,' 'expansion,' or 'reputation' would operate to extend plaintiff's trade area beyond the locale where its products are sold, we are obliged to limit plaintiff's protection to just that area of sale").

Plaintiffs have not in any way demonstrated that the restaurant business in Brooklyn is a market into which they might naturally expand. *See Tally–Ho,* 889 F.2d at 1023 (rights limited to territories of actual use or natural expansion). In order for New York to be considered to be within plaintiffs' zone of expansion, the public in New York must be familiar with plaintiffs as providers of restaurant services under the "Brooklyn Dodgers" mark. *See also Stouffer Corp. v. Winegardner & Hammons, Inc.,* 502 F.Supp. 232, 236 (S.D.Ohio 1980) (protection requires secondary meaning in area such that public associates name with services in that area) (citation omitted); *Hot Shoppes, Inc. v. The Hot Shoppe, Inc.,* 203 F.Supp. 777, 783 (M.D.N.C. 1962) (necessary for substantial section of purchasing public to identify name with services). *See generally* RUDOLF CALLMANN, THE LAW OF UNFAIR COMPETITION, TRADEMARKS AND MONOPOLIES, v. 3, § 19.19–23 (1983) (discussing zones of protection); *William Jay Gross, The Territorial Scope of Trademark Rights,* 44 U.MIAMI L.REV. 1075 (1990) (discussing various categories of zones of protection).

For example, even if plaintiffs' post–1981 uses indicate that Brooklyn is within plaintiffs' zone of expansion for novelty items, plaintiffs only post–1981 restaurant related use—permitting a third party to use photographs as wall decorations in New Jersey— does not demonstrate that plaintiffs' zone of expansion includes using the "Brooklyn Dodgers" name in the context of commercial restaurant services in Brooklyn. *See also Coffee Dan's, Inc. v. Coffee Don's Charcoal Broiler,* 305 F.Supp. 1210, 1213 (N.D.Ca.1969) (in context of motion for preliminary injunction, defendant's San Francisco restaurant was sufficiently far from plaintiff's Los Angeles restaurant to preclude finding of infringement). *Compare McDonald's Corp. v. McBagel's, Inc.,* 649 F.Supp. 1268 (S.D.N.Y.1986) (where plaintiff had national chain, as opposed to a single use, defendants' name McBagel's infringed restaurant chain's mark using the formatives "Mc" and "Mac") *with National Automobile Club v. National Auto Club, Inc.,* 365 F.Supp. 879, 886 (S.D.N.Y.), *aff'd without op.,* 502 F.2d 1162 (2d Cir.1974) (while both plaintiff and defendant rendered national services, the type of services rendered by defendant were sufficiently distinct to be outside plaintiff's zone of expansion).

[47]  This court holds that plaintiffs' failure to utilize the "Brooklyn Dodgers" mark for any significant, commercial trademark use between 1958 and 1981 constituted an abandonment of that mark and dramatically limits the protection to which that mark is entitled since its resumption. *See, e.g. Mission Dry Corp. v. Seven-up Co.,* 193 F.2d 201 (CCPA 1951) (Lanham Trademark Act of 1946 "provides for the cancellation of a registration of any mark which has been so abandoned . . . whether or not there was confusing similarity between the marks of the parties"). Although there was evidence of a very limited number of food services and food items (Dodger Dogs, etc.) in plaintiffs' stadium in Los Angeles and training camp in Florida, no evidence was introduced by plaintiffs on this critical issue to prove that this mark, "Brooklyn Dodgers," has been used by plaintiffs or licensed by plaintiffs for a restaurant such as the singularly nostalgic restaurant defendants operate in Brooklyn. Accordingly, the court declines to enjoin defendants' very limited use of the "Brooklyn Dodger" mark by defendants for use in connection with its local restaurants directed toward older Brooklyn Dodgers fans in the Brooklyn community in the city of New York. The court also declines to cancel any registration of the "Brooklyn Dodgers" mark by plaintiffs for use of that name for the sale

of goods such as T-shirts, caps, memorabilia, etc.

### 3. Laches

Because this court concludes that defendants prevail on their affirmative defense of abandonment, it is not necessary to address defendants' second affirmative defense of *laches.*

### D. *Plaintiffs' State Law Claims*

#### 1. Unfair Competition

[48] Plaintiffs claim for unfair competition under New York State law shares many common elements with the Lanham Act claims of false designation of origin and trademark infringement, including necessary proof of actual confusion before an award of damages may be granted. *See W.W.W. Pharmaceutical,* 984 F.2d at 576 (citations omitted). This court has concluded that the marks used by Los Angeles when it was located in Brooklyn and defendants' mark is not confusingly similar. This court has also concluded that plaintiffs abandoned the mark. The findings provide defendants with an effective affirmative defense to plaintiffs' claim of unfair competition. *Saratoga Vichy Spring Co. v. Lehman,* 625 F.2d 1037, 1043 (2d Cir.1980) ("Since New York state law on the issue of abandonment, even if applicable, is not particularly well-developed, it is appropriate to apply federal law by analogy, with respect to both the state and federal claims"). *See Charvet S.A. v. Dominique France, Inc.,* 736 F.2d 846 (2d Cir.1984) (in action involving Lanham Act and state unfair competition and dilution claims, abandonment by appellant precluded appellants' use to the extent of its abandonment and defeated its claims, state and federal, concerning abandoned markets).

#### 2. Dilution Claim

Plaintiffs' also claim that defendants have violated New York's anti-dilution statutes. N.Y.Gen Bus.L. § 368–d (McKinney 1984).[23]

23. The statute provides:
Likelihood of injury to business reputation or of dilution of the distinctive quality of a mark or trade name shall be a ground for injunctive relief in cases of infringement of a mark regis-

"A claim for dilution rests on the allegation that a defendant is attempting to "feed[ ] upon the business reputation of an established distinctive trade-mark or name." *W.W.W. Pharmaceutical,* 984 F.2d at 576 (quoting *Allied Maintenance Corp. v. Allied Mechanical Trades, Inc.,* 42 N.Y.2d 538, 545, 399 N.Y.S.2d 628, 369 N.E.2d 1162 (1977)).

[49,50] In this circuit, the test for dilution has consisted of three elements:

(1) distinctiveness of the mark, either that the mark is "truly of distinctive quality" or has acquired secondary meaning in the eyes of the public; (2) likelihood of dilution, either as the result of blurring of product identification or the tarnishing of an affirmative association that a mark has come to convey; and (3) predatory intent.

*W.W.W. Pharmaceutical,* 984 F.2d at 576–77 (citing *Lobo Enters., Inc. v. Tunnel, Inc.,* 693 F.Supp. 71, 79 (S.D.N.Y.1988)) (quoting *Sally Gee, Inc. v. Myra Hogan, Inc.,* 699 F.2d 621, 625–26 (2d Cir.1983)); *Mead Data Central, Inc. v. Toyota Motor Sales, U.S.A., Inc.,* 875 F.2d 1026, 1030 (2d Cir.1989). Because the court has concluded that plaintiffs abandoned their right to the "Brooklyn Dodgers" mark when they left Brooklyn, any right that they may have established upon resumption is significantly diminished and remote. Therefore, given the dramatic dilution caused by plaintiffs' own actions, plaintiffs have failed to prove distinctiveness, likelihood of dilution, or predatory intent necessary to prevail on a claim of dilution.

### E. *Defendants' Counterclaims*

[51] In their Amended Answer, defendants' counterclaimed for the cancellation of various trademark registrations for "Brooklyn Dodgers" file by plaintiffs after defendants' application to register the "Brooklyn Dodger" servicemark was filed on April 28, 1988. These cancellations are sought on the ground that plaintiffs' registrations: a) falsely and deceptively suggest and imply a con-

tered or not registered or in cases of unfair competition, not withstanding the absence of competition between the parties or the absence of confusion as to the source of goods or services.

nection between plaintiffs and the Borough of Brooklyn which has not existed since 1958; b) inherently and directly misrepresent the origin of plaintiffs' goods and services as Brooklyn, New York when this is allegedly untrue in violation of 15 U.S.C. § 1052; and c) plaintiffs' use of a "Brooklyn Dodgers" mark suggests an association with defendants which does not exist, in violation of 15 U.S.C. § 1125(a).

Defendants' counterclaims are denied. As discussed above, plaintiffs resumed use of the "Brooklyn Dodgers" mark prior to defendants' use. Plaintiffs, therefore, have acquired the right to use and register the mark to the extent of their resumed use (i.e. clothes, novelty items, and promotional features) or to the extent that it does not infringe upon the prior uses of others.

Submit order on 10 days notice.

PITTSBURGH ATHLETIC CO. et al. v.
KQV BROADCASTING CO.

No. 3415.

District Court, W. D. Pennsylvania.

Aug. 8, 1938.

I. Literary property ⬯2

Owner of professional baseball team which maintained baseball park and paid players who participated in game had property right in news value of games played by team, which right could be sold to advertisers as advertising mediums for their merchandise.

2. Trade-marks and trade-names and unfair competition ⬯68(1)

Advertisers, which by contract with owner of professional baseball team were given exclusive right to broadcast description of game played by the team, acquired a property right and could restrain interference with such right amounting to unfair competition by radio station which to cultivate good will broadcast description of games from information procured by paid observers stationed at vantage points outside the ball field.

3. Trade-marks and trade-names and unfair competition ⬯68(1)

Where advertisers were by contract with owner of baseball team given exclusive right to broadcast play-by-play account of games played by the team, unauthorized broadcasting of description of games by radio station which obtained information concerning games played by team through paid observers stationed at points outside of baseball field, was an interference with the property right acquired by the advertisers and amounted to unfair competition, notwithstanding that radio station received no compensation from a sponsor or otherwise from its baseball broadcasts.

4. Literary property ⬯5

Where advertisers were by contract with owner of professional baseball team given exclusive right to broadcast play-by-play account of games played by the team, owner or advertisers did not destroy property right to control news of games by broadcasting, since such communication of news of the ball games was not a general publication.

**5. Telegraphs and telephones ☞29**

Where advertisers were by contract with owner of baseball team given exclusive right to broadcast description of games played by the team, unauthorized broadcasting of descriptions of games by radio station which obtained information concerning games from paid observers stationed outside of baseball field was a violation of the Communications Act. Communications Act of 1934, 47 U.S.C.A. § 151 et seq.

**6. Trade-marks and trade-names and unfair competition ☞79**

Where advertisers were by contract with owner of baseball team given exclusive right to broadcast description of games played by the team, and broadcasting of descriptions of games by radio station which obtained information concerning games from paid observers outside of baseball field was unauthorized, advertisers had no adequate remedy at law, as regards right to injunction.

———◆———

In Equity. Suit in equity by the Pittsburgh Athletic Company and others against the KQV Broadcasting Company to restrain defendant from broadcasting play-by-play reports and descriptions of baseball games played by the "Pirates," a professional baseball team owned by named plaintiff. On motion for a preliminary injunction pendente lite.

Decree in accordance with opinion.

Shoemaker & Eynon, of Pittsburgh, Pa., and Miller, Owen, Otis & Bailly, of New York City (George L. Eynon, of Pittsburgh, Pa., and Louis F. Carroll, of New York City, of counsel), for plaintiff Pittsburgh Athletic Co.

Thorp, Bostwick, Reed & Armstrong, of Pittsburgh, Pa., and Webster & Garside and Louis M. Treadwell, all of New York City (Roy G. Bostwick, of Pittsburgh, Pa., and Bethuel M. Webster, of New York City, of counsel), for plaintiffs General Mills, Inc., Socony-Vacuum Oil Co., Inc., and National Broadcasting Co., Inc.

Reed, Smith, Shaw & McClay, of Pittsburgh, Pa. (Elder W. Marshall and Henry Eastman Hackney, both of Pittsburgh, Pa., of counsel), for defendant.

SCHOONMAKER, District Judge.

This is an action in equity in which plaintiffs ask for a preliminary injunction to restrain defendant from broadcasting play-by-play reports and descriptions of baseball games played by the "Pirates," a professional baseball team owned by Pittsburgh Athletic Company, both at its home baseball park in Pittsburgh, known as "Forbes Field," and at baseball parks in other cities.

The plaintiffs have moved for a preliminary injunction pendente lite. This motion was heard on the bill of complaint, injunction affidavits, and counter-affidavits.

The bill of complaint was filed July 6, 1938. At the first hearing on this motion held July 12, 1938, defendant disclaimed any intention to broadcast the news of any games played by the "Pirates" in cities other than Pittsburgh during the current season; and by affidavit filed in this case stated that no news had been broadcast by it of such "away" games since May 26, 1938. For that reason there appears to be no such danger of imminent injury to the rights of the plaintiffs as to justify a preliminary injunction, so far as concern any games played by the "Pirates" in cities other than Pittsburgh.

As to the games played, and to be played at Forbes Field in Pittsburgh, defendant admits it has broadcast play-by-play news of the Pittsburgh games, and asserts its intention to continue so to do, averring it secures the news thus broadcast and to be broadcast by it in the future from observers whom it has stationed at vantage points outside Forbes Field who can see over the enclosure of that field and observe the plays as they are made. It asserts it has a legal right to continue this practice.

The essential facts are not in dispute. The question at issue is primarily a question of law. Is the defendant within its legal rights in the practices thus pursued by it? The essential facts of the case may be briefly summarized as follows:

The plaintiff Pittsburgh Athletic Company owns a professional baseball team known as the "Pirates," and is a member of an association known as the "National League." With the several teams of the members of the League, the "Pirates" play baseball both at its home field and at the home fields of the other members of the League in various cities. The home games are played at a baseball park known as "Forbes Field" which is enclosed by high fences and structures so that the public are admitted only to the Park to witness the games at Forbes Field by the payment of an admission ticket, which provides that the holder of the admission ticket agrees not to give out any news of the game while it is in progress.

The Pittsburgh Athletic Company has granted by written contract, for a valuable consideration, to General Mills, Inc., the exclusive right to broadcast, play-by-play, descriptions or accounts of the games played by the "Pirates" at this and other fields. The National Broadcasting Company, also for a valuable consideration, has contracted with General Mills, Inc., to broadcast by radio over stations KDKA and WWSW, play-by-play descriptions of these games. The Socony-Vacuum Oil Company has purchased for a valuable consideration a half interest in the contract of the General Mills, Inc.

The defendant operates at Pittsburgh a radio broadcasting station known as KQV, from which it has in the past broadcast by radio play-by-play descriptions of the games played by the "Pirates" at Pittsburgh, and asserts its intention to continue in so doing. The defendant secures the information which it broadcasts from its own paid observers whom it stations at vantage points outside Forbes Field on premises leased by defendant. These vantage points are so located that the defendant's observers can see over the enclosures the games as they are played in Forbes Field.

On this state of facts, we are of the opinion that the plaintiffs have presented a case which entitles them under the law to a preliminary injunction.

[1] It is perfectly clear that the exclusive right to broadcast play-by-play descriptions of the games played by the "Pirates" at their home field rests in the plaintiffs, General Mills, Inc., and the Socony-Vacuum Oil Company under the contract with the Pittsburgh Athletic Company. That is a property right of the plaintiffs with which defendant is interfering when it broadcasts the play-by-play description of the ball games obtained by

the observers on the outside of the enclosure.

[2, 3] The plaintiffs and the defendant are using baseball news as material for profit. The Athletic Company has, at great expense, acquired and maintains a baseball park, pays the players who participate in the game, and have, as we view it, a legitimate right to capitalize on the news value of their games by selling exclusive broadcasting rights to companies which value them as affording advertising mediums for their merchandise. This right the defendant interferes with when it uses its broadcasting facilities for giving out the identical news obtained by its paid observers stationed at points outside Forbes Field for the purpose of securing information which it cannot otherwise acquire. This, in our judgment, amounts to unfair competition, and is a violation of the property rights of the plaintiffs. For it is our opinion that the Pittsburgh Athletic Company, by reason of its creation of the game, its control of the park, and its restriction of the dissemination of news therefrom, has a property right in such news, and the right to control the use thereof for a reasonable time following the games.

[4] The communication of news of the ball games by the Pittsburgh Athletic Company, or by its licensed news agencies, is not a general publication and does not destroy that right. This view is supported by the so-called "ticker cases" Board of Trade v. Christie Grain & Stock Co., 198 U.S. 236, 25 S.Ct. 637, 49 L.Ed. 1031; Hunt v. New York Cotton Exchange, 205 U.S. 322, 27 S.Ct. 529, 51 L.Ed. 821; Moore v. N. Y. Cotton Exchange, 270 U.S. 593, 46 S.Ct. 367, 70 L.Ed. 750, 45 A.L.R. 1370; McDearmott Commission Co. v. Board of Trade, 8 Cir., 146 F. 961, 7 L.R.A.,N.S., 889, 8 Ann.Cas. 759; Board of Trade v. Tucker, 2 Cir., 221 F. 305.

On the unfair competition feature of the case, we rest our opinion on the case of International News Service v. Associated Press, 248 U.S. 215, 39 S.Ct. 68, 63 L.Ed. 211, 2 A.L.R. 293. In that case the court enjoined the International News Service from copying news from bulletin boards and early editions of Associated Press newspapers, and selling such news so long as it had commercial value to the Associated Press. The Supreme Court said (248 U.S. at page 236, 39 S.Ct. at page

71): "* * * Regarding the news, therefore, as but the material, out of which both parties are seeking to make profits at the same time and in the same field, we hardly can fail to recognize that for this purpose, and as between them, it must be regarded as quasi property, irrespective of the rights of either as against the public.

'In order to sustain the jurisdiction of equity over the controversy, we need not affirm any general and absolute property in the news as such. 'The rule that a court of equity concerns itself only in the protection of property rights treats any civil right of a pecuniary nature as a property right, (In re Sawyer, 124 U.S. 200, 210, 8 S.Ct. 482, 31 L.Ed. 402; In re Debs, 158 U.S. 564, 593, 15 S.Ct. 900, 39 L.Ed. 1092); and the right to acquire property by honest labor or the conduct of a lawful business is as much entitled to protection as the right to guard property already acquired. * * *"

And again at pages 239, 240, 39 S.Ct. at page 72: "* * * The right of the purchaser of a single newspaper to spread knowledge of its contents gratuitously, for any legitimate purpose not unreasonably interfering with the complainant's right 'to make merchandise of it, may be admitted; but to transmit that news for commercial use, in competition with complainant—which is what defendant has done and seeks to justify—is a very different matter. * * *"

In Twentieth Century Sporting Club, Inc., v. Transradio Press Service, Inc., 165 Misc. 71, 300 N.Y.S. 159, the New York Supreme Court applied the principles of unfair competition to a broadcast of the Louis-Farr fight and entered an injunction.

In Associated Press v. KVOS, Inc., 9 Cir., 80 F.2d 575, a preliminary injunction was granted to restrain Station KVOS from appropriating and broadcasting news gathered by the Associated Press on the ground that the broadcasting station was in competition with the Associated Press in the business of publication of news for profit.

Defendant contends it is not unfairly competing with any of the plaintiffs because it obtains no compensation from a sponsor or otherwise from its baseball broadcasts. It concedes, however, that KQV seeks by its broadcast of news of baseball games to cultivate the good will of the public for its radio station. The fact that no revenue is obtained directly from the broadcast is not controlling, as these broadcasts are undoubtedly designed to aid in obtaining advertising business. See Waring v. WDAS Station, Inc., 327 Pa. 433, 435, 194 A. 631; Witmark & Sons v. Bamberger & Co., D.C., 291 F. 776; Remick & Co. v. Automobile Accessories Co., 6 Cir., 5 F.2d 411, 40 A.L.R. 1511; Irving Berlin, Inc., v. Daigle, 5 Cir., 31 F.2d 832; Herbert v. Shanley Co., 242 U.S. 591, 37 S.Ct. 232, 61 L.Ed. 511; Associated Press v. KVOS, Inc., 80 F.2d 575.

Defendant seeks to justify its action on the ground that the information it receives from its observers stationed on its own property without trespassing on plaintiffs' property, may be lawfully broadcast by it. We cannot follow defendant's counsel in this contention for the reasons above stated. The cases cited by them we have carefully studied and are unable to accept as authority. In the Australian case, Victoria Park Racing, etc., v. Taylor, 37 New South Wales 322, where the information broadcast was obtained from a tower adjoining a race track, the court refused an injunction, because there was neither a trespass on plaintiff's race track, or a nuisance created by defendant.

The doctrine of unfair competition is not recognized under the English Common Law. Therefore this decision is not an authority.

In the case of Sports and General Press Agency v. Our Dogs Publishing Company, [1916] 2 K.B. 880, which involved the taking of photographs from a point outside the dog-shows grounds, is likewise a case for the application of English law. The question of unfair competition was not considered at all, and could not be recognized under the English law.

The case of National Exhibition Company v. Tele-Flash, Inc. (D.C.S.D.N.Y. 1936) 24 F.Supp. 488, presents a case somewhat similar to the case at bar. However, we are unable to follow the court's ruling, because we do not believe that the District Judge correctly interpreted the law as to unfair competition as applicable to cases of this kind.

### Conclusions of Law.

1. This Court has jurisdiction of this cause by reason of diversity of citizenship and the amount in controversy.

2. The right, title and interest in and to the baseball games played within the parks

of members of the National League, including Pittsburgh, including the property right in, and the sole right of, disseminating or publishing or selling, or licensing the right to disseminate, news, reports, descriptions, or accounts of games played in such parks, during the playing thereof, is vested exclusively in such members.

3. The actions and threatened actions of the defendant constitute a direct and irreparable interference with, and an appropriation of, the plaintiffs' normal and legitimate business; and said action is calculated to, and does, result in the unjust enrichment of the defendant at the expense of the plaintiffs and each of them.

4. The defendant's unauthorized broadcasts of information concerning games played by the Pittsburgh team constitute unfair competition with the plaintiffs and each of them.

5. The defendant wrongfully deprives the plaintiffs and each of them of the just benefits of their labors and expenditures in respect of the baseball games and the public dissemination of news thereof as alleged in the complaint; and the action, threatened action and practice of the defendant constitute a fraud on the public.

6. The actions and threatened actions of the defendant herein alleged constitute a wrongful interference with the contractual rights and obligations of the parties.

[5] 7. The defendant's action as herein described constitutes a violation of the Communications Act of 1934, 47 U.S.C.A. § 151 et seq.

[6] 8. The plaintiffs have no adequate remedy at law.

9. The plaintiffs are entitled to and are hereby granted a preliminary injunction.

# PART 6

## TORTS AND BASEBALL: LOVE HURTS

There are an endless array of tort cases concerning injuries arising out of the playing or watching of baseball. Unfortunately, the vast majority of these cases are uninteresting and repetitive discussions of the standard duty, negligence, proximate cause, injury, and assumption of risk issues that clog our courts and law school casebooks. The editors therefore have limited this section to three items. The brief note, entitled "Baseball and the Law," sets forth the correct propositions that spectators assume a certain amount of risk when they attend a game, but that team and stadium owners have a duty of care to provide and maintain such helpful items as foul ball screens behind home plate. For a more modern tort case involving defective foul ball screens, see *Yates v. Chicago National League Base Ball Club, Inc.*, 230 Ill. App. 3d 472, 595 N.E.2d 570 (1st Dist. 1992), briefly discussed in chapter 9.

The editors have selected two interesting cases for the readers' consideration. The first is the only known reported decision where a fan has recovered for being hit by a wild pitch, thrown from the bullpen of Wrigley Field. The second involved the "Dave Winfield" of bat-throwing high school ball players. Both cases provide anecdotal support for the editors' suspicion that the language of baseball and the lore of the major leagues has fundamentally infected the American legal system.

## BASEBALL AND THE LAW

The game of baseball, which derived its origin from the old schoolboy game of "rounders," has nearly reached the century mark of its existence, having been first played in Philadelphia in 1833. Since that time public interest in the game has steadily increased, until it is now termed the "national pastime"—and properly so, thousands of golf addicts to the contrary notwithstanding. Its hold on the American people is demonstrated by the fact that the attendance at professional games has increased during the present economic depression; one reason being, perhaps, the comparative inexpensiveness of baseball as a form of diversion.

In view of the vast number of persons who attend games each season, and sit in stands unprotected from batted or thrown baseballs, it is somewhat surprising that there are so few injuries sustained—but such seems to be the case, if one is to judge from the small amount of litigation on the subject which has reached the courts of record in the various jurisdictions.

Can one who has paid to see a baseball game recover from the management for injuries sustained as a result of being struck by a batted or thrown baseball? A review of the authorities indicates generally that no such recovery may be had in the absence of extenuating circumstances.

The question was presented in the recent case of *Lorino v. New Orleans Baseball & Amusement Co., Inc.,* (La. App. 1931) 133 So. 408, an action to recover for injuries inflicted by a batted ball during the batting practice immediately preceding the game. It appeared that the plaintiff, in order to save the additional charge for a seat in the grand stand, had purchased a ticket for the "bleachers." These seats were uncovered and unprotected save for a wire screen about five feet in height, whereas the grand stand seats were covered and fully protected from the dangers from batted or thrown balls. The plaintiff had entered the "bleachers" and was looking around to determine just which seat would suit him best when he was struck by a foul ball, suffering a fractured jaw. It was contended on his behalf that since the defendant maintained the small wire screen in front of the seats, he was justified in assuming that such screen was all that was required to afford him complete protection, and that if there were danger of balls being knocked over that screen, the defendant should have erected a higher one. The court, however, denied a recovery, saying: "It is well known, as the evidence demonstrates, that it is not possible, at baseball games, for the ball to be kept at all times within the confines of the playing field. Errors must inevitably occur and foul balls must frequently be knocked, and on any such occasion there is danger that the ball may enter that portion of the park occupied by the spectators. Those who fear such dangers may, as we have said, secure protection in those seats in front of which screens are erected, and which screens extend from the ground to the roof and afford complete safety. Those who do not elect to take advantage of such protection assume the risks of such obvious dangers. That plaintiff was familiar with the possibilities of such an occurrence is shown by his testimony to the effect that he had attended other baseball games and had been in this particular park on at least two prior occasions. . . . Whether plaintiff was guilty of negligence in standing in an unprotected section without keeping his attention focused on the players is a matter which we find it unnecessary to determine, since we believe that the fact that plaintiff, by selecting a seat in that section, assumed the risk of all such accidents; but, since it is undisputed that such occurrences are most frequent, it would seem to be a more or less dangerous practice to fail to pay attention to the play."

And it was held in *Kavafian* v. *Seattle Baseball Club Assoc.*, (1919) 105 Wash. 219, 181 Pac. 679, reversing (1919) 105 Wash. 215, 177 Pac. 776, that one familiar with baseball, who, instead of taking a seat on the grand stand, protected by a screen, to which his ticket entitled him, took a seat outside of the screened area, was guilty of contributory negligence, or assumed the risk, so as to be precluded from recovery for injury through being struck by a foul ball. It was said: "Conscious of the fact that balls are often hit 'foul,' and that wild throws sometimes result in the ball falling among the spectators, and conscious of the fact that there was no protection between the balls and himself, he continued to occupy a seat in that unscreened portion until he received his injury. It matters not whether one designates his act in this regard contributory negligence, or views it as in the nature of assumption of risk, the result is the same. The place in which he could have taken a seat would have fully protected him against the ordinary and usual hazards incident to witnessing the game in question, but he chose to sit elsewhere and substitute for that safety the compensating facility of vision. If there was a chance of danger, the respondent voluntarily took it. Having purchased a ticket which offered him a choice of two positions, he, with full knowledge of the risk of injury, chose the more dangerous position."

In *Crane* v. *Kansas City Baseball, etc., Co.*, (1913) 168 Mo. App. 301, 153 S. W. 1076, it appeared that the grand stand of the ball park in which the injury occurred was partially protected from batted balls by means of wire netting. The plaintiff paid for admission to the grand stand and had the option of seating himself at some place behind the netting or in an unprotected seat. He chose one of the latter and during the course of the game was struck by a foul ball and injured. His contention was that the defendants were negligent in not screening in the whole of the grand stand, and that such negligence was the proximate cause of the injury. In denying a recovery, the court said: "Defendants were not insurers of the safety of spectators; but, being engaged in the business of providing a public entertainment for profit, they were bound to exercise reasonable care, i.e., care commensurate to the circumstances of the situation, to protect their patrons against injury. . . . In view of the facts that the general public is invited to attend these games, that hard balls are thrown and batted with great force and swiftness, and that such balls often go in the direction of the spectators, we think the duty of defendants towards their patrons included that of providing seats protected by screening from wildly thrown or foul balls, for the use of patrons who desired such protection. Defendants fully performed that duty when they provided screened seats in the grand stand, and gave plaintiff the opportunity of occupying one of those seats. . . . So in the present case plaintiff, doubtless for the purpose of avoiding the annoyance of the slight obstruction to vision offered by the netting, voluntarily chose an unprotected seat, and thereby assumed the ordinary risks of such position. And if it could not be said that he assumed the risk, still he should not be allowed to recover, since his own contributory negligence is apparent and indisputable. One invited to a place, who is offered a choice of two positions, one of which is less safe than the other, cannot be said to be in the exercise of reasonable care if, with full knowledge of the risks and dangers, he chooses the more dangerous place."

In *Wells* v. *Minneapolis Baseball, etc., Assoc.*, (1913) 122 Minn. 327, 142 N. W. 706, Ann. Cas. 1914 D 922, 46 L. R. A. (N. S.) 606, it appeared that a portion of the defendant's grand stand was protected by a screen, there being some dispute whether the plaintiff was seated within the screened portion or outside thereof when she was struck by a foul ball. The plaintiff claimed that she was sitting about 10 feet within the end of the screen and about 12 feet in the rear thereof, and that the ball curved around the edge of the screen. Other evidence tended to show that she was seated beyond the end of the screen. The court held that if she were seated in accordance with her testimony, the defendant baseball association had performed its full duty with regard to her protection, saying: "It is inconceivable that a baseball, when fouled by a batter, could curve around the end of the screen in the manner this ball is said by her to have curved and reached her. No one claims that it glanced from striking any post or object after the time it touched the bat and before it struck plaintiff. The defendant was not an insurer against all perils, nor was it guilty of negligence in failing to guard against improbable dangers." It was further held that if the plaintiff were seated beyond the end of the screen, and if she knew and appreciated the dangers of baseball, she assumed the risk of being struck, the defendant having provided a choice between a screened in and unprotected seat. A new trial was granted because of the fact that the plaintiff's knowledge of the dangers of the game did not conclusively appear.

A somewhat similar state of facts was presented in *Curtis* v. *Portland Baseball Club*, (1929) 130 Ore. 93,

279 Pac. 277, an action to recover damages for injuries sustained by the plaintiff as a result of being struck by a foul ball. The evidence showed that the defendant had erected a screen in front of the grand stand 40 feet high and 150 feet long, and that the plaintiff occupied a seat about 6 feet behind the screen and on the extreme end. The plaintiff was injured, he alleged, by a foul-tipped ball which had been pitched with great speed and which curved around the end of the screen and struck him on the nose. The defendant was charged with negligence in failing to extend a wing of the screen back into the grand stand for a distance of 8 or 10 feet in order to protect spectators from foul balls. A judgment for the plaintiff was reversed, the court holding that the defendant had exercised reasonable care and diligence commensurate with the danger involved to protect its patrons from injury, and that the accident was one which could not reasonably have been anticipated.

A quite different situation was presented in *Cincinnati Baseball Club* v. *Eno,* (1925) 112 Ohio St. 175, 147 N. E. 86, which appears to be the only reported "big league" case dealing with the point under discussion. There the evidence showed that the plaintiff occupied a reserved box seat in the grand stand at a "double header" between the Cincinnati and New York teams. During the intermission between the games one of the defendant's players batted a thrown ball which struck the plaintiff in the face, it being alleged the player was batting from a point near the grand stand where the plaintiff was sitting and not from the diamond proper. It was contended that the defendant was negligent in not providing a screen or other protection for the spectators and in permitting its players to bat balls from such a point. The court, after reviewing a number of cases which denied recovery, stated that it concurred in the soundness of the views expressed therein with regard to injuries incurred by balls thrown or batted during the course of a baseball game. In this case, however, the injury was incurred during practice when a number of balls were being thrown and batted by the various players. In holding that the question of the defendant's negligence and the plaintiff's contributory negligence was one of fact for the jury, the court said: "When several balls are simultaneously in play upon the field, it is impossible for the spectator to protect himself by watching the ball, for more than one ball is being thrown or batted at once. During the course of the game itself the spectator can watch the ball. During the course of the practice he cannot follow the maneuvers of all of the possible groups. . . . We do not think that a court should say as a matter of law that a spectator assumes the risk of every batting or throwing of the ball permitted upon the field by the management, no matter how near the grand stand, no matter how many groups were engaged in the practice, and no matter whether the batting or throwing is a part of the game itself. Under the facts set out in this case, which differ so essentially from those in the cases cited, we are of the opinion that the contributory negligence of the plaintiff should have been submitted to the jury."

And the fact that the equipment of the baseball park is defective may result in a different holding. Thus, in *Edling* v. *Kansas City Baseball, etc., Co.,* (1914) 181 Mo. App. 327, 168 S. W. 908, the evidence showed that the plaintiff, after paying the regular fee charged by the defendant for a seat in the grand stand, took a seat in the section behind the catcher's box, which section was screened in with chicken netting. During the progress of the game a foul ball passed through a large hole worn in the netting and struck the plaintiff, breaking his nose. The inference from all of the plaintiff's evidence was that the screening was old, worn, and rotten, and had not been repaired in either that or the preceding season. The court held that the plaintiff was entitled to recover, saying: "One of the natural risks encountered by spectators of a professional baseball game is that of being struck by a fouled ball, and it goes without saying that defendant was not required by law, and did not undertake, to insure the patrons of the screened-in portions of its grand stand immunity against injury from such source, but, being in the business of providing a public entertainment for profit, defendant was bound to exercise reasonable care to protect its patrons against such injuries. . . . Defendant recognized this duty by screening that part of the grand stand most exposed to the battery of foul balls, and impliedly assured spectators who paid for admission to the grand stand that seats behind the screen were reasonably protected. None of those seats was closed to patrons, and when plaintiff entered the grand stand he was invited to seat himself where he pleased, with the assurance that reasonable care had been observed for his protection. It was the duty of defendant to exercise reasonable care to keep the screen free from defects, and, if it allowed it to become old, rotten, and perforated with holes larger than a ball, the jury were entitled to infer that it did not properly perform that duty, but was guilty of negligence. In seating himself where he did plaintiff did not assume the risks resulting from such negligence." With regard to a suggestion that the plaintiff was negligent in not attempting to catch or dodge the ball, the court said: "His explanation that he was watching the game, but failed to see the course the ball had taken from the bat, is reasonable and natural. The uncertainty in the direction, speed, and force of a batted ball is one of the interesting and often exciting features of the game, and frequently it is difficult for even the trained eye to follow the course of the ball. As is aptly observed by counsel for plaintiff: 'If the Kansas City Blues had kept their eyes on the ball with the accuracy defendant says plaintiff should have displayed, they would have attained a higher place in the race for the pennant.' "

It is customary for owners of baseball clubs to stipulate against liability for injuries incurred by batted and thrown balls. For example, the holder of a ticket to any game presented by the New York club of the American League will find on the back of the "rain check" (which is retained by the patron) the following stipulation: "Important Notice. The holder of this ticket assumes all risk and danger incidental to the game of baseball, including specifically (but not exclusively) the danger of being injured by thrown and batted balls, and agrees that the management is not liable for injuries resulting from such causes." Other clubs, the Brooklyn National League club, for example, do not make such a stipulation.

That such a stipulation will in itself prevent liability on the part of the management is extremely doubtful. It does seem, however, that such provisions would be admissible in evidence as tending to prove a precaution taken by the management to warn spectators of the perils of the game. See *Wells* v. *Minneapolis Baseball, etc., Assoc.,*

(1913) 122 Minn. 327, 142 N. W. 706, Ann. Cas. 1914 D
922, 46 L. R. A. (N. S.) 606, wherein the court, with
reference to signs conspicuously placed by the management
of a baseball club and stating that the management would
not be responsible for injuries received from thrown or
batted balls, said: "Conceding that the defendant may not
escape liability by merely stating it will not be responsible,
nevertheless we do think the signs convey information that
injuries are apt to happen from thrown and batted balls,
and are therefore in the nature of a precaution to prevent
injury."

JOSEPH T. BUXTON, JR.

80 Ill.App.2d 336

**David M. MAYTNIER, Jr., by David M. Maytnier, his father and next friend, Plaintiff-Appellant,**

v.

**Robert RUSH, Defendant-Appellee,**

and

**Chicago National League Ball Club, Inc., a corporation, Defendant.**


**David M. MAYTNIER, Jr., by David M. Maytnier, his father and next friend, Plaintiff-Appellee,**

v.

**CHICAGO NATIONAL LEAGUE BALL CLUB, INC., a corporation, Defendant-Appellant,**

and

**Robert Rush, Defendant.**

**Gen. Nos. 50780, 50781.**

Appellate Court of Illinois. First District, Second Division.

March 6, 1967.

Rehearing Denied April 5, 1967.

---

James A. Dooley, Chicago, for David M. Maytnier, Jr., by David M. Maytnier, his father and next friend.

Hinshaw, Culbertson, Moelmann & Hoban, Chicago, for Chicago National League Ball Club, Inc., and Robert Rush; Perry L. Fuller, Thomas J. Weithers, Chicago, of counsel.

LYONS, Presiding Justice.

This is a consolidation of appeals from judgments, after the return of jury verdicts, entered in favor of plaintiff against defendant, Chicago National League Ball Club, Inc. (hereinafter referred to as defendant, Chicago Cubs) for $20,000.00 and in favor of defendant, Robert Rush (hereinafter referred to as defendant, Rush). General No. 50780 is an appeal by plaintiff from the judgment for defendant Rush and General No. 50781 is an appeal by defendant Chicago Cubs from the judgment for the plaintiff.

On September 13, 1957, plaintiff, David M. Maytnier, Jr., purchased a ticket to a Chicago Cubs doubleheader specifically requesting a seat as close to the Cubs dugout as possible so that he could get a better view of the players. He received and occupied a seat in the front row, approximately ten to fifteen seats to the outfield side of the Cubs dugout. Plaintiff had been to Wrigley Field six to twelve times over the previous two to three years. He knew a protective screen was provided behind home plate and that none was so provided in the area where his seat was located.

During the sixth inning of the second game, plaintiff was struck and injured on the left side of his head by a ball thrown from the bullpen by defendant Rush. This warming up area or bullpen was located on the field of play between the third base foul line and the grandstand at a point about midway between the Cubs dugout and the left field wall. Pitchers warming up therein would throw in approximately the same direction as would the pitcher in the game itself. Plaintiff knew of the bullpen's proximity to the grandstand, and that it was not uncommon for some warming up activity to take place there. The seat occupied by plaintiff was in such a position that it required him to look to his right to see the pitcher and batter in the game and to his left to see the bullpen activity. In just which direction plaintiff was looking when struck by the ball was much controverted.

Testimony was elicited which showed that Cub pitchers may warm up of their own volition or by the specific direction of a manager, and that a pitcher may, on occasion while warming up, experiment with a new pitch. It was proffered that defendant Rush was having a bad year and that when a pitcher is having a bad year, he attempts to correct his pitching rhythm. The warm up catcher, Gordon Massa, testified that the pitch in question went up to his left beyond his reach. Massa was six feet three inches tall.

Evidence was offered to show that there exists a substantial benefit, to be able to throw warm up pitches in the same direction as the pitcher in the game and also thus be able to examine the opposing batters as they come to bat. Testimony was also introduced to support the contention that

there existed no other feasible location in Wrigley Field for such a bullpen. Defendant Rush admitted that he had thrown "wild pitches" while warming up on prior occasions.

It is defendant Rush's theory of the case in No. 50780 that plaintiff's appeal should be dismissed for want of timeliness under the Supreme Court Rules.

It is defendant Chicago Cubs' theory of the case in No. 50781: (1) that it was under no duty to screen off its entire park and is, as a matter of law, not liable to spectators at a game, who are struck by baseballs; (2) that plaintiff assumed the risk of injury; and (3) that the trial court erred in not directing a verdict in its favor.

It is plaintiff's theory of the case in No. 50781: (1) that defendant Chicago Cubs violated the duty an owner-occupier of premises owes to invitees present thereon by establishing and maintaining a dangerous facility in proximity to the grandstand; (2) that defendant Chicago Cubs was negligent in allowing defendant Rush to experiment with new pitches while in the bullpen; (3) that defendant Rush was negligent in throwing the ball into the grandstand; and (4) that the verdict returned for defendant Rush was against the manifest weight of the evidence.

In case No. 50780 plaintiff appeals from a judgment entered below in favor of defendant Rush. Defendant Rush filed a motion to dismiss the appeal, (which was taken with the case) on grounds that the appeal was not perfected within the time permitted by Supreme Court Rule 35. A judgment was entered upon the verdict on January 14, 1965. Plaintiff and both defendants filed post trial motions which were denied on April 28, 1965. Defendant Chicago Cubs filed notice of appeal 16 days thereafter on May 14, 1965, and plaintiff filed notice of appeal from the judgment in favor of defendant Rush on June 25, 1965, 58 days after the judgment had become final. Supreme Court Rule

35(1), Ill.Rev.Stat. (1965) Ch. 110, Par. 101.35(1) stated:

> Each appellee who desires to prosecute a cross appeal from all or any part of the judgment, decision, order or decree, and each co-party who did not join in the notice of appeal but who desires to join as appellant or to prosecute a separate appeal shall, within 10 days after service upon him of notice of appeal, serve a notice upon each party or attorney or firm of attorneys who signed the notice of appeal, and upon each appellee, person or officer entitled to receive notice of an appeal, and file a copy thereof in the trial court.

[1] It is defendant Rush's position that once defendant Chicago Cubs filed its notice of appeal 16 days after the judgment became final, it then became incumbent upon plaintiff to file his notice of cross appeal within 10 days thereafter, or within a sum total of 26 days after the judgment became final notwithstanding the general provision found in the Civil Practice Act, Ill.Rev.Stat. (1965) Ch. 110, Par. 76, allowing 60 days for the filing of notice of appeal. Plaintiff contends that as to defendant Rush, he is neither an appellee nor a co-party who did not file a separate notice of appeal within the meaning of the statute. In addition, plaintiff points out that separate judgments were entered from the verdict in the trial court. This court is of the opinion that plaintiff's reasoning, if accepted here, would operate to defeat the intent of Supreme Court Rule 35.

In case No. 50781, we find that plaintiff entered the premises of defendant Chicago Cubs as a business invitee. Reciprocal benefits were derived as a result. Plaintiff, by accepting the public invitation held out by the defendant Chicago Cubs, was entertained by the performance of professional athletes, and defendant Chicago Cubs in consideration therefor, received pecuniary benefit.

[2-5] It is well established law in this State that the owner-occupier of lands is not an insurer of the safety of invitees on his premises, but he is under a duty to exercise reasonable care for their protection. An owner-occupier's liability to an invitee for injuries not intentionally inflicted must be predicated upon negligence, and no presumption of negligence on the part of the owner-occupier arises merely by showing that an injury has been sustained by one rightfully upon the premises. Altepeter v. Virgil State Bank, 345 Ill.App. 585, 104 N.E.2d 334 (1952). Moreover, this duty of reasonable care owed to an invitee does not require a complete fencing of the spectators present at a baseball game to protect them from stray baseballs. As stated in Brisson v. Minneapolis Baseball & Athletic Association, 185 Minn. 507, 240 N.W. 903 (1932):

> In our opinion they exercise the required care if they provide screen for the most dangerous part of the grandstand and for those who may be reasonably anticipated to desire protected seats, and that they need not provide such seats for an unusual crowd, such as the one in attendance at the game here involved.

[6-8] It does not necessarily follow, however, that once an owner of a ballpark has provided an adequate fenced-in area for the most dangerous part of the grandstand he has thereafter exculpated himself from further liability as defendant Chicago Cubs contends. To the contrary see Restatement of the Law of Torts, 2d, 344 (1964), which states:

> A possessor of land who holds it open to the public for entry for his business purposes is subject to liability to members of the public while they are upon the land for such a purpose, for physical harm caused by the accidental, negligent, or intentionally harmful acts of third persons * * *, and by the failure of the possessor to exercise reasonable care to

(a) discover that such acts are being done or are likely to be done, or

(b) give a warning adequate to enable the visitors to avoid the harm, or otherwise to protect them against it.

In speaking of the independent negligent acts of a third person while on the premises of the owner which result in injury to an invitee present thereon, the court in Altepeter v. Virgil State Bank, 345 Ill.App. 585, 104 N.E.2d 334 (1952) said:

> \* \* \* no liability attaches to the latter (owner) unless the circumstances are such that liability can be predicated on the theory of the existence of a public nuisance or of a dangerous condition, known to the owner or occupant, which he failed to take reasonable precautions to alleviate. (Insert supplied.)

The court went further stating that the basis of an owner's liability for injuries to an invitee rests upon the owner's superior knowledge of the danger. Moreover, proof that the owner had actual knowledge of the dangerous condition is not a prerequisite to his liability. Reichmann v. Robertson's, Inc., 264 Ill.App. 537 (1932).

[9] In Ratcliff v. San Diego Baseball Club, 27 Cal.App.2d 733, 81 P.2d 625 (1938), the court said that the park owner would not have been carrying out its duty of ordinary care if such an accident could reasonably have been foreseen and nothing was done to protect the patrons from such possible injury. Plaintiff here clearly avers a breach of this duty owing to him in paragraph 7(a) of his fourth amended complaint at law, to wit;

> \* \* \* carelessly and negligently permitted and caused to permit and maintain the location of its bullpen at a place in the park which was dangerous to the plaintiff, situated nearby, who was watching the game.

Defendant Chicago Cubs contends that the only evidence presented by plaintiff to sustain his charges of negligence by defendant Chicago Cubs was that in 1957 the Chicago White Sox and New York Yankees of the American League and two of eight National League ball clubs situated their respective bullpens in areas off the playing field. We do not believe this to be a correct appraisal of the evidence offered by plaintiff. Relative to the issue of negligence, plaintiff offered the following: (1) that protective screens are positioned in front of both the first baseman and pitcher during batting practice as more than one ball is simultaneously being played; (2) that protective plastic helmets were worn by some, if not all, batters in the National League in 1957; (3) that Wrigley Field has remained substantially unchanged since its construction in 1916; (4) that the ball in question struck the plaintiff on the fly from his left while he was, at the same moment, looking to his right at the pitcher and batter in the game; (5) that a baseball is a hard ball, oft times thrown at speeds near ninety miles per hour, by a pitcher, from a point sixty feet, six inches away from its intended destination; (6) that pitchers pitching in the bullpen, whether by direction of the team manager or of their own volition, is not an abnormal occurrence during a ball game; (7) that when a pitcher is having a bad year he attempts to correct his pitching rhythm, and he may also possibly experiment by throwing new pitches in practice; (8) that pitchers warming up in the bullpen are eventually throwing as hard as they would in the game itself; (9) that plaintiff was not, as a result of the focus of his attention on the game in progress, in a position to see the ball that struck him; (10) that the defendant Rush, had thrown "wild pitches" during warm up sessions on prior occasions; and (11) that no protective screening was provided by the defendant Chicago Cubs in the area in proximity to said bullpen.

[10, 11] Admittedly, defendant Chicago Cubs is correct in contending that evidence to the effect that another method was used by others in performing a certain task does not, of itself, establish negligence.

Watts v. Bacon & Van Buskirk Glass Co., 18 Ill.2d 226, 163 N.E.2d 425 (1959), Rotche v. Buick Motor Co., 358 Ill. 507, 193 N.E. 529 (1934), Turner v. Chicago Housing Authority, 11 Ill.App.2d 160, 136 N.E.2d 543 (1956), Peterson v. Feltenberger, 102 Pa.Super. 6, 156 A. 621 (1930), Kelly v. Loft, Inc., 124 N.J.L. 185, 11 A.2d 58 (1940), Kahn v. Werbel, 4 N.J.Super. 184, 66 A.2d 559 (1940). It must be pointed out, however, that this evidence is not the only evidence presented by plaintiff, as defendant Chicago Cubs maintains. The aforementioned evidence offered by plaintiff, though seriously questioned by opposing counsel, clearly raises triable issues of fact of sufficient credibility and probative value to warrant the court's refusal of a directed verdict in favor of defendant Chicago Cubs.

Defendant Chicago Cubs further argues that the only question raised by plaintiff as to its alleged negligence is a question of law and not fact and as such should not have been submitted for jury determination. It claims that the owner of a baseball stadium is under no duty to screen the entire baseball park area occupied by the spectators, and as a matter of law, is not liable to spectators at a baseball game who are struck by baseballs. In support of this contention, defendant Chicago Cubs cites eighteen cases, all of which are clearly distinguishable from the facts of the instant case. These cases all dealt with injuries to a spectator from a batted or thrown ball that was the ball actually in play in the game or from a batted or thrown ball when no game was, in fact, in progress.

The facts here in issue evidence an entirely different situation in which the plaintiff was struck by a ball, not in play in the game, coming from his left at a time when the spectators' attentions were focused on the ball actually in play in the game, to plaintiff's right. Furthermore, defendant Chicago Cubs relies on Jones v. Alexandria Baseball Ass'n., La.App., 50 So.2d 93 (1951) as authority for its non-

225 N.E.2d—6½

liability, yet there the court specifically attributed the plaintiff's denial of recovery to his failure to "keep his eye on the ball," a ball that was in play it might be added. The case at bar presents factual circumstances quite different from those held applicable to the general rules concerning non-liability of ball park owners to spectators. This court cannot say, therefore, that defendant Chicago Cubs has not breached a duty as a matter of law.

[12, 13] It is not the province of this court to substitute its judgment for that of a jury. Niman v. Pecatonica Livestock Exchange, Inc., 13 Ill.App.2d 144, 141 N.E. 2d 327 (1957). Furthermore, the sole question presented on a defendant's motion for a directed verdict or judgment notwithstanding the verdict is whether the evidence in favor of plaintiff, admitting it to be true, together with all the legitimate conclusions drawn therefrom, fairly tends to sustain plaintiff's cause of action and thereby support the verdict of the jury. Elbers v. Standard Oil Company, 331 Ill.App. 207, 72 N.E.2d 874 (1947), Seeds v. Chicago Transit Authority, 409 Ill. 566, 101 N.E.2d 84 (1951). It is the opinion of this court that the evidence in favor of plaintiff, assumed to be true, together with reasonable inferences drawn therefrom, that as a matter of law, the motions for a directed verdict and judgment notwithstanding the verdict made by defendant Chicago Cubs was properly denied. We cannot say that an opposite conclusion was clearly manifest or that the jury's verdict was erroneous and unwarranted.

Defendant Chicago Cubs further argues that it was error for the court to refuse his motion for a directed verdict because plaintiff was barred from his action by the affirmative defense of assumption of risk. It contends that plaintiff, then a boy 13 years old, familiar with the game of baseball and the hazards attendant thereto, specifically requested a seat behind the Cub dugout, an area known by him to be unscreened and adjacent to the bullpen, thereby assuming the risk of the injury he incurred. Plaintiff strongly questions the applicability of assumption of risk as a defense beyond the scope of master-servant relationships from which it originated. Defendant Chicago Cubs relies on four decisions as persuasive authority that the doctrine applies equally to contractual relationships as well and possibly any relationship whatsoever in Illinois. They are, Macabee v. Miller, 316 Ill.App. 157, 44 N.E.2d 341 (1942); Campion v. Chicago Landscape Co., 295 Ill.App. 225, 14 N.E. 2d 879 (1938); Stickel v. Riverview Sharpshooters' Park Co., 159 Ill.App. 110, aff. 250 Ill. 452, 95 N.E. 445, 34 L.R.A.,N.S., 659 (1910); Altepeter v. Virgil State Bank, 345 Ill.App. 585, 104 N.E.2d 334 (1952).

The *Macabee* and *Stickel* cases, when analyzed, simply held that the question of assumption of risk, where a master-servant relationship did not exist, was properly submitted to the jury, as a question of fact, for their determination. The court in the *Campion* case, where a golfer was struck by a golf ball while playing on a public course, pronounced that the doctrine was no longer limited to master-servant relationships. This ruling, however, must be afforded little weight by this court as the pronouncement was obiter dictum, as the court there reversed a decision for the plaintiff for his failure to prove any negligence by defendant. Clearly, the question of assumption of risk was not a determinative issue. Similarly in the *Altepeter* case, plaintiff was barred from recovery, not because he assumed the risk, but rather because of his failure to state a cause of action. Again here, the court's discussion of the doctrine was not germane to the outcome of the case.

[14] It is plaintiff's contention that, notwithstanding the position taken by other states, the doctrine is still strictly limited to master-servant relationships in Illinois as promulgated by this State's highest court in Shoninger Co. v. Mann, 219 Ill. 242, 76 N.E. 354, 3 L.R.A.,N.S., 1007 (1906),

Conrad v. Springfield Consolidated Railway Company, 240 Ill. 12, 88 N.E. 180 (1909) and O'Rourke v. Sproul, 241 Ill. 576, 89 N.E. 663 (1909). These cases evidence the traditional limitation placed on the application of the doctrine of assumption of risk in Illinois which its judiciary continues to adopt. Davis v. Springfield Lodge No. 158, Benevolent and Protective Order of Elks, 24 Ill.App.2d 102, 164 N.E.2d 243 (1960); Hensley v. Hensley, 62 Ill.App.2d 252, 210 N.E.2d 568 (1965). Even assuming arguendo that the doctrine were applicable to other than master-servant relationships, it must be remembered that, unlike contributory negligence, it is defendant Chicago Cubs, not plaintiff, who bears the burden of proof on the issue. Moreover, after arguments had been offered by each party in support of their respective positions, it was defendant Chicago Cubs' instruction, which was accepted by the court and given to the jury on the subject.

[15, 16] Dean Prosser on Torts (3rd Ed.) (1964) at page 462 points out:

Knowledge of the risk is the watchword of assumption of risk. Under ordinary circumstances the plaintiff will not be taken to assume any risk of either activities or conditions of which he is ignorant. Furthermore, he must not only know of the facts which create the danger, but he must comprehend and appreciate the danger itself.

and at page 464:

Even where there is knowledge and appreciation of a risk, the plaintiff may not be barred from recovery where the situation changes to introduce a new element, such as several balls in the air at one time in a baseball park.

Plaintiff, in this conjunction, relies on Cincinnati Baseball Club Co. v. Eno, 112 Ohio St. 175, 147 N.E. 86 (1925) where plaintiff was injured by a stray batted ball during a practice session in between games of a doubleheader, at a time when several balls were in use simultaneously. The Ohio Supreme Court reasoned in allowing recovery, that when several balls are simultaneously in play upon the field, it is impossible for the spectator to protect himself by watching the ball, for more than one ball is being batted or thrown at once. The court explained that actual game play is done at a greater distance from the spectators to minimize injury, whereas this practice was within fifteen to twenty feet away from the plaintiff. Defendant Chicago Cubs urges that this case is distinguishable on several points, to wit; (1) that the ball came from an area other than the bullpen at a time when there was no game in progress; (2) that numerous balls were in use, whereas in the instant case only two were in use; and (3) that in the *Eno* case the players had ample space to practice away from the grandstands unlike the instant case. We agree with defendant Chicago Cubs' contentions on these points, but have, nonetheless, made the following observations: (1) this is a case of first impression and (2) the *Eno* case, though distinguishable, clearly stands for the proposition that a spectator at a baseball park does not assume the risk of being hit by a baseball he does not see, when more than one ball is being used, regardless of whether the game is in progress or not. As the Ohio court said:

We do not think that a court should say as a matter of law that a spectator assumes the risk of every batting or throwing of the ball permitted upon the field by the management, no matter how near the grand stand, no matter how many groups were engaged in the practice, and no matter whether the batting or throwing is a part of the game itself.

The subsequent Ohio cases of Ivory v. Cincinnati Baseball Club Co., 62 Ohio App. 514, 24 N.E.2d 837 (1930) and Hummel v. Columbus Baseball Club, 71 Ohio App. 321, 49 N.E.2d 773 (1943) do not distinguish the *Eno* decision as defendant Chicago Cubs maintains. These two cases did not involve situations in which more than one ball was in use simultaneously and furthermore, do not represent decisions of equal or superior authority, being from the Appellate Court.

[17, 18] Defendant Chicago Cubs next contends that the issue of assumption of risk raises a question of law, not fact, and as such it should not have been submitted to the jury. We can find no foundation to this proposition, for even if assumption of risk were made applicable to the instant case, the doctrine's underlying premise is appreciation of the danger itself, not mere knowledge of a defect or condition by which danger is created, thereby necessarily raising a question of fact for the jury. Hopkins v. Kraft Foods Company, 44 Ill.App.2d 373, 194 N.E.2d 680 (1963), Cincinnati Baseball Club Co. v. Eno, 112 Ohio St. 175, 147 N.E. 86 (1925). Moreover, defendant Chicago Cubs submitted the jury instruction on assumption of risk. Having been submitted to the jury, this court will not disturb their finding in absence of manifest error.

For the above reasons, the judgment in case No. 50781 against defendant Chicago National League Ball Club, Inc. is affirmed, and the motion by defendant Robert Rush to dismiss the appeal in case No. 50780 is granted.

As to Appeal No. 50780 the appeal is dismissed.

As to Appeal No. 50781 the Judgment is affirmed.

BURKE and BRYANT, JJ., concur.

**4** STEVEN M. MARLOWE, an Infant, by His Parent and Natural Guardian, STEVEN L. MARLOWE, et al., Respondents, v RUSH-HENRIETTA CENTRAL SCHOOL DISTRICT et al., Appellants. —Order reversed on the law without costs, motion and cross motion granted. Memorandum: Plaintiff, a 17-year-old student at defendant school district, was participating in a baseball game when he was struck in the face and mouth by a baseball bat thrown by defendant Nesmith, a fellow student, after hitting the ball. The game occurred during a gym class voluntarily joined by plaintiff during his lunch break. The court erred in denying defendant Nesmith's motion and defendant school district's cross motion for summary judgment dismissing plaintiff's complaint. Plaintiff assumed the risk that a bat might be thrown accidentally and there is no allegation that Nesmith's conduct was intentional or reckless *(see, O'Bryan v O'Connor,* 59 AD2d 219; *see, e.g., Sutfin v Scheuer,* 145 AD2d 946, *affd* 74 NY2d 697; *O'Neill v Daniels,* 135 AD2d 1076, *lv denied* 71 NY2d 802; *see generally, Turcotte v Fell,* 68 NY2d 432, 439). The school district breached no duty to protect plaintiff from "unassumed, concealed or unreasonably increased risks" *(Benitez v New York City Bd. of Educ.,* 73 NY2d 650, 658).

All concur, except Dillon, P. J., and Lawton, J., who dissent and vote to affirm, in the following memorandum.

Dillon, P. J., and Lawton, J. (dissenting). We must dissent. The majority concludes, as a matter of law, that plaintiff assumed the risk of being struck by a bat thrown at least 35 feet by defendant Nesmith. A participant in a sporting activity assumes only risks that are known, apparent or reasonably foreseeable *(see, O'Neill v Daniels,* 135 AD2d 1076, 1077). Further, whether a risk is assumed is generally a factual question to be determined based on plaintiff's skill, experience and awareness of the risk *(see, Benitez v New York City Bd. of Educ.,* 73 NY2d 650, 657; *Jackson v Livingston Country Club,* 55 AD2d 1045; *Dillard v Little League Baseball,* 55 AD2d 477, 480, *lv denied* 42 NY2d 801). Here, plaintiff admitted that he knew that bats are occasionally thrown during baseball games, but stated that he had never seen a bat "travel in the air anywhere near the distance" thrown by defendant. Further, defendant has failed to produce any evidence that throwing a bat that distance was a known and reasonably foreseeable risk inherent in the game. Since a question exists whether the risk was apparent or reasonably foreseeable, summary judgment must be denied.

Further even if we were to find that plaintiff assumed the risk, summary judgment is still not warranted. Defendant Nesmith does not assert that the bat slipped from his grasp, but rather admitted he "let the bat go". Because of Nesmith's improper conduct the bat traveled in the air at least 35 feet. The record establishes that Nesmith had a history of bat throwing and because of this behavior was referred to by the other players as the "Dave Winfield" of Roth High School. Further, plaintiff stated that when he previously observed Nesmith batting, Nesmith upon hitting the ball would release the bat, causing it to fly in a trajectory parallel to the ground. Plaintiff in his complaint alleged in part that Nesmith threw the bat and that his conduct was in deviation of the rules of the game.

In reviewing a summary judgment motion, we must accept as true the evidence presented by the nonmoving party and the motion must be denied if there is even arguably any doubt as to the existence of a triable issue *(see, Hourigan v McGarry,* 106 AD2d 845). Here, given Nesmith's history of bat throwing in clear contravention of the rules of baseball and his admission that he "let the bat go", a triable issue exists whether his conduct was reckless or wanton, which precludes summary judgment *(see, Turcotte v Fell,* 68 NY2d 432, 439).

Finally, since the employees of defendant school district allegedly knew of Nesmith's history of bat throwing and there is no showing that they adequately enforced safety rules to prevent such conduct or instructed Nesmith as to proper conduct, the issue of whether their actions were reasonable or constituted a breach of their duty of care may not be resolved summarily *(see, Merkley v Palmyra-Macedon Cent. School Dist.,* 130 AD2d 937). (Appeals from order of Supreme Court, Monroe County, Willis, J.—summary judgment.) Present—Dillon, P. J., Boomer, Pine, Lawton and Lowery, JJ.

# PART 7

## THEORY AND METAPHOR

This book analyzes the many uses of baseball as a metaphor and model for American law. We began with articles that show how the infield fly rule developed from traditional common law doctrines and how baseball is replete with issues of construction as troubling as any in constitutional law or statutory interpretation. This chapter stretches the analysis even further to show how baseball is both a metaphor and model for legal theory and more generally a component of American society.

While baseball continues to supply a metaphor for American law it may, oddly enough, also provide the vehicle for transmittting the ideas of legal academics and other scholars to the general public. A seemingly mundane conversation between a pitcher and a manager can inform how lawyers and juges perform their professional roles. Three strikes and you're out is the way to sell criminal justice reform. Knowing a baseball fan's allegiance can simplify jury selection. Knowing the difference between a superstar and an also-ran is just as important for the Supreme Court as it is for the Hall of Fame.

How can one best explain the debate over strict construction and original intent to the American public? The debate over the judicial philosophy of Judge Bork may have been enlightening to very few non-lawyers. But reduce strict constructionism to the game of baseball and the question of the dimensions of the strike zone, and anyone who has been"out" on a called third strike can appreciate the significance of the issue. The Supreme Court has replicated in many contexts the story of a discussion between three umpires about calling balls and strikes. The first umpire says: "I call 'em like I see 'em." The second umpire says: "I call 'em like they are." The third merely says: "They ain't nothing *until* I call 'em."

The history of baseball is also a component of larger aspects of American history. The Black Sox scandal presaged an age of excess in the 1920s. The integration of baseball in the 1940s helped set the stage for the larger integration of American society in the next two decades. Baseball's apparent continuing tolerance of racist statements by owners and other officials may be part and parcel to a national decline in support for civil rights.

Many of the essays in this section will illuminate the place of baseball for the scholar. We included the rest of the articles because we thought they were fun.

# BASEBALL, THE COURTS, AND SOCIETY
### Paul Finkelman

The internal dynamics of baseball have led many scholars to use the game as a metaphor for the legal world. Thus some articles in this book compare the "infield fly rule" and the "strike zone" to our own common law, statutory, and constitutional development. Moreover, in the first Supreme Court case dealing with baseball, *Federal Baseball League v. National League*, 259 U.S. 200 (1922), Justice Oliver Wendell Holmes compared baseball players to lawyers. In his opinion, Justice Holmes stated that professional baseball is not an aspect of interstate commerce; rather, "the business of giving exhibitions," as Holmes called baseball games, "are purely state affairs." Holmes asserted that interstate travel of ballplayers, to play against the home team in another state, was a "mere incident" to the game and "is not enough to change the character of the business." Arguing from analogy, Holmes asserted that the travel of a baseball player from a one state to the next was the same as "a firm of lawyers sending a member out to argue a case." In such a situation the lawyer did not "engage in such [interstate] commerce because" he went "to another state."

*Federal Baseball* notwithstanding, as an industry baseball has spawned its own law. Cases involving player status, collective bargaining, team mobility, and the meaning of antitrust show that baseball is as much a business as a sport. Nevertheless, the response of courts to many suits emanating from baseball shows how our jurists have been overwhelmed by their reverence for the national game. Supreme Court opinions abound with references to the game. Justices have even taken time to dress up their opinions with lists of great players, something that no other sport or cultural institution has achieved.[1]

As noted above, since *Federal Baseball League v. National League*, professional baseball has remained exempt from the antitrust laws. This fact is still one of the mysteries of American law, especially to lawyers and law professors who fail to understand the deeper meaning of baseball for American culture. Yet, Justice Holmes's opinion in *Federal Baseball* was probably not motivated by his love of the sport.[2] Rather, it seems to have been based on a curious and narrow misreading of the antitrust laws and his misunderstanding of the nature of the business of baseball. Despite Holmes's odd opinion, the Supreme Court has consistently upheld *Federal Baseball* as applied to baseball but the fact that the Court has refused to apply the logic or implications of *Federal Baseball* to any other sport[3] suggests that the Court fully understands that Holmes's decision was erroneous.

Why then, has the Court not overturned *Federal Baseball*? One possibility is that the court wants to provide law professors with the perfect example of a "mindless" implementation of *stare decisis*. The Court, however, is rarely so solicitous of the professoriat. Other, strictly legal explanations, are perhaps more plausible.

There is also, however, an important cultural explanation for the Court's behavior. The Supreme Court continues to hold that baseball is not a form of "interstate commerce," because to do otherwise would imply that the national pastime—the national game—is not a game at all. In a world of self-conscious fictions, as law often is, it makes perfect sense to assert that professional baseball is "just" a sport. The Court notes that Congress is, of course, free to change the law. But Congress, like the Court, seems reluctant to undermine the special status of the national pastime.

Baseball's special treatment may be justified, though. At one crucial moment in our history, baseball stood out and did the right thing. The reintegration of major league baseball by the Brooklyn Dodgers altered the landscape of the sport.[4] More importantly, it helped alter the landscape of American culture and law. Branch Rickey hired Jackie Robinson *before* the "*Brown* Revolution" of 1954. No court or judge ordered the integration of the sport. Rickey claimed he hired Robinson only because he thought his new player would help the hapless Dodgers finally win a World Series. Robinson helped them do just that.[5] Brooklyn won pennants and finally, in 1955, a championship in the years after Robinson arrived. Significantly, the first American League team to have black players—the Cleveland Indians—also began winning with black players. Indeed, Larry Doby, the American League's first black player, and Satchel Paige were major contributors to the Indians' 1948 World Series Championship.

Whatever Rickey's motivations, the reintegration of baseball was a critical step toward the integration of America. If blacks could play in the National League on an integrated basis, they could serve in the national army on an integrated basis. If African Americans could play in the American League, surely they could go to any American school. Most baseball owners were aghast at Rickey's action. Integration was the last thing they wanted. Some teams resisted integration for nearly a decade. But, in the end baseball showed all Americans, on black and white television, that blacks and whites could play together and cooperate with each other.

Ironically, then, baseball helped set the stage for our legal system to overcome segregation. Jackie Robinson, Satchel Paige, Monte Irvin, Larry Doby, and Branch Rickey were, in their own ways, as critical to the civil rights revolution as Thurgood Marshall, Spottswood Robinson, Jack Greenberg, and Linda Brown. Baseball made a difference. It was the national sport. In an age before the Super Bowl or televised NBA playoffs, the World Series was *the* sporting event of the year. Thus, black players on World Series teams brought integration into most American homes.

As a sport, baseball was also the perfect vehicle for teaching Americans about racial harmony. Baseball, like all team sports, requires team-work and cooperation; but unlike most team sports, baseball allows for individual effort that is clearly distinct from team play. The batter, the pitcher, the fielder, the base-stealer are all in a position to display stunning individual effort. This combination of individualism and team effort is something of a metaphor for much of American culture: as a society we praise teamwork and the "team player," but we love and worship the individual hero. Baseball allows both. Thus, the earliest black players—Robinson, Paige, Doby, Campanella—proved they could be both team players and individual heros. In other words, they demonstrated to the entire nation that blacks could be equal in both team spirit *and* individual effort. By the time Congress debated the 1964 Civil Rights Act, a generation of Americans had emotionally accepted equal rights by adopting a generation of black players—such future Hall of Famers as Hank Aaron, Willie Mays, and Ernie Banks—as their personal heroes.

The best argument for baseball retaining a privileged place in American culture and law may be rooted in this history. Baseball was the first great national institution—private or public—to dismantle segregation following World War II. It would be too much to argue that baseball set the stage for Truman's civil rights plank of 1948, the integration of the Army, or *Brown*. But, it is nevertheless clear that Branch Rickey, Jackie Robinson, and, through his silent support, baseball commissioner "Happy" Chandler certainly deserve more credit than they have been given for helping America move from a segregated society to one where all people have full legal equality. Jules Tygiel says "one can best describe Chandler's role as endorsement by abstinence."[6] However, compared to Commissioner Landis's adamant opposition to integration, this was a major step forward. The silent support of Chandler, a former Senator from a largely segregated state (Kentucky), may have been just what was necessary.

Baseball integrated because Branch Rickey ignored the wishes of the other owners, and brought Robinson up from his Montreal farm team. The other owners, while largely opposed, were an independent lot who could not or dared not stop a fellow owner from choosing his team. The obvious success of the experiment led other owners, some enthusiastically and others reluctantly, to integrate their teams. Perhaps opposition from a strong and determined commissioner might have delayed integration, but such opposition was not forthcoming from Chandler. Although a southerner, and no great friend of integration, he nevertheless told Branch Rickey, "I'm going to have to meet my maker someday. If he asks me why I didn't let this boy play and I say it's because he's black, that might not be a sufficient answer."[7]

If the actions of Rickey and Chandler give baseball a claim to special treatment, the actions of many team owners tend to undermine that claim. When Rickey brought Robinson to the majors, the owners attacked him. Led by the Yankee's Larry MacPhail, the "Report of the Major League Steering Committee" opposed integration with classical racist arguments, economic arguments (which proved to be totally wrong), and cold war appeals to patriotism implying that supporters of integration were subversive.

Those owners lost their battle, and the field was integrated. But the actions and attitudes of baseball owners suggest that the war is not over. From the dugout to the front office baseball leadership remains overwhelmingly white. Moreover, in the past few years there have been more racist statements emanating from baseball's front offices than at any time since Robinson left the playing field.

In a 1987 interview, Nightline's Ted Koppel asked Al Campanis, the third-highest ranking member of the Los Angeles Dodger's organization, why at the time there were no black managers and so few black executives in professional baseball. Campanis answered "I don't believe it's prejudice. I truly believe that they may not have some of the necessities to be, let's say, a field manager or perhaps a general manager." Two days later Campanis resigned from the Dodgers. While the Dodgers and baseball executives distanced themselves from Campanis's remarks, no one in major league baseball seemed to have a good answer to Koppel's question. Perhaps this is because, as Frank Robinson, baseball's first black manager, noted: "Someone from in the inner circle had let out what we had known all along" about the attitudes of baseball's highest echelon of power.[8]

In response to Campanis's statements, professional baseball promised to do better. But five years later the *New York Times* titled an article on minorities in baseball "Too Few Changes Since Campanis." The article noted that in the previous five years 48 managers had been hired, but only 6 were minorities. While blacks and Hispanics made up 32 percent of all players, they were only 19 percent of all managers, coaches, scouts, trainers and instructors. Moreover, only one black had ever been the general manager of a major league team and only three had made it to assistant general manager. Clearly, the beliefs of Al Campanis mirrored the reality of hiring decisions by baseball's owners.

More recently came the revelations concerning Marge Schott. In 1992 complaints surfaced about the language, views, and attitudes of Ms. Schott, the owner of the Cincinnati Reds. Ms. Schott allegedly referred to some players as "millions-dollar niggers" and to some agents and lawyers as "money-grubbing Jews." She was said to keep Nazi paraphernalia in her home, and showed little remorse for her views or her statements. She had no apology for the fact that only 1 of her 45 front-office employees was black. She more than echoed Campanis: "I once had a nigger work for me," she said, "I would never hire another nigger. I'd rather have a trained monkey working for me than a nigger." When asked if she had made such statements she answered "Sure."[9]

Faced with a call for a boycott of baseball by blacks, the owners responded. They barred Schott from the game for a year and a day, but she still holds her franchise.

While statements of Al Campanis and Marge Schott can be attributed to a few racist individuals, baseball's dismal record on hiring minorities cannot be dismissed so easily. More than any other profession, major league sports have proved that racial integration can work. On the field, race seems not to matter. Moreover, the percentage of blacks and Hispanics in major league baseball more-or-less reflects their percentage in society, and blacks and Hispanics have been among the greatest stars of the game. In the eleven seasons from 1949 (when there were only a handful of black players) through 1959, blacks won the National League's most valuable player award nine times. The first generation of black players—Robinson, Mays, Aaron, Banks—are now in the Hall of Fame. But, despite their skill and their baseball knowledge, black players do not go on to become black managers, scouts, and general managers in anywhere near their proportion as players.

However imperfect, baseball remains a crucible for social change. The ball field will still be a place for dreams that integrate our increasingly diverse society. The major leagues will probably gradually move towards integration of front offices and field staffs. And, it is likely that legal scholars will continue to see important connections and parallels between baseball and law.

Paul Finkelman

## NOTES

1.  See Flood v. Kuhn (p. 120). I know of no court opinions listing great musicians, artists, authors, or hockey, football, or basketball players.
2.  There is no indication Holmes enjoyed any organized sports, either as a fan or a player.
3.  See for example, *Radovich v. National Football League*, 352 U.S. 445 (1957).
4.  Blacks played professional baseball in the 19th century, before whites forced them out of the emerging major leagues in the 1880s. Blacks, of course, also played in their own professional leagues throughout the first half of the 20th century. There were also "barnstorming" exhibitions between white and black stars in the 1920s and 1930s. See for example, Michael Santa Maria, "One Strike and You're Out," 5 *American Visions* 16–21 (No. 2, 1990).
5.  The best study of the integration of baseball is Jules Tygiel, *Baseball's Greatest Experiment* (New York: Oxford University Press, 1983).
6.  William J. Marshall, "A.B. Chandler as Baseball Commissioner, 1945–51: An Overview," 82 *Register of the Kentucky Historical Society* 358 (No. 4, 1984). Jules Tygiel, *Baseball's Greatest Experiment*, p. 82.
7.  Marshall, "A.B. Chandler as Baseball Commissioner," 376.
8.  Robinson quoted in Claire Smith, "Too Few Changes Since Campanis," *New York Times*, August 16, 1992, Section 8, p. 1.
9.  "Baseball's Very Big Problem," *New York Times*, Dec. 3, 1992, p. A24; "Winking At Baseball's Racism," *New York Times*, Feb. 5, 1993, p. A26.

# Dennis Martinez and the Uses of Theory

Stanley Fish†

## I.

On June 24, 1985, Dennis Martinez, then a pitcher for the Baltimore Orioles, was caught by journalist Ira Berkow in the act of talking to his manager, Earl Weaver, shortly before the beginning of a game with the Yankees. Berkow, sensing a story, approached Martinez and asked him "what words of wisdom had been imparted by the astute Weaver."[1] Now Martinez is a pitcher who is unlikely ever to make it into the Baseball Hall of Fame, if only because he seems to experience every pitch as a discrete event, unrelated to either its predecessor or its successor; but if his baseball skills are suspect, his philosophical skills would seem to be beyond dispute. In response to Berkow's question, Martinez offered a two-stage narrative. In the first stage he reports the event. "He [Weaver] said, 'Throw strikes and keep 'em off the bases,' . . . and I said, 'O.K.' " This is already brilliant enough, both as an account of what transpires between fully situated members of a community and as a wonderfully dead-pan rebuke to the outsider who assumes the posture of an analyst. But Martinez is not content to leave the rebuke implicit, and in the second stage he drives the lesson home with a precision Wittgenstein might envy: "What else could I say? What else could he say?" Or, in other words, "What did you expect?" Clearly, what Berkow expected was some set of directions or an articulated method or formula or rule or piece of instruction, which Martinez could first grasp (in almost the physical sense of holding it in his hand or in some appropriate corner of his mind) and then consult whenever a situation seemed to call for its application. What Berkow gets is the report of something quite different, not a formula or a method or a principle—in fact, no guidance at all—simply a reminder of something that Martinez must surely already know, that it is his job to throw a baseball in such a way as to prevent opposing players from hitting it with a stick.

Of course, there is more to it than that, but Weaver made no effort to "impart" that more, and indeed it would have been totally inappropriate for him to have done so. Were he either to explain the principles of pitching or to enumerate the possible situations that might arise during the

---

† Arts and Sciences Distinguished Professor of English and Law, Duke University.
1. Berkow, *The Old and New Manager*, N.Y. Times, June 26, 1985, at B13, col. 1.

1773

game and suggest strategies to deal with those situations, Martinez would be understandably incredulous and justifiably resentful. What Martinez is saying to Berkow is something like this: "Look, it may be your job to characterize the game of baseball in terms of overriding theories, but it's my job to play it; and playing it has nothing to do with following words of wisdom, whether they are Weaver's or Aristotle's, and everything to do with already being someone whose sense of himself and his possible actions is inseparable from the kind of knowledge that words of wisdom would presume to impart." In short, what Weaver says amounts to "Go out and do it," where "do it" means go and play the game. That is why both Weaver's counsel and Martinez' response must be without content. What they know is either inside of them or (at least on this day) beyond them; and if they know it, they did not come to know it by submitting to a formalization; neither can any formalization capture what they know in such a way as to make it available to those who haven't come to know it in the same way.

Let me extend the point by assuming that Martinez has walked the first batter (an all too possible occurrence) and the second baseman trots up to say to him, "There's a man on first base." What could he possibly mean? Certainly he does not think that Martinez has already forgotten what he did only a few seconds ago. Rather he is prompting Martinez to remember what having a man on first base involves: the repositioning of both outfielders and infielders to deal with eventualities that have just become more likely, the narrowing of the options available to the batter who may now adjust his stance or choke up on the bat or steel himself to be more patient and discriminating than he might otherwise have been; the necessity of keeping in mind the next and then the next batter who, even though they have not appeared, are already factors in the situation. All of this and more is, in a sense, contained in "There's a man on first base," although those simple words will only convey that information to someone who literally carries it in his bones.[2] One can imagine Berkow approaching the second baseman to ask him what counsel he gave to Martinez, and hearing in response, "I said, 'There's a man on first base,' and he said, 'O.K.' What else could he say? What else could I say?"

This doesn't mean that there's never anything else to say, in a formal or theoretical sense, about baseball; only that it is not always appropriate to say it, although there are times when it would not be appropriate to say anything else. Presumably, as the second baseman says what he says, an

---

2. In saying this I am arguing as I often do against the availability of a literal level of language. Meaning is always a function of the interpretive condition of production and reception and never a function of formal linguistic structures. The case against theory and the case against formalism are one and the same. *See* S. Fish, Is There a Text in This Class? 225-84 (1980).

announcer up in the radio or television booth—more than likely a former player—is saying just the kind of things that someone like Berkow expects. That is, in the announcer's account of what has just happened, both the pitcher and the second baseman are in the act of consulting and applying a set of underlying rules or formal principles that underlie the skills of baseball in general and the skillful exercise of judgment in this situation in particular; and it is often the announcer's claim to know even more about these rules than the players themselves know. And, in fact, that is, I think, a justifiable claim, but it is a justifiable claim because knowledge of the rules is the game he is in (and, of course, it follows that he would be an expert in his own game), while the players are in quite another game which has, I would contend, only an oblique relationship to the announcer's account of it. My claim, in short, is that in this imagined scenario there are two distinct activities—playing baseball and explaining playing baseball—and that, in a strict sense (which I shall soon elaborate), there is no relationship between them whatsoever.[3]

The point may be clearer if we turn to another example, taken this time from the world of industrial research as reported by Donald Schön.[4] It seems that a research and development team was experimenting with a paintbrush made of synthetic bristles. The bristles were superior in many ways to the old natural kind, but in one respect they were unsatisfactory: They did not deliver paint to a surface smoothly. The team tinkered with the bristles in an attempt to improve them, but to no avail, until someone suddenly said, "You know, a paintbrush is a kind of a pump."[5] In fact no one (including the speaker) did know that until it was hazarded as an observation; but once hazarded it constituted a suggestion: "Let's think of a paintbrush as a pump and see where it get us." Where it got them was to a reconception of the entire problem which now appeared to be one not of individual bristles, but of the channels formed by bristles, channels

---

3. At this point, someone might raise what I call the "Charlie Lau Objection." Lau, now deceased, was a renowned batting coach who regularly turned .260 hitters into .300 hitters and whose "theories" were widely quoted and praised. How does one explain his success if not by reference to the theory with which he apparently taught so many? Of course, I was not myself privy to the Lau experience, but I am sure that part of that experience involved Lau regularly repeating pieces of his theory to his students. I would contend, however, that such repetition served less as instructions one was to follow than as reminders that something wasn't being done "just right." I would also contend that knowledge of that something was not *produced* by Lau's theory; nor could it be recovered by invoking the theory. Rather the theory operates as a verbal place-marker for a knowledge that develops in the context of a trial-and-error attempt to match an example (e.g., Ted Williams' swing). In other words, the articulation of the theory refers to knowledge acquired independently of it, and it serves as a mnemonic and exhortative device. Listening to theory talk may be a part of the experience of becoming a practitioner but not because theory talk would in any strong sense be generating the practice. *See* Fish, *Fish v. Fiss*, 36 STAN. L. REV. 1325, 1329-30 (1984).

4. Schön, *Generative Metaphor: A Perspective on Problem-Setting in Social Policy*, in METAPHOR AND THOUGHT 254 (A. Ortony ed. 1979).

5. *Id.* at 257.

whose properties were hydraulic and which could therefore be interrogated with the familiar vocabulary of mechanical engineering.[6] In the end, the result was just the kind of paint flow the researchers were looking for and the new paintbrush was promptly dubbed a "pumpoid."[7]

After rehearsing the story, Schön turns to the problem of describing what had happened and remarks that it would be tempting to conclude "that the researchers mapped their descriptions of 'pump' and 'pumping' onto their initial descriptions of 'paintbrush' and 'painting' ";[8] but this would be incorrect, says Schön, because it would make a groping developmental process into a formal and explicit program. Rather than beginning with two lists of the formal properties of brushes and pumps and mapping one onto the other, the researchers began with what Schön calls "an unarticulated perception of similarity"[9] which then provoked them to questions and experiments that elaborated and deepened the similarity to the point where it could be the object of an analytic description. "It is important to note," says Schön, "that the researchers were able to see painting as similar to pumping before they were able to say 'similar with respect to what.' "[10] That is, the formalization that one might think served as their guide in doing what they did was available to them only after they had done it. The similarity that now could be reduced to a list of matched components was the product and not the cause of the process of discovery. Only later and after the fact, Schön insists, did the researchers "develop an explicit account of the similarity, an account which later still became part of a general theory of 'pumpoids,' according to which they could regard paintbrushes and pumps, along with washcloths and mops, as instances of a single technological category."[11] Moreover, he concludes, "to read the later model back onto the beginning of the process would be to engage in a kind of historical revisionism."[12] It would be to confuse a retrospective account of what they had done—an account in which the characteristics and capabilities of pumps and paintbrushes are matched up so as to illustrate their membership in a single category—with an account of how they had done it. Insofar as there is now something in the world called the "theory of pumpoids" it would be a mistake to think of that theory as guiding the process by which pumpoids emerged as a solution to the problem the researchers originally faced. The solution—provoked by the intuitive, non-theoretical suggestion that we try thinking of paint-

---

6. *Id*. at 258.
7. *Id*. at 260.
8. *Id*. at 259.
9. *Id*. at 260.
10. *Id*.
11. *Id*.
12. *Id*.

brushes as pumps—came first and the theory followed in response to whatever pressures prompted them to present their achievement in terms more orderly and rule-governed than their actual experience of it.

One can imagine a situation in which the pressures flowed from the need for funds: They now have built a model of a pumpoid, but they need four and one-half million dollars to develop and manufacture it. What do they say in the application to the National Science Foundation or the Exxon Corporation? Well, one thing they wouldn't say—at least if they really wanted the money—would be, "Hey, one day Marty and Ellen and I were sitting around trying to make those bristles deliver paint, and out of the blue Ellen said, 'You know, you can think of a paintbrush as a kind of a pump.'" Rather, they would eliminate from their presentation all traces of the fumbling, groping process by which they came to their triumph, and offer only their conclusions, now dressed up in the vocabulary of hydraulic flow and presented in terms as formal and mathematical as possible.

At this point, there would be those who would fault the researchers for falsifying their experience. They would be accused, in a word, of being dishonest, of suppressing what they knew to be the truth about the matter in order to secure monetary gain. But that would be much too harsh a judgment, and indeed it would be incorrect, for it would assume that the practice of applying for grants was or should be continuous with the practice of discovering or inventing. Think of the two practices as different answers to a single question: What do we have to do in order to reach our goal? When the goal is making the paint flow and flow smoothly, then what you have to do is eliminate the condition (the researchers called it "gloppiness") that now impedes flow, and your procedure is to look around for ways to do that. Presenting theories is not going to be one of those ways, any more than it would be a way of preventing the runner on first base from scoring. But when the goal is to get money from a foundation, then representing yourself as having followed or applied a theory is a very good way, and when you have recourse to it you are not being dishonest, you are being effective—just as you are being effective when you try out the suggestion that a paintbrush is similar to a pump in the absence of any theory of what the similarity is. I call this the "thesis of the plural honesties," and what it says is that in one case you are honestly attempting to get the brush to deliver paint and in the other you are honestly trying to get the foundation to deliver money.

You might reasonably be wondering what this all has to do with the discourse of law. Before I tell you, let me consolidate what I take to be the gains of my two examples: First, what they together suggest is that performing an activity—engaging in a practice—is one thing and discoursing

1777

on that practice another. Second, the practice of discoursing on practice does not stand in a relationship of superiority or governance to the practice that is its object.[13] There are some baseball players who can talk about their craft in an analytic fashion, but that does not make them better baseball players than they would be if they couldn't; and there are some researchers who are good at thinking up ex post facto accounts of their accomplishment, but those accounts are not to be understood as recipes for that accomplishment. Even if the practitioners happen to be in possession of a theory of the activity in which they are engaged, the shape of that activity is not the result of the application of that theory. They do not use their account of what they are doing (assuming that they have one) in order to do it. They can, however, use their account of what they are doing to do something else, to perform as a play-by-play analyst or apply for a grant.

What is at stake here are two uses of the word "use": on the one hand, "use" in the sense of "making use of" as a component of a practice; on the other, "use" in the sense of using in order to generate a practice. It is in the first sense that baseball analysts and grant applicants use theory, and it is in the second sense that no one (this, at least, is my thesis) uses theory. That is, no one follows or consults his formal model of the skill he is exercising in order properly to exercise it. This should not be understood as a distinction between activities that are theoretical and activities that are not. No activity is theoretical in the strong sense of unfolding according to the dictates of a theory, and this includes the activities (for example) of analyzing baseball or applying for grants; for while they are to be distinguished from playing baseball and inventing pumpoids precisely by the self-conscious recourse to a theoretical mode of talk, that talk no more generates the shape of their own enactment than it generates the shape of what the talk is about (playing baseball and inventing pumpoids). As activities, analyzing baseball and applying for grants are just like playing baseball and inventing pumpoids in that those who are engaged in them make use of whatever comes to hand in the effort to achieve a practice-specific goal. Even if the skill one exercises in a practice is the skill of talking theory, this does not make the practice theoretical; it just means that in the judgment of the practitioner who wants to get something done, talking theory is one of the resources he employs in the course of doing it. Again, this does not mean that the skill depends on (in the

---

13. This argument, in its broader contours and with slight variations, is traced in Fish, *Consequences*, 11 CRITICAL THEORY 433 (1985); Knapp & Michaels, *A Reply to Richard Rorty: What Is Pragmatism?*, 11 CRITICAL INQUIRY 466 (1985); Knapp & Michaels, *Against Theory*, 8 CRITICAL INQUIRY 732 (1982); Michaels, *Response to Perry and Simon*, 58 S. CAL. L. REV. 673 (1985). Some of these essays are compiled in AGAINST THEORY (W.J.T. Mitchell ed. 1985).

1778

sense of flowing from) theory talk; it means simply that one expression of the skill is knowing when theory-talk will or will not be useful. While it is certainly the case that the successful performance of a skill will sometimes require the invocation of theory—even of a theory of that particular skill—it is never the case that the theory thus invoked is acting as a blueprint or set of directions according to which the performance is unfolding.

I should acknowledge here that what I intend by "theory" may seem to some to be excessively narrow.[14] I reserve that word for an abstract or algorithmic formulation that guides or governs practice from a position outside any particular conception of practice. A theory, in short, is something a practitioner consults when he wishes to perform correctly, with the term "correctly" here understood as meaning independently of his preconceptions, biases, or personal preferences. To be sure, the word "theory" is often used in other, looser ways, to designate high order generalizations,[15] or strong declarations of basic beliefs, or programmatic statements of political or economic agendas, or descriptions of underlying assumptions. Here my argument is that to include such activities under the rubric of theory is finally to make everything theory, and if one does that there is nothing of a *general* kind to be said about theory. When I assert the lack of a relationship between theory and practice I refer to the kind of relationship (of precedence and priority) implied by the strongest notion of theory; the relationships that *do* exist between theory and practice (and there are many) are no different from the relationships between any form of talk and the practice of which it is a component.

Philosophers, after all, are like anyone else; they want people who don't do what they do to believe that what they do is universally enabling. They want us to believe that the only good king is a philosopher-king, and that the only good judge is a philosopher judge, and that the only good baseball player is a philosopher baseball player. Well, I don't know about you, but I hope that my kings, if I should ever have any, are good at being kings, and that my judges are good at being judges, and that the players on my team throw strikes and keep 'em off the bases.

14. This argument is further developed in Fish, *supra* note 13, at 442–43.
15. *See id.* at 442 (distinguishing "empirical generalizations" from "theory").

# On Eurocentric Myopia, The Designated Hitter Rule and "The Actual State of Things"*

## Robert Laurence**

Under the rules set out by the editors of this *Review*, who insist that this sort of thing is fun, I am entitled to a short final essay. Time is of the essence. Footnotes are to be kept to the barest essentials. Brevity is demanded.

O.K. Return to *Eurocentric Myopia*,[1] Professor Williams' defense of the *Algebra*. Read footnote thirteen. I agree that *that* is the problem. On nearly every scale that might measure social instability, hopelessness and oppression Indian reservations rank near the bottom of American society. It hurts me that this is so. It diminishes my optimism about American democracy that this is so. It makes me do what I can so that it will no longer be so. One never knows how one's words will be read by strangers, but if *Learning to Live* reads to suggest that I can learn to live with footnote thirteen, it should be ripped out of this *Review*. Right now. Tell the librarian to send me the bill.

Likewise, now read the list of injustices listed in the text of *Eurocentric Myopia* at footnotes six through eleven. Just as I did not intend to suggest in my essay that I can live with the state of the world given in footnote thirteen neither did I want to say that learning to live with the plenary power requires that one swallow without objection every exercise of that power. The Sioux and the others have problems because my fathers acted without good faith and with a divine arrogance that is, indeed, hard either to forget, to forgive or to live with. Enduring those problems is not required by *Learning to Live*. Solving them is in order.

So, what is the solution? I have little patience with the one that goes: "O.K., all you white guys—back to Europe." I am impatient with that approach not because it wouldn't be fair to send us all home (it would be, at least under my own notions of fairness—"the iniquities of the fathers" and so forth), nor because it wouldn't be fun to see what would happen on both continents (that would be, too). My impatience with the "back to Europe" solution is that it is not a lawyer's solution. As much as it may appeal to

---

*   *"Editors' Note*: The Editors of the *Arizona Law Review* invited Professor Laurence to write this rejoinder to Robert Williams' preceding paper which appears in this issue at page 439.
**   Professor of Law, University of Arkansas; Visiting Professor of Law, Florida State University.
    1.   Williams, *Learning Not To Live with Eurocentric Myopia*, 30 ARIZ. L. REV. 439 (1988). References in the text are to page numbers and footnotes in that article.

utopian science fiction writers, hippies, law professors and other believers in celestial convergence, that solution has little, if anything, to do with the way things are likely to turn out. It is not the kind of advice that an attorney would give to a tribe. Without suggesting that the only valuable writing is lawyers' writing, I sought to say in *Learning to Live* that a tribal advocate's energies are better spent seeing that the plenary power is exercised in a friendly way than in chartering boats to send us all home, or at least all of us too numerous to allow coexistence in the Gus-Wen-Tah sense. I sought to urge, in other words, that the Sioux and their attorneys go to Congress, not the United Nations, to argue for the return of their land. As Professor Williams notes in footnote nine of *Eurocentric Myopia*, that is just what the Sioux and their allies are doing; *that* is living with the plenary power of Congress.

Now read footnote forty-four in *Eurocentric Myopia*. Notwithstanding any short-term success the Sioux might have this time before Congress, Professor Williams has no faith that justice will be done in the long run. The Indians, he notes, are playing against the house with its unlimited resources. An ebb and flow of the plenary power will surely result, he feels, in an eventual depletion of tribal sovereignty from which the concept will never recover, even under a later, friendlier regime. He may be right. But given the choice between the unlikely and the impossible, I choose the unlikely and will direct my energies and those of my students toward beating and, to some small extent perhaps, changing the odds.

Professor Williams suspects that, were I an advisor to Thurgood Marshall in the '40s and '50s, I would have counselled him to learn to live with a segregated south. That a desegregated school system was a "back to Europe" solution. That to suggest a real right for black people to vote or ride the bus in the front was folly. Perhaps he is right; I admit that the accusation makes me squirm. It is true enough that my "actual state of things" jurisprudence can lead to a comfortable predisposition to the hard issues; it is true enough that as a white, unold, unhandicapped, unpoor, not particularly religious, not particularly irreligious, not particularly gay, mostly apolitical male it is easy enough to advocate the "actual state of things." I am not entirely comfortable with the notion that in the division of people who are happy with the way things are from those who dream of the way things might be, that I am in the former group.

Consider, for example the case of *United States v. Montana*.[2] That case involved the ownership of the bed of the Big Horn river and the Crow Tribe's power to control the hunting and fishing, by whites, on the river and throughout the reservation. In holding that the tribe did not have the power, Judge Sneed of the Ninth Circuit wrote:

> We recognize that in this case, as in others in which we are required to fix the rights and powers of Indians in the latter part of the twentieth century in the light of treaties of an earlier century, our task is to keep faith with the Indian while effectively acknowledging that Indians and non-Indians alike are members of one Nation. Both seek power and

---

2. 604 F.2d 1162 (9th Cir. 1979), *rev'd*, 450 U.S. 544 (1981).

gain through identical processes *viz.* commerce, politics, and litigation. *We must, however, live together, a process not enhanced by unbending insistence on supposed legal rights which if found to exist may well yield tainted gains helpful to neither Indians nor non-Indians.*[3]

The emphasized sentence is a troublesome one for me. Life in my 1988 America would be very different if a similar sentence were found in *Brown v. Board of Education*[4] or *Roe v. Wade.*[5] On the other hand, the sentence seems to harken to *Lynch v. Donnelly*[6] and *Bowers v. Hardwick.*[7] And as Judge Sneed seems to be expressing what appears to him to be "the actual state of things", I do not find it encouraging to note these comparisons— comparisons, of course, that Professor Williams points out. "Unbending insistence on legal rights", "supposed" or not, is surely required if progress is to be made and justice done. For whatever value Judge Sneed's admonition may have as a tactical matter of concern to the litigating or advising attorney, it has little to offer as a matter of bedrock principle. *Eurocentric Myopia* will henceforth sit near my elbow on that shelf over there tó remind me to avoid a Sneedian view of "the actual state of things."

I wrote another essay this spring besides *Learning to Live*, an essay about baseball.[8] That essay has been subject to attacks from friends, colleagues and strangers, attacks so withering as to make "eurocentric myopia" pale in comparison. It risks being thought flippant, I know, to write about sports in the same essay where one writes about Indians, but I really think that there is a jurisprudential point to be made, so bear with me if you will.

Baseball is a game in which substitutions are limited. Once a player is removed from the game, he may not play again in that game. It is difficult to imagine what baseball would be like without this basic rule. The player most commonly involved in substitutions is the pitcher, who might be removed from the lineup because he is not pitching well or because he does not hit well. Once removed, he may not return.

In the realm of major league baseball there are two independent but related organizations, known everywhere as the American League and the National League. Until recently, and with only minor exceptions, the rules of the game were the same in both leagues. Some short time ago as such things are reckoned the American League amended the essential rule of the game. Changed, though not abandoned, was the rule that a player could not be removed from the lineup and later return to the field. The change, called the Designated Hitter—or DH—rule, allows that one player on each team may play defense without batting and that one other player—the "designated hitter"—may bat without playing defense. While the DH rule does not require it, it is always the case in the American League that the pitcher does not bat. Exceptions are so rare as merely to prove the rule.

---

3. United States v. Montana, 604 F.2d 1162, 1169 (9th Cir. 1979) (emphasis added).
4. 347 U.S. 483 (1954).
5. 410 U.S. 113 (1973).
6. 465 U.S. 668 (1984).
7. 478 U.S. 186, *reh'g denied*, — U.S. —, 107 S. Ct. 29 (1986).
8. Laurence, *A Short Essay in Praise of Non-Traditionalism in the Structure and Performance of Baseball*, 7 MPLS. REV. OF BASEBALL 29 (No. 3, 1988).

In the essay called *In Praise of Non-Traditionalism* [9] I wrote in favor of the DH rule, generally a touchy proposition. The details of the praise I will leave to the cognoscenti who may track down the Minneapolis Review of Baseball. For now it is enough only to note that, in defense of my article in subsequent discussions and correspondence, I found myself quoting John Marshall: "[w]e proceed, then, to the actual state of things . . . ." I argued that the DH rule was required not because it was an especially attractive change but because the actual state of baseball required it. Most pitchers have, at best, minor league batting skills and to require them to stand up to 95 m.p.h. fast balls and inside-out curves is folly and mocks the true nature of the game.

Note, now, that here I am using "the actual state of things" jurisprudence to *promote* change, not to oppose it. As trivial as the DH rule may be, it was a happy coincidence that I was writing and defending *Learning to Live* and *In Praise of Non-Traditionalism* at the same time this spring and began to quote John Marshall in defense of both. And it seems to me that the *progressive* innovation of the DH rule, justified by the changing "actual state of things", shows that the philosophy set out in *Learning to Live* need not necessarily be regressive. Perhaps the evolution of the designated hitter rule and my support of it will cause Professor Williams to rest a little easier with *Learning to Live.*

Furthermore, a jurisprudence tied to "the actual state of things" focuses the legal inquiry out of the ivory tower and into the law office. I am generally suspicious of the notion that we professors, as law review writers, have much real impact on the law as it is felt by the residents of Indian reservations. Among all the many things that do not put bread on Indian tables, footnotes hold a prominent position. The influence that we professors— most of us, anyway—*I*, anyway—have on the law and its practice is much greater, I think, in our classrooms than in our law reviews. Professor Williams seeks "cataclysmic irruptions altering the course [of history]" through his scholarship. I teach lawyers and I answer the phone. A jurisprudence that recognizes the "actual state of things" is one less likely to be confined to theoretical obscurity and, I think, more likely to get things done.

None of this is to suggest that all of us "actual state of things" thinkers will agree on what that "state" is. My discussions of the DH rule show that, if nothing else. Many fans disagree with my view of the world of baseball; many scholars disagree with my view of the world of Indian law. "Eurocentric myopia," indeed. But the discussion at least becomes framed in the terms of lawyering and that, to me, is a sensible first step. An "actual state of things" jurisprudence may deny—or at least find uninteresting—the right of the Jicarilla Apache Tribe to international recognition as a truly independent sovereign. It may think it too late to question the power of the United States to limit Jicarilla sovereignty. It may find hopelessly theoretical a search for the precise source of that power. But "the actual state of things" also requires that Indian tribes be accepted by our nation as something a good deal more than private voluntary organizations. The sover-

---

9. *Id.*

eignty of the tribes—even if it is not exactly the sovereignty of Bolivia, nor Georgia—*is* a mainstay of Indian law, as Professor Williams points out and as was one of my seven propositions. Tribal sovereignty has been recognized as such from John Marshall to Felix Cohen to Thurgood Marshall, it was then and is now part of "the actual state of things", and it must be advocated with all of our lawyerly skills.

Recently Professor Williams has published an essay evaluating the Critical Legal Studies movement as it applies or might apply to American Indian law.[10] That article both praises the techniques of the Crits and attacks them. The praise essentially restates, in short form, the *Algebra*.[11] The criticism warns that while "rights" may be deprecated with quotation marks by white male law professors, they are real, tangible, important, day-to-day matters to Indians and other oppressed people and their lawyers.[12] It is not the case that *Taking Rights Aggressively* refutes the *Algebra*, but it does balance it. I feel much more comfortable with the *Algebra* when it is sitting side-by-side with *Taking Rights Aggressively*. Had that article appeared before the *Algebra* I doubt that I would have written *Learning to Live*. Readers are invited to decide whether that would have been good.

My allotted "last word" space is running out. I will end with a number of short reactions to Professor Williams' reactions to my reactions:

1. [p. 441] I did not intend to deride the Gus-Wen-Tah by calling it "charming". On rereading, the word *does* ring false and I am sorry that I used it. "Attractive" or "inviting" would have been better.

2. [p. 447] Tribalism is indeed an important concept in Indian law; without the recognition of tribal sovereignty there is nothing left. This was my third proposition. To the extent that I departed elsewhere in the essay and spoke of "communities" and "individuals" it was because I thought I had covered myself as a *tribal* advocate—though concededly not the tribal advocate that Professor Williams is[13]—in point 3.

3. I think Professor Williams overstates his case on page 447: ". . . the 'right' to a tribal existence, has never been protected by the white man's law or courts." He means, I think, the "right" ". . . has never been protected *absolutely* by the white man's courts." There are many Supreme Court cases recognizing and protecting tribal sovereignty, but they are spoiled for Professor Williams by recognizing the coexistent power of Congress to limit tribal sovereignty.

---

10. Williams, *Taking Rights Aggressively: The Perils and Promises of Critical Legal Theory for Peoples of Color*, 5 L. & INEQUALITY 103 (1987).

11. *Id.* at 127-34.

12. *Id.* at 121-27, and especially at 123.

13. Professor Williams writes on page 447 that: "[w]hen Indian tribal people talk about important 'rights', the word possesses a whole different meaning. Their focus is on protection and perpetuation of their people's tribally-oriented existence." As I will discuss below, it is unclear to me how this quotation applies to Julia Martinez and other Indian peoples who have been plaintiffs under the Indian Civil Rights Act. While I am a tribal advocate, I am not one to the extent of telling Ms. Martinez that her right to be free of sex discrimination and her childrens' rights to be Santa Claran must fall to the Pueblo's "tribally-oriented existence." *See* Laurence, *Martinez, Oliphant and Federal Court Review of Tribal Activity under the Indian Civil Rights Act*, 10 CAMPBELL L. REV. — (1988).

4. [p. 449] There is no "air-tight" argument that the Court won't avoid the role of savior for Indian tribes in the future.

5. I like the word "closer" ten lines down on page 449.

6. [pp. 452-54] Professor Williams and I remain in disagreement over the Indian Civil Rights Act, and, I suppose, always shall be. I understand and respect his arguments on pages 452-54. I have heard them made by other scholars and friends whose work I also admire. But two words are missing: "Julia Martinez". It is hard for me to understand how one can have a meaningful discussion of the ICRA in the abstract; Professor Williams has ignored his own lesson from the first half of *Taking Rights Aggressively*.[14] Perhaps it is necessary that the right—or should I say "right"—of Ms. Martinez's children to be Santa Claran must give way to the Pueblo's "right" to be sovereign. Perhaps freedom from discrimination based upon sex is a "right" that the Pueblo needs time to evolve on its own, or more likely to rediscover following European domination. Perhaps Ms. Martinez's grievance is real but singular and must be lived with for the sake of the greater Indian good. Perhaps her forum is in Strasbourg, not Albuquerque, and the resulting inconvenience to her makes sense because the Pueblo is a sovereign nation. Whatever the explanation is, it seems to me that she, her children and Professor Williams' readers deserve to be told what his thinking is. She is a real person, a real woman, and her children are denied real rights based on the not surprising fact that their mother *is* a woman. The theoretical, detached answer seems to say "Too bad. Now, excuse me, ma'am, I'm busy." She deserves a better explanation.

7. [pp. 454-55] The United States is not Nicaragua.

8. [p. 455] In fact, my taxation hypotheticals were not ones I "obviously would regard as irrational." Like a good teacher, I tried to pose a range of hypos, some objectionable (the anti-Semitic one), some not (the hiring program), some in between (the *ad hoc* tax). Making the inquiry an ICRA one for a federal judge does not mean that the tribe will automatically lose in federal court; the pre-*Martinez* cases show that.

9. [p. 456] My vision is decidedly *not* of "reservation governmental decision-makers run amok without Anglo-American values imposed upon their decision making." I know too well (is this name-dropping? Forgive me.) the Paiute-Shoshone and Devils Lake Sioux tribal chairmen, the Navajo Attorney General, the tribal judges of the Cheyenne River Sioux Tribe, the Laguna Pueblo and Turtle Mountain Chippewa Tribe—all former students of mine[15]—to have that vision. I respect those tribal decision makers

---

14. The reason why leftist and neo-leftist law professors feel little remorse or fear over the abandonment of rights discourse is that for them 'rights' represent a concept, rather than a phenomenon. It is easy to 'trash' a concept. One cannot experience the pervasive, devastating reality of a 'right,' however, except in its absence. One must first be denied that seat on the bus, one must see the desecration of one's tribe's sacred lands, one must be without sanitary facilities in a farm field, to understand that a 'right' can be more than a concept. A right can also be a real, tangible experience.
Williams, *Taking Rights Aggressively, supra* note 11, at 123.

15. At Arkansas? Florida State? No. The American Indian Law Center at the University of New Mexico, as part of its Special Scholarship Program in Law for American Indians, holds a summer session for Indians entering as first-year students at law schools around the nation. I have been on the faculty there for the sessions in 1977, '79, '81, '83, '85 and '88.

and their counterparts in other tribes. But that respect is real, not romantic. I do not imagine that they are immune from the circumstances and forces that result in the occasional denial of important rights and freedoms. Nor do I imagine that they all agree with me regarding the ICRA.

10.   [p. 456] I took and reported my student's "So what?" not as a dismissal of the importance of the fact that the Indians were here first, but as an honest question of "What exactly follows from that fact, and why?"

11.   I agree wholeheartedly with the last two sentences of Professor Williams' sixth point on page 456. Unamended, unedited, unconditionally. And on that happy note, I end this debate, for now.

*THE NEW YORK TIMES, THURSDAY, APRIL 5, 1979*

# Your Law-Baseball Quiz

by Robert M. Cover

The names of four major league baseball personalities appear after the name of a Supreme Court Justice. Circle the name of the baseball figure who bears the same relationship to baseball as the Justice bears to law.

**EXAMPLE:**

**1. John Marshall**

**(a) Enos Slaughter**
**(b) Babe Ruth**
**(c) Dizzy Dean**
**(c) Cookie Lavagetto**

The correct answer is (b) Babe Ruth. Both Marshall and Ruth transformed the games they played. Both became symbols of their institutions, and both are understood to be originators of their professions' modern age. This judgment holds regardless of whether their records are ever broken.

## QUESTIONS

1. Earl Warren
(a) Yogi Berra
(b) Roberto Clemente
(c) Tris Speaker
(d) Willie Mays

2. Byron White
(a) Tommy Fenrich
(b) Don Newcombe
(c) Jackie Jensen
(d) Steve Garvey

3. Oliver Wendell Holmes Jr.
(a) Stan Musial
(b) Mickey Mantle
(c) Ty Cobb
(d) Casey Stengel

4. Felix Frankfurter
(a) Ted Williams
(b) Wayne Terwilliger
(c) Bobby Mercer
(d) Cleon Jones

5. Robert Jackson
(a) Joe DiMaggio
(b) Marty Marion
(c) Duke Snider
(d) Ernie Banks

6. Louis Brandeis
(a) Pie Traynor
(b) Lou Gehrig
(c) Jim Rice
(d) Clyde Vollmer

**ANSWERS**

1. Earl Warren. The correct answer is (a) Yogi Berra.

Both Warren and Berra were enormously effective performers on teams with many stars. Despite the presence of players such as Mantle, Maris, Frankfurter, Douglas and Black in the same lineup—all of whom appeared to have a more elegant swing or style—Berra and Warren were the truly most valuable players. Both would frequently swing at bad pitches, but both were capable of hitting them for extra bases, especially in the clutch. Both saw through excessive thought to the true essence of their game.

"Theorists beset us with other definitions of law: . . . But the idea of justice survives all such myopic views, for as Cicero said, 'We are born to it,'" said Warren. Or as Yogi said more succinctly, "How can you think and hit at the same time?"

2. Byron White. The correct answer is (c) Jackie Jensen.

Both were better as running backs. Despite a Golden-Boy buildup, Jensen failed to win a place on the great Yankee dynasty teams. However, on the mediocre and poor Washington and Boston Red Sox teams of the 50's he was a star. Similarly White, despite a big buildup, failed to achieve special distinction on the Warren Court. But in the context of the Burger Court he has achieved a measure of real stardom.

3. Oliver Wendell Holmes Jr. The correct answer is (d) Casey Stengel.

Both Holmes and Stengel had enormously varied and long careers, in each case serving the game for 50 years. Despite the great success in purely legal or baseball terms, each achieved immortality for his use of the English language. Both men put the game they loved in the perspective of the skeptic's view of the eternal search for truth:

"Logical method and form flatter that longing for certainty and for repose which is in every human mind. But certainty is illusion and repose is not the destiny of man. . . .

"So it's possible a college education doesn't always help you if you can't hit a left handed changeup as far as the shortstop. . . ."

4. Felix Frankfurter. The correct answer is (c) Bobby Murcer.

Frankfurter was in reality a rather ordinary Justice with good skills. However, many so-called experts had expected him to follow in the footsteps of the Mantles and DiMaggios of the law. Some people think Frankfurter was really Ted Williams. This kind of failure of expertise simply *cannot* happen in baseball and this demonstrates a weakness of this Law-Sport Aptitude Test. Experts may argue Mantle v. Mays or Williams v. Musial but there cannot be disagreement over whether Bobby Mercer is really Ted Williams.

5. Robert Jackson. The correct answer is (c) Duke Snider.

Both Jackson and Snider had the classic swing and style much appreciated by purists of the game. Both were men of enormous ability who were outstanding performers in their day. Yet, both also seemed to disappoint their fans in failing, somehow, to achieve all-time super-star status. It has been written of Snider that he was always relieved to get a base on balls and Jackson is perhaps best remembered for his opinion in the Japanese-relocation cases that it would be best for the Court not to decide the case at all.

6. Louis Brandeis. The correct

answer is (b) Lou Gehrig.

Brandeis and Gehrig had enormous ability and belong on the all-time All-Star team. Both had careers marked by outstanding, iron-man diligence. Gehrig's record of playing in 2,130 straight games may never be broken. Similarly, the Court may never have another Justice of whom it would be suggested that recreational reading consists of the reports of the Interstate Commerce Commission.

*Note:* Some have argued that this Law-Sport Aptitude Test discriminates against women. Unquestionably there are few opportunities for women to identify with and become interested in either major league baseball or the Supreme Court. Neither game has ever had a woman player. Unfortunately, given the Court's role in the legal order, knowledge of such exclusively male preserves may be a bona fide job-related necessity for a career as a lawyer.

*Robert M. Cover is professor of law at the Yale Law School and quondam fan of the Boston Red Sox ("because they let Luis Tiant go").*

## What Do Babe Ruth and John Marshall Have in Common?

This is one set of baseball cards your mother won't throw out. What's more, she probably wouldn't even want to.

They aren't cardboard playing cards; they're HyperCard stacks. And the back-of-the-card information features data, not on players from the National or American Leagues, but on the court system's own major league, the Supreme Court.

The "Hitchhiker's Guide to the U.S. Supreme Court" is the invention of Northwestern University political science professor Jerry Goldman, a devotee of both the Supreme Court and the national pastime. According to Goldman, "It's a computer tour of the Supreme Court built on a baseball theme;" it includes information on each of the 106 justices in the High Court's history, in baseball-card format, as well as texts of more than 500 significant constitutional opinions written between 1789 and 1982.

And to liven up the guide even more, users can test their knowledge with a law baseball quiz, which poses questions that compare the contributions of baseball players to their game with the contributions of justices to the law.

"It has a measure of whimsy generally missing in the study of law," Goldman remarks wryly.

The guide, expected to be released this fall, opens with a bird's-eye view of the Court. By picking a year, the user is faced with a panel of judges. Any selection will produce a profile of that justice, beginning with a computer-generated portrait and progressing to baseball-card-style information: "batting order," political party, appointing president, years of service, reasons for leaving the bench, the justice's "team" (by Chief Justice), and "minor league experience" (previous judicial, attorney general, or Senate service).

From a justice card, the user can access summaries of that justice's significant constitutional opinions; it's also possible to go backwards and forwards to investigate the justice's predecessors and successors. Justice cards also can be reached in alphabetical order, and constitutional decisions can be called up directly. The first information on decisions includes a summary of the facts, conclusions, and the vote of the Court; the user then can link to the full text.

But to test your ability to assess the stature of each justice and that individual's impact on the court, you need to turn to the law baseball quiz. You're challenged to compare the contributions of individual justices and baseball players, with relevant information on the ball players provided.

So, for example, you're asked to name the player whose contribution most closely parallels John Marshall's; your choices are Enos Slaughter, Mike Schmidt, Roy Campanella, or Babe Ruth. If you pick Ruth, a sound clue signals that you're right, explaining in part: "Ruth's slugging style and Marshall's 'discovery' of judicial review transformed the games they played. [Both] became symbols of their institutions, and both were originators of their professions' modern age."

Or try to find the baseball match for William J. Brennan, Jr.: Lou Boudreau, Ozzie Smith, Shawon Dunston, or Larry Bowa. The answer is Ozzie Smith, since both were "true wizards of their respective games. They knew what it takes to win and they perfected the skills to do it, on defense and on offense. . . [Smith's] long string of fielding records supports the claim that his glove alone saved the Cardinals 75 runs a year. Much the same could be said for Brennan, who managed to craft important liberal opinions when conservatives dominated the Court. . . ."

Goldman points out that the quiz

can be fun and illuminating even for those not conversant with the history of baseball, because it provides "hints and important pieces of information, so you don't feel like you're a failure when you strike out, but you actually learn something along the way."

But is baseball really an apt metaphor for a subject as weighty as the actions of the highest court in the land? Goldman argues that it is: Baseball is a true American sport, just as the Supreme Court is an essential American institution, and the reach of baseball in American life is extensive.

Not all justices warrant an entry in the quiz. "Just like baseball players, so many [justices] are forgettable," he says. "Both justices and baseball players may have had a moment of glory, but [for some justices] it's hard to find a moment of constitutional glory."

The law baseball quiz was the brainchild of the late Yale Law School professor Robert Cover, who made the Supreme Court/baseball analogy and gave a few sample questions in a 1979 *New York Times* op-ed piece. Goldman decided to build on that and incorporate it into the larger project, "The Hitchhiker's Guide to the U.S. Supreme Court," which takes its name from Douglas Adams's 1980 novel, *The Hitchhiker's Guide to the Galaxy,* which features an electronic book.

Goldman, who is director of Northwestern's Program in American Culture, assembled his "Hitchhiker's Guide" as a companion to *The Challenge of Democracy,* the widely-used American government text he coauthored with Kenneth Janda and Jeffrey M. Berry. The decision to focus on individual justices seemed logical.

"Understanding the justices and the responsibilities of their office is an important element in understanding the Constitution," Goldman says. "To a large extent, the Constitution is a product of the justices."

"The Hitchhiker's Guide" is written for Macintosh users and will be distributed on CD-ROM. It will include a video tour of the Supreme Court building and audio selections of oral arguments from key cases.

Goldman, who worked with Northwestern computer specialist and avid baseball fan Richard Barone, says the guide will initially be a resource for media and computing labs in universities, high schools, and libraries. The program makes the information available to a broad audience, including those without ready access to a law library.

And although he's uncertain whether law schools generally have sufficiently advanced computer technology to accommodate the guide, he thinks it would be valuable to law students as well.

"This is the 'Cliff notes' of constitutional law," he says.

*Contributing editor Sandra Goldsmith is a Boston writer.*

ESSAY

# The Great Gatsby, the Black Sox, High Finance, and American Law

*Allen Boyer**

*The Great Gatsby,* by F. Scott Fitzgerald, is the great novel of America in the 1920s. It is about someone pursuing a girl, and, more than that, it is about someone pursuing a dream. Jay Gatsby is someone who believes in the American dream of success. His life plays out the most famous piece of repartee between Fitzgerald and Hemingway — that the rich are very different from you and me, because they have more money. Gatsby is a man who thought that if he had the money, he would be rich, and could therefore be different.

After reading *Gatsby,* one remembers the parties which its hero threw: dusk-to-dawn galas peopled by financiers, Broadway stars, and the polo-playing aristocracy. But behind the glitter there are occasional glimpses of darkness. Gatsby is a man with no background. Some say he is the Kaiser's nephew, some have heard that he once killed a man. He has unsavory connections — perhaps even criminal connections. His past is a mystery, and there is something in his present which he wants to conceal.

What Gatsby's connections are, where he made his money, Fitzgerald keeps vague.[1] Nick Carraway, the narrator, asks Gatsby what business he is in. Gatsby replies, brusquely, "That's my affair" — then apologetically realizes his rudeness, and says that he was in the drug business for a while, and that he was in oil for a while.

It is just barely possible, given the timing, that Gatsby was involved with Teapot Dome. And his pharmaceutical business meant bootlegging: he owned part of a chain of drug stores which sold grain alcohol over the counter. Tom Buchanan, his rival for Daisy Buchanan, reveals this bootlegging connection near the end of the

* Special Counsel, Division of Enforcement, New York Stock Exchange. B.A. 1978, Vanderbilt University; J.D. 1982, University of Virginia; Ph.D. (English) 1984, University of St. Andrews, Scotland. — Ed. Thanks are due, for their contributions, to Kathleen Dicks, Eliot Asinof, Robert Ferguson, Daniel M. Gray, John R. Herrmann, James Kirby, Joel Lee, Brook Thomas, and Daniel Tritter. Opinions expressed in this essay are not necessarily those of the New York Stock Exchange or any of its officers.

1. *See generally* Randall, *Jay Gatsby's Hidden Source of Wealth,* 13 Mod. Fict. Stud. 247 (1967).

novel. But there is something else Gatsby is involved with. Even Tom Buchanan can't identify it, because his sources are too scared to talk. All we know is that, as Tom says, compared to it, the bootlegging is "just small change."

Two shadows fall directly across Gatsby's career. We know that he is involved with stolen securities. He sounds out Nick, a bond salesman, about working for him:

> "[I]f you'll pardon my — you see, I carry on a little business on the side, a sort of side line, you understand. And I thought that if you don't make very much — You're selling bonds, aren't you, old sport?"
> "Trying to."
> "Well, this would interest you. It wouldn't take up much of your time and you might pick up a nice bit of money. It happens to be a rather confidential sort of thing."[2]

At the novel's end, when Nick answers a phone call in Gatsby's empty house, he finds out what this sketchy invitation meant. The man on the long-distance line from Chicago tells him: "Young Parke's in trouble. They picked him up when he handed the bonds over the counter."[3]

We also know that Gatsby is the business partner of Meyer Wolfsheim — and that Wolfsheim is the man who fixed the 1919 World Series. Nick remembers their introduction:

> "[H]e's a gambler." Gatsby hesitated, then added coolly: "He's the man who fixed the World's Series back in 1919."
>
> . . . .
>
> The idea staggered me. I remembered, of course, that the World's Series had been fixed in 1919, but if I had thought of it at all I would have thought of it as a thing that merely *happened*, the end of some inevitable chain. It never occurred to me that one man could start to play with the faith of fifty million people — with the single-mindedness of a burglar blowing a safe.[4]

Both of these scandals — securities fraud and the Black Sox — trace back in fiction to Meyer Wolfsheim. In life they trace back to Wolfsheim's real-life counterpart, Arnold Rothstein.

## I.  CAPITAL AND THE UNDERWORLD

Arnold Rothstein was the first great financier of organized crime. Rothstein talked very little about himself. Others, however, called him "the Brain" and "the Big Bankroll." His attorney, William Fal-

---

2. F.S. FITZGERALD, THE GREAT GATSBY 83 (Hudson River ed. 1980).

3. *Id.* at 167.

4. *Id.* at 74. For the best history of the Black Sox scandal, see E. ASINOF, EIGHT MEN OUT: THE BLACK SOX AND THE 1919 WORLD SERIES (1963).

lon — unsurpassed for courtroom eloquence, but so crooked that he makes Roy Cohn look like a saint — described Rothstein as "a man who dwells in doorways. A mouse standing in a doorway, waiting for his cheese."[5]

We will not discuss Rothstein's role as the contact man between Tammany Hall and the New York City underworld. We will not discuss his role in labor union racketeering. We will not discuss his role as mentor to John T. Nolan, Arthur Flegenheimer, and Charles Lucania — who would later be known, respectively, as Legs Diamond, Dutch Schultz, and Lucky Luciano. We will not discuss his interests (financial, not personal) in heroin and cocaine. We will mention only briefly his role as the man behind New York's first bootlegging operations — briefly, because the point requires no particular explanation. We *will* discuss his role as a gambler and a mastermind of securities fraud.[6]

Fixing the World Series was only one episode in Rothstein's career. He played the horses, played high-stakes craps and higher-stakes poker, and sometimes cut cards at $40,000 a cut. He would bet on literally anything, from the serial numbers on dollar bills to the license plates on passing cars. He owned and managed gambling houses. On and off the race-course, he was to ordinary bookies what reinsurance companies are to the insurance trade.

As an underworld financier, Rothstein was the man who probably masterminded (or fenced) the Liberty Bond thefts of 1918-1920, in which $5 million of bonds were stolen.[7] He was an insurance broker, appreciating the value of a business which offered a steady flow of cash and checks.[8] In the years bracketing World War I, moreover, he was the man who stood behind the bucket-shops of New York City.

A bucket-shop was a discount retail securities house. Some bucket-shops were legitimate; many others were not. These buck-

---

5. *See* L. KATCHER, THE BIG BANKROLL: THE LIFE AND TIMES OF ARNOLD ROTHSTEIN 8 (1959).

6. On Rothstein's career, see generally D. CLARKE, IN THE REIGN OF ROTHSTEIN (1929); G. FOWLER, THE GREAT MOUTHPIECE: A LIFE STORY OF WILLIAM J. FALLON (1931); L. KATCHER, *supra* note 5; C. ROTHSTEIN, NOW I'LL TELL (1934) (memoir of Rothstein's widow).

7. *See* L. KATCHER, *supra* note 5, at 179. Arrested for these thefts, but never convicted, was Nicky Arnstein, then the husband of Fannie Brice. Arnstein insisted that he had been framed, which may well be true. *Id.* at 174-75, 180.

8. By some accounts, Rothstein used insurance as an enforcement mechanism. By requiring those who borrowed from him to take out insurance and name him as the beneficiary, he let his debtors know that they were funding the price he would put on their heads, should they default. *See* L. MORRIS, INCREDIBLE NEW YORK: HIGH LIFE AND LOW LIFE OF THE LAST HUNDRED YEARS 346 (1951). It seems as likely, if less dramatic, that Rothstein made himself his clients' insurer to prevent them from obtaining an independent source of capital by burning down their properties.

eteers were not above advertising their house stocks, knowing them to be worthless. A common practice was to make a phone solicitation, pocket the money, and postpone filling the order. If the customer's stock went down, the bucketeer could buy the shares at that lower price and keep the difference. If the stock went up, he would persuade the customer to roll over the money into a new investment.

Leo Katcher, Rothstein's biographer, wrote:

> No official total of bucket-shop "take" has ever been compiled. Nat J. Ferber, the New York *American* reporter who did more to expose bucketeers and their activities than any other newspaperman, estimated their take in his book, *I Found Out*, as $6,000,000,000. . . .
>
> This much is on the record. In New York State, in one five-year period, bucket shops went into bankruptcy owing their customers more than $212,000,000![9]

To stay in business, the bucketeers needed protection, which Rothstein provided. When circumstances caught up with them, he was indispensable in providing bondsmen and lawyers.

In 1922 and 1923, the biggest of the bucketing scandals was constantly in the press. E.M. Fuller & Company, the largest brokerage house on the Consolidated Exchange, had gone into bankruptcy, owing its customers an amount estimated at $5 million. The trials that followed — no fewer than four of them — brought out Rothstein's involvement with New York's bucket-shops. Edward M. Fuller awaited arrest in Rothstein's house, and Fuller's attorney was William Fallon. The firm's papers revealed that Rothstein had taken some $425,000 out of the Fuller company's coffers.[10]

For the rest of Rothstein's life, attorneys kept asking him questions about his ties to Fuller. William Chadbourne, the receivers' attorney, grilled Rothstein intensely over whether he had bet with Fuller on the 1919 World Series. Chadbourne sought to show that Rothstein had bet on a fixed Series. This meant, he argued, that Rothstein had acquired the money under false pretenses, so that it therefore could be recovered for legitimate creditors.

Rothstein's answers suggested that he used gambling to launder money. Paying off fictitious bets was an easy way to pass dirty money from one hand to another. But in this case, the wager had been legitimate; triumphantly waving a canceled check, Rothstein proved that he had bet on the White Sox.[11] All Chadbourne could do was snap

---

9. L. KATCHER, *supra* note 5, at 181.

10. *See generally* H.D. PIPER, "THE GREAT GATSBY": THE NOVEL, THE CRITICS, THE BACKGROUND 171-84 (1970).

11. L. KATCHER, *supra* note 5, at 200.

back that perjury obviously had no terrors for the witness.[12]

Here we find the connection to *Gatsby.* Scott Fitzgerald, after the success of *This Side of Paradise,* had become acquainted with the celebrities of New York City — a group that included the town's most prominent gambler. He would later recall that "[i]n *Gatsby* I selected the stuff to fit a given planned mood or 'hauntedness' . . . always starting from the *small* focal point that impressed me — my own meeting with Arnold Rothstein for instance."[13] In Great Neck, Long Island, where Fitzgerald wrote much of *Gatsby,* one can trace down another parallel. His neighbor, a man known for his society connections and his interest in aviation, was Edward M. Fuller — of E.M. Fuller & Co.

## II. AMERICAN PASTIMES

It is easy to gather why Fitzgerald decided that Gatsby would be involved with bootleg liquor and with stolen bonds. These were the most notorious crime waves of the day. A more revealing question is why Fitzgerald named fixing the World Series as the third of the crimes with which Gatsby is connected.

This may have been because he knew Rothstein and Fuller. While Fitzgerald was writing *Gatsby,* he saw Ring Lardner almost daily, and Lardner had been involved in uncovering the Black Sox scandal. But the most important reason is that Fitzgerald was a student of history, and recognized what baseball had come to mean to America.

Baseball, during the Progressive Era, had become more than a game.[14] It had become emblematic of America's social structure. Its teamwork showed democracy in action; its fans were found among all classes of society; it taught America's traditional values to successive waves of immigrants; and it served as an annual ritual which united cities behind their teams. Walt Whitman called it "the hurrah game," and continued:

[W]ell — it's our game; that's the chief fact in connection with it:

---

12. *See* D. CLARKE, *supra* note 6, at 113-40. Stock-bucketeering and baseball gambling intersected at other points. Charles Stoneham, the owner of the New York Giants, was alleged to be a sleeping partner in E.M. Fuller & Co. Stoneham had made his money as a stock-bucketeer, and he would later handle the Havana end of a rum-running operation which Rothstein directed. It may not be coincidental that the Giants hired first baseman Hal Chase, who had been dropped from the Cincinnati Reds for trying to fix a game, and that Giants Manager John McGraw paid for the coffin in which William Fallon was buried. *See* L. KATCHER, *supra* note 5, at 192-93; H.D. PIPER, *supra* note 10, at 182-84; A. HYND, DEFENDERS OF THE DAMNED 182 (1960); *see also* E. ASINOF, *supra* note 4, at 14-15.

13. A. TURNBULL, SCOTT FITZGERALD (1962) (quoting Fitzgerald).

14. Chief among the social historians who have made this point is Steven Riess. *See* S. RIESS, TOUCHING BASE: PROFESSIONAL BASEBALL AND AMERICAN CULTURE IN THE PROGRESSIVE ERA (1980).

America's game: has the snap, go, fling of the American atmosphere —
belongs as much to our institutions, fits into them as significantly, as our
constitutions, laws: is just as important in the sum total of our historic
life.[15]

Literature added sports heroes to the American pantheon. In dime
novels, youngsters read of Frank Merriwell, the only man ever able to
throw the double curve. In real life, they could read of baseball mar-
tyr Christy Mathewson. Mathewson, after the close of a legendary
pitching career, resigned as manager of the Cincinnati Reds to go
overseas in World War I. In a training accident, he became a victim of
poison gas. This led to his death, from tuberculosis, in 1925.

The 1919 Series had been the first major sporting event in post-war
America, and Fitzgerald had a life-long passion for sports. His first
love was football (in particular, Princeton football), and he helped tie
*Gatsby* together with motifs drawn from the athletic world. Jordan
Baker is a professional golfer, about whom hangs a suspicion of cheating. Tom Buchanan was once one of Yale's most powerful ends, and
the Buchanans' social environment is "wherever people played polo
and were rich together."[16] The Black Sox scandal fit his fictional
rhetoric.

If cheating and fixed games hover in the background of *Gatsby,*
and securities fraud is just off-stage, so too is another shadow which
marked the Twenties. Gatsby's role as a bootlegger casts him as a
peripheral figure in one of America's boldest experiments in social and
constitutional history: the short, unsteady life of the eighteenth
amendment, better known as Prohibition.

Prohibition, nowadays, is remembered ironically; pronouncing the
word carries the implication that it was foolish to try to ban the sale of
alcohol. It is only later, intellectually, that one appreciates that Prohibition was an issue of constitutional magnitude. On July 17, 1919, the
Constitution of the United States was amended to prohibit the sale of
intoxicating beverages — and yet the people of the United States continued to buy intoxicating beverages. The law of the land was a popular nullity. To understand what this failure meant, in terms of
American law, one must look back far before the Twenties.

## III. AMERICAN LAW: OLD FAILINGS AND NEW VISIONS

For American jurisprudents, the original definition of law came
from that suggested by Sir William Blackstone: law was a force which

---

15. Folsom, *America's "Hurrah Game": Baseball and Walt Whitman,* 11 IOWA REV. 68, 77
(1980) (quoting Walt Whitman).

16. F.S. FITZGERALD, *supra* note 2, at 6.

commanded the right and forbade the wrong.[17] Law and morality were related, perhaps even coextensive.

In 1897 — when Scott Fitzgerald was one year old, and Arnold Rothstein turned fifteen — Oliver Wendell Holmes, Jr., proposed a radically different view. "I think it desirable," Holmes wrote, "to point out and dispel a confusion between morality and law. . . ." He went on to urge that the two be divorced:

> If you want to know the law and nothing else, you must look at it as a bad man, who cares only for the material consequences which such knowledge enables him to predict, not as a good one, who finds his reasons for conduct, whether inside the law or outside of it, in the vaguer sanctions of conscience. . . .
>
> . . . .
>
> . . . The prophecies of what the courts will do in fact, and nothing more pretentious, are what I mean by the law.
>
> . . . .
>
> . . . The duty to keep a contract at common law means a prediction that you must pay damages if you do not keep it, — and nothing else. If you commit a tort, you are liable to pay a compensatory sum.[18]

And by logical extension, if an act is criminalized, this means only that those who commit it run the risk of being jailed.

Holmes' comments laid the foundation for Legal Realism. During the early decades of this century, while this school of thought raised controversy within law schools, it seemed (with an odd, cynical precision) to restate the popular attitude. In the Twenties, to judge by the American people's response to Prohibition, morality seemed to have no part in law. No matter that Prohibition was enshrined in the Constitution; the population ignored this super-legal commandment. It was as if Holmes' bad man, who cared nothing about morality, but only about penalties, now defined the public's view of law.[19]

---

17. Blackstone wrote: "[T]he primary and principal objects of the law are RIGHTS, and WRONGS. . . . I shall follow this very simple and obvious division; and shall, in the first place, consider the *rights* that are commanded, and secondly the *wrongs* that are forbidden." 1 W. BLACKSTONE, COMMENTARIES *122 (1783), *quoted in* D. BOORSTIN, THE MYSTERIOUS SCIENCE OF THE LAW 92-93 (1958).

18. Holmes, *The Path of the Law*, 10 HARV. L. REV. 457, 459 (1897). Holmes found other influences to replace morality. Historical understanding was one; hence *The Common Law*'s historical aspects. Holmes' amorality, too, bowed to social science and quasi-science. He himself was a Social Darwinist, willing to let law be rewritten by emerging social groups. If law did not embody morality, it should reflect the evolutionary struggle. *See* Gordon, *Holmes' "Common Law" as Legal and Social Science*, 10 HOFSTRA L. REV. 719 (1982).

19. To be sure, other voices echoed Holmes. Roscoe Pound would talk about sociological jurisprudence. Charles Beard would frame the United States Constitution in an economic context, arguing with a great number of tables that it had been written by upper-class white men *for* upper-class white men. Jerome Frank would insist that judges decide cases on the facts, and that lower courts overruled the Supreme Court every day. *See* Hopkins, *The Development of Realism in Law and Literature During the Period 1883-1933: The Cultural Resemblance*, 4 PACE L. REV.

It was acceptable, the American people seemed to feel, to violate the Constitution. The result of the Black Sox trial, held in Chicago in the summer of 1921, seemed only to compound the irony. All eight of the White Sox players involved were acquitted. By the decision of that court, fixing the World Series, tampering with the faith of fifty million people, was not a crime.[20]

In *Gatsby,* one senses a similar moral vacuum. Characters muddle right and wrong, often willfully. People dislike dealing face-to-face with Myrtle Wilson, but they condone Tom Buchanan's keeping a mistress. Despite Nick's self-proclaimed honesty, he romanticizes Gatsby, although Gatsby is linked to the underworld and is obsessed with a woman married to someone else. Even on Wolfsheim (who talks matter-of-factly of gangland killings, and whose cuff buttons are made of human teeth), Nick speaks with moral detachment, as if lunching with gangsters were the same as watching strange beasts in a national park.

The law, not surprisingly, plays little part in Fitzgerald's novel. Only two policemen actually appear. One flags down Gatsby for speeding, then salutes and apologizes when Gatsby flashes the police commissioner's personal card. The second officer appears after Myrtle Wilson's death. Seriously but impotently, he takes down information, opening a case which will never be solved. Even retribution miscarries. At the novel's end, George Wilson desperately tries to avenge his honor and his wife's death; but Wilson is misled by the man who wronged him, and shoots Gatsby instead. Tom Buchanan, the cause-in-fact of a fatal accident and a murder-suicide, bears no legal responsibility for any of these deaths. Faced with this, Nick flees the East — and although this is hardly a solution, Fitzgerald suggests no better one.

## IV.  FROM MORALISM TO REGULATION

From the Black Sox scandal, baseball emerged as a hitter's game, thanks to a livelier ball, which made it possible for Babe Ruth to hit scores of home runs every season. The same years were a turning

---

29 (1983); *see also* Golding, *Jurisprudence and Legal Philosophy in Twentieth-Century America — Major Themes and Developments,* 36 J. LEGAL EDUC. 441 (1986).

20. The trial was flawed by design; the prosecuting attorneys agreed to try the case only on the flimsiest possible theory. *See* E. ASINOF, *supra* note 4, at 197-275. Even without this knowledge, a Chicago editorial writer cut through to a conclusion reminiscent of Justice Holmes:

> The law and the jury seem to say that the question in such a conspiracy is not what you do but what you can get away with. . . . A case like this might seem unimportant in comparison with disarmament, or world commerce, or the race problem, or prohibition. But at the bottom of every issue lies the national character.

Chicago Herald and Examiner, *cited in* E. ASINOF, *supra* note 4, at 274.

point for American law.[21] If law no longer meant morality, it would be reborn as governmental administration. If courts would not give justice, justice *would* be established — by other institutions, found throughout society.

Ten years after *Gatsby,* the modern superstructure of federal regulatory agencies would cover the American economic landscape.[22] Under this new regime, the test for legality would not be morality or justice; it would be technical compliance, whether one had followed directions. The income tax is the best example. Al Capone was jailed not because he ran bootleg liquor, or ordered the massacre of his enemies, or corrupted the politics of the city of Chicago; Al Capone went to Alcatraz because he omitted to pay his taxes.[23]

The Securities Act of 1933 also fell into this category. It brought the issuance of securities under the scrutiny of the federal government — not by establishing a police force, but by prescribing a process to be followed, securities registration. In creating causes of action, this statute made liability hinge upon an objective standard: misstatements of fact. No longer did one hunt for a conman's scienter; no longer did a plaintiff have to prove reliance. Good faith and betrayal had been factored out of the legal calculus.[24]

Regulation also ended the high-flying era of open gambling. The parallel is worth considering: the gambling and securities communities had largely overlapped.[25] Formerly, independent bookies had made their own odds and paid off bettors at different rates — but now all stakes were held by the track, a neutral party, and all bets were paid off at the closing odds. "Undesirable elements" might still be

---

21. Stephen Jay Gould makes this connection in his foreword to *Eight Men Out. See* Gould, *Foreword* to E. ASINOF, *supra* note 4.

22. It has been argued that Legal Realism, with its pragmatic approach, allowed American lawyers to accommodate themselves to administrative law as installed by the New Deal. B. ACKERMAN, RECONSTRUCTING AMERICAN LAW 17-38 (1984).

23. This would eventually have brought down, probably, Arnold Rothstein, who boasted of never having paid more than $150 a year in federal income tax. *See* D. CLARKE, *supra* note 6, at 303.

24. *See* Securities Act of 1933 §§ 11, 12, 17 (codified at 15 U.S.C. §§ 77k, 77l, 77q (1982)). Of course, scienter and reliance found their way back into the Securities Exchange Act of 1934 — but even here one finds § 16(b), which inexorably recaptures all profits made by corporate insiders on trades made within six months. Section 16(b) was enacted to curb an abuse favored by one of Gatsby's regular guests, James B. "Rot-Gut" Ferret: "[T]hey came to gamble, and when Ferret wandered into the garden it meant he was cleaned out and Associated Traction would have to fluctuate profitably next day." F.S. FITZGERALD, *supra* note 2, at 62.

25. When Joseph "Sport" Sullivan sought to place a bet on the 1919 Series, he headed for the Chicago Board of Trade. E. ASINOF, *supra* note 4, at 36-37. In 1920, when gamblers spread rumors that the Yankees team had been involved in a train wreck, with Babe Ruth injured, this disinformation arrived over the private wire of W.E. Hutton & Co. *Id.* at 153. And this leaves to one side the Havana casino into which Charles Stoneham put much of his money.

involved, but now they had to work indirectly, facing the risks involved in public scrutiny.

Gaming commissions turned casinos into quasi-utilities. Just as government employees found their powers constrained by administrative procedures, so casino employees had their discretion limited. In Nevada's casinos, "dealers were instructed to play according to fixed rules set by the house so that they never matched wits against the players."[26] As much as any government regulation, these new standards were meant to ensure certainty and predictability — and the casinos, like the government, flourished.

The old idea of law had been fallaciously simple. (How did one know exactly what rights were commanded, or what was so wrong that it had to be forbidden?) This new-model law avoided that problem, but it placed too much faith in complexity and detail. Eventually, it was bound to go too far. Within two decades, its capacity for contradiction and paradox would be satirized by Joseph Heller, whose *Catch-22* presented a world where rules prevented action.[27] No matter how sophisticated the administrative schema, Heller would observe, there was bound to be a catch somewhere — and, inevitably, there *would* be.

## V.   LAW OUTSIDE LAW: THE RISE OF SELF-GOVERNING INSTITUTIONS

And as for the other shape which the new law took:

The Legal Realists argued that law was only a system which imposed sanctions. If that is true, the converse must also be true: any system which imposes sanctions has a claim to be recognized as law. Here the Realists found themselves poaching on another discipline's terrain. Rejecting law's ties to morality and religious revelation, the Realists studied it as an aspect of human behavior — and so found themselves working side-by-side with social anthropologists. It is no accident that *The Cheyenne Way,* a study of American Indian jurisprudence, was written by anthropologist E.A. Hoebel and arch-Realist Karl Llewellyn.[28]

Hoebel and Llewellyn wrote other books — certainly less idiosyncratic books — but *The Cheyenne Way* is noteworthy as a study in legal anthropology. While confessing how hard it was to define law, the two jurisprudents tried yet again. It was wrong, Hoebel and Llew-

---

26. D. BOORSTIN, THE AMERICANS: THE DEMOCRATIC EXPERIENCE 74 (1973).

27. J. HELLER, CATCH-22 (1961).

28. E. HOEBEL & K. LLEWELLYN, THE CHEYENNE WAY (1941).

ellyn thought, to say that law necessarily involved action by "officials of the political state." Functionally, "the vital difference [lay] between that deviation which is rebuked and that breach which is not."[29] Where sanctions were enforced, there one found law. Statutes passed by legislatures and decisions handed down by judges were only part of the total: "The total picture of law-stuff in any society includes, along with the Great Law-stuff of the Whole, the sublaw-stuff or bylaw-stuff of the lesser working units."[30]

In America, private institutions had taken on a quasi-legal role. The rise of the press illustrated the point. Once, newspapers had called themselves The Advertiser or The Democrat, admitting that they were commercial listings or political organs. By the turn of the century, however, they had declared their independence. (Or, at least, their headstrong self-will.) Now newspapers were political watchdogs. They would lobby for their chosen causes, rake muck against any candidate — even start wars, if their publishers chose. Their power was recognized with the sobriquet of the Fourth Estate, which implied that they were constitutional bodies.[31]

Even baseball found itself growing into this role. Before becoming baseball commissioner, Kenesaw Mountain Landis had been a federal judge. In assuming this new jurisdiction, he may have felt compelled to fill a vacuum. The very next year, Justice Holmes would declare that baseball was not interstate commerce, and so not subject to the antitrust laws.[32] The contract which Landis wrote for himself (with lifetime tenure, financial security, and absolute power, above the politics of baseball leagues) duplicated his previous status. Technically, Landis remained a private citizen, and baseball remained only a popular pastime — but as its organization became effective, it increasingly mirrored the structures of political government.

---

29. *Id.* at 23-24.

30. *Id.* at 28.

31. This point is captured wonderfully in the classically Progressive motto of Joseph Pulitzer's St. Louis *Post-Dispatch,* which still appears on its editorial page each day:

THE POST-DISPATCH PLATFORM

I know that my retirement will make no difference in [the *Post-Dispatch's* ] cardinal principles, that it will always fight for progress and reform, never tolerate injustice or corruption, always fight demagogues of all parties, never belong to any party, always oppose privileged classes and public plunderers, never lack sympathy with the poor, always remain devoted to the public welfare, never be satisfied with merely printing news, always be drastically independent, never be afraid to attack wrong, whether by predatory plutocracy or predatory poverty.

April 10, 1907                                                                    Joseph Pulitzer

32. Federal Baseball Club of Baltimore v. National League of Prof. Baseball Clubs, 259 U.S. 200 (1922). Or was Landis trying to take the sport outside the sphere of government regulation? Before the scandal, as a judge, he had himself stalled action on antitrust suits against organized baseball.

With this in mind, one should look at how the Black Sox scandal finally found its resolution. The day after the verdict in the Chicago trial, Commissioner Landis issued this edict:

> Regardless of the verdicts of juries, no player who throws a ball game, no player that undertakes or promises to throw a ball game, no player that sits in conference with a bunch of crooked players and gamblers where the ways and means of throwing a game are discussed and does not promptly tell his club about it, will ever play professional baseball.[33]

Landis spoke with the finality of formal government; none of the Black Sox ever again played professional baseball.

The Commissioner's findings were challenged (implicitly) in lawsuits brought by Buck Weaver and Shoeless Joe Jackson. Both sued White Sox owner Charles Comiskey for the balance due on their employment contracts — arguing that they had always played to the best of their ability, and so had not breached their agreements with him. Neither prevailed. Weaver lost his suit (although he badgered Comiskey into a settlement). Jackson won a jury verdict, which the judge set aside.[34] Outside the court, Weaver met repeatedly with Landis, urging mitigating circumstances, and Jackson's fans petitioned to have the case reviewed. Neither of these approaches changed one syllable of the decree.

As Hoebel and Llewellyn remind us, *law* is not only formal law; it can be found in the customs, traditions, and other value structures of a society. In this broader meaning, as Fitzgerald sensed, what the Black Sox did violated the law. Their suspension by Landis was a rebuke of this violation. The legitimacy of this decision — and the legitimacy of the new order of law — is shown by the fact that the order was never undone by any court. Eventually, even federal courts, even when constitutional rights were involved, would explicitly defer to the judgment of sports officials.[35]

---

33. E. ASINOF, *supra* note 4, at 273 (quoting Landis).

34. Although substantive law had proved unable to handle the Black Sox affair, adjective law took an inexorable vengeance. Weaver's case was dismissed when his lawyers failed to appear in court. Jackson's verdict was set aside because, the judge said, the plaintiff had perjured himself, telling one story to the grand jury that had indicted the Black Sox, and another on the witness stand. E. ASINOF, *supra* note 4, at 279-92.

35. In 1961, for example, Judge Irving Kaufman would find that a professional sports league "could reasonably conclude that in order to effectuate its important and legitimate policies against gambling, and to restore and maintain the confidence of the public . . . it was necessary to enforce its rules strictly." The reason, at bottom, was that "every league or association must have some reasonable governing rules." Molinas v. National Basketball Assn., 190 F. Supp. 241, 243-44 (S.D.N.Y. 1961). Witness also the dispute over where constitutionally implied rights of privacy should yield to the need to keep sports clean by policing drug use. *See, e.g.,* Cochran, *Drug Testing of Athletes and the United States Constitution: Crisis and Conflict,* 92 DICK. L. REV. 571 (1988).

In 1989, organized baseball eked out a victory over both state courts (too eager, perhaps, to please local voters) and a federal bench drilled to respect due process and individual rights.

## VI. THE NEW METROPOLIS

Looking back to Scott Fitzgerald, it is eerie how well *The Great Gatsby* predicted the end of the Twenties. Arnold Rothstein died in 1928, mortally wounded as he left a poker game in a Manhattan hotel. Documents found among his papers showed the connection between Tammany Hall and the underworld. These scandals brought to office the reform administration of Fiorello LaGuardia, and brought to national prominence New York Governor Franklin Delano Roosevelt.

The Liberty Bond boom of the early 1920s touched off the stock-market speculation which characterized the rest of the decade. This helped cause the Great Depression, and led, in turn, to the securities legislation of 1933 and 1934.

In the middle of the Jazz Age, Fitzgerald had foreseen that the music was bound to stop. The political and financial elites had been humbled; the old order had been brought low. And the new metropolis, even while Fitzgerald was writing *Gatsby,* was already rising.

Part of *Gatsby*'s modern appeal is its portrait of vanished Long Island: a working countryside, set off from New York by the growing town of Queens. The roads are nineteenth-century lanes. In investigating the deaths that close the novel, the police can ascertain which cars took a given route, and when. Yet within one generation, modern highways would criss-cross Long Island, and its villages would become New York City's suburbs — thanks to Robert Moses, America's greatest builder of public works.

In 1923, Moses was surveying parkway routes across Long Island. In the next four decades, he would change the shoreline of Manhattan Island, link the outer boroughs with bridges and tunnels, blast expressways through miles of apartment houses. Moses gave New York City its parklands and beaches; he tore down old neighborhoods and raised up new ones; he created Lincoln Center and the South Bronx.[36]

Moses controlled New York's public authorities: the Triborough Bridge Authority, City Tunnel Authority, City Housing Authority, City Planning Commission, State Public Works Department, State Power Authority, State Council of Parks, and other government boards. He would be known as "the Coordinator." This referred to

---

Commissioner A. Bartlett Giamatti, after a free-wheeling jurisdictional squabble, cut short a case which seemed bound for months of litigation by banning Cincinnati Reds Manager Pete Rose from the game for life for allegedly betting on games. *See* Chambers, *Pete's Fans Learn What Lawyers Do,* Natl. L.J., Sept. 11, 1989, at 13; *He's Out!,* N.Y. Post, Aug. 24, 1989, at 1.

36. *See* R. CARO, THE POWER BROKER: ROBERT MOSES AND THE FALL OF NEW YORK 2-21 (1974).

his position as City Construction Coordinator, and acknowledged his role as the man who shaped the new New York.

Public authorities, originally, had performed the ministerial work of government. They covered only single projects (if a bridge or a turnpike were needed, an authority would be set up to build it), and they went out of existence when those projects were paid for. Moses changed all that. He won for public authorities the power to refinance their bonds, which gave them perpetual existence. He won for them the right to keep collecting commuters' dimes and quarters, even after every project had been paid off. Finally, he made authority decisions unreviewable by sealing them with bond indentures, agreements which the Contracts Clause protected against governmental second-guessing.

To build Long Island's parkways, Moses assumed the power to acquire acreage without a prior hearing and without prior payment — simply and literally, by sending men onto land, declaring it confiscated, and telling the owner to apply for compensation. This was comprehended by the legislative declaration that the Long Island State Park Commission might acquire land by appropriation "in the manner provided by section fifty-nine of the conservation law."[37] The power to construct thoroughfares "connecting" with the Triborough Bridge, the power to build and operate public projects "not inconsistent" "with the use" of the Triborough Bridge — these elastic terms gave Moses the power to plan an entire city, which he ruthlessly exercised.[38]

In an age of statutes and regulations, those people rule who know the laws' hidden meanings — those people who have mapped out, through a circuit of obscure connections, the lines along which power flows. Moses showed how draftsmanship could be cryptography and how personal control could be relayed through the forms of government administration. Rothstein had worked in the gaps of law; Moses worked behind its structures.

In Middle Queens, in the days when he was building parks, Robert Moses found 127 vacant acres — part of the estate of Arnold Rothstein. Rothstein's money had vanished. The land remained, the only tangible portion of his legacy, but it lay under a heavy tax lien. So Moses, his biographer wrote, worked out a typically double-handed arrangement

> under which the city "bought" 74 of the 127 acres for $334,000 but the estate paid the $334,000 back to the city to clear the tax deficiency on all 127 acres, leaving the estate with 53 acres free and clear — and the city

---

37. *Id.* at 174.

38. *Id.* at 627. *See generally id.* at 615-36.

with a 74-acre "Juniper Valley" park which it had acquired without a cent of cash outlay.[39]

The new model of law had succeeded the old. Symbolically and functionally, the Coordinator became the gangster's heir.

---

39. *Id.* at 377.

# ERROR BEHIND THE PLATE AND IN THE LAW[†]

RICHARD LEMPERT*

Casey Stengel, the great manager of the New York Yankees, and later the New York Mets, once dreamed, or so he said, that he had died and gone to heaven. The Lord greeted him personally as he walked through the Pearly Gates. "Casey," he said, "I'm so glad you're here. I want you to form a baseball team." Casey looked around him. He saw Babe Ruth, Lou Gehrig, Ty Cobb, Tris Speaker, Christy Mathewson, Walter Johnson, Grover Cleveland Alexander, and others—all of baseball's immortals—and he said, "I'll see what I can do." Obviously, one can do a lot with such talent, and, Casey soon had a team of all-stars at the peak of their talents. The only question was who they could play.

Casey didn't have to wait long for an answer. No sooner was the team in top playing condition when the dugout phone rang. It was Satan

† Professor Brilmayer's article, *Wobble, or the Death of Error*, 59 S. CAL. L. REV. 363 (1986), is different in many respects from the paper she presented at the conference giving rise to this symposium issue. By rethinking and refining elements of her earlier position, Professor Brilmayer has acted as a good scholar should. Nevertheless, this puts me in a quandary. In commenting on Professor Brilmayer's previous version, I used what she originally had written to identify my own position on the issues. As I am more interested in advancing my own views than in criticizing Professor Brilmayer's, I present my original response largely unchanged. I hope Professor Brilmayer and the reader will indulge me and treat those views attributed to her but not reflected in the current text of her article as "strawmen," valuable only insofar as they help clarify my position on the matters we both discuss. Ultimately, we remain apart in the thrust of our analyses, for the primary purpose of my paper is to differ fundamentally with the conclusion of her current version: "Methodologically, error cannot exist in the legal system in the commonsensical meaning of the word. At most, it means departure from the norms of a more authoritive institution that is itself an indeterminate decisionmaker." *Id.* at 389.

I shall use footnotes to indicate other ways in which my analysis contrasts with the positions Professor Brilmayer espouses in the final version of her article. To avoid confusion, all page citations to Professor Brilmayer's article refer to the article as it appears in this symposium issue. References to Brilmayer without page citations specifically respond to her earlier version. The reader may judge their applicability to the current version.

I am grateful to my colleague Fred Schauer for his comments on an earlier version of this paper. They were wise and helpful, exhibiting the discernment one would expect from a Yankee fan.

* Professor of Law and Sociology, University of Michigan. A.B. 1964, Oberlin College; J.D. 1968, University of Michigan Law School; Ph.D. in Sociology 1971, University of Michigan.

calling to challenge the Lord's team to a baseball game. "But you don't understand," said Casey. "You don't have a chance. I've got all the players." "No—*you* don't understand," said Satan, "I've got all the umpires."

It seems to me that the basic message Professor Brilmayer conveys in her article, "Wobble, or the Death of Error,"[1] is that the law, as enunciated by the ultimate decisionmaker, is the umpire.[2] If baseball is defined solely as a game played in accordance with the judgment of the umpires, then the umpires cannot be wrong. Similarly if law is defined solely as the will of the ultimate legal decisionmaker, then final judgments of law cannot be wrong. The question is, however, whether either baseball or the law are, in fact, so defined.

Baseball is not defined solely as the will of the ultimate decisionmaker. There are rules, which can be found in a book; and, by reference to them, one could criticize an umpire for being wrong if he called a batter out on the second strike or ruled that a pop fly caught by the shortstop was a home run. A manager confronted by an umpire who ruled in such a manner might pull his team off the field, declaring, "This isn't baseball."

Errors of this order—those that tend to transform the game of baseball into something else—are unlikely. The rules are too clear. The target, to use Professor Brilmayer's metaphor, is too large and easy to hit. What does occur, however, are mistakes that seem equally inconsistent with baseball's rules, at least as they are written. A pitch can be called a strike although the ball curves outside of the strike zone; a batter can be called safe even though the throw beats him to the bag; and a batter can be called out although his sinking line drive touched the ground before the center fielder's apparently brilliant catch. In these instances, a manager might argue about the umpire's call, and, if he is sufficiently unrestrained while doing so, the same umpire who made the bad call might eject him from the game.

---

1. Brilmayer, *supra* note †.

2. I see this position in Professor Brilmayer's discussion of hierarchy. After advancing what I understand to be her preferred conception of error, Professor Brilmayer writes that the supreme decisionmaker in the hierarchy is, by definition, incapable of committing error. *Id.* at 379–80. She also argues, "An individual who takes the political structure seriously and recognizes the legitimacy of the decisionmaking hierarchy will define error in conformity with the ultimate decisionmaker in the hierarchy." *Id.* at 382.

To one who only knows the written rules of baseball, there is no obvious difference between these two types of errors. Both errors—holding that a team is retired after its second out and holding that a batter is retired when a ball touches the ground just before entering the fielder's mitt—violate the rules of baseball. Yet the first error might lead an experienced fan to question the umpire's sanity or, perhaps, to demand that he be barred from ever again officiating. The second error, however, would probably not result in so much as a raised eyebrow, unless it occurred in an especially important game or were too often repeated.

The reason for such different responses is not difficult to discern. The first mistake has no obvious cause, and there is no reason to expect that such errors will ever be made.[3] The second mistake is statistically inevitable.[4] Over the long run, some line drives that are trapped will appear as if they are caught. Such mistakes are unavoidable unless we change the way baseball is judged. As long as baseball's procedural rules, which require immediate rulings by human judges, remain unchanged, even certain knowledge that a mistake occurred will not reverse the outcome. Thus, instant replay cameras may show from ten different angles that a ball was trapped, but if the umpire called the batter out, the batter will be out. It is this respect accorded an umpire's judgments that leads to the aphorism, "The umpire is always right."

But note the limited sense in which this aphorism is true. People can talk meaningfully of the umpire's error. Fans might boo, announcers might mention it, and even the umpire might, after viewing the videotape, admit "I blew it." The result of the game, however, will not change. Even if the correct call would have changed the outcome of the game (e.g., assume it was the bottom of the ninth inning with two outs, and the winning runs had already scored from second and third before the ball was trapped) the result remains the same. In this sense, the umpire's decisions are constitutive of the baseball game. Rather than being right or wrong, these decisions become part of the game, integral to its outcome. But the umpire's erroneous rulings are not constitutive of the *game of baseball*; they have no necessary implications for it. Even if

---

3. In this respect, it is analogous to a clear mistake of law; anyone who understands the language of the rule would recognize the error.

4. In this respect, it is analogous to a mistake of fact. Since there is no perfect fact-finding system in law, such errors must occur. Both this footnote and the preceding one refer to expectations. There are, of course, mixed questions of law and fact, and difficult interpretative questions can arise when purely legal questions are posed. In the latter situation, the concept of error may be of limited utility, although it is the language a higher court uses when reversing a lower court's decision.

large numbers of batters are retired each year by trapped balls, the rule that a batter is not out on a trapped ball remains unchanged. It is this fact that allows us to criticize the umpire's ruling and call it erroneous, even though the rule is final and disposes of the game (the case, so to speak). The fact that we cannot or will not change a final score does not mean that we cannot spot error.

This description of umpire behavior looks very much like Professor Brilmayer's "wobble." Umpires tend to center around the target, but occasionally they miss, sometimes in one direction and sometimes in another. Wobble carries little pejorative connotation, for it captures the inevitable and minor nature of the deviations that ordinarily occur. But the fact that we can describe an umpire's errors as wobble does not preclude us from also saying that the umpire is occasionally wrong. Moreover, our ability to speak of error does not turn on the possibility of an appeal to a higher authority, such as the Baseball Commissioner. Here my knowledge of baseball fails me. I do not know whether appeals of such a mundane matter as a ruling that a ball was trapped are allowed, but my very ignorance is evidence that if such appeals are allowed, they almost never succeed. It is not the existence of an appellate hierarchy that allows us to declare decisions at the field level erroneous. Rather, we can take such action because field level decisions can be contrasted with the implications of clear and consensually validated norms: the rules of baseball.

Law is filled with wobbles of the kind that umpires make, wobbles that are properly called error. Indeed, error is often what the law *does* call them. When a trial court misapplies the hearsay rule, for instance, the jury's verdict may be reversed for error below; or, in the more usual case, the appellate court will, if it chooses to address the issue at all, characterize the trial judge's ruling as "harmless *error*." Similarly, a lower court decision will be reversed for error if there are insufficient facts to support the decision or if the lower court has misinterpreted the law.

Professor Brilmayer recognizes that error of this sort exists in the law. If she and I differ at all, it is that she apparently believes that such error is possible only because there is a hierarchy of courts, each of which can reverse those below it for mistakes of these kinds. Presumably, when a case is not appealed or when an appellate court sustains a decision below without identifying harmless error, Professor Brilmayer would argue that no error, only wobble, exists.[5]

My view is that in law, as in baseball, it is the presence of a reasonably well-defined normative code, not an appellate hierarchy, that is necessary and sufficient to allow us to speak of error, at least where norms are clearly violated. Thus, in cases where an appeal is not taken, or in courts, such as small claims courts, from which appeals are not practicable or perhaps not allowed, it is still reasonable to talk of error when the law's precepts have been violated.

Suppose, for example, a small claims court judge rejects a consumer's suit to have a defective toaster repaired or replaced in accordance with the provisions of a full warranty because no negligence was shown in the manufacture or sale of the toaster. Surely we could call this decision erroneous, even if no appeal was taken or permitted. In reaching such a conclusion, we are judging the result in light of an internal or distinctively legal standard[6]—here, a rule which dictates that full warranties provide for the repair or replacement of defective merchandise without regard to the manufacturer's negligence.

This contrasts with situations in which we might judge a legal decision by a standard external to the law. Here, Professor Brilmayer's insistence on the impossibility of *legal* error is, as I understand it, correct. Suppose, for example, that in a prosecution for the possession of burglary tools the state's evidence is insufficient to find the defendant guilty beyond a reasonable doubt, because certain tools found through an illegal search were deemed inadmissible. While the defendant has in fact committed the crime charged, a jury acquittal would not be legally erroneous. This is true both because there is no internal legal standard that allows us to characterize the exclusionary rule as wrong and because the jury verdict was reasonable given the admissible evidence. A similar situation exists when a jury convicts a defendant based on evidence sufficient to find guilt beyond a reasonable doubt, but reliable exculpatory evidence that was never presented at trial (e.g., proof that the defendant was in jail at the time of the crime) later convinces us that the verdict was mistaken.

---

5.   Brilmayer, *supra* note †, at 376-82.

6.   In discussing the possibility of error, we must keep in mind the perspective from which or standard by which we can call something erroneous. Internal standards reflect substantive norms, institutionalized in the legal system and procedural or reasoning constraints (like requirements for logical consistency) that the law recognizes as valid. An external standard holds the law up to the standards of some nonlegal, normative order. An internal standard allows us to identify legal error, while an external standard allows us to characterize laws or other legal action as morally, pragmatically, or factually wrong and in these senses erroneous.

Given the legal norms and the evidence before it, the jury did nothing wrong. Nor does the analysis change if the exonerative evidence is discovered while the case is on appeal and the appellate court remands the case or enters an acquittal. The appellate court would not say that an error occurred below, but rather that there had been a miscarriage of justice which should be rectified. In short, we must recognize that not all decisions that are factually, morally, or otherwise mistaken are legally erroneous. To be legally erroneous, a norm internal to the legal system must have been breached.

It is interesting to consider the kinds of "cognitive illusions" Professors Edwards and von Winterfeldt discuss in their paper[7] with the foregoing discussion in mind. Suppose a jury falls prey to a cognitive illusion and convicts the defendant when the true probative value of the evidence does not justify a conviction. If the jury's understandable, but inaccurate, weighing of the evidence is sufficient for a finding of guilt beyond a reasonable doubt, should we call the decision "erroneous," as in the warranty example, or should we call it simply an injustice without legal error, as in the case of a defendant who is found guilty because exonerative evidence was never presented?

In my view, we can properly speak of legal error in situations where jurors fall victim to cognitive illusions, even though such mistakes are both systematic and inevitable. The reason is that built into the rules of evidence is the expectation that fact finders will rationally evaluate the information they are given. The law does not allow for legal fact finders victimized by cognitive illusions, even though such victimization is inevitable.[8] The law does not expect, although it may presuppose, that a

---

7. Edwards & von Winterfeldt, *Cognitive Illusions and Their Implications for the Law*, 59 S. CAL. L. REV. 225 (1986). Cognitive illusions create intellectual error and are defined briefly as follows: "The first half of that phrase emphasizes the intellectual nature of the tasks; the second is intended to suggest that these phenomena are quite similar to a variety of perceptual illusions extensively studied by psychologists." *Id.* at 226.

8. *See* Lempert, *Modeling Relevance*, 75 MICH. L. REV. 1021 (1977). We see this in the basic rules of relevance and in rules that exclude evidence which is likely to appeal to emotions rather than to reason and/or be improperly weighed. Professor Brilmayer's discussion of her fourth case suggests that she would agree that error exists in this situation. Brilmayer, *supra* note †, at 365. We part company when she says, "attention to process values . . . may greatly confuse the central question of whether a particular decision is an error." *Id.* I think we must understand process values in order to characterize certain legal outcomes as either erroneous or error free. It is, in part, because process values do not give to the adversary system the justificatory scope that Brilmayer sketches (or caricatures) that legal error can be recognized. *Id.* at 376-78. Even when a lawyer is responsible for a verdict that does not accord with the facts or law, this does not mean the decision is error free. Freedom from error depends upon the process norms and the legal values which underlie them. Thus if a plaintiff loses a case because counsel failed to offer the best available evidence, no legal error will have occurred because the law's norms give the parties the choice of what admissible

party will offer all the necessary, probative evidence available.

If a juror, for example, intentionally ignores relevant information, like complicated statistical evidence, because it is cognitively easier to do so, the law's norms concerning rational fact-finding will have been breached, and we can say the juror made an error. If, however, a party chooses not to present favorable evidence or fails to discover the best available evidence, the law's norms do not suggest that the party acted improperly or made a mistake. Thus, injustice attributable to such failures is not considered legal error. The fact that most verdicts hover around the "truth" for just these sorts of reasons appears to be an instance of Professor Brilmayer's wobble. If so, wobble is more than just another name for error or a way of characterizing theoretically indeterminate decisions. It implies that some decisions which appear to contravene legal norms are not really wrong and that other decisions which accord with legal norms are, from the standpoint of the legal system, not quite correct.

The fact that judicial decisions are or may be final does not change this analysis. There are often good reasons for finality, both where there is legal error and where there is an unjust result or one which is mistaken from some extralegal perspective such as the perspective of an observer aware of evidence not presented to the court.[9] Thus, the fact that a decision is final does not mean that it cannot be described as wrong according to the legal system's standards. As with an umpire who has called a trapped ball an out, errors which enter into final judgments may be constitutive of the law of the case (the judgment to be enforced) without being constitutive of the law of the land. This situation is most obvious when a conflict exists among the various federal circuits that the Supreme Court chooses not to resolve. Here, at least one circuit's decision is incorrect, yet the parties' rights turn on it.

As long as case decisions are not necessarily constitutive of more general law, the law provides a perspective from which to criticize the outcome of the case. When wobble consists of deviations from a legal

---

evidence to offer. However, if the plaintiff loses because counsel mistakenly construes precedent as less favorable than it is, and the judge accepts counsel's interpretation, error will have occurred: a judge is supposed to decide questions of law correctly regardless of counsel's input. The fact that an appellate court might not grant a reversal where counsel is in part responsible for a judge's error does not change the analysis.

9. Professor Brilmayer recognizes the importance of other values, such as the importance of law as a dispute resolving process. Brilmayer, *supra*, note †, at 368. As she also notes, a decision that we might respect on the basis of values other than truth (e.g., the need for finality) is not, because it is respected, necessarily error free. *Id*.

norm, the fact that a deviation is small or that such deviations are statistically inevitable does not mean we cannot fairly call wobbling judgments wrong. Nor is our decision to treat such judgments as error necessarily inconsequential. Criticism may mean that a wrong judgment will not guide future cases; it may preclude repetition of the error, and it may prevent the allocation of greater responsibility to the perpetrator of the error.

At the opposite extreme from wobble of this sort, which can and should ordinarily be called error, there is a class of wobbling which cannot be called wrong, because relevant norms allow for some inconsistency. In baseball, for example, a pitcher can request that a scuffed ball be exchanged for a fresh one, but the umpire decides whether the ball is so marred that a new one is needed. If the scuffing is minor, the umpire cannot make a mistake. Indeed the umpire would not have erred even if on one day the game continued with a ball that was more scuffed than one which had been replaced the previous day. The rules of baseball allow such discretion, and not just with respect to trivial matters like replacing scuffed balls, but also with respect to matters that touch the core of the game. Thus, while both the National and American Leagues have identical rules defining the strike zone, conventions are such that marginal pitches that are strikes in one league are balls in the other. Similarly, it may be said without criticism that the umpire is "giving pitchers the outside corner." This is possible because rules identifying the strike zone allow for indeterminacy around the edges, permitting an umpire to call certain pitches balls or strikes without error.

This general observation must, however, be qualified in two important ways. First, if the defined range of discretion is exceeded, we may again speak of error. For instance, it would be an error for an umpire not to provide a new ball when the cover is falling off the old one. Similarly, a pitch above the batter's head must be called a ball, whatever leeway the umpire has when the ball flutters around the armpits. Second, while discretion suggests that neither of two opposing decisions is wrong, and may even permit inconsistent decisions across games (cases), consistency norms permit us to speak of error when different decisions are rendered on similar facts within the same game. Thus, when a particular pitch hovers around the armpits, it may not be wrong to call it either a ball or a strike. However, if the pitch is called a ball when the Dodgers are at bat, a similar pitch should not be called a strike when the Yankees are hitting. Thus, normative systems not only provide absolute rules for evaluating behavior, they also provide rules for evaluating relationships between actions. We may speak of error when relationships do not correspond with such norms.[10]

Again, analogies abound in the law. Many of the rules which relate to the conduct of a trial are of this character, including the fundamental rule of relevance.[11] This rule requires a judge to balance the probative weight of potential evidence against its prejudicial effect, its tendency to confuse the jury, the specter of wasted time, and similar considerations. Discretion resides in the judge: within broad limits there can be no error, whatever the judge decides. As with an umpire, however, a judge can exceed the range of permissible discretion. Thus, a decision to allow the testimony of only one of a defendant's alibi witnesses on the grounds that additional testimony would be cumulative should ordinarily be reversed as an abuse of discretion, since testimony from two consistent witnesses is likely to be substantially more believable than the testimony of one. If, on the other hand, six alibi witnesses had already testified to the same thing, decisions excluding or allowing a seventh witness' testimony might be equally correct.

We can most easily see that the area within which an action is error free (i.e., discretionary) is limited when a disagreement regarding what is discretionary leads a court (or legislature) to establish bounds. For example, in most jurisdictions trial judges have complete discretion to admit or deny a psychologist's expert testimony concerning eyewitness identification. A judge will not be perceived as having acted wrongly if the testimony is admitted nor will the trial court's decision be reversed if the testimony is disallowed. Thus, a judge deciding whether to allow such testimony cannot err; no legal norm constrains the judge's action. However, in two states, California and Arizona, supreme courts have recently held[12] that under certain circumstances it is an abuse of discretion—perhaps a constitutional violation—to preclude an eyewitness

---

10. The consistency criteria which Professor Brilmayer uses as evidence of indeterminacy in law exist because the law regards certain kinds of relational indeterminacy as error. Brilmayer, *supra* note †, at 371-73. For example, under Erie Railroad Co. v. Tompkins, 304 U.S. 64 (1938), it is error for a federal court in a diversity action to differ with the forum state's highest court on a question of state law. Unlike Brilmayer, I do not view the indeterminacy of legal decisions, whether theoretical or practical, as suggesting the impossibility of legal error. *See* Brilmayer, *supra* note †, at 369-71. As I argue in the text below, the indeterminacy which the law allows is typically confined. Decisions which exceed these confines may be called error. If Professor Brilmayer wishes to confine her conception of wobble to decisional variation within areas of permitted discretion, I will readily admit that legal decisions wobble; but if wobble is used in this sense, the indeterminacy which underlies it does not call the possibility of legal error into question.

11. For example, Rule 403 of the Federal Rules of Evidence and its state counterparts.

12. *See* People v. McDonald, 37 Cal. 3d 357, 690 P.2d 709, 208 Cal. Rptr. 236 (1984); State v. Chapple, 135 Ariz. 281, 660 P.2d 1208 (1983). In holding that specific judges abused their discretion

expert from testifying. These courts have created a possibility of error which did not formerly exist.

Thus far, the thrust of my comments and the contrast with Professor Brilmayer's observations reflect, I think, the different perspectives from which we approach the law. As a social scientist and teacher of evidence, I approach law from the bottom up: action lies in the streets and in the lower courts. Because Professor Brilmayer has had a special interest in jurisdictional issues and the conflicts of law, she is accustomed to looking at law from the top down. Her work focuses on appellate decisions. When we examine the question of legal error at the appellate level, the problem becomes more interesting, and we must leave the analogy to baseball behind.

As we have seen, the finality of an umpire's decisions does not preclude judgments of error because the umpire's rulings, although constitutive of the baseball game, are not constitutive of the *game of baseball*. The norms of the *game* provide a standard by which we can judge the umpire's rulings (including erroneous ones) although they are inextricably bound up with a result we respect (e.g., the Yankees won 6-5 only because the umpire did not realize that Gene Woodling trapped the ball for the last out, but it is a Yankee victory nonetheless). The trial judge's situation is similar. Even if judge's rulings shape a jury verdict, they do not shape the law generally and can be criticized if they are discrepant. Indeed, if an appeal is taken, the trial judge's decisions and the verdict they influenced can be reversed for error.

Appellate courts engaged in lawmaking are in a different situation. High court decisions are constitutive not only of the "law" of the case, but also of the law in general, for they make up a body of rules binding on lower courts. Thus, it is plausible to suggest that high court decisions cannot be in error. For example, it is difficult to conclude that the Supreme Court's decision upholding six-person juries is wrong as a matter of law, since, as a matter of law juries, after the decision, need only contain six persons. Nevertheless, I believe there are several bases from which one may conclude that decisions which are constitutive of the law are wrong. Before I do, however, I would like to agree partially with Professor Brilmayer and suggest that often—perhaps always, in certain

---

in disallowing expert testimony, the California and Arizona supreme courts did not take away all trial court discretion to pass on the admissibility of eyewitness expert testimony, but they identified certain circumstances in which the decision was no longer discretionary.

senses—one cannot find error in this situation.[13]

The law embodies value judgments that need not accord with the values that predominate in other sectors of society and are not incorrect simply because they fail to do so. Social science experts often think the law is mistaken when it does not attend to the scientific information they offer or incorporate scientific standards in the decisionmaking process. But the law, not science determines the values law embodies, and these values encompass judgments about the modes and standards of proof that may properly inform legal decisions. I have previously suggested that, given the law's assumptions about fact finder rationality, decisions distorted by cognitive illusions may be considered wrong without moving beyond the vantage point provided by the law's own standards. It does not follow, however, that the law is wrong to bar either person-machine procedures of the kind Professor Edwards and others have explored[14] or certain kinds of expert testimony that might decrease cognitive errors or make fact-finding more accurate. The law may recognize rational fact-finding as a value, but the law also recognizes other values, such as individuality and the importance of jury trials. These values may outweigh incremental gains in verdict accuracy. Scientists encountering the legal process often seek to impose not only the techniques of their disciplines on the legal system, but also the values which underlie them, and they may criticize the legal system when it responds to nonscientific values. But it is the legal system which properly tells the scientist what is relevant, not the other way around. Simply because a legal rule does not make economic sense or a legal procedure accepts incorrect statistics does not mean the law has erred.[15]

It does not follow, however, that we must accept Professor Brilmayer's claim that there is no error in the law. At best, her claim is

---

13. It is in reference to high courts that Professor Brilmayer's indeterminacy argument has its bite, for while it is easy to see that the indeterminacy allowed lower courts is confined to regions of discretion, the bounds which confine high courts are not as obvious. Nevertheless, as I shall argue below, I think there are both internal norms and external moral positions which allow one meaningfully to say that a supreme court decision is wrong. With respect to supreme courts I might accept Professor Brilmayer's suggestion that indeterminacy may be theoretical and that "the premise that there is a right answer might be rejected altogether," Brilmayer, *supra* note †, at 370, but it does not follow from the absence of a "right answer" that there are no wrong ones. And it is the possibility of wrong answers we are discussing.

14. Person-machine procedures include procedures in which humans make certain value judgments or estimates of probabilities and computers calculate the implications of these judgments for the decisionmaking task in question. *See* Edwards & von Winterfeldt, *supra* note 7, at 264-67 (discussing the boundary between human cognition and the use of tools).

15. *See, e.g.*, Lempert, *Statistics in the Courtroom: Building on Rubinfeld*, 85 COLUM. L. REV. 1098 (1985).

true only in a tautological way and actually undercuts one of her basic perceptions. If we say that the law cannot be wrong, and if we define law as any authoritative decision that changes a legal rule, a decision which is constitutive of the law cannot, by definition, be erroneous. However, this argument rules out the idea of wobble as well. Far from wobbling, a court whose decisions appear inconsistent and varied is picking precisely those principles which constitute the law. To spot wobble requires a vantage point from which a pattern is visible.[16] But if we have such a vantage point, then we may spot error as well.[17]

I will refer to external vantage points when I discuss Professor Brilmayer's observations on legal scholarship, but first I shall consider internal perspectives. There are two internal vantage points from which we can criticize lawmaking decisions as wrong. Both rely on consistency criteria. First, I believe (or at least I am willing to argue) that the law presupposes that judicial law makers will adhere to certain kinds of interpretive consistency. Court-made law should be consistent with the meanings naturally or fairly attributable to acknowledged sources of law

---

16. Wobble implies that a legal decision differs somewhat from an apparently appropriate decision either because it deviates from a decision in a similar case or because it deviates from the decision apparently implied by a legal rule. (I assume that this is what Professor Brilmayer means when she speaks of the "amount of scatter that occurs when different decisionmakers each resolve a problem independently" and of the "extent to which systems depart from existing inputs, empirical facts, and legal reasons." Brilmayer, *supra* note †, at 389). Yet if we look in sufficient detail, every case is factually unique. Deviations from similar cases or rules can be seen only because there is a consensus that certain characteristics which make a case unique (ranging from trivial factors, such as a party's first name to ordinarily important considerations such as a party's intent) do not count when particular legal questions are at issue. Absent this consensus, we could not say that particular decisions wobble because each decision can be mapped onto one and only one set of facts (case). With such a consensus we can spot deviations from similar cases or from the apparent implications of apposite legal rules, and we can call them "wrong." If we take an external moral perspective, the earlier cases or apposite rules may be similarly labeled "wrong."

17. Professor Brilmayer argues that the law has procedural rules, like those of res judicata and collateral estoppel, which implicitly acknowledge the existence of wobble. I question the implication. Such rules may be designed to decrease error by encouraging parties to invest heavily the first time they litigate a case; they may reflect nonlegal values, such as cost savings; and they may recognize that where discretion exists and neither of two reasonable decisions would be erroneous, it would nonetheless be wrong for inconsistent outcomes to be reached on essentially the same facts. Professor Brilmayer uses a methaphor in the revised version of her paper that was not in the original. She refers to "a machine that projects pellets" against a wall. Brilmayer, *supra* note †, at 368. The virtue of this metaphor is that it discards the idea that a target exists around which the pellets scatter. The target idea undercut Professor Brilmayer's original argument because it suggested that, despite her language, even she believed there was something out there to hit. However, I do not think her argument is substantially strengthened by using the methaphor of pellets tossed against a wall. Even if no target exists, the eye will impose one as pellet marks accumulate on the wall near the same place. Arguably, this is what interpreters of the common law do. From a scattering of specific cases, they identify general principles which become the bases for determining correct decisions in future cases.

and with related aspects of the legal corpus. Assume, for example, that the Supreme Court were to decide that the sixth amendment right to jury trial was satisfied by a "jury" of one person chosen from a group the prosecutor selected for jury duty. Such a decision could be labeled erroneous even if it changed the law forever, because it enunciates a standard which cannot plausibly be derived from the body of law (i.e. the sixth amendment and cases under it) the Court purports to be interpreting.

The criterion of consistency with related law also affords a position from which one can argue that a particular decision is erroneous. This claim is most visible in the pedagogical philosophy of Christopher Columbus Langdell. Langdell believed that one could identify a string of leading cases which embodied the core principles of the common law.[18] Working from these principles one can criticize officially authoritative but inconsistent court decisions as erroneous. It is unclear, however, whether the criterion of consistency with core cases can operate without an external ethical perspective to complement it. In particular, without the guidance of some ethical perspective, there is no unique or consensually valid way to choose the set of cases which are authoritative.[19]

The other internal stance which allows one to characterize decisions constitutive of the law as wrong focuses on the quality of the lawmaking opinion. If the opinion is internally inconsistent, or if the conclusion does not follow from the premises, then one has a basis for calling it wrong. Consider the portion of *Williams v. Florida*[20] which holds that the sixth amendment permits six-member juries in criminal cases. Had the Court said only that the sixth amendment permits six-member juries, one could not say the Court erred unless one subscribed to a jurisprudence which binds courts to original understandings of meaning. Although the constitutional framers almost certainly thought that juries would have twelve members,[21] a six-member jury, unlike the one-person jury I described above, does not do violence to the term "jury." The Court in *Williams* would be similarly immune from claims that it had erred had it followed the lead of Justice Harlan's concurrence and held that six-member juries were allowed because they did not contravene the

---

18.  C. LANGDELL, A SELECTION OF CASES ON THE LAW OF CONTRACTS, preface (1871).

19.  The validity of the ethical perspective is always questionable, but there might well be widespread agreement on the set of core principles. Without an external ethical guide one has little basis to choose key cases from among cases that appear equally authoritative on their face. Such possible bases as "Massachusetts cases," "Judge X's opinions," "9-0 decisions," or "what I like best" are all unsatisfactory; and, while these suggestions may seem like caricatures, I do not think they can be improved upon unless an external ethical perspective is introduced.

20.  399 U.S. 78, 86-103 (1970).

21.  *Id.* at 99-100.

due process guarantees of the fourteenth amendment.[22]

However, the Court took a third approach. It addressed the issue of jury size in functional terms, making the issue appear to turn on an empirical question: whether a six-member jury is functionally equivalent to a twelve-member jury with respect to the verdicts it returns.[23] The majority concluded that there is no discernible difference between the verdicts of six- and twelve-person juries and thus upheld the Florida law. To support this empirical conclusion, the Court cited a finding by Solomon Asch which the justices read as suggesting that a lone dissenter in a six-member criminal jury is as likely to hold out for acquittal as two dissenters in a twelve-member jury.[24]

However, the Court misinterpreted Asch. Asch found fundamental differences between the ability of one dissenter and the ability of two to resist pressures to acquiesce in a majority's views. Moreover, Asch found that a holdout with an ally is more likely to resist in a group of twelve than is a lone holdout in a group of six.[25] Thus, what the Court presents as a crucial justification for its holding points toward the opposite result. The Court's assumption that there are no discernible differences between the verdicts of six-person juries and those of twelve-person juries is also mistaken, particularly with respect to the likelihood of "hung" juries.[26]

Thus, if we abstract the rule in *Williams* from the case that gave rise to it and treat it simply as a legal pronouncement, we cannot call the Court's holding wrong. To this extent I agree with Professor Brilmayer. However, if we accept the Court's judgment that the constitutionality of six-person juries is contingent on the absence of any discernable difference between the verdicts of six- and twelve-person juries, we have in the Court's misreading of Asch and its ignorance of other relevant research a basis for saying that the Court erred, even though its decision is law. A similar critique could be made if a lawmaking pronouncement revealed a failure of logic rather than faulty empiricism.

---

22. Such a decision might, however, have been open to criticism under one branch of our first consistency criterion—consistency with the body of related law—since by the time of *Williams* the sixth amendment right to jury trial had been applied to the states.

23. *Id.* at 100.

24. *Id.* at 101-102 n.49.

25. Asch, *Effects of Group Pressure Upon the Modification and Distribution of Judgments*, in GROUP DYNAMICS 189 (D. Cartwright & A. Zander 2d ed. 1960). Asch was examining problems that were cognitively quite simple and quite unlike the task jurors face.

26. *See* Lempert, *Uncovering "Nondiscernible" Differences: Empirical Research and the Jury-Size Cases*, 73 MICH. L. REV. 644, 673-76 (1975).

These criteria for spotting legal error assume that a would-be critic must adopt a stance internal to the legal system, validated by the norms of the law or by canons of reasoning that courts purport to follow. This assumption is at the core of Professor Brilmayer's interesting conclusion, in which she argues that scholars cannot use some legal decisions as a basis for criticizing other decisions which are equally valid with respect to finality and enforceability. Instead, legal scholars are limited, on the one hand, to descriptive scholarship or trivial doctrinal criticisms and, on the other, to criticisms unabashedly based on external norms.

To my mind, the most interesting legal criticism involves an external normative perspective, and this is entirely appropriate, for law is the business of enforcing norms which are right by some ethical standard. Professor Brilmayer appears not only to deny that this counts as *legal* criticism, but also to suggest that it is strategically unwise: "It may not, however, always be a good strategy to concede that one's chosen norms are not embodied in the law already. Such approaches will invariably be more controversial for being so clearly value-laden."[27]

This suggests that a possibly good strategy—but one which makes for dishonest scholarship—is to justify criticism by pretending it is based on the identification of a true legal norm. Nonconforming cases are criticized for deviating from this norm (the law) when, in fact, the critic has imported an external normative standard without acknowledging it. If I understand Professor Brilmayer's critique, this is what she accuses Ronald Dworkin, Richard Posner, and Brainerd Currie of doing.

Yet, there is another way to regard their scholarship and the mission of legal criticism in general. It is to integrate internal legal norms (which themselves have ethical content) with external ethical ones. Such scholarship seeks to define what law is by identifying what law aspires to be. The task is not to catalogue all law but to identify central ethical tendencies which unify a diverse set of cases. Outliers, that is, cases which do not fit the core characterization, do not threaten the validity of this approach any more than the fact that some women are taller than some men invalidates the observation that men are generally taller than women. However, as with statistical averages, central tendency information is considerably more informative if one has some sense of the dispersion around the mean value. Perhaps the authors Professor Brilmayer cites may be criticized for not providing sufficient dispersion information, or,

---

27.  Brilmayer, *supra* note †, at 384.

as she suggests of Posner, for misjudging where the law's central tendency lies. I do not think they can be criticized for presenting their ethical views as if they were grounded only in the law,[28] for each author seeks openly to justify his claim by reference to external normative systems as well as by his reading of the law.

Legal scholarship of this sort is, of course, more than an exercise in descriptive statistics. Legal scholars commonly identify certain core legal norms of which they approve and, in light of these norms, criticize cases as both wrong (the external normative view) and aberrant (the internal consistency criterion view). If I understand her correctly, Professor Brilmayer would allow the former but not the latter. It is not clear, however, whether she would call the former "legal" scholarship. I would allow both. High court wobble may be inevitable in the law, but there are also central tendencies. If the core legal principles are not morally justified, they are properly criticized from an external normative perspective. If they are morally justified, legal scholarship serves society by pointing out when the bull's-eye has been missed, for this helps future decisionmakers come closer to the target.

The contrast between the positions Professor Brilmayer and I espouse is sharp, but at a practical level, the debate between us hardly matters. Legal scholarship will continue to serve society by criticizing court decisions whether there is, in some abstract sense, error in the law or not. All that is necessary is that there be error in the eyes of the beholder.

---

28. Professor Brilmayer's criticism is fair when she suggests that, on occasion, these scholars fail to distinguish between the criticism that internal and external perspectives allow. Moreover, these scholars and most others cannot avoid being influenced by external ethical views when deciding what the law really means.

# Baseball and the Legal Profession

## Howard W. Brill

The practice of law, of which you have dreamed, for which you have prepared, and into which you are about to enter, can best be compared to a baseball game. Let me briefly suggest nine similarities, nine comparisons, between the great American pastime and the legal profession.

(1) When the game starts, only 25 players are there. Many players in T-ball and Little League and Babe Ruth dreamed of making the big leagues, but they never made it. Likewise, when you were in the fifth grade in Texarkana or Hot Springs, and all the fifth graders went down to the courthouse on Law Day, many of your classmates said, "I'd like to be a lawyer," but they're not here today. Similarly, many students sat in dorm rooms or fraternity houses and watched "Perry Mason" or "L.A. Law" and said, "It sure would be exciting to be a lawyer," but they're not here today. Even three years ago 150 of you started, but not all have survived; those of you here today have made the big leagues.

(2) A baseball game starts with everyone in attendance standing. The traditional words of the national anthem are heard and the umpire, dressed in black, cries out, "Play ball." Court commences in the same fashion. The bailiff announces the arrival of the judge, everyone stands, traditional words are recited, and the judge, dressed in black, cries out, "This Court is now in session." Another traditional start to another traditional activity.

(3) The players are dressed in traditional, outmoded, non-functional uniforms—useless stirrups, knickers, cold weather clothes in the heat of the summer. In the legal profession, we may no longer dress in robes, we may no longer wear the wigs of colonial days, but we have a traditional uniform of dark blue and gray in somber attire. For some of you, that will mean a major change in the way you have dressed in the past three years. For example, for those of you who came to Remedies and sat in the front row and took off your shoes and socks to relax, I have sad news: you can't take off your shoes and socks in the courtroom.

(4) Baseball has a unique vocabulary. We speak of Texas leaguers and southpaws. The legal profession has its own vocabulary. We read of rules against perpetuities, holders in due course, and even mysterious Latin phrases such as *res judicata*.

81

Baseball has its rules that are vague and open-ended and leave justice to the eye of the umpire, such as the balk. The legal profession has its rules that are vague and open-ended and leave justice to the eye of the judge, such as contempt.[1] Baseball has its rules that many of us view as foolish, such as the designated hitter.[2] The legal profession has rules that you probably view as foolish, such as bar exams.[3]

(5) A visitor to Cooperstown, who walks through the gallery where the plaques of the greatest baseball players hang, soon realizes that one vital piece of information is missing from each plaque. The plaque that honors a pitcher for the St. Louis Cardinals who won thirty games in the 1930s doesn't say that Dizzy Dean started in Lucas, Arkansas; and the plaque that memorializes an All Star third baseman for the Detroit Tigers in the 40s and 50s doesn't tell us that George Kell began in Swifton, Arkansas. Their plaques hang in the Hall of Fame because of what they accomplished, not where they started.

From this day forward in the legal profession, you're starting with a clean slate. Your career will depend upon what you accomplish from this day forward. When clients come into your office next year to decide whether to retain you or not, they will ask you many questions. But they are not likely to ask, in deciding whether to hire you, what your GPA was. When you present an argument in court and the judge is trying to decide whether to rule for you or against you, that judge is not likely to ask, "Counselor, I need to know—were you on the Law Review?" You're starting over on equal ground and whether you make the lawyer's Hall of Fame depends upon what you accomplish from this day forward.

(6) A baseball player suddenly wins 20 games, bats .300, hits 40 home runs and he's an expert: an expert on religion, on politics, on credit cards, on fast-food restaurants, and deodorants. When you hang out the shingle, when you join the civic club, when you go to the PTA at the school where your son is enrolled, and someone points you out and says, "She's the new lawyer in town"; you're the expert. You're supposed to know, certainly about religion and politics, perhaps even about credit cards and deodorants. The public will turn to you, and you're in the limelight. Like the proverbial

city on a hill,[4] your influence will reach farther because you're an attorney. But the down side is if your influence or your light grows dim or even becomes dark, those all around will see it.

(7) Baseball occasionally has players of unparalleled ability, an enthusiasm for the game and a sense of tradition, but who can't live by the rules. In baseball they go by names like Pete Rose.[5] Likewise, in the legal profession, occasionally there are those who can't or won't live by the rules. They practice in large cities and small towns; they've graduated from every law school in the nation; they are in private practice and corporate practice and even in government service. Just as the Pete Roses are removed from baseball, those lawyers need to be removed from the legal profession.

But there is another danger and a greater warning to us. Seventy years ago, baseball expelled a player, not because he threw a game and perhaps not even because he took a bribe, but Shoeless Joe Jackson was expelled from baseball because he knew his teammates did and he kept quiet.[6] In the legal profession, we take that principle, we codify it, we make it a rule, we even give a number (8.3), and through it we say to the public that we will police ourselves.[7] The rule that says that we will act against members of the profession who fall beneath the minimum standards is not an easy rule to follow. No attorney in this room will tell you that it is pleasant, but the rule is essential. The public demands it, the profession demands it, your inner sense of honesty should demand it.

(8) The game nears the end. Some fans cheer; some fans boo. Bill Russell, not the Dodger shortstop but the Celtic center, was once asked how he felt when he heard the boos. Bill Russell responded by saying he never heard the boos, and he never heard the cheers.[8] In the practice of law, you will hear boos and cheers. You can deal with the boos—the boos that come from defending an unpopular client, from telling a client that an action he desires is not permitted. You can respond to those because you have survived the first semester of law school.

But the greater danger, it seems to me, is with the cheers. The cheers will come from winning big cases, from blazing new law, from being recognized as a leader in the profession or in the com-

82

munity. The danger is that those cheers, though rightfully deserved, may lead to pride or to greed, or in some other way start you on the road to tragedy. Don't forget where you started three years ago. Don't forget those in this room who have supported you and who have sacrificed for you. Don't forget those in society who may not be hearing the cheers.

Bill Russell played ball according to his own standard of excellence, regardless of the crowds. You have to practice law according to your own standards of excellence, regardless of those around you.

(9) It's the ninth inning, the fans leave, the infield is covered with a tarp, the lights are turned off, the players go home. It is the end of the game, perhaps the end of a season, perhaps the end of a career, but the players must learn that life goes on. When you leave the office, when you leave the courtroom or the library, you must learn that life goes on. In the practice of law, there are too many temptations to lose sight of life—of children, of family, of the needs of others, of your own beliefs and values and standards. In the rush to succeed and to excel, don't lose sight of life or where you started.

As we walk through the fields of life, we all dream dreams, we all see visions,[9] we all hear voices.[10] Some of us, some of you, may have dreamed of playing major league baseball, and that dream probably will not be achieved. But all of you graduates have dreamed of being attorneys and that dream is coming true. Congratulations!

# NOTES

*This commentary is based on a commencement speech at the School of Law, University of Arkansas, May 12, 1990.*

1. *E.g.*, Clark v. State, 291 Ark. 405, 725 S.W. 550 (1987) (court divided, 4–3, on whether in–court statements of a litigant constituted criminal contempt); Morrow v. Roberts, 250 Ark. 822, 467 S.W.2d 393 (1971) (contempt finding against witness for refusing to have his hair cut, reversed). *See also* Arkansas Gazette, April 13, 1990 (municipal judge held woman in contempt for not wearing proper undergarments).

2. *Compare* Laurence, *On Eurocentric Myopia, The Designated Hitter Rule and "The Actual State of Things,"* 30 ARIZ. L. REV. 459 (1988); Laurence, *A Short Essay in Praise of Non-Traditionalism in the Structure and Performance of Baseball,* 7 MPLS. REV. OF BASEBALL 29 (No. 3, 1988).

3. *E.g.*, Taylor v. Safly, 276 Ark. 541, 637 S.W.2d 578 (1982) (challenge to procedural fairness of bar examination process).

4. Matthew 5:14.

5. Rose v. Giamatti, 721 F. Supp. 906 (S.D. Ohio 1989).

6. Kirby, The Year They Fixed the World Series, 74 A.B.A. 64 (February 1988).

7. *See* Preamble, ARKANSAS RULES OF PROFESSIONAL CONDUCT. *"The legal profession is largely self-governing." See also* Ark. Const., amend. 28: "The Supreme Court shall make rules regulating the practice of law and the professional conduct of attorneys at law."

8. Rosenblatt, Essay, TIME (June 29, 1987).

9. Joel 2:38.

10. In W. P. Kinsella's novel SHOELESS JOE (1982) and the subsequent movie *Field of Dreams*, an Iowa farmer hears a voice which says to him, "If you build it, he will come."

83

The New York Times
May 25, 1983
Wednesday, Late City Final Edition

Simplified Voir Dire
To the Editor:

A close if overlooked relationship exists between Ira Glasser's apologia for the Brooklyn Dodgers (Op-Ed May 3) and the current dispute over permitting lawyers to continue to conduct the voir dire of juries in criminal cases. Before 1957, New York lawyers chose juries inexpensively and expeditiously by asking just one question: What baseball team do you root for?

If the juror answered, "Yankees," the defense exercised a peremptory challenge. If the juror said, "Dodgers," the prosecution exercised the challenge. But Giants fans were eminently acceptable to both sides, under a tacit understanding that they were the only reasonable people in town.

Burt Neuborne
Legal Director, A.C.L.U.
New York, May 17, 1983

# The Bases are Loaded and it's Time to Get a Restraining Order:  The Confounding Conflation of America's Two National Pastimes

**Paul A. LeBel**[*]

Time might begin on opening day and life might imitate the world series, according to one of our finest contemporary sports writers,[1] but it is arguable that too little attention has been paid to the relationship between America's leading pastimes, litigation and baseball.

Some points of comparison are apparent.  The top performers in each receive compensation that seems to many to be grossly disproportionate to their value to society at large, and many of the participants in both enterprises wear pin stripes while they are working.

Still, there are significant differences.  Ball players get to spit and scratch in public a lot more than lawyers, and their pin stripes are bottomed off with spikes instead of wingtips or tassel loafers.  And when it comes down to it, baseball knows how to handle an appeal a lot more efficiently than the legal system.  When was the last time you heard of a successful protest of an umpire's decision in the major leagues?  As far as I can tell, the official league response to a protesting manager has been, "Shut up." (Although, come to think of it, that sounds an awful lot like the current Supreme Court's standard response to petitions for certiorari.)

Baseball and litigation have been linked in such matters as challenges to the exemption that baseball enjoys from the antitrust laws,[2] particularly in connection with attacks on the reserve clause,[3] a libel action by an umpire and the umpires' association against a manager who accused the umpire of bias against his team,[4] and most recently, the challenge to the re-alignment of the teams in the National League.[5]  The law has not always

---

[*]  James Goold Cutler Professor of Law, College of William and Mary.

1.  THOMAS BOSWELL, WHY TIME BEGINS ON OPENING DAY (1984); THOMAS BOSWELL, HOW LIFE IMITATES THE WORLD SERIES (1982).

2.  Toolson v. New York Yankees, Inc., 346 U.S. 356 (1953); Federal Baseball Club v. National League of Professional Baseball Clubs, 259 U.S. 200 (1922).

3.  Flood v. Kuhn, 407 U.S. 258 (1972).

4.  Darling v. Piniella, No. 91-5219, 1991 U.S. Dist. LEXIS 13546 (E.D. Pa. Sept. 27, 1991).

5.  Chicago Nat'l League Ball Club, Inc. v. Vincent, 1992 U.S. Dist. LEXIS 14948 (N.D. Ill. Sept. 24, 1992), *withdrawing and vacating* 1992 U.S. Dist. LEXIS 11033 (N.D. Ill. July 23, 1992).

come off as a particularly impressive performer in these encounters. That last lawsuit, for example, set up the potential for a definitive judicial statement that Chicago is east of Atlanta.

Still, things could be worse. Garrison Keillor once said that folks in Lake Wobegon were waiting to celebrate the Minnesota Twins (well-deserved, I might note[6]) victory in the 1987 World Series until they were sure that there would not be a lawsuit.

Imagine if you will a state of affairs such that the most perceptive of baseball fans turn each week not to *The Sporting News* or *USA Today Baseball Weekly* but rather to the sports pages of *The Legal Times*. A typical news report from the era when litigiousness runs amok in baseball might look like this:

Washington, September 17, 199?—A surprisingly large number of games were played through to completion yesterday in the major leagues. The Florida Marlins, temporarily playing in the Northwestern Division of the National League in order to accommodate the move of the Tampa Bay Giant-Mariners into the Southeastern Division, were able to wrap up a lawsuit-shortened game that was begun on April 25th. In that contest, New York Mets manager Gary Carter secured a restraining order in the eighth inning after Marlins pitcher Bob Milacki threw a pitch behind the head of Mets pinch hitter Eddie Murray. The Marlins front office was able to get an emergency stay of further play from Mario Cuomo, the Supreme Court Associate Justice with jurisdiction over the National League, pending consideration of the matter by the full court. (Murray's own civil suit against Milacki for assault was dismissed in May on a motion for summary judgment. The trial judge ruled that no reasonable juror could conclude that Milacki's fast ball was capable of causing an imminent apprehension of a harmful contact. No appeal is expected from that ruling.) Yesterday's action on the field saw the Marlins complete the sweep of the Mets, winning 2-1 and thereby improving the team's record for the year to 11 and 5. Marlins reliever, Jeff Reardon, has tentatively been credited with the save, but the team's newly-acquired set-up pitcher has filed an action in the Dade County Circuit Court alleging that his retiring of two batters

---

6. *See* PAUL A. LEBEL, JOHN BARLEYCORN MUST PAY: COMPENSATING THE VICTIMS OF DRINKING DRIVERS 336 (1992).

after coming into the game when the bases were loaded and no one was out was demonstrably more significant than Reardon's getting the final out when the only batter he faced hit a weak pop-up to short. The class action, filed on behalf of "non-winning pitchers who do not finish games that their teams win," is calling on the state court to exercise its equitable power to correct the injustice of the save rule and "to award to the plaintiff class adequate credit and such other compensation as the court might deem proper for the substantial contribution that they make to the victory."

In other action around the majors, the Atlanta Braves defeated the Colorado Rockies 12-0, in a three-inning game that was shortened by the Rockies' invocation of the Eighth Amendment prohibition against cruel and unusual punishment. This is the first time that the rule was successfully invoked since the constitutional provision was incorporated into the official rules of major league baseball by a United States Supreme Court ruling last term. Early this season, a claim that an opposing team's use of a suicide squeeze play was unusually stressful for the catcher was dismissed with prejudice by the court in which it had been filed.

In the only complete game in the American League yesterday, the Cleveland Indians continued their division-leading season with a 9-0 defeat of the Oakland Athletics. The Indians' victory came as a result of an Oakland forfeit under the new "excessively wearying travel" clause of the players agreement. The Athletics were unable to field a team due to the failure of the club to arrive in Cleveland with sufficient time for the players to rest, catch up on their shopping, and have a chance to have their laundry done after having traveled across one timezone boundary following the completion in late August of its last series in Chicago. The club traveling secretary declined to comment on the matter, saying that a majority of his attorneys had advised him to make no statement until the completion of arbitration on the question of whether the appropriate starting time for the running of what has come to be known as "the statute of leisure" was the beginning or the ending of an extra-inning game.

Elsewhere yesterday, the Minnesota Twins stopped play in the second inning and marched in protest to the federal courthouse in Minneapolis when White Sox television announcer Ken "Hawk" Harrelson again criticized the playing conditions in the Hubert H. Humphrey Metrodome. The complaint, filed late yesterday afternoon, states that Harrelson has repeatedly made reference to the fact that the team had never won a World Series game on the road, and alleges that his taunting has caused the players and their families to suffer "physical manifestations of severe emotional distress." The complaint further alleges that "Harrelson's statement is false and defamatory, as the clear implication of the words employed by Defendant suggested that Plaintiffs were unable to win a World Series game without the home field advantage and that as a result thereof the World Championships obtained by the Plaintiffs in 1987 and 1991 were less legitimate than similar World Championships obtained by diverse other ball clubs in years other than the aforesaid." Last night's CNN Sports & Courts Center broadcast reported that famed media lawyer Floyd Abrams is flying to Minneapolis to defend Harrelson. When reached for comment, Abrams expressed outrage at this latest attack on the free speech principles that made this country what it is today, and vowed to resist these lawsuits that threaten the very integrity of the social fabric.

In a related action, the Minnesota chapter of the Audubon Club continued to picket the WGN broadcast truck, alleging that Harrelson was giving unfavorable publicity to the eponymous creature he had adopted for his nickname. In explaining why they were picketing, the chapter president pointed to the legislation introduced earlier in this term of Congress to remove the hawk from the endangered species list. That legislation has (not coincidentally) been co-sponsored by members of Congress from every district in which the White Sox play road games.

# The All-Supreme-Court-Opinion Baseball Team

**Patric M. Verrone**[*]

Randy "Ex Parte" MILLIGAN, First Base[1]

Rod "Dred" SCOTT, Second Base[2]

Willie "Read 'em Their Rights" MIRANDA, Shortstop[3]

Bill "Clear and Present Danger" SCHENCK, Third Base[4]

Clyde "Necessary and Proper" McCULLOCH, Catcher[5]

Gates "Board of Education" BROWN, Left Field[6]

Joseph "Plessy" V. FERGUSON, Center Field[7]

Claudell "International Shoe Versus" WASHINGTON, Right Field[8]

---

[*] © 1993 Patric M. Verrone. More of Mr. Verrone's insights are permanently fixed at *supra* p. 733.

1. Ex Parte Milligan, 71 U.S. (4 Wall.) 2 (1866). Milligan played for the New York Mets, Pittsburgh Pirates, and Baltimore Orioles, 1987 to Present.

2. Scott v. Sanford, 60 U.S. (19 How.) 393 (1857). Scott played for the Kansas City Royals, Montreal Expos, Oakland A's, Chicago Cubs, and New York Yankees, 1975-82.

3. Miranda v. Arizona, 384 U.S. 436 (1966). Miranda played for the Washington Senators, Chicago White Sox, St. Louis Browns, New York Yankees, and Baltimore Orioles, 1951-59.

4. Schenck v. United States, 249 U.S. 47 (1919). Schenck played for the Louisville Eclipse, Richmond Virginians, and Brooklyn in the American Association, 1882-85.

5. McCulloch v. Maryland, 17 U.S. (4 Wheat.) 316 (1819). McCulloch played for the Chicago Cubs and Pittsburgh Pirates, 1940-56.

6. Brown v. Board of Educ., 347 U.S. 483 (1954). Brown played for the Detroit Tigers, 1963-75.

7. Plessy v. Ferguson, 163 U.S. 537 (1896). Ferguson played for the Los Angeles Dodgers, St. Louis Cardinals, Houston Astros, and California Angels, 1970-83.

8. International Shoe Co. v. Washington, 326 U.S. 310 (1945). Washington played for the Oakland A's, Texas Rangers, Chicago White Sox, New York Mets, Atlanta Braves, and New York Yankees, 1974-88.

Preacher ROE & Ben WADE, Starting Pitchers[9]

Byron "Appointed Counsel" GIDEON, Relief Pitcher[10]

Curt "Free Agent" FLOOD, Designated Hitter[11]

---

9. Roe v. Wade, 410 U.S. 113 (1973). Roe played for the St. Louis Cardinals, Pittsburgh Pirates, and Brooklyn Dodgers, 1938-54. Wade played for the Chicago Cubs, Brooklyn Dodgers, St. Louis Cardinals, and Pittsburgh Pirates, 1948-55. They were teammates with the Dodgers from 1952 to 1954.

10. Gideon v. Wainwright, 372 U.S. 335 (1963). Gideon played with the Pittsburgh Pirates in 1987.

11. Flood v. Kuhn, 407 U.S. 258 (1972). Flood played with the Cincinnati Reds, St. Louis Cardinals, and Washington Senators, 1956-71.

# STRICT CONSTRUCTIONISM AND THE STRIKE ZONE

Douglas O. Linder*

The Commissioner of Baseball was nearing the end of his long tenure, but there remained one major goal he wished to accomplish before leaving office. He wanted to make baseball a pitcher's game again. "If I see one more 13-10 game, I think I'll just ride my horse off into the sunset. It's really gotten out of hand, hasn't it? All this scoring, I mean? Isn't there *something* we can do about it?"

The Commissioner's assistant thought for a while. "Why yes, maybe there is something," he said finally.

"What's that?" asked the Commissioner. "I'll try anything."

"The problem," said the assistant, "is not so much corked bats of lively balls or indoor stadiums—it's the umpires. The umpires are interpreting rules to favor hitters."

"They are? Why would they do that?"

"It began in the 1960's, that period of licentiousness and misplaced rebellion. Umpires began lowering the strike zone, inch by inch. Some people say that the strike zone was lowered to fit pitches. As this theory has it, when pitchers began throwing more low pitches, mostly sinkers and sliders, and fewer high pitches, down went the strike zone. Personally, I think it more likely pitchers started throwing pitches lower because the high pitches weren't being called strikes anymore. Umpires shrunk the strike zone to please fans who wanted more scoring."

"How could umpires lower the strike zone? Doesn't there have to be a change in the rules for that to happen?"

"You'd think so, wouldn't you, sir? Actually what happened was that umpires began *making* the strike zone, not interpreting it. The strike zone was the same as it always had been. The rulebook says that the strike zone extends from the batter's armpits to the top of his knees, over the width of the plate. That's what the rulebook says, but no umpire in the last twenty years has called a pitch crossing the plate as high as the batter's armpits a strike. The strike zone has moved lower, even though the rulebook remains unchanged. The strike zone now runs roughly from the batter's waist to the bottom of his knees."

"You mean to tell me that our umpires are ignoring the clear language of the rulebook and the intentions of its framers?," asked an obviously incensed Commissioner.

---

* Professor of Law, University of Missouri-Kansas City; Stanford University (J.D.); Gustavus Adolphus College (B.A.).

117

"Exactly," answered his assistant. "The umpires have made up their own strike zone and the result is clear for all to see: our national pastime has been transformed into a run-scoring circus."

"Why, then, let's fire all the umpires!"

"We can't, sir. Their contract, you know."

"Yes, of course. Well, then, what can we do? Didn't you say you had an idea?"

"There's this umpire named Bork working down in Triple A ball. He used to be a professor of Physical Education at a prestigious Eastern University. Bork wrote some scathing attacks on umpires back in his academic days. He espoused what I call 'strict constructionist' principles: an umpire's job is merely to interpret the rules, not change them. I like that Bork, he's not afraid to call that third strike, even when it's rib-high."

"So he's doing a good job in the minors?"

"I think so. Of course the batters disagree. And so do many of the fans. Bork presides over a remarkable number of 1-0 games, some involving fastball pitchers who not long ago were throwing the ball around sand lots. You see, batters have forgotten how to hit high pitches. Batters like Ted Williams, who used to feast on fastballs above the waist, don't exist anymore. The lowered strike zone has produced a league full of pantywaist lowball hitters."

"So we bring this fellow Bork up to the majors. Can he put an end to this runaway scoring and coddling of hitters?"

"He may be able to do it. He's not just one umpire—he's a man of considerable intellectual force."

Moving Bork to the majors wasn't accomplished without a fight. A lot of people *liked* the game as it was. "This Bork fellow is going to set the game back thirty years," one person objected. Finally, however, Bork got the job. Thousands of people who knew little about baseball came to Bork's defense. "Better to have Bork calling major league games than, say, sitting on the Supreme Court where he could have done some real damage," they argued. "Besides, since he'll be wearing a protective mask, no one has to look at his beard."

Bork eventually took his place behind the plate in his first major league game. When a fastball whizzed over the plate, rib-high, Bork yelled, "Stiii-riiike One!"

"Strike?" the batter asked, incredulous. "You've gotta be kidding! That ball was a foot above my waist."

"Check the rulebook, Buddy. The strike zone goes up to your armpits."

"Armpits? Armpits! *No one* calls pitches at the armpits strikes."

"Someone does now."

In the locker room after the game, Bork was asked about his "new" strike zone. "It's not *my* strike zone and it's not new," he said. "It's the rulebook's and it's been around for decades. As long as the book says the strike zone extends to the armpits, that's the way I'll call it. If baseball wants the strike zone lowered, they can change the rule. But until they do, I'll apply the rule as it was written, and as it was interpreted until umpires in the 1960's began thinking that their own notion of what a strike zone should be was better than the books.''

If Bork was the only umpire in the major leagues calling high strikes, perhaps the game wouldn't have changed much. After all, pitchers had been trained to throw low pitches, and they probably wouldn't change their pitching styles just for one umpire. But Bork's argument had its effect. A number of other umpires began to question whether it was legitimate for them to ignore the language of the rulebook and the clear intentions of the rulebook's framers. Soon many pitchers were getting the rib-high strike. Pitchers began adding high pitches to their sinker-slider games. Batting averages dropped. Run production plummeted. Fans began to complain. "Baseball is getting boring", they said. "Who wants to watch a bunch of batters swatting air?'' Support began to grow for a rule which would lower the strike zone.

When the old Commissioner of Baseball retired he was replaced by a Commissioner anxious to satisfy the growing number of fans demanding that baseball become "exciting again.'' The new Commissioner appointed a rule revision committee. Many meetings later a rule change was proposed: the strike zone should extend from the waist to the knees. It did not go unnoticed that the new strike zone was precisely where the old strike zone had been in fact, if not in law, before umpire Bork began applying his strict constructionist principles.

Once the new rule was adopted, the game began to change back into what it was before the day Bork arrived behind the plate. Baseball again became a game of sinker-slider pitchers, lowball hitters, and moderate-to-high run production. Fans were happy again. Only the pitchers, and a few oldtimers who still remembered Ted Williams, grumbled.

Umpire Bork is still calling balls and strikes. Pitches above the waist no longer get his right hand now: he applies the new rule as it is written. Privately, he complains that the game is weighed too heavily in favor of the hitters.

Old men on porches still talk about the early days of Bork's umpiring career. "Those were interesting times—all that debate about where the strike zone should be. Some umpires following Bork's strict constructionist views, and others sticking to the zone that had evolved during the sixties. No one knew where the strike zone would be on any given night—whether to expect a 10-9 game or a 2-0 game.''

Umpire Bork believes baseball is better now for having a strike zone that matches the rulebook's. A lot of other people wonder what difference it all makes. "Everybody *knew* where the strike zone was before he came along, so who cares what the rulebook said?'' they argue. It matters to Umpire Bork, who says that without a guiding principle of fidelity to the rulebook, an umpire might begin calling eyeball-high pitches, or pitches rolled across the plate on the ground, or even pitches thrown behind the batter, strikes.

Other baseball philosophers scoff at Bork's suggestion. "Umpires understand the value of consistency,'' they say. "This business about umpires calling eyeball-high pitches strikes is baloney. Just because an umpire isn't a strict constructionist doesn't mean that he'll call a strike whenever the urge hits him. Umpires are constrained by peer pressure, by fear of ridicule, and by their own love for the integrity of the game. When the strike zone was lowered in the sixties, it wasn't lowered because the umpires said, 'Hey, just for kicks, let's lower the strike zone!' It was lowered in response to various demands of the game and, primarily, the demands of the fans. Baseball was better for the change, which took place more gradually and with less disruption than it ever could have had we depended upon rules committees to revise the strike zone downward an inch or two a year.''

Some debates never end. Perhaps the debate over strict constructionism and the strike zone is one of those. The wisest observation on the whole subject may have been made by a crusty old manager. When asked who was right—the umpires of the 1960's that took it upon themselves to lower the strike zone, or the umpires of the 1980's that raised it again, the manager said "they both were." He explained, "the strike zone got lowered when it needed to be, then umpires like Bork came along to make the rule match the strike zone—like it should."

## BASEBALL JURISPRUDENCE.

In this day of combinations and consolidation of small enterprises into one corporate body, to the mutual profit of all, it is not surprising to find that the amalgamator of corporations has taken up baseball with a view to both pleasure and profit.

Possibly there is no corporate body, if one may say such of the National Association of Professional Baseball Clubs, with which the public comes into closer and more sympathetic contact than this association, and it possibly knows less of its inner nature and working machinery than of other bodies which live and move and have their being away from the limelight.

Baseball has been popular for years, not only as a means of physical development, but as a diversion, and, few are unfamiliar with the game as it is played today, at least with some of the earlier forms from which the present game has been evolved. It has long been a source of large revenue to players and those who promote baseball enterprises.

Prior to ten years ago baseball was played regularly only in the large cities, there being a league, comprising eight or ten clubs, playing in a circuit embracing the larger cities of the North and East, according to a fixed schedule of games, the whole under a single corporate management. The ownership of such clubs had become very valuable at that time, because the games were patronized largely by the public, and the progress of each club, as it advanced or fell behind in its winning, attracted as much attention as if the interests of the National Government were involved. Each city wanted to patronize a winning team, and the demand for skilful players began to exceed the supply. The game had caught the public fancy so surely that it only remained for a man to write "Kelley at the Bat" to spring overnight into public prominence, and an actor who first recited this poem has been a Broadway star ever since.

Other promoters of baseball enterprises, observing the comfortable profits of the larger clubs, entered the field by this time and formed smaller leagues, designed to cater to that portion of the public which was not in reach of the games played by the larger clubs, and these were scattered all over the country, each independent of the other, operating under rules of their own, and settling or attempting to settle their own disputed games and interdissensions of other nature.

At that time a corporation would be formed to own and operate, say an amusement park in each of four or more cities or towns, each park having a ball team of its own, employed to engage in games one against the other, but such clubs had no assurance that they could keep their players from one season to the other, or that they would not be hired away over night by some rival club just when a player's services were needed most, and thus the investment was on a somewhat precarious basis.

These conditions existed about ten years ago when the amalgamator waved his wand and created what is known as the National Agreement of Professional Baseball Clubs. In 1901 representatives of all the important leagues of the country got together and formed this agreement, which, by resolution, was created for ten years, and which, today, is the means by which every ball team in the country is not only governed, but the personnel thereof is kept together, at the will of the club owner, with an invisible and indissoluble tie that exists, not by the force of any common or statute law, but simply by the mandate of the agreement. Indeed the tie which binds is in the very teeth of the law, and it is in this that the business of baseball is peculiar.

Other corporate promoters have carefully studied how close they may sail their ventures to the invisible line which binds their efforts into a compact whole and breathes the breath of legal immortality into it; but this amalgamation was conceived in legal sin, as it were, born of a desire to create an artificial body which should govern and control itself by its own decrees, and enforcing them without the aid of the law, and answerable to no power outside its own. I do not know the name of the promoter who fathered this enterprise, but certain it is that an infant industry was born in that year, with no bar sinister of tariff protection upon its ancestry, that has waxed hale and hearty since then, and whose interest in the eyes of the public today is great; it is said, so great as, just recently, even to over-shadow the public concern in the greatest of all issues of this Republic, the election of its President.

The object of the National Agreement, as stated therein, is "to perpetuate baseball as the national game of America, and to surround it with such safeguards as to warrant absolute public confidence in its integrity and methods; and to promote and afford protection to such professional baseball leagues and associations as may desire to operate under its provisions."

A governing body called the "National Board of Arbitration" was created, composed of five representatives selected by the National Association of Baseball Leagues, and such other members as might be admitted to membership on the board thereafter by the board itself.

The board's duty, and it has full and final jurisdiction in such matters, is to "hear and determine all disputes and complaints between associations and clubs, between one club and another, members of the same or different associations; between club and players or managers, and, in addition thereto, all disputes or complaints arising under, and all matters pertaining to and involving the interpretation of the National Agreement, or the disposition of the rights thereunder." It has the power to pass upon any question brought before it by a club member or members of any organization, where unjust discrimination has been made against any club or clubs, and, if, upon a hearing, the board finds that such charges are true, it has the power to impose such fines or penalties as it deems proper, or to forfeit or terminate the privilege of such organization under the agreement, and it also may make assessments upon the members of the organization to pay necessary expenses in performing its duties and enforcing the agreement.

An association of baseball clubs, which desires to be protected under the terms of this agreement, must make application in writing, stating the name of the league, the cities comprising the circuit or territory embraced therein, the monthly salary limit and a pledge for the maintenance thereof, and the faithful performance of its obligations under the agreement. Having once been admitted, a club's officers, playing grounds, salary limit, constitution, by-laws, agreements and pledges cannot be changed without the consent of the Board of Arbitration.

The leagues are classified by the board according to the average population of the cities composing the league. Class A, comprising cities of 1,000,000; Class B, 400,000 to 1,000,000; Class C, 200,000 to 400,000, and Class D, up to 200,000, and each club has exclusive control of its own territory, no club from any other league, party to the agreement, being allowed to play a game in any city of the circuit, nor within five miles of such city, without the consent of the home club.

The object of the agreement is to tie the player up with his club so that he shall not be able to play with any other club, except with the consent of his employer. This is accomplished by giving the board absolute control of the players and the clubs.

Under the form of contract prescribed by the board, and under which all players work, the player agrees for a stated sum per month, to devote his entire time and services, as a ball player, to his club during the period of the contract, and to conform to all the rules and regulations which his club has, or may thereafter, adopt, appertaining to his services. He also agrees not to render such services, during the time of the contract, to any other club without his employer's consent in writing. He also agrees that all the provisions of the National Agreement are a part of his contract and binding upon him, and in consideration of the foregoing, the club agrees to pay him his salary and necessary expenses when away from home.

It is further provided that should the player fail to comply with his agreement, or the provisions of his club in regard to his services, or if he should be at any time intemperate, immoral, careless, indifferent, or conduct himself in such a manner, whether on or off the field, as to endanger or prejudice the interests of his club, or become ill, or otherwise unfit from any cause, or prove incompetent in the judgment of his employer, then his employer has the right to discipline him, suspend, fine or discharge him in any manner he shall see fit, and is to be the sole judge of the sufficiency of the cause for any such proceeding, and, in case of fine imposed, it may be withheld from his salary as liquidated damages.

At the close of the contract, it is provided that if the player's services should be desired for any period of time, after the date mentioned in the contract for the expiration of the term thereof, or mentioned in any renewal of said contract, the employer shall have the right to the same, upon paying compensation to the player at the rate of one-thirtieth of the amount therein specified as the monthly salary of the player.

Under the agreement all of these contracts must be filed with the secretary of the Board of Arbitration, who keeps a list of the players so signed, and a club, once having contracted with a player, no other club can contract with him that season.

On or before September 25, of each year, the club owner proceeds to get his house in order for the next season's work. If any of the players then working for him seem desirable for the next year, he notifies the secretary of his league of their names, not exceeding fourteen in number, and this list is forwarded to the secretary of the Board of Arbitration, who promulgates it to all the other clubs. In addition to this, a list is sent of the players reserved in any prior annual reserve list, who have refused to contract, as. well as a list of all players ineligible. Upon approval of these lists by the board, these players are ineligible to contract with any other club, unless their club should be in arrears in salary with them, or unless they fail to present them with a contract for the ensuing season by the first of March, of that year, which contract, of course, contains the reservation clause.

Should a player under reserve contract with or play with any other club, without his employer's written consent, he is disqualified from playing ball with any club, member of the agreement, and all members are barred from playing with or against him. Should he desert his club, he must return to it—he cannot play with any other.

In other respects his freedom of contract is curtailed. A club of a higher class has the right, with the consent of the board and the player, after October 1, in each year, to select or draft players from a lower class, upon payment to the club from which the player is taken, for Class B, $300, for Class C, $200, and for Class D, $100. The period within which the various classes may draft players is so fixed that Class A gets the first choice, Class B the second choice and so on. The purpose of this stipulation, as stated in the agreement, is to assist the players to advance in their profession and to build up the leagues, and from this point of view this stipulation is a good one. Should a player be released by his club, except in the case of drafting, his services are at the absolute disposal of the board, which places him with any club applying for him within ten days from the date of his release. Not until after then can he contract with a club of his choice. So that a club, having once secured a good player, may keep him for life in Class A league, from which there is no drafting, or as long as he may be useful by simply exercising the right of reservation of his services from year to year, and invoking the aid of the board to make him either recognize this right or quit playing ball. And, with this power over him, the amount of his salary is more or less subject to the control of the employer. These are the main provisions of the baseball code, and the fact that there are very few reported decisions

of baseball litigation would indicate that it has proven successful as a means of controlling the players, and preserving
the investments of club owners on a profitable basis.

The framers of this agreement were not without a guide
as to the probable construction which the courts would put
upon some of the phases of this contract, for as early as
1882 the Allegheny Baseball Club brought suit against a
player named Bennett, reported in 14 Fed., 257.

In August of 1882, Bennett signed an agreement with
plaintiff, binding himself to sign a contract with the club
in October of that year, covering his services for the next
season. He refused later to sign the contract for the next
season and engaged his services to the Detroit team. The
bill was to compel him to execute his agreement, and to enjoin him from playing with Detroit, or any other club, during the season of 1883.

A demurrer to the bill was sustained, on the ground that
the contract of August was a mere preliminary arrangement and not a final agreement, and that it did not appear
that such an agreement, when executed, would be a mutual
one, its terms certain, or its enforcement practical, and that
plaintiff was not without an adequate remedy at law. It
could have employed some other player of Bennett's skill,
and the damage, if any, would have been the excess of his
salary over that contracted to be paid Bennett.

The next case came up in March, 1900, the case of the
Philadelphia Ball Club v. William Hallman et al., decided
in the Court of Common Pleas of Philadelphia, in which
the same question was involved and treated similarly.

On the 24th of October, 1888, Hallman entered into an
elaborate written contract, consisting of nineteen different
articles, by which he bound himself to play baseball for the
plaintiff for a period of seven months from April 1, 1889.
The eighteenth article of the agreement provided that the
plaintiff had the right to reserve the defendant's services
for the season next ensuing the term mentioned in the contract. In October, 1889, it requested defendant to sign a
written contract for the season of 1890, similar in tenor,

form and terms to the contract for 1888, including article 18. He refused to sign this contract, and, the contract of 1888 having expired, he went to play for another club. This action was to enjoin him from so doing.

The court found that the contract gave the plaintiff the right only to *"reserve"* the defendant's services as a ball player. It did not require the defendant to renew the contract upon the same terms and conditions. He did not covenant to serve for the same salary, but only for some salary to be agreed upon, not less than the amount he had received formerly. The Court said:

"The failure to designate the terms and conditions of the new engagement, under which he is to be reserved, rendered the contract of the reservation wholly uncertain, and therefore incapable of enforcement, especially by a proceeding which is a substitute for a decree of specific performance, for specific performance is never decreed of a contract, the terms of which are uncertain."

"Now, if, on the contrary," the court continues, "it be said as was assumed by plaintiff's counsel, on the argument, that the fair meaning of article 18 is that the defendant should enter into another contract for the season of 1900, precisely similar in all respects to the contract executed in 1888, and embracing all its provisions, then it follows, of course, that he must bind himself afresh by article 18, to renew the contracts for 1891, and again in 1891 for 1892, and in 1892 for 1893, and so on from year to year, so long as it may suit the pleasure of the plaintiff to insist upon the reservation clause, and its annual renewal; for there is no more reason for dropping out article 18 from the new contract, if the new contract is required to be the same in all respects as the old, than from dropping out of it any of the original nineteen articles. In the meantime article 17, of the agreement, provides that the plaintiff may discharge the defendant from its services at any time and without any cause whatever, upon ten days' notice to that effect. So that if the proper construction of the contract is that which the plaintiff put upon it, the necessary result is that while the defendant has sold himself for life to the plaintiff for $1,400 per annum, if it chooses to hold him that time, he has no hold upon them for any period longer than ten days. He is absolutely at their mercy, and may be set adrift at the beginning or in the middle of the season, at home or 2,000 miles from it, sick or well, at the mere arbitrary discretion of the plaintiff, provided only they give him ten days' notice.

"Truly, a defendant may be excused from insisting that he did not intend to so contract, but if this denial of the contract be overruled, and it is determined that that is the real meaning of the contract, then it is perfectly apparent that such a contract is so unfair, and so wanting in mutuality, that no court of equity would lend its aid to its enforcement.

The result of the whole case is that the plaintiff has shown no such case in its bill as would justify us in affording them the extraordinary remedy which they ask."

In January of the same year the question raised in the above case was raised in the First District of the New York Superior Court, in the case of Metropolitan Exhibition Company v. Ward.[1] In this case Mr. Joseph Choate was counsel for the plaintiff. The defendant was the ex-short-stop of the New York Club, and is now a practicing lawyer of New York City, and counsel for the National Association of Professional Baseball Clubs. In this case the defendant had signed a contract with the New York Club for the season of 1889. The contract gave the plaintiff, on certain conditions, the right to "reserve" the defendant for the next ensuing season. Ward played the season of 1889 with New York. At the close of that season, he entered into negotiations with another club for the next season, and declined to play with plaintiff. The action was brought to enjoin defendant from playing with any other club except its own.

One of the principal questions discussed in the argument was the meaning of the word "reserve," as used in the contract. The plaintiff claimed that the meaning of the word was clear, being used in the ordinary sense of "to hold, to keep for further use." The defendant claimed that the word had a history, and with that history both parties to the contract were well acquainted—that it had always been used in a particular sense, and, in order to ascertain that meaning, reference must be had to the history of the word; and that if resort is had to that history, it will result in a construction to be given to the contract, which shall determine that when the defendant accorded the right to reserve his services, that it was not hereby meant that he was absolutely pledged or bound to plaintiff, but that his services were reserved to the exclusion of any other member of the league of ball clubs. In other words, the word "reserve," defendant contended, referred only to the right and practice of reservation previously exercised under the National

---

[1] 24 Abbott's New Cases, p. 393.

Agreement, and did not prohibit a player from contracting with or playing for any club outside the purview of the National Agreement.

The Court held that the reserve clause only gave plaintiff the right to contract with Ward for the next season, as the contract did not say that it was to be renewed upon like terms.

The Court said in this connection: "The failure in the existing contract to expressly provide the terms and conditions to be made for 1890, either renders the latter indefinite and uncertain, or we must infer that the same terms and conditions are to be incorporated in the one now to be enforced, which necessarily includes the reserve clause, for no good reason can be suggested, if all the others are to be included, why this should be omitted. Upon the latter assumption, the want of fairness and mutuality, which are fatal to its enforcement in equity, are apparent, as will be seen when we consider to what extent, under such circumstances, each of the parties is bound. A player who signs such a contract is bound for the current playing season and also for the ensuing playing season, and is obliged at the close of the first season, to make another contract with the same terms and conditions, binding him for the second season and so long as plaintiff elects, the player being always bound one year in advance."

This contract provided for discharge on ten days' notice.

"In thus considering," continues the court, "the obligations, which under the plaintiff's construction of the contract each has assumed, we have the spectacle presented of a contract which binds one party for a series of years and the other party for ten days, and the party who is itself bound for ten days, coming into a court of equity against the party bound for years."

A preliminary injunction was granted in this case, it appearing that a final hearing could be had before the playing season of 1890 opened. On the 31st of March, however, Judge Lawrence filed a memorandum opinion, dismissing the case for the reason that the contract was not such an one as equity would enforce.

It does not appear from this decision how much effect the argument that the word "reserve" had a special significance, as used by the parties in the contract, had upon the Court; but in a case decided in March, 1890, in the Federal Court in the Southern District of New York, Metropolitan Exhibition Co. v. Ewing,[2] the meaning contended for in the Ward case was conceded by the Court. In this case the action was brought to restrain a threatened breach of contract for the performance of personal services, which required special skill, aptitude and experience. Ewing had signed a contract to play ball for New York for the season of 1889, which contract was in the usual form, with the right of reservation. This right was exercised, but defendant refused to recognize it and went to play with another team for that season. Mr. Choate was counsel in this case also. The Court held that the word "reserve" did not indicate any definite understanding of the parties as to their reciprocal rights and obligations, under the new contract that was to be signed, but, by referring to other contracts which the parties had made in respect to the same subject-matter, and apparently in pursuance of the same general purpose, it found that the word was used in the sense that obtains in baseball nomenclature, and that it was intended to signify an option, the character of which was well understood by baseball clubs and professional players when the contract was made.

"The effect of this provision," says the court, "is that when the club has exercised its privilege of reservation, no other club is permitted to negotiate with the player but the club which has reserved him, and no other is then at liberty to enter into a contract with him to obtain his services for an ensuing year. It is a prior and exclusive right, as against the other clubs, to enter into a contract securing the player's services for another season." But it said "until the contract is made which fixes the compensation of the player, and the other conditions of his service, there is no definite or complete obligation on his part to engage with the club. He engages not to negotiate with any other club, but enjoys the privilege of engaging with the reserving club, or not, as he chooses. As a coercive condition which places the player practically, or at least measurably, in a situation where he must engage with the club that has reserved him, or

[2] 7 L. R. A., 381.

face the probability of losing any engagement for the next season, it is operative and valuable to the club. But as a basis for an action for damages, if the player fails to contract, or for an action for specific performance, it is wholly nugatory. In a legal sense it is merely a contract to make a contract, if the parties can agree. It may be that heretofore the clubs have generally insisted upon treating the option to reserve as a contract, by which they were entitled to have the services of the party for the next season, upon the terms and conditions of the first season, and even requiring him to enter into a new contract containing the option for reservation; and it may be that the players have generally acquiesced in the claim of the club. However this may be, the players were not in a position to act independently, and if they had refused to assent to the terms proposed by the clubs they would have done so at the peril of losing an engagement. The facts are not such, therefore, as to permit any weight to be given to the acts of the parties as evincing their own construction of the contract. It follows, therefore, that the act of the defendant in refusing to negotiate with plaintiff for the season of 1890, while a breach of contract, is not a breach that the plaintiff can enforce."

In the case of Baltimore Baseball Club and Exhibition Co. v. Pickett,[3] decided in 1894, the defendant, a player, had been discharged for inefficiency upon ten days' notice.

He brought suit for damages for breach of contract. The defense was inefficiency, and that there was a universal custom observed by all professional baseball clubs that the club shall have the right, upon ten days' notice, to discharge a player who does not come up to the requirements of his position and play satisfactorily.

The Court found that it did not appear that defendant was wanting in skill, and held that the usage of discharging upon ten days' notice was inadmissible in evidence, inasmuch as it varied the terms of a contract for a definite time and destroyed its mutuality.

It is readily seen from these cases that at the time the National Agreement was formed, it had been judicially determined that the right to reserve players from season to season, under the "reserve clause" of the contract, which is the backbone of organized baseball today, and the prime object to be attained by the agreement at that time, would not be upheld in the courts, though the Court said in the

[3] 22 L. R. A., 690.

Ward case: "Between an actor of great histrionic ability
and a professional ball player of peculiar fitness and skill
to fill a certain position, no substantial distinction in applying the rule that they, like actors and actresses, should be
held to a true and faithful performance of their engagements, can be made. Each is sought for his peculiar and
particular fitness; each performs in public, and each possesses for the manager a means of attracting an audience.
The refusal of either to perform, according to contract,
must result in loss to the manager, which is increased in
cases where such services are rendered to a rival."

If the opinion of authorities upon the efficiency required
of baseball players today is any criterion, the comparison
made by the Court in the Ward case, just quoted, is not
far wrong. Perhaps the best posted authority on baseball
in the South today likens the members of a professional
ball team to the wheels of a car, so long as they work together, each one doing his best, but so combining their joint
efforts that a harmonious whole results, the maximum of
efficiency obtains and the team wins, but if one player should
fall behind in his work or does not co-operate fully with
the work of his teammates, it is as if one wheel of a car were
smaller than the others, or was not running perfectly true
upon the rail, or as if it bound the rail. Today and for
some time past the result of contests for supremacy between
the clubs, under the National Agreement, has developed a
ball team into a highly organized piece of machinery. Not
mere physical effort suffices to make a team a serious rival.
There must be, in addition, a mental capacity of high order.
The conditions of a game are constantly changing during
its progress. No two games are alike, nor, for that matter,
is the ball ever struck by the batter twice exactly in the
same way; the trajectory of the flight of the ball, its speed
and the direction and speed with which the ball twists as
it flies through the air, are all different each time, and these
differences must be observed by the player between the
time the ball is struck and the time it reaches him, in some
cases involving only the lapse of a second in time; and only

by years of constant practice, perfect physical condition and concentrated mental effort, can a player arrive at that stage of perfection when he may be said to be finished in his work. In addition to this, he must observe and remember the peculiarities of play of each member of rival clubs, as closely and intelligently as one business concern observes the actions of a neighboring house.

Another authority on baseball compares the members of a team to the movements of a fine watch, unerringly accurate, sensitive, supple, well oiled. He declares that the whole team must be an instrument of precision.

As an instance of the closeness with which opposing players are studied and their weakness noted, and the efficiency with which what is known as ''team-play'' is employed, this authority cites an instance which occurred once in a game between Boston and Chicago, in which a young player appeared with the Boston club who had never played against Chicago before. In the third inning of the game he made a hit and reached second base. On the first ball being pitched to the next batter, he started to run to third base. The catcher motioned as if to throw the ball to second base. The second baseman was playing off his base, and the shortstop ran to cover that position. The runner, at first made a jump toward second base, and, seeing that the catcher had not thrown, he slowed up. The shortstop walked away from second base, and, as he passed the runner, he attracted his attention with some remark. The latter turned to make some retort to the remark, and at that instant the catcher threw to second base. The second baseman met the ball the instant it reached there, and, before the runner knew what had happened, he was out. The whole play appeared to have been made just on the spur of the moment, and yet all of its details had been worked out and agreed upon between these three players upon their having looked this new player over and seen him run the bases once.

This authority gives another instance which shows the mental capacity required of a player which occurred in a game that was played between New York and Boston. New York needed one run to tie the score. Brown, one of its speediest base runners, was on second base, and Doyle, a hard hitter, was at the bat. It seemed certain that if Doyle hit the ball safely, as he usually did, the runner on second would score, on account of his exceptional speed. Doyle hit the ball straight into left field. Brown started for third base, Doyle started for first base and Boston's left fielder, MacCarthy, started after the ball. He reached it on its first bound, grabbed it and without stopping or looking, threw it with terrific force and perfect aim across the diamond straight into the first baseman's hands.

Brown had stopped at third, but Doyle, who had reached first and turned with intention of running to second, was caught standing still, ten feet from first base. The next batter went out on a fly and Boston won the game. This authority asked MacCarthy, after the game, concerning the play: "Well," he explained, "Brown is a quick thinker. He saw how hard that ball was hit, and knew that I could throw him out at the home plate, if he tried to score, unless I fumbled the ball. Doyle doesn't think very fast, and, knowing that he would turn at first and stop to see if I was throwing home, I threw across to first and caught him. He figured that out while the ball was coming through the air toward him, probably reaching his conclusions and making the decisions in four-fifths of a second."

In 1902 the profession of baseball had approached this degree of perfection when the case of Philadelphia Ball Club v. Napoleon LaJoie was decided in Pennsylvania,[4] in which nearly all the cases noted in this paper were cited in the brief before the Supreme Court. This was a case involving a breach of a player's contract of the kind before noticed. The defendant had played part of the season, and had then contracted to play with a rival organization. The action was to restrain him from so doing during the life of his contract. The court below refused the injunction, hold-

[4] 202 Pa. 210.

ing that to warrant the relief prayed, the defendant's services must be unique, extraordinary and of such a character that it was impossible to replace him, so that his breach of contract would result in irreparable loss to plaintiff, and found from the evidence that his qualifications as a player did not measure up to this standard. It also held that the contract was wanting in mutuality, in that the plaintiff had the right to discharge defendant on ten days' notice, without a reciprocal right on the part of the defendant. The court, on appeal, took a different view of the case. As to the qualifications as a player of defendant is said:

"He has been for several years in the service of the plaintiff club, and has been re-engaged from season to season at a constantly increasing salary. He has become thoroughly familiar with the actions and methods of other players in the club, and his own work is peculiarly meritorious as an integral part of the team work which is so essential. In addition to these features, which renders his services of peculiar and special value to the plaintiff and not easily replaced, LaJoie is well known, and has a great reputation among the patrons of the sport, for ability in the position which he filled, and was thus a most attractive drawing card for the public. He may not be the sun in the baseball firmament, but he is certainly a bright particular star. We feel therefore that the evidence in this case justifies the conclusion that the services of the defendant are of such a unique character, and display such a special knowledge, skill and ability, as renders them of peculiar value to the plaintiff, and so difficult of substitution that their loss will produce irreparable injury, in the legal sense of that term."

The eighteenth paragraph of this contract reads: "In consideration of the faithful performance of the conditions, covenants and undertakings and promises herein by the said party of the second part, including the concession of the option of release and renewal prescribed in the seventeenth and nineteenth paragraphs, the said party of the first part, for itself and assigns, hereby agrees to pay him the sum of $2,400."

On the point of mutuality the court said:

"The term 'mutuality' or 'lack of mutuality,' does not always convey a clear and definite meaning. As was said in Grove v. Hodges:[5] 'The legal principle that contracts must be mutual does not mean that in every

[5] 55 Pa. 51t

case each party must have the same remedy for a breach by the other.'
In the contract now before us, the defendant agreed to furnish his professional services to the plaintiff for a period, which might be extended
over three years by proper notice, given at the end of each current year.
Upon the other hand, the plaintiff retained the right to terminate the
contract upon ten days' notice and the payment of salary for that time
and the expense of getting defendant to his home. But the fact of this
concession to the plaintiff is distinctly pointed out as a part of the consideration for the large salary paid to the defendant, and is emphasized
as such; and owing to the peculiar nature of the services demanded by
the business, and the high degree of efficiency which must be maintained,
the stipulation is not unreasonable. Particularly is this true, when it is remembered that the player has played for years under substantially the
same contract. We are not persuaded that the terms of this contract
manifest any lack of mutuality in remedy. Each party has the possibility
of enforcing all the rights stipulated for under the contract. It is true
that the terms make it possible for the plaintiff to put an end to the
contract in a space of time much less than the period during which the
defendant has agreed to supply his personal services; but mere difference
in the rights stipulated for does not destroy mutuality of remedy. Freedom of contract covers a wide range of obligation and duty as between
the parties, and it may not be impaired as long as the bounds of reasonableness and fairness are not transgressed."

The court then held that inasmuch as the damages caused
by the breach of the defendant's contract not to play with
any other club were not susceptible of admeasurement by
any "certain pecuniary standard," they were irreparable
in a legal sense, and injunction would issue.

In commenting on this case, Prof. John D. Lawson says
that up to the time of this decision the relief prayed for in
cases of this kind had been granted only in contracts involving the exercise of mental and intellectual powers, authors,
singers, actors, and the like.

About a month later the identical questions and the construction of identically the same contract came up in the
Circuit Court of St. Louis, in the case of American Baseball
and Athletic Association v. Harper, reported in an able article by Professor Lawson in the *Central Law Journal* of
June 6, 1902. That court held that the evidence did not warrant the finding that the defendant's services were special,
unique, extraordinary and artistic in the degree that the
plaintiff's loss of them would be an irreparable one. The

court also held that the contract was wanting in mutuality, for the reason that the defendant was bound for the entire period, while plaintiff might release him at its discretion upon ten days' notice. The reasoning of the LaJoie case is disapproved of, and the court adds that, as the plaintiff was a member of an association of baseball clubs whose objects were, in part, to control the salaries of players, the price of admission to the game to be played by the different clubs, and the method and terms of employment of players, it had no standing in a court of equity to restrain the breach of a contract made with it by one of its players, and that under the provisions of the Missouri Constitution, declaring that all persons have the natural right to life, liberty and the enjoyment of the natural gains of their own industry, and prohibiting slavery and involuntary servitude, except as a punishment for crime, a court has no power to enforce the performance of personal services due by one person to another under a contract.

In this article Professor Lawson seems inclined to support the Missouri court. He finds that such a contract is fatally lacking in mutuality, and also that the plaintiff, by reason of being connected with a trust, might have no standing in equity in a controversy of this kind. He finds that such a contract is an indefinite contract for personal services, and void, as against public policy, by reason of its imposing a condition of involuntary servitude. He says, further, that one who has made a contract by which his services are promised to another for a certain term, and who, before the end of that term, discovers that he has made a bad bargain, or that his services, for some reason, are obnoxious, or that he may secure better pay elsewhere, has a right to elect either to perform or break his contract and pay damages therefor, adding that to say that damages in money could not be assessed in the LaJoie case would be absurd, citing numerous authorities for his contentions.

An article by Mr. Henry W. Bond, commenting on Professor Lawson's article, appeared in the *Central Law Jour-*

*nal* of July 25, 1902. In dealing with mutuality of contracts, Mr. Bond said: "Although mutuality of obligation is essential to the creation of a contract, yet such mutuality does not require identity of redress. Obviously, the injury to the respective parties, arising from the breach of their agreement, may differ most widely. Indeed, it can hardly ever be the same. The proximate loss of the two parties must always depend upon the nature, kind and subject matter of the contract and its results as reasonably contemplated. Not only does the measure of compensation of the two parties, for breach of the contract, often differ in extent, but in many cases totally different remedies may be employed by them to enforce their respective rights upon the breach of the contract by the other." As in the case of Ackstein v. Downing,[6] where it was held that, in an agreement to exchange stock for a yacht, that one party was entitled to specific performance, while the other was not, and in Baumgardner v. Leavitt,[7] where a contract to convey shares of stock, though not generally enforceable, was enforced, the stock having a unique and special value to the plaintiff, the loss of which could not be fully compensated at law, and other cases cited, deducing the rule from the cases that the mutuality necessary to sustain such a contract may co-exist with inequality of compensation and essential differences of remedy, according as the breach is by one or the other of the parties, which he submits, was what was determined in the LaJoie case.

Since 1902 there has been no reported cases involving the construction of players' contracts, and this silence would indicate that the national agreement was conceived in wisdom, from a business point of view, and that it has been successful in enforcing its decrees and in preserving the investments in baseball clubs upon a firm financial basis. And this investment is no small one. There are about forty organized leagues in the United States, composed of from four to eight clubs each, acting under the national agree-

[6] 64 N. H. 248.          [7] 35 W. Va. 194.

ment, and from the 1st of April to the 31st of October of this year games will be played all over the country. If the figures of last year's attendance are trustworthy, and may be taken as a guide, over seven million people will witness the games played in New York City, Chicago, Philadelphia, Boston, St. Louis, Pittsburgh, Cincinnati, Brooklyn, Detroit, Cleveland and Washington alone, with probably a like number attending the games in other parts of the country, scheduled for about 240 other clubs. Probably a million dollars a month is a conservative estimate of the earnings in baseball during the season, while the amount invested in the business will probably reach ten millions.

The skilled players draw large salaries. Most of the clubs of the largest cities maintain two or more players, who draw not less than $5,000 each. New York pays one of its pitchers $10,000.

In view of the facts and of the recent authorities, cited herein, it is not unlikely, should a case similar to the LaJoie case arise in the future, that the courts would follow the decision of the Pennsylvania court. I do not know whether Mr. Justice Potter, who rendered that decision, is a baseball enthusiast or not. From his fervent description of LaJoie's prowess as a player, it may be inferred that he not only attended the games in Philadelphia, but that he was an ardent and consistent supporter of the home team, and it may be that because he investigated the game from the spectator's point of view he was the more able to grasp the argument of the employer in that case as to the necessity of its control of its players. And it might do no harm if the judiciary, following such an example, as well as that of an eminent executive of this country, should indulge in original research into baseball from the grand stand, and thus get a practical point of view of the player's contract, which will enable them to demonstrate, when the time shall come, that the law progresses along with human events, and that its remedies are administered with intelligence and according to the conditions that control a case.

Newport, Ark.                                    John W. Stayton.

# PART 8

## THE CHICAGO CUBS:
## POST-SEASON PLAY ISN'T EVERYTHING

The question of the unique cultural significance of the Chicago
Cubs and the club's relationship to both the instrinsic nature of
baseball and the law has produced an irreconcilable split among
the editors of this volume. Professor Waller believes that day
baseball, the Cubs, and Wrigley Field occupy a sacred and special
place in the ethos of America and the myths of our national
pastime. Not surprisingly, this editor was raised within sight of
Wrigley Field. Professor Cohen, who was raised in Cleveland,
thinks this is all nonsense. Professor Finkelman, who attended
graduate school on the south side of Chicago (closer to the Chicago
White Sox), understands Professor Waller's position, but does not
wholly endorse it.

The editors agree that the question of the presence and absence of lights in Wrigley Field has produced some of the most
fascinating litigation involving major league baseball. By the
1960s, Wrigley Field had long been the only stadium without
lights or night baseball. During that decade, the Cubs were forced
to defend the business justification for this refusal to play night
baseball against a shareholder's derivative suit brought by one of
the most active litigants in the annals of Illinois corporate law.

By the 1980s, the Chicago Cubs had been sold by the Wrigley
family to the Tribune Corporation, which proceeded with plans to
install lights. The Illinois legislature responded to intense community pressure and passed a narrowly-tailored noise pollution statute which had the practical and intended effect of prohibiting
night baseball in Wrigley Field. Now it was the Cubs who sought
the protections of the law to invalidate the ordinance on constitutional grounds and allow them to proceed with what they had so
vigorously resisted in the past.

In the end, limited night baseball came to Wrigley Field. But
not Professor Waller. To this day, he refuses to attend night games
at Wrigley Field as a matter of principle. This has included turning

down free tickets for the 1990 All-Star Game. Professor Cohen thinks this is nonsense. Again, Professor Finkelman understands Waller, but thinks this is mostly nonsense.

stadium for night baseball games. The Circuit Court of Cook County, Chancery Division, Daniel A. Covelli, J., dismissed stockholder's complaint and he appealed. The Appellate Court, Sullivan, J., held that complaint was properly dismissed for failure to state cause of action based upon fraud, illegality or conflict of interest and also that complaint was defective in failing to allege damage to the corporation.

Affirmed.

**1. Corporations ⟨⟩320(7)**

Complaint alleging that directors of baseball corporation refused to install lights for night baseball games resulting in financial loss though funds were available, that president refused installation of lights believing baseball to be daytime sport, and that directors acquiesced in his views failed to state cause of action based upon fraud, illegality or conflict of interest.

**2. Corporations ⟨⟩320(1)**

Unless conduct of corporate directors borders on fraud, illegality or conflict of interest, stockholder's derivative suit will not lie.

95 Ill.App.2d 173

William SHLENSKY, on Behalf of and as a Representative of Chicago National League Ball Club (Inc.), Plaintiff-Appellant,

v.

Philip K. WRIGLEY, William Wrigley, William J. Hagenah, Jr., George F. Getz, Philip H. Erbes, Gilbert H. Scribner, Arthur E. Meyerhoff, John Holland, Jack Brickhouse and Chicago National League Ball Club (Inc.), Defendants-Appellees.

Gen. No. 51750.

Appellate Court of Illinois.

First District, Third Division.

April 25, 1968.

Stockholder's derivative suit against baseball corporation and its directors for negligence and mismanagement and for an order that defendants install lights in their

**3. Corporations ⟨⟩320(7)**

Complaint in stockholder's derivative suit against baseball corporation and its directors alleging negligence and mismanagement on part of directors for failure to install lights for night baseball games but which did not allege that there would be a net benefit to corporation from such action failed to allege damage to the corporation.

**4. Pleading ⟨⟩214(2, 4, 5)**

Well-pleaded facts must be taken as true for purpose of judging sufficiency of complaint, however conclusions drawn by pleader need not be accepted.

**5. Pleadings ⟨⟩34(4)**

Pleadings are construed most strongly against pleader prior to verdict or judgment on merits.

**6. Pleading** ⟐⟹8(20)

Allegation that minority stockholders and corporation were seriously and irreparably damaged by wrongful conduct of baseball corporation directors in failing to install lights for night games was mere conclusion and not averment of fact.

**7. Corporations** ⟐⟹310(2)

Failure to follow example of other major league clubs in scheduling night games did not constitute negligence on part of directors of baseball corporation.

**8. Corporations** ⟐⟹310(1)

In absence of clear showing of dereliction of duty on part of specific directors, courts will not require directors to forego their business judgment and follow decisions of directors of other companies.

———◆———

Milton I. Shadur, Neil H. Adelman, Chicago, Robert Plotkin, Ronald S. Miller, David J. Krupp, Abner J. Mikva, Chicago, of counsel, for appellant.

Samuel W. Block, Kenneth S. Broun, Chicago, for defendant-appellee Chicago National League Ball Club, (Inc.).

Sidley, Austin, Burgess & Smith, Chicago, for defendants Philip K. Wrigley, William Wrigley, Gilbert H. Scribner, Jack Brickhouse.

Arthur Morse, Chicago, for defendants William J. Hagenah, Jr., Philip H. Erbes, Arthur E. Meyerhoff, John Holland; James E. S. Baker, Edward Slovick, Alexander C. Allison, Chicago, of counsel.

SULLIVAN, Justice.

This is an appeal from a dismissal of plaintiff's amended complaint on motion of the defendants. The action was a stockholders' derivative suit against the directors for negligence and mismanagement. The corporation was also made a defendant. Plaintiff sought damages and an order that

237 N.E.2d—49½

defendants cause the installation of lights in Wrigley Field and the scheduling of night baseball games.

Plaintiff is a minority stockholder of defendant corporation, Chicago National League Ball Club (Inc.), a Delaware corporation with its principal place of business in Chicago, Illinois. Defendant corporation owns and operates the major league professional baseball team known as the Chicago Cubs. The corporation also engages in the operation of Wrigley Field, the Cubs' home park, the concessionaire sales during Cubs' home games, television and radio broadcasts of Cubs' home games, the leasing of the field for football games and other events and receives its share, as visiting team, of admission moneys from games played in other National League stadia. The individual defendants are directors of the Cubs and have served for varying periods of years. Defendant Philip K. Wrigley is also president of the corporation and owner of approximately 80% of the stock therein.

Plaintiff alleges that since night baseball was first played in 1935 nineteen of the twenty major league teams have scheduled night games. In 1966, out of a total of 1620 games in the major leagues, 932 were played at night. Plaintiff alleges that every member of the major leagues, other than the Cubs, scheduled substantially all of its home games in 1966 at night, exclusive of opening days, Saturdays, Sundays, holidays and days prohibited by league rules. Allegedly this has been done for the specific purpose of maximizing attendance and thereby maximizing revenue and income.

The Cubs, in the years 1961–65, sustained operating losses from its direct baseball operations. Plaintiff attributes those losses to inadequate attendance at Cubs' home games. He concludes that if the directors continue to refuse to install lights at Wrigley Field and schedule night baseball games, the Cubs will continue to sustain comparable losses and its financial condition will continue to deteriorate.

Plaintiff alleges that, except for the year 1963, attendance at Cubs' home games has been substantially below that at their road games, many of which were played at night.

Plaintiff compares attendance at Cubs' games with that of the Chicago White Sox, an American League club, whose weekday games were generally played at night. The weekend attendance figures for the two teams was similar; however, the White Sox week-night games drew many more patrons than did the Cubs' weekday games.

Plaintiff alleges that the funds for the installation of lights can be readily obtained through financing and the cost of installation would be far more than offset and recaptured by increased revenues and incomes resulting from the increased attendance.

Plaintiff further alleges that defendant Wrigley has refused to install lights, not because of interest in the welfare of the corporation but because of his personal opinions "that baseball is a 'daytime sport' and that the installation of lights and night baseball games will have a deteriorating effect upon the surrounding neighborhood." It is alleged that he has admitted that he is not interested in whether the Cubs would benefit financially from such action because of his concern for the neighborhood, and that he would be willing for the team to play night games if a new stadium were built in Chicago.

Plaintiff alleges that the other defendant directors, with full knowledge of the foregoing matters, have acquiesced in the policy laid down by Wrigley and have permitted him to dominate the board of directors in matters involving the installation of lights and scheduling of night games, even though they knew he was not motivated by a good faith concern as to the best interests of defendant corporation, but solely by his personal views set forth above. It is charged that the directors are acting for a reason or reasons contrary and wholly unrelated to the business interests of the corporation; that such arbitrary and capricious acts constitute mismanagement and waste of corporate assets, and that the directors have been negligent in failing to exercise reasonable care and prudence in the management of the corporate affairs.

[1] The question on appeal is whether plaintiff's amended complaint states a cause of action. It is plaintiff's position that fraud, illegality and conflict of interest are not the only bases for a stockholder's derivative action against the directors. Contrariwise, defendants argue that the courts will not step in and interfere with honest business judgment of the directors unless there is a showing of fraud, illegality or conflict of interest.

The cases in this area are numerous and each differs from the others on a factual basis. However, the courts have pronounced certain ground rules which appear in all cases and which are then applied to the given factual situation. The court in Wheeler v. Pullman Iron and Steel Company, 143 Ill. 197, 207, 32 N.E. 420, 423, said:

"It is, however, fundamental in the law of corporations, that the majority of its stockholders shall control the policy of the corporation, and regulate and govern the lawful exercise of its franchise and business. * * * Every one purchasing or subscribing for stock in a corporation impliedly agrees that he will be bound by the acts and proceedings done or sanctioned by a majority of the shareholders, or by the agents of the corporation duly chosen by such majority, within the scope of the powers conferred by the charter, and courts of equity will not undertake to control the policy or business methods of a corporation, although it may be seen that a wiser policy might be adopted and the business more successful if other methods were pursued. The majority of shares of its stock, or the agents by the holders thereof lawfully chosen, must be permitted to control the business of the corporation in their discretion, when not in violation of its charter or some public law, or corruptly and fraudulently subversive of the rights and interests of the corporation or of a shareholder."

The standards set in Delaware are also clearly stated in the cases. In Davis v. Louisville Gas & Electric Co., 16 Del.Ch. 157, 142 A. 654, a minority shareholder sought to have the directors enjoined from amending the certificate of incorporation. The court said on page 659:

"We have then a conflict in view between the responsible managers of a corporation and an overwhelming majority of its stockholders on the one hand and a dissenting minority on the other—a conflict touching matters of business policy, such as. has occasioned innumerable applications to courts to intervene and determine which of the two conflicting views should prevail. The response which courts make to such applications is that it is not their function to resolve for corporations questions of policy and business management. The directors are chosen to pass upon such questions and their judgment *unless shown to be tainted with fraud* is accepted as final. The judgment of the directors of corporations enjoys the benefit of a presumption that it was formed in good faith and was designed to promote the best interests of the corporation they serve." (Emphasis supplied)

Similarly, the court in Toebelman v. Missouri-Kansas Pipe Line Co., D.C., 41 F. Supp. 334, said at page 339:

"The general legal principle involved is familiar. Citation of authorities is of limited value because the facts of each case differ so widely. Reference may be made to the statement of the rule in Helfman v. American Light & Traction Company, 121 N.J.Eq. 1, 187 A. 540, 550, in. which the Court stated the law as follows: 'In a purely business corporation * * * the authority of the directors in the conduct of the business of the corporation must be regarded as absolute when they act within the law, and the court is without authority to substitute its judgment for that of the directors.'"

Plaintiff argues that the allegations of his amended complaint are sufficient to set forth a cause of action under the principles set out in Dodge v. Ford Motor Co., 204 Mich. 459, 170 N.W. 668. In that case plaintiff, owner of about 10% of the outstanding stock, brought suit against the directors seeking payment of additional dividends and the enjoining of further business expansion. In ruling on the request for dividends the court indicated that the motives of Ford in keeping so much money in the corporation for expansion and security were to benefit the public generally and spread the profits out by means of more jobs, etc. The court felt that these were not only far from related to the good of the stockholders, but amounted to a change in the ends of the corporation and that this was not a purpose contemplated or allowed by the corporate charter. The court relied on language found in Hunter v. Roberts, Throp & Co., 83 Mich. 63, 47 N.W. 131, 134, wherein it was said:

"Courts of equity will not interfere in the management of the directors unless it is clearly made to appear that they are guilty of fraud or misappropriation of the corporate funds, or refuse to declare a dividend when the corporation has a surplus of net profits which it can, without detriment to its business, divide among its stockholders, and when a refusal to do so would amount to such an abuse of discretion as would constitute a fraud or breach of that good faith which they are bound to exercise toward the stockholders."

From the authority relied upon in that case it is clear that the court felt that there must be fraud or a breach of that good faith which directors are bound to exercise toward the stockholders in order to justify the courts entering into the internal affairs of corporations. This is made clear when the court refused to interfere with the directors decision to expand the business. The following appears on page 684 of 170 N.W.:

"We are not, however, persuaded that we should interfere with the proposed expansion of the business of the Ford Motor Company. In view of the fact that the selling price of products may be increased at any time, the ultimate results of the larger business cannot be certainly estimated. *The judges are not business experts.* It is recognized that plans must often be made for a long future, for expected competition, for a continuing as well as an immediately profitable venture. * * * We are not satisfied that the alleged motives of the directors, in so far as they are reflected in the conduct of business, menace the interests of the shareholders." (Emphasis supplied)

Plaintiff in the instant case argues that the directors are acting for reasons unrelated to the financial interest and welfare of the Cubs. However, we are not satisfied that the motives assigned to Philip K. Wrigley, and through him to the other directors, are contrary to the best interests of the corporation and the stockholders. For example, it appears to us that the effect on the surrounding neighborhood might well be considered by a director who was considering the patrons who would or would not attend the games if the park were in a poor neighborhood. Furthermore, the long run interest of the corporation in its property value at Wrigley Field might demand all efforts to keep the neighborhood from deteriorating. By these thoughts we do not mean to say that we have decided that the decision of the directors was a correct one. That is beyond our jurisdiction and ability. We are merely saying that the decision is one properly before directors and the motives alleged in the amended complaint showed no fraud,

illegality or conflict of interest in their making of that decision.

[2] While all the courts do not insist that one or more of the three elements must be present for a stockholder's derivative action to lie, nevertheless we feel that unless the conduct of the defendants at least borders on one of the elements, the courts should not interfere. The trial court in the instant case acted properly in dismissing plaintiff's amended complaint.

[3-5] We feel that plaintiff's amended complaint was also defective in failing to allege damage to the corporation. The well pleaded facts must be taken as true for the purpose of judging the sufficiency of the amended complaint. (Highway Insurance Co. v. Korman, 40 Ill.App.2d 439, 442, 190 N.E.2d 124.) However, one need not accept conclusions drawn by the pleader. (Nagel v. Northern Illinois Gas Co., 12 Ill.App.2d 413, 420, 139 N.E.2d 810.) Furthermore, pleadings will be construed most strongly against the pleader prior to a verdict or judgment on the merits. New Amsterdam Casualty Co. v. Gerin, 9 Ill.App. 2d 545, 133 N.E.2d 723.

There is no allegation that the night games played by the other nineteen teams enhanced their financial position or that the profits, if any, of those teams were directly related to the number of night games scheduled. There is an allegation that the installation of lights and scheduling of night games in Wrigley Field would have resulted in large amounts of additional revenues and incomes from increased attendance and related sources of income. Further, the cost of installation of lights, funds for which are allegedly readily available by financing, would be more than offset and recaptured by increased revenues. However, no allegation is made that there will be a net benefit to the corporation from such action, considering all increased costs.

Plaintiff claims that the losses of defendant corporation are due to poor attendance at home games. However, it appears from the amended complaint, taken as a whole, that factors other than attendance affect the net earnings or losses. For example, in 1962, attendance at home and road games decreased appreciably as compared with 1961, and yet the loss from direct baseball operation and of the whole corporation was considerably less.

The record shows that plaintiff did not feel he could allege that the increased revenues would be sufficient to cure the corporate deficit. The only cost plaintiff was at all concerned with was that of installation of lights. No mention was made of operation and maintenance of the lights or other possible increases in operating costs of night games and we cannot speculate as to what other factors might influence the increase or decrease of profits if the Cubs were to play night home games.

[6]   Nagel v. Northern Illinois Gas Co., supra, was a stockholder's derivative action for the recission of a contract of the corporation. The court said on page 421 of 12 Ill.App.2d, on page 815 of 139 N.E.2d:

"They allege that by these transactions 'Edison gave to Northern assets, rights and benefits of a value in excess of $5,000,000' and received in return, under the Final Separation Contract, assets, rights and benefits of a net value of less than $50,000. These allegations are mere conclusions of the pleader and not an averment of the fact of gross inadequacy of consideration, unless warranted by the provisions of the contract and the well pleaded facts in the amended complaint consistent with the contract."

Similarly, in the instant case, plaintiff's allegation that the minority stockholders and the corporation have been seriously and irreparably damaged by the wrongful conduct of the defendant directors is a mere conclusion and not based on well pleaded facts in the amended complaint.

[7, 8]   Finally, we do not agree with plaintiff's contention that failure to follow the example of the other major league clubs in scheduling night games constituted negligence. Plaintiff made no allegation that these teams' night schedules were profitable or that the purpose for which night baseball had been undertaken was fulfilled. Furthermore, it cannot be said that directors, even those of corporations that are losing money, must follow the lead of the other corporations in the field. Directors are elected for their business capabilities and judgment and the courts cannot require them to forego their judgment because of the decisions of directors of other companies. Courts may not decide these questions in the absence of a clear showing of dereliction of duty on the part of the specific directors and mere failure to "follow the crowd" is not such a dereliction.

For the foregoing reasons the order of dismissal entered by the trial court is affirmed.

Affirmed.

DEMPSEY, P. J., and SCHWARTZ, J., concur.

108 Ill.2d 357
91 Ill.Dec. 610

The **CHICAGO NATIONAL LEAGUE BALL CLUB, INC.,** Appellant,

v.

James R. **THOMPSON,** Governor, et al., Appellees.

No. 61630.

Supreme Court of Illinois.

Oct. 3, 1985.

---

Don H. Reuben, William J. Campbell, Jr., Samuel Fifer, Steven A. Weiss, Eileen A. Kamerick, Reuben & Proctor and Lawrence Gunnels, Chicago, for plaintiff-appellant.

James D. Montgomery, Corp. Counsel of City of Chicago, Chicago, (Philip L. Bronstein, Chief Asst. Corp. Counsel, Mary K. Rochford and Lynn K. Mitchell, Asst. Corp. Counsel, of counsel), for City of Chicago, defendant-appellee.

Neil F. Hartigan, Atty. Gen., Jill Wine-Banks, Sol. Gen. (Michael J. Hayes, Director of Advocacy Divisions, Russell R. Eggert, Administrative Asst. to the Atty. Gen., Chicago, of counsel), for defendant-appellee Governor Thompson.

Alan R. Borlack, Chicago, (Malcolm H. Brooks, Stewart H. Diamond, Robert J. Krull and Richard M. Lipton, Chicago, of counsel), for defendant-intervenor-appellee.

WARD, Justice.

The Chicago National League Ball Club, Inc., is a corporation which owns and operates the Chicago Cubs, the major league baseball team, and the Cubs' home ball park, Wrigley Field. On December 19, 1984, the corporation (the Cubs) filed a complaint in the circuit court of Cook County seeking a declaratory judgment that a 1982 amendment to the Environmental Protection Act (Ill.Rev.Stat.1983, ch. 111½, par. 1025) and a Chicago city ordinance (Chicago Municipal Code sec. 104.1–14.1)

violate the separation-of-powers constitutional provisions, the State and Federal assurances of due process and equal protection (U.S. Const., amend. XIV; Ill. Const. 1970, art. I, sec. 2), and the special-legislation clause of the Constitution of Illinois (Ill. Const.1970, art. IV, sec. 13). The Cubs asked that the Governor of Illinois, James R. Thompson, be enjoined from enforcing the statutory amendment, which makes certain nighttime professional sporting events subject to the nighttime-noise-emission regulations of the Pollution Control Board, against Wrigley Field, and the city of Chicago from enforcing the ordinance, which prohibits night athletic contests and other amusements at certain stadia, against the Cubs' ball park. The Lake View Citizens Council (LVCC), a nonprofit corporation composed of individuals who reside and certain organizations which are active in the community surrounding Wrigley Field, was granted leave to intervene as a defendant in support of the statute and ordinance. On March 25, 1985, the circuit court, after argument on motions by the Cubs and by the LVCC for judgment on the pleadings, held the statute and ordinance to be reasonable exercises of the police power. The court granted the motion of defendant-intervenor LVCC and entered judgment for the Governor, the city of Chicago and the LVCC. We allowed motions of LVCC and the city for a direct appeal to this court under our Rule 302(b) (87 Ill.2d R. 302(b)).

The statute, which amends title VI, section 25, of the Environmental Protection Act, provides:

"The [Pollution Control] Board shall, by regulations under this Section, categorize the types and sources of noise emissions that unreasonably interfere with the enjoyment of life, or with any lawful business, or activity, and shall prescribe for each such category the maximum permissible limits on such noise emissions. * * *

　　*　　*　　*　　*　　*　　*

No Board standards for monitoring noise or regulations prescribing limitations on noise emissions shall apply to any organized amateur or professional sporting activity except as otherwise provided in this Section. Baseball, football or soccer sporting events played during nighttime hours, by professional athletes, in a city with more than 1,000,000 inhabitants, in a stadium at which such nighttime events were not played prior to July 1, 1982, shall be subject to nighttime noise emission regulations promulgated by the Illinois Pollution Control Board." Ill.Rev.Stat.1983, ch. 111½, par. 1025.

The provisions of the Chicago ordinance are:

"It shall be unlawful for any licensee or other person, firm, corporation or other legal entity to produce, present or permit any other person, firm, corporation, or other legal entity to produce or present any athletic contest, sport, game or any other amusement as defined in Chapter 104, if any part of such athletic contest, sport, game or any other amusement as defined in Chapter 104 takes place between the hours of 8:00 p.m. and 8:00 a.m., and is presented in a stadium or playing field which is not totally enclosed and contains more than 15,000 seats where any such seats are located within 500 feet of 100 or more dwelling units." Chicago Municipal Code sec. 104.1–14.1.

The Cubs challenge the constitutionality of the statute, apparently considering that night baseball games at Wrigley Field would violate the nighttime-noise-emission regulations of the Pollution Control Board. Those regulations are codified in the Illinois Administrative Code. (35 Ill.Adm. Code sec. 901.) The parties, however, are agreed that the ordinance would have the effect of prohibiting night games at Wrigley Field. Wrigley Field is located on the north side of Chicago in the Lake View area. The park is bordered by Sheffield, Waveland, Seminary, Addison and Clark streets. It was built in 1914 and has served as the exclusive home playing field of the Chicago Cubs since 1926. It is an open-air ball park with a seating capacity of slightly over 37,000, and it is the only

park in the major leagues that, because it does not have lights, does not have night games. In the 1984 season, the Cubs played 81 games at Wrigley Field.

The area surrounding Wrigley Field is predominately residential, with some light industry to the south and west of the ball park. Most of the buildings in the area are multi-unit dwellings, which gives Lake View a highly concentrated population. There are no expressways in close proximity to Wrigley Field to accommodate the influx of spectators on days when games are played at the field, and there are few off-street parking facilities in the area. In general, only the neighborhood streets are available for parking.

The Cubs first argue that the statute and ordinance violate the separation-of-powers principle and deprive the Cubs of their right to due process by "declaring as law the conclusive presumption that night baseball at Wrigley Field alone constitutes a private nuisance." The Cubs say that this determination should only be made by means of a civil suit where allegations of a private nuisance would be brought by an aggrieved party, and the Cubs given rights to discovery, cross-examination and an opportunity to defend.

[1] It is clear that the legislature has broad discretion to determine not only what the public interest and welfare require, but to determine the measures needed to secure such interest. (*People v. McCarty* (1981), 86 Ill.2d 247, 253, 56 Ill.Dec. 67, 427 N.E.2d 147; *Tometz v. Board of Education* (1968), 39 Ill.2d 593, 600, 237 N.E.2d 498; *Thillens, Inc. v. Morey* (1957), 11 Ill.2d 579, 593, 144 N.E.2d 735.) Here the legislature amended section 25 of the Environmental Protection Act to establish guidelines for protecting the interests, including property interests, of residents who live near stadia from intolerable noise from nighttime sporting events. In *Rockford Drop Forge Co. v. Pollution Control Board* (1980), 79 Ill.2d 271, 37 Ill.Dec. 600, 402 N.E.2d 602, this court stated:

"The objectives stated in section 25 may reflect in general terms the same concerns as those which underlie the common law. The legislative purpose, however, was to vindicate those concerns through a comprehensive regulatory system. Such an approach might well be thought to require that noise be limited on the basis of an objective, quantitative standard, rather than by its qualitative impact upon a particular affected individual as would be done under the common law method." 79 Ill.2d 271, 280, 37 Ill. Dec. 600, 402 N.E.2d 602. See also *Illinois Coal Operators Association v. Pollution Control Board* (1974), 59 Ill.2d 305, 319 N.E.2d 782.

The city of Chicago as well has, under the home rule provisions, the constitutional authority to regulate, through the police power, for the protection of the public health, safety, morals, and welfare. (Ill. Const.1970, art. VII, sec. 6(a).) Too, the city council has been given the specific statutory authority to define and abate public nuisances. Ill.Rev.Stat.1983, ch. 24, pars. 11–60–2, 21–20.

[2] The Cubs contend also that the classifications made by the legislature and city council do not define a public nuisance. They say that because the enactments apply only to Wrigley Field, the classifications are a legislative attempt to correct a private nuisance. The determination of whether land use constitutes a private nuisance, and whether the nuisance should be abated, the Cubs argue, are judicial questions. It is true that a private nuisance is a civil wrong involving a disturbance of an individual's rights and that its abatement rests with the person or persons whose rights have been disturbed. A private nuisance, however, that interferes with public rights can also constitute a public nuisance. *Village of Wilsonville v. SCA Services, Inc.* (1981), 86 Ill.2d 1, 21–22, 55 Ill.Dec. 499, 426 N.E.2d 824; Prosser, Torts sec. 88, at 572–73 (4th ed. 1971).

[3] The enactments here were within the power and judgment of the legislature and city council. They were designed and enacted for the proper purpose of providing against a specific public nuisance and protecting the public against that nuisance.

In a related argument the Cubs contend that Wrigley Field is the only stadium affected by the statute and ordinance, and therefore the enactments violate the State and Federal equal protection clauses and the provision of the Constitution of Illinois prohibiting special legislation. They say that the legislative classifications serve to impose a burden on Wrigley Field but, contrary to the constitutional guarantees, do not subject other sports and entertainment enterprises to the same restrictions.

To support this contention, the Cubs would have us consider comments made in the legislature and city council which the Cubs say sustain their claim that the motive for enacting the statute and ordinance was to prohibit night games at Wrigley Field only and not at other stadia or parks. The contention, however, even if gratuitously assumed to be true, does not have legislative relevance. The plaintiff does not charge that either enactment is ambiguous and the legislative intention unclear. When the language of a statute or ordinance is clear courts will give effect to the legislation without resort to unnecessary means of statutory interpretation, such as comments by legislators. *People v. Singleton* (1984), 103 Ill.2d 339, 341, 82 Ill Dec. 666, 469 N.E.2d 200.

[4–6] To be constitutional, the Cubs argue, the enactments would have to apply equally to all stadia in the State and not have exclusive application to Wrigley Field. But, of course, the equal protection clauses of our constitution and of the Constitution of the United States do not require uniform treatment in legislative classifications for all persons. (*City of New Orleans v. Dukes* (1976), 427 U.S. 297, 96 S.Ct. 2513, 49 L.Ed.2d 511; *Friedman & Rochester, Ltd. v. Walsh* (1977), 67 Ill.2d 413, 418, 10 Ill.Dec. 559, 367 N.E.2d 1325.) That other stadia in the State might have been, but were not, affected by the legislation is not decisive on whether the legislation was intended to apply to Wrigley Field only, particularly when any stadia constructed in the future will have to comply with the legislation. The legislature need not choose between legislating against all evils of the same kind or not legislating at all. Instead it may choose to address itself to what it perceives to be the most acute need. (*Tometz v. Board of Education* (1968), 39 Ill.2d 593, 601–02, 237 N.E.2d 498; *Rockford Drop Forge Co. v. Pollution Control Board* (1980), 79 Ill.2d 271, 281, 37 Ill.Dec. 600, 402 N.E.2d 602.) An entire remedial scheme will not be invalidated " 'simply because it failed, through inadvertence or otherwise, to cover every evil that might conceivably have been attacked.' " *Friedman & Rochester, Ltd. v. Walsh* (1977), 67 Ill.2d 413, 421–22, 10 Ill.Dec. 559, 367 N.E.2d 1325, quoting *McDonald v. Board of Election Commissioners* (1969), 394 U.S. 802, 809, 89 S.Ct. 1404, 1409, 22 L.Ed.2d 739, 746.

[7–9] The provision in the Constitution of Illinois prohibiting special legislation states: "The General Assembly shall pass no special or local law when a general law is or can be made applicable. Whether a general law is or can be made applicable shall be a matter of judicial determination." (Ill. Const.1970, art. IV, sec. 13.) Special legislation confers a special benefit or privilege on a person or group of persons to the exclusion of others similarly situated. It discriminates in favor of a select group without a sound, reasonable basis. (*Fireside Chrysler-Plymouth, Mazda, Inc. v. Edgar* (1984), 102 Ill.2d 1, 4, 79 Ill.Dec. 677, 464 N.E.2d 275 citing *Illinois Polygraph Society v. Pellicano* (1980), 83 Ill.2d 130, 137, 46 Ill.Dec. 574, 414 N.E.2d 458.) A denial of equal protection, on the other hand, is different. It is an arbitrary and invidious discrimination that results when government withholds from a person or class of persons a right, benefit or privilege without a reasonable basis for the governmental action. (*Jenkins v. Wu* (1984), 102 Ill.2d 468, 477, 82 Ill.Dec. 382, 468 N.E.2d 1162.) Legislation which confers a benefit on one class and denies the same to another may be attacked both as special legislation and as a denial of equal protection (*Wilson v. All-Steel, Inc.* (1981), 87 Ill.2d

28, 56 Ill.Dec. 897, 428 N.E.2d 489), but under either ground for challenge it is the duty of courts to decide whether classifications are unreasonable (*Illinois Polygraph Society v. Pellicano* (1980), 83 Ill.2d 130, 46 Ill.Dec. 574, 414 N.E.2d 458). Though the constitutional protections involved are not identical, a claim that the special-legislation provision has been violated is generally judged by the same standard that is used in considering a claim that equal protection has been denied. *Illinois Housing Development Authority v. Van Meter* (1980), 82 Ill.2d 116, 123, 45 Ill.Dec. 18, 412 N.E.2d 151; *Friedman & Rochester, Ltd. v. Walsh* (1977), 67 Ill.2d 413, 422, 10 Ill.Dec. 559, 367 N.E.2d 1325.

[10–14] Unless legislation operates to the disadvantage of a suspect classification or infringes upon a fundamental right, the legislation, to be upheld as constitutional, must simply bear a rational relationship to a legitimate governmental interest. (*Illinois Housing Development Authority v. Van Meter* (1980), 82 Ill.2d 116, 119–20, 45 Ill.Dec. 18, 412 N.E.2d 151; *San Antonio Independent School District v. Rodriguez* (1973), 411 U.S. 1, 93 S.Ct. 1278, 36 L.Ed.2d 16; *Dandridge v. Williams* (1970), 397 U.S. 471, 90 S.Ct. 1153, 25 L.Ed.2d 491.) It is clear that in the exercise of the police power, government may act to regulate, restrain or prohibit that which is harmful to the public welfare even though the regulation, restraint or prohibition might interfere with the liberty or property of an individual. (*People v. Warren* (1957), 11 Ill.2d 420, 424–25, 143 N.E.2d 28; *City of Carbondale v. Brewster* (1979), 78 Ill.2d 111, 34 Ill.Dec. 838, 398 N.E.2d 829.) There is a presumption in favor of the validity of any legislation, including of course a legislative act enacted under the police power. (*People v. Brown* (1983), 98 Ill.2d 374, 75 Ill.Dec. 216, 457 N.E.2d 6; *Illinois Gamefowl Breeders Association v. Block* (1979), 75 Ill.2d 443, 453, 27 Ill.Dec. 465, 389 N.E.2d 529.) The burden of showing legislation to be an unreasonable exercise of the police power is on the party challenging it. (*Tometz v. Board of Edu-*

*cation* (1968), 39 Ill.2d 593, 237 N.E.2d 498.) When a classification under a statute is called into question, if any state of facts can reasonably be conceived to sustain the classification, the existence of that state of facts at the time the statute was enacted must be assumed. *Thillens, Inc. v. Morey* (1957), 11 Ill.2d 579, 594, 144 N.E.2d 735.

The declared purpose of title VI of the Environmental Protection Act is "to prevent noise which creates a public nuisance." (Ill.Rev.Stat.1983, ch. 111½, par. 1023.) Forming a background to the legislation we consider here, section 25 directs the Pollution Control Board to "categorize the types and sources of noise emissions that unreasonably interfere with the enjoyment of life, or with any lawful business, or activity, and shall prescribe for each such category the maximum permissible limits on such noise emissions." (Ill.Rev. Stat.1983, ch. 111½, par. 1025.) The purpose of this amendment to the Act was to protect, within the comprehensive regulatory scheme, the property and other rights of residents who live near stadia by making the nighttime use of the stadia subject to the regulations of the Pollution Control Board. (See *Rockford Drop Forge Co. v. Pollution Control Board* (1980), 79 Ill.2d 271, 37 Ill.Dec. 600, 402 N.E.2d 602.) We consider that the classifications in the statute are reasonably related to this purpose.

Only stadia in cities with more than one million inhabitants are subject to the regulations. Chicago is the only city in our State that has a population of more than one million. A legislative classification based upon population will be sustained "where founded on a rational difference of situation or condition existing in the persons or objects upon which [the classification] rests and there is a reasonable basis for the classification in view of the objects and purposes to be accomplished." (*People v. Palkes* (1972), 52 Ill.2d 472, 477, 288 N.E.2d 469, quoting *Du Bois v. Gibbons* (1954), 2 Ill.2d 392, 118 N.E.2d 295.) Considering the terms of this amendment, there is a rationally founded difference between a less populous city and a city with a greater population. It might be reasonably

anticipated that in a typical urban setting more people would be affected in the larger city by the noise from spectators in a stadium for a nighttime event. The problems attending a densely populated area would be exacerbated: limited areas for parking would become overburdened; neighborhood streets would become busier and thus potentially more dangerous to residents of the area and their children; and thoroughfares to and from the area would become more congested. Too, a rational basis may be found in the concern that there would be less open space in an area with a highly concentrated population that could serve as a buffer zone against the noise generated.

The same considerations serve as a proper basis for the distinction made by the legislature between nighttime and daytime sporting events. The General Assembly well might have concluded that the evening hours are traditionally spent in restful and quieter pursuits and should be protected by closer regulation. More residents would be at home during the evening hours, and there are variations in traffic patterns and in police patrol deployment between night and day hours which might have served as reasonable considerations by the legislature in enacting the statute. See *Gibbons v. City of Chicago* (1966), 34 Ill.2d 102, 108, 214 N.E.2d 740 (incidence of crime is a reasonable legislative concern for ordinance prohibiting night operation of self-service laundry); *People ex rel. Skokie Town House Builders, Inc. v. Village of Morton Grove* (1959), 16 Ill.2d 183, 157 N.E.2d 33 (traffic conditions considered in zoning ordinance which excludes future residences from industrial area).

[15] The amendment distinguishes between professional and amateur sporting events. Amateur sports generally have shorter seasons than their professional counterparts and often attract fewer spectators. There also is a widely entertained opinion that amateur athletics benefit the public, and the legislature may therefore have decided to limit the applicability of the statute to professional sports, which are

profit-oriented enterprises. Finally, a provision exempts stadia where nighttime events were held prior to July 1, 1982. A legislature may, if it finds remedial measures necessary, address problems one step at a time. "The legislature may select one phase of one field and apply a remedy there, neglecting the others." (*Williamson v. Lee Optical of Oklahoma, Inc.* (1955), 348 U.S. 483, 489, 75 S.Ct. 461, 465, 99 L.Ed. 563, 573.) We are unwilling to strike down as constitutionally infirm a classification because the legislature may have chosen to regulate expectant interests and not established interests. *Minnesota v. Clover Leaf Creamery Co.* (1981), 449 U.S. 456, 466, 101 S.Ct. 715, 725, 66 L.Ed.2d 659, 670; *Katzenbach v. Morgan* (1966), 384 U.S. 641, 86 S.Ct. 1717, 16 L.Ed.2d 828.

[16] An ordinance adopted by the governing body of a city must satisfy the same requirement of reasonableness that is applicable to statutes enacted by the General Assembly. (*City of Carbondale v. Brewster* (1979), 78 Ill.2d 111, 115, 34 Ill.Dec. 838, 398 N.E.2d 829.) Here the ordinance distinguishes between the hours of use, whether the stadia are open-air or enclosed, the seating capacity of the stadia and the proximity to dwelling units. As we observed earlier in discussing the statute, a regulatory scheme intended to abate public nuisances may reasonably distinguish between the hours of permissible use of land when that use may operate to interfere with property and other rights of the community. The distinction between open-air stadia and enclosed stadia may be rationally based on the different volumes of decibels of noise coming from open and enclosed stadia. The noise from an enclosed stadium is muted and less intrusive on area residents.

[17–19] The city council established 500 feet as the required distance between a stadium and the nearest dwelling unit. There is, of course, a reasonable relationship between the distance from the source of noise and the effect that the noise will have on the surrounding community. The city council also decided to restrict the ordi-

nance's reach to stadia with seating capacities in excess of 15,000. The noise from smaller stadia with fewer spectators would not have the same intrusive effect on a neighborhood as the noise from larger stadia. The discretion of the council to create legislative classifications includes the authority to set permissible boundaries. The creation of classifications is for the judgment of the legislature, and their amendment or modification is not for courts to decide. (*Thillens, Inc. v. Morey* (1957), 11 Ill.2d 579, 593, 144 N.E.2d 735.) Classifications are not required to be precise, accurate or harmonious so long as they accomplish the legislative purpose. *Illinois Housing Development Authority v. Van Meter* (1980), 82 Ill.2d 116, 123, 45 Ill.Dec. 18, 412 N.E.2d 151; *Schiller Park Colonial Inn, Inc. v. Berz* (1976), 63 Ill.2d 499, 512, 349 N.E.2d 61.

[20] Simply, the Cubs have failed to meet the burden of showing the unconstitutionality of the legislative actions.

Accordingly the judgment of the circuit court is affirmed.

*Judgment affirmed.*

# PART 9

## TRIPLE-A MATERIAL

In life and in baseball one has to make choices. Each major league team has no more than twenty-four players. We as editors only have room for a limited number of articles and cases in this book. Many deserving contenders were cut at the last minute. We present for you our Triple-A articles and cases, both promising youngsters waiting for their big break and grizzled veterans looking for one more chance at glory. The dedicated student of baseball and the law may wish to consult these additional materials on the subjects that we have covered in the book.

Much relevant and amusing material has been omitted or overlooked in the making of this volume, and new material is being generated by lawyers, judges, and law professors everyday. If you know of other enlightening or entertaining law and baseball articles, please bring them to our attention. Perhaps a second volume will be indicated.

### ANTITRUST

Michael S. Jacobs and Ralph K. Winter, "Antitrust Principles and Collective Bargaining by Athletes: Of Superstars in Peonage," 81 Yale L.J. 1 (1971).

*Fleer v. Topps*, 501 F.Supp. 485 (E.D. Pa. 1980). Antitrust consequences of exclusive contract for baseball cards.

*Radovich v. National Football League*, 352 U.S. 445 (1957). Football is not baseball, and therefore not entitled to antitrust immunity.

*National League of Professional Baseball Clubs v. Federal Baseball Club of Baltimore, Inc.*, 269 F. 681 (D.C. Cir. 1921). Lower court opinion leading to Supreme Court's *Federal Baseball* decision immunizing baseball from the reach of the antitrust laws.

## Labor

Note, "A Critical Perspective on Baseball's Collusion Decisions," 1 *Seton Hall Journal of Sport Law* 109 (1991).

"Baseball Law," *Law Notes* 207 (February 1914). Surveying early labor cases.

*Weeghman v. Killifer*, 215 F. 289 (6th Cir. 1914). Denying owners of Chicago Federal league franchise temporary restraining order to prevent player from changing clubs.

*Rose v. Giamatti*, 721 F.Supp. 906, 924 (S.D. Ohio 1989). Should be self-explanatory for any serious baseball fan.

Basic Agreement between the American League of Professional Baseball Clubs and the National League of National Baseball Clubs and Major League Baseball Players Association, Effective January 1, 1990. Most recent collective bargaining agreement for major league baseball prior to 1994 strike, available from the offices of Major League Baseball.

## Intellectual Property

Bruce H. Little, "Who Owns That Picture (And Other Issues for the Next Players' Strike)," 7 *Minneapolis Review of Baseball* 4 (No. 4 1988).

Shelley Ross Saxer, *"Baltimore Orioles, Inc. v. Major League Baseball Players Association:* The Right of Publicity in Game Performances and Federal Copyright Preemption," 36 *U.C.L.A. L. Rev.* 861 (1989).

## Tort

*Yates v. Chicago National League Base Ball Club, Inc.*, 230 Ill App. 3d 472, 595 N.E.2d 570 (1st Dist. 1992). Fan recovers damages for injuries from foul ball when struck while sitting in improperly screened area behind home plate in Wrigley Field.

## General

*Baseball and the Law, Total Baseball* (Harper Perrenial, New York, New York 1993).

Gerald W. Scully, *The Business of Major League Baseball* (University of Chicago Press, Chicago, Illinois 1989).

Donald J. Rapson, "A 'Home Run' Application of Established Principles of Statutory Construction: U.C.C. Analogies," 5 *Cardozo L. Rev.* 441 (1984).

# Acknowledgments

Aside. "The Common Law Origins of the Infield Fly Rule." *University of Pennsylvania Law Review* 123 (1975): 1474–81. Reprinted with the permission of the *University of Pennsylvania Law Review* and Fred B. Rothman & Company. (Copyright 1975 by the University of Pennsylvania.) Courtesy of Yale University Law Library.

Flynn, John J. "Further Aside: A Comment on 'The Common Law Origins of The Infield Fly Rule.'" *Journal of Contemporary Law* 4 (1978): 241–7. Reprinted with the permission of the *Journal of Contemporary Law*. Courtesy of Yale University Law Library.

Cochran, Mark W. "The Infield Fly Rule and the Internal Revenue Code: An Even Further Aside." *William and Mary Law Review* 29 (1988): 567–77. Reprinted with the permission of the College of William and Mary. Courtesy of Yale University Law Library.

Berger, Margaret A. "Rethinking the Applicability of Evidentiary Rules at Sentencing: Of Relevant Conduct and Hearsay and the Need for an Infield Fly Rule." *Federal Sentencing Reporter* 5 (1992): 96–97, 99–100. Reprinted with the permission of the University of California Press. Courtesy of Yale University Law Library.

Finkelstein, Jared Tobin. "*In re Brett*: The Sticky Problem of Statutory Construction." *Fordham Law Review* 52 (1983): 430–40. Reprinted with the permission of the *Fordham Law Review*. Courtesy of Yale University Law Library.

Clancy, Christopher H., and Jonathan A. Weiss. "A Pine Tar Gloss on Quasi-Legal Images." *Cardozo Law Review* 5 (1984): 411–40. Reprinted with the permission of the *Cardozo Law Review*. Courtesy of Yale University Law Library.

*Federal Baseball Club of Baltimore v. National League of Professional Baseball Clubs.* U.S. Reports 259 (1922): 200, 207–9. Courtesy of Yale University Law Library.

*Gardella v. Chandler. Federal Reporter* Second Series 172 (1949): 402–15. Courtesy of Yale University Law Library.

*Toolson v. New York Yankees. U.S. Reports* 346 (1953): 356–57. Courtesy of Yale University Law Library.

"Conclusions." Organized Baseball: Report of the Subcommittee on Study of Monopoly Power, House Committee on the Judiciary, 82nd Congress, 1st Session on H. Res. 95 (1952): 228–32. Courtesy of Yale University Seeley G. Mudd Library.

Statement of Casey Stengel, Manager of the New York Yankees. Organized Professional Team Sports Hearings before the Subcommittee on Antitrust and Monopoly, Senate Committee on the Judiciary, 85th Congress, 2nd Session persuant to S. Res. 231 (1958): 11–24. Courtesy of Yale University Seeley G. Mudd Library.

*Salerno v. American League of Professional Baseball Clubs. Federal Reporter* Second Series 429 (1970): 1003–5. Courtesy of Yale University Law Library.

*Flood v. Kuhn. Supreme Court Reporter* 92 (1972): 2099–2119. Courtesy of Yale University Law Library.

*Finley v. Kuhn. Federal Reporter* Second Series 569 (1978): 527, 530–541. Courtesy of Yale University Law Library.

Ross, Stephen F. "Preserving Baseball's Antitrust Exemption: Interview with Professor Gary Roberts." *Antitrust* 7 (1993): 17–21. Reprinted with the permission of the American Bar Association. Courtesy of *Antitrust*.

Waller, Spencer Weber, and Neil B. Cohen. "Run Baseball Just Like Any Other Business? That's the Last Thing the Owners Should Want." *Elysian Fields Quarterly* 12 (1994). Reprinted with the permission of the *Elysian Fields Quarterly*. Courtesy of *Elysian Fields Quarterly*.

*American League Baseball Club v. Chase. Miscellaneous Reports* 86 (1914): 441–67. Courtesy of Yale University Law Library.

*Philadelphia Ball Club v. Lajoie. Pennsylvania Reports* 202 (1902): 210, 214–222. Courtesy of Yale University Law Library.

*Metropolitan Exhibition Company v. Ward. Abbott's New Cases* 24 (1890): 393, 407–419. Courtesy of Yale University Law Library.

*Metropolitan Exhibition Co. v. Ewing. Federal Reporter* 42 (1890): 198–205. Courtesy of Yale University Law Library.

M.L.C. "Baseball and the Law—Yesterday and Today." *Virginia Law Review* 32 (1946): 1164–77. Reprinted with the permission of the University of Virginia, School of Law. Courtesy of Yale University Law Library.

McCormick, Robert A. "Baseball's Third Strike: The Triumph of Collective Bargaining in Professional Baseball." *Vanderbilt Law Review* 35 (1982): 1131–38, 1150–69. Reprinted with the permission of Vanderbilt University, copyright holder. Courtesy of Yale University Law Library.

Rosenberg, Norm. "When the Commissioner Was the Law *or* When Czardom Was in Flower." *Minneapolis Review of Baseball* 21 (1988): 21–26. Reprinted with the permission of the author. Courtesy of Spencer Weber Waller.

Cozzillio, Michael J. "From the Land of Bondage: The Greening of Major League Baseball Players and the Major League Baseball Players Association." *Catholic University Law Review* 41 (1991): 117–48. Reprinted with the permission of the *Catholic University Law Review*. Courtesy of Yale University Law Library.

Ayers, Deanne L. "Random Urinalysis: Violating the Athlete's Individual Rights?" *Howard Law Journal* 30 (1987): 93–96, 109–115. Reprinted with the permission of the Howard University School of Law. Courtesy of Yale University Law Library.

Uniform Player's Contract, the National League of Professional Baseball Clubs. Courtesy of Spencer Weber Waller.

*Piazza v. Major League Baseball. Trade Cases* (CCH) 1993–2 70,315 (1993): 70,633–36, 70,644–50. Courtesy of Spencer Weber Waller.

Jarvis, Robert M. "When the Lawyers Slept: The Unmaking of the Brooklyn Dodgers." *Cornell Law Review* 74 (1989): 347–357. Reprinted with the permission of *Cornell Law Review*. Copyright 1989 by Cornell University. All rights reserved. Courtesy of the *Cornell Law Review*.

Garrett, Robert Alan, and Philip R. Hochberg. "Sports Broadcasting and the Law." *Indiana Law Journal* 59 (1984): 155–161. Copyright (1984) by the Trustees of Indiana University. Reprinted by permission. Courtesy of Yale University Law Library.

*Major League Baseball Properties v. Sed Non Olet Denarius. Federal Supplement* 817 (1993): 1103, 1108–1136. Courtesy of Yale University Law Library.

*Pittsburgh Athletic Co. v. KQV Broadcasting Co. Federal Supplement* 24 (1938): 490–94. Courtesy of Yale University Law Library.

Buxton, Joseph T., Jr. "Baseball and the Law." *Law Notes* 35 (1931): 90–93. Courtesy of Yale University Law Library.

*Maytnier v. Rush. North Eastern Reporter* Second Series 225 (1967): 83, 85–91. Courtesy of Yale University Law Library.

*Marlowe v. Rush-Henrietta Central School District. Appellate Division Reports* Second Series 167 (1991): 820–2. Courtesy of Yale University Law Library.

Fish, Stanley. "Dennis Martinez and the Uses of Theory." *Yale Law Journal* 96 (1987): 1773–79, 1800. Reprinted by permission of The Yale Law Journal Company and Fred B. Rothman & Company. Courtesy of Yale University Law Library.

Laurence, Robert. "On Eurocentric Myopia, the Designated Hitter Rule and 'The Actual State of Things.'" *Arizona Law Review* 30 (1988): 459–65. Copyright (1988) by the Arizona Board of Regents. Reprinted by permission. Courtesy of Yale University Law Library.

Cover, Robert M. "Your Law-Baseball Quiz." *New York Times* April 5, 1979. Reprinted with the permission of the *New York Times*. Courtesy of Yale University Sterling Memorial Library.

Goldsmith, Sandra. "What Do Babe Ruth and John Marshall Have in Common?" *Student Lawyer* 21 (1993): 6–7. Reprinted with the permission of the American Bar Association. Courtesy of *Student Lawyer*.

Boyer, Allen. "*The Great Gatsby*, the Black Sox, High Finance, and American Law." *Michigan Law Review* 88 (1989): 328–42. Reprinted with the permission of the Michigan Law Review Association. Courtesy of Yale University Law Library.

Lempert, Richard. "Error Behind the Plate and in the Law." *Southern California Law Review* 59 (1986): 407–22. Reprinted with the permission of the *Southern California Law Review*. Courtesy of Yale University Law Library.

Brill, Howard W. "Baseball and the Legal Profession." *Arkansas Law Notes* (1990): 81–83. Reprinted with the permission of the *Arkansas Law Notes*. Courtesy of *Arkansas Law Notes*.

Neuborne, Burt. "Letter to the Editor, Simplified Voir Dire." *New York Times* May 25, 1983. Reprinted with the permission of the

*New York Times.* Courtesy of Yale University Sterling Memorial Library.

LeBel, Paul A. "The Bases Are Loaded and It's Time to Get a Restraining Order: The Confounding Conflation of America's Two National Pastimes." *Nova Law Review* 17 (1993): 813–16. Reprinted with the permission of the *Nova Law Review*. Courtesy of *Nova Law Review*.

Verrone, Patric M. "The All-Supreme-Court-Opinion Baseball Team." *Nova Law Review* 17 (1993): 933–34. Reprinted with the permission of the *Nova Law Review*. Courtesy of *Nova Law Review*.

Linder, Douglas O. "Strict Constructionism and the Strike Zone." *University of Missouri-Kansas City Law Review* 56 (1987): 117–20. Reprinted with the permission of the *University of Missouri-Kansas City Law Review*. Courtesy of Yale University Law Library.

Stayton, John W. "Baseball Jurisprudence." *American Law Review* 44 (1910): 374–93. Courtesy of Yale University Law Library.

*Shlensky v. Wrigley. North Eastern Reporter* Second Series 237 (1968): 776–81. Courtesy of Yale University Law Library.

*Chicago National League Ball Club v. Thompson. North Eastern Reporter* Second Series 483 (1985): 1245, 1247–52. Courtesy of Yale University Law Library.

**Spencer Weber Waller** is an associate professor at Brooklyn Law School where he teaches in the areas of antitrust and international business law. He also serves as the associate director of the Brooklyn Law School Center for the Study of International Business Law. A native Chicagoan, Professor Waller attended law school, clerked for a seventh Circuit judge, and practiced with the U.S. Department of Justice and Freeborn & Peters, all in Chicago, prior to joining the Brooklyn Law School faculty in 1990. A lifelong Cubs fan, Professor Waller participated in the 1987 Chicago Cubs Fantasy Camp at Wrigley Field where he batted .500, had an E.R.A. of 0.00, but was thrown out at the plate trying to score from third on a sharply hit ball to the shortstop.

**Neil B. Cohen** is a professor of law at Brooklyn Law School where he teaches courses in commercial law, corporate law and constitutional law and is the reporter for the American Law Institute's Restatement of the Law of Suretyship. He is co-author with Gerald T. McLaughlin and Barry Zaretsky of the *Commercial Law and Practice Guide* and the monthly *Commercial Law Report* and with McLaughlin writes a monthly commercial law column for the *New York Law Journal*. He has written numerous law review articles in areas as diverse as commercial law, bankruptcy, medical malpractice, and probability and statistics. Professor Cohen received an S.B. from the Massachusetts Institute of Technology and a J.D. from New York University School of Law where he was a Root-Tilden Scholar. As a lifelong Cleveland Indians fan, he knows that there is more to baseball than postseason play.

**Paul Finkelman** teaches legal and constitutional history at Virginia Tech. As a visiting professor at Brooklyn Law School (1990–1992) he played intellectual stick ball with Professors Waller and Cohen and coached a championship moot court team. He received his B.A. from Syracuse University and his M.A. and Ph.D. from the University of Chicago. He was a Fellow in Law and Humanities at Harvard Law School. Finkelman was born in Brooklyn (and continues to root for the Brooklyn Dodgers), but grew up in very far upstate New York without any access to live professional baseball. Later living in Chicago, Boston, and New York, he learned to cope with agony and futility watching the Cubs, Red Sox, and Mets.